STUDIES IN CHRISTIAN HISTORY AND THOUGHT

Life in Christ

**Union with Christ and Twofold Grace
in Calvin's Theology**

STUDIES IN CHRISTIAN HISTORY AND THOUGHT

A full listing of all titles in this series
will be found at the close of this book.

STUDIES IN CHRISTIAN HISTORY AND THOUGHT

Life in Christ

Union with Christ and Twofold Grace in Calvin's Theology

Mark A. Garcia

Foreword by David F. Wright

WIPF & STOCK · Eugene, Oregon

Wipf and Stock Publishers
199 W 8th Ave, Suite 3
Eugene, OR 97401

Life in Christ
Union with Christ and Twofold Grace in Calvin's Theology
By Garcia, Mark A.
Copyright©2008 Paternoster
ISBN 13: 978-1-55635-865-4
Publication date 2/20/2008

This Edition Published by Wipf and Stock Publishers
by arrangement with Paternoster

STUDIES IN CHRISTIAN HISTORY AND THOUGHT

Series Preface

This series complements the specialist series of *Studies in Evangelical History and Thought* and *Studies in Baptist History and Thought* for which Paternoster is becoming increasingly well known by offering works that cover the wider field of Christian history and thought. It encompasses accounts of Christian witness at various periods, studies of individual Christians and movements, and works which concern the relations of church and society through history, and the history of Christian thought.

The series includes monographs, revised dissertations and theses, and collections of papers by individuals and groups. As well as 'free standing' volumes, works on particular running themes are being commissioned; authors will be engaged for these from around the world and from a variety of Christian traditions.

A high academic standard combined with lively writing will commend the volumes in this series both to scholars and to a wider readership.

Series Editors

Alan P.F. Sell, Visiting Professor at Acadia University Divinity College, Nova Scotia, Canada

David Bebbington, Professor of History, University of Stirling, Stirling, Scotland, UK

Clyde Binfield, Professor Associate in History, University of Sheffield, UK

Gerald Bray, Anglican Professor of Divinity, Beeson Divinity School, Samford University, Birmingham, Alabama, USA

Grayson Carter, Associate Professor of Church History, Fuller Theological Seminary SW, Phoenix, Arizona, USA

For my wife, Jill
"Many women do noble things,
but you surpass them all."
(Proverbs 31:29)

and

The Rev. Dr Richard B. Gaffin, Jr
Ephesians 2:8-10

Contents

Foreword by David F. Wright   xv
Preface   xvii
Abbreviations   xxi

Introduction   1

Part One

Chapter 1
Calvin, Union with Christ, and the *Duplex Gratia*: Paradigms of Interpretation and Methodological Considerations   11

Reading Calvin on Saving Union with Christ   11
"Central Dogma" Model   15
Form-Method Models   19
From General to Specific: *Duplex Cognitio Dei* and *Unio Christi-Duplex Gratia*   19
From General to Specific: Dialectical Structure and Justification and Sanctification in Juxtaposed Tension   21
Revelational-christocentric or "Neo-orthodox" Model   24
Unio Christi and *Duplex Gratia* in Trinitarian Perspective   24
Redeemed Humanity in Christ? The Incarnation and the "Strata" of Union with Christ   26
Questions Posed by the Literature   28
Justification and Sanctification in Covenantal Relationship   28
Calvin's Spirituality   30
The Place of this Study   32
Methodological Considerations   35
A Limited Scope of Interest   35
The Case Studies: Romans, the Sacraments, and Osiander   36
Calvin's Romans Commentary   36
Salvation, Sacrament, and the Strata of Union with Christ   42
Calvin *contra* Osiander   43

Conclusion 45

Chapter 2
Union with Christ and Saving Righteousness: Anticipations,
Proposals, and Trajectories 47
Introduction: The Diverse Prehistory of Calvin's Construction 47
An Overlooked First Question: Taxonomies of Union
with Christ 48
Unio *and* Communio *in the* Dictionnaire de Spiritualité *and
Altenstaig's 1517* Lexicon Theologicum 48
Union, Conjunction, Communion, and Divinization/Deification
in the *Dictionnaire de Spiritualité* 49
"Communio" in Altenstaig's *Lexicon Theologicum* 51
*Late Medieval Taxonomies: Oberman's Penitential, Marital, and
Eucharistic Mysticisms* 53
*Late Medieval Taxonomies: Manifold Marital Union(s) with
Christ in Medieval Marriage Sermons* 53
Justification by Marriage with Christ: Union with Christ and
Saving Righteousness from Late Medieval Theology
through Luther 56
Iustitia Christi, Iustitia Dei, *and the Late Medieval Soteriological
Dilemma* 56
Luther and Mystical Union with Christ 61
Justification and *Unio Mystica* in Mystical Theology and
in Luther 61
Luther's "Marital" Mysticism in Reformation Form 64
Calvin, the Reformers, and Saving Union with Christ 68
Calvin and Unio Mystica 69
Calvin and Luther: Justification and the Place of Good Works 74
*Relating Justification and Renewal: Some Contemporaries
and Regensburg* 78
Martin Bucer: Threefold Justification 78
Peter Martyr Vermigli: Regeneration as the Context for
Justification and Good Works 79
Melanchthon: Luther's "Necessary" Joined to an Emphasis on
Objectivity 81
Regensburg Colloquy, Article 5 81

Conclusion 85

Part Two

Chapter 3
In Christ, Like Christ: Union with Christ, Good Works and Replication in Calvin's *Romans* 89
Introduction 89
The Texts 90
Union with Christ, Justification, and Sanctification
in Calvin's *Romans* 93
The Argumentum 94
*Obedience and Eternal Life: The Conditional Language
of Romans 2 in Light of Romans 8* 98
Sixteenth-Century Approaches 100
Melanchthon: Law, Not Gospel 103
Calvin: *Ordo*, Sequence, and Eternal Life 106
Reward, Not Merit 106
The Hermeneutical-Theological Priority of Romans 8 108
Extra Nos *and* In Nobis *in Augustine, Trent,
and Romans 3:20-31* 113
Calvin: Union with Christ and Merit in Justification 114
Aristotle's Causes in Calvin's Model 117
Divine Engrafting, Death, and Resurrection in Christ: Romans 6 119
Interpretations: Erasmus and Lefèvre 120
Melanchthon's Syllogistic Reading 122
Calvin: Engrafting into the Crucified and Risen Christ 125
Engrafting and Imitation 128
Light from Romans 4 131
New Life in Christ by the Spirit: Romans 8 133
Joined to Christ by the Spirit 133
The Christ-Pattern of Salvation: Suffering to Glory, Obedience to
Eternal Life 136
Concluding Analysis and Proposal: Calvin's
Replication Principle 140
The Replication Principle: A Summary 140
The Organic and the Sequential 143

Replication, Not Imitation	144
Causation, Good Works, and Spirit-Replication	145
A Taxonomical Proposal	146

Chapter 4
Christ and the Spirit: Sacraments, Salvation, and the Strata of Union with Christ

	149
Salvation and Sacrament	149
Calvin vs. the Lutherans: A Brief Publication History	153
Patterns and Parallels	160
Augustinian Signification and "Distinction without Separation"	161
The Spirit as "Bond"	163
Christ and His Benefits	165
The Charge of Fabrication	165
Christ and the Spirit: Calvin and the *Manducatio Impiorum*	170
Of Mice and (Unbelieving) Men: The Question	170
The Spirit of the Anointed Mediator	174
The Theological Crux: Union with Christ Necessarily Enlivening Non-Eating to Destruction? 1 Corinthians 11 and the Problem of Unworthy Participation	176
	180
Correspondence with Soteriological Structure	184
The Strata of Union with Christ	185
The Functional Equivalence of Signa-Res *and Incarnational-Saving Union with Christ: Calvin's Soteriological Language in Eucharistic Context*	185
Redemptive, Incarnational Union with Christ?	191
Conclusion	193

Chapter 5
Applied Christology: Calvin versus Osiander in Light of the Eucharistic Controversy

	197
Polemic and Theological Interplay	197
Andreas Osiander: Reformer, Theologian, Controversialist	198
The Tradition Question: Luther and the Lutheran Response	200
The Struggle for Luther's Authority	200
The Theology of the Lutheran Response	202
Calvin's Response	208

Preliminary Observations	209
Interpretations	209
The Theology of Calvin's Response: A Summary	210
1 Corinthians 1:30 as Exegetical Epicenter	217
Osiander's Use of 1 Corinthians 1:30	217
Calvin's Use of 1 Corinthians 1:30	219
Excursus: A Patristic Parallel	226
The Metaphorical Shorthand for an Unio-Duplex *Soteriology*	228
Analysis: The Theology and Interpretation of Calvin's Polemical Strategy	241
Conclusion	250

Part Three

Conclusion	**255**
A Recapitulation	255
Implications	257
Calvin and Unio Mystica	257
Calvin and Luther(anism)	258
Calvin and Sola Fide	262
The Way Forward	264
Concluding Observations	267
Appendix A	
A Witness to Calvin's Paulinism: 1539 *Institutio* **Marginalia to Chapter Six, "On Justification by Faith and Works of Merit"**	**269**
Appendix B	
Calvin, Vermigli, and the Strata of Union with Christ: A Closer Look at their 1555 Correspondence	**273**
Bibliography	**289**
Scripture Index	**341**
General Index	**345**

Foreword

It is a great pleasure to welcome a book by a young theologian which not only tackles a central subject of continuing debate in both the church and the academy – a subject which can be broadly summarised in traditional terms as the relationship between justification and sanctification – but does so by focussing on the still-contested thought of a theologian of the very first rank. Readers of this volume will learn a great deal about the fundamental theology of one of the most influential shapers of the Protestant tradition of Christianity. If they read sensitively, they will find in Dr Garcia an interpreter of John Calvin who does justice to both the systematic and the historical dimensions of his corpus of works. No one who laboured for almost a quarter of a century over what we know as the *Institutes* can be regarded as less than systematic, at least in intention. (It is another question how far Calvin succeeded in creating a truly unified and coherently articulated body of teaching. The same question, of course would inevitably arise concerning any theologian whose productive career lasted three decades and covered so many different literary genres in two languages.) The important thing is that modern systematicians allow Calvin to be systematic on his own terms, as it were.

Part of what this will entail is respecting both the number and the diversity of Calvin's extant writings, and having no truck for any endeavour to understand his mind on any topic as though he were the author of the *Institutes* alone. At the same time, the origins of these numerous works at particular stages and in specific contexts during Calvin's lifetime must be factored into any responsible attempt to interpret his thought. One of the special strengths of this study by Mark Garcia is the close attention it gives to Calvin's late engagement with the maverick doctrine of justification espoused by the independent Lutheran, Andreas Osiander. This phase of his research has enabled the author to highlight Calvin's distinctiveness on justification by comparison not with the Roman Church but with the emerging Lutheran tradition which he might be expected to find peculiarly congenial.

Key to making sense of what this book identifies as a widening dissonance between Calvin and his Lutheran contemporaries is its basic theme of union with Christ. Dr Garcia joins a growing chorus of students of the Genevan Reformer – not all by any means otherwise singing from the same hymn-sheet – who hail *unio Christi* as basic to understanding his soteriology and much more besides. One devoutly hopes that this study will contribute to the rising profile of this motif in the working theology of both the academic and the more popular reaches of at least evangelical Christianity. It labours under certain disadvantages compared with the staple fare of regeneration, justification and sanctification – even if such terms are decreasingly used in local church life and no less decreasingly understood. Union with Christ does not come packaged, even in Latin, in a single word, although not being dependent, like justification et al., on a similar multi-syllabic Latinized technical term must be in its favour. On the other hand, the generally low estate in evangelical and other brands of modern Christianity of baptism, with which union with Christ is inseparably related in Pauline teaching, must count against optimism for its recovery. All that matters for the present is that Mark Garcia here does handsome justice to the significance of union with Christ in John Calvin, and does so in book which displays a masterful familiarity with contemporary Calvin scholarship, alongside other grounds for high praise.

D. F. Wright
Edinburgh, 2007

Preface

This is a study in historical, not systematic theology, and the difference, for me anyway, is worth noting. Among other things this has meant that I, as one more at home in biblical and systematic theology, have had to resist the temptation to enter into critical assessment of Calvin's theology and exegesis. Very often I have wanted to explain, exegetically and theologically, why Calvin is right when he says something, and occasionally why he is likely mistaken. It hardly needs to be stated, moreover, that "historical, not systematic theology" also means that my goal has been descriptive, not prescriptive, the analysis of what a man said about Scripture rather than what Scripture says to man, though I should hope that those who regard Calvin as a father in the faith, and many more besides, will listen attentively to what he had to say.

At the same time, it would be dishonest not to admit that, especially as the whole picture slowly came into view, I have found what Calvin has to say not only instructive but timely. In my own case at least, it has been an invaluable experience to draw deeply from the wells of the Reformed tradition in order to appreciate what gave her a distinctive voice in her defining years. In the process, much more than learning facts and models takes place, of course, as I have found Calvin the preacher as enriching as Calvin the teacher.

As I suspect is usually the case, this study has ended up covering a lot fewer corners of the subject than I originally intended, indeed, than I think I probably should have. If this book were not long enough already, I could easily write a fresh chapter on all that one should do in treating this subject but that I have not. Instead, some general suggestions in my Conclusion below will have to suffice. Obviously, then, no claim is made for comprehensiveness, far less of exhausting the subject. In its fullest sense, this study is not viewed by its author as an end but, it is hoped, a beginning: I sincerely hope that I have pursued lines of inquiry that will stimulate further work in similar directions. If future analyses follow these lines and come to far better conclusions, I will be delighted to acknowledge the limitations of my own work and to praise those who are more skilled at using these methods than I.

This book is a light revision of a thesis completed at New College, University of Edinburgh, and accepted for the PhD in 2004. While I have endeavored to follow the relevant literature published since early 2004, I have not attempted in my revision to update my investigation everywhere I could. This is partly due to the fact that I have not found that the recent literature poses difficulties for the arguments advanced here.

There are five main chapters. The first (after the Introduction) is an analysis of the literature and the "state of the question," and can be passed by, if necessary, by those without interests in the sometimes bewildering world of Calvin scholarship. The second chapter provides historical-theological background and sets up the heart of the book: Chapters 3-5. While these chapters are in some ways independent of one another, as becomes clear near the close of the investigation the argument presented in the fifth chapter has important cumulative features. So I would recommend the reader read Chapters 3-5 in the order in which they appear. Lastly, I would mention that brief selections from Chapters 4 and 5 were included in my "Imputation and the Christology of Union with Christ: Calvin, Osiander, and the Contemporary Quest for a Reformed Model," *Westminster Theological Journal* 68:2 (2006): 219-51.

In his *Catechism of the Church of Geneva*, Calvin once explained that whatever blessings we receive from others ought to be regarded as coming from God. Through our fellow man, God himself often sends us gifts from "the inexhaustible fountain of his liberality." We are thus under obligation to these instruments of God's generosity. Indeed, says Calvin, "he, therefore, who does not show himself grateful to them by so doing, betrays his ingratitude to God." For this reason, happily recognizing that "every good and perfect gift comes from above," it is a delight to record a small measure of my gratitude to those whom God has lovingly and providentially used to help bring this book to completion.

First mention must be made of Dr Susan Hardman Moore, my PhD supervisor at New College, University of Edinburgh. Susan patiently and deftly guided this project from infancy to maturity. My examiners, Professors David F. Wright and A. N. S. Lane, provided informed, penetrating analyses of my work and did so with generosity and enthusiasm. I have the greatest respect for their own work which is widely recognized as being of a very high standard, so it has been a privilege to benefit from their sustained interaction with my ideas. I am also particularly grateful to Prof. Wright for writing the Foreword and to those who have commended the book so enthusiastically.

Many others helped this project along by granting me access to rare resources. During the course of my research, I was privileged to benefit from the considerable collections in Geneva because of the generosity of the Bourse Française who supplied me with a grant for a month's stay. To Prof. Irena Backus and the staff at the *Institut d'Histoire de la Reformation*, University of Geneva, I owe my sincerest thanks for hospitality and unbridled access to great texts. Likewise I gladly note a debt of gratitude to the H. Henry Meeter Center for Calvin Studies, Calvin Theological Seminary, Grand Rapids, Michigan, USA, for a research fellowship that allowed me to use the largest collection of secondary sources on Calvin. Dr Karin Maag provided valuable and friendly direction and even stopped a day's work to walk me through some sixteenth-century French paleography. I also wish to thank New College, University of Edinburgh for a Divinity Faculty Scholarship in 2002-2003 and 2003-2004 which alleviated some of our financial burden.

There is of course no research without great libraries, and I am particularly indebted to the staffs of the New College Library, Edinburgh University Library, National Library of Scotland, the Munby Rare Books Room at Cambridge University Library, H. Henry Meeter Center and Hekman libraries at Calvin College and Calvin Theological Seminary, Montgomery Library at Westminster Theological Seminary (Philadelphia), and the *Institut d'Histoire de la Reformation* collection and Bibliotheque Publique et Universitaire in Geneva. The Rev. Dr Chad and Emily Van Dixhoorn graciously provided hospitality and great company during my trips to the Cambridge library. At the *Institut*, I should like to record my thanks to Mr Pierre-Olivier Lechot who promptly satisfied my request for further photocopies from Calvin's commentaries on 1 Corinthians after I had left Geneva.

I have also been extraordinarily blessed with eminent scholars who showed an interest in my work and kindly read through portions of it. Prof. Irena Backus carefully read through my discussion of Osiander at a relatively late stage and made a number of valuable comments, only a fraction of which I was able to incorporate in this book. Very early on in this project I also had the honor and pleasure of meeting with Prof. T. H. L. Parker and Prof. A. N. S. Lane to discuss my ideas. I am thankful not only for their insight and advice but also for their hospitality in welcoming me into their homes. In addition, I am particularly eager to record my thanks to the Rev. Dr Chad Van Dixhoorn, Dr Jason Rampelt, and Mrs Christina Rampelt, all of whom not only provided engaging interaction throughout but also meticulously proofread this study at various stages, saving me from a long, unsightly list of mistakes.

It has been a delight to serve Immanuel Orthodox Presbyterian Church as her pastor, and one could not hope for a more supportive congregation. One of her members, medievalist Mrs Atria Larson, kindly compiled the General Index for this volume; and one of her friends, Mrs Barbara Kuhn, prepared a useful Scripture Index. Robin Parry, Anthony Cross, and Jeremy Mudditt of Paternoster were most helpful, and I thank them for their assistance throughout the publishing process. Special mention should be made of my parents, the Rev. and Mrs Rigo Garcia, and my parents-in-law, Dr and Mrs David Head, for unfailing support and encouragement which reaches back long before the first letter of this book. I sincerely hope they will count any success connected to this book as their own. Finally I record my profound gratitude to anonymous donors who made possible the research that gave rise to this study, and in turn a life of ongoing research, writing, and ministry in service to Christ and his Church. It is because of God's generosity through them that this book exists, and much besides. To God be the glory for their "partnership in the gospel from the first day until now" (Phil 1:5).

My wife, Jill, is a woman of remarkable gifts, and from our first day in Edinburgh I have searched for the right words to use in this testament to her help. I know now I may never find enough words to thank her, but still wish to express to her my sincere gratitude and admiration. Jill has endured countless difficulties for my sake from the very beginning of my academic trek down to the present, and has done so with a grace and patience that reflects the abundance of God's grace in her. Only she knows what she has sacrificed for me and, though she has not tried to explain Calvin to me, there is no possible exaggeration of her contribution to this study. Dedicating this book to her is but a small symbol of a debt of gratitude too great to repay.

It is a delight to dedicate this book also to the Rev. Dr Richard B. Gaffin, Jr, Charles Krahe Professor of Biblical and Systematic Theology at Westminster Theological Seminary (Philadelphia). For more than a generation of ministerial students he has faithfully opened up the Scriptures to unfold its riches. A wise counselor and penetrating thinker, Prof. Gaffin has also served as an eminent example of the churchman-theologian. Personally, his influence upon my thinking is reason enough to dedicate this project to him. But to those who know him and his work, the dedication to Prof. Gaffin of a book on Calvin and union with Christ will also seem a fully appropriate, though small token of appreciation for his contribution to Reformed theology and the life of the Church.

Abbreviations

Principal Calvin Editions

CO	*Ioannis Calvini opera quae supersunt omnia...* (59 vols = CR 29-87)
COR	*Ioannis Calvini Opera Omnia Denuo Recognita...* (Geneva: Librarie Droz, 1994-)
COR II	*Ioannis Calvini Opera Omnia Denuo Recognita..., Series II. Opera exegetica*
COR III	*Ioannis Calvini Opera Omnia Denuo Recongita..., Series III. Scripta ecclesiastica*
Inst. (1536)	*Christianae religionis institutio...* (Basel, 1536)
Inst. (1539)	*Institutio christianae religionis...* (Strasbourg, 1539)
Inst. (1543)	*Institutio christianae religionis...* (Geneva, 1543)
Inst. (1559)	*Institutio christianae religionis...* (Geneva, 1559)
Inst. (1560)	*Institution de la religion chrestienne...* (Geneva, 1560)
OS	*Calvini Opera Selecta...*, 5 vols, ed. P. Barth, W. Niesel, and D. Scheuner (Münich: Chr. Kaiser, 1926-52)
SC	*Supplementa Calviniana: Sermons inédits* (Neukirchen: Neukirchener Verlag, 1936-)
TT	*Tracts and Treatises*, trans. and ed. H. Beveridge (Grand Rapids: Eerdmans, 1958)

Calvin Studies Collections

ACC	*Articles on Calvin and Calvinism*, 14 vols, ed. R. Gamble (New York and London: Garland Publishing Company, 1992)
CED	*Calvinus Ecclesiae Doctor*, ed. W. Neuser (Kampen: J. H. Kok, 1978)
CEGC	*Calvinus Ecclesiae Genevensis Custos*, ed. W. Neuser (Frankfurt am Main: Peter Lang, 1984)
CSRV	*Calvinus Sincerioris Religionis Vindex*, ed. W. Neuser and Brian Armstrong (Kirksville: Sixteenth Century Publishers, 1997)
CSSP	*Calvinus Sacrae Scripturae Professor*, ed. W. Neuser (Grand Rapids: Eerdmans, 1994)
CPE	*Calvinus Praeceptor Ecclesiae*, ed. H. Selderhuis (Geneva: Librarie Droz, 2004)

Other

ARG	*Archiv für Reformationsgeschichte/Archive for Reformation History*
ASD	Erasmus, *Opera omnia, recognita et adnotatione critica instructa notisque illustrata*, ed. L.- E.- Halkin, F. Bierlaire, and R. Hoven (Amsterdam: North Holland Publishing Company, 1969-)
BC	*Bibliotheca Calviniana*, 3 vols, vols 1-2 ed. R. Peter and J.-F. Gilmont (Geneva: Librairie Droz, 1991-1994); vol. 3 ed. R. Peter and J.-F. Gilmont with Christian Krieger (Geneva: Librairie Droz, 2000)
CC	*The Creeds of Christendom*, ed. P. Schaff, 3 vols (New York: Harper & Brothers, 1877; rep. Grand Rapids: Baker, 1998)
CCL	*Corpus Christianorum, Series Latina* (Brepols: Turnhout, 1953-)
CD	Karl Barth, *Church Dogmatics*, 14 vols, ed. Geoffrey W. Bromiley and Thomas F. Torrance; trans. G. T. Thomson and Harold Knight (rep. Edinburgh: T. & T. Clark, 2004)
CH	*Church History*
CNTC	*Calvin's New Testament Commentaries*, 12 vols, ed. David W. Torrance and Thomas F. Torrance (Grand Rapids: Eerdmans, 1960)
ConcTrig	*Concordia Triglotta*, ed. F. Bente (St Louis: Concordia Publishing House, 1921)
CR	*Corpus Reformatorum...*, 59 vols, ed. W. Baum *et al.* (Brunswick and Berlin: C. A. Schwetschike, 1863-1900)
CTJ	*Calvin Theological Journal*
CTS	Calvin Translation Society
CWE	*The Collected Works of Erasmus*, ed. R. J. Schoeck, B. M. Corrigan, *et al.* (Toronto: University of Toronto Press, 1969-)
EQ	*Evangelical Quarterly*
OER	*The Oxford Encyclopedia of the Reformation*, 4 vols, ed. H. Hillerbrand (New York: OUP, 1996)
ICC	International Critical Commentary
JHI	*Journal of the History of Ideas*
KD	*Kerygma und Dogma*
LCC	Library of Christian Classics
LW	Martin Luther, *Luther's Works*, 55 vols, ed. J. Pelikan and H. Lehman (St Louis: Concordia Publishing House; Philadelphia: Fortress Press, 1955-75)

LWZ	*The Latin Works and Correspondence of Huldreich Zwingli*. 3 vols, ed. Samuel Macauley Jackson (New York: G. P. Putnam's Sons, 1912-)
MSA	*Melanchthons Werke in Auswahl (Studienausgabe)*, 7 vols, ed. R. Stupperich (Güttersloh: C. Bertelsmann Verlag, 1955)
NPNF	*Nicene and Post-Nicene Fathers*, 28 vols (rep. Peabody: Hendrickson, 1994)
PG	*Patrologiae cursus completus. Series Graeca*, 166 vols (Series II) (Paris: Migne, 1857-66)
PL	*Patrologiae cursus completus. Series Latina*, 221 vols, ed. J. P. Migne (Paris: Migne, 1844-55)
PML	Peter Martyr Library
REAug	*Revue des etudes augustiniennes*
SCJ	*Sixteenth Century Journal*
SHCT	Studies in the History of Christian Thought
SJT	*Scottish Journal of Theology*
SMRT	Studies in Medieval and Reformation Thought
ST	Thomas Aquinas, *Summa Theologiae*, 61 vols (London: Blackfriars, in conjunction with Eyre & Spottiswoode, 1964-81)
TRE	*Theologische Realenzyklopädie*, 24 vols, ed. Gerhard Krause and Gerhard Müller (Berlin: Walter de Gruyter, 1977-)
WA	*Luthers Werke: Kritische Gesamtausgabe*, 108 vols (Wiemary: H. Böhlau, 1883-1993)
WTJ	*Westminster Theological Journal*
ZKG	*Zeitschrift für Kirchengeschichte*
ZTK	*Zeitschrift für Theologie und Kirche*

INTRODUCTION

First, we must understand that as long as Christ remains outside of us, and we are separated from him, all that he has suffered and done for the salvation of the human race remains useless and of no value for us.

Calvin, *Inst.* (1559) 3.1.1[1]

This study revisits familiar territory, familiar not only on account of the legacy of the individual under examination, Jean Calvin (1509-1564), but also on account of the persistence in theological discourse of the question under investigation. One contemporary theologian has stated that the problem in theology "has always been how to affirm at once the gratuity and the reality of the righteousness or holiness that God gives in the church."[2] In the sixteenth century, this

---

[1] "Ac primo habendum est, quamdiu extra nos est Christus, et ab eo sumus separati, quicquid in salutem humani generis passus est ac fecit, nobis esse inutile nulliusque momenti." John Calvin, *Institutio christianae religionis...* (Geneva, 1559) 3.1.1; OS 4.1 (N.B.: "quamdiu" for OS "quandiu") (LCC 20.537). I will cite the *Institutes* from the Latin followed by the edition in parentheses with footnoted references to the *Joannis Calvini opera selecta...* (OS), ed. Peter Barth, et al. 5 vols (Munich: Chr. Kaiser, 1926-68). When I cite the English text of Calvin's *Institutes*, I have ordinarily used the translation provided by Battles for the 1536 text, cited as *Inst.* (1536). For the 1559 edition I have again normally cited from Battles (Library of Christian Classics [LCC], vols 20-21) but I have also consulted Beveridge's translation, and have noted the page number(s). In quotations I have occasionally thought it necessary to modify an existing translation, in which case indication of this will be provided in the footnotes. In the citation of Calvin's commentaries, I have used the Old Testament Commentaries by the Calvin Translation Society (*Calvin's Commentaries*, 22 vols; rep. ed. [Grand Rapids: Baker, 1996], henceforth CTS); and the New Testament Commentaries edited by David W. Torrance and Thomas F. Torrance (*Calvin's New Testament Commentaries*, 12 vols [Grand Rapids and Carlisle: Eerdmans and Paternoster, 1959–], henceforth CNTC). Other Calvin citations are from *Ioannis Calvini opera quae supersunt omnia...*, ed. G. Baum, et al. in *Corpus Reformatorum* (Brunsvigae: C. A. Schwetschke et Filium, 1876), vols 29-87, henceforth CO and CR, respectively. For other abbreviations used in the notes, consult the abbreviations list above.

[2] Robert W. Jenson, *Systematic Theology*, vol. 2: *The Works of God* (Oxford: Oxford University Press, 1999), 294.

question was laden not only with religious but also with social and political significance, and yet the theology that surrounds it has largely outlasted the civil structures it so deeply affected. Using the then-developing theological parlance, the question was raised in these terms: how, in the divine economy of salvation, is "justification," understood as the reckoning of Christ's righteousness and the consequent forgiveness of sins, related to "sanctification," the Spirit-effected renewal of the sinner in holiness after the image of Christ? If, according to many sixteenth-century reformers, they should be held together but distinguished, what then is the nature of their relationship? How can a definitive pardon, freely bestowed on the basis of a righteousness imputed from outside us (*extra nos*), be tied meaningfully to the divine promise and demand of a holy life, understood as something very much within us (*in nobis*)? Is the charge of "antinomianism" or of a "legal fiction," directed against the idea of a justification *sola fide*, inescapable? Or, in terms of the colorful history of Protestant-Catholic dialogue as well as modern Lutheran theology, is saving grace "forensic" and analytic or "personal" and synthetic, "imputed" or "imparted"?

This study is an investigation into Calvin's response to these questions, a response regularly expressed in terms of one specific concept. In his vigorous engagement with the teaching of Andreas Osiander on justification, for example, Calvin stated with strikingly graphic language: "Just as one cannot tear Jesus Christ into pieces, so also these two are inseparable since we receive them together and conjointly in him, namely, righteousness and sanctification."[3] This statement well encapsulates Calvin's meticulously considered and variously argued reply to that question. More than that, however, it also reflects an important theme in Calvin's thought, namely, that the two basic saving benefits (justification and sanctification) are

---

[3] Calvin, *Inst.* (1559) 3.11.6; OS 4.187 (LCC 20.732): "Ut probet illud primum, Deum non tantum ignoscendo sed regenerando iustificare, quaerit an quos iustificat, relinquat quales erant natura, nihil ex vitiis mutando. Responsio perquam facilis est: sicut non potest discerpi Christus in partes, ita inseparabilia esse haec duo, quae simul et coniunctim in ipso percipimus, iustitiam et sanctificationem." In context, "percipimus" is better translated "we receive" rather than "we perceive" (cf. LCC 20.732). The image of tearing Christ into pieces (which receives sustained attention in Chapter 5 below) is a favorite of Calvin's for emphasizing the inseparability of justification and sanctification which results from the work of the Spirit in uniting us to the Christ who is in himself both righteousness and sanctification. See, e.g., *Comm.* on 1 Cor 1:30 (CO 49.330-32; CNTC, 46); *Comm.* on Rom 8:13 (*Comm. Epist. ad Romanos* [COR II/13], 163; CNTC, 166-7); and *Inst.* (1559) 3.16.1; OS 4.249 (LCC 20.798).

distinct and yet inseparable precisely because of a reality still more basic or fundamental: the believer's Spirit-effected *unio cum Christo*. This model, which will be called Calvin's *unio Christi-duplex gratia* soteriology, is a prominent feature in Calvin's theology, whether expressed in positive, polemical-disputative, ecclesiastical (catechetical and sacramental), or pastoral (sermonic) form.

The choice of terminology here reflects an unfortunate confusion in the literature. Calvin's basic model is regularly referred to as a *"duplex gratia"* model. Both contemporary with and after Calvin, however, one finds numerous theological expositions of salvation which may be described as teaching a basic *duplex gratia* of justification and sanctification, and yet differ materially from Calvin's model in that they do not use or understand union with Christ in a way analogous to Calvin. This renders Calvin's own relationship to these other, nominally similar models ambiguous. Thus, for the purpose of clarification within an exceedingly broad category of description, it appears both the formal and the functional importance of Calvin's union idea within his soteriology is better reflected if his framework is referred to as an *unio Christi-duplex gratia* rather than simply a *duplex gratia* framework.[4]

Calvin insists on the indispensability of this union with Christ perhaps most emphatically when he makes the "profitability" of Christ's redemptive work to depend wholly upon it. He writes, "We know, moreover, that he benefits only those whose 'Head' he is, for whom he is 'the first-born among brethren,' and who, finally, 'have put on him'." He concludes, "This union alone ensures that, as far as we are concerned, he has not unprofitably (*inutiliter*) come with the name of Savior."[5]

---

[4] It is hoped that, by the close of this study, the justification for this modification in traditional terminology will be clear. The specific term *"unio Christi-duplex gratia"* may not be the best to serve this purpose, but it is probably sufficient for our purposes as shorthand for Calvin's model.

[5] Calvin, *Inst.* (1559) 3.1.3; OS 4.5 (LCC 20.541): "Scimus autem non aliis prodesse nisi quorum est caput et primogenitus inter fratres, qui denique eum induerunt. Facit *sola* haec coniunctio, ne inutiliter, quoad nos, cum Salvatoris nomine venerit." Italics mine. Because a distinction is not made in the Battles/McNeill edition of Calvin's *Institutes* between biblical references noted explicitly by Calvin and those inserted by the editors, I will not incorporate these references into quotations in order to avoid confusion. See the helpful discussion in Richard A. Muller, *The Unaccommodated Calvin: Studies in the Foundation of a Theological Tradition* (New York: Oxford University Press, 2000), 140-42.

For Calvin, justification and sanctification comprise the *duplex gratia Dei* which flows to us from Christ by his Spirit through faith.[6] Sanctification, therefore, as much as justification, is the application of the redemption accomplished by Christ. Distinct from justification, sanctification (or "repentance")[7] is further distinguished as including both *mortificatio* and *vivificatio*. These twin sides of sanctification describe and correspond to union with Christ in his death and resurrection, respectively.[8] Both justification and sanctification, in their relationship to each other in terms of union with Christ, express what it means to be a child of God. Both are therefore necessary to a proper conception of salvation. As Rainbow correctly observes, "Sanctification is not for Calvin an afterthought, or a problem, or an implication, or a psychological response to justification. Sanctification is *salvation*, just as much as justification is *salvation*. It is grace. Nor is it optional, or dispensable, but necessary and inevitable."[9] Justification is indeed *sola fide*, "by

---

[6] Calvin often refers to this twofold grace in his *Institutes*. See, e.g., *Inst.* (1559) 3.3.1; OS 4.55 (LCC 20.592); 3.3.1; OS 4.55-6 (LCC 20.593); 3.3.19; OS 4.76-7 (LCC 20.613); 3.11.1; OS 4.181-2 (LCC 20.725-6); 3.24.8; OS 4.419-20 (LCC 20.974). Note that *gratia* is singular, not plural. This is Calvin's standard way of referring to salvation, i.e., as one gift (Christ, specifically in terms of union with Christ) rather than as many gifts (justification, sanctification, adoption, etc.). The difference here with much contemporary reflection on salvation, including readings of Calvin, is noteworthy.

[7] In the sixteenth century, "sanctification" and "regeneration" were basically synonymous and "repentance" also frequently had this comprehensive idea in view. Calvin frequently uses "sanctification," "regeneration," and "repentance" interchangeably, with only occasional preference for one term in a given context. In this study, I use the standard term of modern usage, "sanctification," unless Calvin evidently employs "regeneration" or "repentance" to indicate something more specific to these terms. It should be noted that in Calvin's usage "justification" also brings into view a complex of terms, including "pardon" or "forgiveness of sins," "innocence," and "imputation," usually negatively as the non-imputation of sins and at times positively as the imputation of Christ's righteousness. See, e.g., *Inst.* (1559) 3.11.2 where justification is defined as the forgiveness of sins and the imputation of Christ's righteousness.

[8] *Inst.* (1539) 3.3.8-9; OS 4.62-5 (LCC 20.600-1). See Chapter 3 below.

[9] Jonathan Rainbow, "Double Grace: John Calvin's View of the Relationship of Justification and Sanctification," *Ex Auditu: An International Journal of Theological Interpretation of Scripture* 5 (1989): 104. Emphasis Rainbow's. See also the comments by Pierre Marcel, "The Relation Between Justification and Sanctification in Calvin's Thought," *EQ* 27 (1955): 135-7. Rainbow devotes his attention to the relationship of the *duplex gratia* in Calvin but does not discuss Calvin's idea of union with Christ.

faith alone," but faith saves "because through it believers possess God by being engrafted into the body of Christ."[10] For Calvin, it is specifically because of union with Christ by the Spirit through faith that "justification" is tied inextricably and necessarily to "sanctification."

These basic themes constitute the theological focus of this investigation. Before proceeding to an analysis of the literature, however, something should be said briefly about the method and texts chosen.[11] It is an especially difficult decision in an exploration of this nature to select the ideas, figures, texts, and events that are most promising for an advance in understanding. Of those *not* focused upon, perhaps the Regensburg Colloquy, at which Calvin was present, is the most conspicuous by its absence. There, a consensus was reached among select Catholics and Protestants on the doctrine of justification. The importance of the *duplex iustitia* idea to this consensus was considerable, and supplies a useful backdrop for appreciating Calvin's own attempt to navigate the treacherous line between the sixteenth-century Scylla of a justification *on the grounds of* good works and the Charybdis of a justification *without* good works. Similarly, Calvin's rejection of the Tridentine formula on justification is also easily defensible, and yet again this receives only limited attention here. In part, my decision to focus upon other texts and events is due to the fact that Calvin's polemical engagement with Trent on justification is well-explored in the literature. With regard to Regensburg, Calvin's silent role at the Colloquy, and our limited understanding of precisely how the theology of justification was discussed, restricts how much we can profitably glean from this solitary event for our rather specific purposes.[12] In the three case studies in this study, I devote attention instead to texts and events insufficiently examined in interpreting Calvin on the function of union with Christ in the relationship of justification and sanctification. In addition, there is an underlying, self-conscious attempt here (discussed more fully below in the

---

[10] Barbara Pitkin, *What Pure Eyes Could See: Calvin's Doctrine of Faith in Its Exegetical Context* (New York: Oxford University Press, 1999), 92.

[11] These methodological considerations are discussed at greater length, with a fuller introduction to the three case studies, below in Chapter 1.

[12] Furthermore, Anthony N. S. Lane, who has devoted considerable attention to justification in the sixteenth century, is soon to publish a major study of Article 5 on justification. It seems defensible, in this case, to await his work before offering what would amount to a highly provisional and tentative analysis in this book. At the same time, it is not ignored: I survey Regensburg in Chapter 2 below, but of necessity my interest is quite narrow.

analysis of existing studies) to move beyond the consensus in the literature regarding the *fact* of the *unio Christi-duplex gratia* relationship in order to explore the *function* of union with Christ in this theological complex.

What follows is divided into three parts. Part One includes an analysis of the literature and a treatment of methodological considerations, as well as a general analysis of the relationship of union with Christ to salvation in select individuals and traditions preceding and contemporary with Calvin.

Part Two consists of the three case studies which form the book's main body. In the first of these case studies, I examine Calvin's handling of the problem of conditional language in the Epistle to the Romans, a real problem for the Reformers posed by their polemical appropriation of the Apostle Paul. In this study, I explore the *unio Christi-duplex gratia* relationship in particular sections of Calvin's *Commentary*. In particular, I investigate Calvin's treatment of the conditional passages in Romans 2 and 8 in order to argue for what I ultimately suggest is a "replication principle" in Calvin. This principle is, in effect, a description of the regular way union with Christ functions for Calvin in the relationship of justification and sanctification. More specifically, Calvin employs the replication idea to defend the necessary presence of good works in the lives of those justified *sola fide*. Beyond simply asserting that justification and sanctification come to us in union with Christ, this hermeneutical-theological principle reveals concretely how union with Christ actually operates in Calvin's theology of salvation.

In the second case study, the relationship between sacrament and salvation in Calvin's teaching on communion with Christ is explored. Starting with the historical observation that the justification and eucharistic controversies of the Reformation period were largely contemporaneous, I investigate the deep structural congruities of Calvin's theology of saving and eucharistic union or communion with Christ. Specifically, the focus here is upon Calvin's rejection of the Lutheran *manducatio impiorum* ("[eucharistic] eating by unbelievers")[13] with an interest in the patterns of argument and expression that surface here to reinforce points Calvin usually made in a more explicitly soteriological context.

---

[13] More accurately "by the impious." However, as the analysis in Chapter 4 below makes clear, in Calvin's usage at least the communicants in view are not the weak in faith or, if possible, "the sometimes impious yet truly believing," i.e., ungodly believers, but strictly those without faith, i.e., the totally unbelieving.

In the third and final case study, I examine Calvin's 1559 refutation of the Lutheran controversialist Andreas Osiander. The strands of Calvin's thought identified in the first and second case studies converge in what is presented here as the single most significant text and event for Calvin's theology of saving union with Christ. Anticipating our final conclusions, it appears the mutual reciprocity of these themes (soteriological and christological-sacramental) requires a fresh sensitivity to the complexity of the sixteenth-century Lutheran-Reformed relationship on the theology of salvation as well as to the complex nature of Calvin's idea of saving union with Christ.

Part Three is the Conclusion in which the principal arguments of each case study are revisited and recast in light of the whole. Here additional questions are also raised about Calvin's thought from the perspective of conclusions reached and some suggestions are made for further work.

I will say more about these case studies in Chapter 1 below, but the observation regarding the Lutheran-Reformed relationship prompts an additional methodological note. The decision not to focus attention extensively upon Calvin's polemic with Rome is joined to a decision to compare Calvin with those who were closest to him on justification in order to appreciate better what features of his teaching are in fact distinctive. This has resulted in considerable attention to the Lutheran tradition, particularly Melanchthon, in order to document the growing divergence between how Calvin and his Lutheran contemporaries understood union with Christ in relation to justification and sanctification. However, it is especially important to note here that, as suggested in several places in the body of this study, while this sixteenth-century Reformed-Lutheran theological divergence should not be glossed over (a particularly problematic reading challenged throughout this study) neither should it be exaggerated. It is simply the nature of this investigation that the weight of the argument falls heavily on the differences, and ultimately the divergence, between these Reformation traditions.

PART ONE

CHAPTER ONE

Calvin, Union with Christ, and the *Duplex Gratia*: Paradigms of Interpretation and Methodological Considerations

Reading Calvin on Saving Union with Christ

Among the challenges facing an interpreter of Calvin is the distance, both historical and theological, that separates his day from our own. The historical distance is bridged somewhat, but never entirely, as more is learned about Calvin's day and life, his texts and conversation partners. In recent decades, as a survey of the bibliographies demonstrates, considerable advances have been made in this direction. The theological distance, however, has proved more stubborn. Simply put, the challenge for a contemporary student of Calvin's works lies in a history of interpretation which has reflected less of the sixteenth century than it has the history and variety of nineteenth- and twentieth-century theological programs.[1] Schleiermacherian, Barthian, existentialist, post-liberal, and Eastern readings of the Reformer are all easily found in this swelling body of literature. Among the problems posed by this state of affairs is the fact that, because Calvin serves so often as a "wax nose" for modern theology, the difficulty of finding a useful entrance into the scholarly literature is also acutely felt.

Despite this situation, however, it is still possible to classify the various perspectives taken on Calvin's soteriology – provided that the distinctions among categories are not taken too sharply, and that plenty of room is left for overlapping models. Of those proposed,

---

[1] This is the problem addressed forthrightly in Richard A. Muller, *The Unaccommodated Calvin: Studies in the Foundation of a Theological Tradition* (New York: Oxford, 2000), and in a number of Muller's earlier publications. Muller argues for a rigorous sixteenth-century contextualization of Calvin's texts and ideas and against the imposition of modern theological grids. This revisionist methodology, for which Muller is one of the most prolific advocates, is similar to that carried out by Heiko Oberman and others in the study of late medieval theology. See, e.g., Oberman, *The Harvest of Medieval Theology: Gabriel Biel and Late Medieval Nominalism* (1963; 3rd ed.; Grand Rapids: Baker, 2000).

the taxonomy used by Cornelis Venema in his 1985 Princeton dissertation is still among the most helpful.[2] Venema skillfully organizes the unwieldy body of scholarship then current, and the analysis of the literature in this chapter may be viewed as in part an updating and narrowing of Venema's treatment.

Much is held in common with regard to what Calvin intends by "justification" and "sanctification," at least by brief definition. But the same cannot be said about the relationship of these two designations or concepts. For his part, with a view to the variety of scholarly interpretations, Venema approaches the problem of the *duplex gratia* creatively as the point of convergence between more general approaches to Calvin's theology and interpretations of justification and sanctification. Unlike our investigation in which attention is concentrated on the function of union with Christ within the *duplex gratia*, Venema's object is primarily in the "representative significance" of the *duplex gratia* for the interpretation of Calvin's theology as a whole.[3]

Approaches to Calvin's teaching on the *unio Christi-duplex gratia* relationship have proceeded along three general lines: (1) the "central dogma" approach which regards union with Christ as the center of Calvin's theological system and spirituality; (2) the form-method approach which identifies the key or entrance into Calvin's theology with its form or method, and then proceeds to interpret the *unio Christi-duplex gratia* construct in its light; and (3) the christocentric-revelation or "neo-orthodox" approach which sees Calvin's theology as a diverse witness endeavoring to "conform to its object, the being and action of God in Christ."[4] This third approach, rooted in the early work of Wilhelm Niesel and Karl Barth, Venema correctly identifies as the most prominent in twentieth-century Calvin scholarship. This general but distinctive

---

[2] Cornelis Paul Venema, "The Twofold Nature of the Gospel in Calvin's Theology: The 'Duplex Gratia Dei' and the Interpretation of Calvin's Theology," Ph.D. diss. (Princeton Theological Seminary, 1985). See pp. 1-34 for a treatment of the secondary literature on the *duplex gratia* beyond what is provided in this chapter. Despite the considerable amount of relevant literature published since the mid-1980s, Venema's is still a useful study. Venema approaches the issue with basic questions similar to those asked in this study, though with an hermeneutical interest in the widest scope of Calvin's thought.

[3] Venema, "The Twofold Nature of the Gospel," 17, 26.

[4] Venema, "The Twofold Nature of the Gospel in Calvin's Theology," 13; see pp. 2-16. Venema notes that his outline is not original to him and cites the one offered by Benjamin Charles Milner, *Calvin's Doctrine of the Church* (Leiden: E. J. Brill, 1970), 2, as another example. My labels for these categories only vary from Venema's inconsequentially.

perspective determined the questions asked and the interpretive grids used in analyses of Calvin's doctrine of union with Christ by Kolfhaus, T. F. Torrance, and Hart as well as the more general investigations of Calvin's thought by Brunner, Jacobs, Kreck, Parker, and others.[5]

Venema has also identified several questions that are frequently asked of Calvin's soteriology. These include (1) the relative importance of justification and sanctification in Calvin's wider theology; (2) the relation of these two redemptive benefits; (3) the relation of union with Christ to the forensicism in his doctrine of justification; (4) the relation of law and gospel in comparison with his Lutheran contemporaries; (5) and the problem of the *syllogismus practicus*.[6] Of those noted, numbers 2 and 3 occupy the center of attention in this study, though numbers 1 and 4, especially the comparison with contemporary Lutheranism, also belong to our discussion.[7] With respect to the question of forensicism in Calvin's doctrine of justification, a persistent argument is that if justification is truly rooted in union with Christ it cannot be strictly forensic or legal for the union itself is personal and dynamic.[8] Furthermore,

---

[5] Wilhelm Niesel's *The Theology of Calvin* (trans. Harold Knight; London: Lutterworth, 1956; rep. Grand Rapids: Baker, 1980) has actually been more influential in Calvin studies, but it is Barth who is chiefly responsible for the theological framework. For only a few examples of a basically Barthian reading of Calvin on union with Christ, see H. Brglez, "Saving Union with Christ in the Theology of John Calvin: A Critical Study," Ph.D. thesis (University of Aberdeen, 1993); Trevor Hart, "Humankind in Christ and Christ in Humankind: Salvation as Participation in Our Substitute in the Theology of John Calvin," *SJT* 42 (1989): 67-84; Graham Redding, *Prayer and the Priesthood of Christ* (Edinburgh: T. & T. Clark, 2003), who is heavily dependent on T. F. and J. B. Torrance; "Introduction," to *The School of Faith: Catechisms of the Reformed Church*, trans. and intro. by T. F. Torrance (London: James Clarke, 1959); and W. Kolfhaus, *Christusgemeinschaft bei Johannes Calvin* (Neukirchen: Buchhandlung des Erziehungsvereins, 1939). For this reading of Calvin in general, see, e.g., Peter Brunner, *Vom Glauben bei Calvin* (Tübingen: J. C. B. Mohr, 1925); Paul Jacobs, *Prädestination und Verantwortlichkeit bei Calvin* (Kasel: Oncken, 1937); Walter Kreck, "Die Eigenart der Theologie Calvins," in *Calvin-Studien 1959*, ed. J. Moltmann (Neukirchen: Neukirchener Verlag, 1960), 26-42; and T. H. L. Parker, *Calvin's Doctrine of the Knowledge of God* (2nd ed.; Grand Rapids: Eerdmans, 1959).
[6] Venema, "The Twofold Nature of the Gospel," 18.
[7] Venema (p. 19) suggests that, "in several respects, these questions [i.e., union with Christ and forensic justification, law and gospel] are but forms of this more basic question [i.e., the precise relation between justification and sanctification]."
[8] E.g., as an early representative, Emile Doumerge, *Jean Calvin, les hommes et les choses de son temps*, Vol. 4: *La pensée religieuse de Calvin* (Lausanne: Georges Bridel

some interpreters have posited a bare juxtaposition of the *duplex gratia*, an ultimate separation with no convincing relationship established.[9] Others have focused upon Calvin's insistence on inseparability to the neglect of his equally strong insistence on distinction.[10] Between these contradictory views lies the position, adopted by many, that Calvin is able to maintain consistently both the distinguishability and the inseparability of these saving gifts.[11] In addition to these, questions are raised as to the precise shape of Calvin's spirituality, in particular his teaching on mortification and vivification in relation to justification and union with Christ.

---

and Cie, 1910), 275, who as Venema notes (p. 21, n. 36), confuses the issue by subsuming union under justification. However, Venema's own reading has been criticized as too extrinsic in the interests of preserving an objective justification *extra nos*, and thus obscuring the intimately personal reality of union with Christ for Calvin. See the discussion, of mixed value, in William Borden Evans, "Imputation and Impartation: the Problem of Union with Christ in Nineteenth-Century American Reformed Theology," Ph.D. diss. (Vanderbilt University, 1996), 6-68, 428-31. The question is dealt with more fully throughout this study, but for the moment it may be said that while Venema properly identifies the issue, Calvin does not resolve it in the same way.

[9] E.g., A. Ganoczy, *Calvin, Théologien de l'Eglise et du Ministère* (Paris: Les Éditions du Cerf, 1964), 95ff.; idem, *Le Jeune Calvin: Genèse et Evolution de sa Vocation réformatrice* (Wiesbaden: Franz Steiner Verlag, 1966); J. Köstlin, "Calvin's *Institutio* nach Form und Inhalt, in ihrer geschlichtlichen Entwicklung," *Theologische Studien und Kritiken* 41 (1868): 465; and Paul Wernle, *Der Evangelische Glaube, Nach Den Haupschriften Der Reformation, Vol. 3: Calvin* (Tübingen: J. C. B. Mohr, 1919), 254. Cf. this and other literature cited in Venema, "The Twofold Nature of the Gospel in Calvin's Theology," 20, n. 33. On pp. 20-25, Venema summarizes these perspectives on the *duplex gratia*.

[10] E.g., Willy Lüttge, *Die Rechtfertigungslehre Calvins und Ihre Bedeutung fur seine Frommigkeit* (Berlin: Reuther and Reichard, 1909), 27, 43, 84ff. Cf. the literature cited in Venema, "The Twofold Nature of the Gospel," 20, n. 34.

[11] E.g., Kolfhaus, *Christusgemeinschaft*, 66ff.; Werner Krusche, *Das Wirken des Heiligen Geistes nach Calvin* (Göttingen: Vandenhoeck and Ruprecht, 1957), 275ff.; Peter A. Lillback, *The Binding of God: Calvin's Role in the Development of Covenant Theology* (Grand Rapids: Baker, 2001); Niesel, *Theology of Calvin*, 127ff.; Venema, "The Twofold Nature of the Gospel"; Ronald S. Wallace, *Calvin's Doctrine of the Christian Life* (Edinburgh: Oliver and Boyd, 1959), 17-27; François Wendel, *Calvin: The Origins and Development of his Religious Thought* (trans. Philip Mairet; New York: Harper and Row, 1963), 256ff. Even among representatives of this last group, however, thought is divided over whether the distinctive christological framework of Niesel and Barth accurately reflects *how* Calvin successfully relates these benefits.

"Central Dogma" Model

That union with Christ is fundamentally important for Calvin's theology has not been lost on his many interpreters.[12] It has long been appreciated that the Calvin corpus contains numerous passages in which the theological, ecclesiological, and practical significance of union with Christ is prominent. Indeed, virtually every study of Calvin's theology to date has concluded, with more or less insight into the matter, that this theme is a highly significant element of his thought.[13] In Wendel's well-respected reading of

---

[12] However, while many have summarized Calvin's teaching on the *unio Christi*-*duplex gratia* relationship, only a relatively small number of focused investigations exists, including: W. Kolfhaus, *Christusgemeinschaft*; H. A. Brglez, "Saving Union with Christ"; and Dennis E. Tamburello, *Union with Christ: John Calvin and the Mysticism of St. Bernard* (Louisville: Westminster/John Knox Press, 1994). The literature on the *duplex gratia Dei* in Calvin (as a wider question) is summarized in Willy Lüttge, *Die Rechtfertigungslehre Calvins*, 1-10; Tjarko Stadtland, *Rechtfertigung und Heiligung bei Calvin* (Neukirchen: Neukirchener Verlag, 1972), 21-6; and Venema, "The Twofold Nature of the Gospel," 3-16. A number of briefer studies are listed below (n. 13).

[13] The literature on Calvin and union with Christ is prohibitively vast. However, most of these studies are brief, often forming part of a broader investigation into Calvin's theology. The more substantial studies are by Kolfhaus, *Christusgemeinschaft*; Brglez, "Saving Union with Christ"; and Tamburello, *Union with Christ*. Richard B. Gaffin, Jr. ("Biblical Theology and the Westminster Standards," *WTJ* 65 [2003]: 165-79) supplies an insightful, succinct discussion. For other brief studies, see: Thomas Gregory, "Union to Christ the Ground of Justification," in *Opening and Closing Addresses to the New College Theological Society, Session 1882-83* (Edinburgh: Lorimer & Gillies, 1883), 33-50; John W. Nevin, *The Mystical Presence* (Philadelphia: J. B. Lippincott & Co., 1846), 54-8; Niesel, *Theology of Calvin*, 120-39; idem, *Reformed Symbolics* (trans. D. Lewis; Edinburgh and London: Oliver and Boyd, 1962), 181-6; Karl Barth, *CD* IV/3.2, ed. G. W. Bromiley and T. F. Torrance; trans. G. W. Bromiley (Edinburgh: T. & T. Clark, 1962), 551-3; Krusche, *Das Wirken des Heiligen Geistes nach Calvin*, 265-72; Wendel, *Calvin*, 234-42; Paul van Buren, *Christ in Our Place* (Edinburgh and London: Oliver and Boyd, 1957), 95-106; Kilian McDonnell, *John Calvin, the Church, and the Eucharist* (Princeton: Princeton University Press, 1967), 177-205; John H. Leith, *John Calvin's Doctrine of the Christian Life* (Louisville: Westminster/John Knox Press, 1989), 98-103; Robert C. Doyle, "The Preaching of Repentance in John Calvin," in P. T. O'Brien and D. G. Peterson, eds, *God Who Is Rich in Mercy: Essays Presented to Dr. D. B. Knox* (Homebush West: Anzea, 1986), 287-321; Willem van't Spijker, "'Extra Nos' en 'In Nobis' bij Calvijn in pneumatologisch licht," *Theologia Reformata* 31 (1988): 271-91; E. David Willis-Watkins, "The Unio Mystica and the Assurance of Faith According to Calvin," in Willem van't Spijker, ed., *Calvin: Erbe und Auftrag, Festschrift für W. H. Neuser* (Kampen: Kok Pharos Publishing House, 1991), 77-84; Charles Partee, "Calvin's

Calvin, for example, union with Christ is "the indispensable condition for our access to the spiritual life";[14] and Wallace likewise observes: "Calvin notes that in defining the means by which we are saved it is better to use the phrase *in Christ* than *by Christ*, for the former phrase has more expressiveness and force and denotes the union with Christ which is such a necessary part of the gospel."[15]

Furthermore, it is not long before the careful reader finds that Calvin's teaching on this theme is multifaceted and rich, weaving together various major topics and ideas and relating them to one another with distinction and nuance as well as metaphor and simile.[16] This doctrinally-synthesizing function or effect of union with Christ in Calvin's soteriology will be our focus throughout, but note for the moment the variety of salvation concepts Tamburello brings within its purview: "Calvin wants to speak of *unio* in relation to faith, the Holy Spirit, the gospel (scripture), the sacraments, and election. It is intimately connected with all of these, but identical with none of them."[17]

If Calvin's teaching on union with Christ is as comprehensive as the literature suggests, moreover, one would expect to detect its influence in studies of other areas of his theology. This is indeed what one finds: the literature reflects the varied nature of Calvin's

---

Central Dogma Again," *SCJ* 18 (1987): 191-9; W. Duncan Rankin, "Carnal Union with Christ in the Theology of T. F. Torrance," Ph.D. thesis (University of Edinburgh, 1994), 166-235, 270-76; Brian G. Armstrong, "*Duplex cognitio Dei*, Or? The Problem and Relation of Structure, Form, and Purpose in Calvin's Theology," in Elsie A. McKee and B. G. Armstrong, eds, *Probing the Reformed Tradition: Historical Studies in Honor of Edward A. Dowey, Jr.* (Louisville: Westminster/John Knox Press, 1989), 135-53; and Jean-Daniel Benoit, *Calvin in His Letters*, trans. R. Haig (Oxford: Sutton Courtenay Press, 1991), 73-81. Further studies focused on sacramental union with Christ are noted in Chapter 4 below.

[14] Wendel, *Calvin*, 238; cf. "Communion with Christ, the *insitio in Christum*, is the indispensable condition for receiving the grace that the Redemption has gained for us" (p. 235). Cf. Leith, *John Calvin's Doctrine of the Christian Life*, 98-9.

[15] Wallace, *Calvin's Doctrine of the Christian Life*, 17-18. Italics Wallace's. Wallace refers in a footnote to Calvin's comment on Rom. 6:11: "Retinere malui Pauli verba: in Christo Iesu, quam cum Erasmo vertere: per Christum: quia illo modo melius exprimitur insitio illa, quae nos unum cum Christo facit" (Calvin, *Comm. Epist. ad Romanos*, OC II/13/124).

[16] What may be called Calvin's "metaphorical flexibility" is, in fact, among the richest features of his writing on union with Christ. A close analysis would appear to be well worth the effort. The examination in Chapter 5 below of Calvin's use of *discerpi in partes* ("to tear into pieces") is an attempt at such a study, though with a specific theological interest.

[17] Tamburello, *Union with Christ*, 85, criticizing Kolfhaus's identification of union with Christ with faith.

application of the doctrine, and this alone reveals indirectly the wide influence it exerts in his thought. Numerous investigations have thus explored the relationship of union with Christ to Calvin's teaching on such topics as the assurance of faith,[18] repentance or sanctification,[19] and the sacraments.[20]

As we will soon discover, moreover, the comprehensive and determinative reality of the believer's union with Christ is a theme running freely not through Book 3 of Calvin's *Institutes* alone but throughout his other writings as well. As Niesel wrote, it is as though Calvin "never tires of emphasising this."[21] In fact it is difficult to identify many major areas in his thought in which this theme is not at least discernible if not clear, latent if not patent, standing in the background if not "out there" in the open. As the various approaches taken in Calvin scholarship indicate, whether in his teaching on salvation, the Church, or the sacraments, the doctrine of union with Christ seems always to play some role. This comprehensiveness is perhaps best captured by Willis-Watkins, who notes that "Calvin's doctrine of union with Christ is one of the most consistently influential features of his theology and ethics, if not indeed the single most important teaching which animates the whole of his thought and his personal life."[22]

---

[18] E.g., Willis-Watkins, "The Unio Mystica and the Assurance of Faith."
[19] E.g., Doyle, "The Preaching of Repentance in John Calvin." See also the underlying thesis, "The Context of Moral Decision Making in the Writings of John Calvin: The Christological Ethics of Eschatological Order," Ph.D. thesis (University of Aberdeen, 1981); Eric Fuchs, *La Morale Selon Calvin* (Paris: Les Éditions du Cerf, 1986), 70-114; Paul C. Böttger, "Die Christusgemeinschaft als Grundlage der Applikation," in Böttger, *Calvins Institutio als Erbauungs buch – Versuch einer literarischen Analyse* (Neukirchen: Neukirchener, 1990), 31-54; Randall C. Gleason, *John Calvin and John Owen on Mortification: A Comparative Study in Reformed Spirituality* (New York: Peter Lang, 1995).
[20] See the studies in Chapter 4 for additional references but note, e.g., B. A. Gerrish, *Grace and Gratitude: the Eucharistic Theology of John Calvin* (Edinburgh: T. & T. Clark, 1993); Wallace, *Calvin's Doctrine of the Word and Sacrament*; McDonnell, *John Calvin, the Church, and the Eucharist*; and Ferguson, "Calvin on the Lord's Supper and Communion with Christ."
[21] Niesel, *Reformed Symbolics*, 182.
[22] Willis-Watkins. "The Unio Mystica," 78; note also Edward A. Dowey, *The Knowledge of God in Calvin's Theology* (1952; 3rd ed. Grand Rapids: Eerdmans, 1994), 204. On the ecclesiastical dimension of Calvin's doctrine, see Geddes MacGregor, *Corpus Christi: the Nature of the Church According to the Reformed Tradition* (London: Macmillan and Co. Ltd., 1959), 43-65; and David N. Wiley, "The Church as the Elect in the Theology of Calvin," in Timothy George, ed., *John Calvin and the Church: A Prism of Reform* (Louisville: Westminster/John Knox, 1990), 96-117. Cf. Bucer (with whom Calvin has a particularly strong

While it will not be pursued here as "the single most important teaching which animates the whole of his thought," it might prove instructive to note that it has not been beyond recent interpreters to do what in contemporary Calvin scholarship might be deemed the unthinkable: propose yet another "central dogma" theory according to which union with Christ is Calvin's central teaching.[23] One might be sympathetic with this view in light of the comprehensiveness of the idea as just described, but the designation of union with Christ as Calvin's "central dogma" fails to deal adequately with other ideas and themes which also may be said to have a controlling and comprehensive character. Recent studies, for example, have investigated Calvin's rich teaching on the knowledge of God with the same kind of comprehensiveness in view.[24] The consensus among Calvin scholars, moreover, appears to be that no single "central dogma" exists in Calvin's theology, but that a number of doctrines and themes are fundamentally important and together make up the whole.[25]

At the same time, however, as the case studies below will demonstrate, the doctrine of union with Christ does appear to stand as a singularly determinative idea in Calvin's *soteriology*. By "singularly determinative" I intend to emphasize the controlling significance for Calvin of the truth that the Holy Spirit unites believers savingly to Christ by faith. It is the *role* of this union-reality in Calvin's exposition of the *duplex gratia* that I suggest is "singularly determinative." This is not a masquerading proposal for, with Partee, making union with Christ Calvin's "central dogma." I simply wish to draw attention to the relative place of union with Christ in Calvin's teaching on the application of redemption. Is it possible to

---

similarity on this subject) in Willem van't Spijker, *The Ecclesiastical Offices in the Thought of Martin Bucer*, trans. John Vriend and Lyle Bierma (SMRT 57; Leiden: E. J. Brill, 1996), 352-66.

[23] So Partee, "Calvin's Central Dogma Again" and, similarly, Doyle, "The Preaching of Repentance in John Calvin." It should be noted, however, that Partee's suggestion is motivated more by pedagogical concerns than by the exposition of Calvin (see his comments, pp. 191-2). Doyle (p. 292) calls union with Christ "the dominant motif in Calvin's theology."

[24] Cf. T. H. L. Parker, *The Doctrine of the Knowledge of God: A Study in the Theology of John Calvin* (London: 1952; rev. ed. Edinburgh: Oliver & Boyd, 1969) with Dowey, *The Knowledge of God*.

[25] T. H. L. Parker, "The Approach to Calvin," *EQ* 16 (1944): 165-72. For analysis of the alleged centrality of predestination to Calvin's and his successors' systems (the more familiar "central dogma" reading), see Richard A. Muller, *Christ and the Decree: Christology and Predestination in Reformed Theology from Calvin to Perkins* (Durham: Labyrinth Press, 1986).

have one ("singular determination") and not the other ("central dogma")? Perhaps by restricting the language of "control" and "determination" to structural and constitutive considerations in Calvin's *soteriology* (not his theology as a whole) – i.e., to the way Calvin understands the *modum percipiendae Christi gratiae*, "the way we receive the grace of Christ"[26] – it will then be possible to preserve the thematic significance of other ideas in Calvin's theology and still give expression to that which appears fundamentally important in his teaching on salvation.

Form-Method Models

FROM GENERAL TO SPECIFIC: *DUPLEX COGNITIO DEI* AND *UNIO CHRISTI-DUPLEX GRATIA*

We turn now to interpretive proposals that attend to Calvin's text as a whole, particularly in its *form* and as this form possibly reflects the author's *method*. In a large-scale analysis of its structure, Edward A. Dowey argued that Calvin's theology as reflected in his 1559 *Institutes* is organized in terms of the *duplex cognitio Dei*, referred to by Dowey as the "twofold knowledge of God."[27] Soon after the publication of Dowey's essay, one from T. H. L. Parker appeared which pointed to the "four-fold ordering of the Apostles' Creed, which Calvin uses as the framework of the book..."[28] Dowey responded to Parker's criticisms in a later article on the subject, but discussion of the question continues unabated.[29]

---

[26] This is the familiar title of Book 3 of Calvin's *Institutes* (1559) which reads: "de modo percipiendae Christi gratiae, et qui inde fructus nobis proveniant, et qui effectus consequantur" (The way in which we receive the grace of Christ: what benefits come to us from it, and what effects follow) (OS 4.1; LCC 20.535).

[27] Dowey, *The Knowledge of God*. This is also the view of Julius Köstlin and B. A. Gerrish. Dowey's identification of Calvin's basic principle as "the twofold knowledge of God" has been fairly criticized by Parker and, following Parker, Muller who correctly identify "the knowledge of God and ourselves" as the actual idea Calvin has in view (Parker, *The Doctrine of the Knowledge of God*, 119; idem, *John Calvin: A Biography* [Philadelphia: Westminster, 1975], 131; Muller, *Unaccommodated Calvin*, 134).

[28] Parker, *The Doctrine of the Knowledge of God*, 6. For a summary of Parker's creedal ordering of the 1559 *Institutes*, see pp. 5-12.

[29] Dowey, "The Structure of Calvin's Theological Thought as Influenced by the Two-fold Knowledge of God" in W. H. Neuser, ed., *CEGC*, 135-48. For an analysis of the Dowey-Parker debate see Muller, *Unaccommodated Calvin*, 72-8, who offers an important discussion of the *duplex cognitio* question from the perspective of Calvin's late sixteenth-century editors. A fresh perspective on the question of structure is provided by Francis Higman, "Linearity in Calvin's

In Dowey's proposal, knowledge of God as Creator and Redeemer, with the former dependent on the latter, is the structuring principle or idea in Calvin's 1559 *Institutes* and therefore of his theology. Accordingly, with a view to Book 3 and Calvin's theology of salvation, Dowey discusses the relation of faith to this knowledge, explaining that "the noetic aspect of faith is imbedded inextricably in a total work of the Spirit that includes both will and intellect and finally body as well as soul."[30] As Dowey points out, Calvin relates this comprehensive work of the Spirit to the question of assurance. In the context of Calvin's rejection of certain "semipapists" who argued that faith always has doubt as its partner, Dowey explains with Calvin's words that one must not pretend to consider oneself "apart from Christ" or ponder him "at a distance," but rather *know* oneself as brought into union with him. The key to the relation between faith and knowledge is therefore the comprehensive work of the illuminating Spirit who unites believers by faith with Christ himself.[31]

This may suggest to some that Calvin endorses an intellectual faith only. "To 'know' Christ, however, does not mean speculative knowledge, but enjoying 'the sacred and mystical union between us and him; but the only way of knowing this is when he diffuses his life into us by the secret efficacy of the Spirit.'"[32] The knowledge of faith *is* the enjoyment of communion with Christ by the Spirit.

Dowey also sees evidence of the formal or structural importance of union with Christ in the controlling nature of Calvin's discussion at the outset of Book 3.

> And so Calvin's Book III on the activity of the Spirit in applying Christ's work to men, having been introduced comprehensively with the teaching about union with Christ, proceeds through illumination, regeneration, justification, election, and culminates in the doctrine of the resurrection of the body (III.xxv). The key term is "faith," "the principal work of the Spirit," and within faith, knowledge, for knowledge is the highest thing in creation. Yet

---

Thought," in Higman, *Lire et Découvrir: La Circulation des idées au temps de la Réforme* (Geneva: Droz, 1998), 391-401. Higman's insightful approach is based upon Calvin's language as reflective of a linear organization of thought.

[30] Dowey, *The Knowledge of God*, 198.

[31] Dowey, *The Knowledge of God*, 199: "The knowledge of Christ is part of a wider, more comprehensive communication of him. It is true that only when 'inwardly instructed' by the 'illumination of the Spirit' is Christ known by 'the experience of faith.'"

[32] Dowey, *The Knowledge of God*, 199, referring to Calvin, *Comm.* on John 14:20; see also *Inst.* (1559) 3.2.

knowledge is but one aspect of the total impartation of life by which the believer begins now in this earthly existence to share in that eternal life that will one day be his completely when the mystical union is perfected.[33]

Like Dowey's investigation, Parker's study also reflects the movement from a perspective on the general form of the *Institutes* to a perspective on the specific doctrine of union with Christ. In his proposal for a creedal patterning of the 1559 *Institutes*, discussion of saving union with Christ occurs, quite properly, under Book 3, thus corresponding to the article on the Holy Spirit. Parker points to Calvin's repeated insistence in this section that it is the Spirit alone who as "bond" unites believers to Christ.[34] Thus Calvin effects the transition from the redemption accomplished by Christ (Book 2) to its application (Book 3) through discussion of the third article, on the Holy Spirit. Hence, the *duplex cognitio* theme "is continued even more plainly in Book III," explains Parker, "where the objectivity of the redemption wrought in Christ is transmuted into the subjectivity of the inward work of the Holy Spirit, *Christus pro nobis* into *Christus in nobis*."[35] Union with Christ thus lies at the intersection of the wider programmatic theme of the *duplex cognitio Dei* and the narrower themes of faith and salvation.

FROM GENERAL TO SPECIFIC: DIALECTICAL STRUCTURE AND
JUSTIFICATION AND SANCTIFICATION IN JUXTAPOSED TENSION

These recent investigations by Dowey and Parker into the structure of Calvin's thought have prompted other, more detailed studies of the subject. One in particular is noteworthy in that the author argues for the basic and central theological significance of union with Christ from his identification of the form, structure, and purpose of the 1559 *Institutes* and Calvin's theology as a whole. Broadly within this perspective, a dialectical reading of Calvin's theology proposed and developed by Herman Bauke has been further developed by Alexandre Ganoczy and more recently by Brian Armstrong who roots the dialectical tension between justification and sanctification in Calvin's historical and philosophical context.[36] It is Ganoczy who

---

[33] Dowey, *The Knowledge of God*, 204. Emphasis mine.
[34] Parker, *The Doctrine of the Knowledge of God*, 121-2.
[35] Parker, *The Doctrine of the Knowledge of God*, 10. Calvin's doctrine of union with Christ is outlined by Parker in pp. 120-23.
[36] Herman Bauke, *Die Problem Der Theologie Calvins* (Leipzig: J. C. Hinrichs'scher Buchhandlung, 1922); A. Ganoczy, *Ecclesia Ministrans* (Wiesbaden, 1968); Brian G. Armstrong, "*Duplex cognitio Dei*," 135-53. See the discussion of Ganoczy in Venema, "The Twofold Nature of the Gospel," pp. 6-11. Significantly,

draws the explicit tie to the question of ontology, arguing, as Venema notes, that Calvin is unable "to provide an ontological mediation for the interaction and communion between God and humanity," and that this problem is particularly evident in his "dialectical juxtaposition of justification and regeneration."[37]

This focus on Calvin's *duplex gratia* as dialectical presents justification and sanctification as existing in a tension of some kind. In this vein, Armstrong aims to move the *duplex cognitio* discussion forward while benefiting in particular from Dowey's work. Methodologically, Armstrong has proposed that instead of focusing on structure *qua* structure, the Reformer's work should be read as the product of one concerned not with theology in any systematic sense but with spirituality, the life of the Church. As he notes often, Armstrong is indebted to William Bouwsma's *Portrait* for his "two Calvins," Renaissance and Reformation, "co-existing uncomfortably" in the same person. This is especially evident in Armstrong's strongly expressed distaste for studies of Calvin which treat him as in any sense a "systematic" theologian. His emphasis on Calvin's concern for the spiritual life of the Church is intended to counter such a reading.[38]

Evidently following not only Bouwsma but principally the earlier work of Bauke modified by Ganoczy and Battles among others, Armstrong argues that there is a patent dialectical structure to the pattern of argument and presentation in Calvin's 1559 *Institutes* which resulted from Calvin's identification with and accommodation to the antithetical principles of Renaissance and Reformation. This dialectical conflict is of such a fundamental character that Calvin's theology reflects, at every point, "two poles, two aspects, two dialectical and conflicting elements."[39] This conflict, moreover, is "at bottom... fundamentally based in a broad, general philosophical dialectic between the ideal and the real."[40] This Renaissance/Reformation, ideal/real dialectic, Armstrong argues, lies at the heart of the four Books of the 1559 *Institutes* and, importantly, shapes the material throughout.

Armstrong is furthering specifically Ganoczy's identification of a dialectic reflected in the un-harmonious union believers have with Christ.

[37] Ganoczy, *Calvin*, 59; cf. Venema, "The Twofold Nature of the Gospel," 10.

[38] Armstrong, "*Duplex cognitio Dei*," 136; cf. William Bouwsma, *John Calvin: A Sixteenth Century Portrait* (New York: Oxford, 1988). For a trenchant critique of Bouwsma's "theologian of piety vs. systematic theologian" reading, see Muller, *Unaccommodated Calvin*, 79-83, 101-17.

[39] Armstrong, "*Duplex cognitio Dei*," 137.

[40] Armstrong, "*Duplex cognitio Dei*," 137.

Again, it is especially important for Armstrong that Calvin's theology is understood to have a strictly spiritual as opposed to systematic-theological purpose. With this conviction in view, Armstrong observes that the Church's worshipful communion with God stands as the goal or end of theology for Calvin. This doxological-communal *telos*, having been thwarted by the Fall, remains the "ideal" throughout Calvin's theology. The "real" world, in which sin brings death and alienation, is the world in which man's purpose in existing – union and communion with God – is stymied. Armstrong recognizes a "hypothetical" pattern of argumentation in Calvin's theology that reflects this ideal/real situation. The way this hypothetical motif is normally expressed is by strategically-placed conditional "if clauses" present in each of the four Books of the 1559 *Institutes*.

Summarizing the hypothetical elements in Book 3, Armstrong draws attention to mystical union as "central and crucial to the fabric of the hypothetical structure of his thought." He continues:

> Indeed, I believe that the nature and force of his use of the hypothetical motif as it relates to his teaching on grace is best perceived and understood when serious attention is given to the role and importance in his theology of the mystical union of the believer with Christ. The entire discussion of soteriology is a working out of the mystical union principle. In Christ we have restored to us the spiritual life which was lost in Adam. When it comes to our restoration to righteousness, "we possess it only because we are partakers in Christ: indeed with him we possess all its riches" (3.11.23).[41]

Armstrong acknowledges that such an interpretation may be thought unwarranted, but substantiates his observation with a reference to the "conditional" or hypothetical transition from Books 2 to 3 offered by Calvin in *Inst.* (1559) 3.2.1. Addressing a specific question raised throughout this study, Armstrong argues that the hypothetical/actual, ideal/real structure of Calvin's thought is "nowhere more clearly seen than in the discussion of the doctrine of justification by faith and its relationship to the doctrine of sanctification."[42]

But does this dialectical reading truly reflect what is at work in Calvin's soteriology? Armstrong's reduction of the justification/sanctification distinction to differing perspectives in light of which believers are, in the one case viewed in Christ

---

[41] Armstrong, "*Duplex cognitio Dei*," 148.
[42] Armstrong, "*Duplex cognitio Dei*," 149.

(justification) and in the other viewed in themselves (sanctification)[43] seems to obscure Calvin's regular insistence that *both* graces reflect on our union with Christ. Even more fundamentally, however, Armstrong's positing of a fundamental tension or conflict between Renaissance and Reformation can be criticized for separating unnecessarily what, perhaps especially in Calvin and in contemporaries like Melanchthon, certainly belong together.[44] Calvin's weaving of distinctly Renaissance methods and Reformation theology in his exegesis would appear to conflict with Armstrong's basic historical-philosophical premise. For the moment, however, it is most important to note that the recent attention given to the structure of Calvin's theology as a whole has, in Armstrong's study especially, served to point to the determinative significance of union with Christ for his soteriology.

Revelational-christocentric or "Neo-orthodox" Model

UNIO CHRISTI AND DUPLEX GRATIA IN TRINITARIAN PERSPECTIVE

Yet another interpretive model needs to be included in this discussion, not least because it held sway in Calvin scholarship for much of the previous century and persists into the present. This model takes its starting point not from the form or method of Calvin's *Institutes* but from his theology, and this theology is understood and framed along revelational-christocentric (or, perhaps even less helpfully, "neo-orthodox") lines. And in many cases this amounts to a particular kind of stress on Calvin's trinitarianism.

It is of course important in any investigation of Calvin's thought to recognize that it is thoroughly trinitarian. Calvin's doctrine of union with Christ lies embedded in a theology governed by trinitarian presuppositions. This trinitarianism, moreover, is coupled with a pneumatic Christology that determines the shape of his soteriology. In other words, Calvin's insistence that salvation is trinitarian does not compromise but strengthens his exhortation to look to Christ alone: salvation comes to us from the Father through Christ by the Holy Spirit. The fact that it is through Christ alone accounts for the shape of his teaching on union with Christ.

These are observations readily apparent in careful readings of the *Institutes*, but perhaps it is also important to emphasize that Calvin's

---

[43] Armstrong, "*Duplex cognitio Dei,*" 149.
[44] As an entrance into the discussion, see the compelling treatment in Muller, *Unaccommodated Calvin*, 39-61, and the literature cited.

trinitarian theology and christocentric language about union with Christ are located within a very specific historical and theological context, one rich with diverse movements and developments that touch on this theme. One important element in this context, for example, is Calvin's own complex reception of ancient christological formulae, particularly the traditional language for the divine-human hypostasis and its role in sixteenth-century eucharistic debates. In this era of eucharistic controversy, the confusion and disagreement among participants rested in part on differing interpretations and appropriations of traditional christological dogma. The Chalcedonian "one person, two natures" was heartily received, but the language employed to explain the relation between the two natures was quickly seen to have great implications for talk of the eucharistic presence.[45]

In an ambitious effort to investigate Calvin's trinitarianism in terms of the divine-human relationship, Philip Butin has explored the pervasive and controlling nature of Calvin's trinitarianism for his theology as a whole.[46] With respect to Calvin's soteriology, Butin brings together Calvin's understanding of trinitarian perichoresis and his language of divine-human relations in order to elucidate the significance of Calvin's language of the Spirit as the "bond" of union with Christ.[47] Butin sees Calvin's soteriology as consistently trinitarian inasmuch as

> throughout Calvin's development of the theme of the Spirit as bond is the explicit qualitative continuity that is implied between Christ's relationship with the Father (in the Spirit), and the church's relationship with Christ (in the same Spirit). In both cases, the Spirit constitutes the relationship, as its bond.[48]

---

[45] The eucharistic debates will be examined in Chapter 4 below, as will the more general significance of christological formulations for Calvin's soteriological emphases.

[46] Philip Walker Butin, *Revelation, Redemption, and Response: Calvin's Trinitarian Understanding of the Divine-Human Relationship* (New York: Oxford, 1995). See Butin's comment on p. 207, n. 23.

[47] Butin, *Revelation, Redemption, and Response*, 82. Though cognizant of Dowey's objections, Butin (pp. 55, 167 n. 1) follows to a great extent Parker's identification of a creedal patterning in the 1559 *Institutes*. Butin builds on the idea of Leith and Armstrong that Calvin's theology is held together by the divine-human relationship. He advances the model by arguing that the Trinity is the integrating paradigm of this relationship. Thus he also could have been discussed under the "form-method" model.

[48] Butin, *Revelation, Redemption, and Response*, 83.

These are noteworthy observations, and at many points Butin's exposition rings true. On some important questions, however, it is evident Butin's reading of Calvin's trinitarian theology moves much too zealously in the direction of a more modern trinitarian schematic and does not reflect what Calvin actually says he is doing. For instance, with specific reference to the justification/sanctification relationship, it is worth questioning whether it is in fact "the Trinitarian pattern of redemption" that necessitates, for Calvin, the distinction of graces, rather than the more proximate, contextual concern to remove good works from the meritorious grounds of justification.[49] While Butin pays more attention to contextual matters than others have, this is a place where the specifics of the sixteenth-century climate of discourse evidently recede from view.[50]

REDEEMED HUMANITY IN CHRIST? THE INCARNATION AND THE "STRATA" OF UNION WITH CHRIST

Butin's robust trinitarian exposition of Calvin is but one instance of the larger revelational-christocentric model of interpretation. Within this broad category, the question has frequently arisen whether or in what sense Calvin located redeeming union with Christ in the incarnation.[51] The impetus for the question often springs from the correlative debate whether Calvin taught a "universal" or "limited" atonement. For those who argue for a universal atonement in Calvin, it is frequently urged that Calvin teaches a redeeming incarnational union between Christ and all who share his human nature. For those who argue against this view, Calvin teaches a non-redemptive relationship with all humanity in the incarnation which serves as the platform on which his redemptive work is carried out

---

[49] Butin, *Revelation, Redemption, and Response*, 73. Cf. the similar criticism in Richard Muller, "Directions in Current Calvin Research," *Calvin Studies IX*, ed. J. H. Leith and Robert A. Johnson (Colloquium... Davidson College and Davidson Presbyterian Church, N.C., 30-31 January, 1998), 82.

[50] In another, more programmatic example, Butin claims that Calvin anticipated Barth (and, to some extent, Rahner) in the view that the Trinity expresses the very being of God in relationship, as opposed to a rational view of God's oneness prior to revelation and redemption. As John Thompson notes (*Expository Times* 107 [1995]: 58), "This is a claim which the facts scarcely justify."

[51] Note, e.g., Hart, "Humankind in Christ and Christ in Humankind;" Brglez, "Saving Union with Christ in the Theology of John Calvin;" Redding, *Prayer and the Priesthood of Christ*; T. F. Torrance, "Introduction," to *The School of Faith*; and J. B. Torrance, "The Incarnation and 'Limited Atonement'," *Scottish Bulletin of Evangelical Theology* 2 (1984): 32-40.

and applied to the elect. Incarnational union differs, both in quality and in scope, from the Spirit-union that comes by faith.[52]

Within this specific set of questions, and also stemming from the interests of modern trinitarian theological perspectives, Calvin has been summoned as a theological revolutionary who anticipated Barth's distinctive program. Employing his reading of Calvin for this purpose, Trevor Hart proposes the need for a paradigm shift in the traditional Western understanding of objective and subjective aspects of salvation.[53] The typical Western understanding, "predominant ever since the writings of Tertullian," has, according to Hart, overlooked the most important dimension of salvation: Christ himself.[54] Calvin is brought forward as one who, in his doctrine of incarnational union with Christ, rejected this Western paradigm and brought soteriology back to its biblical shape. As discussed below in Chapter 4, Hart's interpretations and conclusions are deeply problematic,[55] but his attention to the importance of union with Christ in Calvin's soteriology, especially the relationship of justification and sanctification, is noteworthy. Ganoczy, with similarities to Hart, argues for a trinitarian-human correspondence on the idea of "grace" in Calvin and points to the importance of Calvin's teaching on union with Christ within this context.[56]

In light of the arguments advanced later in this study, it is useful to approach this particular problem as one of relating accurately the discernible degrees, what one might call the various "strata," of Calvin's doctrine of union with Christ. In his brief study, Willis-Watkins argues that Calvin teaches two "levels" of union. The first level is incarnational, "the hypostatic union of the eternal Word with the humanity which believers share with every other person." Whereas this first level is universal in scope the second is particular

---

[52] This reading is not restricted to those who argue strictly for a "limited" atonement in Calvin but also includes those who regard the question itself as anachronistic and reflective of later Reformed polemical concerns. It should be noted that the view that the question is anachronistic does not nullify the option that Calvin's teaching can be said to stand in basically positive relationship to the later, more technical formulation. More will be said concerning this in Chapter 4 below.
[53] Trevor Hart, "Humankind in Christ and Christ in Humankind."
[54] Hart, "Humankind in Christ and Christ in Humankind," 70.
[55] See Chapter 4 below. More generally, see the section "Calvin Versus Barthianism" in Tony Lane, "The Quest for the Historical Calvin," *EQ* 55 (1983): 95-113, which summarizes the contrast in terms of the knowledge of God, predestination, faith, and monocovenantalism.
[56] Alexandre Ganoczy, "Observations on Calvin's Trinitarian Doctrine of Grace," in McKee and Armstrong, eds, *Probing the Reformed Tradition*, 96-107.

and concerns the "union of Christ with believers which comes about by the Holy Spirit who is the bond by which we are united to Christ... the eternal Word made flesh."[57] This second union presupposes the prior union.

This division by Willis-Watkins into two levels, incarnational and spiritual, has been critiqued by Duncan Rankin who, based on an examination of Calvin's 1555 correspondence with Peter Martyr Vermigli, argues in favor of three unions: (1) incarnational, (2) mystical, and (3) spiritual.[58] The "incarnational union," a legitimate implication of the hypostatic union, is indeed universal in extent. But this union shared by all humanity is "general and weak."[59] This union is *in itself* non-redemptive. "Spiritual" union, however, is the progressive enjoyment of the communion definitively established in "mystical" union, the fount of Christ's blessings that flow to believers through the Holy Spirit.[60]

In light of the fact that Calvin's delimitation of the various unions or strata of union with Christ occurs in the midst of the eucharistic controversies (and is found in correspondence with a fellow defender of what would come to be identified as the Reformed view) it is at least curious that this controversial and polemical context has not been pursued sufficiently in the interpretation of these strata. The debate over the nature and character of eucharistic communion with Christ is deeply relevant to appreciating what Calvin intends, and this context furthermore promises insight into the viability of a Barthian or generally neo-orthodox reading of the incarnation in Calvin.

Questions Posed by the Literature

JUSTIFICATION AND SANCTIFICATION IN COVENANTAL RELATIONSHIP

In contrast to the views that Calvin insufficiently distinguishes them or merely places them in dialectically juxtaposed tension, the majority opinion is that Calvin is successful in relating justification and sanctification. However, just as the discussion above of the various interpretive models would lead us to expect, there is a wide variety of reasons given for this success. In a monograph largely

---

[57] Willis-Watkins, "The Unio Mystica," 78.
[58] Rankin, "Carnal Union with Christ," 167; see the wider discussion in pp. 166-235.
[59] Rankin, "Carnal Union with Christ," 235; Rankin is referring to the 1555 Calvin-Vermigli correspondence examined in an appendix to his thesis (Appendix 12, incorrectly referred to as Appendix 13 on p. 175 n. 35).
[60] Rankin, "Carnal Union with Christ," 235.

concerned with this question, for example, Peter Lillback interprets Calvin's thought through the idea of covenant, an idea more frequently associated with post-Calvin Reformed developments but which in fact has a much deeper and wider history. Lillback has argued, against recent arguments to the contrary, that Calvin holds a rich "covenantal" theology and that that theology also bears a positive relationship to later developments within the Reformed tradition. Specifically with respect to salvation, Lillback has argued that for Calvin "Christ's redemptive work is fully integrated with the covenant," and that "Calvin... sees a relationship of Christ and the covenant in the application of redemption in such areas as faith, sonship, union with God and Christ, good works, and the sacraments."[61] Furthermore, Lillback has highlighted the logical priority for Calvin of the covenant to Christ, inasmuch as "[u]nless the covenant precedes, the atonement of Christ would not be applied."[62] If Lillback is correct, one should expect Calvin's language of union with Christ to sit very much within a "covenantal" context, indicating that union has an indispensably "covenantal" character.

And this is in fact what Lillback has found. Calvin speaks of the two principal benefits of salvation, the *duplex gratia*, as the "two members of the covenant," as *covenantal* benefits.[63] It is the indissoluble tie between Christ and the covenant which renders justification and sanctification inseparable.[64] In this sense, the covenant "helps to organize the benefits of salvation."[65] Justification and sanctification are consequently simultaneous and inseparable yet distinguishable benefits that come through the covenant by union with Christ.[66] It is this covenantal matrix of Calvin's soteriology, Lillback argues, which sets him apart from Luther on the question of the value of the good works of believers.[67]

The distinct value and advantage of Lillback's investigation is his effort to place Calvin's doctrine of saving union with Christ firmly

---

[61] Lillback, *The Binding of God*, 177-8.
[62] Lillback, *The Binding of God*, 178.
[63] *Inst*. (1559) 3.20.45; OS 4.359 (LCC 20.910); Lillback, *The Binding of God*, 180.
[64] Lillback, *The Binding of God*, 182.
[65] Lillback, *The Binding of God*, 183. Lillback also recognizes (p. 183) the polemical significance of Calvin's formulation in his critique of Rome and the Libertines.
[66] See the table in Lillback, *The Binding of God*, 190. Note the subtle but significant difference between Lillback's and Gleason's reading of Calvin: for Lillback, sanctification is "simultaneous" with justification; for Gleason, mortification and vivification (as sanctification) "follow upon" justification.
[67] See Lillback, *The Binding of God*, 183-93, and the relevant sections in Chapter 2 below.

in the covenantal context Calvin himself emphasizes, an effort in which previous scholarship had shown little real interest. As Lillback's extensive footnotes indicate, Calvin does indeed refer to the covenant often, especially in his commentaries. The result for Lillback is that Calvin's teaching on union cannot be examined with profit outside this covenantal context. Calvin's understanding of union with Christ (and, consequently, the benefits of that union) as "covenantal" in character explicitly sets the parameters of his teaching on saving union with Christ. However, despite the force of Lillback's argument for the frequency of the covenant idea in Calvin, it is not as clearly apparent that Calvin's covenant idea is in fact as pervasive and, most importantly, as structurally determinative as Lillback suggests. Lillback is fully correct that Calvin's covenant theology relates positively to later Reformed developments. Despite Calvin's frequent use of the covenant idea, however, it is not necessary to grant Calvin a more sophisticated covenantal theology than he actually had in order to vindicate its importance.

Even more importantly, Lillback's effort to accent the differences between the emerging Lutheran and Reformed attitudes toward good works is salutary in light of the need for this clarification – a need which is addressed somewhat more directly in the present book. But it may be argued that he has restricted the question too narrowly to several quotes by Luther on the law. Here, as elsewhere, Lillback's argument for a positive, soteriological place for good works in Calvin's theology is certainly a helpful advancement in understanding, but arguably still lacks the clarifying comparative analysis that would move beyond more general categorizations. Despite these outstanding questions, however, in Lillback's discussion one does have valuable insight into the broad theological framework within which Calvin understood union with Christ as the central saving benefit.

CALVIN'S SPIRITUALITY

But in both the Eastern and Western theological traditions, to reflect on union with Christ is also to reflect on Christian spirituality. Thus, for the relationship of the *unio Christi* and the *duplex gratia*, Calvin's teaching on the Christian life would seem to be perhaps the most promising area of investigation. Especially in light of the burden of demonstrating that justification *sola fide* does not marginalize the necessity for personal holiness, the connection between Calvin's pervasive union idea and his exposition of the life of sanctification is intriguingly suggestive.

Despite this promise, however, the theological relationship of Calvin's teaching on union with Christ with his teaching on sanctification has not yet been adequately explored with reference to the *duplex gratia* and the Reformation dilemma. In studies of Calvin's spirituality, for instance, Calvin's patterning of Christian experience as mortification-then-vivification after the prototype of Christ's own transition from death to resurrection has often been subjected to strictly genealogical interest. Interest in Calvin's teaching here has frequently been restricted to the complicated pursuit of Calvin's relationship to the general *Devotio Moderna* or the more specific *imitatio Christi* traditions, and has thus suffered a preoccupation with questions of pedigree.[68] While these are worthy and necessary concerns, and indeed still await the definitive treatment, not enough attention has been given to how the imitation theme actually functions within Calvin's soteriology in light of his doctrine of union with Christ and the questions of his day, most especially the necessity of good works in light of justification *sola fide*.

In a helpful look at one feature in this matrix of ideas, Robert Doyle focuses specifically on the relationship of union with Christ to the preaching of repentance in Calvin. Doyle's study has a number of positive features, one of which is the occasional attention given to the influence of Calvin's environment and contemporaries. Doyle notes, for example, that an important aspect of Calvin's teaching on repentance – the legal/evangelical distinction – is borrowed from Bucer and Melanchthon.[69] We are also reminded of the significance of such contextual factors as the Anabaptist teaching on regenerational perfection and, more generally, "the controversial sixteenth century context within which he worked" as a possible reason for Calvin's emphasis on the redemptive importance of the humanity of Christ.[70]

Doyle observes that the concept of repentance in Calvin is intimately tied to and flows from his teaching on union with Christ in that both parts of repentance have that union as their source. Looking at Calvin's 1559 *Institutes*, Doyle notes: "Both parts of repentance only 'happen to us by participation in Christ.' Thus we

---

[68] This is the case, e.g., in Lucien Richard, *The Spirituality of John Calvin* (Atlanta: John Knox Press, 1984) and Hae Yong You, "Bonaventure and John Calvin: The Restoration of the Image of God as a Mode of Spiritual Consummation," Ph.D. diss. (Fordham University, 1992). Clive S. Chin, "*Unio Mystica* and *Imitatio Christi*: The Two-Dimensional Nature of John Calvin's Spirituality," Ph.D. diss. (Dallas Theological Seminary, 2002), provides a useful synthesis of the existing literature and argues for a distinctively Erasmian influence upon Calvin's spirituality.
[69] Doyle, "The Preaching of Repentance," 291.
[70] Doyle, "The Preaching of Repentance," 293, 296; cf. 297.

are brought to the dominant motif in Calvin's theology, *coniunctio per Christum*, union with Christ..."[71] Again, however, though a "dominant motif," one is left without a clear discussion of the way this motif functions to shape sanctification as participation in Christ's death and resurrection.

Similarly, Gleason has also pointed to the controlling nature of union with Christ for Calvin's theology of the Christian life, in particular his teaching on mortification.[72] Union with Christ, says Gleason, is the "channel of grace" in Calvin's spirituality, the reality which makes sanctification possible.[73] The twin aspects of sanctification (mortification and vivification) Gleason describes as "dependent" on justification, itself a grace dependent on union with Christ.[74] Yet one is not provided with an analysis of Calvin's theology beyond this limited description.

Before proceeding further, I would add a word here to clarify from the start what this study will *not* involve. These needs in the scholarly literature will not be addressed here by revisiting "union with Christ in Calvin," or "justification" or "sanctification" in Calvin. Rather, attention will focus upon the *function* of union with Christ within Calvin's *duplex gratia* soteriology. Our question, then, is a specific one, and one which touches on but does not exhaust many other important ideas in Calvin. Justification, for example, will receive attention, but one will not find here anything arriving at a full treatment of Calvin's doctrine of justification; rather, only the way in which Calvin's doctrine of union with Christ functions in shaping his understanding of the distinct-but-inseparable relationship of justification and sanctification. The same holds for other facets of Calvin's thought. This is a study, then, of the interpenetration of ideas and concerns in Calvin's theology of salvation, and of the specific role and impact of Calvin's doctrine of union with Christ in this theological interplay.

The Place of this Study

Where then does the present study fit into the existing body of literature, and is there really a need for it? It was noted above that

---

[71] Doyle, "The Preaching of Repentance," 292.
[72] Gleason, *John Calvin and John Owen on Mortification*, 45-77.
[73] Gleason, *John Calvin and John Owen on Mortification*, 52-3.
[74] Gleason, *John Calvin and John Owen on Mortification*, 59. The extent to which sanctification may be accurately described as "following upon," "flowing from," or "subsequent to" justification in Calvin's thought will be addressed later in this study.

Calvin interpreters agree that the theme of union with Christ is especially important for Calvin, so this is an entirely fair question. The easiest response is to point out the bibliographical need: there is a sizeable gap in the literature and, more importantly, in our understanding of Calvin's theology of union with Christ. Notwithstanding several essays on some aspect of the theme, only a few full-length studies have been devoted to the subject of union with Christ in Calvin to date. Tamburello's book aims to compare Calvin with Bernard on the topic, but, because he adopted a broad, comparative approach, he ends up working with Calvin only in a limited way.[75] While pertinent observations are often made, the most important questions with respect to the context and structure of Calvin's ideas are not investigated in sufficient depth. Kolfhaus's study, while perceptive and helpful, is considerably dated and differs from the present investigation both in orientation and method. On the other hand, surveys highlighting the significance and richness of Calvin's union doctrine abound. But they remain surveys. Historical-theological, contextually-sensitive investigations into the function of the union idea in relation to Calvin's *duplex gratia*, with focused reflection on the texts which are most central to the subject, remain a glaring omission in the otherwise robust corpus of Calvin scholarship.

Furthermore, when we survey the recent literature, there is an indefinable impression that, notwithstanding great advances in our knowledge of the details of Calvin's life and times, the precise shape and force of his theology, especially union with Christ, still eludes us. As demonstrated in our opening discussion, the prevailing uncertainty in the existing studies confirms this impression. Recalling the question of the scope of saving union makes the problem still clearer: Hart argues that Calvin's idea of saving union with Christ is focused on the event of the incarnation and consequently extends to all who share his humanity, while Rankin insists that saving union with Christ is reserved for the elect who are ushered into this relation by faith, and then Brglez, perhaps throwing his hands in the air as well as assuming a distinctly Barthian understanding of what should be, claims to find both views in the reformer and so concludes that he contradicted himself.

---

[75] Tamburello, *Union with Christ*. Tamburello's interpretation of Calvin is also heavily dependent upon Kolfhaus's 1939 work. To illustrate, he cites or refers to Kolfhaus in one-fourth of his footnotes to Chapter 5, "John Calvin on Union with Christ" (pp. 84-101). The other three-fourths of the footnotes to this chapter are mostly references to Calvin himself, usually from the 1559 *Institutes*.

But there is yet another consideration that we need to keep in view. On the question of the *unio Christi-duplex gratia* relationship, the general observation that the former is the context for the latter certainly stands as the consensus view. It is widely agreed that union with Christ is of fundamental importance for Calvin's soteriology, that it plays a vital role in his basic concern with the knowledge of God, that it is a rich and flexible concept embracing and characterizing aspectivally a number of other major elements in his thought, and that it rests upon trinitarian and christological presuppositions which serve to shape its significance as a soteric idea. However, there exists an immense need to move beyond the "that" of the *unio Christi-duplex gratia* relationship to the concrete "how" of union with Christ within that theological complex. Understanding this "how" is inextricably tied up with Calvin's exegesis, his polemical environment, his pedagogical interest, and the specific theological questions he intended to address, i.e., his multifaceted context. In particular, there is a need for the kind of study which, through a context-sensitive investigation of those specific texts which touch directly on the question, exegetical as well as theological and polemical, in light of the event-history of the period, would serve to illuminate further the nature of this complex of ideas in Calvin's soteriology.[76] The bibliographical need in view here is thus patently both theological and historical. And it proceeds self-consciously upon the perceptive and crucial observation by Willis-Watkins that "[e]valuating Calvin's use of the doctrine of union with Christ is a matter of tracing the way it functions differently in different contexts..."[77]

---

[76] Venema provides a useful treatment of union with Christ and appreciates its importance for Calvin's *duplex gratia* formulation. In my view, however, further, more concentrated attention, beyond that offered in Venema's study, is not only desirable but necessary. At several points in this investigation, the textual, contextual, and theological arguments put forward serve to advance, clarify, and occasionally correct Venema's more general assertions. The present thesis, therefore, functions as a focused investigation of something Venema, among others but perhaps more carefully, has recognized as a significant element of Calvin's soteriology. For his part, Brglez's thesis ("Saving Union with Christ in the Theology of John Calvin") is wholly confined to the contradiction the author purports to find in Calvin's doctrine of union with Christ.

[77] Willis-Watkins, "The Unio Mystica," 78.

Methodological Considerations

A Limited Scope of Interest

It should be added that a careful analysis of the scholarship reveals more than a gap in the literature, however. Other Calvin or Reformation studies, usually of an historical and methodological nature, supply fresh insights that clarify the most fruitful way to approach this question. Recent historical-theological studies on the complicated problem of late medieval and Reformation theological relations have prompted a new appreciation for the distinctive nature and character of both. From a methodological point of view, moreover, recent arguments for a historically, contextually sensitive reading of Calvin have fundamentally challenged the direction Calvin studies have often headed for the better part of the last century. Within this methodological shift, the attention to Calvin's theological and exegetical method as indispensable for a proper study of his theology is especially noteworthy.[78]

Predictably, the way forward lies in the sources, the texts which stand as witnesses to the culture and theological climate of a man and a day long behind us. Our approach may be described as contextual as well as theological. This means that the questions asked of Calvin and his theology will be those which serve to illuminate the significance of his ideas in their sixteenth-century context with attention to preceding and contemporary constructs. Calvin's language of union with Christ and salvation must be located in the wider context of his own maturing thought as well as the thought of his contemporaries. It is necessary throughout our investigation, therefore, to bring Calvin's exegesis and theology into conversation, when relevant, with the exegetical and theological tradition with which he was familiar and upon which he was often dependant, as well as attend to Calvin's ongoing conversation with the work of contemporaries, whether Roman Catholic, Lutheran, or Reformed.

In contrast, therefore, with a Calvin-only type of investigation, we need to operate with the assumption that if Calvin is really to be understood, it is important that we attend to his contemporaries and to their handling of the same theological problems. This is necessary not only in order to understand Calvin correctly but also to identify accurately which elements of his teaching, if any, are truly original or unique to him.

In contrast also to dominant strands in recent Calvin interpretation, the object here is to investigate the function of union

---

[78] See Muller, *Unaccommodated Calvin*, 21-38, 101-17, 140-58, for discussion.

with Christ with specific reference to the questions sixteenth-century theologians regularly addressed. In terms of the *duplex gratia* in Calvin, this means the function of union with Christ in his rejection of the charge of a "legal fiction" and in his theological defense of the necessity of good works must take on a greater prominence than questions far more reflective of distinctive twentieth, or indeed twenty-first century theological concerns.

The Case Studies: Romans, the Sacraments, and Osiander

CALVIN'S ROMANS COMMENTARY

Methodologically, the number of potentially profitable avenues of inquiry for studying Calvin on the *unio Christi* is a chief difficulty for every careful student. Because of the challenges inherent in investigating a subject of such immense scope with sufficient depth and thoroughness, it has seemed the wisest course of action to narrow the field of possible texts and events to the three deemed most directly relevant and potentially illuminating. As a result, through a series of three case studies, we will explore texts and events in which union with Christ is brought into positive relation with the *duplex gratia* in order to conclude as to the structural and formative function of union with Christ within this over-arching facet of Calvin's thought. Picking up from the opening discussion of these case studies in the Introduction, we can now say a bit more about these investigations and their importance for our question. The first of these is Calvin's commentary on the Apostle Paul's Epistle to the Romans.

Subsequent to publishing the first edition of his *Institutes* in 1536, Calvin wrote a French Catechism in 1537 and translated it into Latin in 1538.[79] More important than these earlier publications, however, are the two major works published in 1539 and 1540, texts Calvin was almost certainly working on concurrently: the second edition (1539) of his *Institutes* and the first edition (1540) of his *Commentary*

---

[79] Calvin, *Instruction et confession de foy dont on use en l'église de Genève...* (Geneva, 1537; OS 1.378-417) and *Catechismus, sive christianae religionis institutio...* (Geneva, 1538; OS 1.426-32), printed on facing pages in COR III/2. Both of these catechisms, as well as the 1536 *Institutes*, have been translated into English: *Instruction in Faith (1537)*, trans. and ed. Paul T. Fuhrmann (Louisville: Westminster/John Knox, 1992); *Catechism 1538*, trans. and ed. Ford Lewis Battles, in I. John Hesselink, *Calvin's First Catechism: A Commentary* (Louisville: Westminster/John Knox, 1997), 1-38; and *Institutes of the Christian Religion* (1536 edition), ed. Ford Lewis Battles (rev. ed.; Grand Rapids: Meeter Center/Eerdmans, 1986).

on *Romans*. Compared with the first edition, the 1539 *Institutes* represents a fundamental and decisive shift in approach. The small, earlier work was expanded to seventeen chapters which would become the basic text for all later revisions. Importantly, Calvin introduced into this second edition something which would appear in every subsequent edition: a prefatory Letter to the Reader. The combination of this prefatory Letter with the Preface to his 1540 Romans commentary provides a wealth of insight into the plan or method he would carry out in his exegetical and theological labors.[80]

In the epistle dedicatory for his *Romans* Calvin distinguishes his approach. In short, whereas Bucer used his commentary both to exegete the text and discuss theological topics or *loci*, and Melanchthon chiefly to expound *loci*, Calvin would separate the two exercises into distinct publications. The discussions in his commentaries would be restricted to exegesis of the text. The *loci* that emerged from this study of the text would be organized and explained in the *Institutes*.[81] For Calvin, the exegesis of the biblical text and the presentation and defense of theological *topoi* are discussed separately. Two distinct but intimately related exercises, mutually dependent and mutually corrective, are in Calvin's writings represented by two distinct genres. This procedure, which has been called Calvin's "twofold division of labor,"[82] has specific implications for how Calvin's theology should be investigated. Rather than examine the 1559 *Institutes* while making only collateral use of the commentaries and sermons, sensitivity to the way this exegetical-doctrinal symbiosis worked out in Calvin's ongoing ministry is essential to a proper interpretation of his thought. As Steinmetz has pointed out, "There is a reciprocal relationship in Calvin's exegetical work between his struggle with the biblical text and the continuous revisions of his systematic position in successive editions of the *Institutes of the Christian Religion*."[83]

---

[80] See Muller, *Unaccommodated Calvin*, 21-38 for an insightful study of Calvin's use of Prefaces, "Arguments," and Letters to the Reader.

[81] Calvin, "To Simon Grynaeus," 18 October, 1539, in *Iohannis Calvini Commentarius in Epistolam Pauli ad Romanos*, T. H. L. Parker and D. C. Parker, eds. (COR II/13; Geneva: Librarie Droz, 1999) (abbreviated herein as "*Comm. Epist. ad Romanos*"), 3-6; CNTC, 1-4.

[82] Muller, *Unaccommodated Calvin*, 21-38; cf. Elsie A. McKee, "Exegesis, Theology, and the *Institutes*: A Methodological Suggestion," in McKee and Armstrong, eds, *Probing the Reformed Tradition*, 154-72; and Muller, *Unaccommodated Calvin*, 28-9.

[83] David C. Steinmetz, *Calvin in Context* (New York: Oxford University Press, 1995), 130.

Calvin was able admirably to carry out this self-imposed "division of labor" for the whole of his career. He was able to comment on nearly the entire Bible and simultaneously bring his *Institutes* to its final, 1559 edition. Because the 1539 *Institutes* may on this basis appear uniquely important, it may be thought that its existence would render the examination of the 1540 Romans commentary unnecessary. This would underestimate the significance of Calvin's *Romans*, however, not only for the study of his thought but also as a published text in his day. A perusal of the important studies by T. H. L. Parker brings us to the provisional conclusion that the genre of Romans commentating was uniquely a mark of the sixteenth century.[84] Parker's list of fourteen separate studies on the Epistle in a span of thirteen years (1529-1542) justifies his question, "Have so many ever been published in a comparable period in any other century?"[85] Indeed, Calvin's own commentary (Strasbourg, 1540) was preceded by the reputed efforts of Melanchthon (1522), Bucer (1536), and Bullinger (1537),[86] to name only a few. Calvin's own remarks in his dedicatory letter to Simon Grynaeus of Basel reveal his appreciation for these recently published ventures as well as his acknowledgement of the potential

---

[84] For a comparison of some of these commentaries, see T. H. L. Parker *Commentaries on Romans 1532-1542* (Edinburgh: T. & T. Clark, 1986). Cf. idem, *Calvin's New Testament Commentaries* (Edinburgh: T. & T. Clark, 1971; 2nd ed. 1993). Particularly helpful is the informative introduction by T. H. L. Parker and D. C. Parker to the critical edition, *Comm. Epist. ad Romanos*. This introduction includes extensive discussion of Calvin's exegetical method, the Greek and Latin texts, and the publication history of the commentary. The text is a scanned copy of a critical text produced earlier under the same title (SHCT 22; Leiden: E. J. Brill, 1981), revised with an expanded introduction according to the format of the new series. This critical introduction should be supplemented with BC 1.74-7.

[85] Parker, *Commentaries on Romans*, viii. Steinmetz lists more than seventy published in the sixteenth century (*Calvin in Context*, 217-20). As Steinmetz notes, Parker's treatment is of limited use for it does not take into account the important editions of patristic and medieval commentators published during the same period. Parker only discusses commentaries published by sixteenth-century authors.

[86] Melanchthon, *Dispositio orat. in Epist. Pauli ad Romanos* (1529; CR 15:443-92); idem, *Commentarii in Epist. Pauli ad Romanos...*, (1532; rev. twice in 1540; cited as "*Commentarii*" from CR 15:493-796); idem, *Epistolae Pauli scriptae ad Romanos Enarratio...* (1556; in CR 15:797-1052); Bucer, *Metaphrases et Enarrationes Perpetuae Epistolarum D. Pauli Apostoli...* (1536); Bullinger, *In Omnes Apostolicas Epistolas... Commentarii Heinrychi Bullingeri...* (1539).

difficulties in bringing yet another Romans commentary before the reading public.[87]

When the content of the Epistle is in view, moreover, the value of Calvin's *Romans* for this investigation is still more self-evident. Because so many of the enormous sixteenth century questions have a place in the body of the Epistle itself – justice and grace, sin and guilt, justification and sanctification, together with predestination, baptism, and union with Christ – Calvin's *Commentary* affords an opportunity to explore his understanding of their relations within the scope of just one publication.[88] A further advantage, of course, is the opportunity to compare and contrast Calvin's own approach and conclusions with respect to specific texts with the approaches and conclusions of his predecessors and contemporaries, some of whom, like Melanchthon and Bucer, would apparently exert no small influence on his thought.

To be more specific, the first and second main sections of the Epistle as identified by Calvin (chapters 1-4 and 5-8) include classic texts on justification, sanctification, and union with Christ, and Calvin relates each of these topics to the others in the body of his *Commentary* in a way that warrants close attention. As his *Argumentum* reveals, for example, Calvin sees justification in Christ as the "main subject" of Romans, introduces sanctification "which we obtain in Christ" as the inextricable partner of justification, and identifies baptism as that by which believers are "admitted into fellowship with Christ" (*per quem in Christi participationem initiamur*), the result of which fellowship or participation is death and life in Christ as well as peace with God.[89] His laudatory language of Romans as an "open door" through which the reader has access "to all the most profound treasures of Scripture,"[90] taken together with

---

[87] One reason for the high number of commentaries may appear to lie in the ecclesiastical and theological turmoil of the day, but, as Parker notes (*Commentaries on Romans*, viii-x), this may not entirely have been the case. Examination of the commentaries reveals that the expected invective between Roman and Reformation exegesis of Paul is, for those published in the 1530s at least, largely non-existent.

[88] For a fuller appreciation of Calvin's soteriology in his early years it is necessary to compare the 1540 *Romans* to the 1536 and especially 1539 editions of the *Institutes*. Such an approach has largely been neglected. See for exceptions, Parker, "Calvin the Exegete: Change and Development," in W. H. Neuser, ed., *CED*, 33-46; and Benoit Girardin, *Rhétorique et théologique* (Paris: Beauchesne, 1979) who compares the commentary with the 1536 *Institutes*.

[89] Calvin, *Comm. Epist. ad Romanos*, 7-10; CNTC, 5-8.

[90] Calvin, *Comm. Epist. ad Romanos*, 7; CNTC, 5.

the above considerations, justifies giving careful attention to this text.

Furthermore, in examining Calvin's exegetical writings, one is able to do so drawing on the considerable work done in this field in recent years. In terms of volume, the sixteenth century was a period marked by the explosion of biblical commentary. The ties that bind this period of biblical interpretation to the one before it are strong indeed, but there were important and far-reaching changes as well, induced by the tumultuous nature of the reforming movement. Because the *sola Scriptura* principle of the Reformation had at its disposal the considerable advances in literary methods yielded by Renaissance scholarship, unprecedented ventures were made into the discovery of the meaning of the sacred text. Appreciating this phenomenon, the sixteenth century is receiving increased scholarly attention as a fertile period of biblical interpretation. Indeed, the essays and monographs form a body of literature so significant that Richard Gamble has rightly spoken of a "renaissance of interest in exegetical history."[91] This applies especially to studies in Calvin's exegesis, studies that vary considerably with topics ranging from his interpretation of specific passages and hermeneutical method[92] to his

---

[91] Gamble, "Current Trends," 93. As Gamble notes, this "renaissance" is amply indicated by the regular meetings at the University of Geneva to discuss sixteenth-century exegesis. Gamble notes the special significance of the volume by Alexandre Ganoczy and Stefan Scheld, *Die Hermeneutik Calvins: Geistesgeschichtliche Voraussetzungen und Grundzüge* (Wiesbaden: F. Steiner, 1983).

[92] See especially the fine studies in Steinmetz, *Calvin in Context*, and the stimulating collection of essays in Richard A. Muller and John L. Thompson, eds, *Biblical Interpretation in the Era of the Reformation: Essays Presented to David Steinmetz in Honor of His Sixtieth Birthday* (Grand Rapids: Eerdmans, 1996). See also Irena Backus, "Aristotelianism in Some of Calvin's and Beza's Expository and Exegetical Writings on the Doctrine of the Trinity with Particular Reference to the Terms *ousia* and *hypostasis*," in O. Fatio and P. Fraenkel, eds, *Histoire de l'exégèse au XVIe siècle* (Geneva: Librarie Droz, 1978), 351-60; Elsie A. McKee, *John Calvin on the Diaconate and Liturgical Almsgiving* (Geneva: Librarie Droz, 1984); idem, *Elders and the Plural Ministry: The Role of Exegetical History in Illuminating John Calvin's Theology* (Geneva: Librarie Droz, 1988); Richard A. Muller, "The Hermeneutic of Promise and Fulfillment in Calvin's Exegesis of the Old Testament Prophecies of the Kingdom," in Steinmetz, ed., *The Bible in the Sixteenth Century*, 68-82; T. H. L. Parker, "Calvin the Biblical Expositor," *The Churchman*, 78 (1964): 23-31; idem, "Calvin the Exegete: Change and Development," in W. Neuser, ed., *CED*, 33-46; Barbara Pitkin, *What Pure Eyes Could See*; Susan Schreiner, "Through a Mirror Dimly: Calvin's Sermons on Job," *CTJ* 21 (1986): 175-93; and David F. Wright, "Calvin's Pentateuchal Criticism:

relationship to the exegetical tradition.[93] As far as Calvin's method is concerned, Gamble concludes that there is a general consensus that "*brevitas et facilitas*" sums up well the reformer's guiding principles.[94]

In addition to Calvin's method, his practice, in several significant instances at least, of returning to his commentaries years later to revise and expand them points to a further avenue of inquiry. Specifically with reference to the Romans commentary, the edition of 1540 was expanded twice, slightly in 1551 but greatly in 1556. Concerning this final edition, Parker notes that Romans 8 receives considerably more comment. He then points to the significance of this expansion in relation to Book 3 of the 1559 *Institutio*, concluding there is a strong relationship between the growth of Calvin's commentary on Romans 8 and the development of Book 3.[95]

This is precisely the kind of relationship with which this study is concerned: how do Calvin's exegetical labors (and the revisions of his publications, such as the *Romans* expansions of 1556) reflect the maturation of his doctrinal ideas within a changing context? Because Calvin was able, between the 1540 and 1551 editions of *Romans*, to comment on all the Pauline letters, do the 1556 revisions indicate a theological sharpening of Calvin's exposition of the Epistle in light of polemical concerns?[96]

Equity, Hardness of Heart, and Divine Accommodation in the Mosaic Harmony Commentary," *CTJ* 21 (1986): 33-50.

[93] The studies noted immediately above also include this element, of course, but here see as examples: A. Ganoczy and S. Scheld, *Herrschaft-Tugend-Vorsehung* (Wiesbaden: F. Steiner, 1982) who argue in favor of Stoic influences on Calvin; for investigations into the influence of Chrysostom upon Calvin's exegesis, see A. Ganoczy and K. Müller, *Calvins Handschriftlighe Annotationem zu Chrysostomus* (Wiesbaden: Steiner, 1983) and John R. Walchenbach, "John Calvin as Biblical Commentator: An Investigation into Calvin's Use of John Chrysostom as an Exegetical Tutor," Ph.D. diss. (University of Pittsburgh), 1974.

[94] Gamble, "Current Trends," 94. See Gamble, "Brevitas et facilitas: Toward an Understanding of Calvin's Hermeneutic," *WTJ* 47 (1985): 1-17; idem, "Exposition and Method in Calvin," *WTJ* 49 (1987): 153-65. See also Steinmetz, "John Calvin on Isaiah 6," 158; and Schreiner, "Through a Mirror Dimly," 191.

[95] Parker, "Calvin the Exegete," 41: "It would be misleading to particularize too closely the nature of the passages in question, for they deal with as many topics as Rom. 8 itself; but there is surely a relationship between the growth of the commentary on this chapter and the development of the material which became Book III of the 1559 *Institutio*."

[96] Parker, "Calvin the Exegete," 34-5. Note Parker's rejection of this possibility is due to his observation that the *Argumentum* remains unchanged throughout the revisions.

SALVATION, SACRAMENT, AND THE STRATA OF UNION WITH CHRIST

The relationship between Calvin's *unio Christi-duplex gratia* soteriology and his eucharistic theology of a "spiritual," non-local communion with Christ is also promising. In particular, this relationship highlights the importance of Calvin's polemical environment for the interpretation of his theology, especially for emphases found frequently in his work in the 1550s. In view of the time spanned by the eucharistic controversies, however, and because Calvin published a number of pieces on the Supper, it is difficult to point to one particular event in this ongoing controversy that proved more decisive than others in revealing how Calvin understood the spiritual communion enjoyed by believers in the Supper. As a result, we will restrict attention in this case study to a series of parallels of expression and argument in which Calvin defines his eucharistic perspective using the language of his soteriological construct. The focus here, as elsewhere, is on how the sacraments serve, as Calvin repeatedly states, to point believers to their union with Christ.

Especially in his debates with Westphal and later with Heshusius, one finds Calvin explaining and defending his views on the real, spiritual presence of Christ in the Supper by qualifying and clarifying the nature of our fellowship with him there by the Spirit. It is in Calvin's refutation of the Lutheran *manducatio impiorum* or *infidelium* (eucharistic "eating by unbelievers"), moreover, that one finds him dealing specifically with the idea of union with Christ in a way that merits close attention. Calvin is adamant in his rejection of this idea, insisting that the faithless "are not united to Christ by the bonds of mystical union nor do they participate in the benefits of his death and resurrection."[97] For Calvin, there is no redemptive blessing that comes to the faithless apart from the union which, by faith, entails their participation in his saving benefits. The prominence of the idea of union with Christ throughout Calvin's engagement with his Lutheran opponents on sacramental questions is noteworthy, inasmuch as christological and pneumatological questions persistently lie in the background of these discussions.[98]

---

[97] Calvin's view is well-summarized in David Steinmetz, "Calvin and His Lutheran Critics," *The Lutheran Quarterly* 4 (1990): 179-94; rep. in Steinmetz, *Calvin in Context*, 172-86. See the latter, p. 180, for this quotation. For Calvin against Heshusius here, see CO 9.477.

[98] The controversy over the *"extra Calvinisticum"* is a fine example. See the important study by E. David Willis-Watkins, *Calvin's Catholic Christology: The Function of the So-Called Extra Calvinisticum in Calvin's Theology* (SMRT 2; Leiden: E. J. Brill, 1966); and the essay by Heiko A. Oberman, "The 'Extra' Dimension in

This points to the inter-connectedness and complexity of these concepts in sixteenth-century discourse.

Recognition of this inter-connectedness and complexity prompts several converging lines of inquiry pursued in this study. For example, is Calvin's 1555 correspondence with Peter Martyr Vermigli, in which he agrees that there is a distinction between "mystical" and "spiritual" union with Christ,[99] reflective of a wider series of distinctions in his thought, or does this distinction stand somewhat alone? In addition, how do these distinct "unions" relate to the *duplex gratia*? In their expositions of this correspondence, Tamburello, Rankin, and Trumper suggest that "mystical" is roughly correlative to "definitive" (i.e., justifying) and "spiritual" to "progressive" (i.e., sanctifying) union.[100]

The combination of Calvin's christological-sacramental-soteriological parallels, his theological response to the specific *manducatio impiorum* theory, and his focused correspondence with Vermigli on the meaning of union with Christ point to the indispensability of accounting fully for the controversial context of Calvin's *unio Christi-duplex gratia* soteriology. Most basically, the justification for pursuing these explicitly sacramental questions in a study concentrated on an explicitly soteriological construction is simply that, for Calvin, "[t]he Sacraments of Baptism and the Lord's Supper were instituted by Christ in order to make this union continually effective in the life of the Church, and to impress upon us continually that this union is the source of our justification and sanctification."[101]

CALVIN *CONTRA* OSIANDER

It is especially in the discussions surrounding the theology of the Lutheran controversialist Andreas Osiander (1498-1552), however, that one encounters Calvin fully involved in defending his soteriology as it relates to union with Christ. Osiander, Reformer of Lutheran Nuremberg, became a professor there after the Leipzig Interim. He would later become a professor on the theological

---

the Theology of Calvin," in Oberman, *The Dawn of the Reformation: Essays in Late Medieval and Reformation Thought* (Edinburgh: T. & T. Clark), 234-58.

[99] Calvin to Vermigli, 8 August 1555, CO 43.722-5.

[100] Tamburello, *Union with Christ*, 86-7; Rankin, "Carnal Union with Christ," 183-5; and Timothy J. R. Trumper, "An Historical Study of the Doctrine of Adoption in the Calvinistic Tradition," Ph.D. thesis (University of Edinburgh, 2001), 38-214.

[101] Wallace, *Calvin's Doctrine of the Christian Life*, 18-19.

faculty at Königsberg and there attacked Melanchthon's imputative doctrine of justification at his inaugural disputation.[102] When Osiander later took up the doctrine of justification at length, he found himself quite at odds not only with Calvin but also with his fellow Lutherans.

Osiander published two critical treatises on justification in 1551 with Melanchthon's forensic doctrine as his chief opponent.[103] Osiander taught a controversial doctrine of justification via the indwelling of Christ's divinity. Calvin strongly opposed several elements in Osiander's teaching but especially the relationship of Christ's divinity to our humanity in justification. The nature of the disagreement was such that the definition and application of saving union with Christ to justification took center stage.

The Calvin-Osiander scholarship has been complicated by the recent entrance of a growing body of literature that argues in Osiander's defense, recasting him as a tragic hero of the Reformation rather than as a schismatic aberration.[104] It is often Osiander's fidelity to Luther or the internal consistency of his development of Luther's theology of justification that receives special attention. In these reassessments, Osiander's fusion of justification and union with Christ in a manner that suggested, at least to his opponents, that the forensic concept was rejected in favor of a more essentialist position is largely defended. The questions for Calvin-Osiander investigations have now become: is Osiander's teaching a more consistent appreciation, as he insisted, of the significance of union with Christ for justification; or is it a departure from Luther and received Reformation orthodoxy as well as a return, in part, to Rome? Is Osiander's theology a defense of the gospel against Melanchthonian objectivism or is it in fact, as Calvin insisted, a "mingling" or "fusion" of what is properly divine and human in the

---

[102] Steinmetz, *Reformers in the Wings*, 94. See pp. 91-9 for Steinmetz's helpful summary of Osiander's life and teaching.

[103] Andreas Osiander, *Ein Disputation von der Rechtfertigung des Glaubens* (Königsberg, 1551); and *De Unico Mediatore Iesu Christo et Iustificatione Fidei: Confessio Andreae Osiandri* (Königsberg, 1551). See fuller publication information in Chapter 5 below.

[104] See, e.g., Gunter Zimmermann, "Die Thesen Osianders zur Disputation 'de iustificatione'," *Kerygma und Dogma* 33 (1987): 224-44; idem, "Calvins Auseinandersetzung mit Osianders Rechtfertigungslehre," *Kerygma und Dogma* 35 (1989): 236-56; and Stephen Strehle, "Imputatio iustitiae: Its Origin in Melanchthon, its Opposition in Osiander," *Theologische Zeitschrift* 50 (1994): 201-19. See the literature noted in Chapter 5 below.

acceptance of sinners and therefore a threat to the doctrine of justification as well as the Person of the Mediator?[105]

Read in light of his controversial context, Calvin's response reveals that the complicated interdependence of ideas involved in the Reformed disagreement with Lutheran Christology and sacramentology extended beyond questions of *modus praesentiae* and the Supper's efficacy. It is this particular facet of Calvin's polemic which is brought to the fore in this case study. In sum, the Calvin-Osiander debate displays with clarity the precise points where Christology, pneumatology, and soteriology intersect in the matrix of Calvin's thought. Throughout his objection to Osiander, Calvin further clarifies *what* union with Christ means and *how* it relates justification and sanctification. The nature of these clarifications needs to be understood if Calvin's interaction with Osiander is, as it may be, the most promising and yet under-examined polemical source for understanding the function or role of union with Christ in the structural relations of his soteriology.

Conclusion

Calvin's doctrine of saving union with Christ is the fruit of his reception (and rejection!) of antecedent and contemporary conceptions, supplemented, re-shaped, and sometimes entirely replaced by the yield of his own exegetical labors as they were undertaken in an historically unique polemical and pastoral environment. Inasmuch, then, as the events and publications which marked Calvin's days of ministry signal a series of developments in which union with Christ lies either at the center or in the background of discussion, one is justified in paying the closest attention to these events and publications in order more precisely to determine the function of this idea within the over-arching twin themes of his soteriology, as well as the shape the idea itself assumes. More specifically, Calvin's multifaceted labors offer an avenue by which one may examine the maturation and employment of this doctrinal construct in the midst of its complicated historical conditionality. In Calvin's extensive involvement in the eucharistic controversies of his day; in his engagement with the controversial teaching of Osiander; in his wrestling with sacred Scripture; in his correspondence with Vermigli and in his opening words to Book 3 of the 1559 *Institutio*; one sees Calvin's orthodox Christology, pneumatological sacramentology, and trinitarian soteriology intersecting frequently at the point of union with Christ and the

---

[105] See Wendel, *Calvin*, 236.

duplex gratia. Behind the most compelling features of Calvin's teaching on justification and sanctification stands a controlling understanding of what it means to be united to Christ and, thus, to enjoy his saving benefits. In view of these considerations, it remains only to describe and catalogue, in brief terms, the models and language of union with Christ leading up to Calvin's day before we are in a position to explore his approach to the problem of conditional language in Romans.

CHAPTER TWO

Union with Christ and Saving Righteousness: Anticipations, Proposals, and Trajectories

Introduction: The Diverse Prehistory of Calvin's Construction

Connecting union with Christ with justification did not, of course, have its origin in Calvin. Early on the twofold Augustinian inheritance of a rich union idea and an essentially *duplex iustitia* model of salvation, the association of incorporation into Christ with the need and promise of saving righteousness had a storied development, a mixed prehistory, leading up to Calvin's day that provides necessary perspective on his thought. At least two distinct but related historical-theological strands converge upon our subject. The first of these strands is the complex development spanning late medieval and Reformation perspectives on the nature of justification and, employing the Reformation distinction, its relation to sanctification. Second is the direction and impact of parallel religious developments in mystical theology and in medieval preaching upon the theological and ecclesiastical uses of *unio Christi* language.[1] The special significance of this second strand rests in the impact of late medieval ruminations on mystical union with Christ upon Luther and the shaping of early Reformation teaching on justification, teaching with which Calvin was intimately acquainted.

However, the development of doctrine from the fifteenth to the sixteenth centuries is notorious for its complexity. In attempting to account for the matrix of ideas floating around in the sixteenth-century "air" in such a way as to provide a specific context for Calvin's soteriology, one inevitably encounters the difficult question

---

[1] The studies by Steven Ozment of the "scholastic" and "spiritual" traditions and by Marcia L. Colish of the medieval intellectual background to subsequent theological systems are immensely helpful for coming to grips with the multifaceted contexts which shaped sixteenth-century thinking. See Ozment, *The Age of Reform 1250-1550: An Intellectual and Religious History of Late Medieval and Reformation Europe* (New Haven: Yale University Press, 1980), 22-134; and Colish, *Medieval Foundations of the Western Intellectual Tradition, 400-1400* (Yale Intellectual History of the West; New Haven and London: Yale University Press, 1997).

of the precise relationship of late medieval and Reformation theologies. Importantly, this complexity prohibits painting this canvas with too wide a brush. Instead, particularly when the idea of salvation is in view, the question becomes one not only of, more broadly, "continuity and discontinuity," but more specifically, contexts and directions. While a full survey would be well worth the effort, attention is necessarily restricted here to select, context-establishing observations. This restriction, moreover, should guard against presenting a survey of ideas which is too general and, thus, ultimately unhelpful.

An Overlooked First Question: Taxonomies of Union with Christ

Again, analyses of "the" late medieval or Reformation doctrine of union with Christ are ordinarily less than useful. Though an important degree of agreement did obtain, the diversity of late medieval spiritual currents resists simple categorization. Indeed, the varieties of mystical theology defined and characterized the nature, manner (*modus*), bond (*nexus* or *vinculum*), and consummation of union with God or Christ in ways that reflected their divergent views on the knowledge of God and the experience of grace. In light of this diversity, instead of moving immediately into an inquiry of Calvin's teaching on union with Christ, it is advisable to ask first what "union" with God or Christ meant to theologians in Calvin's and the preceding generations. Omitting this exercise risks confusing sixteenth-century understandings with one's own, a step that leads decisively away from the goal of a faithful interpretation.

Unio *and* Communio *in the* Dictionnaire de Spiritualité *and Altenstaig's 1517* Lexicon Theologicum

This taxonomical problem can be alleviated somewhat by using two uniquely useful resources. A revealing index to the theology of late medieval nominalism (and particularly Gabriel Biel's place in it), Johannes Altenstaig's 1517 *Lexicon theologicum* supplies a much-needed contemporary witness to the various uses of the terminology of union with Christ.[2] In Altenstaig, the often subtle distinctions

---

[2] Johannes Altenstaig, *Vocabularius theologiae complectens vocabulorum descriptiones...* (Hagenau, 1517); reprinted as *Lexicon theologicum quo tanquam clave theologiae fores aperiuntur...* (Cologne, 1619). Altenstaig's *Vocabularius theologiae* was printed in Hagenau and Mindelheim (1517), Lyon (1579 and 1580), Venice (1579, 1580, and 1583), Antwerp (1576), and Cologne (1619). From 1619 it was usually reprinted as *Lexicon theologicum*. For use here, I have

among terms are arranged alphabetically with regular reference to the quintessential nominalist, Biel, and the highly regarded late medieval mystic, Jean Gerson (the two cited most frequently by Altenstaig),[3] as well as Augustine, Aquinas, Bonaventure, Scotus, Gregory of Rimini, and others. Combining Altenstaig with Michel Dupuy's article "union à Dieu" in the impressive seventeen-volume *Dictionnaire de Spiritualité* serves as a useful and reliable point of departure.[4]

UNION, CONJUNCTION, COMMUNION, AND
DIVINIZATION/DEIFICATION IN THE *DICTIONNAIRE DE SPIRITUALITÉ*

Dupuy provides a catalog of four *"perspectives chrétiennes"* which focuses upon pre-Reformation models. First, in Athenagoras, Irenaeus, and Gregory of Nyssa, the language of "union" or "unification" (*henosis*) typically belongs to christological discussion of the relation of Christ's divinity and humanity, or, more generally, the possibility of a union of humanity with the eternal Word. As a

---

consulted the 1517 (Hagenau) edition but will cite from the more accessible reprint, *Lexicon Theologicum* (Hildesheim: Georg Olms Verlag, 1974), referred to hereafter as "Altenstaig, *Lexicon theologicum*." On Altenstaig, see Jan Noble Pendergrass, "Humanismus und Theologie in Johannes Altenstaigs *Opus pro conficiundis epistolis* (1512)," Paper for the 2001 Munich conference, "'Germania latina - latinitas teutonica': Politics, Science, and Humanist Culture from the Late Middle Ages to the Present;" and the useful essay by Friedrich Zoepfl, *Johannes Altenstaig: Ein Gelehrtenleben aus der Zeit des Humanismus und der Reformation* (Münster in Westf.: Verlag der Aschendorffschen Verlagshandlung, 1918). For biographical information, see *Die Neue Deutsche Biographie*, I, 215-6 and *Dictionnaire d'Histoire et de Géographie Ecclésiastiques*, II, 797-8. H. Oberman also discusses the importance in late medieval nominalism of Altenstaig's *Vocabularius* in *The Harvest of Medieval Theology: Gabriel Biel and Late Medieval Nominalism* (Harvard, 1963; rep. Grand Rapids: Baker, 2000), 18-20.

[3] As Oberman notes (*Harvest of Medieval Theology*, 18), Altenstaig's use of Biel indicates both Biel's importance in late medieval theology and the fact that Altenstaig evidently favored and was influenced by Biel's nominalism. As Oberman also notes (p. 332, n. 25), the fact that Gerson, a mystical theologian, is cited second only to Biel demonstrates the compatibility of nominalism with mysticism. Altenstaig uses Gerson as the main authority for such mystical terms as "assimilatio" and "abyssus."

[4] Michel Dupuy, "Union à Dieu," s.v., *Dictionnaire de Spiritualité Ascétique et Mystique Doctrine et Histoire*, 17 vols, orig. ed. M. Viller, et al., cont. ed. A. Derville, et al. (Paris: Beauchesne, 1994), vol. 16, cols. 40-61. A fuller examination would require an investigation, certainly involving Altenstaig, into the wider range of mystical and spiritualist vocabulary. Also, in addition to Altenstaig and Dupuy, the reader will find that numerous articles on mysticism and the spiritualist traditions often use different taxonomies or categorizations.

mystery beyond comprehension, this union is supremely a matter of faith.[5] The same term is also used, however, to describe an intimate experience offered to the faithful which appears to be modeled after the christological relation. Here, as in Neo-Platonism, "union" signifies the inner unity in which one rejects the external and separates from that which is "below" to be a part of, involuntarily, that upon which one meditates. In early Christian theology, Athanasius saw this union as an imitation of the union enjoyed by the divine persons of the Trinity, and it seems Cyril pointed to a similarly understood union in the Spirit not possible through the Law but through the Son.[6] This perspective is more commonly associated with Pseudo-Dionysius, however, and brings into view a most intimate union with God, an eschatological union with the eternal Logos made possible by the redemptive work of the Son.[7]

Second, "junction" or "conjunction" (*synapheia*) is found frequently in Basil. It also is christological, and typical of the Antiochene perspective on how the flesh is assumed – "joined" (or "conjoined") – to divinity in Christ's person.[8]

A third term, "communion" (*koinonia*), brings us closer to what would become a more standard concept. *Koinonia* too is used to refer to the relationship of the Father and the Son or of divinity with human flesh in Christ, but is more frequently used for the fellowship enjoyed by the faithful with God or Christ. Usage would seem to indicate this is the term most often used in Christian literature to designate this relationship, whereas "union" is, as Altenstaig's *Lexicon* also indicates, more frequently (though not exclusively) used for christological purposes.

The last term introduced by Dupuy is "divinization" or "deification," also termed *theosis*. This is of course the concept connected with Eastern literature, and refers, following the language of 2 Peter 1:4, to communication with the divine nature. Like the

---

[5] Dupuy, "Union à Dieu," col. 45; cf. Athenagoras, *Legatio pro christianis* 10.3 (PG 6.909b); Gregory of Nyssa, *Or. Cat.* 10 (PG 45.41d). All citations noted in this summary of the *Dictionnaire* are listed by Dupuy.

[6] Dupuy, "Union à Dieu," col. 45; cf. Cyril of Alexandria, *In Os.* 28.3 (PG 72.52d).

[7] For more on *henosis*-union see the noteworthy study by Ysabel de Andia, *Henosis: L'Union à Dieu chez Denys l'Aréopagite* (Philosophia Antiqua 71; Leiden: E. J. Brill, 1996).

[8] Dupuy, "Union à Dieu," col. 46; cf. Basil, *In Is.* II, 66 (PG 30.233b, etc.). Note also (col. 46): "Ce terme de conjunction indique plus clairement que celui d'union la relation à un autre. Aussi le complete-t-il souvent pour éviter qu'on pense seulement à l'unification de la vie intérieure et suggérer l'union a Dieu. En bien des cas, tout comme 'union,' 'conjonction' est pris dans un sens abstrait où la reference à l'expérience ne paraît plus."

previous terms, it also is used to refer to the christological relationship of humanity and divinity, but is more often applied to the faithful who are "deified," e.g., in Clement of Alexandria, and Athanasius. Usage varies considerably, but what is evidently intended in the patristic literature is an eschatological transformation to the divine resemblance and to incorruptibility and immortality, frequently described as a quasi-ontological participation in the divine attributes or in the divine life of the Trinity.[9]

In addition to the terminology used, however, appreciating the various understandings of the mode of union is also important. Is union with God or Christ a union of knowledge as in Pseudo-Dionysius, Gregory of Nyssa and possibly Augustine who paralleled an attachment to truth (*inhaerere veritati*) with an attachment to God (*inhaerere Deo*)?[10] Or is it a union of desire and fruition as in Hugh of St. Victor and Thomas Aquinas (love as greater than knowledge) or Duns Scotus (the *visio Dei* as fruition)?[11] Or is it rather a union of wills, or is it a physical union?[12]

"COMMUNIO" IN ALTENSTAIG'S *LEXICON THEOLOGICUM*

The entry under *unio* in Altenstaig's *Lexicon* collates the opinions of Augustine, Biel, Gerson, Brulefer, and others. Though largely concerned with christological distinctions, the term is distinguished into *corporalis* and *spiritualis*, with mystical experience discussed only with reference to the latter.[13] Gerson and Bonaventure are cited twice each under *communio*, which treats the communion among believers and of the Church with Christ.[14] In Bonaventure communion is threefold (*triplex*). The first is a *spiritualis oratio* with reference to inner desire, the second is *corporalis* and has to do with externals, and the third, *quaedam medio modo*, is sacramental.[15]

---

[9] Dupuy, "Union à Dieu," cols. 46, 48; cf. Clement of Alexandria, *Prot.* 9 (PG 8.197c); Athanasius, *De Incarn.* 54; Basil, *De Spiritu Sancto* (PG 32.110); and Gregory Naz., *Or.* 31 or *Theol.* 5.4. See Kenneth Paul Wesche, "Eastern Orthodox Spirituality: Union with God in Theosis," *Theology Today* 56 (1999): 29-43.
[10] Dupuy, "Union à Dieu," cols. 52-4; cf. Pseudo-Dionysius, *Noms divins* 7.4 (PG 3.872); Gregory of Nyssa, *In Cant.* 6; Maximus the Confessor, *Scholia in... Divinis Nominibus* (PG 4.353c).
[11] Dupuy, "Union à Dieu," cols. 54-5; cf. Hugh of St. Victor, *Exp. in Hier. coel.* (PL 175.1038-9); Thomas Aquinas, *ST* 1a IIae, q. 28, art. 1.
[12] See Dupuy, "Union à Dieu," cols. 55-7.
[13] Altenstaig, *Lexicon theologicum*, fols. 967b-8b.
[14] Altenstaig, *Lexicon theologicum*, fols. 161b-2a.
[15] Altenstaig, *Lexicon theologicum*, fol. 161b: "Communio est triplex secundum S. Bona. d.18.p.2.q.1.*lib*.4. Quaedam spiritualis oratio, et haec est quantum ad

A summary of Gerson receives more attention. There is a natural union which is universal, a union which equips all pilgrims (*viatores*) for glory, and a union of predestination and final grace.[16] Eck is listed at comparative length with a fourfold union model: first, a faith-sacramental union in the blood of Christ; second, a communion of grace in which the faithful communicate with their Head, Jesus Christ, in a fellowship all the righteous have in the grace of God; third, a communion of merit, of which love is the bond; and, fourth, a communion of glory belonging to the church triumphant in heaven.[17]

---

dilectionem interiorem. Quaedam corporalis, et haec est quantum ad exteriorem conversationem. Quaedam medio modo: et haec est quantum ad sacramentorum susceptionem, et praecipue quantum ad sacramentum altaris. Et a prima nullus potest nec debet excludi (ut inquit *Bona*.) quamdiu est viator: nec excommunicatio dicit privationem illius communionis. Quantum ad sacramentalem excluditur quilibet qui dicitur excommunicatus maiore vel minore excommunicatione. Quantum ad conversationem exteriorem attenditur excommunicatio maior, in qua communicatio negatur secundum actus legitimos, qui attenduntur in quinque, scilicet in osculo, in colloquio, in convivio, in oratorio, in valefaciendo. Haec *Bona*. videatur *Alex*.p.2.q.181.m.10."

[16] Altenstaig, *Lexicon theologicum*, fols. 161b-2a: "Est communio naturae, a qua nullus excipitur: Est communio secundum aptitudinem ad gloriam, et ab ista nullus viator excipitur, quia Deus vult omnes homines salvos fieri. Est communio praedestinationis et gratiae finalis, et ab illa omnes reprobi vivi et mortui excommunicantur vel excipiuntur. Est et communio aliqua in gratia meritis secundum praesentem iustitiam tantummodo, etc. sic est aliqua excommunicatio secundum praesentem iniustitiam et demeritum. Rursus aliqua est secundum praesentis Ecclesiae inrinsecum iudicium per sententias irregularitatum et excommunicationum initiate. Haec Gers. Et communio sanctorum dicitur societas quae est in coelo, vel sanctorum communio, hoc est susfragia, quae communicamus, vel communio, id est, Eucharistia (ut idem Gers.p.2.*de art.fid.expos.9.art*)."

[17] Altenstaig, *Lexicon theologicum*, fol. 162a: "Vel adhuc clarius potest dici ut *Ioan*. Eckius scribens ad Dominum Leonardum Abbatem Ottenburensem de communione sanctorum, ponit hanc divisionem. Communio fidei et respicit sacramenta, sic dicitur unus Dominus, una fides, et haec est communis omnibus fidelibus unum baptisma participantibus, uno charactere insignitis, eodem sanguine Christi redemptis, et haec communio magna est. Alia est communio gratiae, quod fideles communicant gratia ab uno capite Iesu Christo, et illa est communis omnibus iustis in gratia Dei existentibus, influens ab uno capite qui est Christus. Tertia est communio meriti: ita ut dum quisque sibi meretur singulariter ex Dei misericordissima liberalitate: meretur alteri universaliter. Hanc communionem intelligit tantum esse charitatis nexum, tanquam benignam Dei misericordiam. Ut cum unus iustus viator aliquod bonum opus meritorium facit, Deus illud acceptat pro eo qui facit ad praemium essentiale, et pro omnibus in gratia existentibus universaliter. Quarta communio est gloriae,

Late Medieval Taxonomies: Oberman's Penitential, Marital, and Eucharistic Mysticisms

Heiko Oberman has drawn from these medieval texts to describe the types of mysticism prominent in late medieval spiritualities. Of particular interest is what Oberman has called "marital" mysticism which is based upon the intimate relationship of husband and wife. This form of mysticism is distinguishable, in Oberman's taxonomy, from "penitential" mysticism on the one hand, in which one pursues a union of wills with God by which all egoism is extinguished; and eucharistic mysticism, or mysticism of the Lord's Supper, on the other hand, which is more ontological, focusing on a union with God that mirrors the disappearance of water into the chalice of Christ's blood.[18] The highest union in marital mysticism, explains Oberman, involves the transfer of goods from one party to another in accord with classical Roman marriage law. It is within this mystical strand that one is able to locate specifically Luther's own early indebtedness to mysticism for his doctrine of justification.[19]

Late Medieval Taxonomies: Manifold Marital Union(s) with Christ in Medieval Marriage Sermons

In anticipation of what Luther says about the connection of marital union with Christ and justification, an example of how various unions with Christ were understood will indicate more concretely the theological concerns and emphases reflected in the medieval distinctions listed in Altenstaig and Oberman. In David D'Avray's pioneering work on the genre of "marriage sermon" in the thirteenth century, we gain a revealing insight into what select

---

quae est praecedentibus longe perfectior. Haec communio habetur duntaxat in aeterna beatitudine in Ecclesia triumphante, et potest dupliciter intelligi. Aut enim ea accipi potest quam habent nobiscum, cum pro nobis orant, aut intercedunt apud Deum. De quo *D.D.* in 4.d.45. Potest et accipi illa communio sanctorum inter se, quod quisque beatus gaudet de quolibet. De hoc quidem per multa Eckius in *expos.art.Communio sanctorum."*

[18] Heiko Oberman, "The Meaning of Mysticism from Meister Eckhart to Martin Luther," in Oberman, *The Reformation: Roots and Ramifications* (Edinburgh: T. & T. Clark, 1994), 86-8. See also Steven Ozment, *Mysticism and Dissent: Religious Ideology and Social Protest in the Sixteenth Century* (New Haven: Yale University Press, 1973), for a nuanced discussion of varieties of mystical spirituality.

[19] This class of mysticism is summarized very briefly by Oberman in "The Meaning of Mysticism," 87, but is developed more fully with a view to Luther in his discussion of the *"iustitia Christi"* and *"iustitia Dei"* (see the relevant sections below).

influential friars taught about marriage.[20] In these sermons, the marital union of husband and wife is described, interpreted, and "theologized" with regular reference to the union of Christ with his bride, the Church. So, for instance, de Reims, preaching on the wedding feast in Cana (John 2:1-25), categorizes four kinds of union with Christ, specifically, "four kinds of marriage, all of which can be understood rather appropriately through this marriage." The first is between God and "human nature," which is analogous to that great condescension in which "our humanity is united in matrimony to the divinity of Christ in the womb of the Virgin," and refers specifically to the co-existence of divinity and humanity in the incarnate Christ.[21] There is, secondly, "a marriage between Christ and the soul: and first in baptism." This "marriage" is identified with the baptismal vows which represent the consent of faith.[22] But because so few "retain their baptismal innocence" God therefore marries us to himself "in justice and judgement," referring to Hosea 2:19. De Reims directly links this marriage union with the purification and restoration of the defiled. It is here, *in this union*, that the impurity of infidelity is made clean: "'And I,' he says, will come 'in mercy and commiserations' (Osee 2:19)... And marvellous is the mercifulness of Christ. /5/ For in carnal marriage virgins are corrupted, but in his marriage those who have lost their integrity are made into virgins, or virginity is imputed to them."[23]

In addition to these three unions (natural or incarnational, baptismal, and justifying or purifying) there is a fourth in which a

---

[20] David d'Avray, *Medieval Marriage Sermons: Mass Communication in a Culture without Print* (Oxford: Oxford University Press, 2001). This volume is the first of a two-part study of "the relation between marriage symbolism and marriage in the literal sense" (p. vii), the first part of which is a critical edition of sermons preached by significant friars prefaced by an informative introduction. The second volume is *Medieval Marriage: Symbolism and Society* (Oxford: Oxford University Press, 2005). In addition, see also the important study by Jane Dempsey-Douglas, *Justification in Late Medieval Preaching: A Study of John Geiler of Kaisersberg* (SMRT 1; Leiden: E. J. Brill, 1966).
[21] d'Avray, *Medieval Marriage Sermons*, 100/101: "/1/ Prime sunt nuptie inter deum et humanam naturam... /3/ Ista mulier fornicaria nomine Gomer, que assumpta interpretatur, Osee, id est, saluatori, coniungitur, quando humanitas nostra diuinitati Christi in uirginis utero matrimonialiter copulatur. /4/ Et tunc bene fuerunt duo in carne una, id est, diuinitas et humanitas in Christo."
[22] d'Avray, *Medieval Marriage Sermons*, 103.
[23] d'Avray, *Medieval Marriage Sermons*, 102/103, 104/105: "'Et ego,' inquid, 'ueniam "in misericordia et miserationibus" (Osee 2:19)'... /4/ Et mira Christi pietas. /5/ Nam in coniugio carnali uirgines corrumpuntur, | sed in suis nuptiis corrupte uirgines efficiuntur, quantum ad reputationem."

burdened conscience is changed into an intimate communion.[24] De Reims then proceeds to interpret the six water jars in John 2 as "the six causes of sadness arising from sin," the first of which is, interestingly, "because she has offended God," her "bridegroom." Because of this offence she cannot recapture joy whether by inheritance (the second jar), good deeds (third), beauty (fourth), friends (fifth), or some other "means of living" (sixth).[25] On the other hand, the three goods of marriage are faith/fidelity, good works, and sacrament "lest the soul ever be separated from Christ, just as Christ should not be from the Church."[26] The idea of union with Christ is here understood as the source both of reconciliation with God and of good works.

This medieval fondness for the marriage metaphor, easily verified by the spate of medieval Canticles commentaries, is consistent with the wide-ranging class of "marital" mysticism, as Oberman has categorized it. An illuminating index to popular thirteenth-century understandings of a Pauline metaphor (Eph 5:21-27), these sermons, with their notable "strata-tization" of union(s) with Christ, also evidence the continuing presence and vitality of the idea of a redemptive union with Christ, as well as provide some indications of the way in which this union was understood approaching the high Middle Ages. Also significant, however, are d'Avray's conclusions concerning the marriage sermon as a veritable "mass medium,"[27] for this observation provide grounds for suggesting that markedly theological ideas about union with Christ, in a metaphorically understood and interpreted marriage context, formed a significant part of the popular late medieval ideological and religious climate.

---

[24] d'Avray, *Medieval Marriage Sermons*, 112/113-4/115.

[25] d'Avray, *Medieval Marriage Sermons*, 107, 109.

[26] d'Avray, *Medieval Marriage Sermons*, 110/111. "Item sacramentum, ne umquam separetur a Christo, sicut nec Christus ab ecclesia. /2/ Quamdiu enim uir uiuit, mulier alligata est ei (cf. 1 Cor. 7:39)." De Reims goes on in this sermon to give a further interpretation of the water jars from the perspective of the *completed* union. They are now (p. 115) "the completion of the works of the active live [sic]; when these have been filled with water, he converts all the labours of the active life into the wine of inward rest and the joy of contemplation." Only de Reim's sermon has been summarized for illustrative purposes but similar observations apply equally to other sermons collected in this volume.

[27] d'Avray, *Medieval Marriage Sermons*, 13-30. The variety of influences upon popular thought on marriage was considerable, but d'Avray suggests (p. 14) that this "genre probably represents the closest thing there was to a dominant discourse about marriage."

Justification by Marriage with Christ: Union with Christ and Saving Righteousness from Late Medieval Theology through Luther

Iustitia Christi, Iustitia Dei, *and the Late Medieval Soteriological Dilemma*

These features of marriage mysticism serve as a natural bridge into a consideration of Luther, in whom both academic and spiritualist strands co-exist and give his Augustinianism a distinctive shape. But to appreciate this dimension of Luther's thought we need to recall that Luther's Reformation doctrine can be appreciated only in light of the mixed Augustinian inheritance of his age. Augustine himself, in his *Tractatus* on the fifteenth chapter of the Gospel of John, had explained the fourth verse – "As the branch cannot bear fruit of itself, except it abide in the vine; no more can you, except you abide in me" – with a rich defense of the need for grace in the presence of the *iustitia Dei*. In this passage (a "grand commendation of grace"), union with the Christ-Vine is the only alternative to proud self-sufficiency. Only those "corrupted in mind, reprobates concerning the faith," explains Augustine, can fail to attribute faith and every good work to the Vine. Indeed, "he who supposes that he has any fruit of himself is not in the vine. He who is not in the vine is not in Christ. He who is not in Christ is not a Christian."[28]

In a classic biblical passage on union with Christ the Vine, Augustine thus freely discussed the divine source of righteousness together with the personal necessity of good works. In this theological complex of special, perennial interest to "Augustinians" of every sort, the ideas of grace and righteousness, self-sufficiency and good works all exist together in Augustine's *Tractatus* on a

---

[28] *Sancti Aurelii Augustini in Iohannis Evangelium Tractatus CXXIV*, tract. 81, sect. 2, ed., R. Willems, *CCL* 36 (1954), 530; *Tractates on the Gospel of John 55-111* (Tractate 81), trans. John W. Rettig in *The Fathers of the Church* 90 (Washington, D.C.: CUA, 1994), 120-21: "Magna gratiae commendatio, fratres mei: corda instruit humilium, ora obstruit superborum. Ecce cui, si audent, respondeant, qui ignorantes Dei iustitiam, et suam uolentes constituere, iustitiae Dei non sunt subiecti. Ecce cui respondeant sibi placentes, et ad bona opera facienda Deum sibi necessarium non putantes. Nonne huic resistunt ueritati, homines mente corrupti, reprobi circa fidem, qui respondent et loquuntur iniquitatem, dicentes: A Deo habemus quod homines sumus, a nobis ipsis autem quod iusti sumus? ... Sed ueritas contradicit, et dicit: *Palmes non potest ferre fructum a semetipso, nisi manserit in uite*...Qui enim a semetipso se fructum existimat ferre, in uite non est; qui in uite non est, in Christo non est; qui in Christo non est, christianus non est."

central Johannine text for understanding the believer's union with Christ.[29] For more than a millennium, followers and interpreters of the *via Augustini* would concern themselves, with mixed results, with the problem of the relations of these several ideas. With respect to the late medieval development of these themes, McGrath's comment is certainly not an overstatement: "The theology of the medieval period may be regarded as thoroughly Augustinian, a series of footnotes to Augustine, in that theological speculation was essentially regarded as an attempt to defend, expand, and where necessary modify, the Augustinian legacy."[30]

This "modification" of Augustine especially included ongoing reflection on his emphasis on the priority of divine grace and action and on his generous use of a particular biblical metaphor, that of the marriage-union between the Redeemer and his redeemed. By the later Middle Ages, the *unio mystica* was a common theme in theological literature whether of the *Devotio moderna* or of the *Via moderna*.

Through a series of penetrating essays, Oberman, among others, has fundamentally challenged the dominant school of interpretation which has seen Reformation theological constructs as wholly incongruous with late medieval ideas.[31] In short, Oberman's thesis is an argument in favor of rigorous textual study marked by

---

[29] Bernard McGinn, who has published extensively on the history of Christian mysticism, argues curiously that Augustine "knows nothing" of union with Christ ("Love, Knowledge, and Mystical Union in Western Christianity: Twelfth to Sixteenth Centuries," *CH* 56 [1987]: 8).

[30] Alister E. McGrath, *Iustitia Dei: A History of the Christian Doctrine of Justification* 2 vol. (Cambridge: Cambridge University Press, 1986; 2nd ed. in one vol., 1998), 17. While such an investigation would take us well beyond the narrow limits of this inquiry, McGrath is still correct to conclude (p. 17) that "[a]n awareness of the leading features of Augustine's doctrine of justification is... an essential prerequisite to a correct understanding of the medieval discussion of the doctrine of justification." For such a discussion, McGrath offers his survey (pp. 17-36) and points us to G. Bavaud, "La doctrine de la justification d'après Saint Augustin et la Rèforme," *REAug* 5 (1959): 21-32; and J. Henninger, *S. Augustinus et doctrina de duplici iustitia* (Mödling, 1935). See also Adolar Zumkeller, "Der Terminus 'sola fides' bei Augustinus," in G. R. Evans, ed., *Christian Authority: Essays in Honour of Henry Chadwick* (Oxford: Clarendon Press, 1988), 86-100.

[31] Formerly, this period of theology from Aquinas and the *via antiqua* to nominalism and the *via moderna* was regularly interpreted in terms of its gradual disintegration and solely speculative character. Perhaps the most concise explanation of Oberman's thesis may be found in his introductory essay ("The Case of the Forerunner") in his controversial *Forerunners of the Reformation: The Shape of Late Medieval Thought Illustrated by Key Documents* (Philadelphia: Fortress Press, 1966 and 1981), 1-49.

contextual sensitivity, one implication of which is the setting aside of romantic portraits which paint Luther as a bolt of light from beyond the blue, as one who rose as a theologian *de novo* from the head of Zeus like the birth of Athena. Scholarly interpretation of Luther's contributions is hence fundamentally challenged to account adequately for the intellectual and spiritual context within which he worked and upon which he was at least partially dependent. According to Oberman, traditional nominalist and Luther scholarship has too often failed to attend closely enough to the primary source materials which, on close examination, reveal identifiable theological trajectories which extend from lines of thought in late medieval theology to and beyond the reforming labors of Luther. Likewise Steven Ozment, whose fine intellectual-historical survey gives considerable attention to the Middle Ages before turning to the Reformation, defends his procedure by appeal to what he rightly sees as a methodological implication of his findings: "This effort," he writes, "to view the Reformation from the perspective of the Middle Ages reflects the conviction that it was both a culmination and a transcendence of medieval intellectual and religious history."[32] Such a statement signals the revolutionary character of this scholarly development.

The fruit of these reassessments touches, predictably, upon our understanding of the early Reformation doctrine of justification by faith. More specifically, Oberman has argued that the nature of Luther's revolutionary theology of justification *sola fide* must be appreciated against the backdrop of late medieval struggles over what he terms the dialectic of the *iustitia Christi* (righteousness of Christ) and the *iustitia Dei* (justice of God).[33] The terms "*iustitia Christi*" and "*iustitia Dei*" are proposed to facilitate the clarification of the *duplex iustitia* Oberman finds at the foundation of all medieval doctrines of justification.[34]

As Oberman explains, the basic problem in late medieval soteriology was how to improve sufficiently, by the performance of good works, one's sacramentally infused grace (the *iustitia Christi*) in order, ultimately, to achieve the full, eschatological reconciliation and restoration before God (the *iustitia Dei*) which lies, one hopes, at

---

[32] Ozment, *The Age of Reform*, xi.
[33] Oberman, "'Iustitia Christi' and 'Iustitia Dei': Luther and the Scholastic Doctrines of Justification," in Oberman, *The Dawn of the Reformation: Essays in Late Medieval and Early Reformation Thought* (Edinburgh: T. & T. Clark, 1986), 104-25.
[34] Oberman, "'Iustitia Christi' and 'Iustitia Dei,'" 110, n. 11.

the end of a lifelong spiritual pilgrimage.³⁵ The *facere quod in se est* ("do what is in you") of the medieval justification process, for which one must be properly disposed, lies at the heart of late medieval soteriology and ethics and stands in the foreground of Luther's theological critique. Notwithstanding the considerable complexity and variation in late medieval theology, there is basic uniformity along these lines.

Luther, as a well-trained monk, was intimately familiar with the themes of medieval theology. In his early, formative years of 1509-1518, he commented on Lombard's *Sentences* (1509-10) and read extensively in Aristotle's *Physics*, *Metaphysics*, and *Ethics*. He annotated works by Augustine (1509-10) and Jacques Lefèvre d'Etaples (1513), as well as Gabriel Biel's *Exposition of the Canon of the Mass* and *Sentences* commentary (1517). He was especially industrious in biblical exegesis, producing lectures on the Psalms (1513-15) and Paul's Epistles to the Romans (1515-16) and Galatians (1516-17). All of this required his familiarity with the medieval exegetical tradition.³⁶

Further illuminating the background of Luther's thought, Oberman refers to the perennial problem which confronted the most sincere of medieval exegetes, one posed by the biblical texts themselves: the apparent elevation in the New Testament of the Old Testament standard of justice.³⁷ It is the problem of the Old Law and the New, Moses and Christ; that is, that the Law of Christ places demands not only on the hands and feet but on the heart and will. Here Oberman points to the solutions proposed by those whom it is known Luther read. Biel pulled together "a multiform collection of quotations from Bonaventure, Thomas, Scotus, and of course from Augustine," not explicitly offering his own view but clearly emphasizing the "law" in the "new law" of Christ.³⁸ This law is, indeed, the fulfillment of the law of Moses, but fulfillment means interiorization, its inward intensification. For the justification of the sinner-*viator*, Christ's merits are insufficient when alone, when they are not joined by the obedience his law requires.³⁹ Scotus, while

---

³⁵ Oberman, "'Iustitia Christi' and 'Iustitia Dei,'" 110, n. 11; 113-4; 119-20.
³⁶ Ozment, *The Age of Reform*, 232.
³⁷ Oberman, "'Iustitia Christi' and 'Iustitia Dei,'" 116.
³⁸ Oberman, "'Iustitia Christi' and 'Iustitia Dei,'" 116-7.
³⁹ It is important to note the debate between Oberman and McGrath concerning the Pelagianism of Biel's covenantal soteriology. Cf. Oberman, *Harvest of Medieval Theology* with McGrath, "The Anti-Pelagian Structure of 'Nominalistic' Doctrines of Justification," *Ephemerides Theologicae Lovanienses* 57 (1981): 107-19. Though unable to discuss the debate more fully here, I am grateful to Dr Chad

working from within a different framework – predestination as the protective guard of justification – maintains the same basic idea: the will is expected to perform those good works the righteousness of God requires. Just as for Biel, to "fulfill" Christ's law is for Scotus to "fill it up" with one's obedience, to complete it.[40] In Aquinas, moreover, the newness of the gospel consists, in part, in the ontological elevation of good works from a natural to a fully meritorious, *de condigno*, state, meritorious wholly apart from a Scotist covenant of acceptance.

As a whole, therefore, even in its complex variety, Oberman contends that the medieval theology of salvation was this at bottom: though one receives in the sacraments the grace of Christ's righteousness (the *iustitia Christi*), the meritorious works of obedience to Christ's law must supplement this gift to meet the holy requirements of God's righteousness (the *iustitia Dei*). Whether the nature of this supplementation is the Thomistic ontological elevation or the Scotist covenantal acceptance of one's works of obedience, in either case "prevenient" grace, however defined and understood, was ultimately insufficient grace.

Oberman concludes that Luther's revolutionary insight, therefore, was not that grace is prevenient (this would only have attacked Ockham), nor that justification comes via the sanctifying grace that is the *iustitia Christi* (this both the Thomists and Scotists knew). Rather, by arguing that in justification both the "*iustitia Christi*" and the "*iustitia Dei*" are granted together, Luther undermined the entire range of scholastic opinion on the question. The *iustitia Dei*, which traditionally stood as the goal, the *telos*, of the *viator*'s journey in grace begun by the spurring of the *iustitia Christi*, Luther brought to the present as the foundation of the pursuit of holiness, of "sanctification."[41]

One can summarize Luther's discovery, therefore, with the following observation:

> [T]he heart of the Gospel is that the *iustitia Christi* and the *iustitia Dei* coincide and are granted simultaneously... It is not the task of those who are justified to implement the iustitia Christi by relating themselves in optimal fashion to the iustitia Dei. The Pauline

---

Van Dixhoorn for access to his unpublished clarification of the issues between Oberman and McGrath.

[40] Oberman, "'Iustitia Christi' and 'Iustitia Dei,'" 117.
[41] Oberman, "'Iustitia Christi' and 'Iustitia Dei,'" 120.

message is the Gospel exactly because the iustitia Dei – revealed at the Cross as the iustitia Christi – is given to the faithful per fidem.[42]

Luther, Oberman states, "radically re-interpreted the 'facere quod in se est,' both as regards the preparation for the reception of the gift of love and as regards the preservation of this gift..." In doing so, "Luther looked beyond the central issue in nominalistic theology, namely the *preparation* for grace, to the problem of the *conservation*, or preservation, of grace."[43]

The nature of Luther's re-direction of the issues will be under-appreciated, however, if a second, correlative element in his doctrine of justification should go unnoticed: his internal critique of the Pelagian tendencies in the mystical soteriology with which he was intimately familiar.

Luther and Mystical Union with Christ

The concerns of the previous section belong largely to the development of "school theology."[44] But the fruit of the academy should not be seen as the whole of pre-Reformation theology. Recent scholarship is showing increasingly that decidedly "non-academic" theological reflection such as the preaching from medieval pulpits (as noted above) and monastic labors formed a substantial part of the medieval ideological climate. In the centuries immediately preceding Calvin's work especially one finds properly "academic" as well as deeply pietistic, "spiritualist" language about union with Christ.

JUSTIFICATION AND *UNIO MYSTICA* IN MYSTICAL THEOLOGY AND IN LUTHER

The marriage sermon, as a mass medium of the thirteenth-century climate of opinion, was but one element in that broad, popular context in which lay and "professional" (monastic) spiritualities supply insight into the ideas that contributed, in part, to the multifaceted background leading up to Luther's theological development. Apart from his well-known monastic experience, the most significant contribution to Luther's spiritual background was probably mysticism or, more properly, mystical theology and theologians, from whom perhaps the most well-known

---

[42] Oberman, "'Iustitia Christi' and 'Iustitia Dei,'" 120 (emphasis Oberman's).
[43] Oberman, "'Iustitia Christi' and 'Iustitia Dei,'" 114.
[44] As representatives such as Gerson and Tauler indicate, however, the academic/scholastic and mystical/spiritual strands did not exist in isolated tension but occasionally overlapped.

contributions to the classic literature on the subject came.[45] It should be remembered, in discussions of Luther's doctrine of salvation, that the extent of Luther's familiarity with medieval thought reaches beyond academic "school" theology to include these spiritual and mystical traditions. It was within his own Order of the Hermits of St. Augustine, for instance, that Luther found the two members for whom he would express his highest praise: Gregory of Rimini, in Luther's eyes the lone scholastic unencumbered by Pelagianism; and Johannes von Staupitz, his superior.[46] In 1515-16, Luther annotated sermons by the mystic Johannes Tauler, and in 1516 he edited part of a mystical treatise and titled it *German Theology*, a work he would later, in 1518, publish in full as a "precedent for the new 'Wittenberg theology.'"[47] As a central theme in mystical theology, the *unio mystica* would recur, in fundamentally different form, as a favorite theme in Luther's distinctive Reformation theology of justification.

The medieval mystical movements had their own sophisticated soteriologies that were intimately bound up with the union idea. As McGinn explains in his survey of Western mysticism, union with Christ or God was the eschatological goal of every *viator*.[48] The pursuit of this goal included a life of contemplation and self-denial. Contemplation was the third stage in the process to union with Christ taught by the greatest of medieval mystics, Bernard, and,

---

[45] On the historical development of mysticism, see the projected five-volume work of Bernard McGinn, *The Presence of God: A History of Western Christian Mysticism* (New York: Crossroad Publishing, 1994-), which includes, to date, vol. 1, *The Foundations of Mysticism: Origins to the Fifth Century* (1994); vol. 2, *The Growth of Mysticism: Gregory the Great through the Twelfth Century* (1996); vol. 3, *The Flowering of Mysticism: Men and Women in the New Mysticism (1200-1350)* (1998); and vol. 4, *The Harvest of Mysticism in Medieval Germany* (2005). See also the fine collection of introductory essays in Jill Raitt, Bernard McGinn, and John Meyendorff, eds, *Christian Spirituality II: High Middle Ages and Reformation* (New York: Crossroad, 1987). See also Dennis Tamburello, *Ordinary Mysticism* (New York: Paulist Press, 1996); and Moshe Idel and Bernard McGinn, eds, *Mystical Union in Judaism, Christianity, and Islam: An Ecumenical Dialogue* (New York: Continuum, 1996).
[46] Ozment, *The Age of Reform*, 232. On Staupitz, see David C. Steinmetz, *Misericordia Dei: the Theology of Johannes von Staupitz in its Late Medieval Setting* (Leiden: E. J. Brill, 1968).
[47] Ozment, *The Age of Reform*, 232.
[48] McGinn, "Love, Knowledge, and Mystical Union," 7: "The classic schools of mystical authors in the Western church from the twelfth through the sixteenth centuries used union with God as a favored way of characterizing the goal of their beliefs and practices."

following Bernard, Gerson and Tauler, influences upon the young Luther.[49]

While Luther's theological relationship with aspects of late medieval scholastic theology is certainly a complicated matter, the question of Luther's relationship to mysticism and mystical theology is especially complex and has proven to function as an impetus to other, more ancillary debates.[50] Nevertheless, progress has been made in recent studies. The study by Ozment on mysticism and the early Luther is among the finest available.[51] Oberman has also offered a series of proposals on the question that serve well to respect this complexity and yet identify, with a measure of precision, those elements of Luther's thought which bear a positive relationship to his knowledge of mystical theology. Importantly, Oberman distinguishes Luther's "mysticism" from movements that sought a quasi-ontological union with the divine. He argues that "there is as yet no reason to assume that Luther rejected mystical theology as such. Rather he opposes the dangers of what [Oberman calls] 'high mysticism.'" He argues that Luther rejected the distinctive characteristics of this "high" mysticism, e.g., the union of soul with body and the "bypassing of Christ in order to rest *in Deo nudo.*"[52]

---

[49] Bernard outlines these three stages or steps – contrition, meditation, and contemplation – in his *De diligendo Deo* (Oberman, "Simul Gemitus et Raptus: Luther and Mysticism," in Oberman, *The Dawn of the Reformation* [Edinburgh: T. & T. Clark, 1986], 134).

[50] Indicative of the scope of importance this debate has had in Luther studies, Oberman ("Simul Gemitus et Raptus," 127) points to the variety of perspectives taken on the reformer which have this debate as their root: "Centuries of controversy are reflected in the varying views presented on Luther's relation to mysticism: the tension between Philippism and Pietism; the differing views on the relation of the young Luther to the mature or – more descriptively – the old Luther; the evaluation of the thesis of "the Reformers before the Reformation"; the Holl-Ritschl debate on justification as impartation (*sanatio*) versus imputation; the intimate interplay of politico-nationalistic and theological factors in the clash of *Deutsche Christen* and the *Bekennende Kirche* reflected in the confrontation of Luther as the spokesman of an endemic "Deutsche" or "Germanische Mystik" (Eckhart-Luther-Nietzsche!) versus an appeal to Luther as the witness to the God who is *totaliter aliter*, without a natural point of contact (*Seelengrund*, etc.) in man; the unclarity regarding the relation of the *Via moderna* to the *Devotio moderna* – and more generally of nominalism to mysticism."

[51] Steven E. Ozment, *Homo Spiritualis: A Comparative Study of the Anthropology of Johannes Tauler, Jean Gerson and Martin Luther (1509-16) in the Context of their Theological Thought* (SMRT 6; Leiden: E. J. Brill, 1969).

[52] Oberman, "Simul Gemitus et Raptus," 142-3.

In contrast, Luther insists that whereas "high" mysticism endorses a *theologia gloriae* (theology of glory) in its pursuit of an *unio*-beatitude in which soul and body coalesce, true spiritual experience comes via the cross, suffering, the *theologia crucis* (theology of the cross).[53] Furthermore, whereas in "high" mysticism Christ *pro nobis* constitutes the bond between Christ and believer, the true embrace of Christ may be enjoyed only when it is joined with the love that the contemplation of this *pro nobis* induces. Luther, on the contrary, turns attention away from *per Christum et charitatem* to *per Christum per fidem*, making faith in Christ alone rather than the combination of Christ and Christ-induced love the presupposition of enjoying union with Christ.[54]

LUTHER'S "MARITAL" MYSTICISM IN REFORMATION FORM

Luther's early association with varieties of mystical theology may lead one to expect its importance only in this period; however, even the "mature" Luther was fond of using marriage imagery to represent the divine reality of the union of Christ and the believer. For example, he writes: "O God who hast created man and woman and hast ordained them for the married estate, hast blessed them also with fruits of the womb, and hast typified therein the sacramental union of thy dear Son, the Lord Jesus Christ, and the Church, his bride..."[55]

The polemical significance of Luther's language should be appreciated. Luther's identification of the "marriage estate" as a type of the "sacramental union" of Christ and the Church accomplishes much more than the rejection of marriage as sacrament: it enriches and widens the scope of his emphasis on the theological significance of a basic Christ-believer relationship, that is, justification by faith. He does this by grounding the estate of marriage in the biblical metaphor for union with Christ and, in so doing, thus re-interprets in distinctively Protestant terms an established institution familiar to both theologian and lay believer.

---

[53] Oberman, "Simul Gemitus et Raptus," 142-3.
[54] Oberman, "Simul Gemitus et Raptus," 143.
[55] Luther, *Traubüchlein* (1529), *LW* 53.115, in Kenneth W. Stevenson, *Nuptial Blessing: A Study of Christian Marriage Rites* (London: S.P.C.K., 1982), 247; cf. discussion pp. 127-8. This text can also be found in English translation in Mark Searle and Kenneth W. Stevenson, *Documents of the Marriage Liturgy* (Collegeville: Liturgical Press/Pueblo, 1992), 213-14. See also Stevenson, *Nuptial Blessing*, 126-8; idem, *To Join Together: The Rite of Marriage* (New York: Pueblo, 1987), 87-9; and B. D. Spinks, "Luther's Other Major Liturgical Reforms: 3. The Traubuchlein," *Liturgical Review* 10 (1980): 33-8.

Therefore, in this recurring theme of Luther's theology an affinity with the "marital" strand of mysticism, reinterpreted to defend a distinctively Reformation theology of justification, is altogether plausible. Yet this recalls the important point that Luther's relationship to mystical ideas of union, via Gerson and Tauler and perhaps Staupitz, while strong, varies at crucial points. With Luther there is a fundamental shift in how this union is conceived: unlike the medieval *viator* who yearns for union at the end of the journey, Luther makes union a present reality and experience. Furthermore, the monastic ideal for which Luther had trained and with which he was therefore so familiar was fundamentally challenged by his extraction of this *unio* from the monastery to the farm. In other words, Luther's soteriology marks a shift in which the *unio mystica* of monasticism, which often belonged exclusively to the spiritual elite, was democratized and universalized as the present possession of every believer.[56]

It is now possible to appreciate something of the function of union with Christ in Luther's thought. This function is tied to his use of *possessio* and *proprietas* language, with which Luther employs the marital union theme to defend his Reformation doctrine of justification. As for the question of sources, Oberman points beyond its legal origins to the marital roots and context of this terminology.[57]

The way Luther uses these ideas is best illustrated by reference to the texts themselves, texts in which the benefits of Christ's work (the *possessio* rather than *proprietas*) belong to the believing sinner brought into marriage union with Christ. The classic text in which Luther extols the glories of marriage union with Christ is his justly famous *The Freedom of a Christian* (1520). "The third incomparable benefit of faith," Luther writes, "is that it unites the soul with Christ as a bride is united with her bridegroom."[58] Luther goes on to explain that Christ and the believer are "one flesh" as a result of this union, citing the bridal imagery in Eph. 5. Here Luther makes the

---

[56] Importantly, Luther's move toward a democratization of union with Christ had medieval precedent (see Oberman, *Harvest of Medieval Theology*, 341-3; idem, "The Meaning of Mysticism," 85). Luther's contribution is the democratization of union with Christ within a distinctively Protestant theological framework.

[57] Oberman, "Simul Gemitus et Raptus," 125, n. 52: "Whereas one root of the understanding of the new righteousness as possessio rather than proprietas is to be found in Roman civil law, the other root can be discerned more specifically in the application of marriage imagery – contractus, sponsalia, consummatio – with the exchange of possession between partners."

[58] Luther, *The Freedom of a Christian* (1520), *LW* 31.351.

significant transition to the redemptive significance of this union in terms of the exchange of possessions between Christ and the soul:

> And if they are one flesh and there is between them a true marriage – indeed the most perfect of all marriages, since human marriages are but poor examples of this one true marriage – it follows that everything they have they hold in common, the good as well as the evil. Accordingly the believing soul can boast of and glory in whatever Christ has as though it were its own, and whatever the soul has Christ claims as his own. Let us compare these and we shall see inestimable benefits. Christ is full of grace, life, and salvation. The soul is full of sins, death, and damnation. Now let faith come between them and sins, death, and damnation will be Christ's, while grace, life, and salvation will be the soul's; for if Christ is a bridegroom, he must take upon himself the things which are his bride's and bestow upon her the things that are his.[59]

As if he felt the redemptive purpose of the union-transfer was not clear enough, Luther goes on to make it explicit:

> By the wedding ring of faith he shares in the sins, death, and pains of hell which are his bride's. As a matter of fact, he makes them his own and acts as if they were his own and as if he himself had sinned; he suffered, died, and descended into hell that he might overcome them all... Thus the believing soul by means of the pledge of its faith is free in Christ, its bridegroom, free from all sins, secure against death and hell, and is endowed with the eternal righteousness, life, and salvation of Christ its bridegroom.[60]

This wondrous and heavenly betrothal, this "royal marriage," Luther further explains, is far beyond our comprehension in that the "rich and divine bridegroom Christ marries this poor, wicked harlot, redeems her from all her evil, and adorns her with all his goodness." She is free from the guilt of sin because, in the exchange of possessions, Christ has "swallowed" her sins and she has received the righteousness of her husband. She can, therefore, in the face of death and hell, say boldly with the bride in the Song of Solomon, that he is hers and she is his.[61] Later in the pamphlet, Luther returns to the exchange of possessions, this time referring to it as the "law...

---

[59] Luther, *Freedom*, *LW* 31.351.
[60] Luther, *Freedom*, *LW* 31.352; cf. Luther's sermon on John 6:57 in *Sermons on the Gospel of St. John Chapters 6-8* in *LW* 23.148-50.
[61] Luther, *Freedom*, *LW* 31.352. Luther's reference to the Song in this context should be recognized as partaking in that long medieval tradition of Canticles commentary in which rich use is made of the marital union imagery.

according to which the wife owns whatever belongs to the husband."⁶²

In short, Luther's understanding of *possessio* as a benefit of the *unio* between Christ and the believer reflects not only Luther's deep understanding of the basic themes of mystical theology and of the scholastic theology of grace but also his ability to adopt the language and forms of the one and use them against the other without embracing either uncritically. Luther would have nothing to do with the incipient Pelagianism in either mystical or nominalist theology, but he did employ their vocabulary, particularly of mystical theology, principally because this was the common vocabulary of contemporary theological discourse. It is not too much to concede the possibility also, however, that Luther recognized the vocabulary of mystical union as the vocabulary of the Church, and not the

---

⁶² Luther, *Freedom*, *LW* 31.354. I cannot enter here into the discussion but do wish to note the importance of the chronology of Luther's development. The issues and literature are discussed concisely in Lowell C. Green, "Faith, Righteousness, and Justification: New Light on Their Development under Luther and Melanchton," *SCJ* 4 (1972): 65-86. The question is important on a number of fronts, not least the relationship of the "early/young" and "late/mature" Luther on justification in light of Melanchthon's doctrine. Green (p. 83, n. 30) employs this distinction in defining his verdict: "In a sense, I reject the doctrine of justification of the Young Luther in favor of Melanchthon's forensic view (which I also find in the Mature Luther in modified form)..." In light of the Finnish proposal, the implications of this shift for associations of Luther's doctrine with *theosis* or deification would seem to be devastating, particularly when it is recognized that the Finnish reading has typically been preoccupied with his early, i.e., "young" texts. Much to be preferred is the assessment of Ozment that, "despite his high praise for the German mystics, Luther consistently showed no noteworthy interest in either their speculation on man's divine powers or their view of man's union with God as deification (*Vergöttung*) – the most distinctive features of German mystical teaching" (*The Age of Reform*, 241). See, in *WTJ* 65 (2003), Paul Louis Metzger, "Mystical Union with Christ: An Alternative to Blood Transfusions and Legal Fictions," (pp. 201-14); Mark A. Seifrid, "Paul, Luther, and Justification in Gal 2:15-21," (pp. 215-30); Carl R. Trueman, "Is the Finnish Line a New Beginning? A Critical Assessment of the Reading of Luther Offered by the Helsinki Circle," (pp. 231-44); and Robert W. Jenson, "Response to Seifrid, Trueman, and Metzger on Finnish Luther Research," (pp. 245-50). See also Reinhard Flogaus, "Luther versus Melanchthon? Zur Frage der Einheit der Wittenberger Reformation in der Rechtfertigungslehre," *ARG* 91 (2000): 6-46, who argues for an agreement between Luther and Melanchthon, in contrast with Franz Posset, "'Deification' in the German Spirituality of the Late Middle Ages and in Luther: An Ecumenical Historical Perspective," *ARG* 84 (1993): 103-25, who argues in support of the Finnish reading.

private possession of mysticism. In his view urged by Scripture and tradition, Luther reveled in the marriage *contractus* between Christ and the soul with its implications for his teaching on justification by Christ's righteousness *sola fide*. At least this much is clear: Luther's revolutionary theology of justification by faith alone included, as an indispensable element, the recasting of traditional teaching on union with Christ in terms of its indissoluble connection to justification.

Calvin, the Reformers, and Saving Union with Christ

In approaching Calvin's day, therefore, one may safely investigate Calvin's own language of union with Christ as an eminently traditional idea, as emerging, to some degree, from a pre-existing framework. With an appreciation for this already-resident matrix of traditional union language – a matrix which bridges the fading chasm between "intellectual" and "social" history – one is at a decided advantage in pursuing Calvin's own contribution in that one is able to do so against a background of *specific* ideas about union with Christ.

The question of the precise context of Calvin's thought from a historical-intellectual perspective, however, and the attendant question of the precise influences upon him, remain among the most difficult and debated issues in Calvin scholarship. In fact, the path to this question has undergone some re-paving in that Calvin's relationship to figures and developments in late medieval scholasticism, as well as to "scholasticism" itself, has recently come under reassessment.[63] In many studies, the idea of Calvin as a "scholastic" is simply unacceptable. Calvin's humanism allegedly serves as sufficient proof of his incompatibility with the adjective "scholastic." His "dynamic christocentric" theology, moreover, has been understood to occupy a position directly opposite the arid logic and speculative superfluity assumed of the whole of scholastic theology. "Calvin" and "scholastic," in this view, are antithetical. In recent studies, however, Calvin's relationship to scholasticism is more complex, and in some respects much more positive, than

---

[63] In particular, the work of David C. Steinmetz and Richard A. Muller is noteworthy. See Steinmetz, "The Scholastic Calvin" in Carl R. Trueman and R. S. Clark, eds, *Protestant Scholasticism: Essays in Reassessment* (Carlisle: Paternoster, 1999), 16-30; and Muller, *Unaccommodated Calvin*, 39-61. See also W. Van Asselt, ed., *Reformation and Scholasticism: An Ecumenical Enterprise* (Grand Rapids: Baker, 2001).

earlier scholarship assumed.[64] In part because of this shift, and in part also because Calvin does not readily disclose his sources, the pursuit of Calvin's pedigree has yet to meet with great success.[65] However, recent attempts have been made to argue a possible area of commonality with, if not an influence of the medieval mystical traditions upon Calvin on the basis of similarities in teaching on union with Christ.

Calvin and Unio Mystica

The literature on union with Christ in Calvin and mysticism, despite some useful discussions, lacked a focused study until recently.[66]

---

[64] See Muller, *Unaccommodated Calvin*, 39-61, for a full discussion and critical interaction with the literature.

[65] This has led to claims based on little or no evidence. Calvin's alleged indebtedness to the thought of Scottish theologian John Major (Mair d. 1550), for example, has been proposed largely on the sole basis of Major's theological lectures in Paris during the time Calvin was an arts student (So Karl Reuter, *Das Grundverständnis der Theologie Calvins* [Neukirchen, 1963]; Thomas F. Torrance, *The Hermeneutics of John Calvin* [Edinburgh: Scottish Academic Press, 1988]), though, as many have objected, there is no clear indication that Calvin ever attended Major's lectures or had any real contact with his ideas (see the discussion by R. Muller, *Unaccommodated Calvin*, 40-41, who points to the critiques of Reuter and Torrance by La Vallee and Ganoczy – criticisms which, after Reuter's subsequent response to Ganoczy, are confirmed by A. N. S. Lane's careful analysis). Others have observed elements of medieval theology in Calvin but disagree on the source(s). McGrath has argued for the general influence of a *via Augustiniana moderna* as a nominalistic *tradition* rather than particular *individuals* (though he does refer to the high likelihood of Gregory of Rimini's impact). This influence is, for McGrath, the particular one within a broader influence of the nominalist *via moderna*, without in any sense ruling out the possibility of Major's influence. See McGrath, "John Calvin and Late Medieval Thought," *ARG* 77 (1986): 77-8; cf. Suzanne Selinger, *Calvin against Himself: An Inquiry in Intellectual History* (Hamden: Archon Books, 1984), who contends for a general impact of nominalism upon Calvin's understanding of human knowledge. H. Oberman has proposed Scotist influences (Oberman, "*Initia Calvini*: The Matrix of Calvin's Reformation" in W. Neuser, ed., *CSSP*, 113-54).

[66] For studies see W. R. Stiktberg, "The Mystical Element in the Theology of John Calvin," Ph.D. diss. (New York: Union Theological Seminary, 1951); Hae Yong You, "Bonaventure and John Calvin: The Restoration of the Image of God as a Mode of Spiritual Consummation," Ph.D. diss. (Fordham University, 1992); Carl-A. Keller, *Calvin Mystique: Au cœur de la pensée du Réformateur* (Geneva: Labor et Fidès, 2001); and Dennis E. Tamburello, *Union with Christ: John Calvin and the Mysticism of St. Bernard* (Louisville: Westminster/John Knox, 1994). See also the literature referred to in Clive S. Chin, "*Unio Mystica* and *Imitatio Christi*:

Dennis Tamburello has compared Calvin and Bernard while Carl Keller has inquired whether Calvin's spirituality fits a narrow or a broad – a "*coincidence avec le Divin sans Nom*" or a "*union avec le Divin Nommé, en l'occurrence avec la Sainte Trinité ou avec l'une de ses 'Personnes'*" – type of mysticism.[67]

Calvin used the terminology of a "mystical union" (*unio mystica*) only twice in the 1559 *Institutes*.[68] Tamburello places considerable weight upon the fact that Calvin uses the term whereas Bernard, a sure mystic, does not.[69] In his comparative study, he proposes that Calvin and Bernard share a basic theology of union with Christ. Tamburello's conclusion summarizes his aim in pursuing this comparison, namely, dialogue between Roman Catholics and Protestants on the basis of Christian experience rather than doctrine. In short, he argues for the ecumenical importance of "stress[ing] the primacy of experience in the construction of a theological worldview" and believes his study "has shown both Bernard and Calvin to be positive resources for this kind of theological reconstruction."[70] Tamburello suggests that Bernard's and Calvin's respective understandings of justification and the Christian life also share strong similarities, most differences being a matter of emphasis.[71]

In his comparison, Tamburello sought to identify major themes both thinkers held in common. In doing so he has helpfully pointed not only to the general contours of Calvin's doctrine of saving union, but also to specific features. Arguing similarities with Bernard, Tamburello recognizes in Calvin the centrality of union with Christ for understanding important elements in the basic fabric of

---

The Two-Dimensional Nature of John Calvin's Spirituality," Ph.D. diss. (Dallas Theological Seminary, 2002). For recent attempts to relate Calvin positively to deification, see Keller, *Calvin Mystique*, part one; and Carl Mosser, "The Greatest Possible Blessing: Calvin and Deification" *SJT* 55 (2002): 36-57.

[67] Keller, *Calvin Mystique*, 13.

[68] *Inst.* (1559) 2.12.7; OS 3.446 (LCC 20.473); and 3.11.10; OS 4.191 (LCC 20.737).

[69] Tamburello, *Union with Christ*, 84. Dowey is sure Calvin "took over" the term from classical mysticism and notes that Jacobs says Calvin adopted this term first in the fight against Osiander. Cf. Dowey, *The Knowledge of God*, 198, with Paul Jacobs, *Prädestination und Verantwortlichkeit bei Calvin* (Kassel: Oncken, 1937), 128.

[70] Tamburello, *Union with Christ*, 110. Tamburello's judgment on the ecumenical value of Calvin's doctrine of union with Christ will not be addressed in this study. His ecumenical aim is important to note, however, because of the discernible effect it has upon the way he shapes his arguments throughout.

[71] Tamburello, *Union with Christ*, 41-63.

salvation. Following the earlier study by Kolfhaus, Tamburello explains:

> Kolfhaus rightly speaks of "engrafting into Christ" as providing the "inner indissoluble cohesion" of Calvin's conception of the salvific work of God. He explains, "Justification and sanctification, faith and morality, are seen [by Calvin] in light of engrafting into Christ. Calvin thinks from this point out, and his thoughts always turn back to it."[72]

As Tamburello notes, Calvin's idea of union with Christ revolves around faith, and he even speaks of union as "simultaneous" with faith.[73] But faith and union with Christ are related because of the work of the Holy Spirit. Faith yields union and yet always depends on union so that there is reciprocity, symbiosis, in their relationship. So Tamburello, again citing Kolfhaus, thus summarizes Calvin's thoughts with the formula: "The Holy Spirit alone, and indeed alone through faith, engrafts us into Christ."[74]

Both Keller and Tamburello are particularly concerned to specify the *kind* of mysticism they see in Calvin: not a broad, inclusive definition but a narrow, specific understanding of mysticism, one that is described in terms of union with God.[75] For Tamburello, the difference between Bernard's and Calvin's mysticism is that Calvin's is "broader in scope," one that "can be enjoyed equally by all the elect, whereas Bernard tends to see the monastery as the unique environment where mysticism thrives." Calvin, explains Tamburello, describes union with "less emphasis on 'esoteric' phenomena such as ecstasies or visions."[76] While the claim that Calvin had any place for "esoteric phenomena" is at least suspect, the question soon becomes whether Calvin's use of *unio mystica* is indeed evidence of an affinity with the mystical traditions and, therefore, indicative of the compatibility of mysticism with Calvin's theology. The impression Tamburello and Keller share is not mistaken: for the most part the literature has indeed responded negatively.[77]

---

[72] Tamburello, *Union with Christ*, 84-5.
[73] Tamburello, *Union with Christ*, 85, incorrectly noting *Inst.* (1559) 3.2.25 when his source is 3.2.35; OS 4.46 (LCC 20.583).
[74] Kolfhaus, *Christusgemeinschaft*, 52; Tamburello, *Union with Christ*, 85.
[75] Tamburello, *Union with Christ*, 7-8; cf. Keller, *Calvin Mystique, passim*.
[76] Tamburello, *Union with Christ*, 8. Keller, on the other hand, proposes his definition of "mysticism" using Denis the Areopagite as a point of departure.
[77] Tamburello, *Union with Christ*, 1-3, 21; and Keller, *Calvin Mystique*, 21-3, who notes the verdict of André Duran (*Le mysticisme de Calvin d'aprés l'Institution chrétienne* [Montauban, 1900], 69-70) and Emil Brunner (*Das Wirken des Heiligen*

The principal difficulties with Tamburello's thesis are those which he himself identifies. First, the denial of a mysticism proper in Calvin by the majority of Calvin scholars is due to Calvin's own negative relationship to mystic-type movements like the *Theologia Deutsch* and to individuals such as Andreas Osiander.[78] Second, the definition of mysticism that Tamburello ends up proposing is arguably so broad as to lose any real significance: it extends eventually to include all in history who expressed any affection for fellowship with God.[79] Thus again the problem of taxonomy: if "mysticism" can be defined so broadly, then Calvin was indeed a "mystic."

Calvin does indeed use what may be designated "the traditional language of mysticism" in describing union with Christ, but the specific question Tamburello raises of influence and agreement is not answered by the presence of this language. Calvin's descriptions of union with Christ in terms of the Ephesians marriage-imagery may just as easily be due to his propensity to follow biblical language and imagery, especially in this case when it is a Pauline

---

Geistes [Zurich, 1935], 38). Niesel (*Reformed Symbolics*, 185), for one, pointedly describes the fundamental differences between mysticism and the "mystical union" spoken of by Calvin and the reformers in terms of the differences between ontology and soteriology: "The mystical union spoken of by Reformed theologians and confessions on the basis of the New Testament, is something quite different. The relationship here is not between created being and Divine being but between the sinner and the Redeemer. It is not a doctrine of being (ontology) but a doctrine of salvation (soteriology). Since man does not merely stand on a level of being below God, but is His creature and, moreover, a creature who runs away from his Creator, the possibility of his submerging or losing himself in God just does not arise." Cf., idem, *Theology of Calvin*, 126; Wendel, *Calvin*, 235; and Krusche, *Das Wirken des Heiligen Geistes nach Calvin*, 265-72.

[78] Calvin's interaction with Osiander involved themes unique to mysticism, such as essential divine participation. Extensive attention is given to Osiander in Chapter 5 below. Tamburello concedes (p. 2) that Calvin's refutation of Osiander can be seen as a critique of mystical themes. Calvin referred negatively to the *Theologia Deutsche* in a letter to the Reformed congregation at Frankfurt (23 February 1559, CO 47.442). Calvin also registered his dislike for Pseudo-Dionysius in *Inst.* (1543) 1.14.4; OS 3.157 (LCC 20.164-5). Cf. Tamburello, *Union with Christ*, 1-2.

[79] While Tamburello criticises such a generalization in others, it could be argued that he has ultimately fallen prey to it as well. He seems somewhat aware of this problem as he closes his study, prompting him to reconsider whether "mysticism" is indeed a profitable way of describing either Bernard's or Calvin's thought. Tamburello, *Union with Christ*, 110.

metaphor.[80] This is not to deny that Calvin was very fond of marriage imagery just as the mystics were. Indeed, it is evident that his affection for this imagery carried over into Genevan church life and liturgy. The suggestion may be true, moreover, that there was a more regular use of the marriage-union imagery made by Calvin (and other reformers) than in the preceding mystical and spiritual traditions. Describing the liturgical transition that took place in the sixteenth century, Kenneth Stevenson sees in the radical changes implemented in Strasbourg and Zurich the beginnings of the marriage reforms instituted by Luther and Calvin. Significantly, Stevenson points in particular to the increase in the Christ-Church union imagery employed by Luther and Calvin in their wedding services, an increase, Stevenson argues, over the customs of their medieval predecessors.[81]

Whether or not Calvin did in fact employ the imagery more often than his spiritualist forebears, his relationship to mysticism, as to any other movement, must be established on more than general similarities in language and piety. Much to be preferred is the approach that adopts a "hermeneutic of suspicion" when investigating the question of Calvin's influences and his ties to antecedent movements.[82] Judgments on Calvin's relation to mystical theologies of union with Christ must be based on case-by-case

---

[80] Note Calvin's heavy reliance on the "bone of his bone and flesh of his flesh" language (Doyle, "Repentance," 315, n. 79) and his extensive use of the Pauline metaphors of "Head," "holy marriage," "members of His body," etc., all of which, while indeed part of the mystical literature, are also prominent features in the Pauline corpus. Cf. *Inst.* (1559) 3.1.3; OS 4.3-5 (LCC 20.540-1); *Inst.* (1559) 3.11.10; OS 4.191-2 (LCC 20.736-8).

[81] On Farel's wedding service, Stevenson comments: "Many of the old customs have disappeared, including the ring. But both these rites show the path to be taken by Luther and Calvin in the future; the centrality of Scripture, and the lush use in new prayers of biblical images of creation, procreation, and the marriage of Christ and the Church. This last image they make much more of than their medieval predecessors." Kenneth Stevenson, *Nuptial Blessing: A Study of Christian Marriage Rites* (New York: Oxford, 1983), 125. While immensely significant, Stevenson's conclusion should probably be balanced with the work of d'Avray, whose critical edition of medieval marriage sermons reveals a rich and regular use of the metaphor made by certain thirteenth-century Parisian priests.

[82] On the Calvin-Bernard literary relationship, see A. N. S. Lane, *John Calvin: Student of the Church Fathers* (Grand Rapids: Baker, 1999), 87-114, 115-50 ("Calvin's Use of Bernard of Clairvaux" and "Calvin's Sources of Bernard of Clairvaux," respectively). See also, idem, *Calvin and Bernard of Clairvaux* (Princeton Theological Seminary: Studies, New Series no. 1, 1996).

examination of the textual sort, involving close attention to matters of context and conversation partners. It seems less than useful, in other words, to make large-scale comparisons using a broad, flexible conception of what qualifies as "mysticism." In light of the fundamental theological differences between Calvin's and Osiander's understanding of the *unio mystica*, one wonders why, again, though Tamburello notes Calvin's criticisms of Osiander, he does not address in detail to what extent Calvin's refutation of the Lutheran controversialist would also apply to mystical conceptions.[83] Such an investigation would seem to be required if the relationship of Calvin's teaching on union with Christ and justification and the mystical traditions is to be clarified.

These criticisms notwithstanding, Tamburello's work does highlight the importance of reading Calvin's teaching on union with Christ against a background of church tradition, part of which is mysticism. Also, to identify problems with Tamburello's thesis is not to deny any influence whatsoever of the mystical tradition upon Calvin. This is especially the case when the basic *imitatio Christi* theme is under examination, which resurfaces, though within a different theological framework, in Calvin's spirituality.[84]

Calvin and Luther: Justification and the Place of Good Works

In light of our observations on the character of Luther's early Reformation soteriology, and the importance of the union idea to both Luther and Calvin, the question that immediately commends itself is that of Calvin's relation to Luther. Calvin, of course, had the highest praise for his German predecessor, praise often expressed with superlatives.[85] As Steinmetz has pointed out, "Among the non-Lutheran theologians of the sixteenth century, none was more reluctant to disagree with Martin Luther or more eager to find

---

[83] Tamburello, *Union with Christ*, 87. Whereas he generally follows Kolfhaus in his reading of Calvin, it is with Kolfhaus's statements regarding mysticism that Tamburello pointedly disagrees (Tamburello, *Union with Christ*, 89; cf. Kolfhaus, *Christusgemeinschaft*, 131).

[84] This theme constitutes an important element in the argument of the Romans case study in Chapter 3 below.

[85] Calvin's praise for Luther is often joined to a negative reference to Zwingli, indicating that Calvin often thought of them together. Cf. Calvin to Bullinger, 25 November 1544 (no. 586), CO 11.774; Calvin to Farel, 26 February 1540 (no. 211), CO 11.24; and *Secunda Defensio...* (1556), CO 9.51. See Karl Barth, *The Theology of John Calvin* (Grand Rapids: Eerdmans, 1922; ET by Geoffrey W. Bromiley, 1995), 118.

common ground with him than John Calvin."[86] But disagree he sometimes did, even on aspects of the theology of salvation. Recent scholarship has at least qualified the earlier approach that tended to over-emphasize the continuity between the two. This has served as a corrective by focusing attention on the nature of their differences, a corrective that has rightly been deemed healthy.[87]

Restricting attention to the question of the relationship of good works of sanctification to justification by faith will clarify to what extent Luther and Calvin did in fact operate with similar yet different theological constructs. In his well-known criticism of Eck, Luther vigorously rejected any language of "acceptance" when good works – even of believers – were under discussion. To speak in any sense of God's acceptance of the believer's good works is to compromise all that the doctrine of justification by faith serves to safeguard. His position on the question is tied to his universal extension and application of a Law-Gospel hermeneutic. The effect of this hermeneutic is the relegation of "conditional" passages of Scripture to the category of Law as distinct from Gospel. Only in light of the controlling character of this idea in his biblical hermeneutic is Luther's puzzling exhortation to believers intelligible:

> The greatest art of Christians is to be ignorant of the whole of active righteousness and of the law; whereas outside the people of God, the greatest wisdom is to know and to contemplate the law... For if I do not remove the law from my sight and turn my thoughts

---

[86] Steinmetz, *Calvin in Context*, 172.
[87] Richard C. Gamble, "Current Trends in Calvin Research, 1982-90," in W. Neuser, ed., *CSSP*, 101-2. Gamble points to T. F. Torrance, *The Hermeneutics of John Calvin* (Edinburgh: Scottish Academic Press, 1988), 159; and A. Ganoczy and S. Scheld, *Die Hermeneutik Calvins* (Wiesbaden: F. Steiner, 1983), 88. Calvin's contribution, when compared with the reforming movement that preceded him (especially the work of Luther), is often described as one of synthesizing the divergent views represented by Luther and Zwingli. Others see in Calvin's relationship to Luther and Zwingli evidence that he was only a "powerful but not a creative thinker." For the former, see Barth, *Theology of Calvin*, 118-20. Barth (p. 119) refers to W. Dilthey ("Das natürliche System der Geisteswissenschaften im 17. Jahrhundert," *Archiv für Geschichte der Philosophie* [1893]: 229) as representative of the latter opinion. Assuming this line of inquiry, the question becomes whether Calvin's "synthesizing effort" is itself "creative" (p. 119) and exactly what is meant by "creative" in the first place.

to grace, as though there were no law and only pure grace, I cannot be blessed.[88]

Rome would recoil from such language, but, as Lillback notes, Rome was not alone in rejecting Luther's view. Lillback proposes to compare Calvin and Luther in terms of covenant and Law-Gospel. Unlike Luther, Reformed covenant theologians like Bullinger would have a much more positive place for the obedience of believers in discussions of covenantal conditionality.[89] It is within this Reformed covenantal framework, says Lillback, that we should locate Calvin's teaching on the subject. While Calvin steadfastly denies the *merit* of any act of obedience apart from Christ's, this does not mean that the good works of obedience performed by believers are unqualifiedly sinful. To the contrary, God "accepts" these works as good. Why? First, because God himself is the source of them. As Calvin explains,

> For the Lord cannot fail to love and embrace the good things that he works in them through his Spirit. But we must always remember that God accepts believers by reason of works only because he is their source and graciously, by way of adding to his liberality, deigns also to show acceptance toward the good works he has himself bestowed.[90]

Second, because "the *covenant of grace* includes perfect obedience to the law as its stipulation."[91] As the indispensable and necessary fruit of the covenant of grace, both justification and obedience together comprise the salvation that flows from that covenant. Consequently, whereas Luther warned believers to avoid the law, Calvin pointed his readers to the biblical imperatives of covenantal obedience. Here, says Lillback, one is able to observe the sharp differences between the way in which Luther and Calvin responded to the Roman Catholic charge that justification by faith alone is a "legal fiction":

---

[88] Cited by Gerhard Ebeling, *Luther*, trans. R. A. Wilson (Philadelphia: Fortress Press, 1972), 123-4, noted in Peter Lillback, *The Binding of God: Calvin's Role in the Development of Covenant Theology* (Texts and Studies in Reformation and Post-Reformation Thought; Grand Rapids: Baker, 2001), 186.

[89] "Bullinger declares that 'the steadfastness and purity of faith, further the innocence and purity of life, that is, the integrity and straight way by which the saints walk before God' are the very conditions of the covenant! One can see why Luther lumped the papists and the Zwinglians together as those who could not accurately teach justification by faith because of their failure to distinguish law and gospel." Lillback, *The Binding of God*, 185, referring to Luther, WA 40.249-53; LW 26.143-5.

[90] *Inst.* (1539) 3.17.5; OS 4.257 (LCC 20.807).

[91] Lillback, *The Binding of God*, 186 (emphasis Lillback's), referring to *Inst.* (1543) 4.13.6; OS 5.243 (LCC 21.1260).

Luther categorized covenant-conditional passages in Scripture as "law" rather than "gospel" while Calvin interpreted such passages in light of the nature of the covenant of grace, the benefits of which are *both* justification and sanctification. As Lillback notes, therefore, the law/gospel distinction is not for Calvin an "irreducible" one.[92] Rather, the gospel differs from law principally in the degree of what may be called redemptive-historical clarity.[93]

At the same time, the inseparability of justification and sanctification does not warrant their confusion. Calvin's *Antidote* to Trent reveals the importance of this clarification for Calvin.[94] While bestowed concurrently, the twin benefits are given in such a way that sanctification is still truly distinct from justification. In other words, the righteousness of the believer must not be confused with the righteousness of Christ. Only the latter is the meritorious ground of the believer's standing before God. The righteousness of works, however, in that they are in reality God's works in the believer, must not be opposed to the righteousness of Christ. The former is a subordinate, not a contrary, righteousness.[95] In short, "Luther's understanding of justification by faith alone had no room for inherent righteousness, while Calvin's view required it as an inseparable but subordinate righteousness."[96]

Appreciating the doctrine of the covenant as a distinguishing mark of Reformed soteriology is certainly helpful in identifying the differences between Luther and Calvin on salvation. Lillback is quite correct to identify a hermeneutical disagreement between Luther and Calvin: Luther's strict use of the law/gospel hermeneutic must not be reconciled simplistically with Calvin's broader and more complicated use of similar language. The question of the value and role of the believer's good works, as Lillback notes, is a still clearer signal of the presence of subtly different models of salvation.

Lillback's conclusions should be combined, however, with a reading of Calvin's own view of Luther's intentions, as expressed for example in Calvin's response to Pighius in 1543:

> When Luther spoke in this way about good works, he was not seeking to deprive them of their praise and their reward before

---

[92] Lillback, *The Binding of God*, 187.
[93] "From this we infer that, where the whole law is concerned, the gospel differs from it only in clarity of manifestation." *Inst.* (1559) 2.9.4; OS 3.401-2 (LCC 20.427).
[94] See *Calvin's Selected Works*, ed. and trans. by Henry Beveridge, (Grand Rapids: Baker, 1983) 3.128; CO 35.458.
[95] For this and related matters see Lillback, *The Binding of God*, 188-90.
[96] Lillback, *The Binding of God*, 192.

God. Nor did he ever say that God does not accept them or that he will not reward them; but he wanted to show only what they are worth if they are considered by themselves apart from God's fatherly generosity.[97]

Relating Justification and Renewal: Some Contemporaries and Regensburg

Among Protestants the heart of Luther's doctrine of justification rang true to the gospel. There remained a concern, however, in view of popular characterizations, that the insistence upon *sola fide* must not be confused with an excuse for moral indifference.

Here a further observation is in order. The focus in this introductory discussion upon Calvin and Luther might suggest, falsely, that they were alone in the attempt at a proper response to the Protestant dilemma. But others discussed union with Christ or justification at much greater length than Calvin. Indeed, Calvin's setting of the *duplex gratia* in a framework of union with Christ is but one of a number of sixteenth-century proposals.[98]

MARTIN BUCER: THREEFOLD JUSTIFICATION

Perhaps the most influential of the early proposals came from Martin Bucer's Strasbourg, where both Calvin and Peter Martyr

---

[97] Calvin, *The Bondage and Liberation of the Will: A Defence of the Orthodox Doctrine of Human Choice against Pighius*, ed. A. N. S. Lane; trans. G. I. Davies (Grand Rapids and Carlisle: Baker and Paternoster, 1996), 26. Lillback's comments on the differences between Calvin and Luther are salutary. His study provides only a part of the picture, however. A focused comparison of Calvin with the more contextually-proximate Melanchthon would have yielded more specific results. A step is taken in this direction in Chapter 3 below.

[98] Though his is easily the more familiar, Calvin's theology is not the sixteenth-century Reformed theology most impacted by the doctrine of union with Christ. This distinction should belong to Jerome (Girolamo) Zanchi (1516-1590) whose treatise *De spirituali inter Christum et ecclesiam, singulosque fideles, coniugio* (Herborn, 1591, drawn from his exposition of Ephesians) applies a marital-type union idea to a wide range of theological questions. This text was translated as *An Excellent and Learned Treatise, of the spirituall marriage betvveene Christ and the Church, and every faithfull man. Written in Latine by that famous and worthie member of Christ his Church H. Zanchius: and translated into English* (Cambridge: Printed by John Legate, printer to the University of Cambridge, 1592). The marital-union *possessio* and *proprietas* model associated with Luther above is also present in Zanchi, *Spirituall Mariage*, 43. Cf. also the discussion in Zanchi's 1585, *De religione christiana fides*, esp. Ch. XII, recently published as *De religione Christiana fides – Confession of Christian Religion*, 2 vols, ed. Luca Baschera and Christian Moser (Studies in the History of Christian Traditions 125; Leiden: Brill, 2007).

Vermigli spent time.[99] Bucer outlined a three-fold schema of justification which wrestles with the various elements of an Augustinian *duplex iustitia*,[100] trying to hold together "imputation" and "impartation." The threefold justification is (1) election, (2) faith and the Spirit as present enjoyment, and (3) full, eternal life.[101] Because good works serve as "causes" of justification (so defined) the reason for their necessity is natural. As Stephens explains, it is Bucer's concern to keep both imputation and impartation together that leads him to use them "almost indiscriminately." "One moment justification can mean to impute righteousness or to forgive, another moment it can mean to impart righteousness or to renew."[102] At the heart of this confusion is the reality that the Spirit is given, and this can only mean that God's righteousness is displayed in us.[103] Significantly, Stephens speculates that the fact that "the believer is in Christ and Christ in him" may account for Bucer's ambiguity.[104]

Peter Martyr Vermigli: Regeneration as the Context for Justification and Good Works

In his study of the development of Vermigli's doctrine of justification, Frank James has demonstrated that the Italian's time in Bucer's Strasbourg was especially important.[105] James documents

---

[99] On Bucer's doctrine of justification, see *Common Places of Martin Bucer, translation and annotations*, ed. D. F. Wright (Courtenay Library of Reformation Classics, 4; Appleford, 1972); and W. P. Stephens, *The Holy Spirit in the Theology of Martin Bucer* (Cambridge: Cambridge University Press, 1970). See also McGrath, *Iustitia Dei*, 221-2, who summarizes Bucer's doctrine. Bucer's doctrine has been heavily criticized. Besides McGrath's criticisms, see Otto Ritschl, *Dogmengeschichte* 3.141-52; Köhler, *Dogmengeschichte*, 362-4, 418; and Müller, *Martin Bucers Hermeneutik*, 16-40, each noted in Stephens, *The Holy Spirit*, 8, n. 2.
[100] Calvin's own soteriology has been described as including a form of "double justification." On this see the comment by Lane in Calvin, *The Bondage and Liberation of the Will*, 26, n. 73; idem, "Calvin and Article 5 of the Regensburg Colloquy," in H. Selderhuis, ed., *CPE*, 231-61.
[101] Stephens, *The Holy Spirit*, 53-4, citing from Bucer's commentary on Romans. As Stephens notes, Bucer also used a twofold justification model, i.e., before the ungodly (Paul) and the godly (James).
[102] Stephens, *The Holy Spirit*, 49.
[103] Stephens, *The Holy Spirit*, 52.
[104] Stephens, *The Holy Spirit*, 49.
[105] Frank A. James III, "*De Iustificatione*: the Evolution of Peter Martyr Vermigli's Doctrine of Justification," Ph.D. diss., (Westminster Theological Seminary, 2000). Cf. James, "The Complex of Justification: Peter Martyr Vermigli Versus Albert Pighius," in Emidio Campi, ed., *Peter Martyr Vermigli: Humanism, Republicanism, Reformation* (Geneva: Librarie Droz, 2002), 45-58; and Vermigli,

how in his Strasbourg years Vermigli adopted the distinctive marks of Bucer's doctrine, including the lack of a clear distinction between justification and regeneration or sanctification. It was only later, near the end of his time at Oxford (and after Bucer's death), that Vermigli abandoned Bucer's threefold model and removed regeneration/sanctification entirely out from under justification.

According to James, regeneration functions for Vermigli in a way similar to how union with Christ functions for Calvin.[106] In Vermigli's model, regeneration by the Spirit serves as the overarching principle of salvation, placing justification and sanctification in positive relationship. In his early discussion of justification, Vermigli, reminiscent of Luther, defends the necessity of good works simply by pointing to the fact that God "requires" obedience and by noting that salvation "demands" that believers are restored to the *imago Dei*. When providing a more theologically self-conscious reason for this necessity, Vermigli consistently refers to Spirit-regeneration by which a *habitus* of good works is developed in the believer.[107]

Importantly, James notes that the comparison with Calvin indicates a "functional parallel" but a "conceptual difference." By grounding justification in the regeneration-work of the Spirit, Vermigli, James argues, holds a "dynamic" view of justification "which allows internal renewal to be linked more intimately to the external forensic pronouncement." Whereas in Calvin union with Christ (as the context for salvation) leads to a clearer distinction between justification and sanctification, Vermigli's construct renders the relationship somewhat ambiguous.[108] Thus, against McClelland who claims union with Christ is a key to Vermigli's understanding of justification, James argues that, despite occasional reference to being "joined to Christ," for Vermigli union is effected "through the Spirit," in other words, through Spirit-regeneration.[109]

Justification and Predestination: Two Theological Loci, ed. and trans. by Frank A. James III (PML 8; Kirksville: Truman State University Press, 2003).
[106] James, "*De Iustificatione*," 337.
[107] James, "*De Iustificatione*," 187-90, 193-7; 339-41; 346-8.
[108] James, "*De Iustificatione*," 337.
[109] James, "*De Iustificatione*," 337, referring to Vermigli, *Romanos*, 523; cf. J. McClelland, *The Visible Words of God* (Grand Rapids: Eerdmans, 1957). On its own terms, of course, this would not distinguish Vermigli sufficiently from Calvin who also teaches that union with Christ comes "through the Spirit." The point made by James is dependent upon his wider argument with regard to Vermigli's understanding of regeneration.

MELANCHTHON: LUTHER'S "NECESSARY" JOINED TO AN EMPHASIS ON OBJECTIVITY

Because Melanchthon's approach is examined in some detail in the Romans case study below, only a sketch is necessary here. Melanchthon is best known for his insistence that justification must be understood forensically and as something grounded in Christ's righteousness *extra nos*. Where there are possible ambiguities in Luther's doctrine, Melanchthon is clear: justification is objective to us, not a subjective renovation of the faithful after the *imago Dei*.[110] With Melanchthon, concern is with preserving this objectivity, and the theological necessity for good works does not receive attention beyond what Luther had repeatedly stated, that is, that they are necessary on account of justification.[111]

REGENSBURG COLLOQUY, ARTICLE 5

The effort to relate the legal and transformative elements of salvation was eventually concentrated in the significant 1540/41 colloquy at Regensburg.[112] Here Roman Catholic and Protestant representatives managed to agree on a statement on justification before the Colloquy ultimately fell apart over the ever-present eucharistic and ecclesiastical differences. Though this agreement on justification was not accounted for when Trent issued its final

---

[110] It is important to remember that Melanchthon's views on justification developed and changed several times over the course of his career. For our purposes, especially in Chapter 3 below, I will focus on those features of Melanchthon's teaching that proved most determinative for, and stand as most reflective of, the position of classical Lutheran orthodoxy with respect to the complex of questions examined in this study.

[111] See the relevant sections in the *Apology of the Augsburg Confession* and the discussion in Chapter 3 below.

[112] The colloquy began in Hagenau in June and July 1540, was adjourned to Worms and then to Regensburg. On Regensburg, see G. Kretschmar, "Der Reichstag von Regensburg 1541 und seine Folgen im protestantischen Lager," 47-91; E. G. Gleason, *Gasparo Contarini* (Berkeley: University of California Press, 1993), 186-256; P. Matheson, *Cardinal Contarini at Regensburg* (Oxford: Oxford University Press, 1972); and the summary of the justification debate and the scholarship interpreting it in Anthony N. S. Lane, *Justification by Faith in Catholic-Protestant Dialogue: An Evangelical Assessment* (London: T. & T. Clark, 2002), 49-60, to whom I am indebted for many of the details concerning Regensburg. For the theological issues, note R. B. Ives, "An Early Effort toward Protestant-Catholic Conciliation: The Doctrine of Double Justification in the Sixteenth Century," *Gordon Review* 11 (1968-70): 99-110; and E. Yarnold, "*Duplex Iustitia*: The Sixteenth Century and the Twentieth," in G. R. Evans, ed., *Christian Authority* (Oxford: Oxford University Press, 1988), 207-13.

verdict several years later, it stands as a revealing index to early efforts to defend theologically the necessity of good works in those justified *sola fide*. As such, the statement should be brought alongside the distinct proposals and statements by Protestants (e.g., Bucer, Melanchthon, and Calvin) relating Luther's *extra nos* idea of justification to the acknowledged necessity for good works, and those of Eck and Sadoleto among Catholics critiquing the Protestant thesis.

Representing the Catholic side at the Colloquy were Eck, Contarini (papal legate for Regensburg), Pflug, and Gropper. Bucer, Melanchthon, and Pistorius represented the Protestants. Calvin was present but did not participate. The Regensburg agreement has to be approached as an ecclesiastical document, with all the specific, limited intentions that belong to this class of documents, rather than with the expectations belonging to a more expansive theological statement. The original form of the fifth article, *De restitutione regenerationis et iustificatione hominis gratia et merito, fide et operibus*, was reworked and revised until all consented to its final form, *De iustificatione hominis*.[113] In short, the article clarifies the distinction between the righteousness which grounds acceptance before God and the righteousness that belongs properly (or inherently) to the believer. Specifically, it describes an *iustitia imputata* and *inhaerens*,

---

[113] Lane, *Justification by Faith in Catholic-Protestant Dialogue*, 51-2. The text of the original article is found in G. Pfeilschifter, ed., *Acta Reformationis Catholicae*, vol. 6 (Regensburg: F. Pustet, 1974), 30-44; the shorter revision by Gropper in *Acta*, 6.44-52; and the final version in *Acta*, 6.52-4. Daphne Hampson, *Christian Contradictions: The Structures of Lutheran and Catholic Thought* (Cambridge: Cambridge University Press, 2001), 64-5, translates a portion of the article, but Lane, *Justification by Faith in Catholic-Protestant Dialogue*, Appendix 1 (pp. 233-7), has provided the only full translation of the article to date. See p. 52, n. 25 in Lane for a list of the literature on the article. On Calvin and Article 5, see Lane, "Calvin and Article 5 of the Regensburg Colloquy," in H. Selderhuis, ed., *CPE*, 233-63. I am grateful to Prof. Lane for allowing me to view a pre-publication version of this essay. See also, idem, "Cardinal Contarini and Article 5 of the Regensburg Colloquy (1541)," in O. Meuffels & J. Bründl, eds, *Grenzgängeder Theologie* (Münster: Lit Verlag, 2004), 163-90; idem, "Twofold Righteousness: A Key to the Doctrine of Justification? Reflections on Article 5 of the Regensburg Colloquy (1541)," in Mark Husbands and Daniel J. Treier, eds, *Justification: What's at Stake in the Current Debates* (Downers Grove: IVP, 2004), 205-24; idem, "A Tale of Two Imperial Cities: Justification at Regensburg (1541) and Trent (1546/7)," in *Justification in Perspective: Historical Developments and Contemporary Challenges*, ed. Bruce L. McCormack (Grand Rapids: Baker, 2006), 119-45. Note that Lane intends to publish a fuller analysis of Article 5 under the title *Compromising Patchwork or Ecumenical Breakthrough? The Regensburg Article on Justification (1541): Introduction, Text and Commentary*.

i.e., justification and sanctification. On account of such statements as (1) one is justified on the basis of "a living and efficacious faith," (2) there is no justification without the infusion of love, and (3) justifying faith is effectual through love, the article has often been described as stating a doctrine of "double justification."[114] This has recently been called into question, however, and for good reason.[115] By the slippery term "double justification" one of two models is usually intended: first, the view that not only the person but one's works are also "justified"; second, the view that justification is *based upon* both "imputed" and "inherent" righteousness. Calvin, as his interpreters have long recognized, taught the first and rejected the second of these views, so the use of "double justification" for both views is at least greatly confusing. The Regensburg article, as Lane argues, clearly *bases* justification on imputed, not inherent righteousness.

Reception of Regensburg was mixed, but mostly negative.[116] For his part, Luther reacted very negatively toward the article, and apparently was most concerned with the potential for Catholic exploitation of its language.[117] In a letter of 29 June to Johann Friedrich, for instance, Luther focused on ideas that were not excluded by the article's language. Significantly, he claimed, as Lane notes,

---

[114] Note from section 4 of the article: "So it is a reliable and sound doctrine that the sinner is justified by a living and efficacious faith, for through it we are pleasing and acceptable to God on account of Christ... But this happens to no one unless also at the same time love is infused which heals the will so that the healed will may fulfil the law, just as Saint Augustine said... Therefore the faith that truly justifies is that faith which is effectual through love..." "Regensburg Agreement (1541), Art. 5," in Lane, *Justification by Faith in Catholic-Protestant Dialogue*, 234-5; pp. 58-9 outlines the article's doctrine on these points.

[115] See C. S. Smith, "Calvin's Doctrine of Justification in Relation to the Sense of Sin and the Dialogue with Rome," M.Phil. thesis (London Bible College, 1993), 140-2, who lists those taking this view. Lane, *Justification by Faith in Catholic-Protestant Dialogue*, 58 and n. 51, rejects it.

[116] Basil Hall, *Humanists and Protestants 1500-1900* (Edinburgh: T. & T. Clark, 1990), 143, and Lane, *Justification by Faith in Catholic-Protestant Dialogue*, 54.

[117] For Luther's response, see Lane, *Justification by Faith in Catholic-Protestant Dialogue*, 53-6; Pfnür, "Die Einigung bei den Religions- gesprächen von Worms und Regensburg 1540/41," 64-8; and von Loewenich, *Duplex Iustitia*, 26-34, 48-55. Luther's judgment that the article did little more than juxtapose opposing positions is echoed in McGrath, *Iustitia Dei*, 247-8, and in Gleason, *Gasparo Contarini*, 227-8 (cf. Lane, *Justification by Faith in Catholic-Protestant Dialogue*, 55-6).

that the two ideas of justification by faith alone without works (Rom. 3) and faith working through love (Gal. 5) had been "zu samen gereymet und geleymet" (thrown together and glued together), whereas one refers to becoming righteous, the other to the life of the righteous. "So they are right, and so are we." This is like sewing a new patch onto an old garment (Matt. 9).[118]

Calvin, on the other hand, was quite positive, describing to Farel his surprise that "our opponents have yielded so much..." While it is not the full, nuanced statement that he would like, still nothing in the article sounded to Calvin inconsistent with "our writings."[119]

Three related observations may be made when comparing Luther's and Calvin's responses to Article 5. First, as Lane remarks,

> since the essence of Calvin's doctrine is precisely to hold these two [i.e., the Augustinian belief in transformation and the idea of imputed righteousness] in balance it is perhaps not so surprising that he was happy with the accord. Neuser has noted that at Worms Calvin was the Protestant theologian most willing to concede a *iustitia operum*. Calvin was able to accept the Regensburg article because he himself had carefully integrated justification and sanctification.[120]

Second, the article states that both imputed and inherent righteousness are promised and appropriated "in Christ" (§4; cf. §8), an idea reflective of Luther's language and which Calvin had already developed in sophisticated form in several publications, most recently in his 1539 revision of the *Institutio* and 1540 Romans commentary. Calvin does not make special note of this point in Article 5 – and indeed the article does not intend to relate

---

[118] Lane, *Justification by Faith in Catholic-Protestant Dialogue*, 53, referring to Luther, Letter of 10/11 May to Johann Friedrich, *WA Br.* 9.406-9, #3616.

[119] Calvin to Farel, 11 May 1541 (CO 11.215-16; CTS 4.260). For Calvin's reaction, see W. H. Neuser, "Calvins Urteil über den Rechtfertigungsartikel des Regensburger Buches," in M. Greschat and J. F. G. Goeters, eds, *Reformation und Humanismus* (Witten: Luther-Verlag, 1969), 176-94; the summary in Lane, *Justification by Faith in Catholic-Protestant Dialogue*, 56-7; and the fuller analysis in Lane, "Calvin and Article 5 of the Regensburg Colloquy." The contrast in Calvin's and Luther's responses is also summarized in Lillback, *The Binding of God*, 190-2.

[120] Lane, *Justification by Faith in Catholic-Protestant Dialogue*, 57, referring to Neuser's discussion in "Calvins Urteil über den Rechtfertigungs- artikel des Regensburger Buches," 178-83, which is based upon Neuser's examination of the manuscript records of the Worms Colloquy. Neuser published these records in Neuser, ed., *Die Vorbereitung der Religionsgespräche von Worms und Regensburg 1540/41* (Lane, p. 57, n. 46).

imputation and renewal in any sophisticated manner – but the phrase "in Christ" does point to Calvin's own effort to clarify the question through a combination of the need for "twofold righteousness" and the idea of union with Christ.

Third, the possibility should be noted here that the difference between Luther's and Calvin's reactions to Article 5 foreshadows the gradual divergence between Calvin and his Lutheran contemporaries on this subject. This divergence would not pertain to the definition of justification (as the forensically characterized imputation of Christ's uniquely meritorious righteousness for the forgiveness of sins) or to the fact of the necessity of good works, on which they were agreed, but to the fuller doctrine, that is, to the relationship of justification to sanctification and the theological rationale for the necessity of good works. At this point, this should only be taken as a suggestion, but I raise the matter with a view to what will soon follow in our study by way of confirmation. Furthermore, this possibility should be recognized as belonging inextricably to the pursuit, common to these sixteenth-century churchmen, of the way to satisfy the concerns for both the peace of conscience belonging to the justified and for the holiness of the Church.

Conclusion

I conclude this survey with three observations. First, in the study of sixteenth-century understandings of union with Christ, sensitivity to the real taxonomical problem is a prerequisite. In the period spanning late medieval mystical theologies and the new Reformation model(s) of salvation, a number of "unions with Christ" – incarnational/natural, justifying, eucharistic, ontological, marital, et al. – belonged to the ordinary discourse of both professional (academic) and popular spiritualities. In this survey, of course, only a taste of this variety has been possible. When attention is not sufficiently paid to historical context, however, then it is natural to expect to find analyses of Calvin's doctrine of justification that conclude, for example, that his forensicism in justification is inconsistent with his doctrine of a personal union with Christ by the Spirit. Even before looking at Calvin, it needs to be asked if this critique is in fact working with a particular conception of union which, by definition, would indeed mitigate forensicism. What "union with Christ" means for one must not be assumed to be the same for another. The possibility should at least be entertained that for the sixteenth-century Calvin, no such tension between forensicism and union existed because "union with Christ" was understood differently. Indeed, the closest idea in the sixteenth-century that would approximate this non-imputative and anti-forensic understanding is found in the theology of Andreas Osiander, whose doctrine of union with Christ Calvin adamantly rejected. More on this below.

Second, the development of Luther's thought attests to the importance of the relationship of union with Christ and justification for the Reformation's first theological steps. While the necessity for good works of obedience is not clearly addressed by Luther from within this framework, it nevertheless stands as evidence of the importance of the union concept to the distinctively Protestant understanding of salvation.

Third, in the complicated variety of early Reformation teaching on justification, the need to relate Christian obedience to justification in a theologically satisfying manner was acutely felt. On the outside, this need was pressed by critics of Protestantism who charged the *Lutheri* with creating a legal fiction. On the inside, however, this need was simply part of Luther's legacy, and belonged as a defining characteristic of a period of transition. Initially, this problem resulted in an astounding variety of models that defies simple categorization. To be understood, Calvin's thought must be located in this rapidly moving stream.

PART TWO

CHAPTER THREE

In Christ, Like Christ: Union with Christ, Good Works, and Replication in Calvin's *Romans*

Introduction

In a classic passage from the 1539 revision of his *Institutio*, Calvin's concentration on the indispensability of union with Christ for salvation is patent and unmistakable. In what is easily one of his most familiar passages, Calvin writes:

> We know, moreover, that he benefits only those whose Head he is, for whom he is the first-born among brethren, and who, finally, have put on him. This union alone ensures that, as far as we are concerned, he has not unprofitably come in the name of Savior. The same purpose is served by that sacred wedlock through which we are made flesh of his flesh and bone of his bone, and thus one with him. But he unites himself to us by the Spirit alone. By the grace and power of the same Spirit we are made his members, to keep us under himself and in turn to possess him.[1]

Significant in this striking assertion of the necessity of union with Christ for the reception of his redemptive benefits (indeed, for the "profitability" of Christ's work as Savior) is Calvin's allusion to several distinctively Pauline ideas drawn from Ephesians (4:15 and 5:30), Romans (8:29), and Galatians (3:27). These Pauline references point to the vital relationship between Calvin's work on Paul and this first revision and major reorganization of his *Institutes*. Calvin's "Paulinism" is arguably clearest at this stage of his career when his work on Paul and his revision of the *Institutio* were concurrent, and

---

[1] Calvin, *Inst.* (1539) 3.1.3; OS 4.5 (LCC 20.541). Where a 1539 passage is retained in 1559, I refer to 1559 and the reference to OS and LCC is noted. For Calvin's Romans commentary, citations are from the critical edition edited by T. H. L. Parker and D. C. Parker, *Commentarius in Epistolam Pauli ad Romanos* (COR II/13; Geneva: Droz, 1999), referred to as *Comm. Epist. ad Romanos*. The 1556 edition is also accessible in CO 49.102-96. Citations in English are from the CNTC translation by R. Mackenzie, with modification where necessary.

the importance of the 1539 revision for all subsequent editions points to its importance in Calvin's maturation.[2] Indeed, close examination reveals that much of the material that would famously become Book 3 of the 1559 *Institutio* has its roots in the final (1556) revision of the commentary on Romans, with many themes tracing back to the first (1540) edition, putting into perspective the scope of the influence of Calvin's reading of Paul beginning in the 1530s and extending through the 1540s.

In what follows we shall explore the *unio Christi-duplex gratia* relationship in Calvin's Romans commentary with concentration on themes that point to his perspective on the role of good works within a distinctly Protestant soteriology. After an introduction to the editions of the commentary, analyses follow of Calvin's comments on the *Argumentum* and on Rom 2:6-7, 13 (conditional language), Rom 3:20-31 (Augustine and Trent), Rom 6 (*imitatio Christi*), and Rom 8 (the Spirit of union). These studies are designed to highlight elements in Calvin's exposition that combine to form what will be termed his "replication principle," a theological-hermeneutical model from the perspective of which various features of his theology of union with Christ may be more clearly understood.

The Texts

First, however, a word about Calvin's *Commentary*. There were two revisions of the 1540 text: a minor one in 1551 and a major one in 1556. At the risk of understatement, the nearly twenty years that spanned the first and final forms of Calvin's *Romans* were not idle,

---

[2] The 1543 revision also reveals the impact of Calvin's *Romans*. For a discussion see Richard A. Muller, *The Unaccommodated Calvin: Studies in the Foundation of a Theological Tradition* (New York: Oxford, 2000), 145-6. On the relationship of the 1539 *Institutio* and the 1540 Romans commentary, see also A. Ganoczy, "Calvin als paulinischer Theologe," in *Calvinus Theologus*, 43-8. On the history of the *Institutio*, among many others see Wilhelm Niesel's discussion in OS 3.vi-l; J. Köstlin, "Calvins Institutio nach Form und Inhalt in ihrer geschichtlichen Entwicklung," *ThStKr* 41 (1868): 7-62, 410-86; B. B. Warfield, "On the Literary History of Calvin's 'Institutes'," *Presbyterian and Reformed Review* 10 (1899): 193-219; and the useful introductions in W. de Greef, *The Writings of John Calvin: An Introductory Guide*, trans. Lyle D. Bierma (Leicester: Apollos/Grand Rapids: Baker, 1993), 195-202; and François Wendel, *Calvin: The Origins and Development of His Religious Thought*, trans. Phillip Mairet (New York: Harper and Row, 1963), 111-49. Cf. also Paul C. Böttger, "Einzelanalyse der Institutio von 1536 und von 1559," in Böttger, *Calvins Institutio als Erbauungs buch: Versuch einer literarischen Analyse* (Neukirchen: Neukirchener, 1990), 55-142.

peaceful ones. Regarding the tumultuous context in which extensive revisions were made, T. H. L. Parker notes:

> The theological situation of 1556 was not exactly that of 1536; nor was the ecclesiastical situation the same. Between these two dates occur the Servetus affair (the reference to him occurs only in 1556 although his two books had appeared in the early fifteen-thirties), the Trinitarian controversies in Geneva, the controversies about predestination and free will involving Bolsec and Pighius and others, and the Council of Trent. These all called forth extended or new treatment of relevant passages.[3]

But, as Parker immediately goes on to note, the changes made do not necessarily indicate a fundamental shift in thinking: "At the outset, however, one point must be made quite clear. The changes made were far-reaching, but there was no change at all in Calvin's general understanding of the Epistle between 1536 and 1556."[4]

Calvin's tortuous relationship with the city of Geneva landed him in Bucer's Strasbourg as an exile during 1538-41. As a recent biographer has noted, it is here, in Strasbourg, that Calvin "became Calvin."[5] From the press of Wendelin Rihel in this city would come arguably the two most important publications in the development of his work: the 1539 revision of the *Institutio* and the *Commentary* published in 1540. The revision of the *Institutio* changed the smaller 1536 version into a full-fledged theological handbook, expanding the work from six to seventeen chapters. This 1539 revision would become the basis of all later revisions, including the final Latin edition of 1559, and, together with the 1543 edition, the text most of his contemporaries would recognize (and with which they would interact) as "Calvin's *Institutio*."[6]

In support of a high estimation of the theological impact of Calvin's Paulinism, David Steinmetz points out that Calvin's *Romans* played an especially prominent role in the successive editions of his *Institutio*. In the first (1536) edition, Calvin cites from Romans 162

---

[3] Calvin, *Comm. Epist. ad Romanos*, xvi. To this list I would add the publication of Andreas Osiander's disputations on justification in 1551, the impact of which I address in Chapter 5 below.

[4] Calvin, *Comm. Epist. ad Romanos*, xvi. Parker's conclusion is based on the largely unaltered form of Calvin's *Argumentum*.

[5] Bernhard Cottret, *Calvin: A Biography*, trans. M. Wallace McDonald (Grand Rapids: Eerdmans and Edinburgh: T. & T. Clark, 2000), 132, following J. Courvoisier, "Les catéchismes de Genève et de Strasbourg. Étude sur le développement de la pensée de Calvin," *Bulletin de la Société de l'Histoire du Protestantisme Français* 84 (1935): 107.

[6] For discussion see Muller, *Unaccommodated Calvin*, 118-39.

times; in the final (1559) revision, this number had swelled to 573.[7] The relatively modest (but growing) number of studies on Calvin's Pauline interpretation, especially his *Romans*, is therefore surprising.[8]

There are no sermons or lectures on Romans extant either before or after the first publication of his *Commentary* in 1540.[9] In light of the careful record made of his lectures beginning in the year 1549, we can be certain that Calvin did not lecture on the Epistle later than that date. Whether he lectured or preached on Romans before 1549 is therefore open to question, and yet there is reason to believe that he did so. Parker cites internal and external evidence to the effect that Calvin lectured on the Epistle upon his return to Geneva from Basel in 1536 in the capacity of *sacrarum literarum doctor*.[10] Parker suggests that the first edition of the *Commentary* was the result of these lectures begun in Geneva (although Basel is a possibility) "and completed in Strasbourg between the early summer of 1538 and October 1539, the date of the dedication."[11]

Calvin's epistle dedicatory is dated October 18, 1539. Calvin, therefore, as Parker has pointed out, must have resolved at an early age to begin his work with Paul and specifically with Romans.[12] Unlike Bullinger and Cajetan who began with Matthew or Bucer who began with the Synoptics, Calvin began with Romans and

---

[7] David C. Steinmetz, *Calvin in Context* (New York: OUP, 1995), 65.

[8] Within this growing body of literature, see H. Paul Santmire, "Justification in Calvin's 1540 Romans Commentary," *Church History* 33 (1964): 294-313; Benoit Girardin, *Rhetorique et théologique: Calvin, le Commentaire del'Epître aux Romains* (Paris: Beauchesne, 1979); T. H. L. Parker, *Calvin's New Testament Commentaries* (Grand Rapids: Eerdmans, 1971; 2nd ed. 1993); idem, "Calvin the Exegete: Change and Development," in *CED*, ed., W. H. Neuser, 33-46; idem, *Commentaries on the Epistle to the Romans, 1532-1542* (Edinburgh: T. & T. Clark, 1986); idem, with D. C. Parker, "Introduction," *Comm. In Epist. ad Romanos* (COR II/13); Fritz Büsser, "Bullinger as Calvin's Model in Biblical Exposition: an Examination of Calvin's Preface to the Epistle to the Romans," in *In Honor of John Calvin, 1509-64* (Montreal: McGill University, 1987), 64-95; David C. Steinmetz, "Calvin and the Patristic Exegesis of Paul," in *The Bible in the Sixteenth Century*, ed. David C. Steinmetz (Durham: Duke University Press, 1990), 100-18.

[9] For my discussion of the publication history of Calvin's *Romans* I am indebted to the details provided by T. H. L. Parker and D. C. Parker in the extensive introduction to their critical edition; to T. H. L. Parker, *Calvin's New Testament Commentaries*, 6-59; and especially to BC 1.74-7.

[10] Calvin, *Comm. Epist. ad Romanos*, xiii.

[11] Calvin, *Comm. Epist. ad Romanos*, xiii.

[12] Parker, *Calvin's New Testament Commentaries*, 9-10.

worked his way through each of the Pauline epistles before turning to the Gospels. Parker speculates that this indicates Calvin's conviction that a "deliberate theological policy" was "demanded by the New Testament itself," one which necessarily begins with Romans as the key to the rest of the New Testament.[13] Parker's speculation finds some justification in Calvin's language about the Epistle's canonical-hermeneutical significance. Like Luther before him Calvin, in his *Argumentum*, locates the Epistle's value in this feature: "if anyone acquires a true understanding of it, he will have doors open into all the most secret treasures of Scripture."[14]

Union with Christ, Justification, and Sanctification in Calvin's *Romans*

The degree to which union with Christ pervades his exposition is astonishing. To a certain extent, it is true, regular attention to the idea is required by his method of commentary which followed the text closely rather than drew out major *loci* for discussion. But the nature of Calvin's handling of the idea suggests that more than the mere union-language of the Epistle – especially in Romans 6 and 8 – is responsible for its pervasiveness. Rather, it is evident that Calvin's comments reflect his understanding that union with Christ is basic to the Apostle's teaching on the application of redemption; and that this reading of the Apostle influenced the maturation of his soteriology as this maturation is evidenced in the revisions of the *Institutes*. Because of the quantity of passages from the commentary that could profitably be examined in detail, however, the following selection of only a few choice examples of Calvin's exegesis should be seen as generally representative of the theology of the whole,[15]

---

[13] Parker, *Calvin's New Testament Commentaries*, 31-5. Parker recognizes (p. 34) that "this thesis has wider implications, in that it undermines the old view that, in contrast to Luther's 'Johannine' Christology, Calvin's was of the 'Synoptic' type..." He notes (p. 34; n. 92) Barth's comments in this regard: "It is in the succession of the Johannine type that we have obviously to see Eutyches' and later Luther's interpretation of Christ, in the succession of the Synoptic type that of Nestorius and of Calvin" (*CD* I/2, p. 24).
[14] Calvin, *Comm. Epist. ad Romanos*, 7; CNTC, 5.
[15] This applies not only to the passages examined but also to the theology discussed. What follows must not be confused, therefore, with a truly comprehensive treatment of Calvin's treatment of conditional language, works/obedience, merit, Trent, or union with Christ. In particular, and as indicated in the introductory chapter, this analysis often assumes the more general work done on Calvin's thought in Wallace, *Calvin's Doctrine of the*

keeping in view, also, the fact that his commentary was published in three recensions. The first indications of Calvin's ideas on the subject occur in the *Argumentum*.

The Argumentum

Calvin's *Argumentum* succinctly states his understanding of the Epistle's principal themes.[16] This *Argumentum* remains essentially unchanged in 1551 and 1556. Here a perspective of the widest possible scope is taken on the Apostle's teaching in the Epistle. Therefore, Calvin's comments on union with Christ in the *Argumentum* serve to indicate his view of the significance of the *unio* idea in the Epistle's overall argument.[17] As will be clear at various points later in this chapter, his comments on the text of the Epistle (the commentary proper) confirm this initial impression.

What in this "methodical" Epistle is the "main argument" (*principale argumentum*), the deduction of which Calvin deems such a fine example of the Apostle's artistic skill? Calvin's observations center on Paul's flow of argument, his rhetoric. Having first proved his apostleship Paul turns to the gospel, but in doing so he must address the disputed topic of "faith" with which any discussion of the gospel is "inevitably accompanied." "Thus he enters on the main subject of the whole Epistle, which is that we are justified by faith." In Calvin's division of the Epistle, justification is the theme to

---

Christian Life; Niesel, *Theology of Calvin*; Wendel, *Calvin*; and Venema, "The Twofold Nature of the Gospel."

[16] While Mackenzie's CNTC translation of *argumentum* as "theme" is legitimate on linguistic grounds, it should be noted that his choice may unintentionally obscure Calvin's intention of introducing an *argumentum* in the specifically humanistic sense. The matter is ultimately a minor one, so while the point should be noted it must not be overstated. For the function of *argumenta* and the humanist stress on the identification of leading themes, see Manfred Hoffman, *Rhetoric and Theology: The Hermeneutic of Erasmus* (Toronto: University of Toronto Press, 1994), 6, 8, 25, 37-8; 145-8; and the discussion of Calvin in Muller, *Unaccommodated Calvin*, 28-9, 31-3, et al. Indicative of its importance, Calvin's *Argumentum* was published separately in French as *Argument et Sommaire de l'Epistre aux Romains* (Geneva: Jean Girard, 1545). See BC 1.176-7.

[17] Note the important observation of Susan E. Schreiner ("Exegesis and Double Justice in Calvin's Sermons on Job," *CH* 58 [1989]: 323): "The history of exegesis requires its students to recognize that premodern exegetes approached a biblical book as a coherent whole. Therefore, their exegesis of particular verses presupposes a comprehensive preunderstanding of how the text coheres and the relation of its message to a whole host of assumed theological and exegetical convictions."

chapter five, the contents of which are summarized thus: "Man's only righteousness is the mercy of God in Christ, when it is offered by the Gospel and apprehended by faith" (*Unicam esse hominibus iustitiam, Dei misericordiam in Christo, dum per Euangelium oblata, fide apprehenditur*).[18] This, in short, is the Epistle's *principale argumentum*.

But all are asleep in their sins and thus "flatter and deceive themselves" by entertaining a "false idea of righteousness," one which lulls them into thinking they have no need for the righteousness of faith. Human beings are "intoxicated" with sin. There is an unqualified necessity, therefore, that all become convinced of their need and state before they will seek the true righteousness. According to Calvin, this is precisely the Apostle's aim in the opening chapters: he convinces them of their sin and awakens them from their slumber. These first chapters thus serve as a principal exegetical resource for Calvin's Augustinian anthropology. Calvin's later criticism of the Augustinian concept of grace in chapter three of his commentary is, in Calvin's presentation, the result of an "Augustinianism" arguably more thoroughgoing than that of the father himself. Men and women think wrongly about grace because they think wrongly about sin.[19]

Calvin then explains how, having emptied all of trust in their own goodness, the Apostle turns to discuss further the righteousness of faith. In chapter four Abraham is summoned as *exemplar* of this faith; he is to be regarded as a "model and general pattern" (*instar regulae et generalis cuiusdam exemplaris*) of the justification which comes by faith. The fifth chapter is devoted to expounding through examples the idea already present in the previous chapters. In the fifth chapter, explains Calvin, Paul argues *a maiori* from the copiousness of the divine love as demonstrated in the gift of the Son.

---

[18] Calvin, *Comm. Epist. ad Romanos*, 7; CNTC, 5. Richard Muller helpfully compares Calvin's division of Romans with Melanchthon's, Bucer's, and Bullinger's in "'Scimus enim quod lex spiritualis est': Melanchthon and Calvin on the Interpretation of Romans 7.14-23," in *Philip Melanchthon (1497-1560) and the Commentary*, ed. Timothy J. Wengert and M. Patrick Graham (Sheffield: Sheffield Academic Press, 1997), 216-37.

[19] The differences between Calvin's and Melanchthon's summaries of this material are largely due to divergent perspectives on the genre of commentary. Thus Melanchthon here introduces the disputed opinions of previous exegetes into his *Argumentum* while Calvin restricts himself to the text. As Muller has observed ("Scimus enim quod lex spiritualis est," 225), "The point is much like Melanchthon's, but it lacks reference either to Origen and Pelagius or to human philosophy – so that Calvin's point, stated with his characteristic sense of rhetorical oppositions, lacks the theological specificity of Melanchthon's point, while at the same time having perhaps a broader hortatory appeal."

To clarify how completely our sins are absorbed or devoured (*absorberi*) by the infinite goodness of God, Paul introduces a series of comparisons: sin and righteousness, Christ and Adam, death and life, law and grace.

Here, however, the importance of Calvin's subsequent comments should be highlighted. In light of the function of *argumenta* in the genre of sixteenth-century commentary, Calvin's identification of the Epistle's principal points and arguments indicates what he deemed its principal theological themes. Thus the role of union with Christ in his connection of the discussion of justification culminating in chapter five with the beginning of sanctification in chapter six should at least be hinted at in the *Argumentum*, and in fact it is. When Calvin turns to this crucial break in the Epistle in order to construct a "bridge," his perspective shifts sharply from the justification-righteousness developed in the previous five chapters to the sanctification-righteousness prominent in the sixth. His highly significant comments on this transition will be examined shortly, but even here in the *Argumentum* one is provided with an indicator of his basic framework. He marks the transition with an important summative statement of the Apostle's soteriological structure:

> In chapter six he turns to discuss the sanctification which we obtain in Christ. As soon as the flesh has had a little taste of this grace, it is liable to gratify its vices and desires without disturbance, as though grace were now ended. Against this Paul maintains here that we cannot receive righteousness in Christ without at the same time laying hold of sanctification. He takes his argument from baptism, by which we are admitted into fellowship with Christ. We are buried with Christ in baptism so that we may die to ourselves and be raised through His life to newness of life. It follows, therefore, that no one can put on the righteousness of Christ without regeneration.[20]

The significance of Calvin's statement must not be overlooked. To prevent indulgence in the vices of the flesh, Paul argues for the *simultaneity* of sanctification and justification from the origin of these

---

[20] Calvin, *Comm. Epist. ad Romanos*, 9; CNTC, 7-8: "Sexto capite descendit ad sanctificationem quam in Christo obtinemus. Siquidem carni proclive est, simul ac levem gratiae huius gustum usurpavit, vitiis ac libidinibus suis placide indulgere, quasi iam defuncta foret. Paulus vero contra hic contendit, non posse nos iustitiam in Christo percipere, quin simul sanctificationem apprehendamus. Argumentatur a Baptismo, per quem in Christi participationem initiamur. Illic Christo consepelimur, ut nobis emortui, per eius vitam suscitemur in vitae novitatem. Sequitur ergo, sine regeneratione neminem posse induere ipsius iustitiam."

graces in Christ. This is signified in baptism, a sign of initiation into Christ-participation (*per quem in Christi participationem initiamur*).[21] But, crucially, how does Paul defend this simultaneity? Calvin is clear: like justification, sanctification is also obtained *in Christo*. Specifically, Calvin's emphasis in the *Argumentum* is on the radical impossibility of experiencing the presence of one and the absence of the other. We cannot receive (*non posse percipere*) righteousness in Christ (justification) without sanctification. Or, "It follows, therefore, that no one can (*neminem posse*) put on the righteousness of Christ without regeneration." Hence the reference to baptism, which Calvin sees as Paul's calculated way of clarifying this specific point. It is in the course of his argument for the necessity of sanctification that Paul recalls baptism. Why? Because it is the very sign of union with Christ. Union with Christ, then, of which baptism is a sign, is that which joins justification and sanctification together in a necessary relationship: when one receives, "lays hold of," Christ, one lays hold of both justification and sanctification. The indissoluble unity of the two graces is the effect of the singularly determinative and presupposed *unio*-reality.

Beyond the Romans 5-6 "bridge" Calvin identifies another place in the Epistle where union with Christ is basic to Paul's sophisticated thesis. In chapter eight, which Calvin sees as devoted entirely to the consolation of weak but believing consciences, Paul commends certain truths to these believers. Against the ungodly prone to unwarranted flattery, it must first be clear that the benefit of a justly pure conscience belongs exclusively to the regenerate, those in whom the Spirit of God "lives and abounds." Then two truths appear:

> All those who have been grafted into Christ our Lord by His Spirit are beyond the danger or likelihood of condemnation, however burdened they may still be by their sins. In the second place, if those who remain in the flesh lack the sanctification of the Spirit, none of them has any share in this great blessing.[22]

---

[21] In this section I refer to baptism as a sacramental "sign" even though Calvin does not use *signa* language here. In my view this is not significant as he does not hesitate to refer to baptism as a sign elsewhere (see, e.g., *Inst*. 4.15-16) and the use of *signa* of course does not sufficiently indicate a particular view on the nature of baptismal efficacy.

[22] Calvin, *Comm. Epist. ad Romanos*, 10; CNTC, 8: "Explicat igitur duo: Omnes qui Domino Christo per eius Spiritum sunt inserti, extra damnationis periculum et aleam esse, utcunque onerati sint adhuc peccatis. Deinde, Omnes qui in carne

According to Calvin, then, divine acquittal belongs only to those who have been grafted (*inserti*) into Christ by the Spirit. Furthermore, only the engrafted have a "share" in this blessing. Thus, already in the *Argumentum*, Calvin sees Paul addressing not only the forgiveness/renewal relationship but also the corresponding divine acquittal/troubled conscience dilemma from the vantage-point provided by union with Christ. Paul goes on in this chapter to show how the troubles of this life, far from disturbing our eternal life actually promote it, since the humiliation-exaltation pattern of Christ's experience belongs to those for whom he is Head. The pattern followed by the Head is necessarily that of the members. This molding or fashioning according to the Christ-exemplar of "first suffering, then glory" is essential to the progress of our wider conformity to him.[23]

In his *Argumentum*, therefore, Calvin locates the heart of the Romans soteriology in the righteousness of God in Christ – not only *extra nos* but also *in nobis* – which is made ours by a faith-union with Christ by the Holy Spirit. Perhaps the point is at its clearest and most forceful when Calvin employs a particular metaphor in service of his soteriology, the metaphor of "tearing Christ into pieces" to which sustained attention is given in Chapter 5 below. In three different passages in the Romans commentary (on 6:1; 8:9, 13), all added in the final, 1556 revision, Calvin says that to contemplate the presence of justification without sanctification, or, in other words, to argue the possibility of one being justified and yet empty of good works, is effectively to "tear Christ into pieces." To what extent this union-idea, already present in the *Argumentum*, is clarified and expanded in the more substantial exegetical section (the commentary proper) now follows. We begin with a crucial, perpetually significant exegetical question that continues to shape perspectives on the nature of saving grace.

Obedience and Eternal Life: The Conditional Language of Romans 2 in Light of Romans 8

In his *Enchiridion*, John Eck, Catholic apologist and vocal opponent of Luther, referred to Romans 2:6, 10, and 13 in his discussion of faith and works, pointing out against the *Lutheri* the reward or merit

---

manent, expertes sanctificationis Spiritus, nequaquam esse tanti boni participes."
[23] Calvin, *Comm. Epist. ad Romanos*, 10; CNTC, 8-9.

In Christ, Like Christ

promised in each verse.²⁴ The full list of verses or passages listed in support for Eck's *Proposition 1*, "That faith does not suffice without works, and works are something meritorious for eternal life, (1532: from divine fore-ordination) and God's accepting grace," is substantial. Occasionally, Eck makes a polemical observation after a reference. For example, after noting Luke 6:23, Eck states, "If reward, therefore, and merit, to whom is reward owed? For these terms are to be interchangeably used in a relative sense, where one cannot be understood without the other." Eck also cites four Pauline passages (and one from Luke) as part of a brief discussion of how good, living works are acceptable to God and worthy of eternal life, as opposed to works done by the impious which the Apostle condemns. Most importantly, however, of a total of fifty-seven biblical citations (including eight apocryphal citations), eighteen are from epistles traditionally regarded as Pauline, not including two from the Epistle to the Hebrews. In almost every case, the passages in Eck's list are *instances of conditional language*, that is, to places where eternal life is conditioned upon obedience or good works.²⁵

Among Calvin's chief concerns, therefore, was the acutely felt obligation to account fully for Paul's conditional language, perhaps especially in Romans 2. Here the Apostle makes the explicit statement that God "will render to every man according to his works" (v. 6), specifically "to those who by perseverance in doing good seek for glory and honor and immortality, eternal life" (v. 7).

---

²⁴ John Eck, *Enchiridion Locorum Communium...* (1529, rev. 1532 and 1541), Cap V, Prop 1, 47ʳ (Prop 1 spans fols. 45ᵛ-48ʳ in the 1541 text). Cf. CC 34.88 and Eck, *Enchiridion of Common Places Against Luther and Other Enemies of the Church* (trans. Ford Lewis Battles; Grand Rapids: Baker, 1979), 52. Reward and merit are not clearly distinguished in Eck.

²⁵ The list is as follows, in order: Gen. 4:4-5, 7 (1529); Gen. 15:1; Is. 40:10; Jer. 31:16; Hos. 10:12; Prov. 11:18; Wisd. 3:15; Wisd. 5:16; Wisd. 10:17; Ecclus. 2:8; Ecclus. 9:10; Ecclus. 16:15; Ps. 17:24-5; Ps. 118:112; Ruth 2:12; 2 Chr. 15:7; Jn. 4:36; Mt. 5:12; Lk. 6:23; Mt. 6:1-2; Mt. 7:21; Mt. 10:42; Mt. 20:4; Mt. 19:17; Mt. 25:35; Mt. 25:34; Jn. 5:29; Jn. 15:14; Rom. 2:6; Rom. 2:10; Rom. 2:13; 1 Cor. 3:8; 2 Cor. 5:10; 1 Cor. 9:17; 1 Cor. 15:58; 2 Cor. 4:17; Gal. 6:8; Col. 3:23-4; Col. 1:10; Phil. 1:21; Phil. 2:12; Heb. 6:10; Heb. 13:16; 2 Jn. v.8; and 1 Jn. 3:7. Subsequently, Eck cites Gal. 5:6; Rom. 11:6; Rom. 4:4; Eph. 5:5; and Lk. 18:10ff. as part of a brief discussion (included in 1529 and 1532 but absent in the 1541 edition) of how good, living works are acceptable to God and worthy of eternal life. A 1532 addition lists Ex. 1:21 (and Augustine, *DCD* 5.12, 15); Ecclus. 3:33 (and Augustine two more times: *Enn. in Ps* 127:23 and *De Poenitentia*, ch. 3); 1 Cor. 13:3 (and [pseudo]Augustine, *De vera et falso poenitentia*); followed by (but also absent in 1541): Ecclus. 12:5f; Dan. 4:24 (and Gregory VII from *Decr.* 2.33.3.5.6); Jn. 7, 8, etc.

The relationship of 2:13 ("for not the hearers of the Law are just before God, but the doers of the Law will be justified") to 3:20 ("because by the works of the Law no flesh will be justified in His sight") poses a similar interpretative problem.

SIXTEENTH-CENTURY APPROACHES

A sampling of contemporary approaches suggests a wide variety of readings. On the Roman Catholic side, Cardinal Grimani's exposition is elaborate, proposing an "easy" solution by way of a distinction at the point of the incarnation. Those who lived before Christ only have their meritorious works justified *after* his death and resurrection. Paul is teaching that these who obeyed the Law could not be justified until this had occurred. After Christ's resurrection, however, "there was conferred on these same works the merit of his death, so that they became meritorious and their doers were justified."[26]

Other approaches are more recognizably Catholic. Guilliaud, for example, resolves the passages into first (3:20) and second (2:13) stages of justification, corresponding to the system of free/unmerited and cooperative/merited grace, respectively. The penitential system, as Parker notes, is also the presupposition of Cajetan's reading.[27] As in Grimani, Haresche's extended exposition of *iustificabuntur* as carrying a four-fold distinction reveals a concern for the centrality of Christ. But, like Grimani but perhaps more explicit, Haresche remains committed to a cooperative understanding of justification. Hence justification is grounded partly on the merit of Christ, partly on the merit of one's obedient act. Parker has summarized Haresche's position, which intimates that "justification is the work of God, that it depends on the merits of Christ, that it also depends on man's cooperation with grace, and that good works flowing from faith working by love are meritorious."[28] It is clear that

---

[26] Marino Grimani, *Commentarii In Epistolas Pauli, ad Romanos, Et Ad Galatas* (Venice, 1542), 22ᵛ, as noted and discussed in Parker, *Commentaries on Romans*, 132. On Grimani and others, see Parker, *Commentaries on Romans*, 125-32, who summarizes a number of sixteenth-century approaches to the dilemma.

[27] Claude Guilliaud, *Collatio In Omnes Divi Pauli Apostoli Epistolas,...* (Lyons, 1542), 15; Cajetan (Thomas de Vio), *Epistolae Pauli et Aliorum ad Graecam veritatem castigatae...* (Paris, 1532), VIII G; in Parker, *Commentaries on Romans*, 131.

[28] Philibert Haresche's four-fold distinction with respect to *iustificabuntur* is *effectivé, meritorié, exequutivé,* and *dispositivé* (*Expositio Tum Dilucida, Tum Brevis Epistolae Divi Pauli Ad Romanos cum definitionibus vocum difficiliorum, et diversarum acceptionum adnotatione,...* [Paris, 1536], xliʳ). For an explanation and

oversimplifications of the late medieval and early Reformation-era Catholic doctrine as, flatly, a salvation by meritorious works, needs to be sufficiently nuanced to account for the complexity in these readings. Almost without exception, an effort is made to make Christ central to the grace of justification without denying the vital human element.

In the view of the Reformers, however, this effort is ultimately unsuccessful. Throughout Lefèvre's exposition of the Epistle stress is placed on the fact that salvation depends on the will and work of God and not on man. However, though as a reform-minded humanist he wishes to emphasize that justification is primarily by grace and not works, Lefèvre, like Erasmus, "values works not only as preparing for justification, but also for retaining and augmenting it."[29] Like Grimani, Lefèvre also reconciles Rom 2:13 with 3:20 by focusing on the future tense (*iustificabuntur*): he interprets Paul as saying "the doers of the law *are* not justified but *will be* justified. For works, if they are good, *prepare for the reception of justification*."[30] Erasmus's single focus, following Origen and Chrysostom, is also on eschatological justification of Christians by works.[31]

Unlike Lefèvre and Erasmus, most Protestant readings stand in stark contrast with Roman Catholic exegesis. Even within this group, however, diversity still obtains. Joel Kok has discussed some of the key differences among Bucer, Melanchthon, and Calvin in the interpretation of these verses, concluding that Calvin's exegesis is indicative more of Melanchthon's than of Bucer's influence.[32]

---

the comparison with Grimani, see Parker, *Commentaries on Romans*, 135, from whom this information comes.

[29] John B. Payne, "Interpretations of Paul in the Reformation," *Encounter* 36 (1975): 202. I include Erasmus under the Reformation readings not because his theology is distinctly Protestant but because he represents the reform-minded humanism with which Calvin was familiar.

[30] See John B. Payne, "Erasmus and Lefèvre d'Étaples as Interpreters of Paul," *ARG* 65 (1974): 70-71; "Interpretations of Paul," 202. Italics mine.

[31] Erasmus, *CWE* 56.76-7. Cf. Payne, "Erasmus and Lefèvre d'Étaples," 75: "Whereas Faber had interpreted these verses as especially applying to the life of the Christian *prior* to faith (works do not justify but prepare for justification), Erasmus sees them as applying to the Christian life *after faith*. But that difference in interpretation does not at all take away from their basic agreement that Paul, however much he may emphasize faith, does not intend to deny the necessity of good works, whether prior or posterior to faith."

[32] Joel Edward Kok, "The Influence of Martin Bucer on John Calvin's Interpretation of Romans: A Comparative Case Study," Ph.D. diss. (Duke University, 1993), 67-74. Kok's thesis is intended as a corrective of the view held by W. van't Spijker, et al., that relates Bucer and Calvin more positively. For

Among the theological essays included at the beginning of his commentary, Bucer provided a full discussion relating 2:6 with 3:20.[33] In all, three *conciliationes* are devoted to the difficult passages in chapter two.[34] Bucer reconciles Paul's statements by careful use of distinctions, particularly that of primary and secondary causation. The language of merit or reward is accordingly regarded as belonging to salvation as its secondary (inferior) cause. The primary cause is the goodness of God.[35] The stress in Bucer's exposition of *iustitia Dei* is clearly on the visible and the transformative rather than on the external and imputative as in Melanchthon. Hence, in his Augustinian definition of *iustitia*, not only justifying faith but also the sanctifying effects of faith are included.[36] The comparative ambiguity of his reading is further indicated by his apparent acceptance of Sadoleto's commentary which had been censured by Paris and banished by Rome for its doctrine of justification. This feature is precisely what Bucer had praised in the commentary, claiming it was consistent with that of the reformers.[37]

Luther, see his discussion of "reward texts" in *De Servo Arbitrio*, pt. III, as well as his distinction of "consequence" from "reward" in Gordon E. Rupp and Philip S. Watson, eds, *Luther and Erasmus: Free Will and Salvation* (Philadelphia: Westminster/John Knox Press, 1969), 208-15.

[33] Bucer, *Harmonization of the verses "God renders to every man according to his works," and "No one will be justified by works,"* in *Metaphrases et Enarrationes*... (2nd ed., Basel, 1562), 99-106. See also, *Harmonization of the verses "... him who justifies the ungodly," and "I will not justify the ungodly,"* (231-2) and Section 8 (on Justification) in his Preface, translated and edited by D. F. Wright, *Common Places of Martin Bucer* (Courtenay Library of Reformation Classics 4; Appleford: Sutton Courtenay Press, 1972), 159-69. These translations of the "harmonizations" are Wright's.

[34] "Conciliatio horum, deus reddit uniquique secundem facta sua, & nemo ex factis iustificabit," "Conciliatio eius, quod Deus personam non recipit, Et quod pollicetur se bene facturum filiis, propter pietatem parentum," and "Conciliatio II Huius, Iustificari eos qui faciunt legem, cum illo, Neminem iustificari ex operibus legis," Bucer, *Metaphrases et Enarrationes*, pp. 115, 126, and 129, respectively. Marijn de Kroon, *Martin Bucer und Johannes Calvin*, trans. Hartmut Rudolph (Göttingen: Vandenhoeck and Ruprecht, 1991), 59-117, provides both discussion and reproduction of some of these texts.

[35] Bucer, *Metaphrases et Enarrationes*, 116, 127. See Kok, "The Influence of Martin Bucer," 69-70.

[36] See Stephens, *The Holy Spirit*, 48-50.

[37] So M. Bernard Roussel, "Martin Bucer et Jacques Sadolet: la concorde possible," *Bulletin de la Société de l'histoire de protestantisme français* 22 (1976): 525-50. See also the discussion by Parker, *Commentaries on Romans*, 27-9, 166, 174-80. Bucer's association of Sadoleto's doctrine with that of the reformers (and thus as possible grounds for reconciliation) is a palpable indicator of the differences

MELANCHTHON: LAW, NOT GOSPEL

The question of good works was a controversial one among the disciples of Luther already in Melanchthon's day. In the course of his career, conflict with Brenz on the question gave way to conflict with Agricola and eventually with Osiander. It is in this controversial setting that Melanchthon's teaching on the subject, in particular his introduction of a third use of the law (as a guide for Christian obedience), should be appreciated.[38]

Melanchthon's exposition is sensitive to uses of the passage to support the Catholic concept of *meritum*, but he is confident that those properly instructed in doctrine will be able easily to harmonize such conditional statements with others that seem to say the contrary.[39] Melanchthon's Law-Gospel hermeneutic then immediately goes to work to explain the passage. The statement "he will reward everyone according to his works" is Law, and means God will reward the righteous and punish the wicked. This word of the Law must be interpreted by the light of the Gospel, however, which teaches us who are the truly righteous and in what way works please God. It is the Gospel and not the Law that instructs us from whom that faith comes which is the highest form of worship and the greatest work, that is, trust in the mercy of God. Besides this divinely-bestowed faith, and after its bestowal, other works are enjoined upon the believer.[40] But Paul's assertion, far from

---

between Bucer and Calvin when it came to the *distinctio* element in Calvin's distinct-but-inseparable formula for clarifying the *duplex gratia* relationship, especially in view of their sharply divergent responses to Sadoleto.

[38] The controversial setting of Melanchthon's teaching on good works is expertly examined in Timothy J. Wengert, *Law and Gospel: Philip Melanchthon's Debate with John Agricola of Eisleben over* Poenitentia (Grand Rapids: Baker and Paternoster, 1997). As the "first public controversy among Luther's students," this exchange is also significant inasmuch as it "profoundly shaped the nature of later Lutheranism by making the distinction between law and gospel one of its distinguishing characteristics" (p. 18). Also, Melanchthon's later introduction of the third use should be noted. Here he still only referred to two uses (see "De duplici usu legis" in *MSA* 5:97.23-98.22). The third use was introduced two years later, in the 1534 *Scholia* (Wengert, *Law and Gospel*, 195). It is from Melanchthon, Wengert concludes, that Calvin received the third use of the law, employed as early as Calvin's first edition of the *Institutes* in 1536 (see CR 29.50).

[39] Melanchthon, *Commentarii*, CO 15.576. When citing Melanchthon in English, I will use the translation by Fred Kramer (*Commentary on Romans* [St. Louis: Concordia, 1992]), always cited *ad loc.*

[40] Melanchthon, *Commentarii*, CO 15.576.

promoting a justification by works actually rules out the possibility since no one in fact fulfills this most basic condition.

At this point one comes to the heart of Melanchthon's understanding of the justification-sanctification relationship in its most familiar form: defending the necessary presence of good works in the justified. The works of Christian obedience, Melanchthon argues, follow faith-imputation as a matter of simple, consequential necessity.[41] Specifically, good works are the *effects* of the imputation of Christ's righteousness, of justification. For Melanchthon, good works are consequentially related to justification and imputation in terms of this principle of necessity. Continuing in his exposition of Rom 2:6, he states: "Afterward also the other works commanded by God, which must of necessity follow faith, are pleasing to Him... And it is necessary that obedience has begun in these." Furthermore, "Although a beginning of obedience must be present, nevertheless faith rests solely on mercy and declares that we are righteous, that is, accepted through mercy."[42]

Summarizing these proposals one should note their variety. Within Catholic exegesis, the reconciliation of good works and justification is fairly straightforward inasmuch as the traditional language of justification contained both elements by definition. As noted, however, this agreement did not preclude substantial

---

[41] By "simple, consequential necessity" I mean that, in this view, the works of Christian obedience are necessary as proper or appropriate expressions of gratitude on the part of the justified sinner in response to grace and mercy shown and as an effect or consequence of justification. This will be clearer by the close of this study. No doubt it is the numerous "conditional" biblical texts promising rewards/eternal life for works of obedience that require such an insistence for Melanchthon upon the *necessary* presence of Christian obedience in the justified. Ultimately, this necessity is based upon a model which regards imputation or justification as the *source* of sanctification, understood in terms of cause and effect. This designation is admittedly simplistic but, I believe, fairly summarizes Melanchthon's animating principle. Cf. Lyle Bierma, "What Hath Wittenberg to do with Heidelberg? Philip Melanchthon and the Heidelberg Catechism," in Karin Maag, ed., *Melanchthon in Europe: His Work and Influence Beyond Wittenberg* (Grand Rapids: Baker, 1999), 103-21, who notes the differences between Reformed and Lutheran approaches to the Law.

[42] Melanchthon, *Commentarii*, CO 15.576-7: "Postea placent et reliqua opera a Deo mandata, quae sequi fidem *necessario debent*... Et in his *necesse est esse incoatam obedientiam*,... Etsi adesse oportet incoatam obedientiam, tamen fides nititur sola misericordia, et statuit nos iustos, id est, acceptos esse per misercordiam." See Carl E. Maxcey, *Bona Opera: A Study in the Development of the Doctrine in Philip Melanchthon* (Nieuwkoop: B. de Graaf, 1980), and Wengert, *Law and Gospel* for fuller discussion.

diversity in interpreting the particulars. Nevertheless, the basic assumption of cooperative grace in justification obtains in each case. Closer to the Protestant perspective in some respects and yet not ultimately very distant from Rome, Lefèvre reconciled Romans 2 and 3 by focusing on the future tense, thus locating justification solely in the eschaton and regarding it as the fruit of lifelong, preparatory obedience. Erasmus's interpretation is similar to Lefèvre's, though with a more explicit relationship drawn between works and justification. Closer to Calvin, both Bucer and Melanchthon still offer sharply divergent views on the proper relationship of works to justification. For Bucer, both personal renovation and forgiveness before God are equally fruits of faith and belong to the definition of justification, with the result, however, that the meaning of justification *sola fide* is arguably rendered ambiguous. Melanchthon avoids the confusion inherent to Bucer's formulation by making sanctification the effect of justifying faith. The result is that they can no longer be confused, but rooting renewal or sanctification in justification as effect to cause exposes Melanchthon anew to the Roman charge that the "Lutheran novelty" leads to licentiousness. Also, by attributing a generative quality to justification (justification produces sanctification), such a schema compromises the strictly forensic, purely declarative notion of justification that is the lifeblood of Melanchthon's (and the classical Lutheran) gospel. Kok has summarized the general situation well:

> The contrasts between Bucer and Melanchthon in dealing with Romans 2 are paralleled by the contrasts between their introductory remarks on justification and faith. While Melanchthon emphasized the imputation of righteousness, Bucer stresses the exhibition of righteousness in the life of believers. While Melanchthon's definitions of justification and faith distinguished these notions from their effects, Bucer is careful to include the effect of being made righteous in his definition of righteousness and the effect of love in his definition of faith. While Melanchthon subordinated renewal to pardon, Bucer consistently parallels renewal and pardon as effects of faith. While Melanchthon distinguishes person and work in order to deal with the issues of merit and reward, Bucer follows Augustine in speaking of merits and rewards as the gifts of God. These differences from Melanchthon lead Bucer to discuss the difficulties of Romans 2 in a much more extended way.[43]

---

[43] Kok, "The Influence of Martin Bucer," 71-2.

In this light, Calvin's own discussion must be identified as a third approach, continuing with the explicit concern to relate compellingly imputation and exhibition, or pardon and renewal.

CALVIN: *ORDO*, SEQUENCE, AND ETERNAL LIFE

Reward, Not Merit

Calvin is also keenly aware of the difficulties connected with the passage, but, like Melanchthon, still remarks both in his commentary and in a parallel passage in the 1539 *Institutio* (in a crucial section devoted to the explanation of merit and reward) that "this sentence, however, is not as difficult as it is generally assumed."[44] First, Calvin argues that Paul is explaining here not the merit of good works accruing to the zealously obedient but is exposing, of necessity, the instability before God of the pseudo-holy, "unseeing pretenders to sanctity" (*illi cum caecis sanctulis negotium est*) who mask their wickedness with a veneer of good works. The purpose of Paul's statement, therefore, is not the commendation of meritorious works as a ground for divine acceptance, but the identification and affirmation of the particular character of the righteousness of which God approves.[45] Therefore the reference to works is not positive but negative: "By punishing the wickedness of the reprobate with just vengeance, the Lord will repay them what they deserve,"[46] despite appearances to the contrary counterfeited by superficial holiness. The argument is similar at Rom 2:13. Calvin has little patience with those who use this passage to support justification by works: they "deserve universal contempt." Probably with a view to Bucer's treatment, Calvin states it is both "improper and irrelevant" to enter into a long discussion of the matter.[47]

---

[44] Cf. Calvin, *Comm. Epist. ad Romanos*, 42; CNTC, 44: "Porro in hac sententia non tantum est difficultatis, quantum vulgo putatur" with *Inst.* (1539), 221: "Quod unicuique dicitur redditurus Deus secundum opera, parvo negotio dissolvitur" (marginal reference to Rom 2:6; translated, "The statement that God will render to every man according to his works is explained with little difficulty" and retained in 1559 as 3.18.1 [LCC 21.821; OS 4.270]). This important section from 1539 would remain in 1559 as *Inst.* 3.18.1-10.

[45] Calvin, *Comm. Epist. ad Romanos*, 42; CNTC, 44. "He has, therefore, pointed out the true righteousness of works which God will value, in case they should confidently assume that it was enough to please Him by bringing words and mere trifles."

[46] Calvin, *Comm. Epist. ad Romanos*, 42; CNTC, 44. "Reproborum enim malitiam iusta ultione si puniet Dominus, rependet illis quod meriti sunt."

[47] Calvin, *Comm. Epist. ad Romanos*, 45; CNTC, 47; cf. Bucer, *Metaphrases et Enarrationes*, 129b-30b (*Conciliatio* II).

In Christ, Like Christ

Instead of supporting justification by works, this passage actually rules out the possibility inasmuch as no one can claim full obedience to the law. At these points, then, Calvin agrees with Melanchthon's basic identification of the statements as Law, not Gospel.[48]

But to leave it there, as some are inclined to do, is to take a tragic misstep as it would neglect the bigger picture Calvin is concerned to keep in view. Does not this passage also teach, positively, that God will reward the works of the righteous? Calvin seems compelled to affirm this as well, explaining in characteristic fashion that this idea is in conflict neither with God's revealed purpose for his people nor with the doctrine of justification. Quite to the contrary, the certainty of eschatological glory, included in God's election of believers, implies and ensures his progressive work of renewal within them: "... because He sanctifies those whom He has previously resolved to glorify, He will also crown their good works..."[49] Still, against the view represented vigorously by Eck, Herborn, and the Sorbonne, Calvin argues that a *meritorious* "crowning" of believer's works is not the intention here since Paul is affirming the reward but not the value due to good works.[50] Calvin then adds, in the first (1551) revision of the commentary: "It is foolish to assume that a thing has merit because it is rewarded."[51] Importantly, however, this

---

[48] Calvin's reading is also reflected in later Reformed exegesis and is sometimes regarded as the traditional Reformed interpretation. See, e.g., Charles Hodge, *A Commentary on Romans* (rep. of 1864 ed.; London: Banner of Truth, 1972), 50; Robert Haldane, *The Epistle to the Romans* (rep. of 1835-39 eds; London: Banner of Truth, 1980), 84. Diverging from this reading and regarding the hope for eternal life expressed by the Apostle as belonging to the believer who trusts in Christ is, e.g., John Murray, *The Epistle to the Romans* (2 vols; NCNT; Grand Rapids: Eerdmans, 1960, 1965), vol. 1, p. 64. See the discussion in Glenn N. Davies, *Faith and Obedience in Romans: A Study in Romans 1-4* (JSNTS 39; Sheffield: JSOT/Sheffield Academic Press, 1990), 53-7.

[49] Calvin, *Comm. Epist. ad Romanos*, 42; CNTC, 44.

[50] Calvin, *Comm. Epist. ad Romanos*, 42; CNTC, 44. In 1556 Calvin adds: "vel quid illis debeatur pretii" ("or the price that is due them"). The editors have noted the comparison with Eck, *Enchir*, Cap V, Prop I (CC 34.88; Battles ET, 50-6) and Herborn, *Enchir* V (CC 12.33[7ff]). They also observe that in the *Art a Fac Paris det*, Art 4, the argument is based on Rom. 6:23 (CO 7.12); cf. Calvin, *Responsio* (CO 7.12-13).

[51] Calvin, *Comm. Epist. ad Romanos*, 42; CNTC, 44. Later, on 2:11, Calvin notes the positive place of regeneration and good works by describing a "twofold acceptance (*duplicem acceptionem*) of men before God." First, God elects us out of his unmotivated goodness alone, not because of anything attractive in our nature; second, the result of his work of regeneration within us and the bestowal of his gifts upon us is that he "shows favor" to the image of Christ

distinction does not preclude connecting good works to the bestowal (reward) of eternal life, as his remarks on v. 7 make clear. Here, where the Apostle says eternal life is granted to those who patiently pursue glory, honor, and immortality, Calvin is concerned to insist that the godly seek only God himself rather than their own aspirations. But to seek God is to seek "to attain the blessedness of His kingdom." Thus Calvin concludes, summing up the Apostle's argument: "The meaning, therefore, is that the Lord will give eternal life to those who strive to attain immortality *by endeavoring to do good works*."[52]

The Hermeneutical-Theological Priority of Romans 8

To understand how Calvin is able to use such strikingly positive language about good works, it is crucial to observe his use of Scripture to interpret Scripture. As will be evident throughout this case study, the ideas of *sequence*, *order*, and *pattern* are of the highest importance to Calvin in his handling of conditional language. First, we are brought into fellowship with Christ by the faith-work of the Spirit. Only then does eternal life "begin" in us and progress to fruition. The exegetical basis for this point, however, is to be found six chapters later than his present concern, in the Pauline *ordo* he locates in Rom 8:29-30. This passage carries an hermeneutical priority over the conditional passages, functioning as a lens through which Calvin reads, in this case, Romans 2. More specifically, Calvin understands the theology of Rom 8:29-30 as the large-scale framework within which Paul's conditional language must be located. The point will be clearer when we examine Romans 8 below, but the basic idea is amply evident from Calvin's comments on 2:6, already quoted, in which he makes a clear allusion to the language of 8:29-30, explaining that God "sanctifies those whom He has previously resolved to glorify" and will, consequently, "also crown their good works..."[53] His abiding concern with the idea of

---

which he sees in us (*Comm. Epist. ad Romanos*, 45; CNTC, 46). This *duplicem acceptionem* of election and image-favor has clear parallels to his more familiar *duplex gratia*, indicating his strong proclivity for the language of *duplex*.

[52] Calvin, *Comm. Epist. ad Romanos*, 43; CNTC, 44. "Quod autem dicit, fideles in bonis operibus persistendo gloriam et honorem quaerere, non significat eos alio aspirare, quam ad Dominum, aut aliquid eo superius praestantiusve expetere; sed ipsum quaerere nequeunt quin simul ad regni eius beatitudinem contendant, cuius descriptio sub horum verborum periphrasi continetur. Sensus ergo est, Dominum vitam aeternam iis redditurum *qui bonorum operum studio immortalitatem meditantur*." Italics mine.

[53] Calvin, *Comm. Epist. ad Romanos*, 42; CNTC, 44. Of note is Calvin's use of the Augustinian idea of the "crowning" of the believer's works. Peter Martyr

merit leads Calvin immediately to add an important qualification, however: *sed non pro merito* ("but not on account of merit").[54] Hence Calvin claims a fully legitimate (and positive) yet non-meritorious place for good works in salvation on the basis of this *ordo*.

The emphasis on the positive place of Christian obedience in God's *ordo* or ordained pattern of salvation is also evident in the 1539 *Institutio*. Here Calvin more explicitly states that Paul in Rom 2:6 intends "an order of sequence rather than the cause." Setting the commentary beside the 1539 *Institutio* is revealing.

Vermigli, in his 1558 commentary, would argue along similar lines: "But works are not of our selves, for they are called the gifts of God, which he works in us. Wherefore Augustine very wisely says: That God doth crown his gifts in us. Now if our works be due unto him (which thing we cannot deny) then undoubtedly the nature of merit is utterly taken away." More notable still is the parallel between aspects of Calvin's replication principle and the way Vermigli relates works to the reward of eschatological life: "Eternal life is sometimes in the holy scriptures called a reward: But then is it not that reward, which Paul writeth to be given according to debt: but is all one as if it should be called a recompensation. Gods will and pleasure was, that there should be this connection, that after good works should follow blessedness: but yet not as the effect followeth the cause, but as a thing joyned with them by the appointment of God" (*In Epistolam S. Pauli ad Romanos commentarii doctissimi...* [Basel, 1558], 40a).

[54] Calvin's chief concern throughout is with *meritum* and *debitum*, i.e., the traditional understanding of merit (*meritum*) with its implication that man, by virtue of his work, places God in his debt (*debitum*). See, within the Romans commentary, his comments on 2:6; 2:25; 3:9; 3:27 (where the *de congruo / de condigno* distinction is in view); 4:4-5; 9:32; 10:5; 11:6. In the 1539 *Institutio*, see Ch. VI.

1540 *Romans*	1539 *Institutes*[55]
This sentence, however, is not as difficult as it is generally assumed. By punishing the wickedness of the reprobate with just vengeance, the Lord will repay them what they deserve; and again because He sanctifies those whom He has previously resolved to glorify, He will also crown their good works, but not on account of any merit. This cannot, however, be proved from the present verse, which, while it declares what reward good works are to have, does not state their value, [added 1556:] or the price that is due to them. [added 1551:] It is foolish to assume that a thing has merit because it is rewarded.	The statement that God will render to every man according to his works is explained with little difficulty. For the expression indicates an order of sequence rather than the cause. But, beyond any doubt, it is by these stages of his mercy that the Lord completes our salvation when he calls those chosen to himself; those called he justifies; those justified he glorifies. That is to say, he receives his own into life by his mercy alone. Yet, since he leads them into possession of it through the pursuit (*studium*) of good works in order to fulfill his own work in them according to the order that he has laid down, it is no wonder if they are said to be crowned according to their own works, by which they are doubtless prepared to receive the crown of immortality.

The sequential and the *ordo* elements in Calvin's teaching on good works are clear in both passages. By "stages of mercy," God, according to his own sovereign design, "completes our salvation" when he calls us to himself, justifies the called, and glorifies the justified. Indeed, making clear the truly soteric value of good works, "he leads them into possession of it [i.e., eternal life] *through the pursuit of good works* in order to fulfill his own work in them according to the order (*ordine*) that he has laid down..." Through

---

[55] In the margin next to this passage Calvin (or possibly his editors) placed references to Rom. 2 and 8 near the quite obvious allusions to these Pauline texts. However, because these were originally marginalia and were not incorporated by Calvin into the *body* of his original text, they are included here in a footnote to avoid confusion. This is a departure from the practice of the editors of OS and CO and, especially, LCC 20-21. For a helpful discussion of the problem, see Muller, *Unaccommodated Calvin*, 140-58, esp. 140-2, 149-50. See Appendix A for a basic tabulation of the marginalia in *Inst.* (1539) Ch. 6.

that diligent performance of the good works which characterize the life of Christian obedience, one is thus *"prepared* to receive the crown of immortality."[56] Though Paul does not include *regeneratio* or *sanctificatio* in the Rom 8:29-30 series, Calvin appears to include it under the aegis of *glorificatio* as its preparatory precursor in the experience of the redeemed. In this divine sequence, good works are therefore indispensable to the ongoing restoration of the divine image in believers and their ultimate salvation. Believers pass from regeneration to eschatological glorification and eternal life *through* the "pursuit of good works."

Elsewhere Calvin's dependence upon this Pauline *ordo* is equally clear. For instance, whereas one finds Calvin distinguishing "sequence" from "cause," even this distinction is not simplistic. After referring to works as "inferior causes" (*causas inferiores*), Calvin ties this to God's "order of dispensation" in a way that is both striking and instructive:

> These do not prevent the Lord from embracing works as inferior causes. But how does this come about? Those whom the Lord has destined by his mercy for the inheritance of eternal life he leads into possession of it, *according to his ordinary dispensation, by means of good works*. *What goes before in the order of dispensation he calls the cause of what comes after*. In this way he sometimes derives eternal life from works, not intending it to be ascribed to them; but because he justifies those whom he has chosen in order at last to glorify them, *he makes the prior grace, which is a step to what follows, as it were the cause*. But whenever the true cause is to be assigned,

---

[56] Calvin, *Inst.* (1539) 3.18.1; OS 4.270 (LCC 20.821): "Quod unicuique dicitur redditurus Deus secundum opera, parvo negotio dissolvitur. Ordinem enim consequentiae magis quam causam indicat ista locutio. Extra dubium autem est, Dominum his misericordiae suae gradibus salutem nostram consummare dum electos a [from 1554: ad] se vocat, vocatos iustificat, iustificatos glorificat. Tametsi ergo sola misericordia Dominus suos in vitam suscipiat: quia tamen in eius possessionem ipsos deducit, *per bonorum operum studium*, ut quo destinavit *ordine* suum in illorum [from 1545: illis] opus impleat: nihil mirum si secundum opera sua dicuntur coronari: quibus haud dubie ad recipiendam immortalitatis coronam praeparantur." One should note the contrast with the more traditional idea, as expressed by Lefèvre, of "preparation" for justification. NB: OS 4.270 n. g notes that *stadium* ("race," in *per bonorum operum stadium*) is *studium* ("pursuit") in 1561, which makes better sense. I have thus used *studium* rather than *stadium* in the translation above and in the Latin text in this footnote.

he does not enjoin us to take refuge in works but keeps us solely to the contemplation of his mercy.[57]

However, does this not suggest a greater estimation of believer's works than is possible within a distinctly Protestant doctrine of salvation? In Calvin's reply to this objection in the 1539 *Institutio* one may note the controlling feature of his perspective: *in Christi consortium*.

> Accordingly, it does not follow that believers are themselves the authors of their own salvation, or that salvation stems from their own works. What then? *Once they are, by knowledge of the gospel and illumination of the Holy Spirit, called into fellowship of Christ, eternal life begins in them.* Now that God has begun a good work in them, it must also be made perfect until the Day of the Lord Jesus. It is, however, made perfect when they resemble their Heavenly Father in righteousness and holiness and so prove themselves to be not degenerates but sons.[58]

Here, moreover, the eschatological character of Calvin's affirmation of the necessity of works, together with its conceptual basis, becomes clear. If God's rewarding of a believer's works with eternal life is not patent evidence of a salvation earned by works, what else could it be? Calvin's idea of sequence is basic to his response.

---

[57] Calvin, *Inst.* (1539) 3.14.21; OS 4.238-9 (LCC 20.787): "Istis nihil obstat quominus opera Dominus, tanquam *causas inferiores* amplectatur; sed unde id? nempe quos sua misericordia, aeternae vitae haereditati *destinavit, eos ordinaria sua dispensatione per bona opera inducit in eius possessionem. Quod in ordine dispensationis praecedit, posterioris causam nominat.* Hac ratione ab operibus interdum vitam aeternam deducit; non quod illis referenda sit accepta: sed quia quos elegit, iustificat ut demum glorificet, *priorem gratiam, quae gradus est ad sequentem, causam quodammodo facit.* At quoties assignanda est vera causa, non ad opera iubet confugere, sed in sola misericordiae cogitatione nos retinet." The whole section is instructive in this regard.

[58] Calvin, *Inst.* (1539) 3.18.1; OS 4.271 (LCC 21.822): "Unde apparet operandi verbum nequaquam opponi gratiae, sed referri ad stadium: ac proinde non sequitur, vel fideles ipsos esse salutis suae authores, vela b ipsorum, operibus eam emanere. Quid ergo? Simul atque per Evangelii notitiam, et Spiritus sancti illuminationem adsciti sunt in Christi consortium, inchoata est in illis aeterna vita. Iam quod in illis bonum opus inchoavit Deus, et perfici oportet usque in diem Domini Iesu. Perficitur porro, quum iustitia et sanctitate Patrem caelestem referentes, se filios eius non degeneres esse probant." Italics mine. I should note here that Calvin's familiar perspective on the Paul-James relationship does not mitigate this in the least. See the summary in Pierre Marcel, "The Relation Between Justification and Sanctification in Calvin's Thought," *EQ* 27 (1955): 140-2.

Eternal life *begins*, Calvin explains, in those who by a Spirit-wrought faith ("knowledge of the gospel and illumination of the Holy Spirit") are brought into union with Christ (*in Christi consortium*). This "beginning" is progressively perfected until the restoration of the divine image ("resembling their Heavenly Father in righteousness and holiness"), the *telos* for which believers have been called, is complete. Only then, at this stage of consummate and eschatological glory, will believers "prove themselves" as God's children, as righteous not only in principle but also in fact.

What is striking here is the very positive place given by Calvin to good works when the eschaton is in view. The chronology is especially significant: the "completion" of the work "begun" in us by God is realized only later at glorification, i.e., when sanctification is completed, when grace becomes glory. That is to say, it is *after* the work begun in us by God has reached its perfection in glorification that believers are "proved" to be adopted sons of God. In fact, according to Calvin, it is precisely in this eschatological vindication of the children of God that the perfection of his redemptive work consists: "It is, however, made perfect when... they prove themselves..."

Extra Nos *and* In Nobis *in Augustine, Trent, and Romans 3:20-31*

We gain further insight into Calvin's model as we move on to examine his comments on Romans 3 in the context of changes made in his first, 1551 revision of his commentary. At issue in the exegesis of Rom 3:20-31 is the relationship of the *iustitia Dei* in Christ to the *iustitia hominis* in justification, a question complicated for Calvin and other reformers by Augustine's reading.[59] The lack of a clear distinction in Augustine between the righteousness *extra nos* and *in nobis* was cited in support by Bucer and criticized by Melanchthon. Augustine regarded the justifying *iustitia Dei* as the free grace of *regeneratio*, free because God by his Spirit renews the unworthy and not on account of the law or good works. Paul is therefore opposing justification on the basis of works performed autonomously, from one's own volition, with the intent to satisfy God. In Augustine's

---

[59] Augustine, *De Spiritu et Litera* 9.15 (PL 44.209); *Contra Duas Epistolas Pelagianorum* 1.8.13 (PL 44.556). Augustine is cited in Erasmus, *Ann*, 576D (*CWE* 56.100). For Augustine's exegesis, see Peter Gorday, *Principles of Patristic Exegesis: Romans 9-11 in Origen, John Chrysostom, and Augustine* (New York and Toronto: Edwin Mellen Press, 1983), 157-8. Parker summarizes many of the sixteenth-century interpretations of Rom 3:20-28 in *Commentaries on Romans*, 142-200.

interpretation, however, the good works produced by the Spirit within believers are not of the same category as those rejected by the Apostle for justification. Put in the terms of late medieval soteriology, it is not the works produced *within* a state of grace as the result of God's Spirit-renewal but those produced *outside* a state of grace for the purpose of gaining divine acceptance that Paul rejects in 3:21ff.

CALVIN: UNION WITH CHRIST AND MERIT IN JUSTIFICATION

In 1551 Calvin adds a lengthy passage to this portion of his commentary, evidently defending his explicitly non-Augustinian reading in light of Trent's affirmation of Augustine's view in the intervening period.[60] Against Augustine, Calvin is confident that the context indicates the Apostle intended to exclude *all* works without exception, including the fruit of God's own work within believers, from the justifying *iustitia Dei*. Regenerate Abraham was not justified by works but by faith; therefore, works are excluded from the justification which comes by faith, whether they be natural/moral or spiritual/believing. Psalm 32:1 provides the definition of justification as the forgiveness of sins, and the widespread acceptance of this definition precludes disputes about the justifying merits of good works; indeed, it "abolishes" this merit and establishes "remission of sins as the cause of righteousness."

Calvin then turns to the specific Tridentine objection that justification "by faith" and justification by works produced by the Sprit are agreeable "because God freely renews us, and we also receive His gift by faith."[61] This is a basic reaffirmation of Augustine's combination of what may be termed, anachronistically before the Reformation, forensic (justifying) and transformative (renewing) aspects of salvation. Calvin's concern is pastoral as well as theological. He claims that Paul's principle that the conscience is never at rest until resting exclusively in the mercy of God undermines Trent's reasoning. For the Apostle, the *modus* of justification is that of "not reckoning unto them their trespasses." With respect to the *effectus* of justification, the Law opposes faith

---

[60] Calvin, *Comm. Epist. ad Romanos*, 68-9; CNTC, 71-2; cf. *Conc Trid, Sess VI Cap 7* with Calvin's *Antidotum* (CO 7.447-8). For Trent, see the important essay by Heiko Oberman, "Duns Scotus, Nominalism, and the Council of Trent," in Oberman, *Dawn of the Reformation*, 204-33. For Calvin and Trent, see Lane, *Justification by Faith in Catholic-Protestant Dialogue*, 17-85; and Theodore W. Casteel, "Calvin and Trent: Calvin's Reaction to the Council of Trent in the Context of his Conciliar Thought," *Harvard Theological Review* 63 (1970): 91-117.
[61] Calvin, *Comm. Epist. ad Romanos*, 68-9; CNTC, 71-2.

because of the Law's comprehensive and intensive demands. Hence is it impossible to allow the merit of works a place in justification.[62]

A survey of Calvin's *Antidotum* may suggest that the whole conflict turned on the meaning of "righteousness" or "to justify." On a more careful reading it becomes clear, however, that the conflict between Calvin and Trent is not exhausted by different interpretations of *iustitia*. At the heart of the disagreement are, first, different estimations of the abilities of the fallen sinner, and, more significantly for our purposes, different conceptions of union with Christ and its implications for justification.[63] With respect to sin, Calvin's repeated insistence on the impossibility of a justification grounded in the meritorious obedience of sinners, even in small part and even in a state of grace – even, it should be remembered, when those works of obedience are the result of God's own operation in them – reflects a fundamentally divergent anthropology which extends the effects of the Fall more deeply and widely than was the case at Trent. In short, Calvin's Augustinian anthropology may be seen as the chief reason for his rejecting the perceived ambiguities inherent in the Augustinian soteriology, at least in terms of this question.

With respect to the importance to Calvin of divergent conceptions of union with Christ, this becomes evident in his 1551 addition to the comment on 3:21, reflecting clearly the Tridentine formulae. Trent had supplied an analytical statement of justification in terms of union with Christ, perhaps intending thereby to deflect the Evangelical charge of a weak christocentrism when it came to justification. It is to this construal that Calvin responds in 1551:

> It follows, therefore, that no merit of works is admitted in the righteousness of faith. It appears evident, therefore, that it is a frivolous objection to say that we are justified in Christ because we are renewed by the Spirit, in so far as we are members of Christ (*sumus Christi membra*); and that we are justified by faith because we are inserted by faith into the body of Christ (*inseramur in Christi corpus*);[64] and that we are justified freely because God finds

---

[62] Calvin, *Comm. Epist. ad Romanos*, 69; CNTC, 72.
[63] See Craig B. Carpenter, "A Question of Union with Christ? Calvin and Trent on Justification," *WTJ* 64 (2002): 363-86, who has pointed to the underappreciated significance of divergent understandings of union with Christ in Calvin and Trent.
[64] Cf. Mackenzie in CNTC, 71, "*united* by faith to the body of Christ" for "quia fide *inseramur* in Christi corpus."

nothing in us but sin.⁶⁵ We are instead *in Christ* (*in Christo*) because we are out of ourselves (*extra nos*); and [justified] *by faith*, because we rest on the mercy of God alone, and on His free promises; and therefore *freely*, because God reconciles us to Himself by burying our sins. Nor can this be confined to the commencement (*initium*) of justification, as they dream,⁶⁶ for this definition, *Blessed are they whose iniquities are forgiven*, was applicable to David after a lengthy period of training in the service of God...⁶⁷

Note that Calvin does not accuse Trent of an under-appreciation of union with Christ. Indeed, in light of the thematic character of the idea in late medieval soteriology, whether mystical or not, such a charge is impossible. Rather, at issue for Calvin is a misunderstanding of its implications for justification. Note also that the differences do not spring from theological vocabulary: both argue a justification that is "in Christ," "by faith," and "free." At issue is the precise meaning of these terms, and this despite Trent's explicit use of the *unio Christi* as an organizing concept.⁶⁸ For Calvin, grounding justification in works springing from one's union with

---

⁶⁵ Cf. *Conc Trid, Sess VI, Cap 7 and 8* with Calvin, *Antidotum* (CO 7.447-53). The editors also note Cajetan (*Epistolae Pauli Et Aliorum Apostolorum...* [1532], X-XI) and Haresche, *Expositio*, lxviiiᵛ (Calvin, *Comm. Epist. ad Romanos*, 69, n. 38).

⁶⁶ Cf. *Conc Trid, Sess VI Cap 8*; with Calvin, *Antidotum* (CO 7.453). Cf. also Eck, *Enchir Cap V Prop VI* (CC 34.97 and Battles ET as cited); and Herborn, *Enchir II.i* (CC 12.19¹²⁻¹³). Calvin, *Comm. Epist. ad Romanos*, 69, n. 39.

⁶⁷ Calvin, *Comm. Epist. ad Romanos*, 69; CNTC, 71-2: "Sequitur ergo, in fidei iustitia nullum operum meritum admitti. Unde constat, frivolam esse cavillationem, nos in Christo iustificari, quia Spiritu renovemur quatenus sumus Christi membra, nos fide iustificari, quia fide inseramur in Christi corpus; nos gratis iustificari, quia nihil in nobis Deus inveniat praeter peccatum. Nam ideo in Christo, quia extra nos; ideo fide, quia in solam Dei misericordiam et gratuitas eius promissiones nos recumbere necesse est; ideo gratis, quia nos sibi reconciliat Deus, peccata sepeliendo. Neque vero ad iustitiae initium id restringi postest, quemadmodum illi somniant. Nam et illa definitio, 'Beati quorum remissae sunt iniquitates', in Davide locum habuit, quum diu se exercuisset in Dei cultu, et Abraham post tricesimum vocationis suae annum, tametsi rarum sanctitatis exemplar fuerit, non habet opera quibus glorietur apud Deum. Atque ideo, quod promissioni credit, illi imputatur in iustitiam. Et quum Paulus tradit, Deum homines iustificare, peccata non imputando, concionem recitat quae quotidie in Ecclesia repetenda est. Et illa pax conscientiae quae operum respectu turbatur, non unius est diei, sed in totam vitam durare debet. Unde sequitur, non aliter nos esse iustos usque ad mortem, nisi quia in solum Christum respicimus, in quo nos Deus adoptavit, et nunc acceptos habet."

⁶⁸ Though, for Trent, "in Christ" here possibly means "in the Church," as Prof. D. F. Wright has suggested to me.

Christ (as opposed to one's nature) does not sufficiently qualify the still-problematic assertion that works, again in any sense, are the meritorious grounds of justification. Because the issue is the meaning of the terms, this three-fold *unio-fide-gratis* model of justification (i.e., *in Christo* because of renewal by the Spirit in accord with our identity as *membra* of Christ, *quia fide* because we are thus inserted into his body, and *gratis* because we have nothing in us but sin) is therefore countered by Calvin's own point-by-point response: we are justified *in Christo* because the grounds of justifying righteousness is *extra nos*; *fide* because we rest exclusively on mercy; *gratis* because of reconciliation through the remission of sins. Presumably, in Calvin's view, Trent's definition is still insufficiently christocentric: justification is still not exclusively *in Christ*. Entailed is not a diminution of the concept of saving union in its relation to justification on Calvin's part, however, but a clarification of its character and implications for justification (here expressed judicially as an act of adoption resulting in a state of acceptance).[69] For Calvin, the reality of union does not compromise the distinctive character of justification; it rather locates it *extra nos* in Christ. Against the backdrop of medieval *unio* concepts the redefinition is not only in its character but also in its "placement," however. Thus in terms similar to Luther before him, the traditional concept of a saving *unio* is relocated from the end or goal, the *telos*, of the journey of the *viator*, where it still fit in Trent's soteriology, to the beginning as its sole presupposition and context.[70]

ARISTOTLE'S CAUSES IN CALVIN'S MODEL

All of Calvin's points thus far belong to his comment on 3:21, originally, in 1540, quite a small exposition.[71] In the exposition of verse 22, Calvin asserts immediately that there is an *ordo* to be followed in discussing the righteousness of God and the righteousness of faith.[72] He then begins a concise statement on justification. First, the cause of our justification is located solely at the tribunal of God, not in the court of public opinion, and God,

---

[69] Cf. Calvin, *Comm. Epist. ad Romanos*, 69; CNTC, 72.

[70] Note also Calvin's subsequent statement, "Nor can this be confined to the commencement (*initium*) of justification, as those interpreters fondly suppose..." (*Comm. Epist. ad Romanos*, 69; CNTC, 72), thus denying a progressive element to justification commensurate with the traditional idea of an exclusively future-eschatological, justifying union with God or Christ.

[71] Parker notes (*Commentaries on Romans*, 193) that the entire exposition of 3:20-28 ran only to approximately two thousand words in the 1540 text.

[72] Calvin, *Comm. Epist. ad Romanos*, 70; CNTC, 73.

unlike men, demands perfect, absolute obedience to his law. Second, and consequently, only Christ can transfer to us the righteousness necessary for justification. Thus the righteousness of faith is the righteousness of Christ. These two points are summarized using the Aristotelian causes: the efficient cause (*causa efficiens*) is God's mercy, the substance (*materia*) is Christ, and the instrumental cause (*instrumentum*) is the Word with faith.[73] But how exactly does Christ "communicate" his righteousness to us (*nobis communicatur*)? Again the idea of union with Christ performs the central role. Specifically, both the reality of the *unio Christi* framework of Calvin's soteriology and its importance as a context for locating good works become patent.

> Faith is therefore said to justify because it is the instrument by which we receive Christ, in whom righteousness is communicated to us. *When we are made partakers of Christ*, we are not only ourselves righteous but *our works also are counted righteous in the sight of God*, because any imperfections in them are obliterated by the blood of Christ. The *promises, which were conditional, are fulfilled in us*[74] also by the same grace, since *God rewards our works as though perfect*.[75]

---

[73] Calvin, *Comm. Epist. ad Romanos*, 70-1; CNTC 73. "Ut ergo iustificemur, causa efficiens est misericordia Dei; Christus, materia; verbum cum fide, instrumentum." On the Aristotelian causes in Calvin and Trent see the discussion by Lane, *Justification by Faith in Catholic-Protestant Dialogue*, 68-71. On the causes see Aristotle, *Physics* 2:3 (Loeb ed. 1:128-31); T. Mautner, *A Dictionary of Philosophy* (Oxford: Blackwell, 1996), 68; Richard A. Muller, *Dictionary of Latin and Greek Theological Terms* (Grand Rapids: Baker, 1985), 61-3. Lane (p. 69, n. 99) notes these and refers also to M. Hocutt, "Aristotle's Four Becauses," *Philosophy* 49 (1974): 385-99, who argues that the causes should be understood as reasons why ("becauses"). On Aristotle in the Reformation period, see Joseph S. Freedman, "Aristotle and the Content of Philosophy Instruction at Central European Schools and Universities during the Reformation Era (1500-1650)," *Proceedings of the American Philosophical Society* 137 (1993): 213-53. On Calvin and Aristotelianism, see Irena Backus, "'Aristotelianism' in Some of Calvin's and Beza's Expository and Exegetical Writings on the Doctrine of the Trinity, with Particular Reference to the Terms οὐσια and ὑποστασις," in Olivier Fatio and Pierre Fraenkel, eds, *Histoire de L'exégèse Au XVIe Siècle: Textes Du Colloque International Tenu à Genève en 1976* (Geneva: Librairie Droz, 1978), 351-60.

[74] Calvin, *Comm. Epist. ad Romanos*, 71. 1551: *In Errata list* in nobis (cf. Mackenzie, "to us").

[75] Calvin, *Comm. Epist. ad Romanos*, 71; CNTC, 73. "Quare fides iustificare dicitur, quia instrumentum est recipiendi Christi, in quo nobis communicatur iustitia. Postquam facti sumus Christi participes, non ipsi solum iusti sumus, *sed opera nostra iusta reputantur coram Deo*; propterea scilicet quia quicquid est in illis

The saving efficacy of faith, that is, its instrumental function for receiving the *communicatio iustitiae*, Calvin argues, is tied to its purpose in uniting the believer to Christ. Calvin resolves the problem of conditional language (though there is no condition other than faith expressed by Paul in Rom 3:22) by appeal to a partaking of Christ in whom both believers and their works are considered righteous for Christ's sake. These works *iusta reputantur coram Deo*, and are thus subject to their own "justification" of sorts (understood as a "considering righteous") inasmuch as they are themselves sanctified by Christ's sacrifice. Through union with Christ the conditional promises are consequently not set aside but fulfilled *in nobis* by this grace. Hence justification *sola fide* is not in tension with the conditional character of God's promises. Rather, union with the Christ who *is* righteousness renders both believers and their works acceptable to God.[76] Such language may surprise some students of Calvin's theology, yet a fuller picture of his model will establish its context as well as its importance. A major step in this direction is taken in Calvin's interpretation of Romans 6.

Divine Engrafting, Death, and Resurrection in Christ: Romans 6

The familiar Pauline statements on righteousness, faith, and the atonement in chapters one to five of the Epistle afforded Calvin the opportunity to defend the Reformation reading of Paul in general as

---

imperfectionis, obliteratur Christi sanguine. *Promissiones, quae conditionales erant, eadem quoque gratia nobis implentur, quatenus opera nostra, ceu perfecta, remuneratur Deus.*" In 1556 Calvin adds "quia defectus gratuita venia tegitur" ("inasmuch as their defects are covered by free favor") to the final sentence.

[76] In his comment on Rom 3:23, Calvin is concerned that this not be misunderstood as analogous to the theory of "half-righteousness": "Since all men are sinners, Paul infers that they are deficient or completely lacking in the praise of righteousness. There is, therefore, [1556: according to his teaching] no righteousness except that which is perfect and absolute. If there were such a thing as half righteousness (*dimidia*), it would not be necessary to deprive man of all glory because he was a sinner." In a 1551 addition, he repeats his point with an addition to his comment, again perhaps because of the intervening Tridentine pronouncement: "The fiction of what is called partial righteousness is hereby sufficiently refuted. If it were true that we are partially justified by works, and partially by the grace of God, this argument of Paul, that all are deprived of the glory of God because they are sinners, would have no force..." (*Comm. Epist. ad Romanos*, 71-2; CNTC, 74). The editors (*Comm. Epist. ad Romanos*, 71, n. 44) attribute this latter addition to the Articles of the Faculty of Paris to which Calvin also responded. Cf. *Art a Fac Paris det, Art IVi* (CO 7.12) with Calvin's *Responsio* (CO 7.12-13).

well as focus on the nature of justification in particular. In the transition to chapter six, however, he is now afforded the opportunity not only to say something about the distinct-but-inseparable character of justification and sanctification, but also more explicitly to relate justification and sanctification without departing from the rhetorical flow of the Epistle. This is possible because of the classic statements in chapter six, first, on the renewal of the believer and, second, on the believer's engrafting into Christ.

Furthermore, adopting Melanchthon's mortification/vivification distinction, Calvin is able to describe the Christian life in terms of mortification and vivification *in Christ*. As a result, the precise union-character of Calvin's idea of sanctification is further clarified in his exposition of divine engrafting in Romans 6. In the Apostle's transition from redemption accomplished to redemption applied, expressed with the grammar of Christian baptism, divine engrafting, and death and resurrection with Christ, Calvin focuses attention on the union language in a way both continuous and discontinuous with the mystical and *imitatio Christi* traditions as well as Melanchthon's reading of Paul. For Calvin, the believer's union with Christ, here articulated in terms of *participatio* and *insitio*, connects the atoning work of Christ to the believer's experience of grace and *determines the shape* of that experience as death and resurrection with Christ.

That relating imputation and transformation coherently is an exercise forced upon any interpreter of the Epistle is clear whenever we consider the exegetical history of relating chapters five and six in the sixteenth century. Traditionally, these chapters are at the exegetical, textual level what justification and sanctification are at the doctrinal level. As such, the analysis of their relationship proposed by commentators often provides, within the context of their wider comments, a unique index to their basic soteriological orientation.

INTERPRETATIONS: ERASMUS AND LEFÈVRE

The spiritualist streams that flowed into the sixteenth century from the fourteenth and fifteenth typically had the themes of Romans 6 at heart. Calvin's contact with representatives of the *Devotio Moderna*, especially through the small French "circle of Meaux" in his early years, has thus led scholars to identify common themes in Calvin's theology and this late medieval spiritual tradition.[77] For our

---

[77] It may be inadvisable to say much about "the" *Devotio Moderna* since this was far from a monolithic movement. Still, the basic themes in the thought of its father, Gerhard Groote (1340-1384), did persist with remarkable resilience in the

purposes, direct comparisons with the humanist and spiritual traditions are made possible by the published works on Romans by Lefèvre, the most famous of the French humanist-mystics, and Erasmus, the humanist *par excellence*.[78] In the exposition of Romans 6, this comparison is perhaps uniquely significant on account of the language of dying and rising with Christ, themes central to *imitatio Christi* spirituality and piety.

Erasmus and Lefèvre share a basically moralistic reading of the chapter, while Erasmus's is more ethical and Lefèvre's has a decidedly mystical bent. Both display great interest in the idea of baptism into Christ. Erasmus stresses the need for progressive sanctification following baptism.[79] For Erasmus baptism into Christ thus has ethical consequences, as chapter six as a whole indicates. For Lefèvre, however, baptism is mystical in significance and is tied to Paul's two-Adam structure. There are two births, the one natural by the first Adam; the other spiritual through baptism into Christ, the second Adam. We have died with Christ "in mystery," have been buried and will rise with him when we experience "that

---

movement's various forms. The *imitatio Christi* form is easily the most recognizable of late medieval currents, although the goal of imitation is not unique to this strand of spirituality. More specifically, Calvin probably would have been at least somewhat familiar with the Erasmian form of this spirituality as it was combined with the mystical bent of Lefèvre. See Lucien Joseph Richard, *The Spirituality of John Calvin* (Atlanta: John Knox Press, 1974), 12-77; P. M. E. Dols, *Bibliographie der Moderne Devotie* (Niemegen, 1941); A. Ganoczy, *The Young Calvin*, trans. David Foxgrover and Wade Provo (Philadelphia: Westminster, 1987); J. Hashagen, "Die Devotio Moderna in ihre Einwirkung auf Humanismus, Reformation, Gegenreformation und spätere Richtungen," *Zeitschrift für Kirchengeschichte* 55 (1936): 523-31; A. Hyma, *The Christian Renaissance, A History of the "Devotio Moderna"* (New York: Hamden, 1924); Heiko A. Oberman, *Forerunners of the Reformation: The Shape of Late Medieval Thought* (New York: Holt, Rinehart, and Winston, 1966; rep. Philadelphia: Fortress, 1981); R. R. Post, *The Modern Devotion: Confrontation with Reformation and Humanism* (SMRT 3; Leiden: Brill, 1968); and the summary of literature in Clive S. Chin, "*Unio Mystica* and *Imitatio Christi*: The Two-Dimensional Nature of John Calvin's Spirituality," Ph.D. diss. (Dallas Theological Seminary, 2002), 69-195.

[78] Though Calvin's familiarity with both Erasmus and Lefèvre is beyond question, this is not a claim as to the extent of their respective influence upon Calvin. As humanists contemporary with Calvin, however, they serve as useful sources for comparison with Calvin's own exegesis as it relates to the moral (Erasmian) and mystical (Lefèvre) strands of sixteenth-century humanist Pauline interpretation.

[79] Payne, "Interpretations," 199.

perpetual beatific vision of God."[80] Because the *visio Dei* is the goal of the human *viator*, all of life must be oriented to *contemplatio* and the experience of praise of God. Thus the Apostle commends the Christian life as one of *Christiformitas*, or the *imitatio Christi*, the pattern of which is not found in the law of God but in the life of Christ as this life partakes of the particular characteristics of self-denial, service, and humility.[81]

As far as the Pauline union or engrafting language is concerned, Lefèvre maintains that the *mortificatio carnis* is effected in union with the untainted flesh and spirit of Christ, which he received from the uniquely blessed Virgin and not from Adam. He explains that "Christ received his flesh not from Adam, who had been preceded by the curse, but from the Virgin, who had been preceded by the blessing. His flesh is therefore not at all tainted by sin or even the possibility of sin.[82] Here, according to Payne, Erasmus strikes a radically different note. Centuries before Edward Irving (and, following him, Barth) taught a "fallen" humanity of Christ, Erasmus claimed "…although he was completely free from the contagion of sin, he nevertheless was clothed with the same flesh with which other sinners are clothed… he walked among sinners as a sinner. Nay, among criminals he was crucified as a criminal."[83]

MELANCHTHON'S SYLLOGISTIC READING

Melanchthon's reading of Romans 6 supplies a still more immediate counterpart to Calvin's own work, however, not only because he is mentioned in Calvin's Preface but also because of the general continuity in their doctrines of justification, at least in terms of their concerns. In Melanchthon's reading of Romans 6, his necessity principle becomes more explicit.[84]

---

[80] Payne, "Erasmus and Lefèvre," 76.

[81] Payne, "Erasmus and Lefèvre," 76, notes the parallel with Nicholas of Cusa.

[82] Payne, "Erasmus and Lefèvre," 77. This union is tied to the Eucharistic event and is based upon this specific christological presupposition.

[83] Payne, "Erasmus and Lefèvre," 77-8. In fact, as Prof. D. F. Wright has suggested to me, perhaps the last clause quoted suggests that Erasmus is not as "modern" as might at first appear. In either case, Payne rightly observes how this difference between Lefèvre and Erasmus anticipates their famous debate concerning the translation and interpretation of Hebrews 2:7, in which their conflicting christologies surface with striking clarity.

[84] Note the significance for Melanchthon of Romans 6 within the rhetorical patterning of the Epistle as a whole, evidenced in the structure of his *argumentum*. Muller, "*Scimus enim quod lex spiritualis est*," 226: "Melanchthon regards ch. 6 as a highly significant *digressio*, to be analyzed in considerable

In Christ, Like Christ

As Calvin would in his own commentary, Melanchthon, at the outset of his exposition of chapter six, associates the cause of the Reformation with that of the Apostle over against their common adversaries.

> The reader will more easily understand these objections of Paul if he will consider the controversies of our time. For just as our adversaries now shout: "If we are not just on account of our works, then what good does it do to do well?," so the Pharisees threw up the same absurdities to Paul. From this is it is sufficiently evident that we are dealing with the very same matter about which Paul is arguing, and that we are giving the genuine and true meaning of Paul.[85]

Not only the godless raise these objections but also the weak-believing who, upon hearing the gospel of an imputed righteousness, become lax in their obedience.[86] The question is therefore immediately one of relating justifying faith to the necessary presence of good works. Melanchthon is clear about Paul's answer. First, by faith the righteousness of Christ is imputed to the believer.

> Thereafter the new obedience is necessary (*deinde nova obedientia est necessaria*) as an effect which necessarily follows the imputation, because with the imputation there comes about renewal, which is the beginning of new and eternal life. The beginning of the new and eternal life is truly new and spiritual obedience. Therefore new and spiritual obedience is necessary. This is the sum and substance of Paul's answer.[87]

The necessity principle thus recurs explicitly here in Melanchthon's exposition as imputation and renewal are related as cause and effect. His subsequent division of renewal into the two parts of *mortificatio*

---

detail, with far greater attention to the technical details of rhetorical form than Calvin would offer."

[85] Melanchthon, *Commentarii*, CR 15.634.

[86] Melanchthon, *Commentarii*, CR 15.634: "The godly should weigh also this here that it is not only the adversaries who raise these objections which I have stated, but there is in all men so great an infirmity of nature that when we hear the teaching about gratuitous imputation, we become less fruitful for doing good and carnal security is strengthened."

[87] Melanchthon, *Commentarii*, CR 15.635: "Deinde nova obedientia *est necessaria*, ut *effectus necessario consequens* illam imputationem, quia cum imputatione fit renovatio, quae est incoatio novae et aeternae vitae. Incoatio vere novae et aeternae vitae est nova et spiritualis obedientia. Ergo nova et spiritualis obedientia *est necessaria*. Haec ipsa est summa responsionis Pauli."

and *vivificatio* is also the result of understanding imputation as the efficient cause.[88] Melanchthon presents the basic theological point in terms of two syllogisms which are illustrated as follows (using Melanchthon's words):

Syllogism 1[89]

Major Premise	Dead nature is not efficacious
Minor Premise	It is necessary (*necesse est*) that the old and corrupt nature in us should be mortified
Conclusion (Ergo)	The old and corrupt nature ought not to be (*non debet esse*) efficacious, nor ought it to be obeyed when it fights against the will of God

Syllogism 2[90]

Major Premise	Living nature ought to be (*debet esse*) working
Minor Premise	We receive the new nature and light when faith raises [us] up and comforts the conscience
Conclusion (Ergo)	This new life ought to have (*debet habere*) works that are in harmony with it, that is, obedience toward God, whom we begin to know already in this new life

The prominence of *debere esse* / *debet habere* language in each of the two conclusions highlights the principle of simple necessity (*necesse est*) in Melanchthon's thinking. Christian obedience is ultimately a matter of the *ergo* springing from the reality of faith-imputation.[91]

---

[88] Melanchthon, *Commentarii*, CR 15.635: "But he divides renewal into two parts, namely, mortification and vivification, and he argues from the efficient causes (*a causis efficientibus*)." Melanchthon then begins the first syllogism.

[89] Melanchthon, *Commentarii*, CR 15.635: "Sed ipse distribuit duo membra renovationis, scilicet mortificationem et vivificationem: et sic argumentatur a causis efficientibus. Prior syllogismus: Mortua natura non est efficax, Necese est in nobis veterem et vitiosam naturam mortificari, Ergo vetus et vitiosa natura non debet esse efficax, nec obsequendum est ei pugnanti cum voluntate Dei."

[90] Melanchthon, *Commentarii*, CR 15.635: "Alter syllogismus est: Viva natura debet esse efficax, Nos concipimus novam vitam et lucem, cum fides erigit et consolatur conscientiam, Ergo haec nova vita debet habere opera consentanea, id est, obedientiam erga Deum, quem iam in hac nova vita incipimus agnoscere."

[91] Girardin notes the contrast with Calvin: "Certes in 213ss, Mélanchthon exhortet-il aux bonnes oeuvres. Toutefois il distend la régénération de

Melanchthon's syllogistic reading of Paul's argument, moreover, provides the framework for his employment of the terms *mortificatio* and *vivificatio*. The gospel set before believers is the gospel of both repentance and the forgiveness of sins, each of which is placarded in the death of Christ. The anger of God against sin, vividly portrayed in the crucifixion of his Son, ought to stimulate the "true terrors and pains" of repentance. The cross should also evoke comfort, however, as this same cross provides the forgiveness of sins. So, corresponding generally to law and gospel, "mortification is genuine terror and pain, and vivification is the faith which comforts us."[92]

CALVIN: ENGRAFTING INTO THE CRUCIFIED AND RISEN CHRIST

The theological significance of the way one relates Romans 5 and 6 has been noted. In the final, 1556 revision of his commentary, Calvin adds a revealing transitional and summative statement to open his interpretation of Romans 6: "Throughout this chapter the apostle maintains that those who imagine that Christ bestows free justification upon us without newness of life shamefully rend Christ asunder (*Christum discerpere*)."[93]

Unlike Melanchthon, therefore, Calvin thus immediately and vigorously locates the relation of Romans 5 to 6, and of justification to sanctification, in the doctrine of union with Christ. To imagine the gift of justification without "newness of life" is to imagine a Christ torn in two.[94] The point made strikingly on 6:1 is restated no less forcibly in a comment on v. 2. For Calvin, the Spirit's renovative

---

l'imputation, les distribuant en deux temps séparés. Calvin, lui, insiste sur les deux parties de la rédemption contenues dans le terme de *gratia*: 'remissio peccatorum qua iustitia imputatur et sanctificatio spiritus per quam ad bona opera regeneramur'" (*Rhétorique et Théologique*, 307, n. 88, citing CO 49.113).

[92] Melanchthon, *Commentarii*, CR 15.636: "Sed sciamus mortificationem esse veros terrores et dolores, et vivificationem ipsam fidem consolantem nos."

[93] Calvin, *Comm. Epist. ad Romanos*, 117; CNTC, 121. "Hoc toto capite disseret Apostolus, perperam eos Christum discerpere, qui gratuitam ab ipso iustitiam nobis donari fingunt absque vitae novitate." The significance of Calvin's metaphor (*discerpere Christum*) will be examined at length in Chapter 5, though in anticipation of that discussion its presence should be noted in this and the following chapter.

[94] Thus Calvin's specific concern to counter the charge of licentiousness is evident again in his exposition of this chapter, starting, as his opening statement indicates, at the earliest possible point. See also his pointed comment on 6:19 where he refers to "the gross and evil slander which imagines that the liberty obtained by Christ gives license to sin" (*Comm. Epist. ad Romanos*, 130; CNTC, 134).

work and the merciful, adopting call of God to fellowship with his Son require that believers are "never reconciled to God without the gift of regeneration."[95] Hence there is "no greater contradiction than to nourish our vices" by the very grace that restores us. Why? Because the Apostle teaches "the efficacy of the fellowship of the death of Christ," in other words, that in Christ's death the believer died to sin.[96]

In the course of his exposition of Romans 6,[97] Calvin clarifies that the salvation offered by the gospel is not only justification but sanctification as well (the *duplex gratia*). When told that one is not under the law but under grace, one should understand by *gratia* both "parts" of salvation: "i.e., the forgiveness of sins, by which God imputes righteousness to us, and sanctification of the Spirit, by whom He forms us anew to good works."[98] Salvation is not

---

[95] Calvin, *Comm. Epist. ad Romanos*, 118; CNTC, 122. This clause is also added in 1556. Here Paul is arguing from the contrary position (*a contrarii positione*). Calvin continues: "Nam qui peccat, eum peccato vivere certum est. Nos mortui peccato sumus per Christi gratiam. Falsum ergo est, peccato quod abolet, vigorem dare. Sic enim res habet, nunquam sine regenerationis dono reconciliari Deo fideles. Imo in hunc finem nos iustificari, ut deinde vitae puritate Deum colamus. Nec vero nos Christus suo sanguine aliter abluit, suaque expiatione Deum nobis reddit propitium, quam dum nos facit Spiritus sui participes, qui nos in sanctam vitam renovat (N.B.: in 1540, 1551: "regenerati, vitae puritate Dominum glorificemus")... Porro memoria tenendum est quod nuper attigi, Paulum non hic tractare quales nos Deus inveniat, dum vocat in societatem Filii sui, sed quales esse nos deceat, postquam nostri misertus, gratis nos adoptavit. Adverbio enim futuri temporis, qualis iustitiam sequi debeat mutatio, ostendit." Calvin refers here to ἔτι (*adhuc*). In light of some popular misunderstanding, it should be noted that by "follow" Calvin intends to distinguish the definitive justification existentially related to faith from the progressive work of sanctification, *not* to indicate causality or theological priority, as this study as a whole demonstrates.

[96] Calvin, *Comm. Epist. ad Romanos*, 117-18 (on 6:3); CNTC, 121-2.

[97] Girardin, *Rhétorique et Théologique*, 375-6, provides a rhetorical analysis of Calvin's exposition of Romans 6 in outline form. In this analysis, Calvin sees Paul move from the Romans 5 *amplificationes* of the theme of chs. 1-4 to a *descendit ad sanctificationem*, the first section of which (vv. 1-11) is summarized as "*iustitia in Christo = sanctificatio*." In this first section of the chapter Calvin reads Paul as dealing first with certain *calumnia* before providing a positive exposition of his doctrine. This doctrine is argued *ab effectu baptismi intentionem suam probat* (vv. 3-4), *confirmat quod iam posuerat argumentum* (vv. 5-6), and then by means of an *argumentum a mortis effectu* (vv. 7-10), concluding in v. 11.

[98] Calvin, *Comm. Epist. ad Romanos*, 127 (on 6:14); CNTC, 130: "Ergo 'non esse sub Lege' significat non tantum mortua litera nobis praescribi quod nos in reatum addicat, quia ad praestandum simus impares, sed etiam obnoxios nos

justification but the *duplex gratia* of justification and sanctification. The gift of God (6:23) is "not a single, unaccompanied gift," says Calvin, "for since we are clothed with the righteousness of the Son, we are reconciled to God, and renewed by the power of the Spirit to holiness. He has added, therefore, *in Christ Jesus*, to call us away from conceit about our own dignity."[99]

Calvin's focuses attention in this chapter on the mortification/vivification of the flesh as expressed in the Pauline language of dying/rising with Christ.[100] The focus is specifically on *efficacious* death/resurrection with Christ, but the underlying reality throughout is the believer's union or fellowship with Christ. At one point, Calvin chooses against Erasmus's translation *per Christum* in favor of the Vulgate *in Christo Iesu* simply because the Vulgate communicates more clearly the union-engrafting idea that Paul intends.[101] Calvin repeatedly emphasizes the real efficacy of the death and resurrection of Christ for mortification and vivification in light of this union-reality.[102] He thus interprets the baptism language

---

amplius non esse Legi, quatenus exigit perfectam iustitiam, edicta morte omnibus qui ab ulla parte declinaverint. Sub 'gratiae' nomine similiter intelligimus utranque redemptionis partem; hoc est, remissionem peccatorum qua iustitiam Deus nobis imputat (1540, 1551: iustitia imputatur), et sanctificationem Spiritus, per quam ad bona opera nos refingit (1540, 1551: regeneramur)." But note his comment on 4:25 where the two parts of "salvation" are expiation of sin and the obtaining of righteousness, correlating to the death and resurrection of Christ, respectively. This is potentially confusing but in light of his specific attention in this passage to the *meritorious cause* of salvation, it is clear that here Calvin has only the twin blessings of justification in view.

[99] Calvin, *Comm. Epist. ad Romanos*, 133; CNTC, 138. Cf. comment on 6:10 where this renewal is specifically conformity to Christ's life in heaven and thus participation in that life.

[100] Calvin's summation of sanctification as mortification and vivification has been well surveyed. See Wendel, *Calvin*, 242-55; Wallace, *Calvin's Doctrine of the Christian Life*, 41-100; and note the observations made on the basis of Calvin's correspondence in Jean-Daniel Benoit, *Calvin in His Letters*, trans. Richard Haig (Appleford: Sutton Courtenay Press, 1991), 73-82.

[101] Calvin, *Comm. Epist. ad Romanos*, 124 (on 6:11); CNTC, 128. In the Latin column of his first, 1516 text Erasmus opted for the locative *in Christo* as a translation of the dative ἐν Χριστῷ Ἰησοῦ but changed this to the instrumental *per Christum* in later editions (1519, 1522, 1527, 1535). Calvin's text reads *In Christo Iesu*.

[102] Cf. comments on Rom 6:4, 5, 6, 7, where Calvin is most adamant. On baptism and engrafting into Christ in Calvin, see Egil Grislis, "Calvin's Doctrine of Baptism," *CH* 31 (1962): 46-65; cf. Bryan D. Spinks, "Calvin's Baptismal Theology and the Making of the Strasbourg and Geneva Baptismal Liturgies

along these lines, arguing that in baptism we put on Christ, a reality that contains two principles: first, we put him on so that we may be one with him; second, we grow up in his body when his death "produces its fruit in us." This fellowship in Christ's death is the central focus of baptism. Thus baptism does not serve to signify a mere washing but a real mortification, a real death *in Christ's death*. It is in baptism that one begins to participate in this grace.[103]

But fellowship with Christ's death, explains Calvin, is inseparable from fellowship in his resurrection; so the efficacy of Christ's death (mortification) is inextricably connected to the efficacy of his resurrection (vivification). The former brings about the overthrow of the depravity of the flesh; the latter, a true renewal of our nature after the pattern of Christ. This is the intention behind the Pauline language of engrafting: just as engrafting into a living tree produces fruit, so engrafting into Christ produces real death and resurrection in us. Indeed, the union is so close and the efficacy so real that one is said to "pass from our nature into his."[104] Because Christ's death is inseparable from his resurrection life, both are received by virtue of this engrafting. Calvin's center of interest is on the *inseparability* of the one from the other, rooted in the historical transition that took place in Christ.

Engrafting and Imitation

The symbolic significance of divine engrafting, moreover, with its effectual mortification/vivification, is not to be confused with a

---

1540 and 1542," *SJT* 48 (1995): 64, who notes that for Calvin "... the main stress... is on the christological dimension of baptism, namely our union with Christ" (cf. p. 72).

[103] Calvin, *Comm. Epist. ad Romanos*, 118-9 (on 6:3); CNTC, 122. Cf. comment on the *duplex gratia* in 4:11: "In conclusion, as now in baptism there are two parts [*duae...partes*], so formerly in circumcision there were the two parts which testified both to newness of life and to forgiveness of sins" (*Comm. Epist. ad Romanos*, 86; CNTC, 89).

[104] Calvin, *Comm. Epist. ad Romanos*, 121 (on 6:5); CNTC, 124). Calvin is continuing his comments on the tree analogy. That he intends by this statement ("passing into Christ's nature") not an ontological confusion but an emphasis on real efficacy is evident from the context in which this statement is set: "In the grafting of trees the graft draws its nourishment from the root, but retains its own natural quality in the fruit which is eaten. In spiritual ingrafting, however, we not only derive the strength and sap of the life which flows from Christ, but we also pass from our own nature into His. The apostle desired to point quite simply to the efficacy of the death of Christ (1551 add: which manifested itself in putting to death our flesh,) and also the efficacy of His resurrection in renewing within us the better nature of the Spirit."

modelling activity of the believer in which one strives to follow Christ's example. Engrafting pertains not primarily to an *imitatio Christi* but to the secret *coniunctio Christi* work of the Spirit. "The comparison which he introduces [i.e., united in the likeness of Christ's death and resurrection (v. 5)] removes all ambiguity, since ingrafting signifies not only conformity to an example," Calvin explains, "but also the hidden union (*arcanam coniunctionem*) by which we grow together with Him, in such a way that He revives us by His Spirit, and transfuses his power to us." The Spirit's work is one of engrafting believers into the *similitudinem* of Christ's death and resurrection.[105] Recalling the themes observed in Calvin's reading of Romans 2 above, it should be noted that a believer's death/resurrection is thus *patterned* after Christ's. The point is further clarified by Paul's choice of language in Rom 6:5 in which believers are said to have "become united" (*insititii facti*) to Christ in this way: "This word has great emphasis, and clearly shows that the apostle is not exhorting us, but rather teaching us about the benefit we derive from Christ." In a 1551 addition, Calvin adds: "He does not require from us any duty which our care or diligence can achieve, but speaks of the engrafting which is accomplished by the hand of God."[106] These clarifying statements should be understood as Calvin's effort to distinguish his view from the semi-Pelagian tendencies inherent in the *imitatio Christi* tradition.[107]

---

[105] Calvin, *Comm. Epist. ad Romanos*, 120 (on 6:5); CNTC, 123-4): "Confirmat verbis clarioribus quod iam posuerat argumentum. Nam similitudo quam adhibet, nihil iam ambiguum relinquit; quia insitio non exempli tantum conformitatem designat, sed arcanam coniunctionem, per quam cum ipso coaluimus, ita ut nos Spiritu suo vegetans, eius virtutem in nos transfundat. Ergo ut surculus communem habet vitae et mortis conditionem cum arbore in quam insertus est, ita vitae Christi non minus quam et mortis participes non esse consentaneum est. Nam si insiti sumus in similitudinem mortis Christi, illa autem resurrectione non caret, ergo nec nostra sine resurrectione erit."

[106] Calvin, *Comm. Epist. ad Romanos*, 121; CNTC, 124: "Magna est vocabuli huius energia, et quae clare ostendit Apostolum non exhortari tantum, sed potius de Christi beneficio docere. [1551 add:] Neque enim quicquam a nobis requirit quod studio industriave nostra praestandum sit, sed insitionem Dei manu factam praedicat."

[107] See Wendel, *Calvin*, 250; cf. also Calvin, *Comm.* on Matt. 16:24 (CO 45.481). Wallace, *Calvin's Doctrine of the Christian Life*, 47, also notes briefly that Calvin's perspective is *unio* rather than *imitatio*. Note Otto Grundler, "John Calvin: Ingrafting in Christ," in E. Rozanne Elder, ed., *The Spirituality of Western Christendom* (Kalamazoo: Cistercian Publications, 1976), 169-87, who, noting well that the "race of righteousness" is for Calvin modeled on Christ as

But if the *imitatio* is not what Calvin has in view, then the question arises as to exactly what he intends to emphasize by the use of language so similar to that used in this tradition. It is not necessary to insist that he is rejecting everything in this tradition in order to show that he has modified it. The evident differences in this respect are, first, those texts, just noted, in which Calvin distances himself from an *exemplar* view of mortification/vivification; and, second, those texts in which he correlates the pattern of Christ's transition from death to resurrection/eternal life with the experience of believers united to him. It is here, in Calvin's emphasis on pattern and sequence as a way of contextualizing the idea of causation in salvation, that his distinctive and animating idea should be identified. On v. 7, for instance, Calvin describes the progressive nature of the duty to bear Christ's cross. He then refers to Paul's argument in 2 Corinthians 4 in which the Apostle speaks of another *communicatio* in the death of Christ in which bearing the cross is followed by participation (*consortium*) in eternal life.

> We may summarize Paul's teaching in the following way: If you are a Christian, there must be evident in you a sign of your communion in the death of Christ (*communionis cum morte Christi*), and the fruit of this is that your flesh has been crucified together with all its desires. Do not assume, however, that this communion is not a real one if you find traces of the flesh still existing in you. But you are continually to strive to increase your communion in the death of Christ, until you arrive at the goal... There is another fellowship (*communicatio*) in the death of Christ of which the apostle often speaks, as in II Cor. 4, viz. the bearing of the cross, which is followed by our participation (*consortium*) in eternal life.[108]

The general observations made above on Calvin's use of Romans 8 to interpret the conditional language of Romans 2 must be remembered here, as it is this principle that operates here as well.

---

exemplar (pp. 182-4), insufficiently discerns Calvin's reinterpretation of the *imitatio* theme.

[108] Calvin, *Comm. Epist. ad Romanos*, 122; CNTC, 125-6. "Sic ergo in summa habeto, 'Si Christianus es, oportere in te signum apparere communionis cum morte Christi; cuius fructus est, ut crucifixa sit caro tua cum suis concupiscentiis omnibus. Caeterum hanc communionem non ideo nullam esse, si reliquias carnis vivere adhuc in te sentias. Sed meditandum assidue eius augmentum, donec ad metam perventum sit.' Bene enim est si mortificatur continenter caro nostra; neque parum profectum est, ubi regnum illi ademptum, Spiritui sancto cessit. Est altera mortis Christi communicatio de qua loquitur Apostolus, quum saepe alias, tum 2. Corint. 4, nempe crucis tolerantia, quam sequitur et vitae aeternae consortium."

Calvin's association of cross-bearing with eternal life is purposely analogous to his association of communion with Christ in his death and his resurrection. These two stages are tied together, so that one follows the other: as Christ's death was followed by his resurrection, so those in fellowship with him die in his death (mortification) and rise with him (vivification), or, more particularly, bear/partake of Christ's cross before partaking of his eternal life. The necessity – and for Calvin, the inseparability – of this pattern is based on what was true in Christ's own historical experience. In particular, Calvin sees in Paul's organic language of engrafting a strict emphasis upon the inseparability of death and resurrection in the experience of the believer grounded in the experience of Christ. Just as in Romans 2, so here in chapter six the transitions from death to life, and from cross-bearing to eternal life, are rooted in the historical transition that took place in Christ's own earthly experience. Calvin has in view a divine *ordo* according to which one brings about the other non-meritoriously. The duty incumbent upon every believer, then, according to Calvin, is naturally one of faithfully representing within himself or herself the image of Christ by mortifying the flesh and living by the Spirit. For "if we return to our own filthiness, we deny Christ, for we can have communion with Him only by newness of life, even as He Himself lives an incorruptible life."[109]

Light from Romans 4

Calvin's remarks on Rom 4:25 ("[Christ] was delivered up for our trespasses and raised for our justification") may help to clarify his comments on resurrection/vivification in Romans 6. For Calvin, the death of Christ effects reconciliation with God and his resurrection results in the obtaining of righteousness.[110] But, together, Christ's death and resurrection are both the single "cause of our salvation,"

---

[109] Calvin, *Comm. Epist. ad Romanos*, 122; CNTC, 126. "Si enim in coenum nostrum revolvimur, Christum abnegamus, cuius nisi per vitae novitatem, consortes esse non possumus, sicut ipse vitam incorruptibilem agit." These themes from Calvin's reading of Romans 6 should be located in the stream of revisions made in the 1537/1538 Catechisms and the 1539 *Institutes* to his 1536 exposition of the Creed. In 1539, the revisions and expansions of the earlier texts are often substantial. Here, as in the *Commentary*, Calvin interprets dying and rising in Christ in terms of mortification and vivification, and also distances himself explicitly from an exemplar or *imitatio* model. The focus throughout, as in his *Romans*, is upon union-participation in Christ's death and resurrection. Examine carefully the text-history of the relevant portions of *Inst.* (1559) 2.16, and note the role of Romans 6.

[110] Calvin, *Comm. Epist. ad Romanos*, 99; CNTC, 102.

and they are distinguished by the Apostle only to accommodate to our ignorance.[111] While Scripture often speaks only of the death of Christ, here the Apostle "give[s] a more explicit account" and thus divides salvation into its "two parts." Because they are both necessary and each brings a distinct benefit to the believer, "The sum is that when we possess the benefit of Christ's death and resurrection, righteousness is fulfilled in all its parts."[112] The analogy is then drawn explicitly between Christ's death and resurrection and the *duplex gratia*, indicating the indispensability of each to salvation:

> Since Christ, however, has made known to us how much He had achieved by His death by rising from the dead, this distinction will also teach us that our salvation was begun by the sacrifice by which our sins were expiated, and finally completed by His resurrection. The beginning of righteousness is our reconciliation to God, and its completion is the reign of life when death has been destroyed...[113]

Calvin retains his focus on justification, however, by stating, *contra* Melanchthon for example, that the following clause ("and was raised for our justification") does not refer to newness of life but to imputed justification.[114] The alternative reading would make Christ's death merely the acquisition of the grace needed for mortification, a "sense which no one admits." Instead, one ought to understand by Paul's statement that just as by his death Christ delivered us from death, so by his resurrection he has "fully restored life to us." In the person of a sinner (*in persona peccatoris*) he was "struck by the hand of God" and was consequently exalted *in vitae regnum* from whence he freely gives us life.[115] Thus the distinction between justification and sanctification is tied to the distinction between Christ's death and resurrection, and their inseparability is based upon the same. The inseparability, moreover, is also due to the necessary presence of each element for salvation. But, as we observed above, the death

---

[111] Calvin, *Comm. Epist. ad Romanos*, 99; CNTC, 102.
[112] Calvin, *Comm. Epist. ad Romanos*, 99; CNTC, 102.
[113] Calvin, *Comm. Epist. ad Romanos*, 99; CNTC, 102. "Sed quia resurgendo patefecit Christus, quantum morte sua profecisset, haec quoque distinctio ad docendum apta est, 'Sacrificio, quo expiata sunt peccata, inchoatam fuisse salutem nostram; resurrectione vero demum fuisse perfectam.' Nam iustitiae principium est, nos reconciliari Deo; complementum autem, abolita morte vitam dominari."
[114] Cf. Calvin, *Comm. Epist. ad Romanos*, 100, with Melanchthon (CO 15.610). The editors of Calvin's text (100, n. 39) also note Lombard (*Collect.*, PL 191.1378A; *Glossa Ordinaria*, 12ra).
[115] Calvin, *Comm. Epist. ad Romanos*, 100; CNTC, 103.

and resurrection of Christ also correspond to the two parts of sanctification: mortification and vivification. In a potentially confusing way, Calvin thus argues that the death and resurrection of Christ requires a particular understanding of both the *duplex gratia* and the *duplex regeneratio*. In the former, emphasis falls on the inseparability of justification and sanctification in Christ. In the latter, emphasis falls on the inseparability of death to sin and newness of life in Christ.

New Life in Christ by the Spirit: Romans 8

Once we reach Calvin's comments on Romans 8, we encounter the final, crucial strands that bring into view the larger fabric of his replication model. For in this section, expanded considerably in his final revision of the commentary in 1556, Calvin's understanding of the Holy Spirit as the integrating Person of his soteriology is given extended attention.[116]

JOINED TO CHRIST BY THE SPIRIT

In 1540 Calvin opens his exposition of Romans 8 by pointing to the consolation of believing consciences afforded by Paul's statement (8:1) that there is no condemnation for those "who are in Christ Jesus, who do not walk according to the flesh but according to the Spirit" (*qui sunt in Christo Iesu: qui non secundum carnem ambulant, sed secundum spiritum*). The assurance of believers who struggle with the flesh and their freedom from the power and curse of death are both certain – provided they live *secundum spiritum* and not *secundum carnem*. Here Calvin notes the unity of justification and sanctification in Paul's thought. Paul, he explains, connects (1) the ongoing imperfection of believers, (2) the mercy of God in pardon and forgiveness (justification), and (3) the regeneration of the Spirit.[117] Elsewhere, the Spirit's work is decidedly a kingdom work, so that Christian denial of the flesh is related to his rule: "the kingdom of the Spirit is the abolition of the flesh." The sharp contrast between

---

[116] It should be noted that virtually the whole of Calvin's comment on Romans 8 is eminently worthy of examination for our purposes. Calvin's convictions regarding the inseparability of justification and sanctification, adoption, inheritance, and the role of suffering/good works in salvation are expressed repeatedly in terms of the Spirit's union-work. See, e.g., his comments on vv. 1, 2, 3, 4, 6, 8, 9, 10, 11, 13, 14, 15, 23, 28, 29, 30.

[117] Calvin, *Comm. Epist. ad Romanos*, 152; CNTC, 156.

being "in/out of the Spirit" is thus rooted in the corresponding "not serving/serving the flesh."[118]

Again, on Rom 8:13, Calvin makes this point sharply and clearly, but this time with explicit reference to the inseparability of justification and sanctification.

> He adds a warning in order to shake off their sluggishness with greater severity. This also provides a useful refutation of those who boast of justification by faith without the Spirit of Christ. Their own conscience, however, more than sufficiently convicts them, since there is no confidence (*fiducia*) in God where there is no love of righteousness. It is, indeed, true that we are justified in Christ by the mercy of God alone, but it is equally true and certain, that all who are justified are called by the Lord to live worthy of their vocation.[119]

This rule of the Spirit is tied to the reality of adoption, for God favors only the elect with the sanctification of the Spirit and sets them alone apart as sons.[120]

This insistence on Calvin's part upon the inseparability of justification and sanctification by the Spirit is rendered still more forceful in the significant additions made to the above expositions in 1556. On Rom 8:2 Calvin adds a note regarding the simultaneity of justification and sanctification in order to nuance and distinguish his view from those who would make justification *dependent* upon renewal. In light of the Epistle's teaching that the life-giving Spirit abolishes the law of sin in us, such a view might seem to be demanded by the text. But Calvin's stress is on the strict contemporaneity and consequent inseparability of justification and sanctification.

> Someone may object that in this case the pardon, by which our offences are buried, depends on our regeneration. This is easily

---

[118] Calvin, *Comm. Epist. ad Romanos*, 160 (on 8:9); CNTC, 164): "He adds this in order to show how necessary it is for Christians to deny the flesh. The kingdom of the Spirit (*regnum spiritus*) is the abolition of the flesh. Those in whom the Spirit does not reign do not belong to Christ; therefore those who serve the flesh are not Christians."

[119] Calvin, *Comm. Epist. ad Romanos*, 163; CNTC, 166-7: "Addit comminationem, quo acrius torporem illis omnem excutiat; qua etiam probe refelluntur qui iustificationem fidei iactant sine Christi Spiritu. Quanquam sua ipsorum conscientia plus satis redarguuntur, quia nulla est in Deum fiducia, ubi non sit et amor iustitiae. Verum est quidem, nos sola Dei misericordia iustificari in Christo. Sed aeque et istud verum ac certum, omnes qui iustificantur, vocari a Domino ut digne sua vocatione vivant."

[120] See Calvin, *Comm. Epist. ad Romanos*, 163; CNTC, 167. Cf. *Comm*. Rom 8:15, 23.

In Christ, Like Christ

answered. Paul is not here assigning the reason (*causam*), but merely specifying the manner (*modum*), in which we are delivered from guilt. He denies that we obtain deliverance by the outward teaching of the law. In being renewed by the Spirit of God, however, we are at the same time (*simul*) also justified by a free pardon, so that the curse of sin may no longer lie upon us. The sentence, therefore, means the same as if Paul had said that the grace of regeneration is never separated (*nunquam disiungi*) from the imputation of righteousness.[121]

Also, in a 1556 addition to his comments on Rom 8:4, the idea is explicated with specific reference to the communication of Christ's righteousness to those joined to Christ by the Spirit. The perfection demanded by the law was "exhibited in the flesh" so that its demand "should no longer condemn us."

> But because Christ communicates His righteousness only to those whom He joins (*coniungit*) to Himself by the bond of His Spirit, Paul mentions regeneration again, lest Christ should be thought to be the minister of sin. It is common for the teaching of the fatherly indulgence of God to be used for the lust of the flesh, while others maliciously slander this doctrine, as if it extinguished the pursuit (*studium*) of upright living.[122]

---

[121] Calvin, *Comm. Epist. ad Romanos*, 152-3; CNTC, 157. "Sententia igitur est, 'Quod Lex Dei homines condemnat, id fit quia quantisper sub Legis obligatione manent, peccati servitute premuntur, atque ita rei sunt mortis. Spiritus autem Christi, dum inordinatas carnis cupiditates corrigendo, legem peccati in nobis abolet, simul a mortis reatu nos vindicat'. Siquis excipiat, veniam ergo qua sepeliuntur nostra delicta, a regeneratione pendere, facilis solutio est, non assignari causam a Paulo, sed modum tradi duntaxat quo solvimur a reatu. Negat autem Paulus externa Legis doctrina id nos consequi, sed dum Spiritu Dei renovamur, simul etiam iustificari gratuita venia, ne peccati maledictio in nos amplius recumbat. Perinde ergo valet haec sententia acsi dixisset Paulus, regenerationis gratiam ab imputatione iustitiae nunquam disiungi." Melanchthon's exposition also relates at least the basic content of a *duplex gratia* as non-imputation/forgiveness of sins and newness of life (CR 15.655-6).

[122] Calvin, *Comm. Epist. ad Romanos*, 156; CNTC, 160. "Sed quia suam iustitiam nullis communicat Christus, nisi quos Spiritus sui vinculo sibi coniungit, additur iterum regeneratio, ne putetur Christus peccati esse minister; sicut proclive est multis ad carnis lasciviam rapere quicquid de paterna Dei indulgentia traditur. Alii autem maligne calumniantur hanc doctrinam, acsi recte vivendi studium extingueret." The contrast with Melanchthon, who focuses on imputation and its effect (newness of life) in contrast to the "opinions of our adversaries" regarding merit and perfection, should be noted (CR 15.656).

Still more explicit are the 1556 additions made by Calvin to the comments on 8:9 and 8:13, in both cases employing (as in the 1556 addition to 6:1) the metaphor of tearing Christ into pieces. In 8:9, those who serve the flesh do not belong to Christ,

> ...for those who separate (*divellunt*) Christ from His Spirit make Him like a dead image or a corpse. We must always bear in mind the counsel of the apostle, that free remission of sins cannot be separated (*disiungi*) from the Spirit of regeneration. This would be, as it were, to rend (*discerpere*) Christ asunder.[123]

In Rom 8:13, already noted briefly above, Paul adds a severe warning to those who think they are justified by faith but are sluggish in loving righteousness. "It is, indeed, true that we are justified in Christ by the mercy of God alone, but it is equally true and certain, that all who are justified are called by the Lord to live worthy of their vocation." Then, Calvin adds in 1556,

> Let believers, therefore, learn to embrace Him, not only for justification, but also for sanctification, as He has been given to us for both these purposes, that they may not rend Him asunder (*lacerent*) by their own mutilated faith.[124]

THE CHRIST-PATTERN OF SALVATION: SUFFERING TO GLORY, OBEDIENCE TO ETERNAL LIFE

As in Calvin's exposition of Rom 2:6-7, the specific character of this saving union with Christ is that of an analogue, in the experience of believers, of the pattern of Christ's own historical experience. In Romans 8, this is expressed with specific reference to the question of Christian suffering and the conditional nature of adoption. This is particularly important since the blessing of adoption entails becoming fellow-heirs with Christ of the eschatological reward of eternal life. For Calvin the key is simple: only those who suffer like Christ are truly God's children. But this suffering is neither a cruel twist of fate nor a mere *imitatio Christi* effort on man's part. It is in

---

[123] Calvin, *Comm. Epist. ad Romanos*, 160; CNTC, 164. "Christum enim a Spiritu suo qui divellunt, eum faciunt mortuo simulachro vel cadaveri similem. Ac semper tenendum est illud Apostoli consilium, gratuitam peccatorum remissionem a Spiritu regenerationis non posse disiungi; quia hoc esset quasi Christum discerpere."

[124] Calvin, *Comm. Epist. ad Romanos*, 163; CNTC, 166-7. "Verum est quidem, nos sola Dei misericordia iustificari in Christo. Sed aeque et istud verum ac certum, omnes qui iustificantur, vocari a Domino ut digne sua vocatione vivant. [1556:] Discant ergo fideles non in iustitiam modo, sed in sanctificationem quoque amplecti, sicuti in utrunque finem nobis datus est, ne mutila sua fide eum lacerent."

fact the Spirit's work of *replication*, something Calvin regards as a *sine qua non* of salvation.

Calvin notes the Apostle's intention to comfort suffering believers and therefore reads the text with this in mind. When the Apostle in Rom 8:28 points sufferers to the divine purpose, he does so "so that we may know that the fact that everything happens to the saints for their salvation depends on the free adoption of God as the first cause." Indeed, Paul's predestination language is specifically referred to suffering so that predestination is specifically predestination to cross-bearing. The source of election is (ultimately) the same as the source of suffering for, in the divine *decretum*, both election and suffering are laid out as the path of conformity to Christ and as the prerequisites of heaven.[125]

Calvin makes the same point earlier in his handling of the conditional language in Rom 8:17: "If truly sons, then heirs, heirs of God and coheirs with Christ: if indeed we share in his sufferings so that we will share his glory" (*Si vero filii, etiam haeredes: haeredes quidem Dei, cohaeredes autem Christi: siquidem compatimur, ut et una glorificemur*).[126] Calvin notes that various interpretations exist but favors the following: we are fellow-heirs of Christ only if we, with a view to our inheritance, follow the pattern of our Leader. Here Calvin sums up the Apostle's chain of reasoning: adoption by grace entails the sure possession of our eschatological inheritance. In support of this, we need only remember that this inheritance already belongs irrevocably to Christ, and we have been united to him. However, Christ came to possess this inheritance *via* the pattern of suffering-then-glory. *Ergo*, so must those who are united to him.

> Paul made this mention of Christ, because he intended to pass on to this exhortation by these steps: "The inheritance of God is ours, because we have been adopted by His grace as His sons. To remove any doubt, the possession of it has already been conferred on Christ, with whom we are made partakers (*consortes*). But Christ went to that inheritance by the cross (*per crucem*). We, therefore, must go to it the same way."

But as Calvin quickly points out, this should not suggest that our suffering/obedience/works cause our eternal glory in an unqualified sense. Paul is identifying the *ordinem* that God follows "in

---

[125] Calvin, *Comm. Epist. ad Romanos*, 175-6; CNTC, 179-81.
[126] Cf. Vulgate: "si autem filii et heredes heredes quidem Dei coheredes autem Christi si tamen conpatimur ut et conglorificemur."

ministering salvation to us, rather than its cause."[127] The first cause of salvation in this divine order is God's sovereign act of adoption in Christ and this act includes the real necessity that suffering conform us to his holy image.[128]

However, if transformation by the Spirit belongs so inextricably to God's work of salvation, does this not suggest a *causal* place for works in the salvation of sinners? God in his good pleasure alone is the author of our salvation and he alone completes it, replies Calvin, renewing us after Christ's image through our partaking of him. The point is made within a passage in the commentary intended to assure the suffering believer that cross-bearing, despite appearances to the contrary, contributes to rather than detracts from their ongoing experience of God's saving grace. He explains, "Every action of the Spirit of God within us tends to our blessedness. There is, however, no reason for attributing salvation to works on this account, for although God begins our salvation, and finally completes it by renewing us after His image, yet the only cause of

---

[127] Calvin, *Comm. Epist. ad Romanos*, 167; CNTC, 171. "Atque ita quod mentionem Christi iniecit, eo quoque voluit ad hanc cohortationem transitum facere, velut his gradibus, Dei haereditas ideo nostra est quia in filios, eius gratia sumus adoptati. Ac ne dubia sit, eius possessio iam Christo delata est, cuius facti sumus consortes. *Atqui eam Christus per crucem adiit. Ergo et nobis eo modo adeunda est.* Neque timendum est quod verentur quidam, ne sic gloriae aeternae causam laboribus nostris transcribat Paulus. Siquidem haec loquendi formula Scripturae insolita non est, sed ordinem potius, quem in salute nobis dispensanda sequitur Dominus, quam causam, denotat. [added 1556:] Nam antehac satis asseruit gratuitam Dei misericordiam contra operum merita. Nunc dum ad patientiam nos hortatur, non disputat unde nobis proveniat salus, sed quo modo suos Deus gubernet." Italics mine. Note also Calvin's integration of the ideas of decree, adoption, and inheritance in his comments on 8:23. Melanchthon's treatment of the conditional language in 8:17 again reflects his principle of simple necessity, this time based on the sufferings of Christ but still explicitly identifying obedience/newness of life as the necessary effect of justification: "What then does the condition, 'if we suffer with him,' say? I answer: Not purchase price or merit, but a necessity, because obedience is the newness itself by which eternal life is begun in believers according to 2 Cor. 5... It is necessary as an effect necessarily following justification (*Vel est necessaria, tanquam effectus necessario sequens iustificationem*)" (CO 15.688).

[128] Calvin, *Comm. Epist. ad Romanos*, 176; CNTC, 179-80. "Scimus enim, ubi de salute agitur, libenter homines a seipsis incipere, fingereque sibi praeparationes quibus Dei gratiam antevertant. Ergo Paulus quos vocavit Dei cultores, eosdem prius ab eo fuisse electos docet. Certum est enim ideo notari ordinem, ut sciamus a gratuita Dei adoptione tanquam a prima causa pendere, quod sanctis omnia in salutem succedunt." I have reproduced the 1556 revision; for the 1540 and 1551 texts, see *Comm. Epist. ad Romanos*, 176, nn. c-d.

our salvation is His good pleasure, by which He makes us partakers (*consortes*) of Christ."[129]

In a passage already noted above in the analysis of Romans 2, it is clear again both how prominent a role the suffering of believers plays in their salvation and how important it is that this role be understood in terms of "replication."

> Paul meant only that God had determined that all whom He has adopted should bear the image of Christ. He did not simply say that they should be conformed to Christ, but to the image of Christ (*imagini Christi*), in order to teach us that in Christ there is a living and conspicuous example (*exemplar*) which is set before all the sons of God for their imitation (*imitationem*). The sum of the passage is that free adoption, in which our salvation consists, is inseparable from this other decree, viz. that He had appointed us to bear the cross. *No one can be an heir of heaven who has not first been conformed to the only begotten Son of God.*[130]

Calvin is therefore not opposed in principle to the language of *exemplar* or *imitatio*, but the distinguishing mark of his doctrine is that this *imitatio* belongs to the Spirit's larger project of replication. It is indeed because of this principle that the works/suffering/obedience of believers do not compromise the reality of a gracious justification *sola fide* as it arguably does in the semi-Pelagian presuppositions of the *imitatio Christi* tradition. Instead they serve to confirm the truth that all of salvation must be

---

[129] Calvin, *Comm. Epist. ad Romanos*, 159; CNTC, 162. "Quicquid enim agit in nobis Dei Spiritus, ad nostram beatitudinem spectat; frustra tamen ideo quis tribuat salutem operibus. Quanquam enim Deus salutem nostram inchoat, et demum absolvit in imaginem suam nos refingendo, unica tamen causa est eius beneplacitum, quo nos facit Christi consortes."

[130] Calvin, *Comm. Epist. ad Romanos*, 177 (on 8:29); CNTC, 181. "Verbum προορίζειν quod 'praedestinare' vertunt, ad circunstantiam huius loci refertur; quia Paulus duntaxat intelligit, Deum ita statuisse ut quoscunque adoptavit, idem Christi imaginem gestarent. Neque simpliciter dixit, 'ut conformes sint Christo', sed *imagini Christi*; ut doceret vivum et conspicuum exemplar extare in Christo, quod omnibus Dei filiis ad imitationem proponitur. Summa porro est, '*Gratuitam adoptionem in qua salus nostra consistit, ab hoc altero decreto inseparabilem esse*, quod nos ferendae cruci addixit: *quia nemo caelorum haeres esse potest, qui non ante unigenito Dei Filio fuerit conformis.*'" Italics mine. This is a 1556 addition. As Parker notes, the reference is to Bolsec, Pighius, and Siculus. See *Congrégation* (CO 98.102); *De aeterna Dei praedestinatione* (CO 8.256, 272; COR III/1, 4-8; 44-6); *Comm. Epist. ad Romanos*, 177, n. 50.

sought in Christ as Head,[131] and that all aspects of a believing response are ultimately the work of his Spirit. Calvin also states that citizenship in heaven is conditioned upon being conformed to Christ. The point is again made that the decree of adoption is inseparable from the decree to bear the cross, so that they must not be separated.

But if it is still unclear that following the Christ-pattern of suffering-glory is indispensably tied to salvation in Calvin's thought, this is settled by his subsequent remark, dating from the original, 1540 text.

> Paul now employs a climax (*gradatione*) in order to confirm by a clearer demonstration how true it is that our conformity to the humility of Christ is our salvation (*illam cum Christi humilitate conformationem saluti nobis esse*). In this he teaches us that our participation in the cross is so connected with our vocation, justification, and finally our glory, that *they cannot in any way be separated*.[132]

Concluding Analysis and Proposal: Calvin's Replication Principle

The Replication Principle: A Summary

Taking a step back from these studies of select sections from Calvin's *Romans*, how should his perspective be described? If one restricts the question to Calvin's defense of the necessary presence of

---

[131] Calvin also employs the Pauline Head-members metaphor in a 1556 addition to his exposition of Romans 8:29. See Calvin, *Comm. Epist. ad Romanos*, 177; CNTC, 181.

[132] Calvin, *Comm. Epist. ad Romanos*, 177-8; CNTC, 181. "Iam ut clariori demonstratione confirmet quam verum sit, illam cum Christi humilitate conformationem saluti nobis esse, gradatione utitur. In qua docet, sic cum vocatione, iustificatione, gloria denique nostra, cohaerere societatem crucis, *ut nullo modo separari queant*." Italics mine. The recognition of the *gradatio* rhetorical device may reflect the influence of Melanchthon who also recognized a *gradatio* in the Apostle's argument in 8:17: "Postquam tradidit doctrinam, quod oporteat existere novam obedientiam, attexit gradationem de glorificatione, quae sequitur iustificationem. Et huic loco admiscet propositionem de afflictionibus, quod illa nova obedientia versetur inter afflictiones, quia repugnat carni, diabolo et mundo, hoc est, toti regno peccati" (CO 15.667-8). On *gradatio* as a rhetorical device see Heinrich Lausberg, *Handbook of Literary Rhetoric: A Foundation for Literary Study*, Foreword by George A. Kennedy; trans. of 2nd German ed. (1973) by Matthew T. Bliss, et al.; ed. by David E. Orton and R. Dean Anderson (Leiden: E. J. Brill, 1998).

good works in those justified *sola fide* and, within this, his positive language about the role of these works in salvation (in particular, what has often been called his doctrine of "double justification" and occasionally *duplex iustitia*)[133] then a certain cluster or matrix of ideas emerges. The preceding analysis indicates that this matrix of ideas includes the following: a divinely appointed *ordo* which includes (1) a sequential pattern; (2) adoption in connection with the inheritance of eternal life; (3) Christ-imitation in terms of death/resurrection and suffering/glory; (4) restoration of the *imago Dei* or *Christi*; and (5) the theme of union/participation/fellowship/engrafting with/in Christ. Basic to this matrix of ideas are two important distinctions intended to distance Calvin's formulation from Rome and particularly Trent: (1) reward, not merit; and (2) sequence, not (primary or meritorious) causation.

In light of the foregoing analysis, this matrix of ideas may be accurately and succinctly described as Calvin's "replication principle," an aspect of his teaching on saving union with Christ without which a great deal is unintelligible. It is the distinctiveness of Calvin's idea of Spirit-replication, as well as the control that it exercises in his theology of salvation, that sets him apart from Rome, Bucer, and Melanchthon, as well as the *imitatio Christi* tradition with which his spirituality is often associated. The central theme of the replication principle is this: by virtue of union with Christ by the Spirit, the progress of eternal life reflects the pattern fleshed out in Christ's own historical experience, which is first humiliation, and only then exaltation. More than a reflection (which would suggest mere resemblance with no existential connection in reality), however, the pattern is a Spirit-created replica in the life of the believer of what was and is true of Christ himself. Within this construct, the obedience of the believer, as the fruit of his union with Christ, is the *necessary* though *non-meritorious prerequisite* to eschatological reception of eternal life. Good works belong to the established *ordo* of salvation as the *via* through which, according to the divine administration, those united to Christ ultimately receive

---

[133] Recall the discussion in Chapter 2, above, in which it was noted that the use in the literature of "double justification" for the idea that not just ourselves but our works are justified or accepted in Christ is fully appropriate. My "replication principle" is intended as a supplement to this accurate understanding of the term and as a description of its wider framework. The use of "double justification" to suggest a dual-grounding of justification (partly Christ's righteousness, partly our works), however, must be rejected as foreign to Calvin's thought.

their inheritance.[134] Calvin's affirmation of secondary or inferior causation in interpreting conditional passages is to be located in this rather sophisticated theological and conceptual framework.

It will be remembered that, in Romans 2, Calvin resolved the problem of Paul's conditional language with recourse to the Pauline *ordo* in Rom 8:29-30, according to which non-meritorious good works belong indispensably to salvation as part of God's appointed *ordo* or pattern of leading his people to their inheritance of eternal life. This divine *ordo* extends from election in eternity past and has in view the ultimate, eschatological glorification of the people of God, the path to which is obedience and the meritorious grounds of which is exclusively the righteousness of Christ with whom believers are united by faith. In Romans 3, Calvin relates the *iustitia Dei* and *iustitia hominis* in terms of this union, and critiques Trent on the grounds that one is righteous only in union with the uniquely righteous second Adam, Christ. Here again Calvin turns to "partaking of Christ" to explain how conditional passages in Scripture are fulfilled in believers by grace, and also distinguishes God's union-administration of grace in Christ, the Second Adam, from the union-administration of nature in the first Adam. In Romans 6, "baptism/engrafting into Christ" means both death and resurrection in Him. Participation in Christ thus entails participation in both stages of his earthly, historical experience. In Romans 8, Calvin again addresses Paul's conditional language of suffering and eternal life with explicit recourse to the *ordo* hermeneutical device, this time, however, with explicit reference to the prototypical nature of the transition in Christ's own experience from suffering to glory. Our inheritance is secure because it has already been bestowed on Christ, who is our Head. But he reached this inheritance *per crucem*, thus those united to him must as well. As singularly expressive of Christian obedience in general, suffering thus has a salutary, soteric influence inasmuch as suffering (when located in this replication

---

[134] Does the sequential then negate the *simul*? It appears not. Calvin's emphasis on simultaneity has the justification-sanctification relationship in view: one cannot receive Christ for justification without at the same time (*simul*) receiving Christ for sanctification, because one is united to the righteous Christ himself and not to his benefits independent of him. The idea of sequence, on the other hand, has the character of sanctification in view: Spirit-renewal is specifically a replication in the believer of the sequence or *ordo* that applied in Christ's earthly experience: humiliation, then exaltation; suffering, then glory; obedience, then reward. In other words, the *simul* element has reference to the relationship of the *duplex gratia*; the sequential element has reference to the character of sanctification as one aspect of the *duplex gratia* which comes in union with Christ. Both are essential to Calvin's argument.

framework) *advances* the progress of salvation. Just as in his experience Christ passed from suffering/obedience to glory/inheritance/eternal life, so those who are united to him pass through the same. The nature of Paul's argument in Romans 8, with the prominence of the Spirit's role in bringing saints from suffering to glory, best accounts for why Calvin's replication principle appears more explicitly here than in his expositions of Romans 2 and 6.

The specific function of the replication principle in Calvin's soteriology, evidently shaped in large measure by the questions raised in Catholic-Protestant polemic, is important to recognize. It is only within this overarching purpose, established in eternity by the divine will, that a positive, indeed saving – yet non-meritorious – regard for good works must be located. Or, to view this from yet another angle, for Calvin Paul's argument in Rom 8:28-30 is such that it requires that one understand God's rewarding of believers' works to be based upon his own ultimate purpose for them, i.e., eschatological glorification, the antecedent progress toward which is the life of sanctification or obedience, itself equally purposed by God.

The various re-emerging themes gleaned from Calvin's exegesis demonstrate how union with Christ (in its various forms) functions at the most basic level in Calvin's reading of the Apostle's soteriology and Calvin's argument for the necessity of good works. The replication principle, in fact, is what it is for Calvin only because union with Christ is what it is. Christian suffering/bearing the cross is necessary, therefore, for the simple yet profound reason that this is what saving union with the only Christ of history and revelation must look like.

The Organic and the Sequential

The importance for Calvin of the historical should be noted. For Calvin, Spirit-replication produces an historical pattern corresponding to the pattern of Christ's own historical experience. Another way of expressing this is to affirm that both the organic and sequential elements are crucial to Calvin. As Calvin's exposition of Romans 8 and the problem of Christian suffering pointedly demonstrates, the believer's engrafting to the resurrected Christ (organic) originates or produces the (sequential) pattern of suffering then glory, or obedience then eschatological life. The idea of transition is crucial. The organic character of this union ensures that the pattern that was true for Christ in history is true for those united to him. As Calvin would subsequently make clear (in 1559), the Spirit, as the "bond" of union with Christ, is the nexus of this relationship as the agent and dynamic of the work of replication. The sufferings of the present life thus belong necessarily to the Christ-pattern of Christian experience, of the sure transition in history from sanctification to glorification. As in Christ it was first humiliation, then exaltation; so for those united to him it is first suffering-obedience, then glory.[135]

Replication, Not Imitation

It may be objected, however, that Calvin's "replication principle" differs only immaterially from the themes of the *imitatio Christi* tradition. Aspects of this objection are correct but a crucial distinction must still be recognized. It is true, for instance, that the *Devotio Moderna* had attached its own importance to the ideas of order or pattern, the historical experience of the human Christ, and imitation. It is also true, as shown above, that Calvin's language often reflects these themes. However, close examination of Calvin's pattern of argument, particularly in the Romans commentary, indicates that Calvin purposely distinguished his principle from that of the *imitatio* tradition. At several points, most notably in Romans 6 where the *imitatio* theme is explored most extensively, Calvin explicitly argues against simple imitation of an *exemplar* and in favor of a replication-type idea. In Calvin's soteriological structure, the idea of *imitatio* is theologically subordinate to and contextualized by the idea of Spirit-replication which is itself the existential form saving union with Christ takes. Imitation of Christ, in other words, is part of the Spirit's larger work of replication.[136] Moreover, further

---

[135] The more sophisticated theology of Christ's states of humiliation and exaltation is admittedly post-Calvin but in light of Calvin's framework I am convinced it is still helpful at the level of description. For more attention to this important theme in Calvin and post-Reformation Reformed orthodoxy, see Marvin P. Hoogland, *Calvin's Perspective on the Exaltation of Christ in Comparison with the Post-Reformation Doctrine of the Two States* (Kampen: J. H. Kok, 1966).

[136] The title of this section ("replication, not imitation") must therefore not be misunderstood as suggesting that Calvin did not teach the *imitatio Christi*. Besides his *Romans*, Calvin expounds the theme at length in *Inst.* (1539/1559) 3.6-10. Instead, I submit that while the "content" of Calvin's idea (imitation of Christ) is basically the same as that found in the spiritual traditions, the framework within which this content is set is fundamentally different and is best understood as "replication." One way of explaining this is to say that, from the perspective of human experience, replication is the imitation of Christ on the path to eternal life. But from the divine perspective, this faith-imitation is the

confirmation of this basic difference lies in his anthropology which sharply conflicts with what is ordinarily found in the preceding spiritual traditions. The *imitatio Christi* tradition in particular assumed a basically positive view of fallen human nature in contrast with Calvin's strictly negative view, and his critique of this line of thinking in general sharply distinguishes his perspective from theirs.

Causation, Good Works, and Spirit-Replication

In this light, one should acknowledge that Calvin often reads the conditional language of Scripture positively as indicative of secondary rather than primary causation. Calvin is thus rather comfortable ascribing soteriological causation to good works, but, once again, this language can only be appreciated within the context established by replication. Specifically, Calvin regards what comes prior in God's appointed *ordo* as "causing" what follows, thus making it possible to insist that Christian obedience, as it comes before the reception of the inheritance of eternal life, yields this reward. Hence, in Calvin's replication principle, the sequential contextualizes the non-meritorious causal.

It is certainly the case for Calvin that the ultimate or primary cause of salvation is to be found exclusively in God himself. In particular, justification is always and only grounded in Christ's righteousness; our works, on the other hand, are always impure on their own. Hence the works of believers do not "contribute" to justification. Christ's righteousness needs no supplementation. But for Calvin justification is not equivalent to salvation, is not itself sufficient for salvation, and is never alone in salvation. While in certain contexts there appears to be a priority of justification in his thought, justification does not assume the role in his theology that it does for Melanchthon and the emerging tradition of Lutheran orthodoxy. Instead, for Calvin the emphasis on justification often serves to elevate Christ's righteousness above any human righteousness rather than make justification central in salvation. Thus, in summary comparison with arguably his closest ally on justification, it should be noted that Calvin, like Melanchthon, also affirms a strong "principle of necessity" when sanctification is in view, though on different grounds and within a different framework. Their difference is thus not in the presence of a

---

work of Spirit-replication bringing many sons to glory. Replication is important not only as a description of Calvin's way of explaining the soteriogical necessity of good works but also in light of Calvin's concern to distinguish his concept from the *imitatio* tradition.

"necessity" idea, but in Calvin's framework within which the life of obedience or sanctification by the Spirit does not flow from the imputation of Christ's righteousness but from Christ himself with whom the Spirit has united believers. In other words, for Calvin sanctification does not flow from justification. They are not related as cause and effect. Rather, together they are "effects" or, better, aspects of union with Christ.

A Taxonomical Proposal

With a view to these observations on Calvin's teaching on good works in his Romans commentary and *Institutes*, it seems plausible to suggest a taxonomical refinement in Calvin scholarship. The conclusions reached in this chapter suggest that it may be more faithful and more helpful in describing Calvin's thought to refer to this matrix of ideas as his "replication principle" and thus to set aside (or at least greatly qualify) the somewhat ambiguous sobriquet, "double justification." Though in its most accurate sense referring to Calvin's teaching that God accepts the good works of believers, the latter carries the potential of obscuring how Calvin typically speaks of justification, that is, in terms of merit and imputation and not with reference to works. There is thus a danger of confusing Calvin's doctrine with other contemporary versions such as Bucer's neo-Augustinian doctrine, from which it should be kept distinct despite occasional, significant similarities. Reference to Calvin's "replication principle" immediately contextualizes his language of causation in a way that "double justification" simply cannot. Ultimately, of course, it is not the term itself but appreciation of the idea that is most important. If, therefore, "double justification" should still persevere in future studies of Calvin's doctrine, it is at least advisable that his "version" of it be properly distinguished in terms of replication. The true features of his doctrine, perhaps uniquely summarized in the following passage (cited in briefer form earlier in this chapter), are best appreciated this way. With another appeal to the traditional scheme of Aristotle's causes, Calvin explains that Scripture's identification of the good works of believers as *reasons* that the Lord blesses them does not compromise what he had just explained about the ultimate cause of salvation resting in God. As he had explained, "the efficient cause of our salvation consists in God the Father's love; the material cause in God the Son's obedience; the instrumental cause in the Spirit's illumination, that is, faith; the final cause, in the glory of God's great generosity (*tantae Dei benignitatis gloriam*)." And what then of good works?

These do not prevent the Lord from embracing works as *inferior causes*. But how does this come about? Those whom the Lord has destined by his mercy for the inheritance of eternal life he leads into possession of it, *according to his ordinary dispensation, by means of good works. What goes before in the order of dispensation he calls the cause of what comes after*. In this way he sometimes derives eternal life from works, not intending it to be ascribed to them; but because he justifies those whom he has chosen in order at last to glorify them, *he makes the prior grace, which is a step to what follows, as it were the cause*. But whenever the true cause is to be assigned, he does not enjoin us to take refuge in works but keeps us solely to the contemplation of his mercy... In short, *by these expressions sequence more than cause is denoted*. For God, by heaping grace upon grace, *from the former grace takes the cause for adding those which follow that he may overlook nothing for the enrichment of his servants*. And he so extends his liberality as to have us always look to his freely given election, which is the source and beginning.[137]

---

[137] Calvin, *Inst.* (1539) 3.14.21; OS 4.238-9 (LCC 20.787-8). Emphases mine.

CHAPTER FOUR

Christ and the Spirit: Sacraments, Salvation, and the Strata of Union with Christ

Salvation and Sacrament

Sacramental theology is layered theology. It rests, as the sixteenth century perhaps uniquely attests, upon certain christological and soteriological premises. The way one understands the person of Christ, particularly in terms of the *communicatio idiomatum*, is tied to one's view of how this Christ has become our salvation, and, further, how this Christ and this salvation are "given" in the sacraments. Especially in its formative Reformation expression, the theology of the sacraments rests upon an explicit relationship of interdependence, a fact that points to the sixteenth-century presupposition of the unity of truth. Naturally, then, and as the polemic of this period proves, an attack on one "layer" is perceived as an attack on them all. From the Reformed literature of the period, one often encounters a line of accusation that typically runs thus: a misunderstanding of Augustine on signification results in the confusion of *signa* and *res*, which leads in turn to a denigration of the real, that is, locally circumscribed humanity of the Mediator. Alternatively: the supposed ubiquity of the humanity of Christ necessarily implies a rejection of Chalcedon, which again obscures the ontological distinction and distance between God and humankind. Yet again: a local, "corporeal" presence of Christ in the Supper marginalizes the indispensable work of the Spirit for salvation.

Christ, salvation, and sacrament thus belong together in the sixteenth-century mind. This interdependence must be recognized in order to caution against the tendency to distinguish too sharply the eucharistic from the justification controversies of the sixteenth century. These controversies were more than merely contemporaneous. Indeed, it is a fact often overlooked in the more modern distribution of *loci*, but there was a strong soteriological motivation underlying the eucharistic controversy. As W. Peter

Stephens has argued with respect to the Marburg Colloquy (1529), the animating concern of both Luther and Zwingli was rooted in their understandings of *salvation*, not the Supper in isolation. For Zwingli, the idea of a physical presence of Christ in the Supper shifted the locus of faith from the spiritual, immaterial, truly saving "reality" – Christ – to a visible, material object incapable of bearing salvation. For Zwingli, Luther's position threatened the central Christian affirmation that salvation is to be sought in Christ alone, *sola fide*, not in anything on this earth.[1] For Luther, Zwingli's rejection of Christ's personal presence in the Eucharist ruled out the only hope for salvation. Recognizing the "poison" of Andreas Bodenstein von Karlstadt, Luther perceived in Zwingli's spiritualism a rejection of the divinely ordained connection between the outer Word and the sacraments as vehicles of inner grace.[2]

We expect to (and do) find a similar inter-connectedness in Calvin. Because the grace of salvation and the grace of the sacraments are the same grace, one anticipates the mutually interpretive language of union with Christ that pervades Calvin's exposition of the sacraments. A sacrament is, says Calvin, using traditional language, a visible or outward attestation of divine benevolence. It is a visible instrument, a sign which figures spiritual grace and seals the promises of God to us.[3]

---

[1] W. Peter Stephens, "The Soteriological Motive in the Eucharistic Controversy," in Willem van't Spijker, ed., *Calvin: Erbe und Auftrag: Festschrift für Wilhelm Neuser zu seinem 65. Geburtstag* (Kampen: Kok, 1991), 203-13. See *LWZ* 2.113, 118. Cf. B. Gerrish, "Eucharist," s.v., in *OER* 2.74a: "If grace were bound to the sacraments, the clergy would have God at their disposal and could grant or withhold salvation at will. Indeed, the very notion of sacramental grace implies another way of salvation, in competition with the *sola fide* ('by faith alone') of the Reformation."

[2] See Luther, *Sermon von dem Sakrament des Leibes und Blutes Christi, wider die Schwarmgeister* (1526), *LW* 36.346-54; and the points made by Gerrish, "Eucharist," 75a-b.

[3] Calvin, *Catechismus ecclesiae Genevensis, ...* (Strasbourg, 1545; Latin trans. of 1541/2 *Le Catéchisme de l'église de Genève*) OS 2.130; TT 2.83-4. For Calvin on the sacraments, see Joachim Beckmann, *Vom Sakrament bei Calvin: Die Sakramentslehre Calvins in ihren Beziehungen zu Augustin* (Tübingen: J. C. B. Mohr, 1926); W. F. Dankbaar, *De Sacramentsleer van Calvijn* (Amsterdam: H. J. Paris, 1941); Thomas J. Davis, *The Clearest Promises of God: the Development of Calvin's Eucharistic Teaching* (New York: AMS Press, 1995); B. A. Gerrish, *Grace and Gratitude: the Eucharistic Theology of John Calvin* (Edinburgh: T. & T. Clark, 1993); Kilian McDonnell, *John Calvin, the Church, and the Eucharist* (Princeton: Princeton University Press, 1967); Ronald S. Wallace, *Calvin's Doctrine of the Word and Sacrament* (Edinburgh: Oliver and Boyd, 1953; rep. Edinburgh: Scottish Academic Press, 1995), who collates many of Calvin's sacramental passages in

For Calvin, union with Christ in his flesh and blood is the *res* of the sacraments; union or communion with him is the blessing for which they were divinely instituted.[4] Furthermore, this central participatory reality of "incorporation" is bound to a correct understanding of the grace(s) in the object or *res* to which the sacramental *signa* refer. Baptism, for Calvin, does not figure "grace" merely, in a general sense, but the specific *duplex gratia* of forgiveness of sins and renewal, or justification and sanctification. In baptism, one has the "sure evidence" that (1) God will be propitious, not imputing our sins against us; and that (2) he will renew us by his Spirit to the end that we will fight against the flesh and "live in the liberty of his kingdom, which is the kingdom of righteousness."[5]

In a fuller exposition of the grace of baptism, Calvin outlines emphases discussed in the preceding study. Regeneration consists of two parts: (1) renouncing ourselves or "mortification" and (2) following the light of God, or the obedience of new life. But the accomplishment of both is *in Christ*

> whose death and passion have such virtue, that in participating in it we are as it were buried to sin, in order that our carnal lusts may be mortified. In like manner, by virtue of his resurrection, we rise again to a new life which is of God, inasmuch as his Spirit conducts and governs us, to produce in us works which are agreeable to him.

These graces are bestowed when believers are incorporated into Christ's church in baptism "for in this sacrament he attests the remission of our sins." Indeed, the reality of grace in believers testifies to them that the "virtue and substance" of baptism is not in them but in Christ. Thus, in the *modus operandi* of God's redemptive activity which involves both the verbal and the sacramental, the blessings of union with Christ are bestowed: "As he communicates

---

summary form; Hughes Oliphant Old, "Biblical Wisdom Theology and Calvin's Understanding of the Lord's Supper," in John H. Leith, ed., *Calvin Studies VI* (Colloquium on Calvin Studies, Davidson College, January 1992), 111-36, who provides an interesting account of Calvin's perspective in light of biblical wisdom literature; and the relevant sections in Leith, *Calvin's Doctrine of the Christian Life*; Niesel, *Theology of Calvin*; and Wendel, *Calvin*.

[4] The basic themes are ably expounded in Sinclair Ferguson, "Calvin on the Lord's Supper and Communion with Christ," in David Wright and David Stay, eds, *Serving the Word of God: Celebrating the Life and Ministry of James Philip* (Edinburgh: Christian Focus and Rutherford House, 2002), 203-17.

[5] Calvin, *Form of Administering the Sacraments*, TT 2.115; cf. *Catechismus Gen.*, OS 2.133; TT 2.86. Also see Wallace, *Calvin's Doctrine of the Word and Sacrament*, 145-6.

his riches and blessings to us by his word, so he distributes them to us by his sacraments."[6]

Furthermore, because Jesus Christ is himself the *substantia* of the grace held out in baptism, believers are properly baptized in his name.[7] In his use of the sacraments the communicant is therefore urged to seek Christ and his grace. With respect to the Supper specifically, communicants are to understand that they truly partake of Christ's body and blood. On this partaking or union our whole salvation depends, for, in order that Christ's obedience unto death should be imputed to us, it is necessary that we possess him. The relationship is inseparable: "Do we therefore eat the body and blood of the Lord? I understand so. For as the whole reliance for our salvation depends on him, in order that the obedience which he yielded to the Father may be imputed to us just as if it were ours, it is necessary that he be possessed by us; for the only way in which he communicates his blessings to us is by making himself ours."[8] Why, Calvin asks, did Christ employ the two signs of bread and wine? So that we learn not to seek any part of spiritual life outside of Christ.[9] God therefore distributes by his sacraments the riches and blessings of union with Christ communicated to us by his Word.[10]

But this union is not a completely realized blessing. For Calvin, the sacraments are intended to nourish faith, and are thus as eschatological in character and orientation as salvation is. In light of Calvin's replication principle, it is noteworthy that the Lord's supper is instituted to teach (*docere*) and assure believers that their souls are being trained in the hope of eternal life (*in spem vitae aeternae*), to confirm and increase their union with Christ. This sacramental sustenance is essential, moreover, for the faithful presently receive Christ only in part, not entirely.[11] Faith merely begun is not sufficient but must be nourished and increased, and it is to this purpose that the Lord instituted the sacraments.[12] It is thus

---

[6] Calvin, *Form of Administering the Sacraments*, TT 2.114-5.
[7] Calvin, *Confession de Foy au nom des eglises reformees de France...*, CO 9.765; TT 2.154. On this Confession, see BC 2.1064-7 and De Greef, *The Writings of John Calvin*, 78-9.
[8] Calvin, *Catechismus Gen.*, OS 2.138; TT 2.89: "Ergone corpore Domini et sanguine vescimur? Ita sentio. Nam quum in eo sita sit tota salutis nostrae fiducia, ut accepta nobis feratur obedientia ipsius, quam patri praestitit, perinde ac si nostra foret: ipsum a nobis possideri necesse est. Neque enim bona nobis sua aliter communicat, nisi dum se nostrum facit."
[9] Calvin, *Catechismus Gen.*, OS 2.140; TT 2.91.
[10] Calvin, *Form of Administering the Sacraments*, TT 2.115.
[11] Calvin, *Catechismus Gen.*, OS 2.137; TT 2.89, 90. Italics mine.
[12] Calvin, *Catechismus Gen.*, OS 2.132; TT 2.85.

beyond doubt that the connection between salvation and sacrament in Calvin is intimate and clear in that the sacraments signify the reality which is the content of the *unio Christi-duplex gratia* construction.

In Calvin's eucharistic thought, and in particular his response to the Lutheran idea of ubiquity, union with Christ is further seen to be the single most important idea for the justification-sanctification relationship. The themes that constitute the whole of Calvin's more general understanding of saving union with Christ are present in concentrated form in his teaching on eucharistic communion with Christ. In particular, the themes of the Christ-Spirit relationship and the necessarily vivifying effect of being united to Christ surface as truly controlling themes both in Calvin's *unio-duplex* construction and in his teaching on eucharistic communion. In this chapter, attention to Calvin's sacramentology functions as a bridge between the studies both preceding and following it in that here Calvin's regular language of union and communion with Christ is located in the context within which he most often used it: the sacraments, whether in straightforward exposition or in polemic. Calvin states repeatedly that the area of difference between him and his opponents has to do not with whether Christ is truly present in the Supper but with the *modus* of his presence. But because, for Calvin, a specific (non-corporeal) view of presence requires a correspondingly similar (spiritual) view of communion, the question of the mode of eucharistic presence naturally involved the question of the mode of eucharistic communion. The two questions – *modus praesentiae* and *modus communionis* – belong together.[13]

Calvin vs. the Lutherans: A Brief Publication History

Calvin's most fateful act was not his role in the execution of Servetus but his simple signature on the *Consensus Tigurinus*. For the rest of his days Calvin would live in the shadow of the *Consensus*. From its publication in 1551 Calvin was engaged in explaining, clarifying,

---

[13] Butin's statement that "For Calvin, the primary issue in the eucharist was not how Christ was present in the elements; rather, it was how God worked in the eucharist to unite believers to Christ by the Spirit, and the benefits that this union brought," (*Revelation, Redemption, and Response*, 114) is potentially misleading as it separates questions that belong together. If the "how" question is not the primary issue in the 1536 *Institutes* (from which Butin quotes) it certainly is, as many have noted, in Calvin's 1550s ubiquitarian polemic. See, e.g., TT 2.401, 411, 414, 528, *et al.* where Calvin identifies the *modus praesentiae* question as the single issue dividing him from his Lutheran opponents.

and defending his relationship to this document. First in the form of a *Defensio* and then in responses to Westphal and Heshusius, Calvin sought to interpret the language of the *Consensus* in accord with his own stated view, and to tie that language positively not only to Augustine, the father of Reformation sacramentology, but also to what he himself had written prior to its composition.[14]

Calvin signed the *Consensus* but later added articles 5 and 23 to the original total of twenty-four. In both additions, as Thomas J. Davis has noted, one finds a fully Calvinian emphasis. Only in article 5 is the language of *exhibere* used and here the idea of union with Christ receives special attention. In article 23, the notions of exhibition and true partaking are tied together by the work of the Spirit.[15] In part because of his use of *exhibere*, the mature, even

---

[14] For Calvin and the *Consensus*, see, beyond those listed in n. 3, the studies of Joseph N. Tylenda who has visited and revisited the Calvin-Westphal exchanges. I have consulted his work often for this summary. See Tylenda, "A Study in the Eucharistic Theologies of John Calvin, Reformer of Geneva, and of Max Thurian, Monk of Taize," Ph.D. diss. (Pontificia Universitas Gregoriana, 1964), pp. 433-41 of which contain a useful, brief summary of Calvin's writings on the Supper; idem, "Calvin on Christ's True Presence in the Lord's Supper," *American Ecclesiastical Review* 155 (1966): 321-33; idem, "Calvin on Christ's Presence in the Supper — True or Real," *SJT* 27 (1974): 65-75; idem, "The Calvin-Westphal Exchange: The Genesis of Calvin's Treatises Against Westphal," *CTJ* 9 (1974): 182-209; idem, "The Ecumenical Intention of Calvin's Early Eucharistic Teaching," in *Reformatio Perennis: Essays on Calvin and the Reformation in Honor of Ford Lewis Battles*, ed. B. A. Gerrish (Pittsburgh: Pickwick Press, 1981), 27-47; idem, "A Eucharistic Sacrifice in Calvin's Theology?" *Theological Studies* 37 (1976): 456-66; idem, "Calvin and Westphal: Two Eucharistic Theologies in Conflict," in Wilhelm H. Neuser, et al., eds, *Calvin's Books: Festschrift dedicated to Peter De Clerk on the Occasion of his Seventieth Birthday* (Heerenveen: J. J. Groen, 1997), 9-21.

[15] See Davis, *The Clearest Promises of God*, 41-2. The question of a Calvinian or Bullingerian bent in the theology of the *Consensus* has been a debated one, with an earlier near-consensus on Calvin's "victory" giving way somewhat, in more recent studies, to a more modest estimate of Calvin's success. See the history of interpretation in Davis, *The Clearest Promises of God*, 15-68, who argues against the earlier view. Also see Irena Backus, "Nicolas Durand de Villegagnon contre Calvin: le *Consensus Tigurinus* et la Présence Réelle," in Olivier Millet, ed., *Calvin et ses Contemporains* (Geneva: Librarie Droz, 1998), 163-78; Timothy George, "John Calvin and the Agreement of Zurich (1549)," in Timothy George, ed., *John Calvin and the Church: A Prism of Reform* (Louisville: Westminster/John Knox Press, 1990), 42-58; Joseph C. McLelland, "Meta-Zwingli or Anti-Zwingli? Bullinger and Calvin in Eucharistic Concord," in Edward J. Furcha, ed., *Huldrych Zwingli, 1484-1531: A Lively Legacy of Reform* (Montreal: McGill University Faculty of Religious Studies, 1985), 179-96; Paul Rorem, "Calvin and

refined thought of Calvin in the 1559 *Institutio* is the product of his repeated refutation of the charge of "sacramentarian," a charge that suggested that partaking of Christ is only a faith-event, not a flesh and blood communication. Calvin vigorously denied the accusation as he heard it from his most vociferous opponent, Joachim Westphal, insisting that he does not regard the sacramental *signa* as bare or empty signs but as instruments of a true participation in Christ's flesh and blood and as a means of saving grace – *signa* not of something absent but of something very present.[16]

Westphal (1510/11-1574), a Wittenberg student of Luther and Melanchthon, was a pastor in his native city of Hamburg.[17] The publication of the *Consensus* in 1551 precipitated his conflict with Calvin. The specific statement that was destined to launch this Reformed-Lutheran disagreement into a frenzy of heated polemic is found in the twenty-fourth article:

> In this way are refuted not only the fiction of the papists concerning transubstantiation, but all the gross figments and futile quibbles which either derogate from his celestial glory or are in some degree repugnant to the reality of his human nature. For we deem it no less absurd to place Christ under the bread or couple him with the bread than to transubstantiate the bread into his body.[18]

Bullinger on the Lord's Supper, Part 1: The Impasse," *Lutheran Quarterly* 2, no. 2 (1988): 155-84; idem, "Calvin and Bullinger on the Lord's Supper, Part 2: The Agreement," *Lutheran Quarterly* 2, no. 3 (1988): 357-89.

[16] Calvin is meeting the charge of an association with Zwingli's identification of "eating" with "believing" or faith and his rejection of presence in any form. Cf. Luther's objection to Zwingli and Oecolampadius, *LW* 37.104-5.

[17] On Westphal, see *Allgemeine deutsche Biographie* (Berlin, 1967-1971) 42:198-201; *Realencycklopädie für protestantische Theologie und Kirche* (3rd ed., Leipzig, 1896-1913) 31:185-9; *The New Schaff-Herzog Encyclopedia of Religious Knowledge* (New York, 1908-1912) 12:328-9. See also C. H. W. Sillem, ed., *Briefsammlung des hamburgischen Superintendenten Joachim Westphal aus den Jahren 1530 bis 1575* (Hamburg, 1903); Carl Mönckeberg, *Ioachim Westphal und Iohannes Calvin* (Hamburg, 1865); J. T. A. Nieter, *De controversia quae de Coena Sacra inter Westphalum et Calvinum fuit, dijudicatio* (Berlin, 1873).

[18] The full title of the *Consensus* is *Consensio mutua in re sacramentaria ministrorum Tigurinae ecclesiae et D. Johannis Calvini ministri Genevensis ecclesiae* (*Mutual Consent in Regard to the Sacraments between the Ministers of the Church of Zurich and John Calvin, Minister of the Church of Geneva*). The text of the *Consensus* is printed in CO 7.689-748 and OS 2.247-53 and is available in English translation in TT 2.212-20. The text of Article 24 reads: "*Contra transsubstantiationem et alias ineptias*. Hoc modo non tantum refutatur Papistarum commentum de transsubstantiatione, sed crassa omnia figmenta atque futiles argutiae, quae vel

Westphal responded with *A Mixture of Confused and Divergent Opinions on the Lord's Supper Taken from the Books of the Sacramentarians*, published about a year after the *Consensus*, in which he contrasted the eucharistic vocabulary used by Calvin, Bullinger, Vermigli, Bucer and others in order to show their confusion.[19] He soon followed the *Farrago* in 1553 with a study of 1 Cor 11 and passages from the Gospels published as *The True Belief in Regard to the Lord's Supper Demonstrated and Taught in the Words of Paul the Apostle and the Evangelists*.[20] There was some discussion over whether or not a response to Westphal should be published, but in 1554 Calvin's reply appeared under the title *The Defense of the Sane and Orthodox Doctrine of the Sacraments*.[21] The *Defensio* consists of Calvin's explanation of the *Consensus* in the form of a letter to the Swiss ministers, the text of the *Consensus* itself, and the defense proper: "Exposition of the Heads of Agreement."

Westphal was not finished, and in 1555 two more treatises were released, though probably too soon to have been intended as responses to Calvin's *Defensio*: one on Cyril of Alexandria and

---

coelesti eius gloriae detrahunt, vel veritati humanae eius naturae minus sunt consentanea. Neque enim minus absurdum iudicamus, Christum sub pane locare vel cum pane copulare, quam panem transsubstantiare in eius corpus."

[19] Westphal, *Farrago confusanearum et inter se dissidentium opiniorum de Coena Domini ex Sacramentariorum libris congesta* (Magdeburg, 1552). Westphal constructed a large table of twenty-eight allegedly different opinions held among the "sacramentarians." I note here that, with the exception of Westphal's and the Saxon ministers' important *Confessio fidei* (see n. 26, below), one copy of which is held in Geneva, I have not had access to the original texts of Westphal or Heshusius referred to in this chapter but rely on descriptions in contemporary texts and in the scholarly literature.

[20] Westphal, *Recta fides de Coena Domini ex verbis apostoli Pauli et evangelistarum demonstrata et communita* (Magdeburg, 1553). Tylenda, "Calvin and Westphal," 10-11, notes that this was published before the prior publication (*Farrago*) had even reached Calvin.

[21] Calvin, *Defensio Sanae et Orthodoxae Doctrinae de Sacramentis*, in CO 9.6-40. See the correspondence between Calvin and Bullinger: Letter 1935 (CO 15.95); and Beza to Calvin: Letter 1926 (CO 15.75-76). For the question of chronology, see the discussion in Tylenda, "Calvin and Westphal," 11-12; idem, "The Calvin-Westphal Exchange," *passim*, esp. p. 185. Note that TT 2.199-244 is printed under the title, "Mutual Consent in Regard to the Sacraments; Between the Ministers of the Church of Zurich and John Calvin, Minister of the Church of Geneva...," when it is in fact a translation of the *Defensio* including the text of the agreement after the prefatory letters. The contents of the *Defensio* are divided as follows: (1) prefatory letters of Calvin to Zurich and Zurich to Calvin, (2) the Heads of Agreement, and (3) Calvin's defense of the Heads of Agreement.

another on Augustine's sacramental teaching.[22] Westphal then directed his attention implicitly to Calvin's *Defensio* with his *Just Defense Against the False Accusation of a Certain Sacramentarian*.[23] Here the charge is made that the sacramentarians have as their only object the denial of a real presence of Christ's physical body and blood in the Supper. All that is left, on this position, are "empty signs."

Not long after Westphal's rejoinder was published, Calvin's *Second Defense of the Pious and Orthodox Faith Concerning the Sacraments in Answer to the Calumnies of Joachim Westphal*, more than three times the size of the *Defensio*, issued from a Genevan press.[24] This time, to summon support for his cause and to demonstrate his good-will toward them, Calvin dedicated the treatise to the ministers of Saxony.[25] As Tylenda observes, this decision would prove a grave mistake. Again Westphal was quick to reply with not one but two more publications. The first, from Westphal, was a *Letter which Briefly Answers the Accusations of John Calvin*. The second was titled a *Confession of Faith on the Sacrament of the Eucharist, in which the Ministers of the Church of Saxony Defend the Presence of the Body and Blood of the Lord Jesus Christ in the Supper by Solid Arguments from Sacred Scripture in Answer to the Book Dedicated to Them by John Calvin*.[26] This text, a copy of which is in the Geneva library, included a substantial collection of supporting letters written by Saxon

---

[22] The treatise on Augustine was a collection of quotations on the Supper published as *Collectanea sententiarum D. Aurelii Augustini ep. Hipponensis de Coena Domini* (Ratisbon, 1555). Tylenda, "Calvin and Westphal," 13, notes: "The treatise contains (1) passages from Augustine which are said to agree with Lutheran teaching, (2) passages which Westphal's adversaries use to support their cause, and finally (3) a refutation of the objection that the nature of material bodies is opposed to ubiquity." These publications almost certainly account for the increased attention given to both Cyril and Augustine in Calvin's final refutation.

[23] Westphal, *Adversus cuiusdam sacramentarii falsam criminationem iusta defensio* (Frankfurt, 1555).

[24] Calvin, *Secunda defensio piae et orthodoxae de sacramentis fidei contra Joachimi Westhpali calumnias* (Geneva, 1556), in CO 9.45-120. This was the immediate result of Laski's urgings. See the correspondence, Letter 2296 (CO 15.774) and Letter 2318 (CO 15.812). Cf. also the further correspondence discussed and documented in Tylenda, "Calvin and Westphal," 14.

[25] See the statement in CO 9.49.

[26] Westphal, *Epistola Ioachimi Westphali qua breviter respondet ad convicia Iohannis Calvini* (1556). *Confessio fidei de eucharistiae sacramento,...* (Magdeburg, 1557), and cited in CO 9.xxi. Tylenda ("Calvin and Westphal," 15) lists Matthäus Judex, Ernhard Schnepff, and Paul von Eitzen as Lutherans besides Westphal who were spurred into action by Calvin's *Secunda defensio*.

ministers with a preface by Westphal. These are the ministers Calvin had hoped to win over to his cause. Instead, they forcefully defended the Westphalian rendering of the Lutheran position and opposed Calvin by associating him with the likes of Schwenckfeld and Osiander.[27] With the opposition growing significantly in number, Calvin resolved to engage Westphal once more and penned his *Last Admonition of John Calvin to Joachim Westphal, who, if he heeds it not, must henceforth be treated in the way which Paul prescribed for obstinate heretics*, published in Geneva in 1557.[28] Predictably, Westphal's response was prompt. He quickly published his *Answer to Some of the Lies of John Calvin* and then an *Apology Concerning the Defense of the Lord's Supper Against the Errors and Calumnies of John Calvin*, both in 1558.[29]

Calvin's *Ultima Admonitio* was indeed his last formal response to Westphal and, as Tylenda notes, this silence "signified that Westphal no longer deserved his attention." Other activities occupied his time and attention, especially the revision of his *Institutes* and his ongoing commentary and sermon writing. As Tylenda also notes, however, the addition of twenty-two new paragraphs to what would become *Institutes* 4.17 functions as an unofficial postscript to his *Ultima Admontio*, publicly restating and defending his position yet once more against Westphal.[30] This was not lost on one Tilemann Heshusius (1527-1588), who successfully coaxed Calvin out of silence with his own attack, *The Presence of the Body of Christ in the Lord's Supper against the Sacramentarians*.[31] Heshusius was not a carbon-copy of Westphal, but retained much of what Calvin found objectionable. Calvin's refutation was published in 1561 under the title, *The Clear Explanation of the Sound Doctrine Concerning the True Partaking of the Flesh and Blood of Christ in the Holy Supper in order to Dissipate the Mists of Tilemann Heshusius*.[32] At the

---

[27] I will return to this text, and specifically to the Osiander association, in the next chapter.

[28] Calvin, *Ultima Admonitio Johannis Calvini ad Joachim Westphalum, cui nisi obtemperet eo loco posthac habendus erit quo pertinaces haereticos haberi iubet Paulus* (Geneva, 1557), in CO 9.137-252. While clearly argued, this much longer treatise is repetitive and at times even tedious.

[29] Westphal, *Confutatio aliquot enormium mendaciorum Johannis Calvini* (Ursel, 1558) and *Apologia confessionis de Coena Domini contra corruptelas et calumnias Johannes Calvini scripta* (Ursel, 1558), both cited in CO 9.xxiv.

[30] Tylenda, "John Calvin and Max Thurian," 440, n. 4.

[31] Heshusius, *De praesentia corporis Christi in Coena Domini: contra Sacramentarios* (1560).

[32] Calvin, *Dilucida explicatio doctrinae de vera participatione carnis et sanguinis Christi in sacra Coena ad discutiendas Heshusii nebulas* (Geneva, 1561), in CO 9.457-

close of this treatise he bows out of the dispute altogether, passing the responsibility of further response to Beza.³³

The Magdeburgians accused Calvin of reasoning that believers are justified by faith alone and thus not by the sacraments. Perhaps surprising to a modern reader, Calvin denies the accusation, saying, "We are not so raw as not to know that the sacraments, inasmuch as they are the helps of faith, also offer us righteousness in Christ... No, as we are agreed that the sacraments are to be ranked in the same place as the Word, so while the gospel is called the power of God unto salvation to every one that believes, we do not hesitate to transfer the same title to the sacraments (*elogium ad sacramenta transferre*)."³⁴ The sacraments do not offer a righteousness other than that offered in the preached Word. Rather, because salvation is not exclusively a past event but an ongoing and eschatological experience, the sacraments serve as divinely appointed aids in the path of salvation and eternal life. Consistent with the replication principle examined in the preceding study, the sacraments serve as means of spiritual nourishment for the believing *viator*, increasing and maturing the union with Christ in which salvation consists. The "true end of the Supper," Calvin explains, is "that being reconciled to God by the sacrifice of Christ we may obtain salvation."³⁵

---

524. In 1562, Heshusius responded with *Verae et sanae confessionis de praesentia corporis Christi in Coena Domini pia defensio adversus cauillos et calumnias* (Magdeburg), in which he lists as culprits, "1. Iohannis Calvini. II. Petri Boquini. III. Theodori Bezae. IIII. Wilhelmi Cleinwitzii."

³³ See Calvin, *De Vera Participatione*, CO 9.524. Beza published *De Coena Domini plana et perspicua tractatio, in quo Ioachimi Westphali calumniae refelluntur* as a final refutation of Westphal. See Beza, *Traités théologiques de Theodore de Bèze* (*TractTh*) (2ⁿᵈ ed.; Geneva, 1572), 1.211-58. Against Heshusius, Beza wrote ΚΡΕΩΦΑΓΙΑ *sive Cyclops, Dialogus de vera communicatione corporis et sanguini Domini, adversus Tilemanni Heshusii commenta* (*TractTh* 1.259-336).

³⁴ Calvin, *Ultima Admonitio*, CO 9.182; TT 2.400: "Longius deinde prosilit calumnia, nos applicationem remissionis peccatorum negare in coena fieri. Quasi vero applicationis nomen proprio et genuino sensu non usurpem. Nam quod ita nos ratiocinari dicunt: Sola fide iustificamur, ergo non per sacramenta: non adeo rudes sumus, *quin sciamus sacramenta, quatenus adminicula sunt fidei, iustitiam quoque nobis in Christo offerre*. Imo quum optime inter nos conveniat, eodem in gradu locanda esse sacramenta, quo verbum: sicuti evangelium vocatur potentia Dei in salutem omni credenti, idem *elogium ad sacramenta transferre non dubitamus*."

³⁵ Calvin, *Ultima Admonitio*, CO 9.182; TT 2.400-1: "Quando autem ubique docemus, verum esse coenae finem, ut per Christi sacrificium Deo reconciliati salutem consequamur, nemini ambiguum esse potest vel obscurum, quam indigne pietatis elementa nobis excutiant."

If what has been argued with respect to the place of Christian obedience in Calvin's wider teaching on union with Christ and salvation, in particular what I have termed his idea of "replication," is correct, one would expect justifiably to find confirmation, even elucidation, of this basic complex of ideas in his theology of sacramental communion with Christ. Not only is this the case, but our understanding of the necessity of Christian obedience or sanctification for Calvin's understanding of salvation finds a highly significant parallel at the more specific sacramental level.

Because of space constraints, attention will be restricted here to specific questions centered on the importance for our purposes of Calvin's polemical engagement with Lutheran ubiquitarianism. In this controversial context, the specifics of the Christ-Spirit, Union-Life, and Chalcedonian "distinction without separation" relationships will be treated in connection with what will be called the "strata" of union with Christ. It will be argued that Calvin's soteriological emphasis on the inseparability of justification and sanctification as a consequence of union with Christ is of a piece with his insistence that the unbeliever does not partake of Christ in the Supper, i.e., there is no *manducatio impiorum* or *infidelium*.[36]

Patterns and Parallels

What does Calvin's teaching on the sacraments, in particular the Supper, reveal about his *unio Christi-duplex gratia* construction? Key to understanding Calvin's line of thought is carefully observing a series of parallels and distinctions that he employs in the course of argument and exposition. Underlying a number of fine distinctions, there exists a series of significant sacramental patterns of expression and argument and parallels of form and structure used by Calvin that correspond to patterns and parallels used in his teaching on salvation. The following list is certainly not exhaustive, and each pattern and parallel is related to the others.

---

[36] The *manducatio impiorum* took confessional status in the Formula of Concord (FC). See FC, Epitome, VIII, "Of the Lord's Supper" in *ConcTrig*, pp. 812-3: "Credimus, docemus et confitemur, quod non tantum vere in Christum credentes, et qui digne ad Coenam Domini accedunt, verum etiam indigni et infideles verum corpus et sanguinem Christi sumant; ita tamen, ut nec consolationem nec vitam inde percipiant, sed potius, ut illis sumptio ea ad iudicium et damnationem cedat, si non convertantur et poenitentiam agant (1 Cor. 11:27-29)." Cf. FC, Thorough Declaration, VII (*ConcTrig*, cols. 992-7). G. C. Berkouwer, *The Sacraments* (Grand Rapids: Eerdmans, 1969), 244-58, provides a useful summary of the issues.

Augustinian Signification and "Distinction without Separation"

The most prominent formal or structural elements in Calvin's doctrine of union with Christ, both soteriological and sacramental, are the Chalcedonian *distinctio sed non separatio* formula and the *signa – res* relationship in Augustinian signification. Calvin's concern with the focus in late medieval piety on objects, on "things" like images and relics, rather than the Gospel reality which comes in the Word preached and heard, carried over into a rejection of an inappropriately lofty view of the sacramental elements, whether in the form of carrying them in lifted hands or gasping when they hit the ground. This perverted state of affairs, thought Calvin, encouraged people to place their trust on the tangible and the visible, the earthly, when by divine institution these are intended to point us away from the visible to the invisible, from the earthly to the heavenly. As G. R. Evans has explained, this debate over the proper place of the sacraments in relation to the preached Word has its roots in "a double medieval heritage: a broad and comprehensive understanding of 'sacramentum'; and Augustinian sign-theory."[37] While rejection of the former was common among the reformers, the latter functioned differently in Reformed and Lutheran teachings on the Eucharist.

Peter Lombard's discussion of the sacraments opens with a reference to Augustine's theory of signification and the relation of *signa* and *res*.[38] A sacrament is "the visible form of an invisible grace" (*sacramentum est invisibilis gratiae visibilis forma*); as a sign of a thing, it is both itself a thing and yet necessarily not the thing referred to.[39] The *signum* aids in grasping the *res*, so that there is a positive, necessary relationship. Calvin focuses attention on the crucial distinction or difference in Augustine's teaching between *signa* and

---

[37] G. R. Evans, "Calvin on Signs: an Augustinian Dilemma," *Renaissance Studies* 3 (1989): 35.

[38] Lombard, *Sententiae*, I.1.2; cf. I.1.1, citing Augustine, *Quaestiones in Pent.*, bk. III, q.84.

[39] Lombard, *Sententiae*, I.1.3, citing Augustine, *De Doctr. christ.*, bk. II., c.1, n.1: "Signum vero est res praeter speciem, quam ingerit sensibus, aliud aliquid ex se faciens in cogitationem venire." Augustine had provided an hermeneutically-oriented discussion of *signa* and *res*. As noted, the basic contours of his view formed the opening discussion in Lombard's *Sententiae* and underwent significant modification in the medieval period. On the primarily hermeneutical development of Augustinian signification in the late medieval period leading up to the Reformation, see Christopher Ocker, *Biblical Poetics Before Humanism and Reformation* (Cambridge: Cambridge University Press, 2002), esp. 31-71.

res. If something is a sacrament it cannot simultaneously be the thing signified.

In Calvin's eucharistic thought, moreover, the Augustinian *signa-res* relationship functions as the sacramental form of the christological "distinction-without-separation" of Chalcedon. In countering Rome and Wittenberg, Calvin's accent is naturally heavy on the *distinctio*, expressing a dominant concern that the ontological distance between God and humankind, or divinity and humanity, must not be obscured. Sacramental signification requires that the *signa* are not confused with the *res*; otherwise their identity as signs rather than reality is lost. Yet this is to be maintained without their separation. For all his concern to keep distinct things distinct, the factor of inseparability is equally crucial to Calvin's position: sacramental signification, as a true identification of the *signa* with the *res* by way of metonymy, indicates the closest possible unity and yet prevents confusion. Repeatedly in Calvin's criticism of ubiquitarianism he alleges that his opponents violate the cardinal rule of signification: there is a sacramental, not substantial identification of the *signa* with the *res*.[40] Thus in the language he employs he regularly objects to the "confusion" and "mixing" of substances, in particular the humanity of Christ with his divinity or the sacramental reality (Christ's body and blood) with its sign (the elements).

In Calvin, however, this Chalcedonian-type language does double service, functioning in soteriological as well as sacramental contexts. The eucharistic controversy is the principal historical matrix in which Calvin clarified the distinct-but-inseparable nature of the justification/ sanctification relationship. To be sure, Calvin had used the formula on numerous occasions prior to the 1550s, but the central role of the Spirit in explicating this formula in the context of salvation was not clarified until he found himself deeply involved in eucharistic polemic with his Lutheran counterparts. Thus while the Chalcedonian principle is the christological presupposition of Calvin's teaching regarding Christ's sacramental presence, it is also clearly paralleled in his soteriological formulation. Indeed, the christological center of Calvin's refutation of Lutheran ubiquitarianism (one must not confuse or blur together the divine and human natures) corresponds exactly to his insistence on the proper soteriological distinction of justification and sanctification. In one, attributes which are properly divine and properly human must

---

[40] See, e.g., Calvin, *Inst.* (1559) 4.17.11; the summary in Wallace, *Calvin's Doctrine of Word and Sacrament*, 159-65; and the discussion in Gerrish, *Grace and Gratitude*, 164-7.

remain so, just as, in the other, that which belongs properly to justification and sanctification must remain so. Again, however, equally important for Calvin is the *inseparability* both of the divine and human natures in Christ and of justification and sanctification.[41]

What, in sum, is Calvin doing? Calvin is evidently appropriating a combination of the traditional christological language of Chalcedon and Augustinian sign theory for use both in his teaching on the spiritual communion with Christ in the Supper and in his soteriological *unio Christi-duplex gratia* construction. Both the Chalcedonian language and Augustinian sign theory are, of course, inherited and common to his contemporaries, thus serving well to aid Calvin in clarifying points about salvation in a context pressured to demonstrate fidelity to the Fathers.

The Spirit as "Bond"

Against the Lutheran criticism that a non-physical presence of Christ in the Supper must imply no real presence at all, Calvin argued that Christ is truly present by the work of the Spirit who, Calvin teaches, is able to unite as bond things otherwise distant. How can we be joined to Christ's body in heaven while we are still "pilgrims on the earth"? By the secret and miraculous agency of the Spirit, "for whom it is not difficult to unite things otherwise disjoined by a distant space."[42] The problem posed to communion by the bodily ascension of Christ is overcome by the Spirit-bond of sacred union who raises our souls by faith and infuses life into us from our living Mediator and Head.[43] The Spirit bridges heaven and earth, bringing believing communicants to heaven to feed on Christ and bringing the virtue of

---

[41] This distinction-without-separation parallel is noted briefly in Niesel, *Theology of Calvin*, 248-9. William M. Thompson ("Viewing Justification Through Calvin's Eyes: An Ecumenical Experiment," *Theological Studies* 57 [1996]: 449) refers to Calvin's "Chalcedonian style of thinking, which appeals, as in Christ, to distinction rather than separation."

[42] Calvin, *Catechismus Gen.*, OS 2.140; TT 2.91: "Verum qui hoc fieri potest, cum in coelo sit Christi corpus: nos autem in terra adhuc peregrinemur? Hoc mirifica arcanaque spiritus sui virtute efficit: cui difficile non est sociare, quae locorum intervallo alioqui sunt disiuncta." Cf. Bucer to Hardenberg, 22 October 1549 (Gorham, *Gleanings*, 121-2), where Bucer notes the necessity that true communion with Christ must be increased continually while believers are pilgrims, and that the sacraments are to be received "BY FAITH ALONE – and that a living faith" (all caps Bucer's).

[43] Calvin, *Ultima Admonitio*, CO 9.174; TT 2.390. The issues are summarized with a view to the importance of the ascension in Gordon E. Pruett, "A Protestant Doctrine of the Eucharistic Presence," *CTJ* 10 (1975): 142-74.

Christ's flesh and blood to believers according to promise. The so-called *extra Calvinisticum* – the idea that "Christ, dwell[ing] in heaven respecting his flesh, still as Mediator fills the whole world" – is specifically intended by Calvin to preserve the reality of the union the faithful enjoy with Christ's person.[44] As the "organ" of Christ's efficacy, it is only by the "agency" of the Spirit that communicants receive God's gifts as they are offered in Christ.[45] The grace of Christ's animating, vivifying flesh and blood reaches believers only by the "virtue" of his Spirit. It is the Spirit who by his "secret agency" (*arcana spiritus efficacia*) makes feeding on Christ a reality.[46] Hence the power and efficacy of the sacraments are not contained in the outward elements but are communicated entirely by the Spirit. In the wisdom of his own design, the Lord has been pleased to exert his energy by these instruments, which is the purpose he destined for them, and he accomplishes this without detracting from the virtue of the Spirit.[47] The Spirit in his Person and activity thus pervades Calvin's exposition of eucharistic communion with Christ and functions as the "bond" between Head and members.

Correlatively, in his teaching on salvation, Calvin famously calls the Spirit the "bond" of union with Christ.[48] He is the *nexus* (or *vinculum*) who effects the communion of Christ and believer that results in the believer sharing not only in Christ himself but, as a consequence, in all his spiritual gifts or graces. Among these gifts, justification and sanctification are the most prominent, and describe distinct benefits belonging to those united to Christ. The role of the Spirit in the Supper and salvation, therefore, provides a still more immediate parallel between Calvin's sacramental and soteriological arguments.

---

[44] Calvin, *Ultima Admonitio*, CO 9.229; TT 2.465: "Sicut ergo tunc aperti sunt coeli: ita discant oculos aperire Magdeburgenses, ut Christum agnoscant, quamvis in coelo sedentem, immensa tamen et incomprehensibili spiritus sui virtute fidelibus in terra esse coniunctum... Nihil in hac doctrina perplexum est, quod Christus secundum carnem in coelis habitans, quatenus mediator est, repleat totum mundum: et vere unum sit cum suis membris, quia communis est vita."

[45] Calvin, *Secunda Defensio*, CO 9.94; TT 2.310: "An dictat communis sensus ab humana carne petendam esse immortalem animae vitam? An fert ratio naturae ut e coelo in terram usque penetret vivifica illa carnis Christi virtus, et in animas nostras admirabili modo influat? An philosophicis speculationibus consentaneum est, mortuum et terrestre elementum efficax organum esse spiritus sancti?" Cf. *Catechismus Gen.*, OS 2.88; TT 2.50.

[46] Calvin, *Ultima Admonitio*, CO 9.172; TT 2.387.

[47] Calvin, *Catechismus Gen.*, OS 2.131; TT 2.84.

[48] Calvin, *Inst.* (1559) 3.1.1.

Christ and His Benefits

But the Spirit is not the only one Personally active, as though it is in reality the Spirit's and not Christ's Supper. In the form of his response to an important Lutheran criticism, the union with Christ effected by the Spirit is indeed a union with *Christ*, not with his benefits or graces (his "virtue") alone. In response to Westphal, Calvin insists that eucharistic communion is "not only in the fruit of Christ's death, but also in his body offered for our salvation."[49] Alongside Calvin's clarification that union is with Christ, not with his benefits, is the explanation that it is precisely because one is united to Christ in his redeeming flesh and blood that one is made, for this reason, partaker in all his blessings.[50] In other words, the bond of union, the Spirit, does not bring himself but Christ, but in doing so brings all of Christ's graces.

Again the parallel argumentation in Calvin's soteriological discussions is noteworthy, and in this case Calvin himself often makes the connection explicit precisely because of the deep connection of sacrament and salvation. Against the objection that, in terms of *sola fide*, one could theoretically receive Christ for justification but not for sanctification – and thus stand forgiven in Christ while devoid of good works – Calvin vigorously rejected the situation as theologically impossible. One does not in practice take Christ for justification *itself* or sanctification *itself* for these are not independent realities to be grasped. One is not united to justification or sanctification. Rather, one receives and is united to Christ, in whom these blessings reside. Therefore, to be united to Christ is necessarily to be made a partaker of all his blessings, not merely a few.[51]

The Charge of Fabrication

Fourth, and in line with Calvin's insistence on union with Christ and not merely his graces, is his response to the different forms of the charge of "fabrication." This is among the most important of the parallels between Calvin's soteriological and sacramental emphases, and belongs to the wider discussion of Calvin's rejection of the Lutheran *manducatio impiorum*.

Calvin's understanding of the non-physical presence of Christ by his Spirit prompted the Lutheran accusation that, by implication,

---

[49] Calvin, *Ultima Admonitio*, CO 9.477; TT 2.517. Cf. TT 2. 376, TT 2.573.
[50] See, e.g., Calvin, *Inst.* (1559) 4.17.33.
[51] This is expressed most concisely in Calvin's comment on 1 Cor 1:30, to be examined below in Chapter 5.

one is only really united with Christ's virtue and not with Christ himself. The *substantia* of the Supper, the *res* signified by the elements, is not in reality Christ in his flesh and blood but his Spirit-grace-virtue. As a result, his Lutheran opponents insisted that Calvin's non-physical presence of Christ is no real presence at all; it is a fabricated presence. They surmised that Christ's promise, "This is my body," could not be taken seriously by Calvin and would on his construction have to be regarded as deceitful on Christ's part. On Calvin's view, one is ostensibly united to a figment, to "naked or empty figures," not Christ's body.[52]

This is an accusation Calvin rejects tirelessly in his responses to Westphal and Heshusius. Addressing this criticism, and again employing the "tearing Christ from his Spirit" metaphor, Calvin writes, "For certainly the reality and substance of the sacrament is not only the application of the benefits of Christ, but Christ himself with his death and resurrection. Wherefore, they are not skilful expositors who, on the one hand, make Christ devoid of the gifts of his Spirit and of all virtue, and, on the other hand, conjoin him with spiritual gifts and the fruit of eating, because *he cannot without insult be separated from his Spirit any more than severed from himself.*"[53] Calvin reacts strongly with the insistence that he maintains no "fallacious exhibition."[54] His understanding of a sacramental communion which is spiritual rather than corporeal in mode does not imply a fictional presence, a "phantasm." Turning the tables on his Lutheran opponents, Calvin argued that an ubiquitous rather than a circumscribed humanity is in reality no humanity at all, at least not by definition, and thus no true presence either.

But are not the sacraments then, on Calvin's non-local theory, reduced to dispensable, empty signs? How can one maintain the

---

[52] See, among very many, the charges met in Calvin, *Ultima Admonitio*, CO 9.182-3; TT 2.401-2.

[53] Calvin, *Optima ineundae concordiae ratio*, CO 9.522; TT 2.578: "Nam certe veritas et res sacramenti non tantum est applicatio beneficiorum Christi, sed Christus ipse cum morte et resurrectione sua. Quare non dextri sunt interpretes, qui ab una parte Christum statuunt vacuum omnibus spiritus sui donis omnique virtute, ab altera coniungunt eum cum spiritualibus donis et manducationis fructu: *quia non potest sine contumelia separari a spiritu suo, non magis quam a se ipso divelli.*" Calvin's refusal to relinquish the slippery term *substantia* is due to this insistence that it is Christ himself, and not something less than the real Christ, who is the *res* of the Supper. See Willis, "Calvin's Use of Substantia," 289-301. The confusion in Calvin's use of *substantia* is noted with a vivid example by G. S. M. Walker, "The Lord's Supper in the Theology and Practice of John Calvin," in *John Calvin* (Appleford: The Sutton Courtenay Press, 1966), 141.

[54] Calvin, *Optima ineundae concordiae ratio*, CO 9.521; TT 2.576.

integrity of the divinely instituted *signa* if one refuses to locate the *res* within (or under, or beside) them? Responding to this frequent accusation, Calvin insists that recognition of the *signa-res* distinction does not relegate the sacrament to a figment or an "empty," "bare" sign. It is not empty or bare because Christ really performs what is held out or "exhibited" in the *signa*: the union between Christ and the communicant is not illusory but a true communion with the real, flesh-and-blood Christ. In short, distinction is not separation. Thus are the *signa* holy not intrinsically or by virtue of their local identity with the *res* but on account of the service they yield as *instrumenta* by Christ's own appointment. Since Jesus is Truth he fulfills the promise he there gives us. As he testifies by words and signs so he makes us partakers of his substance so that we have one life with him.[55] As visible, tangible aids, the sacraments are thus God's gracious way of accommodating to our weaknesses. If we were spiritual we could spiritually behold him, says Calvin, but living in bodies of clay we need figures and mirrors to exhibit a view of spiritual, heavenly things in an earthly manner; otherwise we could not attain to them.[56]

The clear affirmation of Christ's human flesh and blood as "life-giving" is an area in which Calvin's eucharistic theology may have developed. Davis argues that in Calvin's early writings, particularly in his 1536 *Institutes*, it is unclear whether union is with Christ himself (in his flesh and blood) or with the virtues or benefits of Christ.[57] Apart from the ambiguous specifics of chronological

---

[55] Calvin, *Catechismus Gen.*, OS 2.140; TT 2.91.
[56] Calvin, *Catechismus Gen.*, OS 2.131; TT 2.84. On accommodation in Calvin, see Jon Balserak, *Divinity Compromised: A Study of Divine Accommodation in the Thought of John Calvin* (Studies in Early Modern Religious Reforms 5; Dordrecht: Springer, 2006). On the relationship of accommodation, incarnation, and sacrament, see Éric Kayayan, "Accommodation, Incarnation et Sacrement dans l'Institution de la Religion Chrétienne de Jean Calvin: L'Utilisation de metaphors et de similitudes," *Revue d'Histoire et de Philosophie Religieuses* 75 (1995): 273-87.
[57] The development in Calvin's thought is explored by Davis, *The Clearest Promises of God*, pp. 100-104, 109-15, 169-78, 181-5, 204-10. The debate between Charles Hodge and John W. Nevin had this question at heart. See Charles Hodge, "Doctrine of the Reformed Church on the Lord's Supper," *Princeton Review* 20 (April 1848): 227, 275-7, 278; John Williamson Nevin, *The Mystical Presence: A Vindication of the Reformed or Calvinistic Doctrine of the Holy Eucharist* (Hamden: Archon Books, 1963; facsimile of original edition, Philadelphia: J. B. Lippincott and Co., 1846); idem, "Doctrine of the Reformed Church on the Lord's Supper," in *The Mystical Presence and other Writings on the Eucharist*, ed. by Bard Thompson and George H. Bricker (Philadelphia and Boston: United

development, at least Calvin certainly has a clear doctrine of Christ's life-giving flesh in the 1550s. Indeed it performs an integral function in his theological response to his Lutheran counterparts. Now, in the 1550s, the union idea which Calvin had insisted upon from his earliest days as the purpose and *res* of the Supper is enriched with a clear emphasis on communion with Christ's substance, the relation of Christ to his benefits, the work of the Spirit as bond of union, and the spiritual *modus* of union.

This places us in a position to appreciate a most important parallel that exists at the level of Calvin's insistence on the distinction without separation of justification and sanctification, on the one hand, and of the sacramental *signa* and *res* on the other. The point was made above, but here another dimension of it requires attention. Against the charge of a legal fiction, to which Calvin was always particularly sensitive, Calvin argued that a truly justifying faith is inextricably joined to, though necessarily distinguished from, renewal in godliness and good works. To separate them so that one can in theory exist independently of the other, the abhorrent charge of which it was suggested the reformers were guilty, was simply unthinkable. Note now how Calvin explains the *signa-res* relationship. The name of the body of Jesus Christ is appropriately transferred to the bread inasmuch as the bread serves as the sacrament and figure of it. "But we likewise add that the sacraments of the Lord should not and cannot be at all separated from their reality and substance. To distinguish, in order to guard against confounding them, is not only good and reasonable, but altogether necessary; but to divide them, so as to make the one exist without the other, is absurd."[58] This is exactly the argument Calvin offers against Sadoleto in 1539 and against the Roman Catholic criticism in general when the meaning of a justification *sola fide* is in question.

Calvin's response to the Lutheran charge of a fabricated presence, therefore, must be associated with his response to the similarly

---

Church Press, 1966; originally published as Vol. 2, no. 5 of the Mercersburg Review, 1850), 267-401. For literature see Brian A. Gerrish, "The Flesh of the Son of Man: John W. Nevin on the Church and the Eucharist," in *Tradition in the Modern World: Reformed Theology in the Nineteenth Century* (Chicago: University of Chicago Press, 1978), 49-70; and Davis, *The Clearest Promises of God*, 15-28.

[58] Calvin, *Petit Traicté de la Saincte Cene*; OS 1.509; TT 2.172: "Mais nous adiousterons pareillement que les sacremens du Seigneur ne se doivent et ne peuvent nullement ester separez de leur verité et substance. De les distinguer à ce qu'on ne les confunde pas, non seulement il est bon et raisonnable, mais du tout necessaire. Et les diviser pour constituer l'un sans l'autre, il n'y a ordre." The Lutheran response, of course, was that Calvin's rejection of a *manducatio impiorum* reflected the very division or separation that he denied.

constructed "legal fiction" accusation. In both cases, Calvin is concerned to demonstrate that he is not describing a "statement contrary to fact" but a reality. Against Rome, Calvin insists that a justifying faith devoid of good works is inconceivable precisely because, just as one is united to the Christ who *is* Righteousness and Life, so one cannot receive Christ for justification without receiving him for sanctification. Against Westphal and Heshusius, Calvin similarly argues that his "spiritual" presence is not a presence without the Person but a true and real presence of Christ by his Spirit. He meets the accusation that the *signa* are but "empty signs" (note the parallel to justification by faith as a legal fiction) by demonstrating that they are inseparably "annexed" to the reality which is promised in them.

Put differently, Calvin's regular response to the Roman charge of a legal fiction is paralleled in the 1550s by his response to Westphal's and Heshusius's critique of his understanding of eucharistic presence. Against Rome, Calvin responded that obedience is necessarily connected to justification because of their relationship as aspects of union with Christ, the real saving reality. Justification is distinguished from sanctification to clarify the *extra nos* ground of justification – the obedient death of Christ – but it has no existence as a grace independent of sanctification. Together they comprise a (singular) *duplex gratia*. In the same way, Calvin met the Lutheran objection to spiritual presence by emphasizing the reality of Christ's presence alongside his rejection of a corporeal presence. Calvin refuses to concede that true presence is contingent upon physical locality. But this does not mean Christ cannot be really and personally present, if one understands presence not to require corporeality. Because christologically the communication of properties is not an alteration or exchange of what is proper to the natures but a denotation of what is true of the Person, the wholeness of Christ, in both his divinity and humanity, is personally present, yet non-physically, by the virtue of the Spirit.[59] One must not confuse or mix justification and sanctification just as one must not confuse or mix the proper humanity and divinity of Christ. Thus whereas Heshusius accused Calvin of "lacerating" Christ because he imagines him present in his divinity alone and not in his flesh, Calvin insists that the flesh of Christ is present but according to a spiritual, non-local mode. To think otherwise, says Calvin to

---

[59] Calvin's understanding of the *communicatio* is dealt with in a variety of studies. A useful introduction is provided by Joseph N. Tylenda, "Calvin's Understanding of the Communication of Properties," *WTJ* 38 (1975): 54-65.

Heshusius, is to depart from orthodox Christology and specifically "to tear the flesh of Christ from his divinity."[60]

In sum, just as Calvin answers the Lutheran charge that his formulation reduces the Supper to a fallacious exhibition by emphasizing that the grace of the Supper lies in a true, not fabricated, participation or communication, so Calvin responds to the charge of a legal fiction by affirming the *reality* of the righteousness belonging to believers by virtue of their union with the righteous Christ. It is a true union, moreover, not with the grace or virtue of Christ's presence but with Christ himself, Christ in his flesh and blood, who is made present by the Spirit through faith.[61]

These general observations, involving the soteriological relationships among familiar elements in Calvin's sacramentology, supply the necessary framework for a crucial, more concentrated inquiry into Calvin's rejection of the Lutheran *manducatio impiorum*.

Christ and the Spirit: Calvin and the *Manducatio Impiorum*

Of Mice and (Unbelieving) Men: The Question

The medieval tradition made official at the Fourth Lateran Council (1215) affirmed a presence of Christ in the eucharistic elements so objective that it is wholly independent of the worthiness or unworthiness of the communicant. This emphasis on objectivity was intended to safeguard God's saving presence from becoming dependent on the creature. For thirteenth-century theologians, however, this also raised an immediate and pressing problem. Is Christ's presence so definite, so *objective*, that his transubstantiated body and blood may be consumed not only by an unbeliever but even by an animal?[62] Thomas Aquinas had provided the definitive

---

[60] Calvin, *De Vera Participatione*, CO 9.509; TT 2.560.
[61] Calvin, *Optima ineundae concordiae ratio*, CO 9.520-1, 522-3; TT 2.576, 579.
[62] John L. Farthing, *Thomas Aquinas and Gabriel Biel: Interpretations of St. Thomas Aquinas in German Nominalism on the Eve of the Reformation* (Durham, 1988), 125; cf. Thomas J. Bell, "The Eucharistic Theologies of *Lauda Sion* and Thomas Aquinas's *Summa Theologiae*," *The Thomist* 57 (1993): 179-83. For a history of transubstantiation, see James F. McCue, "The Doctrine of Transubstantiation from Berengar through Trent: The Point at Issue," *Harvard Theological Review* 61 (1968): 385-430. The reader should note the distinctions, drawn from Alexander of Hales, Thomas, and Scotus (cf. Altenstaig, *Lexicon Theologicum*, fols 139^v, 140^r, s.v. "*manducatio*"), among (1) *manducare sacramentum et non sacramentaliter* or *impiorum*, (2) *manducare sacramentaliter* or *indignorum*, (3) *manducare sacramentum spiritualiter*, and (4) the *manducare corpus Christi* summarized in Heiko Oberman,

answer to the *manducatio peccatorum* question, and the related *manducatio brutorum* speculation, explaining that Christ's corporeal presence necessarily persists as long as the accidents of bread and wine remain. Aquinas, then, grants the speculation: if a crumb of consecrated bread should fall to the floor and be eaten by a mouse, then the body of Christ will in fact have been eaten by a mouse. However, though Christ's body would have been consumed, it would have been eaten *corporeally*, not *spiritually*. For to use the elements spiritually is to use them properly, that is, to one's spiritual benefit, something of which a mouse is naturally incapable.[63]

Consequently, just as the body and blood of Christ remain joined to the elements as sacramentally present, even though in a mouse, so Christ must be said to be truly eaten by unbelievers, though not spiritually. Otherwise, if a true eating of Christ by unbelievers is rejected, the objective sacramental union of *signa* and *res* is irreparably severed.[64] "Should even an unbeliever receive the sacramental species, he would receive Christ's body under the sacrament: hence he would eat Christ sacramentally, if the word 'sacramentally' qualify the verb on the part of the thing eaten..."[65] Both the worthy and unworthy therefore truly partake of Christ in the consecrated elements: an unbeliever receives without positive effect whereas the believer eats spiritually to his benefit. Or, put differently, both the *pii* and the *impii* share a real sacramental eating of Christ, one "perfectly" and the other "imperfectly."[66]

Though joined with a rejection of transubstantiation, this is the line of reasoning Calvin was convinced he encountered in his Lutheran opponents. In his *Second Defense*, Calvin addresses Westphal's explanation that communion in the sacramental substance is common both to believer and unbeliever while the effect differs with respect to the presence or absence of faith. Hence both believer and unbeliever partake of the substance of Christ but with differing effects, one to life but the other to destruction. Calvin objects to this separation of the *substantia* from the *effectus* of Christ arguing that, on this view, "Christ is rendered lifeless and is severed

---

"The 'Extra' Dimension in the Theology of Calvin," in Oberman, *The Dawn of the Reformation*, 243.
[63] Aquinas, *ST* III q.80 a.3.
[64] Aquinas, *ST* III q.80 a.3. For Thomas, nothing prevents true feeding on Christ except a conscious act of mortal sin (*ST* III q.80 a.6 and *ST* III q.79 a.3).
[65] Aquinas, *ST* III q.80 a.3.
[66] Aquinas, *ST* III q.80 a.1. Cf. *ST* III q.80 a.4.

by sacrilegious divorce from his Spirit and all his virtue."[67] A careful reading of this argument, which Calvin uses often against Westphal, points to the consistent christological-pneumatological *sine qua non* of Calvin's thought: in their functional or economic identity, Christ *must not* be separated from his Spirit. The importance for Calvin of this specific theological point is evidenced in the fact that he framed his disagreement with the ubiquitarians in precisely these terms: "The matter now controverted between us, viz. whether unbelievers receive the *substance* of the flesh of Christ *without his Spirit*, is peculiarly applicable to the Supper."[68] This, it is important to recognize, is the anti-ubiquitarian (and generally sacramental) form of Calvin's soteriological argument that justification cannot be separated from sanctification. In both cases, the argument rests on the presupposition that the Christ-Spirit relationship *necessitates* a vivifying, transformative effect in all who are truly united to Christ. To confirm the parallel one needs only to recall his comment on Rom 8:9:

> ...those who separate (*divellunt*) Christ from His Spirit make Him like a dead image or a corpse. We must always bear in mind the

---

[67] Calvin, *Secunda Defensio*, CO 9.89; TT 2.303: "Quid? an ut mortuum Christi corpus edant increduli? Omnino, inquit: quia licet nullam spiritus gratiam percipiat quisquis non rite utitur sacramento, Christi tamen carne et sanguine fruitur. Quis non videt exanimem fieri Christum, et sacrilego divortio a spiritu suo, totaque virtute avelli?"

[68] Calvin, *Secunda Defensio*, CO 9.90; TT 2.305: "In coenam peculiariter competit quod nunc inter nos controvertitur, an increduli carnis Christi substantiam recipiant sine eius spiritu." The distinction is essentially the same as the distinction in later Reformed orthodoxy of a *manducatio sacramentalis* or *symbolica* from a *manducatio spiritualis* (R. Muller, *Dictionary of Latin and Greek Theological Terms*, 183-4). "Sacramental" or "symbolical" eating pertains to all who eat the bread and drink the wine, believer or unbeliever; real, "spiritual" eating, i.e., a true partaking of Christ's flesh and blood by the operation of the Spirit, however, belongs exclusively to those with faith. This seemed to Calvin's Lutheran critics to be a denial of the real presence of Christ, understood in the ordinary sense of presence, for if Christ is truly present he is present independent of the communicant's faith or unbelief. To argue otherwise is to make Christ's promise and God's work entirely dependent on man, and thus to do dishonor to the glory of Christ. On their view, the unbeliever truly partakes of the flesh and blood of Christ (by way of a *manducatio oralis*, which is not a carnal eating but a *manducatio hyperphysica sive supernaturalis*) but to his condemnation rather than blessing (because the spiritual body and blood are not "digested" in a similar sense that bread and wine are not digested), while the believer by faith receives, through the *manduatio sacramentalis* or *spiritualis*, the merits and graces of Christ.

counsel of the apostle, that free remission of sins cannot be separated from the Spirit of regeneration. This would be, as it were, to tear (*discerpere*) Christ apart.[69]

In this parallel faith occupies a central place. Intrinsic to Calvin's objection to the Lutheran *manducatio impiorum* is his insistence on the prerequisite of faith for union with Christ. Just as in his soteriology there is no union with Christ apart from the instrumentality of a Spirit-wrought faith, so in Calvin's sacramentology there is no true participation in Christ's flesh and blood by the unfaithful, unbelieving communicant. How does the effect follow the use of the sacraments, asks Calvin? When we receive them in faith, seeking Christ alone and his grace in them.[70] A momentary faith will not do, however; it is necessary that faith is nourished continually and increases daily. This nourishing work belongs to the divinely ordained purpose of the sacraments.[71]

It was this insistence on faith for true communion that exacerbated the rift with his Lutheran opponents. The *Consensus* had declared that "the signs are administered alike to reprobate and elect, but the reality reaches the latter only."[72] This distinction often appears in Calvin as *offer* and *receive*: the grace exhibited in the sacraments is truly offered to all but communion with Christ is only truly received by those with faith.[73] Calvin's distinction between *offer* and *receive* corresponds to the distinction between *signa* and *res*: the *signa* offer the *res* which is only received by faith.

The Christ-Spirit argument that figures so prominently in his relating justification and sanctification through union functions here with equal effect. Put concisely, to argue for an unbelieving union with Christ is to tear Christ from his Spirit. As the Living Bread, Christ cannot enter a body void of his Spirit.[74] As in his more

---

[69] Calvin, *Comm. Epist. ad Romanos*, 160; CNTC, 164. "Christum enim a Spiritu suo qui divellunt, eum faciunt mortuo simulachro vel cadaveri similem. Ac semper tenendum est illud Apostoli consilium, gratuitam peccatorum remissionem a Spiritu regenerationis non posse disiungi; quia hoc esset quasi Christum discerpere." Cf. Calvin, *Catechismus Gen.*, OS 2.95; TT 2.55.
[70] Calvin, *Catechismus Gen.*, OS 2.132; TT 2.85.
[71] Calvin, *Catechismus Gen.*, OS 2.132, 138-9; TT 2.85, 89-90.
[72] *Consensus*, Art. 17, TT 2.217.
[73] *Consensus*, Art. 18, TT 2.217.
[74] Calvin, *De Vera Participatione*, CO 9.485; TT 2.527: "Ergo his cavillis ne minimum quidem apicem labefactat mei axiomatis: Non posse Christum, quatenus est panis vivificus, et victima in cruce immolata, spiritu suo vacuum in corpus hominis intrare." For a discussion of contemporary ontological issues in the exegesis of John 6, see Irena Backus, "Polemic, Exegetical Tradition, and Ontology: Bucer's Interpretation of John 6:52, 53, and 64 Before and After the

explicitly soteriological statements so in his denial of a *manducatio impiorum*: because a true union or "feeding" on Christ *necessarily* vivifies, it is impossible that an unbeliever truly partakes of Christ in the Supper. As in salvation there is no saving union with Christ apart from faith, so in the Supper there is no true feeding (partaking, union) on, of, or with Christ apart from faith. It must ever be remembered, however, that it is not faith *per se* but the fact that faith unites us to Christ, our "faith-union," that warrants the exclusivity of *sola fide*. So Calvin explains that the "manner of receiving" the grace of Christ "consists in faith." But this is not only believing that he died and was raised for us but "recogniz[ing] that he dwells in us, and that we are united to him by a union the same in kind as that which unites the members to the head, that *by virtue of this union* we may become partakers of all his blessings."[75]

The Spirit of the Anointed Mediator

Calvin's polemical clarification of the Christ-Spirit relationship merits still further attention. The familiar opening section to Book 3 of the 1559 *Institutio* – the Spirit as the "bond" of union with Christ – is new to 1559, published in the heat of Calvin's controversy with the Lutherans, especially Westphal. Here Calvin ties the work of the Spirit in uniting believers to Christ to Christ's own anointing with the Spirit.[76] The Father bestowed the Spirit liberally upon the Son to be minister to us of his own liberality. He "laid up" the gifts of the Spirit in Christ in order then to give them to us.[77]

Richard Muller has noted Calvin's use of the western christological perspective as rooted in Hilary, Ambrose, and Augustine, in which the distinction rather than inseparability of the natures is emphasized in contrast with the divinization idea of the East. This generally western perspective carried with it a natural orientation into soteriological matters. In particular, Calvin's modification of the traditional person-work use of the Anselmic model in the direction of a whole-person structure functions to clarify that Christ as Mediator "must be considered in and through

---

Wittenberg Concord," in David C. Steinmetz, ed., *The Bible in the Sixteenth Century* (Durham: Duke University Press, 1990), 167-80.

[75] Calvin, *Catechismus Gen.*, OS 2.138; TT 2.89-90: "… sed in nobis quoque habitare agnoscimus, nosque illi coniunctos esse eo unitatis genere, quo membra cum capite suo cohaerent: ut huius unitatis beneficio omnium eius bonorum participes fiamus."

[76] Calvin, *Inst.* (1559) 3.1.1; OS 4.1-2 (LCC 20.538).

[77] Calvin, *Inst.* (1559) 3.1.2; OS 4.2-3 (LCC 20.538-9).

his office."⁷⁸ In accord with this official-Mediatorial focus, Calvin's frequent emphasis on Christ's humanity is concentrated specifically on his humanity *as sanctified by the Spirit* or *as gifted by the Spirit* in distinction from the *communicatio idiomatum*.⁷⁹ Christ's investiture with the Spirit is the underlying motif of Calvin's teaching on the Christ-Spirit relationship, and this is reflected in the way Calvin understands Christ's *munus triplex* (Prophet, Priest, and King) as Mediator to be underlined with the Spirit.

The idea of the Mediator's "office" is based upon the biblical terminology of "Christ" and "Messiah" which indicate anointing to a specific work and which furthermore require a redemptive-historical and "official" identification of the eternal Son of God with the name "Christ."⁸⁰ Christ is anointed in his whole divine-human Person, not only his humanity, for the specific redemptive purpose ordained in the eternal plan of God. The Spirit bestows upon him the gifts requisite to performing his mediatorial function or role, and these gifts then "belong to the entire person by reason of the *communicatio idiomatum*."⁸¹ In each mediatorial function Christ therefore performs his work *in the power of the Spirit*, by virtue of his anointing as Mediator, so that there is already, on this christological presupposition, no possibility of separating the intent and effect of Christ's redemptive work from the person and work of the Spirit. Christ, Calvin writes, "was filled with the Holy Spirit, and loaded with a perfect abundance of all his gifts, that he may impart them to us, – that is, to each according to the measure which the Father knows to be suited to us. Thus from him, as the only fountain, we draw whatever spiritual blessings we possess."⁸²

---

⁷⁸ Richard Muller, *Christ and the Decree: Christology and Predestination in Reformed Theology from Calvin to Perkins* (Durham: Labyrinth Press, 1986), 28, noting also Wendel, *Calvin*, 216-20; Pannenberg, *Jesus – God and Man*, 124, 221-3. It also points to the basically Scotist strain in Calvin's explanation of the necessity of a Mediator: it is not an *absolute* necessity but one resulting from God's ordained will regarding our salvation.

⁷⁹ Muller, *Christ and the Decree*, 28. See the discussion in Paul Timothy Jensen, "Calvin and Turretin: A Comparison of Their Soteriologies," Ph.D. diss. (University of Virginia, 1988), 107-29.

⁸⁰ Muller, *Christ and the Decree*, 31. See the discussion, pp. 31-3.

⁸¹ Muller, *Christ and the Decree*, 32. Muller notes (p. 32) that this is not yet the twofold anointing subsequently described by Ursinus, Perkins, and Polanus, though Calvin's idea "does, however, contain the germ of the later conception." See also, idem, "Christ in the Eschaton: Calvin and Moltmann on the Duration of the Munus Regium," *Harvard Theological Review* 74 (1981): 31-59.

⁸² Calvin, *Catechismus Gen.*, OS 2.80; TT 2.42-3: "Spiritu sancto repletus, perfectaque omnium eius donorum opulentia cumulatus fuit, quo nobis ea

In this light what Calvin writes about the Spirit and union in *Institutes* Book 3 reflects what he had explained previously in *Inst.* 2.15.2 about Christ's office of Mediator.[83] For Calvin, the relationship between Christ and the Spirit is not only ontological, due to a shared divine essence, but economical precisely because of Christ's mediatorial identity and anointing. As Calvin states, "he is called the 'Spirit of Christ' not only because Christ, as eternal Word of God, is joined in the same Spirit with the Father, but also from his character as the Mediator... In this sense he is called the 'Second Adam', given from heaven as 'a life-giving spirit'."[84] The "life-giving" quality of Christ's whole Person is thus bound inextricably to his identity as Mediator anointed with the Spirit, according to both natures.

Accordingly, this inseparability of Christ and the Spirit applies to both the universal and the redemptive aspects of the Son's activity.[85] The thread which runs through Calvin's thought here, what Willis has called his "Filioque–Christology," is the pneumatological, and ultimately *trinitarian* way in which Calvin conceives of the redeeming work of Christ, most explicit in the so-called "*extra Calvinisticum*."[86] Christ himself is truly present in his vivifying activity by the virtue and efficacy of his Spirit; the Spirit "diffuses the virtue of Christ's substance."[87] This functional, economic identity of Christ and the Spirit in Calvin's theology lies at the heart of his distinctive soteriological emphasis on union with Christ as requiring the inseparability of the graces. And it is because of this identity, which reflects back upon Christ's own Spirit-anointing, that whenever Christ is "eaten" the Spirit is present in his vivifying work, making efficacious the union of the Head and members where there is inevitably and ineluctably *life*.

The Theological Crux: Union with Christ Necessarily Enlivening

These structural and theological observations supply the needed framework for understanding Calvin's criticism of the Lutheran

---

impertiat, cuique scilicet pro mensura, quam nobis convenire novit pater. Ita ex eo, tanquam unico fonte, haurimus quidquid habemus bonorum spiritualium."
[83] Gary D. Badcock, *Light of Truth and Fire of Love: A Theology of the Holy Spirit* (Grand Rapids and Cambridge: Eerdmans, 1997), 102-3.
[84] Calvin, *Inst.* (1559) 3.1.2; OS 4.2-3 (LCC 20.539).
[85] See Werner Krusche, *Das Wirken des Heiligen Geistes nach Calvin* (Göttingen: Vandenhoeck & Ruprecht, 1957), 128-9.
[86] Willis, *Calvin's Catholic Christology*, 82-3.
[87] Calvin, *Confession de Foy au nom des eglises reformees de France*, CO 9.769; TT 2.160.

manducatio impiorum. In his objection to the Lutheran construct, one discovers the identical complex of ideas and arguments that gives rise to his distinctive *unio-duplex* understanding of salvation. Specifically, and most significantly, Calvin objects to the *manducatio impiorum* on the specific grounds that *there is no union with the Spirit-anointed Christ that is less than vivifying or life-giving*. Union with the Christ who *is* Life by the Spirit cannot but enliven: "Let [Westphal] now say whether the bread of the Supper vivifies the wicked. If it does not bestow life, I will immediately infer that they do not have the body of Christ."[88]

Those who truly eat the flesh and blood of Christ thus do so only to their nourishment. Because Christ is only truly present when he is present with his Spirit, his flesh cannot but vivify. Is this similar to the Thomist explanation of "definitive" presence, according to which an immaterial essence or substance is present if it produces a local effect despite a non-spatial locality?[89] In fact, this view is actually closer to the Lutheran position Calvin rejected. On the basically Thomist view, a causal, definitive eucharistic presence implies a substantial presence. In Calvin's view, however, substantial presence is to be steadfastly rejected for it requires a qualification on Christ's spatial, locally-circumscribed humanity and the presence of this humanity in heaven.[90] Instead, for Calvin, Christ's eucharistic presence is spiritual and the true partaking of Christ by believers is therefore necessarily spiritual.[91] This line of argument points to a desire for consistency on Calvin's part, for if Christ's eucharistic presence and our eucharistic feeding are indeed spiritual (i.e., effected by the Spirit), an unbeliever, who by definition does not have the Spirit, cannot truly partake of Christ in

---

[88] Calvin, *Ultima Admonitio*, CO 9.159; TT 2.368-9: "Respondeat nunc ergo, impiosne vivificet panis coenae: quia si vitam non confert, mox inferam, neque illis esse Christi corpus."

[89] As Richard Cross notes ("Catholic, Calvinist, and Lutheran Doctrines of the Eucharistic Presence: A Brief Note towards a Rapprochement," *International Journal of Systematic Theology* 4 [2002]: 302, n. 1), Aquinas technically denies a definitive presence because it restricts presence to one place at one time, and Christ is in fact present in the Eucharist in many places at one time (see *ST* 1.52.2 c and 3.75.2 c). The basic concept in Aquinas, however, that distinguishes "definitive" presence from "circumscriptive" or "spatially local" presence is retained and developed after Aquinas in Ockham and notably in Luther. See Ockham, *Quodlibet* 1.4, art. 2; and Luther, *Vom Abendmahl Christi. Bekenntnis* (*WA* 26.327-8; *LW* 37.215), both cited by Cross.

[90] Calvin, *Secunda Defensio*, CO 9.73; TT 2.281; cf. CO 9.86; TT 2.298.

[91] Calvin, *Secunda Defensio*, CO 9.74; TT 2.283; cf. Calvin, *Ultima Admonitio*, CO 9.162; TT 2.373-4.

the Supper.[92] The role of the Spirit in transferring the believer to Christ and Christ to the believer thus excludes a faithless eating of Christ's body.

Against the idea Calvin perceived in Westphal, there is thus no real contact with or feeding upon the flesh of Christ that is not life-giving. With a characteristically Anselmic focus on Christ's death, Calvin explains that the flesh offered and given in the Supper is the same flesh sacrificed for our redemption and which has become the source of life for all who are united to Christ. The Christ-Spirit bond is perhaps most visible when Calvin suggests that Christ's flesh is life precisely because it is not merely fleshly but spiritual. It is through the Spirit's active role as *vinculum* that the flesh of Christ nourishes and feeds. The Spirit raises us up to heaven where the "vigor" of Christ's flesh vivifies us like the rays of the sun. Simultaneously, Christ also descends to us by his vivifying energy.[93]

Calvin's equating of Christ with life is important to his argument. Calvin frequently describes Christ as the source of life, indeed as Life itself. In this connection, Calvin's rejection of a sacramental context for John 6 should not be understood as suggesting that the referent (Christ's flesh as life) is for Calvin *non*-sacramental. Rather, unlike much of the preceding exegetical tradition, Calvin interprets the passage as *pre*- or, perhaps better, *sub*-sacramental in significance. Calvin identifies the union with Christ of John 6 as the

---

[92] It appears that Cross' difficulty with Calvin's view (pp. 308-11) may be due to his overlooking the Mediator-centered Christ-Spirit relationship with which Calvin is operating. Cross does not see a real difference between the definitive (immediate) presence view and Calvin's spiritual (mediate) presence view. According to Cross, "[t]he trouble is that [Calvin] cannot see a way of avoiding an argument from *bodily* presence to *spatial* presence" (p. 310). Cross' criticism, reflective of the Lutheran objection, is that "there is no reason to accept Calvin's inference from bodily to spatial presence... The counterargument of mine... is that the substantial presence of a body entails its bodily presence" (p. 310). Cross' own proposal for rapprochement among the conflicting eucharistic traditions is thus predicated on his rejection of Calvin's presupposition of a necessarily circumscriptive humanity, apart from which the definition of "human" fails, and should be evaluated in this light. With a view to our specific interest in this chapter, and the discussion above regarding the medieval speculation about mice eating Christ's body in the consecrated wafer (*manducatio brutorum*), Cross concedes (p. 315) that on his view the unbeliever "and sometimes mice" could consume Christ's body. But because God can withhold his presence at will, this is not required; indeed, for Cross, the question is ultimately irrelevant.

[93] This ascent/descent pattern is of course patristic, but it appears Calvin tends to emphasize the descent element.

more general union of which eucharistic communion is a specific, special event. In the institution of the Supper, Calvin explains, the Lord "spoke briefly," whereas in the sixth chapter of John "he discourses copiously and professedly of that mystery of sacred conjunction of which he afterwards held forth a mirror in the Supper."[94] The body of Christ, Calvin writes, *is* "vivifying bread to us."[95] But this is true both in and apart from participation in the Supper; the divine intention of the Supper is directed to the nurture of faith and eschatological progress toward the reception of eternal life.[96]

In sum, the pneumatic character of Calvin's Christology requires so close a relationship of Christ and the Spirit that to violate this economic unity by arguing the *manducatio impiorum* is to separate Christ from his Spirit, to disjoin the Spirit and faith from the sacraments. To claim a non-spiritual eating is to suggest that Christ can be sacramentally present for salvation without the Spirit, with the unacceptable result that "the chief earnest of eternal salvation will be unaccompanied by the Spirit."[97] Rather, Christ is never present as Mediator without the Spirit of holiness. One cannot separate Christ from his Spirit (and his spiritual gifts) any more than one can separate Christ from himself.

In an appeal to Augustine, Calvin thus insists on the connection rather than separation of Christ's substance and fruit by appeal to the same principle: the distinction of *signa* and *res* requires that we recognize the life that issues to all who partake of it by faith.

> If Christ is our head, and dwells in us, he communicates to us his life; and we have nothing to hope from him until we are united to his body. The whole reality of the sacred Supper consists in this – Christ, by engrafting us into his body, not only makes us partakers of his body and blood, but infuses into us the life whose fullness resides in himself: for his flesh is not eaten *for any other end than to give us life*.[98]

---

[94] Calvin, *Ultima Admonitio*, CO 9.200; TT 2.425.
[95] Calvin, *Ultima Admonitio*, CO 9.193; TT 2.415: "Certe dum nos externis signis ac terrenis pignoribus contenti certo credimus corpus Christi panem nobis esse vivificum..."
[96] For eucharistic communion as a special instance of a more general spiritual union with Christ, see, e.g., Calvin, *Ultima Admonitio*, CO 9.162; TT 2.374.
[97] Calvin, *De Vera Participatione*, CO 9.479; TT 2.520.
[98] Calvin, *Ultima Admonitio*, CO 9.165; TT 2.377: "...si Christus caput nostrum sit, et in nobis habitans vitam nobis suam communicat. Neque enim ab eo quidquam nobis sperandum est, donec in eius corpus coaluerimus. Atque haec integra est sacrae coenae veritas, ut Christus nos inserendo in corpus suum, non

Thus, when it is claimed that the patristic writings pointed to the hypostatic union as requiring ubiquity and a *manducatio impiorum*, Calvin writes that "...ancient writers, when they say that the flesh of Christ, in order to be vivifying, borrows from his Divine Spirit, say not a word of this immensity, because nothing so monstrous ever came into their thoughts."[99]

Non-Eating to Destruction? 1 Corinthians 11 and the Problem of Unworthy Participation

But what about the *locus classicus* for the *manducatio impiorum* view in 1 Cor 11? Calvin agrees that the unbeliever cannot benefit from the Supper because he is without faith, but he does not concede that the disputed language of the Apostle in 1 Cor 11:27-29 (to eat and drink unworthily brings judgment) implies a true but destructive partaking of Christ. Adopting not only the reading of Augustine but of Chrysostom, whom Calvin used frequently for his commentary on 1 Corinthians, Calvin locates the judging action of God not in the elements (through an unbelieving partaking) but in the faithless communicant (through his rejection of what is offered). Judgment belongs to those who hold the Supper in abusive contempt, who insult the Christ who is truly offered there.[100] In his commentary on the passage, Calvin's rejection of the *manducatio impiorum* idea rests explicitly upon the basis of his pneumatologically characterized Christology. Commenting on unworthy eating in 1 Cor 11:27, Calvin notes the questions to which this verse gives rise: do the unworthy truly partake of Christ's body? Did Peter receive no more than Judas at the first supper?

Because his comment dates from the first, 1546 edition, before the Reformed-Lutheran controversy really took shape, it is difficult to identify those Calvin has in view. He explains that "some were led, by the heat of controversy, so far as to say" that true partaking was indiscriminate; further, many others "at this day maintain tenaciously *(pertinaciter)* and most noisily *(magnis clamoribus)*" the same idea.[101] The culprits of the past may be safely identified as those figures representative of late medieval, especially post-Fourth

---

modo participes faciat corporis et sanguinis sui, sed vitam, cuius in ipso residet plenitudo, in nos inspiret: quia non alium in finem comeditur eius caro, nisi ut sit vivifica."
[99] Calvin, *De Vera Participatione*, CO 9.508; TT 2.559.
[100] Calvin, *Comm. in Priorem ad Corinthios* [11:27], CO 49.491; CTS, 386. See Chrysostom, *Hom.* 28.2; PG 61.230-1.
[101] Calvin, *Comm. in Priorem ad Corinthios* [11:27], CO 49.491; CTS, 386.

Lateran Council, transubstantiation theory. The tenacious and noisy adherents of Calvin's own day are not named by Calvin, but may also lie in Rome.

The theological themes observed thus far are applied by Calvin in his explanation of this problem passage, confirming their importance. Calvin denies an indiscriminate eating, saying, "I hold it, then, as a settled point, and will not allow myself to be driven from it, that Christ cannot be disjoined from his Spirit. Hence I maintain, that his body is not received as dead, or even inactive, disjoined from the grace and power of his Spirit."[102] In his sermon on the passage in question, one finds the same theology and the same metaphors but in a more lively form. Proving the importance of the Christ-Spirit line of argument, it is significant that Calvin uses this argument in both his commentary and sermon on the verse. In his commentary, the Christ of the Supper is not the dead but the risen Christ. Therefore, one cannot be united to Christ as an unbeliever because union with the risen Christ *necessarily* vivifies. Not only is saving union contingent upon the presence of faith, argues Calvin, it is always – as a union with the resurrected, Spirit-anointed Christ – a vital union with necessarily vital effects. To support this first point Calvin clarifies it by explaining that because "Christ is never where his Spirit is not," one *cannot* partake of Christ without at the same time being renewed or vivified by the Spirit. Likewise in his sermon,

> Quand la table sera mise pour recevoir la Cene, ie prononceray les promesses: Voila Iésus Christ qui nous déclare qu'il nous fait participans de son corps et de son sang, sous les signes visibles, que nous prenons ici. Et bien, en prononçant cela, ie ne m'adresse point ni à trois, ni à quatre, c'est à tous sans exception. Voyla donc Iésus Christ qui présente son corps à tous, mesmes aux incredules et aux meschans. Voire, mais c'est à leur condamnation. A sçavoir maintenant s'ils le reçoyvent? Et comment le reçoyvent-ils? *Car il faudroit que le corps de Iésus Christ fust separé de son Esprit: ils sont possedez de Satan, il a toute puissance sur eux, ils n'ont rien de commun avec Iésus Christ, et cependant ils fourreront son corps et son sang en leur ventre?*[103]

Perhaps unexpectedly, however, the Christ-Spirit and life-giving emphases in Calvin's commentary are not new to the third and final, 1556 revision of his commentary on 1 Corinthians. One would expect a new emphasis in light of the chronology of the Reformed-Lutheran eucharistic controversy. Instead, the central text of

---

[102] Calvin, *Comm. in Priorem ad Corinthios* [11:27], CO 49.491; CTS, 386.
[103] Calvin, *Serm. Cor., ad loc.*, CO 49.815-6. Italics mine.

Calvin's exposition is virtually unchanged from 1546, suggesting that the clarifications made during the 1550s eucharistic controversy should be understood precisely as such – as clarifications, and not as signaling a new development in his thought.[104]

The question naturally arises as to the admonition directed toward believers. What of the elect, not the reprobate, who partake "unworthily"? What happens in and with them? In his comment on v. 27 Calvin states that there are some who truly receive Christ in the Supper, though unworthily because of weak faith. Brian Gerrish rightly notes that for Calvin there is a difference between absence of faith and weakness of faith.[105] The key to Calvin's line of thought here is to recall the eschatological dimension of the sacrament: the Supper is designed for nourishment, for progress in the path of eternal life, for advancing in faith. Far from detracting from its use, the eschatological dimension of sacramental grace in fact presupposes the presence of imperfect yet real faith; it is *for the weak* that it was instituted, to strengthen them and seal Christ to them. Importantly, however, this does not mitigate Calvin's sharp rejection of a *manducatio impiorum*: while he acknowledges that the weakest of believers partake of Christ unworthily in the Supper, yet he will not admit "that those who bring with them a mere historical faith, without a lively feeling of repentance and faith, receive anything but the sign. For *I cannot endure to maim Christ*, and I shudder at the absurdity of affirming that he gives himself to be eaten by the wicked in a lifeless state." Then, using a statement by Augustine found frequently in his writings against Westphal, Calvin continues: "Nor does Augustine mean anything else when he says, that the wicked receive Christ merely in the sacrament, which he expresses more clearly elsewhere, when he says that the other Apostles ate the bread the Lord (*panem Dominum*), but Judas ate only the bread of the Lord (*panem Domini*)."[106]

---

[104] Cf. *Iohannis Calvini Commentarii in Priorem Epistolam Pauli ad Corinthios* (Strasbourg: Wendelin Rihel, 1546), 187^v-8^r with *Ioannis Calvini in omnes D. Pauli epistolas, atque etiam in epistolam ad Hebraeos commentaria luculentissima...* (Geneva: John Gerard, 1551), fol. 198, and the 1556 text in CO 49.491-2. The only exceptions are slight changes, e.g., in spelling or in the substitution of a synonym.

[105] Gerrish, *Grace and Gratitude*, 172-3.

[106] Calvin, *Comm. in Priorem ad Corinthios* [11:27], CO 49.492; CTS, 386-7: "Sicut ergo fateor quosdam esse, qui vere simul in coena et tamen indigne Christum recipiant, quales sunt multi infirmi: ita non admitto, eos, qui fidem historicam tantum sine vivo poenitentiae et fidei sensu afferunt, aliud quam signum recipere. *Neque enim Christum mutilare sustineo*, et illam absurditatem reformido, quod se impiis quasi examinem edendum tradat. Neque aliud sentit

Does this distinction not denigrate the glory of God, however, by making the efficacy of his sacraments dependent upon something in the creature? Calvin denied this argument, little modified from its medieval form. "Many preclude its entrance by their depravity and make it void to themselves. Hence the benefit extends to believers only, and yet the sacrament loses nothing of its nature."[107] His opponents equated true presence with indiscriminate participation as necessary correlatives (if Christ is truly present at all then he is present to all), but Calvin is content that the glory of God is preserved if the body and blood of Christ is truly presented or offered indiscriminately. If this obtains, then the efficacy of the sacraments and the faithfulness of God to his covenant word of promise is secure.[108]

These concerns are woven together in an interesting exchange with Heshusius. Calvin rejects Heshusius's assumption that "fixture to a place implies exclusion, unless the body is enclosed under the bread." Heshusius's point rests upon an important and sound christological rationale: the saving "virtue" of Christ does not come to us *extra carnem*, apart from his flesh, or, the Spirit is not present without the Son. By this Heshusius intends the Son's flesh and bones, suggesting that, on Calvin's position, Christ's local absence from the Supper must necessarily imply the absence of his grace. Remove Christ's flesh and you remove his virtue as well; you cannot have one without the other. This is a line of reasoning far from foreign to Calvin, of course, who had himself insisted on the inseparability of the two. But, denying Heshusius' argument, Calvin focuses on the implications of Heshusius' own reasoning for the *manducatio impiorum*: "But he says, the Spirit is not without the Son, and therefore not without the flesh. I in turn retort that the Son is not without the Spirit, and that therefore the dead body of Christ by no means passes into the stomach of the reprobate."[109] On the grounds of the inseparability Heshusius had himself emphasized, Calvin

---

Augustinus, quum malos dicit Christum recipere in coena sacramento tenus. Quod alibi clarius exprimit, quum tradit reliquos apostolos edisse panem Dominum, Iudam vero nonnisi panem Domini." Italics mine.

[107] Calvin, *Catechismus Gen.*, OS 2.134; TT 2.87: "Multi dum illi sua pravitate viam praecludunt, efficient ut sibi sit inanis. Ita non nisi ad fideles solos pervenit fructus. Verum, inde nihil sacramenti naturae decedit."

[108] See Calvin, *Comm. in Priorem ad Corinthios* [11:27], CO 49.492; CTS, 387.

[109] Calvin, *De Vera Participatione*, CO 9.509-10; TT 2.560-1. "In quo nimis stulte hallucinatur Heshusius, dum loco affixus exclusionem somniat, nisi sub pane corpus sit inclusum. At spiritus, inquit, non est sine filio: ergo non sine carne. Ego autem vicissim retorqueo: non esse filium sine spiritu, ideoque mortuum Christi corpus minime transmitti in ventrem reproborum."

thus argues for the impossibility of an unbelieving participation in or feeding upon Christ in the Supper.

Correspondence with Soteriological Structure

The continuity of this sacramental structure with Calvin's soteriological structure, perhaps evident at this point, is striking. The underlying theme of Calvin's soteriology, the *unio Christi-duplex gratia* construct, should be recalled: one cannot be united to Christ for justification and not for sanctification. As noted in Chapter 3 above, in his 1556 revision of his Romans 8 commentary Calvin added that to claim otherwise is "to tear Christ into pieces." Elsewhere, after denying any place to our merit in procuring favor rather than wrath from God, and locating the righteousness by which we are acceptable to God in Christ alone, Calvin moves to his characteristic clarification of this point. "Meanwhile, however," he says, "I acknowledge that Jesus Christ not only justifies us by covering all our faults and sins, but also sanctifies us by his Spirit, so that the two things (the free forgiveness of sins and reformation to a holy life) cannot be severed and separated from each other."[110] As argued in the preceding study, the theological reason for this *non posse* is the work of the Spirit who unites believers to the righteous Christ. In the sacraments also, it is this Spirit who nourishes with Christ, or, rather, Christ who nourishes through his Spirit.

But we must recall also the specific christological underpinnings of this emphasis, also referred to in the Romans case study: from his earliest texts, Calvin presents his *unio Christi-duplex gratia* construction as a necessary implication of the Christ-Spirit relationship. In Calvin's anti-ubiquitarian polemic of the 1550s (and early 1560s) one finds the identical point made in a different context, verifying its importance in the underlying fabric of Calvin's thinking. Union with Christ or, more specifically, union with the risen Christ is necessarily vivifying or sanctifying. One *cannot* be united to the Christ who is Life without being sanctified. Its presence as a crucial element in his doctrine of the Supper indicates both the importance of the point to Calvin as well as his cross-application of it to different questions. Finally, it reveals the extent to which the idea of union with Christ, and not justification *per se*, controlled his understanding of salvation, especially when the question of good works is raised.

---

[110] Calvin, *Brief Confession of Faith*, TT 2.132.

The Strata of Union with Christ

The Functional Equivalence of Signa-Res *and Incarnational-Saving Union with Christ: Calvin's Soteriological Language in Eucharistic Context*

The sacramental-soteriological parallels that surface most visibly in Calvin's rejection of the Lutheran *manducatio impiorum* should be supplemented by another set of documents. It was during the eucharistic controversy that Calvin exchanged correspondence with a fellow defender and expositor of what would be known as the "Reformed" position. The subject of discussion was union with Christ, and the exchange makes explicit a number of the implicit connections in Calvin's eucharistic and soteriological thought.

Calvin's exchange with Peter Martyr Vermigli in 1555 is almost entirely devoted to clarifying the idea of union with Christ. Its significance as an index to the early Reformed understanding of union with Christ is beyond question, and it has recently generated a small body of literature. Of existing studies, Duncan Rankin's doctoral thesis has devoted the most extensive attention to this correspondence, employing these letters in his critique of T. F. Torrance's reading of Calvin on incarnational union.[111] Here it is possible only to highlight its most relevant points.[112]

---

[111] Duncan Rankin, "Carnal Union with Christ in the Theology of T. F. Torrance," Ph.D. thesis (University of Edinburgh, 1997), 170-235. This use by Rankin is appropriate, given that this correspondence is uniquely valuable for addressing questions posed in the literature by those adopting Torrance's general perspective. See the entire chapter for a more detailed critique of the incarnation/atonement question in modern Calvin scholarship (in particular Torrance's use of Calvin). Others have pointed to the importance of this correspondence for interpreting Calvin on union with Christ. See, e.g., Kolfhaus, *Christusgemeinschaft*, 24-35; following Kolfhaus, Tamburello, *Union with Christ*, 86-7; 89-90; 143 nn. 18, 19; 144 n. 36; and B. A. Gerrish, *Tradition and the Modern World: Reformed Theology in the Nineteenth Century* (Chicago and London: University of Chicago Press, 1978), 63. Wallace notes the letter in passing in *Calvin's Doctrine of the Word and Sacrament*, 146, n. 5. Tim J. R. Trumper, "An Historical Study of the Doctrine of Adoption in the Calvinistic Tradition," Ph.D. thesis (University of Edinburgh, 2001), has revisited the correspondence with an interest in adoption (pp. 38-214). For the Calvin-Vermigli correspondence in general, see Marvin W. Anderson, *Peter Martyr: A Reformer in Exile (1542-1562)* (Nieuwkoop: B. De Graaf, 1975), 186-95; idem, "Peter Martyr, Reformed Theologian (1542-1562): His letters to Heinrich Bullinger and John Calvin," *SCJ* 4 (1973): 41-64; and J. C. McLelland, *The Visible Words of God* (Edinburgh and London: Oliver and Boyd, 1957), 88, 14-147.

[112] A fuller analysis is included as Appendix B below.

In his response to an earlier letter from Vermigli,[113] Calvin expresses his agreement with Vermigli's description of union with Christ, stating his goal in writing is simply to show the Italian that "we entirely agree in sentiment."[114] Confusion in the raging eucharistic controversy over communion with Christ had led Vermigli to ask Calvin specifically about the mode of the "communion which we have with the body of Christ and the substance of his nature."[115] Both Calvin and Vermigli agree that there are three different kinds of union with Christ: natural/incarnational, mystical, and spiritual. Most importantly, they agree that natural/incarnational union is, in itself, "very general and feeble" (*communis admodum... et debilis*), i.e., not redemptive.[116]

---

[113] Peter Martyr Vermigli to Calvin, CO 15.492-7; cf. the printing in the *Epistolae* of the *Loci Communis Petri Martyris Vermilii Florentini Theologi Celeberrimi* (Geneva: Pierre Aubert, 1627), 767-9. An early translation into English may be found in Vermigli, *Common Places of the most famous and renowned Divine Doctor Peter Martyr, divided into foure principall parts*, with Appendix, trans. Anthony Marten (London: H. Denham and H. Middleton, 1583), (Appendix) 96-9. G. C. Gorham translated a large portion of both letters into English for his *Gleanings of a Few Scattered Ears and of the Times Immediately Succeeding: A.D. 1533 to A.D. 1558* (London: Bell and Daldy, 1857), 340-4 and 349-52; but a more recent (but also partial) English translation of a portion of Vermigli's letter is included in J. C. McLelland and G. E. Duffield, eds, *The Life, Early Letters & Eucharistic Writings of Peter Martyr* (Appleford: Sutton Courtenay Press, 1989), 343-8.
[114] Calvin to Vermigli, CO 15.724.
[115] Vermigli to Calvin, CO 15.494.
[116] Vermigli to Calvin, CO 15.494: "Quum enim pueri carni et sanguini communicarint, et ipse voluit horum esse particeps. Verum nisi aliud communionis genus intercederet, *communis admodum haec esset et debilis*. Nam quotquot humana specie comprehenduntur, hac ratione iam cum Christo communicant: sunt quippe homines, ut ipse fuit." Italics mine. In his discussion of union with Christ drawn from his commentary on Romans 8 and included in his posthumously compiled *Common Places*, Vermigli explains (Ch. 3, pt. 3, sect. 35, pp. 77b-8a) that natural union is "general and weak, and onlie (as I may terme it) according to the matter..." (78a). Cf. Calvin's agreement in CO 15.722-3, esp. his concern with the "new fusionists" who envision a *substantiae commixtione*: "Crassis interea commentis de substantiae commixtione adytum praecludo: quia mihi satis est, dum in coelesti Gloria manet Christi corpus, vitam ab eo ad nos defluere, non secus ac radix succum ad ramos transmittit" (p. 723). Calvin had expressed his agreement in an earlier letter to Vermigli (18 January, 1555, in Beveridge, *Letters*, 125-9 [no. 382]). Nick Needham ("Peter Martyr and the Eucharist Controversy," *Scottish Bulletin of Evangelical Theology* 17 [1999]: 5-25) notes the relationship of Vermigli's three unions to his eucharistic theology but fails to recognize Vermigli's negative view of

Hence Calvin and Vermigli agree that a further, "spiritual" union is necessary, one in which believers are united to Christ by the Spirit through faith which is "breathed into the elect." The result is twofold: (1) their sins are forgiven and they are reconciled to God; and (2) they are renewed by the Spirit after Christ's image. In addition to these two unions, a mystical, intermediate (*mediam*) union serves as "the fount and origin" of likeness to Christ.[117]

Noteworthy here is the continuity of Calvin and Vermigli with the tradition, recounted in a limited way in Chapter 2 above, of recognizing various "union(s)" with Christ. In Calvin and Vermigli, however, this traditional idea seems to function more like *strata* in that "natural" union lies behind the "mystical" and "spiritual" unions.[118] The way in which Calvin's distinction in this

---

incarnational union. This is likely because he follows McLelland, whom he notes.

[117] See Vermigli to Calvin, CO 15.493-4; and Calvin's agreement in CO 15.722-4.

[118] Note that Vermigli, in a letter to Beza, described his three unions, saying (referring to the second, mystical union): "Credo nostrae communionis cum Christo *tres gradus*, atque illum medium, arcanum, mysticumque metaphora membrorum et capitis, viri atque uxoris in divinis literis exprimi animadverto" (*Correspondance de Théodore de Bèze*, vol. 1 [1539-1555], ed. Hippolyte Aubert; pub. Fernand Aubert and Henri Meylan [Geneva: Librarie Droz, 1960], 153-5, here 155). Italics mine. Vermigli here lists the three unions as natural, eternal (through the resurrection), and mystical (by faith and the sacraments). One common denominator in both of Vermigli's lists is the negative assessment of the redemptive efficacy of natural/incarnational union: "Non tamen Christianis est propria, sic enim Judaei, Turcae, et quotquot hominum censu comprehenduntur, cum Christo coniunguntur" (p. 154). Furthermore, if Calvin and Vermigli also agree, as Rankin suggests, that mystical communion or union "grounds justification, while spiritual communion appears to ground sanctification," then the apparent correspondence between the various *strata* of union with Christ with the *benefits* of that union – namely, justification and sanctification – signals a possible note of dissonance within Calvin's thought as it has been investigated thus far. See Rankin, "Carnal Union with Christ," 183-4. Again (Rankin, p. 185), "[Calvin] distinguishes between mystical and spiritual communion in the same way he distinguishes Christ and his gifts, or justification and sanctification." Rankin is following Tamburello (*Union with Christ*, 86-7) and is followed on the point in a fuller study by Timothy J. R. Trumper, "An Historical Study of the Doctrine of Adoption in the Calvinistic Tradition," PhD thesis (University of Edinburgh, 2001), 117-48, who suggests that mystical union corresponds to the adoptive act while spiritual union corresponds to the adoptive state. However, in my view the argument for a correspondence of mystical union to justification and spiritual union to sanctification is less than convincing, and appears to be based upon the arbitrary division of Calvin's letter into two paragraphs in the translation by G.

correspondence between the non-redemptive "incarnational" union and the redemptive "mystical" and "spiritual" union(s) reflects the pattern of distinctions in Calvin's sacramental thought is significant. In short, Calvin evidently regards incarnational union as functionally equivalent to the sacramental *signa*. Again, when not joined with faith, the *signa* are "useless" to the communicant, not truly communicating Christ with his redemptive grace. When joined with faith, however, they are *instrumenta* for a true partaking of Christ. Importantly, the Spirit works through the *signa* as instruments. Without his activity they bear no grace; taken up by his power, however, they become efficacious for salvation. The *signa* are useful, therefore, only when God makes them efficacious, when Christ operates inwardly by his Spirit in order to do his work. When separated from this Spirit-faith union with Christ, the sacraments are but "empty shows." Thus it is the Holy Spirit who brings the *effectus* to the sign, who as the *nexus* or *vinculum* of participation with Christ makes the Supper an effectual means of grace.

This sacramental-soteriological parallel in Calvin's language is unmistakable. For instance, among his numerous appeals to Augustine, Calvin argues the "uselessness" of the crucified flesh of Christ if not joined to the Spirit and "eaten" in faith.

> Augustine thinks that we ought to supply the words "alone," and "by itself," because it ought to be conjoined with the Spirit. This is consonant to fact: for Christ has respect simply to the mode of eating. He does not therefore exclude every kind of utility, as if none could be derived from his flesh, but he only declares that it will be useless (*inutilem*), if it is separated from the Spirit (*si a spiritu separetur*). How then has flesh the power of vivifying, but just by being spiritual? Whosoever therefore stops short at the earthly nature of flesh will find nothing in it but what is dead; but those who raise their eyes to the virtue of the Spirit with which the flesh is pervaded, will learn by the result and the experience of faith, that it is not without good cause said to be vivifying."[119]

C. Gorham (*Gleanings of a Few Scattered Ears*, 349). See Appendix B below for a full discussion of the problem.

[119] Calvin, *De Vera Participatione*, CO 9.511; TT 2.562-3: "Augustinus subaudiendum putat Solam, et per se, quia debeat cum spiritu coniungi... Non ergo quamvis excludit utilitatem, quasi nulla percipi ex carne sua possit: sed ita demum inutilem fore pronunciat, si a spiritu separetur. Unde enim habet caro ut vivificet, nisi quia spiritualis est? Ideo quisquis in terrestri carnis natura subsistit, nihil in ea reperiet nisi mortuum: sed qui oculos attollent ad spiritus virtutem, qua perfusa est caro, non frustra vivificam dici ipso effectu et fidei experientia sentient."

Similarly, the sacramental signs communicate the reality only if and when God gives effect through the Spirit.[120]

Indeed, Calvin has good reason to cite Augustine in support of the strata enumerated elsewhere in the Vermigli correspondence. Augustine identified a qualitative difference between the sinful flesh in which all mankind are guilty before God, and the Flesh fashioned "after the likeness of sinful flesh" (citing Rom 8:3) in which all are freed from condemnation. This, however, is "by no means" suggestive, says Augustine, that all who are born in the first class are cleansed by the One in the second class: the two humanities are not equivalent in scope. The difference is faith, which signals a different *kind* of union. Only those born "from the spiritual union" are cleansed by the second Flesh which is "in the likeness of sinful flesh": "In other words, those of the former class are in Adam unto condemnation, the latter are in Christ unto justification."[121] Calvin does not explicitly cite Augustine in support here, but the mirrored pattern of argument is noteworthy as an indication of the received Augustinian understanding.

Moreover, this pattern of argument is further paralleled by Calvin's use of the Lombardian sufficiency/efficiency distinction to clarify the infinite sufficiency of Christ's atoning work together with its efficacy restricted to the elect.[122] This also points to Calvin's wide-ranging application of the Chalcedonian principle (distinction without separation) in combination with Augustinian sign theory (the relationship of *signa* and *res*), and must not be isolated from the eucharistic context in which these distinctions and patterns, as well

---

[120] Calvin, *Confession De Foy au nom des eglises reformees de France*, CO 9.764; TT 2.152: "Toutesfois nous disons qu'ils ne sont utiles sinon là où Dieu les fait valoir, et y desploye la vertu de son Esprit, comme par ses organs. Ainsi il faut que l'esprit de Dieu y besongne pour nous en faire sentir l'efficace à nostre salut."

[121] Augustine, *De Peccatorum Meritis et Remissione*, bk. 1, ch. 28, sect. 55, PL 44.140-41; ET cited from NPNF, 1st series, vol. 5, *Anti-Pelagian Writings*, Chap. 55, pp. 36b-37a. Cf. Augustine, *Tractatus* on John 13:1-5, para. 1, in which he refers to "unbelievers, who stand altogether apart from this Head and His members..."

[122] Cf. Calvin, *Comm.* on 1 Jn. 2:2; CO 55.310 ("Qui hanc absurditatem volebant effugere, diserunt, *sufficienter* pro toto mundo passum esse Christum: sed pro electis tantum *efficaciter*." Italics mine. [cf. *Inst.* 2.16.16 and 3.22.1]), with Lombard, *Sententiae*, III, d. xx, c. 51, as discussed in R. Muller, *Christ and the Decree*, 33-5 (note the wider discussion in pp. 17-38); and, idem, *Unaccommodated Calvin*, 55-6. This distinction would lie at the heart of the later Reformed teaching of a "limited" atonement.

as this set of correspondence, occur. The parallels may be summarized thus:

"Natural" Union

Signa
- ▶ incarnational union and sacramental signs are soteriologically *instrumental*, i.e., indispensable to salvation when connected with the Spirit-faith bond, but "useless" to the faithless when alone
- ▶ functional equivalence with *unlimited sufficiency*

"Mystical" Union
- ▶ Spirit-faith is a prerequisite for saving union and establishes the relationship

"Spiritual" Union

Res
- ▶ Spirit-faith brings the graces of justification and sanctification, i.e., forgiveness of sins/reconciliation with God and renewal in the form of an eschatological *Christiformia*: this is the grace (the *duplex gratia*) that the sacraments signify but only communicate by the Spirit through faith
- ▶ functional equivalence with *limited efficiency*

Redemptive Incarnational Union with Christ?

In this light, we are in a position to address briefly a question raised on occasion within Calvin scholarship. What is the relationship of Christ's humanity, specifically the event of the Incarnation, to the nature and scope of Christ's atoning work? To use the concrete form in which the issue is usually raised, does Calvin teach an "unlimited" or "limited" atonement and, conversely, a "redemptive" or "non-redemptive" incarnational union with Christ? In some of the literature, one reads, for instance, about the "new humanity" Calvin finds established in the *redeeming* incarnational union Christ shares with all mankind, of the incarnation *as* atonement, and therefore of the hypostatic union as itself an atoning union.[123]

For two reasons, the treatment of the question here must be brief. First, the question is actually further afield from our immediate interest than the literature might suggest. Second, this is territory well-covered by existing studies, studies which address the question in greater length and detail than is desirable here. Indeed, the hermeneutical and theological perspectives at the heart of the most influential proposals of what is known as the "Barthian" (or neo-Barthian) reading of Calvin, represented by T. F. and J. B. Torrance, Charles Bell, and Trevor Hart among others, have been subjected to considerable scrutiny.

The result has been twofold. On the one hand, many have objected to what is perceived as anachronistic paradigms and assumptions that have distorted the sixteenth-century meaning of Calvin's texts. Representative in this regard is the work of Richard A. Muller, the most prolific of a growing number of scholars who have examined, at considerable length and from various perspectives, the problems with the Barthian reading of Calvin.[124] On the other hand, studies from the Barthian-Torrancian perspective continue to appear, but the absence in this body of literature of sustained interaction with criticisms makes it difficult to engage it beyond what has already been done. The recent studies by Brglez,

---

[123] So Trevor Hart, "Humankind in Christ and Christ in Humankind," 79-84.
[124] R. Muller, *Christ and the Decree*, 33-5; idem, "Calvin and the 'Calvinists': Assessing Continuities and Discontinuities Between the Reformation and Orthodoxy," (revised) in Muller, *After Calvin*, 63-102; and, idem, *Unaccommodated Calvin*, 55-6. See the literature cited by Muller for further studies.

Kennedy, and Redding,[125] furthermore, have done little more than repeat the heavily criticized model in a reorganized and re-presented form. Still, it appears appropriate to make one observation regarding the implications of the soteriological-sacramental relationship in Calvin's theology for this discussion.

On the basis of the themes investigated in this second case study, it is evident that Calvin's pattern of argument and expression renders the assertion that Christ in the incarnation established a *redemptive* union with all humanity deeply problematic. This is in fact the idea explicitly rejected in Calvin's response to Vermigli. Furthermore, the host of Calvin's positive statements about the redemptive significance of Christ's full humanity may be regarded as entirely natural for one who similarly insisted on the integrity and indispensability of the sacramental *signa*. Against the charge of fabrication, Calvin has the burden of demonstrating that he does indeed insist on a union with the flesh-and-blood Christ, not merely his graces. Yet to read into Calvin a redemptive or atoning natural or incarnational union is not only to fail to account for his most explicit rejection of the idea (in his Vermigli correspondence) but also, significantly, to fail to account for Calvin's wider pattern of argument and expression, in particular the Lombardian sufficiency/efficiency distinction as well as the offer/receive and *signa/res* distinctions, each of which is functionally equivalent to his natural/mystical-spiritual union distinction. Ultimately, it would appear Calvin's line of thinking bears a more positive relationship to the later terminology of a limited atonement than some have wished to perceive. It is not insignificant that it is within this eucharistic context – and specifically the *manducatio impiorum* question – that Calvin states:

> ...the first thing to be explained is how Christ is present with unbelievers, as being the spiritual food of souls and, in short, the *life and salvation of the world*. And as [Heshusius] adheres so doggedly to the words, I should like to know how the wicked can

---

[125] H. Brglez, "Saving Union with Christ in Calvin: A Critical Study," Ph.D. diss. (University of Aberdeen, 1993); Kevin Dixon Kennedy, *Union with Christ and the Extent of the Atonement in Calvin* (New York: Peter Lang, 2002); and Graham Redding, *Prayer and the Priesthood of Christ in the Reformed Tradition* (Edinburgh: T. & T. Clark, 2003). Apart from these recent inquiries, I do not here list the essays and articles which are accessible in most treatments and are listed fully (to the year 2000) in Muller, *Unaccommodated Calvin*.

eat the flesh of Christ *which was not crucified for them*, and how they can drink the blood *which was not shed to expiate their sins?*[126]

More positively, however, the common function of union with Christ in Calvin's sacramental and soteriological texts points unmistakably to corresponding concerns to preserve the presence of spiritual life as a necessary implication of participation in Christ. The common denominator in Calvin's rejection of the Roman charge of a legal fiction and of the Lutheran *manducatio impiorum* is the single christological-pneumatological assertion that Christ cannot be separated from his Spirit.

Conclusion

What, in sum, does Calvin's teaching on the sacraments reveal about the function of union with Christ in his *duplex gratia* understanding of salvation? This series of observations, determined as they are by attention to the theological rationale assumed in Calvin's polemic, vindicates the view that his conception of union with Christ controls his manner of relating justification and sanctification. Also, in connection with his replication principle, it further substantiates the claim that union with Christ functions in order to relate forgiveness and renewal in a way that distinguishes Calvin and the Reformed not only from Rome but also, especially in his later years, from the pattern of early Lutheran thinking. The strictly soteriological difference in Calvin's argument for the necessity of good works recurs here as a rejection of the Lutheran *manducatio impiorum* – to Calvin an instance of failing to view vivification as a necessary effect of union with Christ.

---

[126] Calvin, *De Vera Participatione*, CO 9.484; TT 2.527: "Sed in primis hoc probandum est, quomodo adsit Christus incredulis, quatenus est spiritualis animarum cibus, vita denique et salus mundi. Et quando tam mordicus verbis adhaeret, scire velim quomodo Christi carnem edant impii, pro quibus non est crucifixa, et quomodo sanguinem bibant, qui expiandis eorum peccatis non est effusus." It is acknowledged that without access to Heshusius's text (not extant) it is impossibly to be confident what he meant. Still, the continuity of Calvin's concern with his wider christological-soteriological framework means his point remains, in my view, sufficiently clear. Apparently validated, then, from another perspective is the judgment by A. N. S. Lane (in response to J. B. Torrance), "The Quest for the Historical Calvin," *EQ* 60 (1983): 113, "The idea of the headship of Christ over all men is a Barthian idea alien to Calvin." J. B. Torrance's view is included in the same issue of *EQ* (pp. 83-94) as "The Incarnation and 'Limited Atonement'." See Rankin, "Carnal Union with Christ," 166-235, for a critique of T. F. Torrance's similar reading of Calvin on incarnational union.

Calvin's regular pattern of expression and argument suggests a conscious attempt to apply the traditional language of Chalcedon and Augustinian sign theory to the relationship of justification and sanctification. More importantly, however, the nature of Calvin's objection to the Lutheran *manducatio impiorum* confirms in a very different context that the necessity of good works or Christian obedience is grounded not in justification but in union with Christ, or, better, in Christ himself with whom believers have been brought into union. The christological-pneumatological basis for this point is clarified in an unprecedented way in Calvin's anti-ubiquitarian polemic, for here the Christ-Spirit relationship is developed to function within his theology in a way previously somewhat ambiguous. Specifically, the inseparability of justification and sanctification is rooted in the inseparability of Christ and the Spirit in their common redemptive activity. Christ who is Life by his Spirit necessarily vivifies those united to him just as a living vine necessarily yields fruit in its branches. The union itself is further defined as substantial and yet non-ontological in the sense of mixing or transfusion of essences; it is instead "spiritual" because it is the secret work of the divine Spirit. Union with Christ is thus fully personal and necessarily vivifying, and yet is described in such a way that the forensic dimension is not compromised by its basis in union: the Righteous Christ is in himself both justification and sanctification.

Furthermore, looking at Calvin and Vermigli together, especially in terms of their 1555 correspondence, suggests a basic consensus on the nature of union with Christ. This agreement was the fruit not of soteriological inquiry independent of other *loci*, but of the eucharistic controversy and the perceived implications of this area of Church life for the doctrine of salvation. Possibly the most interesting element of the Calvin-Vermigli agreement on the Supper, however, is this: Vermigli's reception of Augustinian sign theory came through its reinterpretation in the hands of Aquinas and yet is strikingly similar to Calvin's, who did not share Vermigli's education in Thomism. The similarities may, in the end, be due simply to a shared reading of Augustine himself or potentially to the influence of Bucer, with his rich pneumatology, during their stays in Strasbourg. It seems a question worth pursing further.

Finally, it should be noted that Calvin's *unio Christi-duplex gratia* construction was clarified in his participation in Reformed-Lutheran polemic. Calvin's vigorous objection throughout the 1550s and the early 1560s to the *mixing* of the divine and the human, the *confusion* of proper qualities, and other objectionable elements of ubiquitarian Christology and sacramentology supplies the contextual framework within which his own teaching on the Spirit should be identified and read. The importance of this final point must not be overlooked. Indeed, it leads naturally into our third and final study where these themes aid in appreciating the significance of the most important event in Calvin's ministry for our question: Calvin's response to the theology of Andreas Osiander. Here, pneumatic Christology, sacrament, and salvation are brought together in an unprecedented way.

CHAPTER FIVE

Applied Christology:
Calvin versus Osiander in Light of the Eucharistic Controversy

Polemic and Theological Interplay

Calvin's participation in the Osiandrian controversy is among the most conspicuous features of his later, exceptionally trying years. But the question should be raised from the outset why Calvin would involve himself to such great lengths in what was really an intra-Lutheran debate. The answer to this question is complex but deeply significant. The evidence bears at least this much out: Calvin's response to Osiander must be understood as interaction with one he did not view only as a rogue thinker. For Calvin, Osiander is ever a Lutheran ubiquitarian, and a close, contextual reading of the texts suggests that Calvin regarded Osiander's doctrine of justification as the logical implication of the Lutheran Christology and sacramentology with which he had been engaged in heated polemic throughout the 1550s. This is more than a matter of mere historical interest. It will soon become clear that this single observation sheds considerable light on Calvin's own theology of saving union with Christ.

To appreciate and weigh the significance of this fundamental thesis, however, the fascinating though sometimes bewildering interplay of traditional, exegetical, and theological factors in the Calvin-Osiander relationship must be understood. *Traditionally* – that is, in terms of the concern to be faithful to received teaching – a basic struggle in the Osiandrian controversy was over the right to claim Luther's support. Hence I assume as beyond question that Luther can at this stage already be regarded as a standard of true reformational teaching, for the role of his authority in intra-Lutheran debate certainly indicates he was.[1] Luther's rhetorical ambiguity,

---

[1] See Robert Kolb, *Martin Luther as Prophet, Teacher, and Hero: Images of the Reformer, 1520-1620* (Carlisle: Paternoster; Grand Rapids: Baker, 1999). Cf. idem, *Nikolaus von Amsdorf (1483-1565): Popular Polemics in the Preservation of Luther's Legacy* (Nieuwkoop: De Graaf, 1978); idem, "Dynamics of Party Conflict in the

however, evident in passages often capable of opposing interpretations, had proved in the years subsequent to his death a principal cause of sharply conflicting views of justification. Considered *exegetically*, the Osiandrian dispute was preeminently a disagreement over the correct reading of the Apostle Paul in 1 Cor 1:30, "It is because of God that you are in Christ Jesus, who has become for us wisdom of God, righteousness, sanctification and redemption," against the background of several OT passages, especially Jer 23:6 where Yahweh promises to become the righteousness of his people. This exegetical element, we will soon recognize, is centrally important for appreciating the complexity of Calvin's involvement. In addition I will give some attention below to a further metaphorical element which is tied to Calvin's role in the exegetical dispute. *Theologically*, Calvin's participation in the Osiandrian controversy involved the somewhat subtle and often-overlooked differences between the emerging Lutheran and Reformed understandings of salvation, differences which while indeed not of the same order as their common differences with Rome (and hence largely obscured in the preceding decades by this common polemic), appear as a major subtext in this exchange. To be more specific, these soteriological differences surface in Calvin's refutation of Osiander as perceived implications of acknowledged differences in eucharistic and christological presuppositions.[2] The perspective on Calvin's refutation of Osiander gained by an appreciation of these various elements is indispensable as an indication of the remarkable complexity of Reformed-Lutheran polemic in the 1550s. This polemic finally involved not only sacramental but soteriological understandings of what it means to be united to Christ.

Andreas Osiander: Reformer, Theologian, Controversialist

Andreas Osiander (1496-1552), an early and active supporter of the Reformation in the Lutheran city of Nuremberg, served as instructor at an Augustinian house until 1548 when the Leipzig Interim took effect. A younger contemporary of Luther, Osiander was a signatory of the 1530 Augsburg Confession and the 1537 Smalcald Articles

---

Saxon Late Reformation: Gnesio-Lutherans vs. Philippists," *The Journal of Modern History* 49 (On Demand Supplement) (1977): D1289-D1305.

[2] To assess Osiander's fidelity to Luther's ideas or the viability of his views is well beyond the scope of this discussion. Instead, our interest here is in what Calvin's refutation of Osiander reveals about Calvin's own understanding of the *unio Christi-duplex gratia* relationship.

and, after leaving Nuremberg, served as a professor on the theological faculty at Königsberg where he was highly esteemed by Duke Albert.³ Much to the chagrin of his more accomplished colleagues, Osiander's appointment, despite his lack of much academic training, appears to have been due entirely to the Duke's regard for him. It was at Königsberg, in his inaugural disputation *De Lege et Evangelio*, that Osiander publicly attacked Melanchthon's forensic and imputative doctrine of justification by giving formal expression to views he had held for some time.⁴ This 1549 disputation served as the official catalyst for what would become a major controversy within Lutheranism, one which had a discernible

---

³ On Osiander and Duke Albert, see Jörg Rainer Fligge, "Herzog Albrecht von Preussen und der Osiandrismus," Ph.D. diss. (Friedrich-Wilhelms University, Bonn, 1972); idem, "Zur Interpretation der osiandrischen Theologie Herzog Albrechts v. Preussen," *ARG* 64 (1973): 245-80. Osiander's niece was married to Thomas Cranmer, and Osiandrian connections also have been argued for Cranmer's theology. See, e.g., Patricia Wilson-Kastner, "Andreas Osiander's Probable Influence on Thomas Cranmer's Eucharistic Theology," *SCJ* 14 (1983): 411-25. Calvin wrote to Cranmer about Osiander's theology (*Orig. Letters*, Parker Society, p. 712). On Osiander, see "Osiander, Andreas," s.v., by Gottfried Seebass in *OER* 3.184-5; David C. Steinmetz, *Reformers in the Wings* (Philadelphia: Fortress Press, 1971), 91-9; and Rainer Vinke, "Osiander, Andreas," in Peter G. Bietenholz and Thomas B. Deutscher, eds, *Contemporaries of Erasmus: A Biographical Register of the Renaissance and Reformation* (Toronto: University of Toronto Press, 1987), 3.35-6 (includes a portrait reproduction). See also Gottfried Seebass, *Das reformatorische Werk des Andreas Osiander* (Nuremberg, 1967); idem, ed., *Bibliographia Osiandrica: Bibliographie der gedruckten Schriften Andreas Osianders d. Ä, 1496-1552* (Nieuwkoop, 1971); idem, "Zwei Schreiben von Andreas Osiander," *Mitteilungen des Verens für Geschichte der Stadt Nürnberg* 57 (1970): 201-15; Martin Stupperich, *Osiander in Preussen, 1549-1552* (Berlin and New York: de Bruyter, 1973). Osiander has become a subject of intensive research in recent decades. The recent completion of a critical edition of his works, including correspondence, has greatly facilitated ongoing examination and reappraisal. See *Andreas Osiander d. Ä. Gesamtausgabe*, 10 vols, vols 1-6 ed. by Gerhard Müller; vols 7-10, commissioned by the Heidelberg Academy of Sciences, ed. by Gottfried Seebass (Gütersloh: Gütersloher Verlagshaus Mohn, 1975-1995), hereafter *GA*.

⁴ Osiander regularly claimed his views were not new to the 1550s but had been maintained since his days with Luther. Of course, Osiander's decision to air his views publicly at a *disputatio* is not an unusual one in the sixteenth century. Note in this connection the observation by George W. Forell, *Luther's Disputations as a Key to His Theology* (University of Iowa, privately printed); noted by Patricia Wilson-Kastner, "Osiander's Theology of Grace in the Perspective of the Influence of Augustine of Hippo," *SCJ* 10 (1979): 79, n. 28, regarding the importance of the university *disputatio* for the spread of Reformation ideas.

impact upon the subsequent era of confession formation in both Lutheran and Reformed traditions. Osiander's 1549 disputation was soon followed in 1550 with *De Iustificatione*[5] and *An Filius Dei fuerit Incarnandus*. The following year saw the publication of his important *De Unico Mediatore Iesu Christo et Iustificatione Fidei: Confessio Andreae Osiandri*. Following Hirsch, François Wendel describes Osiander as "of a disposition easily carried away to extremes," one who had "always confessed doctrines of a marked originality," an impression quite in keeping with the views of his contemporaries who recognized him as a gifted but volatile man, eloquent in speech but boisterous in temperament.[6] One theologian of the day regarded Osiander's attacks as but one more sign of the times, when it had become increasingly popular to attack Wittenberg.[7] As a result of the "Osiandrian controversy" within Lutheranism that continued beyond his death in 1552, his ideas were officially rejected in the 1577 Formula of Concord, Article III, "Of the Righteousness of Faith."

The Tradition Question: Luther and the Lutheran Response

The Struggle for Luther's Authority

In 1552, the year of his death, Osiander wrote a brief defense in response to an anonymous critic and curiously titled it "Against the Night-loving and Light-fleeing Crow, who with one sheet of paper has tried to arouse the false impression that my teaching of justification is contrary to that of the Blessed Doctor Luther" (*Wider den Liechtflüchtigen Nacht-Raben, der mit einem einigen Bogen Papiers ein falschen Schein zu machen, unterstanden hat, als solt mein Lehr, von*

---

[5] See the study by Gunter Zimmermann, "Die Thesen Osianders zur Disputation 'de iustificatione'," *Kerygma und Dogma* 33 (1987): 224-44.

[6] Wendel, *Calvin*, 235, citing from Emanuel Hirsch, *Die Theologie des Andreas Osiander* (Göttingen: Vandenhoeck and Ruprecht, 1919). If this is the case, at least to the extent described by Wendel, it is unclear why the Lutherans did not reject him early on. On Osiander's reputation, note, for example, that in an early, 1527 letter to Bucer Erasmus includes Osiander with the contentious Luther and Zwingli. See No. 1901, *Erasmi Epistolae* 7.231 in P. S. Allen and H. M. Allen, eds, *Opus Epistolarum Des. Erasmi Roterodami* (New York: Oxford University Press, 1928; rep. 1992). According to Beza, Calvin and Melanchthon called him "Pericles" (TT 1.lxxxv), which reflects well Osiander's reputation for combining eloquence with arrogance, and we know Calvin told Farel Osiander was "altogether mad" (see Gorham, *Gleanings*, 268).

[7] John À Lasco to Hardenberg, 25 August 1551, in Gorham, *Gleanings*, 272.

der Rechtfertigung des Glaubens, Doctor Luther's seligen Lehr entgegen und gantz widerwertig sein).[8] As it would be during the years of controversial turbulence within Lutheranism spanning Luther's death and Orthodoxy, an important factor in the Osiandrian controversy was the struggle for Luther's support issuing from the widespread recognition of his authority.[9]

This traditional-authoritorial element among those who proudly bore Luther's name became the chief motivation for much of the vituperation that was exchanged. But how this became such a struggle, and the reason this question was only resolved with great difficulty, evidently lies in obscurities in Luther himself. As Kolb has shown, one of the reasons the Formula of Concord failed to cite Luther as a secondary authority was the simple fact that his writings admitted of various, often diametrically opposed interpretations. "Luther's corpus," Kolb explains, "was simply unwieldy as a source of secondary authority for determining public teaching – not only because of its size, but also because of the diversity of issues and perspectives which determined his particular expression of doctrine in varying situations."[10] Consequently, as in the other intra-Lutheran disputes over adiaphora, original sin, and synergism, one side (the Osiandrians) used Luther to defend their doctrine of justification while the other side (the Philippists and Gnesio-Lutherans, most prominent among them various representatives of the Musculus and Flacius circles) used Luther to refute the opposition. This normally took place in the form of published collections of Luther quotations, carefully selected, circulated, and employed by Osiander in support of his views and by his opponents against him.[11] This intra-Lutheran

---

[8] Osiander, *Wider den lichtflüchtigen Nachtraben* (*GA* 10.398-413); cf. Henry P. Hamann, "The Righteousness of Faith Before God," in Robert D. Preus and Wilbert H. Rosin, eds, *A Contemporary Look at the Formula of Concord* (St. Louis: Concordia Publishing House, 1978), 139.

[9] Hirsch (*Die Theologie des Andreas Osiander*), drawing on a broad range of Osiander's texts, narrates the Osiandrian controversy in the context of the justification disputes of the sixteenth century, concluding that Osiander was close to Luther. Stupperich (*Osiander in Preussen*) highlights the differences between them.

[10] Kolb, *Martin Luther as Prophet, Teacher, and Hero*, 66; see also p. 66 nn. 72, 188.

[11] See Osiander, *Etliche schon Spruche von der Rechtfertigung des Glaubens Des Ehrwirdigen Hochgelerten D. Martini Luther...* (*GA* 9.582-601); idem, *Excerpta quaedam dictorum de iustificatione...* (*GA* 9.574-81); and idem, *Christlicher und Gru[e]ndtlicher bericht Von der Rechtfertigung des Glaubens Einwonung Gottes und Christi in vns... D. Martini Luthers... Johannis Brentzii... Urbani Regij....* For collections published by Osiander's opponents, see Bernhard Ziegler, *Zwo Predigten des Ehrwirdigen herren Doctoris Martini Lutheri...* (Leipzig: Hantzsch,

polemical use of Luther's works extended not only to published collections of citations, however, but also to newly-published exegetical works, such as the commentaries on Galatians by Heshusius, Selnecker, and Wigand, who summoned Luther's 1535 commentary against Osiander's reading.[12]

The Theology of the Lutheran Response

The controversy revolved specifically around Osiander's theology of justification by union with Christ in his divine justice or righteousness.[13] As Pelikan explains, the 1529 Marburg agreement

---

1551); two anonymous publications, *Drei Sermon D. Martini Lutheri, darin man spueren kan wie ein Herlicher Prophetischer Geist in dem manne gewesen ist,...* (Frankfurt/Oder: Eichorn, 1552) and *Christlicher und Gruendtlicher bericht, Von der Rechtfertigung des Glaubens, Einwonung Gottes und Christi in uns...* (n.p., n.d.), both noted in Robert Kolb, *For All the Saints: Changing Perceptions of Martyrdom and Sainthood in the Lutheran Reformation* (Macon: Mercer University Press, 1987), 131 n. 62. Musculus, or his circle, published *Drei Sermon D. Martini Lutheri darin man spu[e]ren kan wie ein Herlicher Prophetischer Geist...* (Frankfurt/Oder: Johann Eichorn, 1552); and Flacius's circle responded with *Tro[e]stliche Gegenspru[e]cht des Ernwirdigen Herren Doctoris Martini Lutheri und Matthie Jllyrici...* (Magdeburg: Rödinger, 1552). See Kolb, *Martin Luther as Prophet, Teacher, and Hero*, 66.

[12] Tilemann Heshusius, *Explicatio epistolae Pauli ad Galatas* (Helmstedt: Jacob Lucius, 1579), 109ᵛ, 270ʳ; Nikolaus Selnecker, *In omnes epistolas D. Pauli apostoli Commentarius plenissimus,...*, ed. Georg Selnecker (Leipzig: Jacob Apel, 1595), 386; Johannes Wigand, *In epistolam S. Pauli ad Galatas annotationes...* (Wittenberg: Johannes Crato, 1580), 110, 120. See Robert Kolb, "The Influence of Luther's Galatians Commentary of 1535 on Later Sixteenth-Century Lutheran Commentaries on Galatians," *ARG* 84 (1993), 167; see n. 41 where these references are found.

[13] For Osiander's theology, see Rainer Hauke, *Gott-Haben – um Gottes Willen: Andreas Osianders Theosisgedanke und die Diskussion um die Grundlagen der evangelisch verstandenen Rechtfertigung* (Frankfurt am Main: Peter Lang, 1999); idem, "Sola Dei iustitia. Die theozentrische Rechtfertigungslehre des Andreas Osiander (1498-1552): Eine misslungene Belehrung der forensischen Rchtfertigungslehre?," in Elke Axmacher and Klaus Schwarzwäller, eds, *Belehrter Glaube, Festschrift für Johannes Wirsching zum 65. Geburtstag* (Frankfurt, 1994), 101-32; Claus Bachmann, *Die Selbstherrlichkeit Gottes: Studien zur Theologie des Nürnberger Reformators Andreas Osiander* (Neukirchen-Vluyn: Neukirchener, 1996); Wilson-Kastner, "Andreas Osiander's Theology of Grace;" Heinz Scheible, "Melanchthon und Osiander über die Rechtfertigung," in Irene Dingel, et al., eds, *Reformation und Recht: Festgabe für Gottfried Seebass zum 65. Geburtstag* (Gütersloh: Christian Kaiser, Gütersloher Verl.-Haus, 2002), 161-75. From the perspective of the FC, see Hamann, "The Righteousness of Faith Before God," 137-62. Attention to Osiander's theology is coming increasingly

had proclaimed that "faith is our justification before God..." on account of which we are regarded as righteous, not for our own sake but "for the sake of his Son, in whom we believe and thereby receive and participate in the righteousness, life, and all blessings of his Son."[14] As Pelikan further notes, "It was this second emphasis [i.e., participation] that Osiander took as his own."[15] This notion of a union-participation in the divine justice or righteousness of Christ was the principal characteristic of justification in Osiander's theology.

---

from those who desire to defend him from caricature or to employ his ideas in the service of modern ecumenism, e.g., to reconcile Lutheranism with Rome by way of the East. See, in its most controversial embodiment, the so-called "Finnish school" of Luther research which revives in basic form an Osiandrian reading of Luther (though note the differences observed in Hauke, *Gott-Haben – um Gottes Willen*, 471-90). For the Finnish school see the work of its head, Tuomo Mannermaa, "In ipsa fide Christus adest," in *Der Im Glauben Gegenwärtige Christus: Rechtfertigung und Vergottung* (Hannover: Lutherisches Verlaghaus, 1989); idem, "Theosis as a Subject of Finnish Luther Research," *Pro Ecclesia* 4 (1995): 37-48; and the collection of essays in Carl Braaten and Robert Jenson, eds, *Union with Christ: The New Finnish Interpretation of Luther* (Grand Rapids: Eerdmans, 1998). For critical responses from within orthodox Lutheranism to this development, see, among others, John F. Brug, "Osiandrianism – Then and Now: Justification through Christ Dwelling in Us," Wisconsin Lutheran Seminary, 2001; idem, "The Lutheran-Catholic Statement of Justification," *Wisconsin Lutheran Quarterly* (Winter, 1984): 66-70; Carl Lawrenz, "On Justification: Osiander's Doctrine of the Indwelling Christ," in *No Other Gospel: Essays in Commemoration of the 400th Anniversary of the Formula of Concord* (Milwaukee: Northwestern Publishing House, 1980), 149-73. Note also the series of *WTJ* articles listed in Chapter 2, n. 63. See also the highly influential presentation by F. Bente, "The Osiandrian Controversy," in *ConcTrig*, 152-9, criticized by Wilson-Kastner as "informative but notoriously biased" ("Andreas Osiander's Theology of Grace," 71, n. 3). Others who seek to defend Osiander from Orthodoxy (in particular, the triumph of Melanchthon's forensicism) include Gunter Zimmermann, "Die Thesen Osianders zur Disputation 'de iustificatione',"; idem, "Calvins Auseinandersetzung mit Osianders Rechtfertigungslehre," *Kerygma und Dogma* 35 (1989): 236-56; and Stephen Strehle, "Imputatio iustitiae: Its Origin in Melanchthon, its Opposition in Osiander," *Theologische Zeitschrift* 50 (1994): 201-19; idem, *The Catholic Roots of the Protestant Gospel: Encounter between the Middle Ages and the Reformation* (SHCT 60; Leiden: E. J. Brill, 1995), 66-85.

[14] Osiander, *Report on the Marburg Colloquy* (Augsburg, 1529), 2v-3r, quoted in Jaroslav Pelikan, *The Christian Tradition: A History of the Development of Doctrine, Vol. 4: Reformation of Church and Dogma (1300-1700)* (Chicago and London: University of Chicago Press, 1984), 151.

[15] Pelikan, *Reformation of Church and Dogma (1300-1700)*, 151.

For the later Luther, and especially in the Melanchthonian formulation, however, it was a decidedly *alien* righteousness that was imputed when grasped by faith. But as Pelikan also observes, it was Luther's adoption of Jeremiah's words, "The Lord is our righteousness" (23:6), as the OT *locus classicus* for justification that became, in the meaning Osiander gave them, the center of controversy. Exactly how is Christ our righteousness? Should this justifying righteousness be understood forensically, as the imputation of Christ's alien righteousness, or quasi-ontologically, as participation in the righteousness belonging to Christ's divine nature? Melanchthon and nearly all Lutherans taught the former; Osiander, however, urged the latter. In a representative statement he explained: "If one asks what righteousness is, one must answer: Christ dwelling in us through faith is our righteousness according to his divinity, and the forgiveness of sins, which is not Christ himself, but is earned by Christ, is a preparation and cause of God's conferring on us his righteousness, which is God himself."[16] This doctrine of justification was tied to Osiander's peculiar teaching on the *imago Dei* in which he explained that the image in which Adam was created was specifically the image of the incarnate Christ.[17]

For Osiander, the distinction between justification and regeneration or sanctification upon which Melanchthon insisted did not even resemble the teaching of Luther. Luther, Osiander thought, "included the renewal of man in justification and understood it as a personal union with Christ."[18] The righteousness according to and on the basis of which we are justified, said Osiander, is indeed the righteousness of Christ. But, *contra* Melanchthon, it is not an imputed righteousness merely; rather, Christ, who lives in us by

---

[16] Osiander, quoted in Pelikan, *Reformation of Church and Dogma (1300-1700)*, 151; see the summary in *ConcTrig*, 152a-161b.

[17] Osiander develops this idea in *Disputatio de Iustificatione* (1550) and *Von dem einigen Mittler* (1551). Calvin's other interaction with Osiander in the 1559 *Institutes* is over this doctrine (see *Inst*. 2.12.4-7; OS 3.440-7). Barry E. Bryant ("Trinity and Hymnody: the Doctrine of the Trinity in the Hymns of Charles Wesley," Paper read at Conference on Trinitarian Theology, Institute of Systematic Theology, King's College, University of London, 26 September 1990, p. 5) claims Osiander's doctrine as the only precedent for Wesley's Trinitarian understanding of the *imago Dei*. On Osiander and Calvin on the *imago Dei*, see the insightful studies of Jelle Faber, "Imago Dei in Calvin: Calvin's Doctrine of Man as the Image of God by Virtue of Creation;" idem, "Imago Dei in Calvin: Calvin's Doctrine of Man as the Image of God in Connection with Sin and Restoration," in *Essays in Reformed Doctrine* (Neerlandia, Alberta, Canada: Inheritance Publications, 1990), 227-50 and 251-81, respectively.

[18] Steinmetz, *Reformers in the Wings*, 95.

faith and according to his divine nature, so fully justifies us by his grace that we become righteous ourselves.

It was not long before Osiander had stirred up heated reactions from his opponents. Taken as a whole, the theology of the Lutheran response consisted of two important elements: (1) a vigorous emphasis on objectivity over subjectivity in justification and salvation; and (2) a pattern of argument in which sanctification or believing good works is regularly rooted in justification or, alternatively, (justifying) "faith" or "imputation," in order to emphasize both the necessary distinction between forgiveness and transformation as well as their inseparability.

There was some variety among these responses, however. Osiander's prioritizing of the indwelling divine nature of Christ was countered by the Lutheran Francesco Stancaro who, like Lombard, argued the other extreme, i.e., that Christ is Mediator only in his human nature.[19] Other equally vigorous but more orthodox critics, representing the standard Lutheran response to Osiander, included Johann Brenz, Joachim Mörlin, Melanchthon, and Matthias Flacius Illyricus who each published extensively against Osiander.[20]

Opposing the elevation of divinity over humanity in Osiander's ontological understanding of justification, and in particular its tie to the language of 1 Cor 1:30, Melanchthon argues that Christ is not our righteousness "because the Son of the Eternal is righteous," but

---

[19] Calvin strongly opposed several elements in Stancaro's teaching but especially the relationship of Christ's divinity and humanity in justification. For Calvin and Stancaro, see Joseph Tylenda, "Christ the Mediator: Calvin Versus Stancaro," *CTJ* 7 (1972): 5-16; idem, "The Controversy on Christ the Mediator: Calvin's Second Reply to Stancaro," *CTJ* 8 (1973): 131-57. See Beza on Stancaro in *Correspondance* III, 86-9 (no. 167, "Bèze au Nom de la Compagnie a Gwalter," 27 February 1561).

[20] Johann Brenz, *Brentij und Osiandri meinung,...* (Magdeburg: Michael Lotther, 1553); Matthias Flacius Illyricus, *Beweisung, das Osiander helt und leret,...* (Magdeburg: Christian Rödinger, 1553); Joachim Mörlin, *Apolgia auff vermeinte Widerlegung des Osiandrischen Schwermers in Preussen,...* (n.p.: n.p., ca. 1552). For Melanchthon, see responses in CR 8.579-87, CR 7.782-4, and *Antwort auff das Buch Herrn Andreae Osiandri von der Rechtfertigung des Menschen* (1552) in Robert Stupperich, ed., *Melanchthons Werke in Auswahl* (*MWA*) (C. Bertelsmann Verlag, 1955), 6.452-61, besides brief responses in his 1555 *Loci Communes*, the 1552 Saxon Confession, and other correspondence. For a study, see Heinz Scheible, "Melanchthon und Osiander über die Rechtfertigung," in Irene Dingel, et al., eds, *Reformation und Recht* (for Gottfried Seebass; Gütersloh: Kaiser Gütersloher Verl.-Haus, 2002), 161-75.

because of the merit of his obedience which is credited to us.[21] Christ is "our righteousness, sanctification, and redemption, namely through his merit, his presence, and his strong activity in us."[22]

Melanchthon understood the issue at the heart of Osiander's theology to be related to the wider question whether or not one is justified through the good works of Christian obedience. Forgiveness of sins, insists Melanchthon, comes "not on account of any infused love or newness, nor on account of the divine activities in us in this life, of which Osiander speaks in his *iustitia essentiali*, but on account of the obedience and merits of Christ, who is the Mediator and Reconciler."[23] In the background here is Melanchthon's ongoing opposition to the antinomianism of Agricola which, at the risk of oversimplification, may be understood as representing the other extreme (opposite Osiander) of sixteenth-century responses to the theological problem of the necessity of good works for justified believers. For Agricola, the solution was to discard the necessity altogether, to substitute "gospel" completely for "law", while Melanchthon repeatedly defended the necessity of obedience (or the virtues of love and hope) as the fruit of justifying faith.[24] In Osiander's turn to the *in nobis* subject rather than the *extra nos* object, Melanchthon, as well as Flacius and Mörlin, perceived a threat to the comfort of believing consciences posed by the confusion of renewal with justification. Osiander's doctrine, Melanchthon explains, is a "legal teaching," one which "deprives us of comfort." For, "if being justified depended on doing what is right, conscience would be without comfort."[25]

Theologically, Melanchthon's specific concern, again a common one for the reformers, was to defend against both Agricola and Osiander a real distinction of justification from sanctification without thereby sacrificing their unity. One way of accomplishing this was through an emphasis on their simultaneity. Using a popular metaphor Melanchthon explains "the world grows bright and warm with the sun; nevertheless, light and warmth are in themselves

---

[21] Melanchthon, CR 12.408-9, thesis 34: "Ita necesse est discerni iusticiam essentialem, quae est in filio, a iusticia nobis communicata per imputationem et effectionem…"

[22] Melanchthon, CR 8.612.

[23] Melanchthon, *Loci Comm.* (1555) XIV.Q3 (ET, 179). When citing from the 1555 LC I will use *Melanchthon on Christian Doctrine: Loci Communes 1555*, trans. and ed. by Clyde L. Manschreck (New York: Oxford University Press, 1965), abbreviated ET.

[24] See Kolb, *Law and Gospel*, for a full discussion of Melanchthon's engagement with Agricola.

[25] Melanchthon, *Loci Comm.* (1555) XIII (ET, 169).

different."[26] In Melanchthon's thought, the "sunlight" is justifying faith; the "warmth" is obedience or virtue, its necessary effect. The "new obedience" of the gospel, in other words, must begin "because we are justified and our sins are annulled, and with that the new and eternal life actually begins in us, which is a new light and obedience toward God."[27]

Despite the constant flow of literature confusion and disagreement persisted. Article III of the 1577 Formula of Concord was designed to clarify the authentic Lutheran position over against Osiander (and Stancarus). Article III does not mention Osiander explicitly but clearly has his theology in view. In connection with this confusion and in support of the Formula's statement, Jacob Andreae preached a sermon refuting Osiander as part of a series devoted to clarifying the issues of contemporary controversy.[28] Andreae notes the special importance to the dispute of the passages in Jeremiah and Daniel in the Old Testament and 1 Cor 1:30 in the New Testament where God or Christ is said to *be* the righteousness of believers. Because the great name of Yahweh must refer to the divine essence, and it is he who is said to be our righteousness, the righteousness of justification, Osiander claims, must come to us in Christ according to his divine nature alone.[29] But, Andreae objects, the Apostle teaches that in justification the Father looks to the Son not in his divinity but as the one "who died," in which phrase all of his obedience to the Law is included. This meritorious obedience,

---

[26] Melanchthon, CR 24.815. Cf. CR 14.86 and *Loci Comm.* (1555) XIII (ET, 166): "And it is true... that where true faith is, there at the same time are many virtues. However, they are not meritorious; they are not *causae iustificationis*; they are not reasons why God accepts us. They result from faith... we receive grace and gift. As the sun has both light and the power to warm, and the two cannot be separated, so wherever there is true faith, a recognition of God's mercy, there also is love, invocation of God, and hope, and a will which willingly subjects itself to God and is obedient. These accompany faith as light and heat accompany a fire."

[27] Melanchthon, CR 13.1342: "Hanc novam et incoatam obedientiam esse necessarium manifestum est, quia ideo iustificamur, et peccatum ideo tollitur, ut vere in nobis incoeter nova et aeterna vita, quae est nova lux, et obedientia erga Deum." See further, on the simultaneity of justification and sanctification in terms of justifying faith, CR 21.442 and CR 28.401.

[28] For an able, short history and analysis of the context of Andreae's *Six Christian Sermons* of 1573, as well as translations of the sermons themselves, see Robert Kolb, *Andreae and the Formula of Concord: Six Sermons on the Way to Lutheran Unity* (St. Louis: Concordia Publishing House, 1977), 9-57. I cite from Kolb's translation.

[29] Andreae, *Sermon on the Righteousness of Faith*, 69-70.

credited to us, is our righteousness.[30] Again in the Formula's statement and in other contemporary texts, the Lutheran response to Osiander takes the form of a greater emphasis on the objectivity of justification and salvation in opposition to the perceived subjectivity of Osiander's doctrine.[31]

Calvin's Response

Calvin, faithful to his commitment to a methodological "division of labor," did not publish a refutation of Osiander's teaching in relevant portions of his commentaries published in the 1550s; instead, he reserved his full response for the 1559 edition of the *Institutes*.[32] Whereas Calvin's engagement with his opponents only occasionally affected substantially the development or expansion of his *Institutes*, the dispute with Osiander is one of the exceptions. Calvin spent page after page in his response, critiquing Osiander's concept of union with considerable detail and dealing at length with what he perceived as the implications of Osiander's theology.[33]

---

[30] Andreae, *Sermon on the Righteousness of Faith*, 71-7.

[31] In this connection the charge of Osiandrianism made by eighteenth-century opponents of Lutheran Pietism is noteworthy. Matthew E. Thompson ("Walther's Anti-Conventical Position: Its Roots in Pietism and Contemporary Application," *Lutheran Synod Quarterly* 42 [2002]: 270) notes that Lutheran theologians from Wittenberg, Leipzig (Benedikt Carpzov), and Greifswald (Johann Friedrich Mayer) "all accused Pietism of Platonism, a Schwaermer spirit, Osiandrianism (mixing Sanctification and Justification), demeaning the efficaciousness of the Word, separating the Word and the Spirit, a faulty theology of regeneration, a legalistic concept of sanctification, and chiliasm."

[32] See Muller, *Unaccommodated Calvin*, 114-15., 152, 237 n. 110, 237-8 n. 116. For Calvin and Osiander, see, among many other brief studies, Ronald Feenstra, "Calvin versus Osiander on Justification," Paper submitted to Seminar on Calvin's *Institutes* conducted by Ford Lewis Battles, Grand Rapids: Calvin Theological Seminary, 1978; Hauke, *Gott-Haben – um Gottes Willen*, 310-20; Kolfhaus, *Christusgemeinschaft*, 59-64; Niesel, *Theology of Calvin*, 133ff.; idem, "Calvin wider Osianders Rechtfertigungslehre," *Zeitschrift für Kirchengeschichte* 46 (1927): 410-30; Stadtland, *Rechtfertigung und Heiligung bei Calvin*, 96-106; Venema, "The Twofold Nature of the Gospel in Calvin's Theology," 223-36; James Weis, "Calvin Versus Osiander on Justification," *The Springfielder* 29 (Autumn 1965): 31-47; Wendel, *Calvin*, 235-7, 258-60; Clive S. Chin, "*Unio Mystica* and *Imitatio Christi*: The Two-Dimensional Nature of John Calvin's Spirituality," PhD diss. (Dallas Theological Seminary, 2002), 254-71; Gunter Zimmermann, "Calvins Auseinandersetzung mit Osianders Rechtfertigungslehre."

[33] Calvin's fullest refutation of Osiander's doctrine of justification is found in *Inst.* (1559) 3.11.5-12.

Exactly why he would go to such great lengths will become clearer below.

Preliminary Observations

INTERPRETATIONS

The theology of Calvin's critique is best appreciated against the background of the Lutheran response just summarized. Despite scholarly agreement over the basic theological contours of his response, there is some disagreement regarding the fundamental concern Calvin has with Osiander. Adopting a helpful, comprehensive perspective, Zimmermann recognizes five fundamental ideas Calvin opposes: (1) Osiander's characterization of union with Christ; (2) his conjunction of justification and sanctification; (3) the identification of Christ and faith; (4) his exaggeration of the "already" and his diminution of the "not yet" in the Christian's present situation; and (5) his idea of justification exclusively by Christ's divine nature.[34] Zimmermann's summary is generally accurate and provides a reliable entrance into Calvin's refutation. For his part, Zimmermann is convinced Calvin misinterprets Osiander, and his study is designed to demonstrate this misinterpretation.

At a more specific level, scholarship is divided over the theological heart of Calvin's objection. Is the sovereignty of grace Calvin's basic disagreement with Osiander, crystallized in the question whether or not justification is the basis of sanctification, as Berkouwer and Smedes suggest?[35] Or is Calvin's principal objection, as Wendel thinks, Osiander's mixing of the divine and human and the resulting deification of man?[36] Or, alternatively, is Calvin's objection rooted not in questions of sovereignty or mixing of divinity and humanity but in his own Mediator-centric theology, as Niesel and Pannenberg understand it?[37] Or, as yet another option, is

---

[34] Zimmermann, "Calvins Auseinandersetzung mit Osianders Rechtfertigungslehre."

[35] G. C. Berkouwer, *Faith and Justification* (trans. Lewis B. Smedes; Grand Rapids: Eerdmans, 1954), 16, 100; Lewis Smedes, *All Things Made New* (Grand Rapids: Eerdmans, 1970), 172. Feenstra notes ("Calvin versus Osiander on Justification," n. 19) that Smedes' agreement with Berkouwer here is likely connected to his serving as Berkouwer's translator for *Faith and Justification*, even though Smedes does not cite Berkouwer.

[36] Wendel, *Calvin*, 259.

[37] Niesel, *Theology of Calvin*, 133-34, 137; cf. Wolfhart Pannenberg, *Jesus – God and Man* (2nd ed.; trans. Lewis Wilckens and Duane Priebe; Philadelphia: Westminster Press, 1977), 222.

Feenstra correct that, while relevant, none of these truly penetrates to the heart of Calvin's critique? For Feenstra, the principal issue is that of *assurance* – or rather, the destruction of it – in Osiander's confusion of justification and sanctification.[38] We will return to these proposals at the close of this chapter.

THE THEOLOGY OF CALVIN'S RESPONSE: A SUMMARY

Though seldom noted, Calvin's refutation of Osiander's doctrine of justification belongs to an important series of expansions introduced in the 1559 *Institutes*. But this delayed response (Osiander died in 1552) should not be misunderstood as indicating a lack of interest on Calvin's part. By 1559 he had already corresponded about the Osiander problem extensively with inquirers, addressed Osiander's theology within his refutations of Westphal, and even supplied a somewhat more formal, albeit brief critique of his views.[39] At the time, Calvin thought his *"brevis admonitio"* would be sufficient, and explained he did not have the time to write at length, nor did he think a lengthy reply particularly useful.[40] The length of the 1559 refutation indicates he must have had a dramatic change of heart.

Moreover, this new, 1559 material on Osiander – which compared to other 1559 additions to the *Institutio* is rather lengthy – should be associated with other revisions carried out in the 1550s which enriched specifically Calvin's teaching on the Holy Spirit. In particular, the emphasis on the work of the Spirit as the *vinculum* or *coniunctio* of union with Christ in the Osiander refutation must not be divorced from (1) Calvin's introduction of an opening discussion of the Spirit (and union) in Book 3 (3.1.1); (2) the ongoing polemic with Westphal and the Lutherans over his doctrine of a true but "spiritual" communion with Christ in the Supper; and (3) the extensive revision in 1556 of his commentary on Romans 8, a chapter devoted to the work of the Spirit. There is a rich intertextuality here that signals the importance of the 1550s for Calvin's doctrine of Spirit-faith union with Christ, and that highlights also the necessity

---

[38] Feenstra, "Calvin versus Osiander on justification." Feenstra interacts with the opinions of Berkouwer, Wendel, Smedes, Weis, Niesel, and Pannenberg.

[39] See Calvin, "Contra Osiandrum," CO 10.165-7. An English translation of this brief refutation is available in *Calvin's Ecclesiastical Advice* (trans. Mary Beaty and Benjamin W. Farley; Edinburgh: T. & T. Clark, 1991), 32-4. Peter and Gilmont note (BC 2.581) that Hermann Vecheld of Erfurt wrote to Calvin on 4 May 1555 to encourage Calvin to respond to Osiander because Osiander could not accept his view on the Supper (CO 15.598-600).

[40] CO 10.167: "Haec brevis admonitio sanis et modestis lectoribus, ut spero, contra Osiandri praestigias muniendis sufficiet. Neque enim longum volumen scribere nunc vacat, nec expedire iudico." Cf. *Calvin's Ecclesiastical Advice*, 33-4.

of keeping this intertextuality, and the history behind it, clearly in view.[41]

In his refutation Calvin's invective is often sharp. Taking issue with Osiander's use of the OT promise that Yahweh will be our righteousness, Calvin replies to Osiander, a professor of Hebrew, that "anyone moderately versed in the Hebrew language, provided he has a sober brain, is not ignorant of the fact..." that justification is legal pardoning.[42] Indeed, as our knowledge of sixteenth-century polemic leads us to expect, Calvin also often does not tell the whole story. For instance, Calvin sharply criticizes Osiander's decision, in the exegesis of Isa 53:11, to take צדק in the active sense. Calvin conveniently fails to mention, however, that he had argued, in his 1559 commentary on the passage, that the verb "may be taken either in an active or passive sense, as denoting either 'the knowledge of him' or 'his knowledge'," and that, "in whichever of these senses it is taken, we will easily understand the Prophet's meaning..." It is most interesting, and rather ironic, that the second edition of Calvin's Isaiah commentary, revised and expanded by his own hand, appeared in the same year in which he published this criticism of Osiander.[43]

---

[41] But note that I am not arguing for the introduction of wholly new ideas, only clarification and enrichment of concepts already present. As I will show, Calvin's theological response to Osiander was expressed in near-exact form as early as 1539.

[42] Calvin, *Inst.* (1559) 3.11.11; OS 4.193 (LCC 20.738): "Nec vero quisquam mediocriter in lingua Hebraica versatus (modo idem sedato sit cerebro) inde ortam esse phrasin hanc ignorat, deinde quorsum tendat et quid valeat." See Peter Matheson, *The Rhetoric of the Reformation* (Edinburgh: T. & T. Clark, 1998), 157-214, on the dynamics of sixteenth-century polemic.

[43] Cf. *Inst.* (1559) 3.11.8 with *Comm. in Isaiam* 53:11 (CO 37.264): "Potest (fateor) hic tam active quam passive legi dictio צדק, id est, cognitio vel scientia. Quocunque modo accipiatur, facile prophetae mentem tenebimus..." (cf. CTS, 3.127). Calvin did not write the first edition of the commentary himself, but he did read and correct for publication the final version of the lecture notes recorded by Nicholas des Gallars (Gallasius). The Latin edition that appeared in 1551 was greatly revised and expanded by Calvin for publication in 1559. The dedication to Queen Elizabeth is dated 15 January 1559, retaining the earlier (1551) dedication to Edward VI who had died in 1553. The 1559 Latin text is accessible in CO 36.19-37.454. For a brief history and description of the Isaiah commentaries, see BC 2.696-700; and De Greef, *The Writings of John Calvin*, 101-4. Peter Wilcox ("'The Restoration of the Church' in Calvin's 'Commentaries on Isaiah the Prophet,'" *ARG* 85 [1994]: 68-95) compares the two editions. On Calvin's role in the production of his OT commentaries, see T. H. L. Parker, *Calvin's Old Testament Commentaries* (Edinburgh: T. & T. Clark, 1986), 23-9, and

Similarly, Calvin's objection to Osiander's identification of the redeeming Yahweh of the Old Testament with the divinity of Christ is less than consistent. John Michael Owen argues for parallels between elements in Calvin's response to Osiander and the Christology of the 1560 *Scots Confession*. In both there is an emphasis on the importance of the humanity of Jesus as the incarnation of the wisdom and righteousness of God, employing the biblical titles "Angel of the Great Counsel" and the "just seed of David." Calvin takes issue with Osiander's identification of the promise respecting "Jehovah our Righteousness" with the divinity of Christ, but in fact Calvin, in a 1559 modification of a 1539 passage designed to demonstrate the divinity of Christ, refers all of the names listed in Isa 9:6 to Christ's *divinity*, and then ties this verse to Jer 23:5-6 ("Yahweh our Righteousness"):

> ... [T]here is no doubt that he is now called "Mighty God" for the same reason as he was called "Immanuel" a little earlier. Yet nothing clearer could be looked for than the place in Jeremiah that this is to be the name by which the shoot of David will be called, "Jehovah our Righteousness". For, since the Jews further teach that other names of God are nothing but titles, but that this one alone which they speak of as ineffable, is a substantive to express his essence, we infer that the only Son is the eternal God who elsewhere declares that he will not give his glory to another.[44]

Again, as in his Isaiah commentary, it is in the same year he publishes his criticism of Osiander that he also introduces a statement (actually an expansion of an earlier statement) that seems to contradict his point of criticism.

The more important unspoken issue, however, is Calvin's near-silence on the apparent affinity of his own theology of union with Christ with Osiander's, an affinity recognized by some of Calvin's sharpest critics but only hinted at in Calvin's refutation. Calvin does

---

p. 25 for Parker's translation of Calvin's letter to Dryander (CO 13.536) regarding his corrections of des Gallars' text.

[44] Calvin, *Inst.* (1559) 1.13.9; OS 3.120-1 (LCC 20.132): "Quare dubium non est quin eadem ratione Deus fortis nunc vocetur, qua paulo ante Immanuel. Nihil autem dilucidius Ieremiae loco quaeri potest, hoc fore nomen quo vocabitur germen Davidis, Iehovah iustitia nostra. Nam quum doceant ipsi Iudaei ultro alia Dei nomina nihil quam epitheta esse, hoc solum quod ineffabile dicunt, esse substantivum ad exprimendam eius essentiam: colligimus Filium unicum esse Deum et aeternum, qui alibi pronuntiat se gloriam suam non daturum alteri." The passage is noted on p. 315 in John Michael Owen, "The Angel of the Great Counsel of God and the Christology of the *Scots Confession* of 1560," *SJT* 55.3 (2002): 303-24, in connection with Calvin on the OT foundations of Christology.

state that he agrees with Osiander on the importance of union with Christ for justification,[45] but does not note any further areas of agreement. In fact there are other important areas, and when appreciated they serve to clarify the specific character of Calvin's objection to Osiander's formulations.[46]

In his controversial *Disputationes*, for example, Osiander stated that "He justifies no one whom he does not also vivify. Likewise, he vivifies no one whom he does not at the same time (*simul*) justify"[47] – a point, already shown in connection with his Romans commentary, that Calvin insists upon repeatedly from his earliest publications. Furthermore, the idea of justification is for Osiander intimately related and inextricably joined to the idea of union with Christ. In the centrality of union with Christ for justification, and in the consequential simultaneity of forensic and transformative elements of salvation as a consequence of this union, Calvin and Osiander agree. Indeed, it was especially this insistence on a simultaneity rooted in union that had been the precise intent of Calvin's *unio Christi-duplex gratia* formula and that had become his characteristic response to the charge of a legal fiction. This area of agreement is also significant, however, inasmuch as Osiander's idea of a simultaneity grounded in union was set opposite the perceived one-sidedness of Melanchthon's forensic doctrine, and, as already observed, it is the relationship of this complex of ideas that distinguished Calvin's from Melanchthon's understanding of salvation as well.

Recognized by some, this apparent affinity with Osiander became a focus of Lutheran polemic against Calvin. In the course of his exchanges with Westphal and Heshusius, Calvin complained of this association, and he took the opportunity to distance himself from one he was convinced "despised" the human, humiliated Christ.

---

[45] Calvin, *Inst.* (1559) 3.11.5; OS 4.186 (LCC 20.730).
[46] Keller notes (*Calvin Mystique*, 137-8) that "La raison de [Calvin's] intérêt pour le Réformateur de Nuremberg et de Königsberg est claire: c'est que sa propre position est dangereusement proche de celle d'Osiander." He fails, however, to account for this in his interpretation which concludes that Calvin's use of *substantia* confused matters when he objected to Osiander's doctrine of a substantial justification. While confusion certainly existed, Keller overlooks the real nature of Calvin's objection which lies, as will be argued here, in the deeper structures of Osiander's Lutheran Christology and sacramentology.
[47] Osiander, *GA* 9.428: "Nihil enim iustificat, quod non et vivificet. Nihilque vicissim vivificat, quod non simul etiam iustificet." See Hauke, *Gott-Haben – um Gottes Willen*, 132-6, for a summary view of the 1551 disputation.

What shall I say in regard to antiquity? It is certain that all ancient writers, for five centuries downwards from the Apostles, with one consent support our view. Here they taint us with the manure of *their own Osiander, as if we had any kind of affinity with him.* Doubtless that Osiander, in his insane pride, *despised a humiliated Christ*, what is that to us, whose piety is too well known to be defamed by such vile falsehoods?[48]

Moreover I say in my *Institutes*, "I am not satisfied with those who, when they would show the mode of communion, teach that we are made partakers of the Spirit of Christ, omitting all mention of the flesh and blood: as if it were said to no purpose, 'My flesh is meat indeed,' etc." This is followed by a lengthened explanation of the subject. Something, too, had been said on it previously. In the Second Book I had refuted, as I suppose, with no less perspicuity than care, the fiction of *Osiander, which* [Heshusius] *falsely accuses me with following.* Osiander imagined that righteousness is conferred on us by the Deity of Christ. *I showed, on the contrary, that salvation and life are to be sought from the flesh of Christ in which he sanctified himself, and in which he consecrates Baptism and the Supper. It also will be seen there how completely I have disposed of his dream of essential righteousness.* I have received the same return from Heshusius that he made to his preceptor Melanchthon…[49]

---

[48] Calvin, *Ultima Admonitio*, CO 9.246 (TT 2.488): "Quid de tota antiquitate dicam? constat enim vetustos omnes scriptores, qui totis quinque saeculis post apostolos vixerunt, uno ore nobis patrocinari. Et hic nobis Osiandri sui stercora aspergunt: quasi ulla unquam inter nos affinitas fuerit. Contempserit sane Osiander pro suo vesano fastu humiliatum Christum, quid hoc ad nos? Quorum pietas notior est, quam ut hac mendaciorum labe foedari queat. Quin optimo iure in eorum capita inanem istum garritum retorqueo: quia Christum humiliatum negant, eos totam salutis nostrae summam exstinguere, et impie abolere incomparabile divini in nos amoris pignus."

[49] Calvin, *De vera participatione*, CO 9.504-5 (*Calvin: Theological Treatises*, 308): "Institutionis porro haec verba sunt: Non satisfacere mihi eos, qui dum communicationis modum ostendere volunt, nos docent spiritus Christi esse participes, praeterita carnis et sanguinis mentione. Quasi de nihilo dictum foret: Caro mea vere est cibus: et quae sequuntur. Prolixa enim huius rei explicatio sequitur et iam ante aliquid dictum fuerat. Libro autem secundo non minore, ut existimo, perspicuitate quam diligentia Osiandri commentum refutaverum: cuius me subscriptorem esse mentitur. Imaginatus est Osiander conferri nobis iustitiam a deitate Christi. Ostendi contra, salutem et vitam a Christi carne petendam esse, in qua se ipsum sanctificavit, et in qua baptismum et coenam nobis consecrat. Alterum quoque somnium de essentiali iustitia quam probe discusserim illic apparet. Merces ab Heshusio mihi refertur, qualem praeceptori suo Melanchthoni rependit."

But since in his complaint Calvin evidently has more than one person in view (note the plural), it may seem unclear who else besides Westphal (and Heshusius) had made this association. If one relies only on the text of Calvin's response, usually cited with a short title, then the answer remains unclear, but if the sixteenth-century editions both of Westphal's pamphlet and of Calvin's response are examined one learns more. Prefaced by Westphal, a volume was published in 1557 the contents of which included (1) a copy of the *Confessio fidei de eucharistiae sacramento* and (2) a substantial collection of supporting letters from Saxon ministers. It is in these letters of the *Magdeburgenses*, some of which are as long as Westphal's opening statement, where the Calvin-Osiander association is also made.[50] This published collection was used by Calvin and explains sufficiently his plural reference, and any remaining doubts are removed when the subtitle of Calvin's *Ultima Admonitio* is read: *"...Refutantur etiam hoc scripto superbae Magdeburgensium et aliorum censurae, quibus caelum et terram obruere conati sunt."*[51] One highly plausible reason, therefore, for the lengths to which Calvin dealt with Osiander may simply have been his desire to distance himself as much as possible from one almost universally regarded as a heretic.

The association did not die, however, either with Osiander in 1552 or Calvin in 1564. Beza, writing against Flacius and dealing with the Osiander legacy, was able to claim that, despite Lutheran attempts to associate Calvin with Osiander's teachings, "Calvin has detected, refuted, and condemned the illusions [of Osiander] more clearly and solidly than anyone else."[52] Elsewhere, in his biography of Calvin, Beza explains the circumstances of the Calvin-Osiander exchange in order to defend his predecessor:

> At this time also, that unhappy dispute concerning the Lord's Supper again crept in, Osiander, a man of haughty and extravagant temper, stirring up the smothered embers. It certainly was not Calvin's fault that this fire was not extinguished... But the

---

[50] *Confessio fidei ministrorum Saxoniae inferioris...* Westphal had accused Calvin of not being fair to this confession, and includes it to reinforce the point. See De Greef, *The Writings of John Calvin*, 193.
[51] The full title of Calvin's *Ultima Admonitio* is included, with a reproduction of the title page and a useful history, in BC 2.652-7. See also the letter of Beza to Calvin regarding the response to the Magdeburgeois, in Bèze, *Correspondance* 2.77.
[52] Beza, *TractTh*. 1.330.

intemperance of that man, whom both Calvin and Melanchthon surnamed Pericles, left no room for their sound advice.[53]

The Osiander question took on grand political dimensions late in Calvin's life and in Beza's career as the conflict over "Crypto-Calvinism" raised visibly the question of Lutheran-Reformed compatibility. With the Reformed churches in Saxony struggling to retain their Reformed identity in the face of a constantly-shifting political situation (will they be allowed to teach and worship *as Reformed*?), the need for Beza to explain just who was to blame for the Osiandrian conflict was strong, as was the need to identify where the Reformed and Lutheran forms of reformation identity were similar and dissimilar.[54]

The contours of Calvin's refutation are familiar, and are marked by strong statements on the necessity of distinguishing justification from transformation and of affirming that Christ is Mediator according to both natures. At the outset, Calvin criticizes Osiander's theory as a *monstrum nescio quod essentialis iustitiae* (strange monster of essential righteousness)[55] because it deprives believers of their experience of grace. In this charge Calvin repeats the general criticism of the reformers against Rome, as well as both Reformed and Lutheran theologians against Osiander. But Osiander's conception is also, Calvin states, the speculative fruit of "mere feeble curiosity."[56] Calvin agrees with Osiander that the believer's union

---

[53] Beza, *Life of Calvin*, TT 1.lxxxv.
[54] On the history of the complicated situation in Calvinist Germany, see especially the work of Heinz Schilling, *Konfessionskonflikt und Staatsbilding* (Gütersloh, 1981); idem, *Religion, Political Culture and the Emergence of Early Modern Society: Essays in German and Dutch History* (Leiden: E. J. Brill, 1992), 205-45 ("Confessionalization in the Empire: Religious and Societal Change in Germany Between 1555 and 1620"); and, idem, "Confessional Europe," in Thomas A. Brady, Jr., et al., eds, *Handbook of European History, 1400-1600*, vol. 2, *Late Middle Ages, Renaissance, and Reformation: Visions, Programs, and Outcomes* (Leiden: E. J. Brill, 1995), 641-81. See also R. Po-Chia Hsia, *Social Discipline in the Reformation: Central Europe 1550-1750* (London and New York: Routledge, 1989), esp. pp. 26-38, 53-185.
[55] Calvin, *Inst*. (1559) 3.11.5; OS 4.185 (LCC 20.730). Cf. his French *Institution* (Geneva: Conrad Badius, 1561), 242ᵛ: "Mais pource qu' Osiander a introduit de nostre temps *un mostre ie ne scay quell de iustice essencielle*..." Italics mine.
[56] Fligge treats at some length the speculative strain in Osiander's theology. See Fligge, "Herzog Albrecht von Preussen und der Osiandrismus"; and, idem, "Zur Interpretation der osiandrischen Theologie Herzog Albrechts v. Preussen." As noted by Roland M. Frye ("Calvin's Theological Use of Figurative Language," in Timothy George, ed., *John Calvin and the Church: A Prism of Reform*

Applied Christology

with Christ and Christ's union with believers is central to a proper understanding of justification. But Osiander has misunderstood this union, believing it to be "essential" rather than spiritual. He does not, in short, observe the *vinculum* ("bond") of union with Christ, the Holy Spirit: "Now it is easy for us to resolve all his difficulties. For we hold ourselves to be united with Christ by the secret power of his Spirit."[57]

1 Corinthians 1:30 as Exegetical Epicenter

OSIANDER'S USE OF 1 CORINTHIANS 1:30

As the exegetical epicenter of the controversy, the Apostle's language in 1 Cor 1:30 became the biblical *locus classicus* of both Osiander's formulation and Calvin's reply. This was the case at least from the early 1550s. In his highly controversial *Disputatio*, for example, in which he laid out his theology of justification, Osiander said of Christ *"ipse enim factus est nobis a Deo sapientia, iustitia, sanctificatio et redemptio,"* quoting the words of this verse.[58] Here Osiander had adopted for the defense of his theology a strain of Luther's occasional language, often found in sermons, in which Christ was said to be our righteousness according to Old Testament promise. In fact, according to Bizer, in Luther's own transitional period Paul's statement in 1 Cor 1:30 aided him in understanding the righteousness of God in Rom 1:17.[59]

[Louisville: Westminster/John Knox, 1990], 189, n. 2), Cicero, *De finibus* 5.18.49 (Loeb, p. 451), also warns against "fruitless curiosity."

[57] Calvin, *Inst.* (1559) 3.11.5; OS 4.185 (LCC 20.730): "Multa quidem Scripturae testimonia accumulat, quibus Christum probet unum esse nobiscum, et nos vicissim cum ipso, quod probatione non indiget: sed quia non observat huius unitatis vinculum, seipsum illaqueat. Nobis vero omnes eius nodos expedire facile est, qui tenemus nos cum Christo uniri arcana Spiritus eius virtute." Cf. 3.11.10 (OS 4.192) where Calvin says Osiander spurns "hac spirituali coniunctione."

[58] Osiander, *Disputatio de Iustificatione/Eine Disputation von der Rechtfertigung*, proposition no. 18 (GA 9.430/431). The German reads, "Dan er ist uns worden zur weisheit von Gott und zur gerechtigkeit, zur heiligung und zur erlösung." Cf. also Osiander, *Disputatio de Lege et Evangelio*, proposition nos. 41 (GA 9.512) and 44 (GA 9.513).

[59] Ernst Bizer, *Fides ex Auditu: Eine Untersuchung über die Entdeckung der Gerechtigkeit Gottes durch Martin Luther* (2nd ed.; Neukirchen: Neukirchner Verlag, 1961), 115ff.

Employing not only this verse but also the OT background recognized by Luther in Jeremiah and Daniel,[60] Osiander regularly appealed to 1 Cor 1:30 in defense of his thesis that it is God himself, Christ in his divine nature, who is the righteousness of justification.[61] Publications from the period indicate that Lutheran opposition to Osiander recognized the significance of this verse to the dispute and summoned the Fathers to make their case. In his published comment on 1 Corinthians, for example, Cyriakus Spangenberg combined quotations of Cyril and Hilary to criticize the notion that God dwells in us by the divine nature. Augustine on the righteousness of justification in Rom 3 served equally well to show that this is not the

---

[60] See, e.g., Osiander, *Von Dem Neu Gebornen Abgott* (GA 9.361-2), where Jer. 23:6 and 1 Cor. 1:30 are brought together: "Als wan er uns durch seinen antichrist wil verfüren, der glaub allein rechtfertige nicht, sonder es mussen gute werck darbey sein, so disputir nicht mit im, welchs gute werck sein, wie, wan und warumb man sie thun musse oder ob sie vor oder nach der rechtfertigung kommen, sonder sprich: *Christus ist unser gerechtigkeit, Jeremie 23[6], 1. Cor 1[30]*, der is in uns, Johan. 17[23], und ist darumb in unser fleisch kommen, das uns sein gerechtigkeit zugerechnet werd, und welcher geist das nicht bekennet, der ist des antichrist geist." Italics mine. For the same combination, see *GA* 9.529, 695; 10.169/170, 205/206 et al. For examples of how Osiander appeals to Luther's works for this combination see his collection of Luther citations, *Etliche Schöne Sprüche* (GA 9.585-6, where the references are to sermons found in WA 2, S. 44.39-45.3 and WA 2, S. 145.9-14, respectively) and *De Unico Mediatore* (GA 10.174/175), where Osiander appeals to Luther's distinction *de duplici iusticia* ("Sermo de duplici iustitia," 1518, in WA 2, S. 143), writing: "Prima iusticia est aliena et ab extra infusa, qua Christus iustus est, sicut 1. Cor. 1[30] dicitur: 'Qui factus est nobis sapientia a Deo, iusticia, sanctificatio et redemptio' etc." Osiander also refers to Augustine behind Luther's use of the verse (GA 9.600). The connection is not unique. When James Ussher, seventeenth-century Archbishop of Armagh, discussed the passage, he also carefully related the Apostle's language to the promise in Jeremiah. See *Praelectiones Theologicae* (1610) in *The Whole Works of the Most Rev. James Ussher, D. D., ...*, vol. 14 (Dublin: Hodges, Smith, and Co., 1864), 477.

[61] See the biblical indexes to vols 9 and 10 in the critical edition of Osiander's works to appreciate how frequently Osiander appealed to this verse. For a discussion of this verse in connection with Osiander's important 1551 work, *Von Dem Einigen Mittler/De Unico Mediatore* (GA 10.49-300; nos. 488/496), see the editor's introduction in GA 10.55-61. One of Osiander's chief Lutheran opponents, Joachim Mörlin, referred (as Calvin would) to the verse in defense of a non-essential (i.e., non-Osiandrian) doctrine of justification. See "Mörlin an Osiander" (no. 454), GA 9.622.

righteousness belonging to the divine essence but a gift to those with faith.[62]

CALVIN'S USE OF 1 CORINTHIANS 1:30

Turning to Calvin one is immediately drawn into the irony of the situation. Under one of the arches at the entrance of the Genevan *College* is an inscription bearing the words, in Greek, of the Apostle Paul in 1 Cor 1:30, "...Christ has been made to us of God wisdom..." This is but one small indication of the importance this verse carried for Calvin who, in the course of his labors, made extensive use of it. From his earliest publications, and increasingly in the 1550s, Calvin made a use of this verse that can scarcely be exaggerated in importance. In fact, observing his pattern of usage one concludes that he employed it as a kind of biblical short-hand for his *unio Christi-duplex gratia* soteriology. When Calvin wishes to clarify the distinct-yet-inseparable character of the saving benefits (the *duplex gratia*) that come in union with Christ, he cites or refers to the language of this verse with striking regularity.[63]

For instance, in the first (1536) edition of his *Institutes*, Calvin's affirmation of Christian holiness is rooted in the implications of the Christ-Spirit relationship for a proper understanding of union with Christ. If Christ, who was and is filled with the Spirit of holiness is made ours, we too share in the same Spirit. So Calvin argues that to be a Christian under the law of grace does not entail moral license. Rather, "By Christ's righteousness we are made righteous and become fulfillers of the law... Thus is fulfilled Paul's statement: 'Christ was made righteousness, sanctification, and redemption for us.'"[64] Later, in his 1537/1538 *Catechism* and in his response to Caroli,

---

[62] For the use of Cyril and Hilary, see Cyriakus Spangenberg, *Die erste Epistel S. Pauli an die Corinthier...* (Frankfurt/Main: Weygand Han and Georg Raben, 1561), L^v; for the use of Augustine, see Spangenberg, *Aüsslegung der ersten Acht Capitel der Episteln S. Pauli an die RO[e]MER* (Strasbourg: Samuel Emmel, 1566), xcv^v. For these and other ways Spangenberg used the Fathers, see Robert Kolb, "Patristic Citation as Homiletical Tool in the Vernacular Sermon of the German Late Reformation," in D. Steinmetz, ed., *Die Patristik in der Bibelexegese des 16. Jahrhunderts* (Wiesbaden: Harrassowitz Verlag, 1999), 155-79 (here, 169).

[63] Discussion in this immediate section is restricted to uses of 1 Cor 1:30 outside Calvin's commentary. His published comment is discussed below.

[64] Calvin, *Inst.* (1536) (CO 1.48-9; Battles ET, 34): "Hanc vero certitudinem nullus assequi potest nisi per Christum, cuius solius benedictione a maledictione legis liberamur, quae omnibus nobis edicta et denunciata est; cum ob imbecillitatem, quam ex patre Adam haereditariam accepimus, legem operibus nostris implere non possimus, ut necesse erat iis, qui sibi iustitiam inde comparare velint, cuius deinde iustitia, iusti ipsi et legis impletores fimus. Hanc enim ut nostram

the same use is made of the Apostle's language.⁶⁵ Consistent with the theme present in 1536, Calvin explains in his *Catechism* why Christ's possession of the Spirit has implications for the nature of our salvation.

> For the Spirit of the Lord has reposed on Christ without measure – the Spirit, I say, of wisdom, of intelligence, of counsel, of strength, of knowledge and reverential fear of the Lord – in order that we may all draw from his fullness and receive grace through the grace that has been given to Christ. As a result, those who boast of having the faith of Christ and are completely destitute of sanctification by his Spirit deceive themselves. For the Scripture teaches that *Christ has been made for us not only righteousness but also sanctification*. Hence we cannot receive through faith his righteousness without embracing at the same time (*simul*) that sanctification, because the Lord in one same alliance, which he has made with us in Christ, promises that he will be propitious toward our iniquities and will write his Law in our hearts.⁶⁶

Similarly, in his important 1539 rebuttal of Sadoleto's charge of licentiousness, Calvin uses this verse to clarify the relationship of justification to sanctification. Again in light of the Christ/Spirit/union relationship, Calvin explains why the

---

induimus, et sane pro nostra nobis a Deo accepta fertur, ut pro sanctis, puris et innocentibus nos habeat. Ita impletur quod ait Paulus: Christum nobis factum esse iustitiam, sanctificationem, et redemptionem."

⁶⁵ Calvin, *Catechismus*, COR III/2/44-5: "Id autem in Symbolo, quod vocant, explicatur; *nempe qua ratione factus sit nobis a Patre Christus sapientia, redemptio, vita, iustitia, sanctificatio.*" In the French, p. 52, "C'est à sçavoir comment Christ nous a esté faict du Pere sapience, redemption, vie, justice, sainctification (*mg*: '1 Cor 1').' Calvin's statement against Caroli does not cite the language of the verse but clearly reflects it (*Confessio Genevensum praedicatorum*, COR III/2/147): "Nam ut nuncupatur vita, lumen, salus, iustitia, sanctificatio nostra, ita fiduciam spemque omnem in ipso reponere et eius nomen invocare docemur." I am grateful to Prof. Irena Backus for this last reference.

⁶⁶ Calvin, *Catechismus*, COR III/2/40: "Siquidem requievit super eum spiritus Domini citra mensuram: spiritus, inquam, sapientiae et intellectus, consilii, fortitudinis, scientiae, timoris Domini: ut de eius plenitudine hauriamus omnes, et gratiam pro gratia. Falluntur ergo, qui fide Christi gloriantur, sanctificatione spiritus eius prorsus destituti. *Christum factum esse nobis non iustitiam modo, sed sanctificationem quoque, Scriptura docet*. Proinde recipi a nobis iustitia eius fide non potest, quin illam sanctificationem *simul* amplectamur. Eodem enim pacto Dominus, quod in Christo nobiscum ferit, se nostris iniquitatibus propitium fore, et legem suam cordibus nostris inscripturum pollicetur." The French text is on p. 41 (facing). Cf. *Calvin's First Catechism*, 19-20; *Instruction in Faith*, 43. Italics mine.

Reformation doctrine of justification, properly understood, does not marginalize the indispensability of good works for the one justified *sola fide*. "We deny that good works have any share in justification, but we claim full authority for them in the lives of the righteous," explains Calvin.

> For, if he who has obtained justification possesses Christ, and at the same time, *Christ is never where his Spirit is not*, it is obvious that free righteousness is necessarily connected with regeneration. Therefore, if you would properly understand how *inseparable* faith and works are, look to *Christ, who, as the Apostle teaches, has been given to us for justification and for sanctification*. Wherever, therefore, that righteousness of faith which we maintain to be free is, there too Christ is, and where Christ is there too is the Spirit of holiness, who regenerates the soul to newness of life.[67]

Citations of or allusions to this verse in connection with a clarification of his soteriological structure are numerous in the *Institutes*, and many of them serve to demonstrate still more unmistakably how central this pattern of expression is for Calvin. One rather lengthy section, dating from 1539, brings together what are possibly the strongest statements by Calvin on the subject. Here he rails against "the Papists" who think that "when faith is so gloriously extolled, works are degraded."

> What if, rather, these were encouraged and strengthened? *For we dream neither of a faith devoid of good works nor of a justification that stands without them.* This alone is of importance: having admitted that faith and good works must cleave together, we still lodge justification in faith, not in works. We have a ready explanation for

---

[67] Calvin, *Responsio* (OS 1.470; TT 1.43): "Opera bona in homine iustificando negamus ullas habere partes: in iustorum vita regnum illis vindicamus. Nam si Christum possidet qui iustitiam est adeptus, *Christus autem nusquam sine suo spiritu est*, inde constat, *gratuitam iustitiam cum regeneratione necessario esse coniunctam*. Proinde si rite intelligere libet, quam sint res individuae, fides et opera, *in Christum intuere: qui, ut docet apostolus, in iustitiam et sanctificationem datus nobis est*. Ubi ergo cunque ista quam gratuitam praedicamus fidei iustitia est, illic est Christus. Ubi Christus, illic spiritus sanctificationis: qui animam in vitae novitatem regeneret." Italics mine. Note Calvin's following statement: "Contra vero ubi non viget sanctitatis innocentiaeque studium, illic nec spiritus Christi nec Christus ipse est. Ubi non est Christus, neque etiam illic est iustitia, imo neque fides: quae Christum in iustitiam, sine spiritu sanctificationis, apprehendere non potest." Italics mine. Note also that in the important sixth chapter added to the 1539 revision of the *Institutio*, "*De Iustificatione Fidei, et meritis operum*," there are two significant allusions, without marginal annotation, to 1 Cor 1:30 (fols. 208, 210). See Appendix A.

doing this, provided we turn to Christ to whom our faith is directed and from whom it receives its full strength. Why, then, are we justified by faith? Because by faith we grasp Christ's righteousness, by which alone we are reconciled to God. Yet you could not grasp this without at the same time (*simul*) grasping sanctification also. *For "he is given unto us for righteousness, wisdom, sanctification, and redemption." Therefore Christ justifies no one whom he does not at the same time (simul) sanctify.* These benefits are joined together by an everlasting and indissoluble bond, so that those whom he redeems, he justifies; those whom he justifies, he sanctifies.[68] But, since the question concerns only righteousness and sanctification, let us dwell upon these. Although we may distinguish them, Christ contains both of them inseparably in himself. Do you wish, then, to attain righteousness in Christ? You must first possess Christ; but you cannot possess him without being made partaker in his sanctification, because he cannot be divided into pieces (*quia in frusta discerpi non potest*). Since, therefore, it is solely by expending himself that the Lord gives us these benefits to enjoy, he bestows both of them at the same time (*simul*), the one never without the other. *Thus it is clear how true it is that we are justified not without works yet not through works, since in our sharing in Christ, which justifies us, sanctification is just as much included as righteousness.*[69]

---

[68] In this statement, recalling the language of what he regards as Paul's *ordo* in Rom. 8:29-30, Calvin is best understood when his "replication principle" is kept in view.

[69] Calvin, *Inst.* (1539) 3.16.1; OS 4.248-249 (LCC 20.798): "*Non enim aut fidem somniamus bonis operibus vacuam, aut iustificationem quae sine iis constet*; hoc tantum interest, quod quum fidem et bona opera necessario inter se cohaerere fateamur, in fide tamen non operibus iustifationem ponimus. Id qua ratione, facile explicare promptum est si ad Christum modo convertamur, in quem dirigitur fides, et unde totam vim accipit. Quare ergo fide iustificamur? quia fide apprehendimus Christi iustitiam, qua una Deo reconciliamur. Hanc vero apprehendere non possis quin et sanctificationem simul apprehendas. *Datus est enim nobis in iustitiam, sapientiam, sanctificationem, redemptionem. Nullum ergo Christus iustificat quem non simul sanctificet.* Sunt enim perpetuo et individuo nexu coniuncta haec beneficia, ut quos sapientia sua illuminat, eos redimat: quos redimit, iustificet: quos iustificat, sanctificet. Sed quia de iustitia et sanctificatione tantum quaestio est, in iis insistamus. Inter se distinguamus licet, inseparabiliter tamen utranque Christus in se continet. Vis ergo iustitiam in Christo adipisci? Christum ante possideas oportet; possidere autem non potes quin fias sanctificationis eius particeps; quia in frusta discerpi non potest. Quum ergo haec beneficia, nonnisi seipsum erogando, fruenda nobis Dominus concedat, utrunque simul largitur: alterum nunquam sine altero. *Ita liquet quam*

Applied Christology

This is just a taste of the extent to which the language of 1 Cor 1:30 structures Calvin's understanding of salvation, as well as the passion Calvin brings to his insistence on the matter. By the Spirit through faith believers are united to Christ who is in himself both righteousness and sanctification. Hence are these graces (1) distinct but inseparable, and entirely out of reach unless we are united to Christ; and (2) simultaneously bestowed – something Calvin is careful to emphasize repeatedly. Consequently it is impossible to entertain either a justification *without* works (works as dispensable for justification) or a justification *through* works (works as instrumental for justification).

Therefore, by the time Osiander had become infamous Calvin had already "adopted" this verse and relied heavily upon it for the clarification of his own ideas. With Osiander now touting a widely-rejected theology of justifying union with Christ that is ostensibly rooted in the language of 1 Cor 1:30, ambiguity inevitably is introduced to Calvin's own theology. His handling of this verse (and its core ideas of union and righteousness) is thus understandably prominent in his 1559 refutation. Explicit references to the verse are actually few in number, but a close reading reveals several clear allusions to it. When Calvin refers to the idea that "Christ is our righteousness," he is usually alluding to this verse, and occasionally in connection with its OT background in Jeremiah and elsewhere.

> He says that we are one with Christ. We agree. But we deny that Christ's essence is mixed with our own. Then we say that this principle is wrongly applied to these deceptions of his: that *Christ is our righteousness* because he is God eternal, the source of righteousness, and the very righteousness of God.[70]

Moreover, while properly speaking it is God who justifies, Calvin explains the same function can be transferred to Christ "because *he*

---

verum sit nos non sine operibus, neque tamen per opera iustificari: quoniam in Christi participatione, qua iustificamur, non minus sanctificatio continetur quam iustitia." For further citations of or allusions to 1 Cor. 1:30, see *Inst.* (1559) 2.15.2; 2.16.19; 3.2.8; 3.3.19; 3.4.30; 3.11.6; 3.11.8; 3.11.12; 3.15.5; 3.13.1.

[70] Calvin, *Inst.* (1559) 3.11.5; OS 4.186 (LCC 20.730): "Dicit nos unum esse cum Christo. Fatemur: interea negamus misceri Christi essentiam cum nostra. Deinde perperam hoc principium trahi dicimus ad illas eius praestigias: *Christum nobis esse iustitiam,* quia Deus est aeternus, fons iustitiae, ipsaque Dei iustitia." Italics mine. Cf. another possible allusion in Calvin, *Inst.* (1559) 3.11.6; OS 4.187 (LCC 20.731-2): "Deinde fortiter negat, quatenus Christus sacerdos peccata expiando, Patrem nobis placavit, *ipsum esse iustitiam nostram,* sed ut est Deus aeternus, et vita." Italics mine.

was given to us for righteousness."[71] Elsewhere, in perhaps his strongest statement in connection with this verse, Calvin objects to Osiander's confusion of justification and sanctification by referring to the verse in order to emphasize their distinctiveness.

> For since God, for the preservation of righteousness, renews those whom he freely reckons as righteous, Osiander mixes that gift of regeneration with this free acceptance and contends that they are one and the same. Yet Scripture, even though it joins them, still lists them separately in order that God's manifold grace may better appear to us. *For Paul's statement is not redundant: that Christ was given to us for our righteousness and sanctification.* And whenever he reasons – from the salvation purchased for us, from God's fatherly love, and from Christ's grace – that we are called to holiness and cleanness, he clearly indicates that to be justified means something different from being made new creatures.[72]

Paul, Calvin explains, is not being redundant (*supervacuum*) when he lists "righteousness" (justification, as both Calvin and Osiander assume) and "sanctification" distinctly in his list. Therefore, they are not identical but must be distinguished. Paul also teaches, moreover, that they both come to believers *in Christ*, with whom they have been brought into spiritual or mystical union. Again as a consequence, these saving benefits cannot be separated. Christ has been made to us of God both righteousness and sanctification. As they are both *in him* and believers are also *in him*, they cannot and must not be separated. Calvin used 1 Cor 1:30 as though it alone sufficiently summarized the whole of his thought on the subject: the distinct-yet-inseparable character of the *duplex gratia* is rooted in union with Christ. Or, put differently, every element in his formula – the distinction without separation, the twofold grace, and union

---

[71] Calvin, *Inst.* (1559) 3.11.7; OS 4.188 (LCC 20.733): "Nos quidem nihil tale imaginamur, sed proprie loquendo Deum unum iustificare dicimus: deinde hoc idem transferimus ad Christum, quia datus est nobis in iustitiam..." Italics mine.
[72] Calvin, *Inst.* (1559) 3.11.6; OS 4.187-8 (LCC 20.732): "In hac duplicis gratiae confusione, quam obtrudit Osiander, similis est absurditas: quia enim re ipsa ad colendam iustitiam renovat Deus quos pro iustis gratis censet, illud regenerationis donum miscet cum hac gratuita acceptatione, unumque et idem esse contendit. Atqui Scriptura, utrunque coniungens distincte tamen enumerat, quo multiplex Dei gratia melius nobis pateat. *Neque enim supervacuum est illud Pauli, datum fuisse nobis Christum in iustitiam et sanctificationem.* Et quoties a salute nobis parta, a paterno amore Dei, a Christi gratia ratiocinatur nos ad sanctitatem et munditiem vocatos esse, aperte indicat aliud esse iustificari quam fieri novas creaturas." Italics mine.

with Christ as the more basic soteric reality – is contained in this one verse.

In this light the function of the verse in Calvin's critique may be summarized. While Osiander assumes, in the course of using this verse, that the hypostatic union implies Christ was "made righteousness for us" according to the divine nature, Calvin argues, using the same verse, that if Christ is "made righteousness" for us according to his divine nature alone, than this saving work is not peculiar to Christ but common to the Father and Spirit as well. For the divine righteousness of the Son is common to the Father and Spirit. On the grounds argued by Osiander, the true referent in Paul's verse would be the whole Trinity and not Christ alone, and the Apostle's statement that the eternally divine Son was "made righteousness for us" by God, in time and still exclusively according to the divine nature, would be nonsensical.[73] In other words, any real distinction between eternal-trinitarian, ontological, and incarnate-historical categories is obscured, and Christ, whose earthly (human) work is by implication made irrelevant, could not be said to have been "made" anything to us by God.

In connection with this last observation one notes the role of this verse in Calvin's affirmation of the indispensability of Christ's incarnate state, without which, as man, Christ could not have been obedient and died as a holy sacrifice. So, whereas Osiander "gloats over" the OT anticipation that Yahweh will be our righteousness, Calvin concludes that Christ was "made righteousness" *when he took the form of a servant* and justifies believers in obedience to the Father.

---

[73] Calvin, *Inst.* (1559) 3.11.8; OS 4.189 (LCC 20.734): "Sed hoc Osiandri placitum est, quum Deus et homo sit Christus, respectu divinae naturae non humanae factum nobis esse iustitiam. Atqui si proprie hoc in divinitatem competit, peculiare non erit Christo, sed commune cum Patre et Spiritu: quando non alia est unius quam alterius iustitia. Deinde quod naturaliter ab aeterno fuit, non congrueret dici nobis esse factum. Sed ut hoc demus, Deum nobis factum esse iustitiam; qui illud quod interpositum est conveniet factum esse a Deo? Hoc certe peculiare est Mediatoris personae: quae etsi in se continet divinam naturam, hic tamen insignitur proprio elogio, quo seorsum a Patre et Spiritu discernitur." Cf. Melanchthon (CR 8.580) who advances a similar argument against Osiander saying he confuses the trinitarian persons and does not discern the necessity of the Mediator for the obedience necessary for justification: "Deinde confusio est personarum: homo est iustus iustitia Patris, Filii et Spiritus S. Hic non discernitur mediator a ceteris personis, cum necesse sit, retineri hanc doctrinam: nos propter solum mediatorem, et quidem propter obedientiam eius iustos id est reconciliatos ac Deo acceptos esse. Sicut 1 Timoth. 2. Dicitur: *Unus Deus, et unus mediator Dei et hominum, homo Christus Iesus*; et Rom. 5.: *propter obedientiam unius iusti constituuntur multi*."

This, Calvin argues, is not accomplished in the divine nature but only "by reason of the dispensation enjoined upon him."[74]

EXCURSUS: A PATRISTIC PARALLEL

Interestingly, the function of 1 Cor 1:30 in Calvin's critique of Osiander bears striking similarities to an earlier use made by Chrysostom. It has been shown by Walchenbach that for Calvin Chrysostom was first among the Fathers as an exegete of the NT and particularly the Apostle Paul. This high regard is reflected, for example, in Calvin's early effort toward editing an edition of Chrysostom for the benefit of his beloved French-reading public.[75] It has also been noted, significantly for our purposes, that Chrysostom is the Father cited most frequently in Calvin's commentary on 1 Corinthians.[76] While there is no explicit reference by Calvin to Chrysostom in connection specifically with 1 Cor 1:30 (whether in Calvin's own proposed edition, in his commentary, or in the course of his other work)[77] the case for Calvin's use of Chrysostom is strengthened both by Calvin's familiarity with Chrysostom's 1 Corinthians homilies and by the nature of Calvin's use of the verse in his response to Osiander.

Commenting on this verse in Homily V of 1 Corinthians, Chrysostom explains the way in which Paul's language ought to be

---

[74] Calvin, *Inst.* (1559) 3.11.8; OS 4.190 (LCC 20.735): "... ac proinde non secundum divinam naturam hoc nobis praestare, sed pro dispensationis sibi iniunctae ratione."

[75] See John Robert Walchenbach, "John Calvin as Biblical Commentator: An Investigation into Calvin's Use of John Chrysostom as an Exegetical Tutor," Ph.D. diss. (University of Pittsburgh, 1974); Alexandre Ganoczy and Klaus Müller, *Calvins Handschriftliche Annotationen zu Chrysostomus: Ein Beitrag zur Hermeneutik Calvins* (Wiesbaden: Franz Steiner, 1981); and W. Ian P. Hazlett, "Calvin's Latin Preface To His Proposed French Edition of Chrysostom's Homilies: Translation and Commentary," in James Kirk, ed., *Humanism and Reform: The Church in Europe, England, and Scotland, 1400-1643: Essays in Honour of James K. Cameron* (Cambridge: Blackwell, 1991), 129-50.

[76] Walchenbach, "John Calvin as Biblical Commentator," 58. But note that Walchenbach's statistics are based on the occasionally erroneous indices in CO. Thus the need for caution, as Walchenbach himself notes (p. 57, n. 1).

[77] Walchenbach ("John Calvin as Biblical Commentator," 58) does not include 1:30 in his list of Calvin's citations of Chrysostom, whether "explicit or implicit..." The edition by Ganoczy/Müller also does not include reference to 1 Cor. 1:30. It is altogether likely, however, that, in the approximately twenty years that span his critical work on Chrysostom and his encounter with Osiander's theology, Calvin in his reading recognizes and incorporates the theological and polemical value of Chrysostom's observation. See n. 79, below.

understood. Here the Apostle speaks of an act of God by which Christ himself is a saving gift to us, complete with wisdom, righteousness, sanctification, and redemption. Chrysostom asks, "But why did he not say, He has made us wise, but 'was made unto us wisdom'? To show the copiousness of the gift. It is as if he had said, 'He gave unto us Himself'." One should note the parallel with Calvin's statement, quoted above: "Yet Scripture, even though it joins them, still lists them separately *in order that God's manifold grace may better appear to us.*" And for Chrysostom the Apostle's order of presentation is significant: "For first He made us wise by delivering us from error, and then righteous and holy, by giving us the Spirit; and He has so delivered us from all our evils as to be 'of Him.'" Then, long before the Osiandrian controversy would raise the question of the divine *essentia*, Chrysostom followed this with a significant distinction: "*non per ipsius essentiam* (οὐσιώσεως), *sed per fidem.*"[78]

Chrysostom's distinction between being and faith, or ontological and spiritual communication, lies at the heart of the disagreement in the 1550s over Paul's language. It is this distinction, moreover, with the crucial factor of the Spirit's role, which is specifically decisive for Calvin in his response to Osiander: Osiander, Calvin argues, does not observe the *nexus* or *vinculum* of union, the Spirit, and thus misunderstands the union itself and its implications for justification. He misreads the Apostle in terms of being or ontological communication rather than in terms of faith and spiritual communication. Ordinarily, in the absence of concrete evidence in favor of Calvin using Chrysostom here, one would hesitate to conclude Calvin is definitely using Chrysostom. Nevertheless, in view of the other relevant data regarding Calvin, Chrysostom, and 1 Corinthians, the connection appears to stand upon evidence that is more than sufficient for a definitive judgment.[79]

---

[78] Chrysostom, *1 Cor. Hom.*, V (PG 61.42): "Cur autem non dixit, Fecit nos sapientes, sed, *Factus est nobis sapientia*? doni ostendens abundantiam, ac si diceret, Seipsum nobis dedit. Et vide quomodo procedat. Prius enim nos sapientes fecit cum ab errore liberavit, et tunc iustos et sanctos, Spiritum largitus, et sic nos a malis omnibus liberavit, ita ut ipsius simus, non per ipsius essentiam, sed per fidem (καὶ οὐ τῆς οὐσιώσεως τοῦτο δηλωτικὸν ἀλλὰ τῆς πίστεως)."

[79] Note the comments of A. N. S. Lane on the significance of the silence in Ganoczy/Müller. In short, the absence of a notation on this specific passage is greatly outweighed by Calvin's citations of other passages in Chrysostom's Corinthian homilies not noted or underlined. In view of the other evidence, Calvin's use of Chrysostom's homilies for other unmarked passages is sufficient

The Metaphorical Shorthand for an Unio-Duplex *Soteriology*

These historical and exegetical observations reveal a great deal about Calvin's critique, but at least one metaphorical element in his work, connected with his use of 1 Cor 1:30, must be examined before a full appreciation is possible. As a journalist once pointed out, "Classic invective demands a vivid figure of speech."[80] For Calvin, that vivid figure was "to tear Christ into pieces," and one finds it at a particularly crucial point in Calvin's refutation.[81] According to Calvin, Osiander argues (1) "to justify" must include not only reconciliation but transformation by union with the indwelling divine essence, and (2) Christ is our righteousness not as expiating Priest but as eternal God. In this way Osiander endeavors to evade the Roman charge that justification by the sole instrumentality of faith compromises the necessity of good works. Calvin responds,

> To prove the first point – that God justifies not only by pardoning but by regenerating – he asks whether God leaves as they were by nature those whom he justifies, changing none of their vices. This is exceedingly easy to answer: as Christ cannot be torn into parts (*discerpi Christus in partes*; 1561 *Inst.*: *deschirer Iesus Christ par pieces*), so these two which we receive in him together and conjointly (*simul et coniunctim*) are inseparable – namely, righteousness and sanctification. Whomever, therefore, God receives into grace, on

---

to remove this objection. See Lane, *John Calvin: Student of the Church Fathers*, 72-3, 168, 194, 222-23, 234.

[80] William Safire, "Invective's Comeback," *The New York Times*, Tuesday 29 April, 2003.

[81] The metaphor is generally that of "tearing to pieces" and is usually found in Calvin as *discerpo* but in some significant places as *lacero*, and in French as *deschirer*. The following analysis should not be regarded as exhaustive but as representative of Calvin's general pattern of usage. On Calvin's use of language see, among a growing number, Francis M. Higman, *The Style of John Calvin in his French Polemical Treatises* (London: Oxford University Press, 1967), 123-64; Éric Kayayan, "La Porteé Epistémologique de *la Métaphore du Miroir* dans l'Institution de la Religion Chrétienne de J. Calvin," *Revue d'Histoire et de Philosophie Religieuses* 77 (1997): 431-51; and Roland M. Frye, "Calvin's Theological Use of Figurative Language." Also, while Calvin does not use the figure of speech against Osiander directly, he uses it in this context, as he regularly does elsewhere, to defend against the Roman Catholic charge of a legal fiction, something basic to his contention with Osiander. Because polemically Calvin's use of the image is simultaneously a defense and an attack on his opponents' Christology and soteriology, it may be viewed as not only defense but "invective."

Applied Christology 229

them he at the same time (*simul*) bestows the Spirit of adoption, by whose power he remakes them to his own image.[82]

Thus, in Calvin's view, Osiander responds to the Roman charge by affirming it, stating that God justifies not only by pardoning but by renewing, and therefore God does not leave in sin those whom he justifies. Calvin replies to Osiander in the same way he had replied to Rome numerous times, which suggests he regarded Osiander as holding a basically Roman Catholic view of justification despite the Lutheran garb.

In its basic form, this violent image of "tearing to pieces" has a rich classical heritage of which Calvin may have been aware. For example, one finds various uses of this language in Cicero, Lucretius, Seneca, and Quintilian.[83] It is also found in Hugh of St. Victor, Isidore of Seville, Clement, and in Augustine's *Treatises* against the Pelagians, where he accuses his opponents of intending

---

[82] Calvin, *Inst*. (1559) 3.11.6; OS 4.187: "Ut probet illud primum, Deum non tantum ignoscendo sed regenerando iustificare, quaerit an quos iustificat, relinquat quales erant natura, nihil ex vitiis mutando. Responsio perquam facilis est: sicut *non potest discerpi Christus in partes*, ita inseparabilia esse haec duo, quae *simul et coniunctim* in ipso percipimus, iustitiam et sanctificationem. Quoscunque ergo in gratiam recipit Deus, simul spiritu adoptionis donat, cuius virtute eos reformat ad suam imaginem." Cf. *Institution* (1561), 242b: "A quoy la response est facile: c'est que comme *on ne peut point deschirer Iesus Christ par pieces*, aussi ces deux choses sont inseparables, puis que nous les receuons ensemble et conioinctement en luy, ascavoir iustice et sanctification." Italics mine. N.B.: Battles (LCC 20.732) "perceive" for *percipimus*, rather than "receive." On the necessity of personal holiness grounded in union with Christ, see also CO 49.375-6 where Calvin explains the confession of the gospel with the tongue must be joined to newness of life. See also *Comm*. Eph 4:20 (CO 51.207; COR II/16/243; CTS, 294) and *Comm*. Col 1:22 (CO 52.90-1; COR II/16/406-7; CTS, 159).

[83] See, e.g., Cicero, *Topica*, 28: "Atque etiam definitiones aliae sunt partitionum aliae divisionum; partitionum, cum res ea quae proposita est *quasi in membra discerpitur*,..."; see also, idem, *De Oratore* III, VI, 24; III, XIII, 49; III, XXXIII, 132; Lucretius, *De Rerum Natura* II, Line 829: "...ut fit ubi *in parvas partis discerpitur austrum*..."; IV, Line 96; Seneca, *Quaestiones Naturales*, II, 7.1: "Quidam aera *discerpunt* et in particulas diducunt ita ut illi inane permisceant."; see also, idem, *Epistolae Morales ad Lucilium*, V, 51 (8); and, idem, *Thyestes*, Line 61; Quintilian, *Declamatio Maior* XII, 1: "...quantalibet ignominia dimittite domo noxium; habet quo eat. non publicis manibus exeuntem *discerpsimus*, non, quoniam semel consveramus et bona fide ferarum esse civitas coeperat,...". I am grateful to Prof. Irena Backus for suggesting this classical line of inquiry. *The Oxford Latin Dictionary* (s.v. "discerpo"; cf. s.v. "lacero") also notes examples in Cicero, Horace, Lucretius, et al.

to "tear in pieces the sheep redeemed at such a price..."[84] But this classical figure of speech became especially popular in the highly-charged atmosphere of sixteenth-century eucharistic polemic. Peter Martyr Vermigli, for example, uses it with great frequency. In his *Dialogus* he accuses the ubiquitarians of "tearing apart," by implication of their Christology, the union of divinity and humanity in Christ. He further says that on their construction, the unity of Christ's Person is "torn asunder" and, elsewhere, that Christ's own body is "torn apart." In Brenz's Lutheran Christology, says Vermigli, the humanity of Christ is "torn" from his divinity.[85] Many other occurrences could be mentioned.[86]

In Calvin, one finds a frequent and calculated use of the metaphor, one that incorporates its common eucharistic function into his soteriological concern for the necessity of good works. In many cases, however, the union idea that gives the metaphor its force is specifically ecclesiastical: because Christ is our Head and the Church is his Body, dissension in the Church is a "tearing apart" of Christ. Sadoleto accuses the Protestants of schism, and thus of attempting "to tear (*discerpere*) the Spouse of Christ in pieces, that the garment of the Lord, which heathen soldiers were unwilling to divide, they attempted not only to divide, but to rend."[87] Calvin retorts that it is actually Sadoleto and "his whole herd of pseudo-

---

[84] Hugh of St. Victor, *Didascalicon* III, cap. IV, 768D; Isidore of Seville, *Etymologiae* I, xxxix (*De Metris*), 4; *Etymologiae* XII, ii (*De Bestiis*), 17; Clement, *Epist. ad Cor.*, cap. XLVI; Augustine, *Treatises Against Two Letters of the Pelagians*, Bk. 1, ch. 2 (PL 44.551): "Cum vero non desinant fremere ad dominici gregis caulas, atque ad diripiendas tanto pretio redemptas oves, aditus undecumque rimari...".

[85] Peter Martyr Vermigli, *Dialogus de utraque in Christo natura* (1562), 12^v (PML 2, *Dialogue*, 27), 25^r (45), 48^r (78), 88^r (135), respectively.

[86] See, e.g., within the *Dialogus*, pp. 10^r (24), 14^r (30), 24^v (44), 27^r (49), 34^r (59, a reference to Cyril), 86^r (133), 87^r (134), 88^r (136, here Martyr argues that the humanity of Christ is not "torn away" from his divinity just because it is confined to a fixed place), 96^v (148), and 104^r (159, quoting Cyril [PG 74.157]).

[87] Sadolet, *Epist. ad Genevates* (OS 1.454): "Atqui, si reliqua istorum omnia aliquo tamen pacto perferri et tolerari possent, hoc quemadmodum ferretur (in quo mihi videtur ne ad ignoscendum quidem illis locum ullum veniae et misericordiae apud Deum dari posse) quod sponsam hi Christi unicam *discerpere* sunt conati? quod tunicam illam Domini, quam profani milites dividere nolverunt, isti ausi sunt, non dividere solum, sed *lacerare*?" He continues, "Sed huius modi scissionem, huiusmodi sanctae ecclesiae dilaniationem, potestne quisquam Christum agnoscens et confitens, et cuius aliquando menti atque cordi spiritus sanctus illuxerit, non intelligere, Satanae, et non Dei propriam operationem esse? Quid imperat nobis Deus? quid praecipit Christus? Nempe ut unum omnes in ipso simus." Italics mine.

bishops" that have "cruelly torn and mutilated" (*disiectam et mutilatam*) the Church through iniquities and incompetence.[88] He later returns in his *Reply* to this charge calling it the "most serious charge of all," "that we have attempted to dismember (*discerpere*) the Spouse of Christ."[89]

Elsewhere, concerned that this charge of schism must not be substantiated by intra-Evangelical strife, Calvin writes to Bullinger in 1544 that conflict gains nothing and "if we tear each other in pieces" (*nos proscindimus*) their enemies will readily exploit the mutual accusations.[90] And appealing in a sermon for the unity of the Church, Calvin reminds his congregation that Christ has called us to be members of his body. We should then "knit ourselves together" to glorify God "with one heart and mind..."

> Let us therefore demonstrate our brotherly love for one another by showing the world that we will not be separated (which would be to divide Jesus Christ himself) (*comme pour deschirer Iesus Christ par pieces*). Instead may we desire that he would unite us so that we

---

[88] Calvin, *Responsio* (OS 1.476; TT 1.50): "Ad extremum enim nequitiae perventum est: ut iam nec vitia sua, nec remedia pati possint adumbrati isti praesules, in quibus stare et perire ecclesiam putas, a quibus nos ipsam dicimus immaniter fuisse disiectam et mutilitatem..."

[89] Calvin, *Responsio* (OS 1.488; TT 1.66-7): "Sed omnium teterrimum est illud crimen, quod sponsam Christi *discerpere* conati sumus. Id si verum esset, merito et tibi et orbi universo haberemur pro deploratis. Atqui non aliter crimen istud in nos recipiam, nisi *discerpi* ab iis Christi sponsam contendas, qui virginem castam exhibere Christo cupiunt; qui sancta quadam zelotypia sollicitantur, quo eam Christo illibatam conservent; qui pravis lenociniis corruptam, ad fidem coniugalem revocant; qui adversus adulteros omnes, quos eius pudicitiae insidiari deprehenderint, contentionem suscipere non dubitant." Calvin continues, passionately, "Scilicet, quia non sumus passi, sacrosanctum Chrisi thalamum tanto haberi a vobis ludibrio, sponsam eius *lacerasse* dicimur. Ego autem dico illam, quam a nobis falso accusas *lacerationem*, apud vos non obscure conspici. Neque in ecclesia id modo, sed in Christo ipso, quem misere *dissectum* esse constat." Italics mine.

[90] Calvin to Bullinger, 25 November 1544 (CO 11.775; Gorham, *Gleanings*, 27-9, here 28): "Deinde nihil vos hostiliter in eum confligendo profecturos, quam ut lusum impiis praebeatis, ut non tam de nobis quam de evangelio triumphent. Si mutuo nos proscindimus, plus satis habent nobis fidei." As Gorham notes, the Latin (*plus satis habent nobis fidei*) is difficult to translate clearly here. Note Sadoleto's remark (OS 1.454; TT 1.59): "Quot enim iam, istis initium facientibus, sectae ecclesiam disciderunt, neque cum istis congruentes, et ipsae inter se discordes? quod manifestum esse falsitatis indicium omnis doctrina confirmat."

may live in him and he in us, and that he would lead us by his Holy Spirit...[91]

Furthermore, with a view to the dissension in Corinth, Calvin explains that as the object of the gospel is that we would all be bound together in Christ, so the Corinthian conflict resulted in Christ being "torn asunder" (*lacerabatur*); indeed, such conflicts prevent acceptable worship for "to glory in his name amid conflicts and parties is to tear him in pieces (*discerpere*)..."[92]

This intimate connection of Christ and his Body has implications for understanding the severity of sexual sins. Paul's admonition is that since the Father has united us to his Son,

> what wickedness there would be in breaking away our body from that sacred connection, and giving it over to things unworthy of Christ!... Hence he has, as if with the view of explaining it, that Christ is joined with us and we with him in such a way, that we become one body with him. Accordingly, if I have connection with a harlot, *I tear Christ in pieces* (*discerpo*), so far as it is in my power to do so; for it is impossible for me to draw Him into fellowship with such pollution... He brings out more fully the greatness of the injury that is done to Christ by the man that has intercourse with an harlot; for he becomes one body, and hence he *tears away a member from Christ's body* (*membrum igitur a Christi corpore avellit*)...[93]

---

[91] Calvin, *Serm. Galat.*, Sermon 11 (CO 50.414; *Sermons on Galatians*, 171): "Ansi donc que nous ayons ceste fraternité pour recommandee en telle sorte que nous monstrions que nous ne voulons pas nous separer comme pour deschirer Iesus Christ par pieces: mais que nous desirons qu'il nous unisse tellement que non seulement il vive en nous, et nous en luy: mais qu'il nous gouverne par son sainct Esprit, en telle sorte qu'un chacun tasche de le servir et honorer en premier lieu, et puis de s'employer au service de ses prochains, selon le moyen qu'il aura." ET from John Calvin, *Sermons on Galatians*, trans. Kathy Childress (Edinburgh: Banner of Truth, 1997).

[92] Calvin, *Comm.* 1 Cor 1:13 (CO 49.316; CTS, 67): "Quum autem pauculi ex Corinthiis, qui aliis erant saniores, Christum retinuerint magistrum, utcunque omnes se Christianos iactarent, ita lacerabatur Christus. Nos enim unum esse corpus oportet, si velimus sub eo, tanquam sub capite, contineri. Quod si in diversa corpora scindimur, ab ipso quoque dissilimus: gloriari ergo eius nomine inter discordias et factiones, est ipsum discerpere, quod fieri nequit." See further *Comm.* Gal 5:12 (CO 50.249; COR II/16/124-5; CTS, 156-7); *Comm.* Col 1:23 (CO 52.91; COR II/16/407-9; CTS, 160-1); *Comm.* Heb 10:25 (CO 55.132; COR II/19/168-9; CTS, 240-1); Ded. Epist. to *Comm.* 1 Pet (CTS, xiv).

[93] Calvin, *Comm.* 1 Cor 6:13, 15-16 (CO 49.397; CTS, 216, 217): "Quod addit et Dominus corpori pondere non caret: nam quum Deus Pater filium aptaverit

Calvin also uses the image of tearing (usually *lacero*) for the intra-trinitarian personal relations. Against Servetus who argued for a simple, undivided trinitarian essence, Calvin complains of those who have "boiled up several sects, which partly tore God's essence to pieces (*quae partim lacerarent Dei essentiam*), partly confused the distinction that exists between the persons." Similarly, against Valentine Gentile who, unlike Servetus, confessed three persons but taught that the Father infused his deity into the Son and Spirit, Calvin writes of false trinitarianisms that would "tear apart the essence of God" (*lacerarent Dei essentiam*).[94] And significantly in light of his association of Osiander with Manichaeism, Calvin explains that "to tear apart the essence of the Creator (*interea Creatoris essentiam lacerare*) so that everyone may possess a part of it is utter folly."[95]

The christological-sacramental use of the image is also frequently found in Calvin's work. Addressing the *signum-res* relationship in a comment on 1 Peter 3:21, Calvin, in a non-polemical passage,

---

nobis, quantum flagitium est corpus nostrum a sacra illa coniunctione abreptum ad res Christo indignas transferri?" (CO 49.397-8): "Itaque tanquam illud exponens dicit, Christum ita nobis aptatum et nos illi, ut in unum corpus coalescamus cum eo. Ideo si me commisceam cum meretrice, Christum, quantum in me est, *membratim discerpo*: quia fieri nequit ut eum in tantae pollutionis communionem traham... Melius exprimit quantam iniuriam Christo inferat qui se cum scorto miscet: unum enim corpus efficitur, *membrum igitur a Christi corpore avellit*." Italics mine. The whole of Calvin's comment on these verses is vividly written in order to draw out the conclusions of the idea that "our connection with Christ is closer than that of a husband and wife, and that the former, accordingly, must be greatly preferred before the latter, so that it must be maintained with the utmost chastity and fidelity" (Hoc ideo adiecit ut doceret arctiorem esse coniunctionem Christi nobiscum quam viri cum uxore: et ideo illam huic esse longe praeferendam, ut summa castitate et fide colatur) (on 6:17; CO 49.399; CTS, 219). Cf. also *Serm.* on Ps 119 (Sermon 18) where Calvin explains that those who defile their bodies deface the image of God in them, pollute his temple, *"divide and pull in pieces the body of Jesus Christ ..."* in *Two and twentie Sermons of Master Iohn Calvin, In which Sermons is most religiously handled, the hundredth and nineteenth Psalme of David,...* (1580; rep. Audubon, N. J.: Old Paths Publications, 1996), 357.

[94] Calvin, *Inst.* (1559) 1.13.22 and 1.13.23, respectively. Cf. 1.13.28 where Calvin opposes the use of Tertullian by his trinitarian opponents, saying, "Contendit enim adversus Praxeam, quanvis in tres personas distinctus sit Deus, non tamen fieri plures deos, neque *discerpi* unitatem" (OS 3.149).

[95] Calvin, *Inst.* (1559) 1.15.5; OS 3.181 (LCC 20.191): "Interea Creatoris essentiam lacerare, ut partem quisque possideat, nimiae amentiae est." Calvin here opposes the re-introduction of the Manichaean derivation of the human soul from the divine essence.

explains that the apparent fruitlessness of the sacramental sign in some is not due to a fault in the thing signified but to the abuse of the sign by the communicant. "Let us then learn not to *tear away* (*divellere*) *the thing signified from the thing*."[96]

This is but a sampling of Calvin's heavy use of this "tearing" language. But it is Calvin's soteriological use of the image that is of greatest significance, for it serves to integrate the christological/eucharistic and soteriological strains of Calvin's thought as this theological complex of concerns was intensified in the polemics of the 1550s. Calvin's use of the image against Osiander parallels his earlier (1539) and practically identical use of it in what would become (in 1559) *Inst.* 3.16.1:

> Do you wish, then, to attain righteousness in Christ? You must first possess Christ; but you cannot possess him without being made partaker in his sanctification, because *he cannot be torn into pieces* (*quia in frusta discerpi non potest*). Since, therefore, it is solely by expending himself that the Lord gives us these benefits to enjoy, he bestows both of them at the same time (*simul*), the one never without the other.[97]

In a Galatians sermon Calvin similarly explains, "Unless we have been sanctified by the Holy Spirit, we cannot be members of the body of the Lord Jesus Christ... The Lord Jesus Christ cannot be divided or fragmented (*ne peut pas ester divisé, ne mis par pieces*), for he is infinite, and has secured forgiveness for our sins through his sufferings and death..."[98]

---

[96] Calvin, *Comm.* 1 Pet 3:21 (CO 55.268): "Discamus ergo rem signatam a signo non divellere."

[97] Calvin, *Inst.* (1539) 3.16.1 (OS 4.249; LCC 20.798): "Vis ergo iustitiam in Christo adipisci? Christum ante possideas oportet; possidere autem non potes quin fias sanctificationis eius particeps; *quia in frustra discerpi non potest*. Quum ergo haec beneficia, nonnisi seipsum erogando, fruenda nobis Dominus concedat, utrunque *simul* largitur: *alterum nunquam sine altero*."

[98] Calvin, *Serm. Galat.*, Sermon 22; CO 50.550 (*Sermons on Galatians*, 331-2): "Ainsi nous n'avons de quoy nous glorifier, quoy qu'il en soit, pour estre en repos: nous ne pouvons pas nous fonder sur nos merites. Vray est que les fideles doivent cercher de s'adonner à Dieu: car nous ne pouvons pas estre membres de Seigneur Iesus Christ, sinon que nous soyons sanctifiez par son sainct Esprit, comme nous verrons en temps et en lieu. Et nostre Seigneur Iesus Christ ne peut pas estre divisé, ne mis par pieces, comme il est infini, d'autant que nos pechez nous sont pardonnez par sa mort et passion, qu'ils ont esté lavez et purgez par son sang: que ce lavementlá nous a esté donné pour nous reformer à l'image de Dieu son Pere: tellement qu'en luy il nous faut estre nouvelles creatures."

Applied Christology

The force of the metaphor depends entirely on Calvin's argument that union with Christ underlies and forms the context of the saving benefits, the *duplex gratia* of justification and sanctification. The desired effect, violent as it is, has this precise theological intention: to demonstrate the danger and folly of a salvation understood only in either its forensic or transformative aspects. Because salvation is union with the Christ in whom all saving benefits reside, to contemplate a justification without sanctification, or a sanctification without justification, is effectively to tear Christ to pieces.

Of special significance is the increase in Calvin's use of this metaphor in the 1550s, together with the apparently calculated way in which he uses it. The final revision of the Romans commentary can be taken as an especially significant example. Taken together with other numerous occurrences of the metaphor in his commentaries and sermons, the introduction of this metaphor three times in the 1556 revision of the Romans commentary to make precisely the same theological point is worthy of the most careful attention. At the crucial transition from Romans 5 to Romans 6, Calvin introduces in 1556 a new opening statement on 6:1: "Throughout this chapter the apostle maintains that those who imagine that Christ bestows free justification upon us without imparting newness of life shamefully tear Christ asunder (*Christum discerpere*)."[99] In two places in chapter eight (vv. 9, 13), Calvin, again in 1556, introduces the following clarifications to his comments:

... for those who separate Christ from his Spirit make Him like a dead image or corpse. We must always bear in mind the counsel of the apostle, that free remission of sins cannot be separated (*disiungi*) from the Spirit of regeneration. This would be, as it were, to tear Christ asunder (*quasi Christum discerpere*).[100]

Let believers, therefore, learn to embrace Him, not only for justification, but also for sanctification, as He has been given to us for both these purposes, that they may not tear Him (*lacerent*) by their own mutilated faith.[101]

---

[99] Calvin, *Comm. Epist. ad Romanos*, 117: "Hoc toto capite disseret Apostolus, perperam eos *Christum discerpere*, qui gratuitam ab ipso iustitiam nobis donari fingunt absque vitae novitate." Italics mine.

[100] Calvin, *Comm. Epist. ad Romanos*, 160: "Ac semper tenendum est illud Apostoli consilium, gratuitam peccatorum remissionem a Spiritu regenerationis non posse disiungi; quia hoc esset *quasi Christum discerpere*." Italics mine. Note the Christ-Spirit relationship in light of the inseparability of Christ/Spirit and justification/sanctification in Calvin's comments on Rom. 8:9.

[101] Calvin, *Comm. Epist. ad Romanos*, 163: "Verum est quidem, nos sola Dei misericordia iustificari in Christo. Sed aeque et istud verum ac certum, omnes

In each case the image is added in the final, 1556 revision; it does not appear before then. In each case, moreover, the metaphor is intended to enforce the idea that justification and sanctification are as inseparable as Christ and the Spirit. Inasmuch as Calvin uses this metaphor to make precisely the same point in criticism of Osiander's proposed way of overcoming the charge of a legal fiction, it is highly likely that the new occurrences of this metaphor in the last revision of the Romans commentary and in the 1559 *Institutes* are related. Indeed, when taken together with the frequent use of the image in sermons and polemical texts of the 1550s, these passages indicate a pattern of expression to which Calvin attached himself more and more over the course of his ministry, and particularly in the 1550s when the christological-eucharistic presupposition underlying its graphic violence served especially well to make his point about the distinction without separation of the saving *duplex gratia*. Therefore, in light of the function and intention of this metaphor in Calvin's usage, and in light of its ability to integrate crucial eucharistic and christological points of dispute, it seems likely that the presence of this metaphor in Calvin's Osiander refutation is far from coincidental. There is yet one more indication, however, that Calvin's increased use of this metaphor, while broadly applicable to Rome, should be closely associated with his refutation of Osiander: Calvin's formal commentary on 1 Cor 1:30, which we have not yet examined and to which we now turn.

In light of the foregoing discussion of the importance of 1 Cor 1:30 as both the biblical shorthand for Calvin's model and the exegetical epicenter of his 1559 refutation of Osiander, it is of great significance that in his comment on this verse, Calvin summarizes his *unio*-soteriology and makes use of the very same metaphor to argue for the simultaneity and inseparability of the *duplex gratia*. It is necessary to quote at length.

> Secondly, he says that he is *made unto us righteousness* (*nobis factum esse in iustitiam*), by which he means that we are on his account acceptable to God, inasmuch as he expiated our sins by his death, and his obedience is imputed to us for righteousness. For as the righteousness of faith consists in remission of sins and a gracious acceptance, we obtain both through Christ.
>
> Thirdly, he calls him our *sanctification*, by which he means, that we who are otherwise unholy by nature, are by his Spirit renewed

---

qui iustificantur, vocari a Domino ut digne sua vocatione vivant. [1556 add:] Discant ergo fideles non in iustitiam modo, sed in sanctificationem quoque amplecti, sicuti in utrunque finem nobis datus est, *ne mutila sua fide eum lacerent*." Italics mine.

unto holiness, that we may serve God. From this, also, we infer that *we cannot be justified freely through faith alone without at the same time living holy*. For these graces are connected together, as it were, by an indissoluble tie, so that *he who attempts to sever them does in a manner tear Christ in pieces (ut qui eas separare nititur, Christum quodammodo discerpat)*. Let therefore the man who seeks to be justified through Christ, by God's unmerited goodness, consider that this cannot be attained without his taking him *at the same time (simul)* for sanctification, or, in other words, being renewed to innocence and purity of life. Those, however, that slander us, as if by preaching a free justification through faith we called men off from good works, are amply refuted from this passage, which intimates that faith apprehends in Christ regeneration equally with forgiveness of sins.

Observe, on the other hand, that these two offices of Christ are *conjoined (coniungi)* in such a manner as to be, notwithstanding, *distinguished (distinguatur)* from each other. What, therefore, Paul here expressly *distinguishes (discernit)*, it is not allowable mistakenly to *confound (confundere)*. Fourthly, he teaches us that he is given to us for *redemption*, by which he means that through his goodness we are delivered at once from all bondage to sin, and from all the misery that flows from it. Thus redemption is the first gift of Christ that is begun in us, and the last that is completed. For the commencement of salvation consists in our being drawn out of the labyrinth of sin and death; yet in the meantime, until the final day of the resurrection, we groan with desire for redemption. If it is asked in what way Christ is given to us for redemption, I answer "Because he made himself a ransom." In fine, of all the blessings that are here enumerated we must seek in Christ not the half, or merely a part, but the entire completion. For Paul does not say that he has been given to us by way of filling up, or eking out righteousness, holiness, wisdom, and redemption, but assigns to him exclusively the entire accomplishment of the whole. Now as *you will scarcely meet with another passage of Scripture that more distinctly marks out all the offices of Christ*, you may also understand from it very clearly the nature and efficacy of faith. For as Christ is the proper object of faith, every one that knows what are the benefits that Christ confers upon us is at the same time taught to understand what faith is.[102]

---

[102] Calvin, *Comm.* 1 Cor 1:30 (CO 49.331-2; CTS 93-4): "Secundo dicit, nobis factum esse in iustitiam: quo intelligit, nos eius nomine acceptos esse Deo, quia morte sua peccata nostra expiaverit, et eius obedientia nobis in iustitiam imputetur. Nam quum fidei iustitia in peccatorum remissione et gratuita

Outside the *Institutio*, this is perhaps the most concise articulation of Calvin's soteriology, incorporating the exegetical shorthand (1 Cor 1:30), the *unio Christi-duplex gratia* formula (with the important particulars of faith and the Spirit), and the *discerpi* metaphor, all in one passage. Calvin himself claims one will "scarcely meet with another passage of Scripture" that is so clear as this, and his comment reflects each of his most basic concerns: the obtaining of righteousness exclusively in Christ, the inseparability of sanctification from justification in light of the controlling significance of union with Christ (in his sermon on the passage this is emphasized with a view to the sinfulness of mankind and the

---

acceptione consistat, utrumque per Christum consequimur. Tertio vocat sanctificationem: quo intelligit, nos alioqui natura profanos, spiritu eius regenerari in sanctitatem, ut serviamus Deo. Unde etiam colligimus *non posse nos gratis iustificari sola fide, quin simul sancte vivamus*. Istae enim gratiae quasi individuo nexu cohaerent: *ut qui eas separare nititur, Christum quodammodo discerpat*. Proinde qui per Christum gratuita Dei bonitate iustificari quaerit, cogitet fieri hoc *non posse* quin *simul* in sanctificationem eum apprehendat: hoc est, eius spiritu renascatur in vitae innocentiam et puritatem. Qui autem nos calumniantur, quasi gratuitam fidei iustitiam praedicando a bonis operibus avocemus homines, abunde hinc refelluntur, quod fides non minus regenerationem in Christo apprehendit quam peccatorum veniam. Rursum observa sic duo ista Christi officia *coniungi*, ut tamen *distinguatur* unum ab altero: quae ergo Paulus nominatim *discernit*, perperam *confundere non licet*. Quarto, in redemptionem datum esse docet: quo intelligit eius beneficio nos tam ab omni peccati servitute, quam omni miseria, quae inde manat, liberari. Ita redemptio primum Christi donum est quod inchoatur in nobis, et ultimum perficitur. Hoc enim salutis est initium, quod ex peccati et mortis labyrintho extrahimur: interea tamen usque ad ultimum resurrectionis diem gemimus desiderio redemptionis, ut habetur Rom. 8:26. Modus autem si quaeritur, quo Christus in redemptionem nobis datus est, respondeo, quia pretium se constituit. Postremo, bonorum omnium, quae hic recensentur, non dimidium aut partem aliquam, sed complementum in Christo quaeramus. Neque enim dicit Paulus, nobis datum esse in supplementum vel adminiculum iustitiae, sanctitatis, sapientiae, redemptionis: sed solidum omnium effectum ei soli assignat. *Quoniam autem vix occurret alius in scriptura locus, qui distinctius omnia Christi officia describat*, ex eo quoque optime poterit vis et natura fidei intelligi. Nam quum proprium fidei obiectum sit Christus, quicunque novit quae sint erga nos Christi beneficia, ille etiam edoctus est quid sit fides." Italics mine. N.B.: Mackenzie's translation of "Istae enim gratiae" as "for these two fruits of grace" changed to "for these graces." This is one of the rare occasions where we find Calvin use the plural, *gratiae*, rather than the singular (e.g., *duplex gratia*) but even here the accent is on their inseparable unity, christologically expressed.

restoration of the *imago Dei* in Christ),[103] the importance of the proper distinction of these benefits, and the consequent indispensability of sanctification or good works to justification ("we *cannot* be justified freely through faith alone without at the same time living holy"). The linking together of these three elements (exegetical, formulaic, and metaphorical) in the span of one comment on 1 Cor 1:30 is arguably the most compressed combination of Calvin's strongest soteriological emphases, and bears an unmistakable, positive relationship to his refutation of Osiander in which the identical combination is present.[104]

But, importantly, the explicit connection of these three elements is not restricted to the commentary on 1 Corinthians. In a sermon on Galatians, for example, Calvin explains why it is necessary to attribute all of our righteousness to Christ, bringing together the language of 1 Cor 1:30 and the metaphor to emphasize the necessity of our justifying righteousness being located in Christ *extra nos*.

> Why? Because it is as if they are dividing Christ, and only attributing to him half of that which is wholly his own. *He is our righteousness* and our peace (1 Cor. 1:30; Eph. 2:14). What does this word "righteousness" imply? It means that God can freely accept us through the Lord Jesus Christ. If we say that we can please God by our merits, and that Jesus Christ simply completes that which we lack, are we not *tearing him in two (deschirer)*, and *dismembering him (desmembrer)* as far as is in our power?[105]

---

[103] *Primier Volume, contenant 58 Sermones faict sur les 9. primers chapitres de la 1 Epistre de Sainct Paul Aux Corinthiens, par M. Jean Calvin*, 1555, 76ʳ-83ᵛ (serm. on 1 Cor 1:30), preached 17 November, 1555, manuscript number: BPU Ms. fr. 26. I have only been able to make limited use of this manuscript here but recommend its incorporation in future work on Calvin and Osiander. Prof. Elsie Anne McKee is presently working on a transcription of these sermons.

[104] An additional connection should be noted. Calvin's states in *Inst*. 3.1.1 (also new in 1559) that the Holy Spirit is the "bond (*sanctum vinculum*) by which Christ effectually unites us to himself." Then Calvin immediately explains that this pertains also to what he taught in Book 2 concerning Christ's anointing. This connection between the Spirit as *vinculum* and the offices of the Mediator is explicit in his statement here that 1 Cor 1:30, more than any other passage, "*distinctly marks out all the offices of Christ*." In light of the function of (1) the Spirit as *vinculum* (central to Calvin's critique), (2) the offices of the Mediator, and (3) the centrality of 1 Cor 1:30 in Calvin's response to Osiander, this threefold complex is a significant indicator of the Christ-Spirit / justification-sanctification relationship in Calvin's thought.

[105] Calvin, *Serm. Gal.*, Sermon 31, CO 50.663-4 (*Sermons on Galatians*, 466): "Or sainct Paul au contraire dit que Iesus Christ ne profite rien, quand nous voulons entrer en telle paction avec Dieu. Et pourquoy? car c'est tout un de partir Iesus

But something must be addressed here. If the increased use of the metaphor in the 1550s points to the Osiandrian controversy, one would expect that, as in the Romans commentary, the metaphor would have been added in the final, 1556 revision of the Corinthians commentary. In fact it is present as early as the first, 1546 edition, functioning much as it did in Calvin's 1539 *Reply* to Sadoleto. In fact, on close examination of the texts, Calvin's comment on 1 Cor 1:30 not only fails to show an addition of the metaphor to his comment in 1556 but does not indicate any change whatsoever from its 1546 form (apart from minor matters of spelling, etc.).[106] Instead, Calvin's comment does not reveal any impact of the Osiandrian controversy upon his exegesis of this pivotal verse. Thus it could be argued that the unchanged commentary undermines the claim advanced above of the unique centrality of this verse to the 1559 Osiander refutation, for surely if this verse is as central to the refutation as I have suggested, at least some effort would presumably have been made by Calvin in 1556 to bring his comment to bear *more explicitly* on the questions at issue.

In reality this objection turns out to be much weaker than it first appears, for while it is true that Calvin did not modify his comment in light of the Osiandrian affair, a careful comparison of his 1546 comment with his 1559 refutation reveals that no modification was necessary. The very argument that Calvin develops in the form of a theological refutation in the 1559 *Institutes* is identical in form and content with the 1546 comment. Indeed, the parallel is remarkable, for it indicates that the theological, exegetical, and metaphorical contours of Calvin's 1559 response were present more than a decade earlier in practically identical form. Just as in 1559, Calvin explained in 1546 that the Apostle's language demanded both a simultaneity – and thus inseparability – of the *duplex gratia* as a consequence of

---

Christ et de luy attribuer à demi ce qui luy appartient du tout et en perfection. Or il nous est donné pour iustice: il est appelé nostre paix: et ce mot de iustice qu'emporte-il? c'est que Dieu nous accepte gratuitement au nom de nostre Seigneur Iesus Christ. Or maintenant si nous disons que par nos merites nous sommes agreables à Dieu, et s'il y a quelque deffaut que Iesus Christ y supplie, n'est-ce pas deschirer Iesus Christ et le desmembrer, en tant qu'en nous est?"

[106] For example, changing "... in Christo vero subsistentia ita non est quod superbiatis" (*Commentarii... ad Corinthios*, 31ᵛ) to "... in Christo vero subsistentia *vestra fundata est,* ita non est quod superbiatis" (*In Omnes Pauli Apostoli Epistolas,* 158; cf. CO 49.330) or "... nos ab omni tam peccati servitute..." (*Commentarii... ad Corinthios,* 32ᵛ) to " ...nos tam ab omni peccati servitute,..." (*In Omnes Pauli Apostoli Epistolas,* 158; cf. CO 49.331). Italics mine. The other changes are still more minor, such as spelling changes or corrections, e.g., "cum" to "quum" and "prophanos" to "profanos."

union with Christ, and the distinction of the graces in light of Paul's manner of speaking in which both righteousness and sanctification are listed, as Calvin says, "without redundancy." In this light, Calvin's use of the *discerpi* metaphor against Osiander is evidence of both (1) the threefold complex of 1 Cor 1:30, the *unio Christi-duplex gratia* construction, and the metaphor; and (2) the long-standing importance of this threefold complex to his soteriology.

Analysis: The Theology and Interpretation of Calvin's Polemical Strategy

In the foregoing analyses, the importance of the exegetical crux of 1 Cor 1:30 was emphasized in order to reveal the complexity which underlay the affirmation, whether by Osiander or by Calvin, that Christ *is* our righteousness. Attention was directed specifically to Calvin's objection to Osiander's ontological or essentialist reading of the Apostle's language, and this concern was clarified by Calvin's regular use of a violent image in which the Chalcedonian presupposition of his own Christology and sacramentology was employed in the service of his *unio-duplex* soteriological model. This image functioned to emphasize, in the most striking way possible, the necessity both of the simultaneity and of the distinct-yet-inseparable character of justification and sanctification. What remains is for us to tie these observations to a reading of the actual text of Calvin's refutation, highlighting the vocabulary and forms of expression in order to demonstrate that he adopted a specific polemical strategy designed to make a point much larger than the commonly recognized claim that Osiander's doctrine of justification was faulty.

By now it is clear that appreciating how Calvin approaches Osiander depends to a great extent on one's ability to recognize what Osiander's proposals meant in the mid sixteenth-century struggle for the authentic language of gospel proclamation. Osiander's theology in particular must be located in the early development of Lutheran responses to Rome. Because justification and salvation were equated so often in the Lutheran literature, a particular difficulty surfaced with respect to objectivity and subjectivity. It has been noted that Osiander sought to emphasize for his fellow Lutherans the real responsibility for Christian obedience, an observation that places his burden (as we have seen) squarely in line with the common Reformation dilemma of defending the necessary presence of good works in the lives of those justified *sola fide*.[107] Put differently, Osiander felt acutely the heat of the charge of a legal fiction. But beyond this common concern, the character of Osiander's ideas is more complex and, importantly, more particularly Lutheran. Indeed, it appears Osiander's proposal is best understood as an effort to reconcile the tension within Lutheran thought between the physical immanence of ubiquitarian sacramental theology and the radical *extra nos* distance of justification. If so, then his idea of a justifying union with the divine nature of Christ effectively tied the physical immanence of ubiquitarianism to the Lutheran primacy of justification on account of Christ alone. His followers regarded this as a positive exposition of Luther's own ideas. For almost all of his Lutheran colleagues, however, this only had the unacceptable effect of confusing justification with personal transformation, the very idea rejected by a distinctly Lutheran theology of salvation. As noted above, the Lutheran response to Osiander, therefore, especially as eventually codified in the Formula of Concord, was manifestly an emphasis on the objectivity of justification, and because of the *de facto* equivalency of justification and salvation, of salvation, too.

These considerations clarify the nature of Calvin's response to Osiander as it incorporates his own discomfort with Lutheran ideas. Important in this connection is the ontological concern Calvin has with Lutheran Christology. As indicated in Chapter 4 above, in the course of polemic with Westphal and Heshusius Calvin often argues that the physical omnipresence of Christ's human nature and its location in the bread and wine only confuses what is properly divine and human. In part acknowledging this context, Marijn De Kroon correctly views the Calvin-Osiander polemic as a struggle over the idea of distance. Calvin saw in Osiander a transgression of the ontological distance between men and God.[108]

These observations aid in the discovery of what is really the theological heart of what Calvin objects to in Osiander: Osiander's distinctly Lutheran idea of Christ and the Supper, which, unlike his controversial doctrine of justification, is *common* to all Lutherans (the

---

[107] Note Feenstra's observation ("Calvin versus Osiander on Justification," 9) that Osiander "wanted to lay a heavier responsibility upon the 'justified' Christian than he found in Lutheran theology in his day…"

[108] Marijn de Kroon, *The Honour of God and Human Salvation: A Contribution to an Understanding of Calvin's Theology According to His* Institutes (trans. John Vriend and Lyle D. Bierma; Edinburgh: T. & T. Clark, 2001), 102-3. Note that de Kroon finds an inconsistency in Calvin here (p. 104). Prof. Irena Backus, in private correspondence, has also referred to Calvin's "allergic" reaction to any transgression of this distance, evident also in Calvin's critique of Servetus.

Philippists perhaps excepted). Upon examination one finds that, though ostensibly only about justification, Calvin in his polemic in reality attacks Lutheran Christology and sacramentology as the cause of which Osiander's heresy is the effect. Indeed, Calvin's pattern of expression and argument suggests it is this crucial subtext of Calvin's response that is in fact the *principal point* of his entire refutation. This is a claim in need of documentation, and the following is offered for consideration.

The points at which Calvin employs the language of the eucharistic controversy in his refutation are numerous. The form they usually take is in Calvin's objection to Osiander's "essential mixing" of natures, human and divine, and, consequently, of the saving benefits. For instance, just as other Reformed theologians attacked the Lutheran *communicatio idiomatum* and ubiquitarianism as a Manichaean error, so Calvin says Osiander is bordering on Manichaeism in "his desire to *transfuse* the *essentia Dei* into men."[109] Osiander's ontological confusion of the physical and spiritual, the human and divine, and his idea of the "essence of communion," i.e., that the "essence of God's righteousness is accidental, present with a man one moment and absent the next,"[110] leads to this Augustinian charge of "bordering" on the error of the Manichees.[111] Moreover, applying the Reformed critique of the Lutheran *communicatio*, Calvin explains that while it is true we are one with Christ, his *essentiam* is not *mixed* with our own (*interea... misceri Christi essentiam cum nostra*).[112] Osiander, Calvin says, is discontented with "the righteousness which has been acquired for us by Christ's obedience and sacrificial death" and prefers instead that we are made righteous substantially by infusion of the divine *essence* and quality

---

[109] Calvin, *Inst.* (1559) 3.11.5; OS 4.185-6: "Conceperat vir ille quiddam affine Manichaeis, ut essentiam Dei in homines transfundere appeteret." Calvin makes this association twice. Cf. with CO 38.166 (*Calvin's Ecclesiastical Advice*, 33): "Adde, quod essentialis illa communicatio ex Manichaeorum deliriis sumpta est." Heshusius accused Calvin of Manichaeism, to which Calvin objected vigorously (*De Vera Participatione*, CO 9.466; cf. *Calvin: Theological Treatises*, 263). Cf. Calvin here with Vermigli, *Dialogus*, 74ᵛ, 81ᵛ; PML 2, *Dialogue*, 116, 126. Flacius made the same accusation of Manichaeism against Osiander, and Calvin makes a near identical point against Menno elsewhere (CO 38.167): "Mennonis doctrina, quam ex deliriis Manichaeorum hausit, mihi non erat incognita."

[110] Calvin, CO 38.166 (*Calvin's Ecclesiastical Advice*, 33): "Nec video quomodo excusari possit hoc absurdum, essentialem Dei iustitiam esse accidens, quod adesse nunc homini possit, nunc abesse."

[111] The editors of OS note Augustine, *Serm.* 182, 4, 4 MSL 38, 986 (OS 4.186, n. 1).

[112] Calvin, *Inst.* (1559) 3.11.5; OS 4.186: "Dicit nos unum esse cum Christo. Fatemur: interea negamus misceri Christi essentiam cum nostra."

(*substantialiter in Deo iustos esse tam essentia quam qualitate infusa*).[113] Osiander claims a *mixture of substances* (*substantialem mixtionem*) by which God *transfuses* (*transfundens*) himself into us, making us a part of himself. Indeed, Osiander regards the Spirit's work as practically useless unless *Christ's essence is mingled with ours* (*nisi eius essentia nobis misceatur*), unless we are united to God *essentialiter*.[114] Calvin explains that had Osiander confined himself to a union by conjunction of essence (*essentiali coniunctione*) insofar as Christ is our Head, or with the essence of the divine nature poured into us, then he would have "fed on these delights with less harm" and the controversy ("the great quarrel") would not have arisen. But Osiander insists instead on understanding the justifying *iustitia* not as free imputation but as a personal righteousness flowing from the indwelling divine *essence* of God (*quam Dei essentia in nobis residens*).[115]

Calvin's approach to Osiander *as a Lutheran* is still more explicit when he criticizes Osiander's confusion of justification and renewal by explaining that "reason itself forbids us to *transfer the peculiar qualities of the one to the other (transferre tamen quod unius peculiare est ad alterum, ratio ipsa prohibet*)," a clear attack on the fundamental ubiquitarian premise. He continues, making the connection with ubiquitarianism clear, that "in this *confusion of the two kinds of grace*

---

[113] Calvin, *Inst.* (1559) 3.11.5; OS 4.186: "...dilucide tamen exprimit se non ea iustitia contentum, quae nobis obedientia et sacrificio mortis Christi parta est, fingere nos substantialiter in Deo iustos esse tam essentia quam qualitate infusa."

[114] Calvin, *Inst.* (1559) 3.11.5; OS 4.186: "Deinde substantialem mixtionem ingerit, qua Deus se in nos transfundens, quasi partem sui faciat. Nam virtute Spiritus sancti fieri ut coalescamus cum Christo, nobisque sit caput et nos eius membra, fere pro nihilo ducit, nisi eius essentia nobis misceatur. Sed in Patre et Spiritu apertius, ut dixi, prodit quid sentiat: nempe iustificari nos non sola Mediatoris gratia, nec in eius persona iustitiam simpliciter vel solide nobis offerri: sed nos fieri iustitiae diviniae consortes, dum essentialiter nobis unitur Deus."

[115] Calvin, *Inst.* (1559) 3.11.6; OS 4.187: "Si tantum diceret Christum nos iustificando essentiali coniunctione nostrum fieri: nec solum quatenus homo est, esse caput nostrum, sed divinae quoque naturae essentiam in nos diffundi: minore noxa deliciis se pasceret, nec forte propter hoc delirium tanta esset excitanda contentio..." In connection with this criticism, one should note Calvin's *Brevis Confessio* in which a similar point is made. There, Calvin explains that justification is by faith inasmuch as it is by faith that the Mediator is savingly grasped and the promises of the gospel are relied upon. "Wherefore I detest," Calvin continues, "the ravings of those who endeavor to persuade us that the essential righteousness of God exists in us, and are not satisfied with the free imputation in which alone Scripture orders us to acquiesce" (TT 2.133).

Applied Christology

(*duplicis gratiae confusione*) that Osiander forces upon us there is *a like absurdity* (*similis est absurditas*)."[116] The connection of a specifically Lutheran Christology and ubiquitarianism with Osiander's mingling of the graces now made explicit, Calvin continues to observe that the correct way of thinking, which sees in Christ's flesh the "sure pledge" (*certum... pignus*) of spiritual life, is seen also in the correct (that is, Calvin's own) sacramentology: "This method of teaching is perceived in the sacraments; even though they direct our faith to the whole Christ and not to a half-Christ, they teach that the matter both of righteousness and of salvation resides in his flesh – not that as mere man he justifies or quickens by himself but because it pleased God to reveal in the Mediator what was hidden and incomprehensible in himself."[117]

In his pattern of expression, then, Calvin appears to parallel Osiander's diminution of the humanity of Christ in justification with his denial of a proper (circumscribed) humanity in his Lutheran sacramentology. This parallel is important, and continues the relationship that Calvin has been highlighting between Lutheran sacramentology and Osiander's doctrine of justification.

To make this relationship firm, Calvin is most explicit near the end of his refutation, where there can no longer be any question about the intention of his strategy and the heart of his theological critique. Osiander, Calvin says, spurning the Spirit-bond (*spirituali coniunctione*) of union,

> forces a *gross mingling of Christ with believers*. And he therefore calls *"Zwinglian"* all who disagree with his *"essential"* righteousness *because they do not say Christ is eaten in the Supper...* Osiander's violent insistence upon *essential* righteousness and *essential* indwelling of Christ has this result: first, Osiander holds that God

---

[116] Calvin, *Inst.* (1559) 3.11.6; OS 4.187: "Verum si solis claritas non potest a calore separari, an ideo dicemus luce calefieri terram, calore vero illustrari. Hac similitudine nihil ad rem praesentem magis accommodum? sol calore suo terram vegetat ac foecundat, radiis suis illustrat et illluminat; hic mutua est ac individua connexio: transferre tamen quod unius peculiare est ad alterum, ratio ipsa prohibet. In hac duplicis gratiae confusione, quam obtrudit Osiander, similis est absurditas..."

[117] Calvin, *Inst.* (1559) 3.11.9; OS 4.191: "Quae ratio docendi in sacramentis perspicitur: quae etsi fidem nostram ad totum Christum non dimidium dirigunt, simul tamen iustitiae et salutis materiam in eius carne residere docent; non quod a seipso iustificet aut vivificet merus homo, sed quia Deo placuit, quod in se absconditum et incomprehensibile erat, in Mediatore palam facere."

pours himself into us as a *gross mixture, just as a physical eating in the Lord's Supper.*[118]

The connections are drawn compellingly by Calvin as he ties Osiander's soteriology to his sacramentology, his idea of justification by essential union with the divine Christ to his Lutheran interpretation of the *communicatio idiomatum* and eucharistic communion.

By way of assessment, it is crucial to observe that Calvin's own *unio Christi-duplex gratia* construction is not at all intended to challenge the *extra nos* character of imputed justification, properly understood. The forensic character of justification is also crystal clear in Calvin's works and stands as one of his chief emphases; it is not in the least relativized by his doctrine of union with Christ. But it is precisely this point, namely, the effect of union with Christ upon justification, which Calvin focuses on in his refutation of Osiander. Instead of solidifying the unity of justification and renewal, Osiander's union-concept only serves to de-forensicize justification and thus obscure the distinction of the graces on which everything Reformational is staked.

The reason this is the case is especially important for appreciating the energy Calvin brings to his refutation. In short, Calvin is convinced that Osiander's *iustitia essentialis* rests upon the presupposition of a Lutheran Christology and sacramentology, in particular the Lutheran *communicatio idiomatum*. This crucial observation comports well with recent Osiander scholarship which has confirmed earlier suggestions that Osiander's doctrine of justification is based upon his christological presuppositions.[119] Not only does it rest upon this presupposition, however. Calvin evidently perceives in Osiander's aberrant doctrine of justification the inevitable soteriological implications of a consistently-held Lutheran Christology and sacramentology. Osiander, in Calvin's eyes, is *effectively the only consistent Lutheran*, and serves therefore as an ideal foil (remember Osiander is widely rejected by his Lutheran colleagues) for demonstrating what he regards as the dangerous

---

[118] Calvin, *Inst.* (1559) 3.11.10; OS 4.192: "Sed Osiander hac spirituali coniunctione spreta, crassam mixturam Christi cum fidelibus urget: atque ideo Zuinglianos odiose nominat, quicunque non subscribunt fanatico errori de essentiali iustitia: quia non sentiant Christum in Coena substantialiter comedi... Quod ergo essentialem iustitiam et essentialem in nobis Christi habitationem tam importune exigit, huc spectat, primum ut crassa mixtura se Deus in nos transfundat, sicuti in Coena carnalis manducatio ab ipso fingitur..."
[119] See Hauke, *Gott-Haben – um Gottes Willen*, 213-36, 258-59.

irrationality at the heart of Lutheran ideas about eucharistic communion with Christ.

The evidence therefore suggests, in light of his regular pattern of expression, that Calvin recognizes a correspondence between (1) the ontological-christological confusion of Lutheran ubiquitarianism and (2) the justification/sanctification confusion in Osiander's doctrine of an essential union with Christ. According to Calvin, the confusion of what is properly divine and human at the level of Lutheran Christology and ubiquitarianism is simply carried through at the soteriological level in Osiander's doctrine of essential union which results in a mixing of what is properly justification and sanctification. Hence Calvin's pattern of argument points to his understanding of the Spirit as the theological safeguard against ontological confusion in salvation, just as for Calvin the Spirit's activity in eucharistic communion safeguards against confusing the divine and human natures of Christ.

To appreciate this anti-ubiquitarian subtext, one must remember that Calvin has been engaged for much of the decade with defending his sacramentology against Lutheran ubiquitarianism, particularly as represented by Westphal and Heshusius. In the course of his attacks on ubiquitarian teaching, he has focused attention on the indispensability of Christ's real (circumscribed) humanity. Christ's humanity is located at the Father's right hand; otherwise his is not a true humanity. Or, as Calvin often puts it, to grant ubiquity to Christ's human nature is to confuse what is properly divine and human. A ubiquitous human nature is a contradiction in terms. The vital elements of Calvin's criticism of Osiander – Christ must be truly man to be Mediator, the proper qualities of justification and sanctification must not be transferred to one another, etc. – must be located within this contemporary polemical setting.

Moreover, inasmuch as Westphal and others had accused Calvin of being theological kin with Osiander, one should appreciate that Calvin is hereby tossing the universally rejected Osiander back to his Lutheran counterparts, claiming in the course of his argument, "No, he really belongs to you. *If you were consistent you would be where he is.*" Note the comment Calvin makes against Westphal in a quotation already noted above:

> Here they taint us with the manure of their own Osiander, as if we had any kind of affinity with him (*Osiandri sui... quasi ulla unquam inter nos affinitas fuerit*). Doubtless that Osiander, in his insane pride, despised a humiliated Christ; what is that to us, whose piety is too well known to be defamed by such vile falsehoods? No, with

the best right I throw back the empty talk at their own heads (*Quin optimo iure in eorum capita inanem istum garritum retorqueo*)...[120]

He "threw back" Osiander to the Lutherans precisely by arguing that Osiander's "monstrous" doctrine of justification by essential union with the divine Christ is implied in Lutheran Christology and ubiquitarianism. Thus Osiander's theology, rejected widely by Lutherans, is only the consistent outworking of distinctive presuppositions held in common by all Lutherans. The evidence suggests that *this* point is the polemical intention of Calvin's explicitly eucharistic pattern of argument and expression. When set alongside Calvin's eucharistic polemic, the Osiandrianism–ubiquitarianism connections in his argument seem quite unmistakable, and a sixteenth-century Lutheran, especially Westphal, certainly would not have missed them.

These observations point, furthermore, to the heart of the differences between Calvin and the Lutheran reactions to Osiander. Whereas Osiander's Lutheran opponents emphasized the objectivity of justification against Osiander's subjective view, Calvin argued for a unity of objective and subjective elements as distinct but inseparable aspects of one saving reality: union with Christ. In other words, Calvin's objection to Osiander is *not*, as Andreae's and Melanchthon's are, that sanctification is grounded in justification or imputation. Contrary to Berkouwer, Calvin's criticism does not have as its underlying dogmatic concern that "justification is the basis of sanctification."[121] To be sure, the peace of conscience that rightly belongs only to the redeemed rests upon the *extra nos* character of the righteousness imputed in justification, but the grace of renewal does not on this account flow from the grace of imputation. Nor is this grace subordinated to it as an ultimately dispensable facet of salvation. Rather, what is evident at the earliest stages in Calvin's work as a theme already cherished is only heightened in significance and clarity in the refutation of Osiander: the rationale for both justification and sanctification is to be identified exclusively with the (spiritual, not essential or ontological) union believers have with Christ, or, rather more accurately, in the righteous Christ himself with whom they have been brought into saving union by the secret or mystical work of the Spirit through the instrumentality of faith.

But what else can we conclude with regard to the significance of the Osiander refutation within the wider Calvin corpus? At the very least the complicated intertextuality is significant. Here again it is

---

[120] Calvin, *Ultimo Admonitio*, CO 9.246; TT 2.488. See n. 49 above for the full quotation.
[121] Berkouwer, *Faith and Justification*, 100.

important to note the addition of the *discerpo* metaphor in the 1556 *Romans* revision. Furthermore, the opening section of Book 3 in the 1559 *Institutes* functions both as the beginning of a Book on the work of the Holy Spirit and as a theological orientation to the work of the Spirit in uniting believers to Christ. The intention of the opening section of Book 3 is clearly to establish the *unio Christi* perspectival construct on salvation developed throughout the rest of the Book. In light of the eucharistic controversial context of the 1550s in which Calvin defends a uniquely "spiritual" understanding of personal communion with Christ in the Supper, the addition in 1559 of 3.1.1 to the *Institutes*, as well as other additions throughout the rest of Book 3, should be appreciated as directly related to Calvin's sustained emphasis on the significance of the Spirit's work. Just as the distance between the ascended humanity of Christ and earthly communicant is bridged by the special operation of the Spirit, so the Spirit is the *vinculum* or *nexus* of saving union with Christ. For Calvin, the ontological confusion of Lutheran sacramentology, evident in the idea of the ubiquity of Christ's human nature, is avoided through the affirmation of the Spirit's secret, mysterious, special work of uniting the believer with Christ by faith. Put in reverse, Calvin substitutes the *Spirit* in union for the ubiquitarian focus on *ontology*. In this light, it is little wonder that of the extensive revisions and additions made to the Romans commentary in 1556, it is in Romans 8, where the Spirit's work is most prominent, that Calvin's expansion is most extensive. The additions made to the commentary on Romans 8 thus bear a positive and direct relationship to the revision of Book 3 of the *Institutes* in 1559. In the light of the whole of Calvin's activities, one can certainly be more at ease with the suggestion raised provisionally above, namely: the addition of the *discerpi* metaphor both in the 1559 *Institutes* and in the Romans commentary is not haphazard or coincidental, but reflects a pattern of thought and expression on Calvin's part that points to the inter-relations of his ongoing labors – polemically, in the eucharistic controversy; theologically, on the doctrine of the Spirit; and textually, in his revision of the *Institutes* and Romans commentary. Only in light of these important intertextual and contextual elements of Calvin's work in the 1550s is it possible to discover that this complex interplay converges ultimately in a single event and text: the 1559 Osiander refutation.

Conclusion

In the Calvin-Osiander debate, therefore, one sees with clarity the precise points where Christology, sacramentology, pneumatology, and soteriology intersect in the matrix of Calvin's thought. Throughout his objection to Osiander, Calvin works with and further defines *what* union with Christ means and *how* it relates to our justification. Thus Niesel is correct that Calvin is not merely juxtaposing justification and sanctification without setting them in immediate relation. But Niesel is mistaken in explaining that the manner of relation, and the heart of Calvin's idea, is a "theology of revelation."[122] Not revelation of the Mediator but Spirit-union with him is the nexus-point of their relation. It is precisely this point which yields the distinct-yet-inseparable Chalcedonian language of Calvin's *unio-duplex* soteriological model, and it is precisely this basic idea which undergirds the insistence in Calvin's thought upon the *simultaneity* of justification and sanctification. Furthermore, it is also this point on which Calvin and Osiander share so much nominally but disagree so fundamentally, and which contributed to the necessity of the clarifications Calvin offers. Indeed, to overlook this construction is to overlook the principal structural element that distinguished subtly Calvin's soteriological framework from Melanchthon's, a distinction, it should be added, which did not serve in the least to compromise the strength of their agreement on the imputation-*character*, the *extra nos* meritorious *grounds*, and the *faith-instrumentality* of justification.

The tendency to read this refutation only in terms of a dispute over justification fails to appreciate the principal point made in the preceding chapter, namely, that the eucharistic controversy had a soteriological orientation. Particularly in Calvin's thought, there is more than a mere historical connection between disputes over sacramental *communion* with the ascended *Christ* by the *Spirit* through *faith* and the crux of his soteriology: *union* with *Christ* by the *Spirit* through *faith*. This parallel is not incidental. Calvin's refutation of Osiander, one must conclude, is much more than a dispute over justification. Rather, in light of the textual and contextual evidence, it is a strategic attack on Lutheran ubiquitarianism, intended to demonstrate not only that Osiander's doctrine of justification is "wrong" but that it is necessarily implied in a distinctly Lutheran understanding of Christ and the Supper. Without an appreciation of these factors, Calvin's refutation is easily misunderstood as just one more occasion in which he defended the evangelical teaching on

---

[122] Niesel, *Theology of Calvin*, 137.

justification against someone who threatened to compromise it, but nothing more.

To the question of the "underlying motif" or basic problem Calvin has with Osiander, therefore, Feenstra's dismissal of Osiander's "mixing" in favor of the question of assurance is now seen to be misguided. Lack of assurance is rather the *effect* of the confusion Calvin perceives in Osiander's theology, not the heart of his objection. The evidence advanced here confirms as well as extends and deepens Wendel's suspicion that Osiander's "mixing" of divinity and humanity lies close to the center. In light of the history behind Calvin's refutation, and the intricate interplay of eucharistic and soteriological concerns in Calvin's writings in the 1550s, the significance of Calvin's mixing-language must be located at the heart of his critique. Indeed, it is the commonality of eucharistic and soteric language employed by Calvin that accentuates the crucial anti-ubiquitarian subtext in his criticisms, and that reveals the connection Calvin perceives between Lutheran christological-eucharistic thought and Osiander's "monstrous" doctrine of justification. As a result, this complexity of issues, historical and theological, also puts in question the assumption that Calvin's handling of Osiander was "aggressive and dismissive."[123] "Aggressive" certainly, but "dismissive" does not sufficiently account for the nuanced strategy Calvin adopts in view of the polemical circumstances.

The reader will recognize that at this point an interesting historical-theological question emerges. If this reading of Calvin's refutation of Osiander is correct, then at least the possibility should be entertained that the Osiandrian controversy, and specifically Calvin's 1559 refutation, marks the inception of an *explicit* divergence between Lutheran and Reformed in the area of salvation. Their sharply divergent perspectives on Christ and the Supper having been established years earlier, it is arguably here, in 1559 at the height of eucharistic controversy, that the soteriological implications of their sacramental differences are for the first time identified and employed at length by an active participant. In other words, this explicit divergence in relating justification and sanctification, evident already in earlier decades as demonstrated in Chapter 3 above, arose out of the simultaneous eucharistic (Supper) and Osiandrian (justification) controversies of the 1550s, but was not related directly to these controversies until Calvin creatively merged them, using Osiander as his foil.

---

[123] Alister E. McGrath, *A Life of John Calvin: A Study in the Shaping of Western Culture* (Oxford: Blackwell, 1990), 146.

That said, it is of the greatest importance to observe again that the Osiandrian affair did not nullify the significant continuity that obtained, and continued to obtain in great measure during the period of Orthodoxy, between Lutheran and Reformed understandings of justification as the imputation of Christ's uniquely meritorious righteousness. But the controversy did clarify what was already evident earlier, that the Lutheran and Reformed strands of the Reformation had in fact adopted distinguishable understandings of the justification/sanctification relationship. Pelikan explains that "Luther's equation of justification with the forgiveness of sins and with salvation became for Osiander, long before the conflict, another way of asserting that the content of justification was Christ the divine Lord himself…"[124] For Calvin, on the other hand, justification, as one aspect of a *duplex gratia*, is not "equated," nominally or functionally, with saving grace. The difference is important. As has been substantiated from different perspectives in this book, it is this subtle but significant difference between Lutheran and Reformed that accounts for their divergent ways of defending, conceptually or theologically, the necessary presence of good works for the salvation of those justified *sola fide*.

---

[124] Pelikan, *Reformation of Church and Dogma (1300-1700)*, 151.

PART THREE

CONCLUSION

The diversity of content and structure in the three case studies which form the heart of this book makes it desirable to pause briefly and recapitulate the major points before raising some final observations for reflection.

A Recapitulation

The analysis of Calvin's Romans commentary highlighted a cluster of ideas that belong to a wide-ranging hermeneutical and theological principle in Calvin's soteriology, his "replication principle." Hermeneutically, Calvin read the conditional passages in Romans, in which eternal life is promised as a reward for good works, through the Pauline *ordo salutis* he found summarized in Rom 8:28-30. Theologically, this *ordo* reflects the union believers have with Christ by the Spirit through faith. Specifically, the Spirit of union replicates in the experience of the faithful what was true of Christ in his own earthly experience. This experience consists primarily of a transition from humiliation to exaltation, suffering to glory, or obedience/good works to eternal life. What precedes in the divinely ordained sequence is called the "cause" of what follows. For Calvin, the good works of believers are on this account properly regarded as causes of salvation, though non-meritoriously. The uniquely meritorious character of Christ's work is safeguarded through Calvin's emphasis on *ordo* and sequence as contextualizing, within the reality of union with Christ, the idea of non-meritorious causation. As this is God's ordinary *via salutis*, there is no justification *without* works just as there is no justification *on account of* works. Thus Calvin's replication principle demonstrates how union with Christ functions in relation to the *duplex gratia* of justification and sanctification.

The force of Calvin's replication principle depends, however, on his pneumatic Christology. The Christ with whom believers are united through faith is none other than the Spirit-anointed Mediator. By virtue of the economic or functional identity of Christ and the Spirit in terms of the application of redemption, one cannot receive Christ for forgiveness without receiving the Spirit of holiness. Indeed, the Spirit is not only the agent of replication; he is also the bond of union with Christ and the presence of Christ among the faithful. These christological-pneumatological (*"filioque"*) underpinnings of Calvin's construct are most evident in his rejection of the Lutheran *manducatio impiorum*. Here Calvin spurns the idea of a faithless partaking of Christ for the christological reason that this would require a severing of Christ from the Spirit, indeed of Christ from himself.

The structure of Calvin's emphasis on a distinction without separation of the *duplex gratia* is clarified through attention to a series of patterns and parallels in his thought. These patterns and parallels signal a functional equivalence in Calvin's theology between corresponding ideas, including the sacramental *signa* and incarnational union on the one hand and the sacramental *res* and mystical/spiritual union on the other. With a view to the implications of this functional correspondence for a redemptive incarnational union with Christ and the *duplex gratia*, our findings confirm that Rupp is certainly on the mark. In his view, if one wishes to "gloss" Calvin's method of relating justification and sanctification, "perhaps it should not be by flanking him with Karl Barth and T. Torrance, but with the vast Common places of Wolfgang Musculus and Peter Martyr – compared with which the Institutes is the third dinosaur, which survived." In doing so, one is able to appreciate how "they show the common stresses of the emerging Reformed tradition...".[1] The interdependence of christological and pneumatological themes within Calvin's wider soteriological construct is thus of the highest importance. For, as Colin Gunton once noted, "the debate about whether, and in what respect, Calvin taught that Christ died for all rather than for the elect is inextricably dependent upon his christology and pneumatology."[2]

The combination of Calvin's replication principle with the more general christological-pneumatological foundations of his soteriology aid in appreciating the importance of Calvin's refutation of Osiander. The circumstances surrounding Calvin's refutation of Osiander may now be viewed as germane to a proper appreciation of how the *non separatio* element in Calvin's *unio Christi-duplex gratia* soteriology (as investigated in his Romans commentary) and the polemical-theological context of heated eucharistic controversy (as

---

[1] Gordon Rupp, "Patterns of Salvation in the First Age of the Reformation," *ARG* 57 (1966): 63.

[2] Colin E. Gunton, *Intellect and Action: Elucidations on Christian Theology and the Life of Faith* (Edinburgh: T. & T. Clark, 2000), 121. This is an important methodological note, though I acknowledge that Gunton may not have agreed with my conclusions. Indeed, it signals the extent to which one's interpretation of a major aspect of Calvin's thought (like Christ and the Spirit) affects one's interpretation of other aspects as well.

detailed in Calvin's rejection of the Lutheran *manducatio impiorum*) converge – theologically as well as historically – in this addition to the 1559 *Institutio*. Indeed, fully appreciating the richness of this convergence may be the single most significant hermeneutical factor in approaching the sixteenth-century complexity of Calvin's *unio Christi-duplex gratia* soteriology.

Implications

Calvin and Unio Mystica

It needs to be asked, however briefly, what implications these findings have for the somewhat ambiguous relationship between Calvin and mysticism. In light of Calvin's repeated emphasis on the reality of union with Christ's flesh and blood, there is no question but that Calvin envisioned a union of the closest intimacy.[3] Indeed, as Kuyper once noted, "although Calvin may have been the most rigid among the reformers, yet not one of them has presented this *unio mystica*, this spiritual union with Christ, so incessantly, so tenderly, and with such holy fire as he."[4] But in the proposals for Calvin's "mysticism" it appears his refutation of Osiander has not yet been sufficiently accounted for. To be sure, Tamburello, for example, notes the importance of this refutation for assessing Calvin's "mystical" union with Christ, but this has little impact on his actual interpretation of Calvin. This is especially true with respect to Calvin's alleged doctrine of deification, which may be viewed as still less moderate than the mystical reading. Indeed, Keller goes so far as to claim of Calvin and Osiander that "les deux théologiens étaient d'un seul Coeur animés par le desire d'expliquer l'indispensable divinization du Chrétien." For Keller, Osiander's *divinité essentielle* is the same as Calvin's *unio mystica*.[5] But one can only conclude this if one overlooks all Calvin has to say in criticism of Osiander's essentialist, divinizing conception. Instead, as De Kroon has correctly remarked, Calvin's vigorous polemic against Osiander demonstrates that Calvin's frequent use of *participatio* must be distinguished clearly from an Aristotelian or essentialist

---

[3] Indeed, Wendel (*Calvin*, pp. 235-9) notes places where Calvin comes dangerously close to language of a too-substantial union: *Comm.* on Jn. 17:21; Eph. 5:29-30; 1 Cor. 6:15; *Inst.* (1545) 3.2.24; *Inst.* (1559) 3.11.10.
[4] Abraham Kuyper, *The Work of the Holy Spirit*, trans. Henry De Vries, with introduction by B. B. Warfield (New York: Funk and Wagnalls, 1900), 324-5.
[5] Keller, *Calvin Mystique*, 141-2; cf. on the topic, Carl Mosser, "The Greatest Possible Blessing: Calvin and Deification," *SJT* 55 (2002): 36-57.

participatio, such as that which belongs distinctively to theosis-type conceptions, and that, as a result, this polemic shows he is "utterly opposed to any form of deification."[6]

At the same time, as De Kroon also notes, translating *participatio* simply as "communion" or "fellowship" is not sufficiently representative of the intimacy in Calvin's idea.[7] The solution, however, is not to move in the direction of an essentialist, ontological model which is not supported by Calvin's texts, but to read Calvin's language in light of his eucharistic and sacramental context. As in his teaching on the Supper, communion with Christ is much more than mental but less than baldly physical or essential. It is real and true not by a miracle of ontological oneness but by the blessing of the Spirit's work who unites Christ and his own. Calvin's striking language for the intimacy of union with Christ must be located, first, in the wider context of his effort to distance himself from Lutheran and Roman Catholic assumptions about real communion and, second, in his teaching regarding the Spirit as the bond of union – whether this union is considered in its sacramental or its specifically soteriological (justification/sanctification) aspects. Though there are clearly places where Calvin and the mystical traditions may be shown to have ideas in common, in the absence of firmer textual evidence conclusions about a positive relationship must be more hesitant than they have been.

Calvin and Luther(anism)

The opening section in Keller's chapter on justification in Calvin is titled "Jean Calvin n'est pas Martin Luther!"[8] And van't Spijker similarly points his readers to the "deep-seated difference" between Calvin and Luther on justification and the *theologia crucis* of which Calvin was not aware. This difference, van't Spijker explains, is rooted in their different ideas about the Holy Spirit and communion with Christ.[9] These assessments are certainly liable to exaggeration

---

[6] De Kroon, *The Honour of God and Human Salvation*, 19-20; cf. Wendel, *Calvin*, 259. As De Kroon also observes (20, n. 135), it is precisely his hesitation with the idea of deification that leads him to be so cautious in his exegesis of 2 Pet. 1:4. Contrast Mosser who adopts the opposite perspective ("The Greatest Possible Blessing").

[7] De Kroon, *The Honour of God and Human Salvation*, 20.

[8] Keller, *Calvin Mystique*, 129.

[9] Willem van't Spijker, "The Influence of Bucer on Calvin as Becomes Evident from the *Institutes*," in *John Calvin's Institutes: His Opus Magnum*, Proceedings of the Second South African Congresss for Calvin Research (Potchefstroom:

and misunderstanding, but our findings clarify the extent to which they are correct.

One cumulative effect of our three case studies is that it is not possible to distinguish Calvin and the Lutherans exclusively along the lines of the Eucharist or predestination. To the contrary, the complex interdependence of christological, sacramental, and soteriological strands in Calvin's theology and polemic requires that the observations made with respect to his rejection of Osiander are taken seriously. If in fact Calvin claimed Osiander as the only consistent Lutheran, as one who alone follows fully the logic of Lutheran Christology, then the differences that obtained between Calvin and his Lutheran counterparts, at least on Calvin's view, must be appreciated as more architectonic and structural. Put differently, the interdependence of ideas on which Calvin concentrates attention, both in his positive expositions of doctrine and in his negative, polemical discussions, suggests a *systemic* divergence, rooted in conflicting understandings of the *modus communionis* with all its christological underpinnings and soteriological implications. To be sure, the implicit, muted nature of this divergence is due in large part to the twin realities of (1) a period still very much in transition, with distinctions only becoming clearer in time; and of (2) a concern for unity in the face of the charge of schism. Calvin does not explicitly criticize Melanchthon, for example, for his understanding of good works.[10]

Do, then, the Lutheran and Reformed branches of the Reformation share a common doctrine of justification? Two things must be noted. First, the Lutheran and Reformed traditions extend well beyond the sixteenth century into our own day, and our attention has been restricted to sixteenth-century considerations. Furthermore, Calvin is not exhaustive of Reformed theology, not even in its sixteenth-century expression. Other important Reformed thinkers from the period must be read and studied with great care. Still, as his place in late sixteenth- and seventeenth-century Reformed thought certainly suggests, Calvin did function as the

---

Potchefstroom University, 1986), 106-32 (here p. 131). He suggests that where Calvin differed from Luther he followed Bucer.

[10] If, however, the warmth of the Calvin-Melanchthon correspondence is taken to suggest that a divergence should not be claimed unless explicitly identified as such, the essay by Timothy Wengert on their "epistolary friendship" contradicts any such assumption. See Wengert, "'We Will Feast Together in Heaven Forever': The Epistolary Friendship of John Calvin and Philip Melanchthon," in Karin Maag, ed., *Melanchthon in Europe: His Work and Influence Beyond Wittenberg* (Grand Rapids: Baker, 1999), 19-44.

principal theologian and systematizer of the tradition in its infancy, often providing the necessary sophistication in theological form and structure.

Second, "doctrine of justification" needs explanation. If agreement on the *definition* of the term "justification" is in view, such as what might be sought at the catechetical level, then the question is easy to answer in the affirmative. Calvin's understanding of "justification" is basically synonymous with the brief definitions found in the classic Lutheran confessions. In his theology as much as theirs justification is a forensic declaration grounded upon the uniquely meritorious righteousness of Christ imputed to a believer by faith, entailing the forgiveness of sins and a righteous standing before God. The effort, it should be said, to pit union with Christ against forensic imputation in Calvin may be seen now to be deeply mistaken.[11]

If, however, "doctrine of justification" means more than a bare-essentials definition such as one finds in a confessional document – if it includes, for example, the *relationship* justification bears to other aspects of God's saving work and the *context* in which justification is to be understood, the discussion of which is naturally involved in any treatment of the theology of justification – then one must answer negatively. Unlike his Lutheran counterparts, Calvin did not ground good works in imputation or justification but in union with Christ. In contradistinction with Melanchthon, for example, Calvin argued a positive, soteric value of good works as the ordinary prerequisite for receiving eternal life. It appears that basic differences exist in their respective understandings of justifying faith: at the heart of the inseparability in Calvin's *unio Christi-duplex gratia* formulation is a justifying faith defined not only passively, as a resting on Christ alone, but actively, as an obedient faith that, resting on Christ alone, perseveres in the pursuit of holiness.

Despite important continuities, then, Calvin's "main hinge on which religion turns" (*Inst.* [1539] 3.11.1) is not identical with the Lutheran "doctrine of the standing or falling church," neither in nature (justification as the *de facto* sum-total of salvation) nor in

---

[11] So William Thompson, "Viewing Justification Through Calvin's Eyes: An Ecumenical Experiment." *Theological Studies* 57 (1996): 451-3. Obscuring the *distinctio* element in Calvin's construct, Thompson also incorrectly claims (p. 452) that for Calvin justification is "already intrinsic and transformative." On union and imputation, see my "Imputation and the Christology of Union with Christ: Calvin, Osiander, and the Contemporary Quest for a Reformed Model," *WTJ* 68:2 (2006): 219-51.

function (justification as theological center or hermeneutical rule).[12] Instead, Calvin's model points to a distancing effort on the part of the Reformed that distinguishes their understanding of justification and salvation from the understanding of their Lutheran counterparts. Indeed, in Calvin one finds only a more sophisticated form of the self-conscious critique of the Lutheran model noted by Frank James in the work of another sixteenth-century theologian, Peter Martyr Vermigli.[13] James's findings should be seen as additional confirmation that this distancing effort was not Calvin's alone but belonged in varying degrees to the emerging Reformed tradition at large.

It might be added, however, that Calvin's formulation is frequently assumed to stand, explicitly or implicitly, as a mediating (though distinctly Protestant) position equidistant between Rome and Luther. Thus he is often praised for his "balance" and avoidance of "extremes." In one case at least he is even accused of "re-Catholicizing" Reformation theology at its most distinctive point: the theology of good works.[14]

However, Calvin's *unio-duplex* formulation is not the result of an Hegelian-type synthesis of the Roman thesis (salvation as transformation) and the Lutheran antithesis (salvation as justification), but the sophisticated theological fruit of his approach to the problem from the fundamentally different perspective of union with Christ. This approach is the fruit of his extensive reflection on the Pauline writings, reflection which reveals itself to be part mediated and part original. It was not arrived at by mediating between both Rome and Wittenberg, for Calvin retained the greater part of Luther's teaching on justification and did not concede any ground to Rome on the crucial question of the merit of human works. Rather, in the ultimately evasive mystery of the precise factors which contribute to any individual's thought at any single point in history, polemical and traditional, but especially exegetical and theological factors prove the most determinative.

---

[12] Which renders still more interesting how, in view of Calvin's *unio Christi-duplex gratia* construction, Niesel (*Theology of Calvin*, 131) can call justification the "supreme gift" of salvation and I. Howard Marshall ("Sanctification in the Teaching of John Wesley and John Calvin," *EQ* 34 [1962]: 77) can counter that "sanctification was in fact the centre of gravity of his theology."

[13] See James, "The Complex of Justification," 58, who points perceptively to Vermigli's self-conscious but non-antagonistic opposition to the Lutheran model of justification.

[14] So Steven Ozment, *The Age of Reform: 1250-1550* (New Haven: Yale, 1980), 374.

In short, Calvin's formulation was, just as with Luther, his reaffirmation of what he was convinced the Apostle Paul taught and the Church had always believed, clothed with expressions and distinctions demanded by the needs of his day. His soteriology, he insisted, was nothing other than Paul's own, obscured if not destroyed by the Roman concept of merit but thrust back into the light in his own day. As McKee perceptively notes, "...modern scholars often find it difficult to take seriously Calvin's claim that the loci of the Institutes were indeed based on scripture, and so they tend to look elsewhere for the 'real' if unconscious influences on the reformer's thought."[15]

Calvin and Sola Fide

Among the most significant elements in Calvin's replication principle is his use of the language of soteriological causation when the good works of the faithful are in view. Within his replication model, good works do not serve as the meritorious grounds of justification, but they belong so necessarily to salvation that there is no justification without them. This positive place for conditional language, therefore, fits nicely with what other studies have concluded with respect to the bilateral side of Calvin's covenantal theology.[16] But it also prompts the question as to Calvin's relationship to *sola fide*.

Calvin's relationship to *sola fide* depends largely on what the modern inquirer understands by the expression, which Calvin, like others, expressly affirmed by using it often. Our appreciation of this fact is deepened by the observations in this study regarding the inseparability of justification and sanctification as derivative aspects of union with Christ. If by *sola fide* one suggests that justification by faith alone is salvation, that our relationship to saving grace is

---

[15] Elsie Anne McKee, "Exegesis, Theology, and Development in Calvin's *Institutio*: A Methodological Suggestion," in Elsie Anne McKee and Brian Armstrong, eds., *Probing the Reformed Tradition*, 155.

[16] See Lyle D. Bierma, *German Calvinism in the Confessional Age: The Covenant Theology of Caspar Olevianus* (Grand Rapids: Baker, 1996), who concludes (p. 183) that *all* sixteenth-century Reformed covenant theologians recognized *both* unilateral and bilateral dimensions of the covenant of grace within a context of a monergistic soteriology; Peter Lillback, *The Binding of God*, 162-75; 264-75; Cornelis Venema, *Heinrich Bullinger and the Doctrine of Predestination: Author of "the Other Reformed Tradition"?* (Grand Rapids: Baker, 2002); and the relevant sections in Andrew Alexander Woolsey, "Unity and Continuity in Covenantal Thought: A Study in the Reformed Tradition to the Westminster Assembly," 2 vols, Ph.D. thesis (University of Glasgow, 1988).

exclusively passive, or that the faith that unites to Christ for justification is devoid of works, then this is not Calvin's *sola fide*. Because for Calvin faith is not exclusively punctiliar, restricted to the moment of definitive union with Christ, but an ongoing, perpetual reality, truly justifying faith is never "alone." Instead, as the faith that unites to Christ, it is always a working faith just as it is always a resting faith. The consequent inseparability of justification and sanctification in Calvin's *unio Christi* construct is designed specifically to counter the allegation that any faith can be truly justifying which is not simultaneously sanctifying.

If, on the other hand, one intends by the expression to remove works from the meritorious ground of justification and to identify the Spirit's work of faith as the sole instrumental means by which one is united to Christ for justification, then one has captured Calvin's *sola fide*. There is thus a sense in which *sola fide* is correct and incorrect, and the difference has the richness of the gospel at stake. If this is still insufficiently clear, Calvin's own treatment of the question in the twilight of his ministry should be noted. In a lecture on Ezekiel 18:17, Calvin explains how "faith without works justifies" is either true or false, depending on the sense it bears. He explains,

> But although works tend in no way to the cause of justification, yet, when the elect sons of God were justified freely by faith, at the same time their works are esteemed righteous by the same gratuitous liberality. Thus it remains true that faith without works justifies, although this needs prudence and a sound interpretation. For this proposition, "faith without works justifies," is true and yet false, according to different senses. "Faith without works justifies when by itself" is false, because faith without works is void (*nulla est*). But if the clause "without works" is joined with the word "to justify," the proposition will be true: therefore faith cannot justify when it is without works, because it is dead, and a mere fiction (*merum figmentum*). He who is born of God is just, as John says (1 Jn. 5:18). Thus faith can be no more separated from works than the sun from its heat yet faith justifies without works, because works do not form a reason (*rationem*) for our justification; but faith alone (*sola fides*) reconciles us to God and causes him to love us, not in ourselves, but in his only begotten Son.[17]

---

[17] Calvin, *Prael. Ezek.* 18:17 (CO 40.439; CTS, 2, 238): "Quamvis autem ad causam nihil afferant opera, tamen ubi gratis fide iustificati sunt filii Dei, vel electi, simul etiam eadem gratuita liberalitate iustificantur eorum opera. Ita verum illud manet, fidem sine operibus iustificare. Quanquam prudentia et sana interpretatione id indiget. Nam haec propositio, Fidem sine operibus

Calvin's relationship to *sola fide*, then, depends on what is meant by the expression. For Calvin, "faith without works justifies" is true, but only in the proper sense. This proper sense has the meritorious basis – the *rationem* – of justification in view: the Spirit unites sinners *sola fide* to the Christ whose righteousness is the sole basis of their acceptance before God. Yet "faith cannot justify without works" precisely because such a "faith" is "dead," a "mere figment," that is, because a truly justifying faith unites to Christ for sanctification as well as for justification and is thus a real, an obedient, enlivened faith. Within Calvin's soteriological model, to make sanctification follow justification as an effect is to concede the theological possibility that one may be truly justified but not yet sanctified, with the result that the legal fiction charge, to which Calvin was always sensitive, would be validated. This is a charge Calvin guarded against with meticulous care and vigor. There is much more than "a little exaggeration," therefore, in the claim that Calvin "sought to show how one could not lead a Christian life and still remain a Christian."[18] To this one should add that rooting sanctification in justification as its cause would also appear to forfeit a cardinal Reformation concern in justification, for it would attribute to justification a generative and ultimately transformative, and thus not purely declarative and forensic, nature.

The Way Forward

These case studies can be multiplied to pursue other legitimate avenues of inquiry, such as the role of the union idea in the morality of Calvin's Geneva in light of the Consistory records and as reflected

---

iustificare, est vere et est falsa, secundum diversos sensus: Fides sine operibus, deinde seorsum iustificat, haec propositio est falsa, quia fides sine operibus nulla est. Atqui si particula, Sine operibus, coniungatur cum verbo iustificandi, vera erit propositio: fides ergo non potest iustificare quum est sine operibus, quia est mortua, vel merum figmentum. Qui natus est ex Deo iustus est, sicuti Ioannes dicit (1 Ioan. 5:18). Ita fides nihilo magis poterit avelli ab operibus, quam sol a calore suo: iam tamen fides iustificat sine operibus, quia opera non veniunt in rationem ubi iustificamur: sed sola fides nos Deo reconciliat, et facit ut nos diligat, non in nobis, sed in filio suo unigenito." This is one of the last of Calvin's lectures (*praelectiones*, and thus not a true commentary), the final one ending February 2, 1564 with Ezek 20:44. They were published in 1565 in both Latin and French. See BC 3.47-53; and De Greef, *The Writings of John Calvin*, 109. The whole of Calvin's comment on the chapter merits special attention. My thanks to Prof. Richard B. Gaffin, Jr for drawing my attention to this passage.

[18] Charles Trinkaus, "Renaissance Problems in Calvin's Theology," *Studies in the Renaissance* 1 (1954): 60.

in Calvin's sermons. A step in this direction may be made by studying the relationship of Calvin's sermons on union with Christ and sexual infidelity in 1 Corinthians 11 and the maintenance of these morals. Extending the relationship to Calvin's counselling activities, a full study of union with Christ in his correspondence also promises fresh insight into its pastoral function. To these may be added more explicitly theological investigations into the nature of union with Christ and the development of the idea in his thought (both treated only indirectly here). Also meriting attention is the degree to which Luther's *theologia crucis* and the concomitant union with Christ through suffering is developed by Calvin in his teaching on *mortificatio* as an aspect of *regeneratio*, itself an aspect of union with Christ as the second of the *duplex gratia Dei*. The conclusions of this study regarding Calvin's replication principle would appear to take such an inquiry in a new and profitable direction.

In addition to these sixteenth-century interests, studies investigating the implications of this study for contemporary theology may be noted. These are questions for which our space and methodological restraints did not permit attention. Especially with respect to Calvin's Christology, it has not been possible to enter into discussions over the contemporary viability of sixteenth-century structures.[19] Nor am I able here to discuss the numerous theological implications of Calvin's response to Osiander but point, as but one example, to the fine observations by Jelle Faber on the criticisms of Barth's anthropology implied in Calvin's critique of the *imago Dei* in Osiander.[20] It should also be said that constructive interest in Calvin's ideas needs greater historical responsibility. In light of our findings, for example, enthusiasm for the linear parallelism in Calvin's pattern of theological argument and expression must be restrained so as not to compromise Calvin's own intentions. The danger is not illusory that Calvin's analogical pattern may be taken

---

[19] This applies to the shift in scientific cosomologies, so that the question whether in fact "the *extra Calvinisticum* depended upon a Ptolemaic cosmology which has been replaced by Copernican and Einsteinian ones..." (George A. Lindbeck, *The Church in a Postliberal Age*, ed. James J. Buckley [London: SCM Press, 2002], 63) must be addressed elsewhere.

[20] Jelle Faber, "Imago Dei in Calvin: Calvin's Doctrine of Man as the Image of God by Virtue of Creation," and, idem, "Imago Dei in Calvin: Calvin's Doctrine of Man as the Image of God in Connection with Sin and Restoration," in *Essays in Reformed Doctrine* (Neerlandia, Alberta, Canada: Inheritance Publications, 1990), 227-50 and 251-81, respectively.

too far and applied inappropriately, as is evident when it is summoned against the "literal infallibility of Scripture" in Calvin.[21]

Looking beyond Calvin, the recent, salutary interest in post-Reformation Reformed theologians might contribute to our understanding of how Calvin's soteriological formulations relate to subsequent constructs. A thorough and wide-ranging investigation would be most welcome, but it should be noted here that several of the themes in this study recur in later Reformed writers. In Ursinus, for example, one finds a similar emphasis on the necessity of good works for salvation (even for justification) and the assertion that one cannot receive the *telos* of one's faith without them.[22] Similarly, Westminster Assembly divine Obadiah Sedgwick used language strikingly similar to Calvin's about the necessity of good works for eternal life within a treatise brimming with language of our union with Christ. His sensitivity in one particular comment to Calvin's concern that pardon might be illegitimately equated with salvation is worth quoting at length:

> The Reasons why God doth promise these two great Gifts of holiness and forgiveness; to sanctifie his people as well as to justify them. There may be these Reasons for their Connexion. First, Both of them have a necessary respect to the salvation of the people of God: A man must be justified if he will be saved; and a man must be sanctified if he will be saved; he cannot be saved without both: he cannot be saved unless he be justified: [Rom. 8:30]… None are justified but such as are called, and none are glorified but such as are justified: [Mark 16:16]… He cannot be saved unless he be sanctified: [John 3:5]… [Heb. 12:14]… Here you see a necessity of both of them in reference to salvation; we many times think that if our sins are pardoned, there needed no more to save us, but we are deceived; for as forgiveness is necessary, so is holiness necessary to salvation; as no unpardoned person, so no unsanctified person shall be saved.[23]

---

[21] As in John McIntyre, *The Shape of Pneumatology: Studies in the Doctrine of the Holy Spirit* (Edinburgh: T. & T. Clark, 1997), 109-33.

[22] Zacharias Ursinus, *Commentary on the Heidelberg Catechism* (rep. Phillipsburg: Presbyterian and Reformed, 1992), 484-5. Ursinus notes that this way of speaking is not incorrect but ambiguous. Cf. *Westminster Confession of Faith* 15.3: "Although repentance be not … any cause of the pardon… yet it is of such necessity that none may expect pardon without it."

[23] Obadiah Sedgwick, *The Bowels of Tender Mercy Sealed in the Everlasting Covenant, wherein Is set forth the Nature, Conditions and Excellencies of it, and how a Sinner should do to enter it, and the danger of refusing this Covenant-Relation. Also the Treasures of Grace, Blessings, Comforts, Promises and Priviledges that are comprized in*

Worthy of careful scholarly attention is the degree to which the soteriological necessity of good works is understood by these writers as the theological fruit of a Calvinian understanding of union with Christ, and how this idea is shaped and employed in subsequent polemical encounters. To this end, attention must be given to the differing contexts – exegetical, polemical, theological, ecclesiastical – within which subsequent formulations arose, noting again that Calvin was not the sole source of later Reformed theology. Perhaps this kind of work will be able to clarify how a Calvinian understanding thrived in some pockets of the Reformed tradition but not in others.[24] These considerations take us to the outside limits of our investigation.

Concluding Observations

In sum, I would draw special attention to the more general theological impact of Calvin's *unio* doctrine. The function of union with Christ within Calvin's *unio Christi-duplex gratia* soteriology points to an influence that is more than merely structural or formal. If the conclusions of this study are granted, then at the very least his replication principle instead illustrates how union with Christ is *constitutive* of the application of redemption. The distinction here is between recognizing the nominal frequency of union language in Calvin and appreciating its constitutive function. Indeed the structural or formal impact evident in his analysis of union with Christ, justification, and sanctification should be understood as the architectonic effect of this constitutive reality.

Furthermore, the texts, read in context, force modern interpreters to come to terms with a theological complex – and a polemical zeal – that reflects the assumption of an underlying unity to all truth. As noted with respect to the eucharistic controversy, it is a matter of recognizing the "layered-ness" of theology, and the fact that an attack on one layer was perceived as an attack on them all. Without

---

the Covenant of Gods Free and Rich Mercy made in Jesus Christ with Believers (London: by Edward Mottershed for Adoniram Byfield, 1661), 490.

[24] In later Reformed theology, a more Melanchthonian (i.e., classical Lutheran) pattern of argument appears to have become standard, resulting in the frequent exposition of justification and good works as cause and effect. See, e.g., what in light of our findings is a rather remarkable statement by Charles Hodge, *Systematic Theology* (1871; rep. Grand Rapids: Eerdmans, 1982), vol. 3, p. 238: "There has never been any real difference of opinion among Protestants... It was universally admitted that good works are not necessary to our justification; that they are consequences and indirectly the fruits of justification, and therefore cannot be its ground."

a sensitivity to this presupposition, it will be difficult to appreciate how Calvin's critique of Osiander has in view not only his aberrant doctrine of justification, but the deeper structures of Lutheran thought as they are set opposite the deeper structures of Calvin's own theology. Otherwise, the significance of christological and eucharistic themes will be set aside in pursuit of more explicit "soteriological" questions, such as neglecting the Christ-Spirit relationship in Calvin's rejection of a "legal fiction." When reading these sixteenth-century texts, this methodological oversight, it might be added, turns distinction into separation.

Our analysis of Calvin's Romans commentary means we can be confident that Bahmann is simply mistaken that in 1539 justification and sanctification are left without an immediate relation.[25] But while Bahmann is incorrect about Calvin in 1539, he is certainly fully correct that, for Calvin, "while it is true that our righteousness is *extra nos*, namely in Christ, it is not true that Christ himself is *procul stans*" (standing afar off). This, indeed, is a central theme of our findings: that Calvin's *extra nos* is greatly liable to confusion with a *procul stans*.

But this observation touches on the differences between popular understandings of Calvin's theology and the image the actual texts reveal. It may not be too simplistic to suggest that in the popular mind the *distinctio* Calvin ("we are not justified by works") has been far more familiar than the *sed non separatio* Calvin ("we are not justified without works"), that the *extra nos* emphasis has tended to overshadow the reality of Calvin's *union* with Christ, a reality which emphasizes that Christ is not *procul stans*. In fact, for Calvin, affirming *extra nos* as a *procul stans*, i.e., failing to appreciate the soteriologically constitutive reality of union with Christ, emasculates the gospel. Modern theological sensibilities, moreover, may deem "in Christ savingly for justification" more central to the gospel than "in Christ savingly for sanctification," if not theologically then at least pastorally. But if the frequency with which both themes are present in his sermons, not to mention his theology, is a fair indication, Calvin would not agree, for he deemed them both to be pastorally indispensable.

---

[25] Manfred K. Bahmann, "Calvin's Controversy with Certain 'Half-Papists'," *Hartford Quarterly* 5 (1964/5): 33. Bahmann is trying to emphasize the significance of the Osiander refutation in the 1550s by minimizing what is present before then.

APPENDIX A

A Witness to Calvin's Paulinism: 1539 *Institutio* Marginalia to Chapter Six, "On Justification by Faith and Works of Merit"

In her studies of Calvin's ecclesiology, Elsie Anne McKee has made extensive use of the marginalia in the original editions of Calvin's texts. In particular, she has observed that the Scripture references in the original editions of Calvin's *Institutes* often function less as "proof-texts" in the modern sense of the term than as cross-references to his expositions in the commentaries.[1] If a point of exposition is dealt with at greater length and detail in his commentary than is appropriate for the *Institutes* (keeping in mind Calvin's division of labor: exegesis and exposition in the commentaries, *loci* or topical discussion in the *Institutes*), then the marginalia would simply refer the reader to the appropriate place in his commentary.

This intertextual relationship serves to underscore not only the strong exegesis-theology relationship in Calvin's method, but also the extent of Calvin's identification with and employment of the Pauline writings. In articulating the justification/sanctification relationship in terms of union with Christ, it becomes clear Calvin is seeking to clarify what he understands and identifies as the heart of the Pauline soteriology.

To complement the investigation of Calvin's Romans commentary in Chapter 3 above, the important sixth chapter of his 1539 *Institutio*, entitled "*De Iustificatione Fidei, et meritis operum*," has been examined for Pauline marginalia. The result is the following tabulation. Statistically, Calvin (perhaps together with his editor) included 60 Pauline references printed as marginalia adjacent to relevant columns of text. Of these 60, nearly half (26) refer to a passage from Romans, on which Calvin was of course then writing a commentary.

---

[1] See Elsie Anne McKee, "Exegesis, Theology, and Development in Calvin's *Institutio*: A Methodological Suggestion," in Elsie Anne McKee and Brian G. Armstrong, eds, *Probing the Reformed Tradition: Historical Studies in Honor of Edward A. Dowey, Jr.* (Louisville: Westminster/John Knox Press, 1989), 154-72, esp. 156. See the discussion in Muller, *The Unaccommodated Calvin*, 107-8.

The importance of the sixth chapter of Calvin's 1539 *Institutio* in relation to his Romans commentary has been noted by Albert Clarke Dean. In his study he has found that of the seventeen chapters in the 1539 *Institutio*, Romans is cited most often in the sixth chapter (46 times).[2]

Chapter 6 spans fols. 186-225. The Pauline marginalia occur among references to Lombard, Ambrose (Ambrosiaster), Augustine, and Chrysostom, as well as to other biblical texts. The total of 60 Pauline references does not include 4 passages from the Epistle to the Hebrews (fols 187, 207, 211, 224) and 2 allusions, without explicit marginal annotation, to the language of 1 Cor 1:30 (fols 208, 210). These two allusions should be regarded as significant in light of the discussion of this verse in Chapter 5 above. Otherwise the Pauline marginalia are listed as follows, with Romans passages highlighted in bold:

1539 *Institutio* Pauline Marginalia

Fol. 187:	Phil. 3; **Rom. 10**; **Rom. 3**
Fol. 188:	**Rom. 10**; Gal. 3; Gal. 3; **Rom. 4**
Fol. 189:	**Rom. 1**; **Rom. 3 and 4**
Fol. 190:	**Rom. 4**; **Rom. 5**; 2 Cor. 5; **Rom. 4**
Fol. 191:	2 Cor. 5; **Rom. 8**; **Rom. 5**
Fol. 192:	2 Cor. 4
Fol. 195:	**Rom. 3**
Fol. 196:	Eph. 1; Eph. 2; **Rom. 4**
Fol. 197:	Gal. 5
Fol. 198:	Eph. 2; **Rom. 4**
Fol. 199:	**Rom. 11**; Eph. 2; 2 Tim. 1; Tit. 3; **Rom. 11**; **Rom. 5**; Col. 1
Fol. 200:	1 Cor. 6
Fol. 203:	Phil. 3; 1 Cor. 9
Fol. 204:	Eph. 1; **Rom. 3**
Fol. 206:	**Rom. 6**
Fol. 208:	1 Cor. 3; Tit. 3
Fol. 209:	Eph. 2; 2 Tim. 2
Fol. 210:	2 Cor. 4; 2 Tim. 2; Phil. 3; **Rom. 8**

---

[2] Albert Clarke Dean, "The Institutes of 1539 and the Letter to the Romans," Th.M. thesis (Union Theological Seminary, 1953), 192. Dean includes (p. 193) a tabulation of the Romans citations in the 1539 *Institutio* by chapter.

Fol. 211:   Tit. 2; 1 Thess. 5; Eph. 2; 2 Cor. 6; 1 Thess. 4; **Rom. 6**; **Rom. 12**; **Rom. 12**; 2 Cor. 9
Fol. 213:   Gal. 2
Fol. 214:   Gal. 5
Fol. 219:   **Rom. 2**
Fol. 220:   2 Cor. 1; 1 Co. 4
Fol. 221:   Eph. 1; 1 Thess. 3 *et alibi*; 2 Cor. 5; **Rom. 2**; 1 Cor. 3; **Rom. 2**
Fol. 222:   Eph. 1; Gal. 4; Col. 3; Col. 1
Fol. 223:   1 Cor. 15; 1 Tim. 6
Fol. 224:   2 Cor. 9; 2 Thess. 1
Fol. 225:   1 Cor. 13; Col. 3

APPENDIX B

Calvin, Vermigli, and the Strata of Union with Christ: A Closer Look at their 1555 Correspondence

In March 1555, the Italian Peter Martyr Vermigli, after responding to Beza's question on the same subject, inquired after Calvin's thoughts on union with Christ. Vermigli asked Calvin for his view by first explaining his own. In August of the same year, Calvin replied with the simple purpose of showing Vermigli that they were in hearty agreement. Our interest in this exchange is justified both by Calvin's enthusiastic agreement with the view articulated by Vermigli and by Calvin's praise for the Italian's explanation of a highly relevant theological corollary, the eucharistic presence and communion.[1] This set of correspondence was discussed briefly as part of our

---

[1] There is also precedent for the use of this correspondence for clarifying the character of Calvin's doctrine of union with Christ. See W. Duncan Rankin, "Carnal Union with Christ in the Theology of T. F. Torrance," PhD thesis (University of Edinburgh, 1997), 166-235 and A-50–A-75 (Appendix 12), whose principal concern is Vermigli's and Calvin's understanding of natural or incarnational union. Others have pointed to the importance of this correspondence for interpreting Calvin on union with Christ. See W. Kolfhaus, *Christusgemeinschaft bei Johannes Calvin* (Neukirchen: Buchhandlung des Erziehungsvereins, 1939), 24-35; following Kolfhaus, Dennis E. Tamburello, *Union with Christ: Calvin and the Mysticism of St. Bernard* (Louisville: Westminster/John Knox, 1994), 86-7; 89-90; 143 nn. 18, 19; 144 n. 36; B. A. Gerrish, *Tradition and the Modern World: Reformed Theology in the Nineteenth Century* (Chicago and London: University of Chicago Press, 1978), 63; and Tim J. R. Trumper, "An Historical Study of the Doctrine of Adoption in the Calvinistic Tradition," PhD thesis (University of Edinburgh, 2001). Ronald S. Wallace notes the letter in passing in *Calvin's Doctrine of the Christian Life* (Edinburgh: Oliver and Boyd, 1959), 146, n. 5. For the Calvin-Vermigli correspondence in general, see Marvin W. Anderson, *Peter Martyr, A Reformer in Exile (1542-1562): A Chronology of Biblical Writings in England & Europe* (Nieuwkoop: B. De Graaf, 1975), 186-95; idem, "Peter Martyr, Reformed Theologian (1542-1562): His letters to Heinrich Bullinger and John Calvin," *SCJ* 4 (1973): 41-64; and J. C. McLelland, *The Visible Words of God* (Edinburgh and London: Oliver and Boyd, 1957), 88, 14-147.

investigation into the patterns and parallels in Calvin's sacramentology and soteriology. In this appendix, attention is focused more specifically on Calvin's delimitation of the strata of union with Christ with a view to recent interpretations of the relationship these strata bear to justification and sanctification.

The Correspondence

A Threefold Union: Vermigli to Calvin

Vermigli is best remembered for his substantial contribution to the articulation and defense of the Reformed perspective on the eucharistic presence. His place in the history of Reformation sacramentology, however, should not obscure his rich teaching on saving union with Christ. Anderson has correctly noted that one who desires to understand Vermigli's years of exile (1542-1562), for example, "ought not concentrate on Vermigli's sacramental disputations and miss his theology of communion with Christ."[2]

Vermigli's letter to Calvin, dated March 8, 1555, opens with an expression of thanks for Calvin's *Defensio* of the 1549 *Consensus*.[3] He quickly moves to his purpose in writing, noting the centrality of the *modus* question in the eucharistic conflict.

> Men do not all agree concerning the communion which we have with the body of Christ and the substance of his nature; for what reason, I suppose you will hear. It is so important that he that is Christ's should understand the mode of his union with him.[4]

---

[2] Anderson, *Peter Martyr*, 61.

[3] Peter Martyr Vermigli, 8 March 1555, CO 15.492-7 (no. 2142); also printed in the *Epistolae* of the *Loci Communis Petri Martyris Vermilii*... (Geneva: Pierre Aubert, 1627), 767-9. An early translation into English may be found in Vermigli, *Common Places of... Peter Martyr...*, trans. Anthony Marten (London: H. Denham and H. Middleton, 1583) [Appendix] 96-9. G. C. Gorham translated a large portion of the letter into English for his *Gleanings of a Few Scattered Ears, During the Period of the Reformation in England and of the Times Immediately Succeeding, A. D. 1533 to A. D. 1588* (London: Bell and Daldy, 1857), 340-44, and a more recent (but also partial) translation of the letter by J. C. McLelland is included in McLelland and G. E. Duffield, eds, *The Life, Early Letters & Eucharistic Writings of Peter Martyr* (Appleford: Sutton Courtenay Press, 1989), 343-8. These translations are cited henceforth as "McLelland" and "Gorham."

[4] CO 15.494; McLelland, 345: "De communione quam habemus cum corpore Christi atque substantia ipsius naturae non omnes eadem dicunt quamobrem [quae?] ipse credam audies. Res magni momenti est, ut qui Christi est qua ratione illi sit coniunctus intelligat."

Appendix B

Vermigli then outlines his own understanding of this union as threefold in kind. First, Vermigli explains, all share the communication with Christ extended universally to the human race by his incarnation. Christ, in order to become true man, took upon himself the human properties of flesh and blood. This physical union, however, as a mere flesh and blood communication derived through our parents, is "very general and feeble." It is a "natural fellowship," in itself non-redemptive. It is the platform upon which God's saving work in Christ takes place but is not independently of redemptive value. Vermigli explains,

> But unless some other kind of communion were offered us, this would be very general and feeble; for the whole human race already has communion with Christ in this manner. They are in fact men as he was [a man].[5]

Vermigli proceeds immediately to the union with Christ that does have redemptive qualities. Faith is "breathed into the elect" with the result that their sins are forgiven and they are reconciled to God (justification) as well as renewed by the Spirit, body and soul, with a view to their eschatological conformity to Christ (renewal as *Christiformia*).[6] On the essence of this union Vermigli is clear: this union with Christ does not involve an ontological but a spiritual communion with Christ, one which yields in effects the plentiful and progressive increase in spiritual likeness to Christ himself.

> Not that they cast aside the substance of their own nature and pass into the very body and flesh of Christ, but that they no less

---

[5] CO 15.494: "Principio quidem video, beneficio incarnationis eius illum (ut ad Hebraeos dicitur) voluisse nobiscum carne et sanguine communicare. Quum enim pueri carni et sanguini communicarint, et ipse voluit horum esse particeps. Verum nisi aliud communionis genus intercederet, communis admodum haec esset et debilis. Nam quotquot humana specie comprehenduntur, hac ratione iam cum Christo communicant: sunt quippe homines, ut ipse fuit." As noted by Rankin ("Carnal Union with Christ," A-52, n. 8), the translation by Gorham (p. 342; later repeated by McLelland, p. 346) of "sunt quippe homines, ut ipse fuit" as "They are in fact *men*, as he was *man*' (emphases Gorham) is potentially misleading. If the final "man" is thought necessary, perhaps the inclusion of an indefinite article is preferable: "... as he was a man." Hence the alteration made in the quotation above.

[6] CO 15.494; McLelland, 346: "Ideo praeter illam hoc accedit, electis destinato tempore fedem adspirari, qua in Christum credant, atque ita illis non tantum condonari peccata et Deo reconciliari, qua in re vera et solida iustificationis ratio sita est, sed etiam spiritus vim instaurantem addi, qua nostra quoque corpora, caro, sanguis et natura immortalitatis capacia fiunt, et Christiformia (ut ita dixerim) indies magis ac magis evadunt."

approach him in spiritual gifts and properties than at birth they naturally communicated with him in body, flesh and blood.[7]

Thus far Vermigli has two communions in view, each with its own character: while one union is natural and feeble, the other comes to us by the Holy Spirit and brims with heavenly vitality. At this point Vermigli introduces an intermediate (*mediam*) union which he locates between the natural and spiritual unions just described. This intermediate union is "the fount and origin of all the heavenly and spiritual likeness which we have with Christ. It is that by which, as soon as we believe, we obtain Christ himself our true Head, and are made his members."[8] This communion, later called "secret" (*arcana*), is logically prior to the spiritual union introduced through renewal (*per instaurationem inducitur*).[9]

"We Entirely Agree in Sentiment": Calvin's Reply

Calvin's response to Vermigli is brief, warm, and enthusiastic.[10] On the "secret communion which we have with Christ," Calvin demonstrates his agreement with Vermigli by outlining his own perspective.

Agreeing that the question is one of "vast importance," Calvin opens his discussion with a passing reference to the common fraternity with Christ established at the incarnation and shared by all. This general brotherhood rests upon the event of Christ's

---

[7] CO 15.494; McLelland, 346: "Non quod substantiam suae naturae abiiciant, et re ipsa in corpus atque carnem Christi transeant, sed quod spiritualibus donis atque propietatibus non minus ad illum accedant, quam corpore, carne ac sanguine cum eo iam ab ipsa nativitate naturaliter communicaverint."

[8] CO 15.494; McLelland, 346: "Habemus itaque hic iam duas communiones cum Christo: una est naturalis quam ab ipsis parentibus per ortum trahimus, altera vero contingit per Christi spiritum quo ab ipsa regeneratione ad speciem eius gloriae innovamur. At credo inter has duas mediam esse, quae sit fons et oro omnis coelestis et spiritualis similitudinis quam cum Christo adipiscimur: et ea est qua statim quum credimus Christum ipsum vere caput nostrum nanciscimur efficimurque ipsius membra."

[9] CO 15.493: "Proinde communio haec nostra cum capite prior est saltem natura, licet fortasse non tempore, illa posteriori communione quae per instaurationem inducitur."

[10] Calvin to Vermigli, 8 August 1555, CO 15.722-5 (no. 2266). Gorham (pp. 349-52) again provides only a partial translation but includes much more than Beveridge/Bonnet. Cf. Calvin, "To Peter Martyr," in Henry Beveridge and Jules Bonnet, eds., *Selected Works of John Calvin: Tracts and Letters*, vol. 6; trans. M. R. Gilchrest (Grand Rapids: Baker, 1983), 217-18. Gorham will be cited unless otherwise indicated.

Appendix B

incarnation, his putting on human flesh "in order that he might become our brother, partaker of the same nature..."[11] Concerning this communion Calvin has chosen not to comment at length in order to discuss the "communion which flows from His heavenly influence and breathes life into us, and makes us to coalesce into one body with Himself."[12]

Calvin affirms that immediately upon the believing reception of Christ one is definitively made a member of Christ his Head. This communion is a sacred unity, a holy engrafting which forms the context of the communication of Christ's benefits. It is accomplished by the secret work of the Spirit "who makes Christ to dwell in us, to sustain us, to quicken us, and to fulfill all the offices of the Head."[13] In this redemptive work of the Spirit, the life of Christ 'flows to us from Him as from our Head. For He reconciles us to God by the sacrifice of His death in no other way than as He is ours and we are one with Him.'[14] For this reason, Calvin explains, Paul in 1 Cor. 1:9 teaches us we are called to the κοινωνίαν (communion) of his Son, not *consortium* (fellowship) or *societas* (society), for these terms are too weak.[15] Calvin, like Vermigli, distinguishes carefully the rich reality of this union from any notion of an ontological confusion, no doubt the confusion perceived in their Lutheran opponents. This union is thus no "mixture of substance"; rather, the analogy of root and branches sufficiently illustrates the way in which the life of Christ is transmitted to us.[16]

A third union is entailed in this second union. It is the "fruit and effect of the former."

> For after that Christ, by the interior influence of His Spirit, has bound us to Himself and united us to His Body, He exerts a second influence of His Spirit, enriching us by His gifts. Hence, that we are strong in hope and patience, that we soberly and

---

[11] CO 15.722; Gorham, 349.
[12] CO 15.722-3; Gorham, 349: "Quod filius Dei carnem nostram induit, ut frater noster fieret eiusdem naturae particeps, de illa communicatione dicere supersedeo. Nam de ea tantum agendum est quae a coelesti eius virtute manat et nobis vitam inspirat, et facit ut in unum cum ipso corpus coalescamus."
[13] CO 15.723; Gorham, 350: "Ergo spiritus est qui facit, ut in nobis habitet Christus, nos sustineat atque vegetet, omniaque capitis officia impleat."
[14] CO 15.723; Gorham, 350: "Dico autem, simul ac fide Christum recipimus qualiter se in evangelio offert, vere nos fieri eius membra, et vitam ab eo non secus atque a capite in nos defluere. Neque enim aliter nos Deo mortis suae sacrificio reconciliat, nisi quia noster est ac nos unum cum ipso."
[15] CO 15.723; Gorham, 350.
[16] CO 15.723; Gorham, 350.

temperately keep ourselves from worldly snares, that we strenuously bestir ourselves to the subjugation of carnal affections, that the love of righteousness and piety flourishes in us, that we are earnest in prayer, that meditation on the life to come draws us upwards, – this, I maintain, flows from that second Communion, by which Christ, dwelling in us not ineffectually, brings forth the influence of His Spirit in His manifest gifts.[17]

Thus Calvin's reply corresponds broadly in structure to Vermigli's letter. Both outline three "unions" or strata of union, the first (incarnational or natural) fraternity-establishing in character and the latter two (mystical and spiritual) effected by the Spirit for salvation. This correspondence to Vermigli's outline is purposeful. As Calvin remarks, "I have glanced at it [the subject, union with Christ] briefly, with the simple view of showing you that we entirely agree in sentiment."[18]

Thus are there three degrees or strata of union with Christ according to Vermigli and Calvin: natural or incarnational, secret and spiritual. Is there a correspondence between these latter strata – secret and spiritual – and the benefits of justification and sanctification?

Justification, Sanctification, and the Strata of Union with Christ

The relationship these strata of union with Christ bear to justification and sanctification has been variously interpreted.[19] Willis, not with a view to this correspondence but to Calvin's theology as presented in the 1559 *Institutes*, has suggested that Calvin distinguishes between two unions: incarnational and spiritual.[20] T. F. Torrance has spoken of a "threefold grafting and

---

[17] CO 15.723; Gorham, 351.
[18] CO 15.724; Gorham, 352.
[19] The short history of interpretation begins with Kolfhaus's attention to the correspondence in his 1939 study (*Christusgemeinshaft*, 24-35). Following this precedent, Gerrish (*Tradition*, 63) and then his student, Tamburello (*Union with Christ*, 86-7; 89-90), both point to its significance for Calvin studies. Butin (*Revelation, Redemption, and Response*, 203, n. 17) calls it "remarkable" as an example of Calvin's ongoing development of the idea of communion with Christ. Rankin's is the most extensive and helpful analysis to date, constituting the better part of one chapter in his thesis as well as an appendix (see n. 2, above).
[20] David Willis-Watkins, "The *Unio Mystica* and the Assurance of Faith According to John Calvin," in Willem van't Spijker, ed., *Calvin: Erbe und Auftrag, Festschrift für W. H. Neuser* (Kampen: Kok Pharos, 1991), 78.

twofold breaking off" in Calvin.[21] Tamburello, who is interacting with this correspondence, also maintains two, albeit different, unions: mystical and spiritual.[22]

In a recent and thorough examination of the correspondence, Rankin points to the three strata that I have outlined: natural or incarnational, secret or mystical, and spiritual. On the relationship these strata bear to the *duplex gratia*, Rankin, following Tamburello in what we will henceforth designate "the traditional reading," has suggested that there is a correspondence between the intermediate, "secret" union and the benefit of justification, and between "spiritual" union and the benefit of regeneration or sanctification.[23] Like Tamburello, Rankin has pointed specifically to the definitive character of the secret "mystical" union and the largely progressive character of the "spiritual" union as evidence of a neat correspondence with justification and sanctification, respectively.

> Both Calvin and Martyr agree that mystical communion must lie behind the daily experience of spiritual communion with Christ in a believer's life. Mystical communion is a definitive event in the lives of the elect, while spiritual communion is an ongoing, progressive relation. Thus mystical communion grounds justification, while spiritual communion appears to ground sanctification... To [Calvin's] mind, they are distinct and yet inseparable concepts, each brought about by a separate influence of the Holy Spirit.[24]

Again,

> [Calvin] distinguishes between mystical and spiritual communion in the same way he distinguishes Christ and his gifts, or justification and sanctification.[25]

---

[21] T. F. Torrance, *Kingdom and Church* (London: Oliver & Boyd, 1956), 102, n. 3. In an interview with Rankin, Torrance explained this "threefold engrafting" as consisting of (1) Christ (in the incarnation), (2) baptism, and (3) faith (Rankin, "Carnal Union with Christ," 169, n. 9).

[22] Tamburello, *Union with Christ*, 86-7. As Rankin observes, the failure on Tamburello's part to discern the first natural or incarnational union is due chiefly to his lack of attention to Vermigli's original letter to Calvin specifically and the Vermigli corpus in general. Rankin includes Gerrish in this criticism ("Carnal Union with Christ," 185, n. 72).

[23] Rankin attributes his identification of a correspondence between the two latter strata of union and the *duplex gratia* to Tamburello's earlier study ("Carnal Union with Christ," 184-5, n. 65).

[24] Rankin, "Carnal Union with Christ," 183-4.

[25] Rankin, "Carnal Union with Christ," 185.

It appears that this interpretation is governed in part by the language surrounding Vermigli's description of "spiritual" communion, the communion which results from faith "breathed into" the elect. It is in this paragraph that Vermigli refers to the saving reception of justification and renewal.

> So besides that [natural] communion this is added, that in due season faith is breathed into the elect whereby they may believe in Christ. Thus are they not only forgiven their sins and reconciled to God (in which the true and solid method of justification consists) but further there is added a renewing power of the spirit, by which our bodies also – flesh, blood and nature – are made capable of immortality, and become daily more and more in Christ's form as I may say.[26]

The correspondence between the strata and the benefits of union with Christ in these letters as observed in this traditional reading does indeed have a certain *prima facie* weight to it. It is only after naming "spiritual" union, for example, that Calvin introduces language descriptive of the Christian life, perhaps suggesting that the latter belongs to the former. And as Rankin explains, "Both Calvin and Martyr agree that mystical communion must lie behind the daily experience of spiritual communion with Christ in a believer's life."[27] Rankin follows Tamburello's suggestion, therefore, that because definitive language accompanies Calvin's description of the secret, "mystical" union and "progressive" language the "spiritual" union, the former must correspond to justification and the latter to sanctification.[28]

Vermigli

To evaluate the traditional reading we begin with a closer look at Vermigli's letter to Calvin. As observed above in Chapter 4, Vermigli first posits a universal union with Christ best described as a fraternal communion of the most basic sort. On the interpretation of this first stratum of union we have no difficulty with Rankin's critique of McLelland and Torrance: Vermigli and Calvin both understand this union as the platform upon which redemption is

---

[26] CO 15.494; McLelland, 346.
[27] Rankin, "Carnal Union with Christ," 183.
[28] Rankin's proposal does not differ from what he learns from Tamburello, making Tamburello the principal source for this perspective although it is Rankin who gives it the most attention. Cf. Rankin, "Carnal Union with Christ," 183-4, n. 65, referring to Tamburello, *Union with Christ*, 86-7.

carried out but not as independently redemptive. As a "very general and feeble" union, it is not co-extensive with the soteric union with Christ effected by the Holy Spirit. Incarnational and soteric union with Christ differ, therefore, both in nature and scope. Far from rendering this fraternal communion unnecessary and ultimately irrelevant, however, Christ's assumption of human flesh to become our brother is, as both Vermigli and Calvin recognize, a necessary precondition of the redemption of human persons.

Vermigli then describes "spiritual" union. Whereas Tamburello and Rankin see in this description the presence only of sanctification, Vermigli evidently intends to include justification as well. His two opening sentences, quoted in full above, lay the relationship bare for our purposes. Here Vermigli presents the two principal redemptive effects of the "faith... breathed into the elect" as justification ("forgiven their sins and reconciled to God") *and* regeneration/sanctification (the "renewing power of the spirit," "*Christiformia*"). The references to justification and renewal are both explicit, and both are made to follow the presence of faith consequentially (*ita*).[29] Furthermore, both benefits are bound *together* as the consequences of faith implying distinguishability yet inseparability arising from their joint source in Christ.

While the proximity of his reference to faith to his reference to justification may suggest that they belong together, a closer reading of the full letter suggests that Vermigli's reference to faith is in reality but an early reference to the intermediate union to be described in the following section. In light of what he will say about this intermediate union, it is altogether appropriate that he mention from the start that the benefits belonging to "spiritual" union or communion have this faith-union as their source.

If both justification and sanctification are the joint effects of the existential reality of faith, to what should we ascribe faith? How, in other words, is faith capable of such saving strength that it issues forth the whole of salvation? The answer is that the faith "breathed into the elect" is the divinely appointed existential entrance into the union with Christ from whom these benefits derive. Here it is important to recall Vermigli's description of the union he identifies as "between these two communions." This intermediate union is "the fount and origin of all the heavenly and spiritual likeness which

---

[29] *Ita* functions as a conditional particle. In short, I am arguing that the definitive faith-union is for Vermigli the logical *protasis* (or premise) of which the saving reception of Christ's benefits, including justification and sanctification, is the *apodosis* (conclusion): *If* (or, since) we are united to Christ by faith, *then* we are justified and sanctified.

we have with Christ." Moreover, "[i]t is that by which, *as soon as we believe*, we obtain Christ himself our true Head, and are made his members."[30]

Vermigli's language here purposely recalls his earlier statement that faith yields justification and sanctification. The faith referred to as the existential starting-point and source of justification and renewal is here tied to a definitive union with Christ which is prior, in some sense, to the divine bestowal of these benefits. This "intermediate union" is thus a faith-union, an engrafting into Christ in which the Head-members relationship is *definitively* established. The relationship of this union to the subsequent union is therefore one of source and fruit, cause and effect, obtaining Christ and thus obtaining his benefits. It is, as Vermigli states, the *"fount* and *origin"* of Christ's graces. Accordingly, one ought to understand Vermigli's statement on the priority of this intermediate union as an emphasis upon the necessity of union with Christ for the enjoyment of his benefits – both justification *and* sanctification.

In short, the strata of union with Christ as outlined in Vermigli's letter may be summarized as follows:

Natural Communion: unless supplemented, "very general and feeble"

Intermediate (Secret or Mystical) Union: the definitive engrafting into Christ by faith through the work of the Holy Spirit
- by faith we obtain Christ our Head and are made his members
- the "fount and origin of all the celestial and spiritual likeness which we obtain, together with Christ"
- prior "in nature at least, if not in time" to spiritual communion

Spiritual Union: the effect of the definitive, intermediate (secret) union is twofold:
- remission of sins and reconciliation with God (justification)
- renovating influence of the Spirit (sanctification)

Rather than viewing the intermediate union with Christ in Vermigli's letter as correlative to justification, there is therefore warrant for viewing this union as the definitively established union of Christ and the believer from which the benefits, i.e., justification and sanctification, flow. The third stratum of union, "spiritual" union, therefore includes both justification and sanctification as well as all other benefits derived by the believer from Christ. In other words, Vermigli's discussion is not markedly different from what I

---

[30] CO 15.494; McLelland, 346.

have described as Calvin's more clearly articulated view: justification and sanctification are distinct but inseparable graces that come to us simultaneously in our union with Christ by faith.

Calvin

A brief look at Gorham's translation may suggest that Calvin, though expressing his agreement with Vermigli, is not working with this same pattern. However, this is due not to Calvin's organization but to Gorham's. Gorham correctly notes that in Beza's printing of the letter there is no division between sections. Gorham, "for the sake of perspicuity," has divided the sections into two.[31] The result in Gorham's text is a mid-sentence break to introduce the first union. Gorham's text appears as follows:

> That the Son of God put on our flesh, in order that He might become our Brother, partaker of the same nature, – is a Communion on which I do not mean to speak here: for I propose to treat only on –
>
> 1. That Communion which flows from His heavenly influence, and breathes life into us, and makes us to coalesce into one body with Himself. But I affirm, that, as soon as we receive Christ by faith, as He offers Himself to us in the Gospel, we are truly made His members, and His life flows to us from Him as from our Head. For He reconciles us to God by the sacrifice of his death, in no other way than as He is ours and we are one with Him...
>
> 2. I come now to *a second Communion*, which, as I think, is the fruit and effect of the former. For after that Christ, by the interior influence of His Spirit, has bound us to Himself and united us to His Body, *He exerts a second influence of His Spirit, enriching us by His gifts.*[32]

Gorham correctly identifies the second section as such; Calvin is indeed moving on to the "second Communion," as he states explicitly. The question, as I see it, lies in Gorham's decision to begin the first communion in mid-sentence. Gorham's text suggests that Calvin begins his discussion of the first communion with "That Communion...," and that this first communion includes all the benefits described until the start of the second communion two pages later. More importantly, however, Gorham's decision also suggests that "That Communion..." effectively serves as a title or summary description of this first communion. In point of fact,

---

[31] Gorham, p. 349.
[32] Gorham, 350-51 (emphasis Gorham's).

however, Gorham's text appears to reflect a misunderstanding of Calvin's discursive summary, and the resulting ambiguity contributes to the potential for misinterpreting his delimitation of the strata of union with Christ. There are several reasons to favor a different perspective on the structure of the text.

First, the flow of the passage points to a natural break after Calvin's "heavenly influence" sentence. In this reading, the first union which Calvin describes begins with the words, "But I affirm…" If this is the case, the pattern of Calvin's presentation is as follows (retaining Gorham's punctuation and capitalization but not italics):

> That the Son of God put on our flesh, in order that He might become our Brother, partaker of the same nature, – is a Communion on which I do not mean to speak here: for I propose to treat only on that Communion which flows from His heavenly influence, and breathes life into us, and makes us to coalesce into one body with Himself.
>
> But I affirm, that, as soon as we receive Christ by faith, as He offers Himself to us in the Gospel, we are truly made His members, and His life flows to us from Him as from our Head.

The first distinction Calvin makes is a broad one between incarnational or fraternal union, in which Calvin suggests the life of Christ does *not* flow to us as from our Head, and a saving union in which we are made members of Christ and his life *does* flow to us. This union is definitive inasmuch as it is brought into existence at the moment of faith. Like Vermigli, Calvin uses the language of "Head" and "members" to describe the nature of this definitive engrafting.[33]

This proposal may seem contradicted by Calvin's next sentence in which he introduces justification during discussion of this first union. If justification does belong to this first union, then our point about presentation is rendered moot and the second and third strata of union with Christ do in fact correspond to justification and sanctification, respectively. A closer look at the texts, however, reveals that this is not the case.

The key to understanding Calvin here is the transitional language used between the sentences in question.

> But I affirm, that, as soon as we receive Christ by faith, as He offers Himself to us in the Gospel, we are truly made His members, and His life flows to us from Him as from our Head. *For* He reconciles

---

[33] CO 15.723; Gorham, 349-50.

us to God by the sacrifice of His death, in no other way than as He is ours and we are one with Him.[34]

If in Calvin's second sentence he is merely continuing in his description of this first union, then he is indeed identifying justification ("He reconciles us to God by the sacrifice of His death") with the union just described as the definitive engrafting into Christ our Head. If, however, the causal particle *enim* introducing the second sentence relates the subsequent statement *consequentially* to the former, then Calvin is merely referring to an illustrative fruit of this definitive, "secret" union. Taking this into account, it is clear that Calvin is only referring to a *benefit* of definitive union (in this case, justification) and not to the *nature* or *character* of the union itself. Calvin is saying, in effect, "We receive life from Christ our Head because we are made his members. For without this union, reconciliation with God on the basis of Christ's sacrifice is not ours." He is *not* saying, "We receive justification in one (definitive) union with Christ, sanctification in another (progressive)." Only in this light is the parallel to Vermigli's letter clear. Just as Vermigli uses "thus" (*ita*) to indicate, perhaps even more explicitly, the same faith-union – saving benefit relationship ("...in due season faith is breathed into the elect... Thus [*ita*] are they not only forgiven their sins and reconciled to God [in which the true and solid method of justification consists] but further there is added a renewing power of the spirit...") so Calvin ties definitive union with Christ to the reception of his benefits consequentially. The definitive union in Calvin's letter corresponds, therefore, to the "secret," "intermediate" union described by Vermigli.

Secondly, Calvin's subsequent discussion of the "spiritual" communion stands in favor of this reading. In a subsequent, illuminating passage he pointedly describes the final communion as

> the *fruit* and *effect* of the *former* (*quae illius prioris mihi fructus est ac effectus*). For after that Christ, by the interior influence of His Spirit, has bound us to Himself and united us to His Body, *He exerts a second influence of His Spirit, enriching us by His gifts.*[35]

We may ask why – if Calvin designates both justification and sanctification as the blessings of a prior, definitive union – he proceeds directly to a moving passage that describes what can only

---

[34] CO 15.723; Gorham, 349-50. Emphasis mine.
[35] CO 15.723; Gorham, 351: "Iam venio ad secundam communicationem, quae illius prioris mihi fructus est ac effectus. Nam postquam Christus interiore spiritus virtute sibi nos devinxit atque univit in corpus suum, secundam spiritus virtutem exserit, donis suis nos locupletando."

be identified as the experience of sanctification. Is his omission of justification in this section proof that only sanctification should be identified with the third, spiritual strata of union with Christ? If justification was not mentioned earlier in the letter than this objection might be strong. As it is, however, Calvin's earlier reference to justification as the saving benefit of our definitive union with Christ renders the later repetition of this point superfluous.

This is the case for at least three reasons. It is not as though, first of all, Calvin disagreed with Vermigli on either union with Christ or justification. If this were the case perhaps a more extensive discussion (and repetition) would be appropriate. Secondly, one must be careful in ascribing too much of a crucial significance to statements made in this context. This is, after all, only a letter (and a brief one at that), and we must not demand of correspondence what we justly expect from full theological discussions. In light of this important genre distinction, we remember with profit what Calvin *does* say in his *Institutes* and elsewhere, where these relations are filled out much more substantially. There, unambiguously, both justification and sanctification are benefits together, the *duplex gratia*, of a single, definitive union with Christ by the Spirit through faith. Lastly, Calvin explicitly states at the close of his letter that he has only looked at the subject briefly, and only to express his agreement with Vermigli's summary. In the interests of brevity, repetition of a point already made is naturally avoided. Thus the "gifts" Calvin has in view are to be understood as the full, comprehensive range of blessings that come in union with Christ, blessings that include both justification and sanctification.

On a concluding note, it seems appropriate to note that the omission on Tamburello's part of not examining Vermigli's letter as the necessary background to Calvin's (which Rankin is careful to point out as his error) appears also to stand as the probable reason Rankin himself has overlooked the structure of the strata inasmuch as this structure is clearest in Vermigli's letter (since it was longer and written first) and Rankin states that he follows Tamburello's reading. In light of our brief inquiry into the problem, the comment by Gerrish appears to reflect a more accurate reading when he describes the intermediate, definitive union as "something subsequent to the union with Christ that was already effected by the incarnation, but antecedent to the communication of his benefits."[36] If indeed it is "antecedent to the communication of his benefits,"

---

[36] Gerrish, *Grace and Gratitude*, 128. Interestingly, this statement is quoted by Rankin ("Carnal Union with Christ," 186, n. 74) though it is not accounted for in his own reading.

then it is antecedent (logically, not chronologically in light of Calvin's stress on simultaneity) to justification since justification is consistently and insistently for Calvin one facet of a *duplex gratia Dei*.

Bibliography

Primary Sources

Manuscript

Primier Volume, contenant 58 Sermones faict sur les 9. primers chapitres de la 1 Epistre de Sainct Paul Aux Corinthiens, par M. Jean Calvin. 1555. Bibliotheque Publique et Universitaire (Geneva), BPU Ms. fr. 26.

Calvin: Latin and French Editions

Institutes of the Christian Religion of John Calvin 1559: Text and Concordance, ed. Richard F. Wevers, 4 vols. Grand Rapids: H. Henry Meeter Center for Calvin Studies, 1988; CD-Rom, 2002.

Institutes of the Christian Religion of John Calvin 1539: Text and Concordance, ed. Richard F. Wevers, 4 vols. Grand Rapids: H. Henry Meeter Center for Calvin Studies, 1986.

Institutio christianae religionis nunc vere demum suo titulo respondens. Strasbourg: Wendelin Rihel, 1539.

Ioannis Calvini Commentarii in Priorem Epistolam Pauli ad Corinthios. Strasbourg: Wendelin Rihel, 1546.

Ioannis Calvini in omnes D. Pauli epistolas, atque etiam in epistolam ad Hebraeos commentaria luculentissima... Geneva: John Gerard, 1551.

Ioannis Calvini Opera Omnia Denuo Recognita. Opera Exegetica. Ioannis Calvini commentarius in Epistolam Pauli ad Romanos, ed. T. H. L. Parker and D. C. Parker. Geneva: Librairie Droz, 1999.

_____. *Commentarii in Pauli epistolas ad Galatas, ad Ephesios, ad Philippenses, ad Colossenses*, ed. Helmut Feld. Geneva: Librairie Droz, 1992.

_____. *Commentarii in secundam Pauli epistolam ad Corinthios*, ed. Helmut Feld. Geneva: Librairie Droz, 1994.

_____. *Commentarius in epistolam ad Hebraeos*, ed. T. H. L. Parker. Geneva: Librairie Droz, 1996.

_____. *In evangelium secundum Johannem commentaries pars prior*, ed. Helmut Feld. Geneva: Librairie Droz, 1997.

_____. *In evangelium secundum Johannem commentaries pars altera*, ed. Helmut Feld. Geneva: Librairie Droz, 1998.

Ioannis Calvini opera quae supersunt omnia, ed. G. Baum, E. Cunitz, and E. Reuss. 59 vols. (= *Corpus Reformatorum* vols 29-88). Brunswick and Berlin: C. A. Schwetschike, 1863-1900.

Ioannis Calvini opera selecta, ed. P. Barth, W. Niesel, and D. Scheuner. 5 vols. Münich: Chr. Kaiser, 1926-1952.

Supplementa Calviniana: Sermons inédits. Neukirchen: Neukirchener Verlag, 1936-.

Calvin: English Translations

Bondage and Liberation of the Will: A Defence of the Orthodox Doctrine of Human Choice against Pighius, The, ed. A. N. S. Lane and translated by G. I. Davies. Carlisle: Paternoster/Grand Rapids: Baker, 1996.

Calvin's Commentaries. 46 vols. Edinburgh: Calvin Translation Society, 1843-1855; rep. in 22 vols. Grand Rapids: Baker, 1996.

Calvin's Commentary on Seneca's 'De Clementia', ed. and translated by Ford Lewis Battles and A. M. Hugo. Leiden: E. J. Brill, 1969.

Calvin's Ecclesiastical Advice. Translated by Mary Beaty and Benjamin W. Farley. Edinburgh: T. & T. Clark, 1991.

Calvin's New Testament Commentaries, ed. David W. Torrance and Thomas F. Torrance. Various translators. 12 vols. Grand Rapids: Eerdmans, 1959-1972.

Calvin: Theological Treatises. Translated by J. K. S. Reid. Philadelphia: Westminster Press, 1954.

Catechism 1538, ed. and translated by Ford Lewis Battles in I. John Hesselink, *Calvin's First Catechism: A Commentary*, 1-38. Louisville: Westminster/John Knox Press, 1997.

Concerning Scandals. Translated by John W. Fraser. Grand Rapids: Eerdmans, 1978.

Concerning the Eternal Predestination of God. Translated by J. K. S. Reid. London: James Clarke, 1961.

Institutes of the Christian Religion, ed. John T. McNeill and translated by Ford Lewis Battles. 2 vols. Library of Christian Classics, vols 20-21. Philadelphia: Westminster Press, 1960.

Institutes of the Christian Religion (1536). Translated by Ford Lewis Battles. Atlanta: John Knox Press, 1975; rev. Grand Rapids: Meeter Center/Eerdmans, 1986.

Instruction in Faith (1537), ed. and translated by Paul T. Fuhrmann. Foreword by John H. Leith. Louisville: Westminster/John Knox Press, 1992.

John Calvin's Sermons on the Ten Commandments, ed. and translated by Benjamin W. Farley. Forward by Ford Lewis Battles. Grand Rapids: Baker, 1980.

Letters of John Calvin. Compiled and edited with historical notes by Jules Bonnet. 4 vols. Translated by David Constable and Marcus R. Gilchrest. New York: Burt Franklin, 1972.
Selected Works of John Calvin: Tracts and Letters, ed. Henry Beveridge and Jules Bonnet. Grand Rapids: Baker, 1983.
Sermons on Galatians. Translated by Kathy Childress. Edinburgh: Banner of Truth Trust, 1997.
Sermons on Melchizedek & Abraham: justification, faith & obedience. Foreword by Richard A. Muller. Rep. Willow Street: Old Paths Publications, 2000.
Sermons on the Epistle to the Ephesians. Rev. ed. Edinburgh and Carlisle: Banner of Truth Trust, 1973.
The Deity of Christ and Other Sermons. Translated by Leroy Nixon and forward by Richard C. Gamble. Rep. Audubon: Old Paths Publications, 1997.
Tracts and Treatises. Translated by Henry Beveridge; historical notes added by Thomas F. Torrance. Grand Rapids: Eerdmans, 1958.
Treatises against the Anabaptists and against the Libertines. Translated, edited, and notes by Benjamin W. Farley. Grand Rapids: Baker, 1982.
Two and twentie Sermons of Master Iohn Calvin, In which Sermons is most religiously handled, the hundredth and nineteenth Psalme of David, by eight verses aparte according to the Hebrewe Alphabet. Translated by "T. S.," 1580. Rep. Audubon: Old Paths Publications, 1996.

Other Pre-Seventeenth-Century Primary Texts, Critical Editions, and Translations

Acta Reformationis Catholicae, Vol. 6, ed. G. Pfeilschifter. Regensburg: F. Pustet, 1974.
Altenstaig, Johannes. *Vocabularius theologiae complectens vocabulorum descriptiones...* Hagenau, 1517.
_____. *Lexicon theologicum quo tanquam clave theologiae fores aperiuntur, et omnium fere terminorum et obsuriorum vocum, quae s. theologiae studiosos facile remorantur, etymologiae, ambiguitates, definitiones, usus, enucleate ob oculos ponuntur, & dilucide explicantur.* Cologne, 1619.
Aquinas, Thomas. *Summa Theologiae.* Latin text and English translation, introductions, notes, appendices, and glossaries. 61 vols. London: Blackfriars, in conjunction with Eyre & Spottiswoode, 1964-1981.
Aristotle, *Physics.* 4 vols. Translated by F. M. Cornford and P. H. Wicksteed. Loeb Classical Library. Harvard University Press, 1927; rev. 1957.

Beza, Theodore. *Correspondance de Théodore de Bèze*. Recueillie par Hippolyte Aubert; publiée par Fernand Aubert, Henri Meylan, et al. Geneva: Librairie Droz, 1964-.

_____. *De Coena Domini plana et perspicua tractatio, in quo Ioachimi Westphali calumniae refelluntur*. In Beza, *Traités théologiques de Theodore de Bèze*. 2nd ed. Geneva, 1572, 1:211-58.

_____. *ΚΡΕΩΦΑΓΙΑ sive Cyclops, Dialogus de vera communicatione corporis et sanguinia Domini, adversus Tilemanni Heshusii commenta*. In Beza, *Traités théologiques de Theodore de Bèze*. 2nd ed. Geneva, 1572, 1:259-336.

Biblia Latina cum Glossa Ordinaria. Facsimile Reprint of the Editio Princeps by Adolph Rusch of Strassburg, 1480/81. 4 vols, ed. Karlfried Frohlich and Margaret Gibson. Turnhout: Brepols, 1992.

Bucer, Martin and Matthew Parker. *Florilegium Patristicum*. Publié par Pierre Fraenkel. Martini Buceri Opera Latina, Vol. III. Leiden: E. J. Brill, 1988.

Bucer, Martin. *Metaphrases et Enarrationes Perpetuae Epistolarum D. Pauli Apostoli,...Tomus Primus. Continens Metaphrasim et Enarrationem in Epistolam ad Romanos...* Strasbourg, 1536.

_____. *Praelectiones doctiss. in Epistolam D. Pauli ad Ephesios*. Basil, 1562.

_____. *Common Places of Martin Bucer*, translation and annotations, ed. and translated by D. F. Wright. Courtenay Library of Reformation Classics 4. Appleford: Sutton Courtenay Press, 1972.

_____. [Selections]. In *Melanchthon and Bucer*, ed. Wilhelm Pauck. Library of Christian Classics, vol. 19. Philadelphia: Westminster Press, 1969.

Bullinger, Heinrich. *In Omnes Apostolicas Epistolas... Commentarii Heinrychi Bullingeri...* Zurich, 1537.

Canons and Decrees of the Council of Trent, The. Translated by H. J. Schroeder. St. Louis: B. Herder, 1941. Rep. Rockford: TAN, 1978.

Cicero. *De Finibus*. Translated by H. Rackham. Loeb Classical Library. Harvard University Press, 1914.

_____. *Topica*. 2 vols. Vol. 1 translated by A. S. Wilkins; Vol. 2 translated by H. M. Hubbell and edited by E. H. Warmington. Loeb Classical Library. Harvard University Press, 1935, 1949.

_____. *De Oratore*. 4 vols. Vols 1-2 edited by A. S. Wilkins; Vols 3-4 translated by H. Rackham and E. W. Sutton. Loeb Classical Library. Harvard University Press, 1922, 1935, 1942.

Concordia Triglotta. St. Louis: Concordia Publishing House, 1921.

Corpus Christianorum Latinorum/Corpus Christianorum, Series Latina. Brepols: Turnhout, 1953-.

Eck, Johannes. *Enchiridion Locorum Communium...* 1529; rev. 1532 and 1541. Translated by Ford Lewis Battles as *Enchiridion of*

Common Places Against Luther and Other Enemies of the Church. Grand Rapids: Baker, 1979.

Erasmus, Desiderius. *Opera omnia, recognita et adnotatione critica instructa notisque illustrata* (ASD). Ed. L.- E.- Halkin, F. Bierlaire, and R. Hoven. Amsterdam: North Holland Publishing Company, 1969-.

———. *Collected Works of Erasmus*, ed. R. J. Schoeck, B. M. Corrigan, et al. Toronto: University of Toronto Press, 1969-.

———. *Opus Epistolarum Des. Erasmi Roterodami*, ed. P. S. Allen and H. M. Allen. New York: Oxford University Press, 1928; rep. 1992.

———. *The Enchiridion of Erasmus*. Translated by Raymond Himilick. Bloomington: n.p., 1963.

———. *In epistolam Pauli Apostoli ad Romanos paraphrasis*. Translated and annotated by John B. Payne, et al., in *Paraphrases on Romans and Galatians*, ed. Robert D. Sider. Complete Works of Erasmus 42. Toronto: University of Toronto Press, 1984.

———. *Annotationes in epistolam ad Romanos*. Translated and annotated by John B. Payne, et al., in *Annotations on Romans*, ed. Robert D. Sider. Complete Works of Erasmus 56. Toronto: University of Toronto Press, 1994.

Gorham, George C. *Gleanings of a Few Scattered Ears, During the Period of the Reformation in England and of the Times Immediately Succeeding, A. D. 1533 to A. D. 1588*. London: Bell and Daldy, 1857.

Herminjard, A.–L., ed. *Correspondance des Réformateurs dans les pays de langue française*. 7 vols. Geneva and Paris: H. Georg, 1866-1886.

Hyperius, Andreas. *In D. Pauli ad Romanos epistolam exegema*. London: Thomas Vautrollerius, typographus, 1577.

———. *The foundation of Christian religion, used in the time of the primitiue church: learnedly & purely expounded (in catechising) out of the 6. chap. to the Hebrews, by Andrewe Hyperius, professor in diuinity, at Marpurge, in the countrie of Hesse. Translated out of Latine into French, and out of French into English. By I. H.* London: printed by Robert Vvalde-graue, 1583.

Kingdon, R. M., ed. *Registres de la Cmpagnie des Pasteurs de Genève au Temps de Calvin*. 4 vols. Geneva: Librairie Droz, 1962-.

Lombard, Peter. *Magistri Petri Lombardi* Sententiae in IV libris distinctae, ed. Ignatius Brady, O.F.M. 2 vols. Spicilegium Bonaventurianum 4-5. Grottaferrata: Editiones Collegii S. Bonaventurae Ad Claras Aquas, 1971-1981.

Lucretius. *De Rerum Natura*, ed. Cyril Bailey. Oxford Classical Texts. Oxford University Press, 1922.

Luther, Martin. *Die Martin Luthers Werke: kritische gesamtausgabe*. Weimary: H. Böhlau, 1883-1993.

———. *Luther's Works*, ed. Jaroslav Pelikan. 55 vols. St. Louis: Concordia Publishing House/Philadelphia: Fortress Press, 1955-75.

———. *The Freedom of a Christian*. Translated by W. A. Lambert; rev. by Harold J. Grimm. *Luther's Works* 31, 327-77. Philadelphia: Muhlenberg Press, 1957.

Lyra, Nicholas of. *Postilla perpetuae in Veteris et Novum Testamentum*. 5 vols. Rome: Conradus Sweynheym and Arnoldus Pannartz, 1471-72.

Melanchthon, Philip. *Phillipi Melanchthonis Opera quae supersunt omnia*, ed. C. G. Bretshneider. [= *Corpus Reformatorum* vols 1-28]. Brunswick and Berlin: C. A. Schwetschike, 1834-1860.

———. *Melanchthons Werke in Auswahl*. Güttersloh: C. Bertelsmann Verlag, 1955.

———. *Melanchthon on Christian Doctrine: Loci Communes 1555*, ed. and translated by Clyde L. Manschreck. New York: Oxford University Press, 1965.

———. *Commentary on Romans*. Translated by Fred Kramer. St. Louis: Concordia, 1992.

Migne, J. P., ed. *Patrologiae Cursus Completus, Series Graeca*. Paris, 1886-.

———, ed. *Patrologiae Cursus Completus, Series Latina*. Paris, 1879-.

Nicene and Post-Nicene Fathers of the Christian Church, A Select Library of. First Series, 14 vols; Second Series, 14 vols. Peabody: Hendrickson, 1994.

Original Letters Relative to the English Reformation, ed. and translated by Hastings Robinson. Parker Society 42. Cambridge: Cambridge University Press, 1847.

Osiander, Andreas. *Andreas Osiander d. Ä. Gesamtausgabe*. 10 vols. Vols 1-6 ed. Gerhard Müller; vols 7-10 commissioned by the Heidelberg Academy of Sciences, ed. Gottfried Seebass. Gütersloh: Gütersloher Verlagshaus Mohn, 1975-1995.

Oxford Latin Dictionary, The. Oxford: Oxford University Press, 1966-82.

Quintilian. *Declamationes XIX Maiores Quintiliano Falso Adscriptae*. Ann Arbor: University of Michigan Press, 1982.

Rupp, Gordon E. and Philip S. Watson, eds. *Luther and Erasmus: Free Will and Salvation*. Philadelphia: Westminster/John Knox Press, 1969.

Sedgwick, Obadiah. *The Bowels of Tender Mercy Sealed in the Everlasting Covenant, wherein Is set forth the Nature, Conditions and Excellencies of it, and how a Sinner should do to enter it, and the danger of refusing this Covenant-Relation. Also the Treasures of Grace, Blessings, Comforts, and Promises and Priviledges that are comprised in the Covenant of Gods Free and Rich Mercy made in Jesus Christ with*

Believers. London: by Edward Mottershed for Adoniram Byfield, 1661.
Seneca. *Quaestiones Naturales*. 4 vols. Loeb Classical Library. Harvard University Press, 1992.
_____. *Epistolae Morales ad Lucilio*. 2 vols. Madrid: Gredos, 1996.
_____. *Thyestes*. Translated by Frank J. Miller and Frank Justus Miller. Loeb Classical Library. Harvard University Press, 1917.
Seripando, Hieronymus. *In Pauli Epistolas ad Romanos et Galatas Commentaria*. Naples, 1601. Rep. Gregg International Publishers Ltd., 1971.
Ursinus, Zacharius. *Commentary on the Heidelberg Catechism*. Rep. Phillipsburg: Presbyterian and Reformed Publishing Company, 1992.
Ussher, James. *The Whole Works of the Most Rev. James Ussher, D. D.,…* Dublin: Hodges, Smith, and Co., 1864.
Vermigli, Peter Martyr. *Justification and Predestination: Two Theological Loci*, ed. and translated by Frank A. James, III. Peter Martyr Library Series 1, Vol. 8. Kirksville: Truman State University Press, 2003.
_____. *In Epist. S. Pauli ad Romanos*, 2 vols, Basil, 1558.
_____. *Commentary on Romans…* Translated by "H.B.," London, 1568.
_____. *In Selectissimam S. Pauli priorem ad Corinth. epistolam D. Petri Martyris …commentari doctissimi …*Tiguri, Christ. Froschoveri, 1551.
_____. *Loci Communes Petri Martyris Vermilii Florentini Theologi Celeberrimi…* Geneva: Pierre Aubert, 1627.
_____. *Common Places of the most famous and renowned Divine Doctor Peter Martyr, divided into four principall parts, with Appendix*. Translated and compiled by Anthonie Marten. London: H. Denham and H. Middleton, 1583.
_____. *Tractatio de sacramento eucharistiae… Disputatio de eodem eucharistiae sacramento*. Translated as *Dialogue on the Two Natures of Christ*, ed. and translated by John Patrick Donnelley, S.J. Peter Martyr Library Series 1, Vol. 2. Sixteenth Century Essays and Studies 31. Kirksville: Thomas Jefferson University Press and Sixteenth Century Journal Publishers, 1995.
_____. *Dialogus de utraque in Christo natura*. Translated as *The Oxford Treatise and Disputation on the Eucharist, 1549*, ed. and translated by Joseph C. McLelland. Peter Martyr Library Series 1, Vol. 7. Sixteenth Century Essays and Studies 56. Kirksville: Truman State University Press, 2000.
_____. "Letter No. 121. To Doctor John Calvin." In *Peter Martyr Vermigli, Life, Letters, and Sermons*, ed. and translated by John

Patrick Donnelly, S.J., 138-41. Peter Martyr Library Series 1, Vol. 5. Kirksville: Sixteenth Century Essays and Studies, 1999.

Westphal, Joachim. *Confessio fidei de eucharistiae sacramento, in qua ministry ecclesiarum Saxoniae solidis argumentis sacrarum litterarum astruunt corporis et sanguinis Domini Jesu-Christi praesentiam in coena sancta et de libro Ioannis Calvini ipsis dedicato respondent*. Magdeburg, 1557.

Zanchi, Girolamo. *De spirituali inter Christum et ecclesiam, singulosque fideles, coniugio, ...* Herborn, 1591.

————. *An excellent and learned treatise, of the spirituall mariage betvveene Christ and the church, and every faithfull man. Written in Latine by that famous and worthie member of Christ his church H. Zanchius: and translated into English*. Cambridge: Printed by John Legate, printer to the Universitie of Cambridge, 1592.

————. *Hieron. Zanchii, de religione Christiana, fides*. London: Excudebat Iacobus Rimeus cum gratia & privilegio Regio, 1605.

————. *H. Zanchius his confession of Christian religion*. Cambridge: Printed by John Legat[e], printer to the Universitie of Cambridge, 1599.

————. *De religione Christiana fides – Confession of Christian Religion*, 2 vols, ed. Luca Baschera and Christian Moser. Studies in the History of Christian Traditions 125; Leiden: Brill, 2007.

Ziegler, Bernhard. *Zwo Predigten des Ehrwirdigen herren Doctoris Martini Lutheri...* Leipzig: Hantzsch, 1551.

Studies

Adams, H. M. *Catalogue of Books Printed on the Continent of Europe, 1501-1600, in Cambridge Librairies*. London: Cambridge University Press, 1967.

Anderson, Luke. "The *Imago Dei* Theme in John Calvin and Bernard of Clairvaux." In *Calvinus Sacrae Scripturae Professor*, ed. W. H. Neuser, 178-98. Grand Rapids: Eerdmans, 1994.

————. "Review of *Union with Christ: John Calvin and the Mysticism of St. Bernard*, by Dennis E. Tamburello." *Princeton Seminary Bulletin* 42 (1996): 116-17.

Anderson, Marvin W. "Trent and Justification (1546): a Protestant Reflection." *Scottish Journal of Theology* 21 (1968): 385-406.

————. "Word and Spirit in Exile (1542-61): the Biblical Writings of Peter Martyr Vermigli." *Journal of Ecclesiastical History* 21 (1970): 193-201.

————. "Peter Martyr, Reformed Theologian (1542-1562): His letters to Heinrich Bullinger and John Calvin." *Sixteenth Century Journal* 4 (1973): 41-64.

_____. "Peter Martyr on Romans." *Scottish Journal of Theology* 26 (1973): 401-20.

_____. *Peter Martyr, A Reformer in Exile (1542-1562): A Chronology of Biblical Writings in England and Europe.* Nieuwkoop: B. de Graaf, 1975.

_____. "Royal Idolatry: Peter Martyr and the Reformed Tradition." *Archiv für Reformationsgeschichte* 69 (1978): 160-200.

_____. "Rhetoric and Reality: Peter Martyr and the English Reformation." *Sixteenth Century Journal* 19 (1988): 451-69.

_____. "*Vista Tigurina*: Peter Martyr and European Reform (1556-1562)." *Harvard Theological Review* 83 (1990): 181-206.

Andia, Ysabel de. *Henosis: L'Union à Dieu chez Denys l'Aréopagite.* Philosophia Antiqua 71. Leiden: E. J. Brill, 1996.

Armstrong, Brian G. "The Nature and Structure of Calvin's Thought According to the *Institutes*: Another Look." In *John Calvin's Institutes: His Opus Magnum*, 55-81. Proceedings of the Second South African Congress for Calvin Research. Potchefstroom: Potchefstroom University for Christian Higher Education, 1986.

_____. "*Duplex cognitio Dei*, Or? the Problem and Relation of Structure, Form, and Purpose in Calvin's Theology." In *Probing the Reformed Tradition: Historical Studies in Honor of Edward A. Dowey*, ed. Elsie Anne McKee and Brian G. Armstrong, 135-53. Louisville: Westminster/John Knox Press, 1989.

Armstrong, E. B. B. "Calvin's Theology of the Lord's Supper Set in Historical Context and With Special Reference to his 'Short Treatise'." M.Th. diss., University of Aberdeen, 1994.

Audisio, Gabriel and Isabelle Bonnot-Rambaud. *Lire le Français d'hier: Manuel de Paléographie Moderne Xve – XVIIIe Siècle.* Paris: Armand Colin, 1991; 2nd ed. 1997.

Augustijn, Cornelius. "Calvin in Strasbourg." In *Calvinus Sacrae Scripturae Professor*, ed. W. H. Neuser, 166-77. Grand Rapids: Eerdmans, 1994.

Aulén, Gustaf. *Christus Victor: An Historical Study of the Three Main Types of the Idea of the Atonement.* Translated by A. G. Hebert. London: S. P. C. K., 1931.

Ayres, Robert H. "Language, Logic and Reason in Calvin's *Institutes*." *Religious Studies* 16 (1980): 283-97.

Bachmann, Claus. *Die Selbstherrlichkeit Gottes: Studien zur Theologie des Nürnberger Reformators Andreas Osiander.* Neukirchen-Vluyn: Neukirchener, 1996.

Backus, Irena. "Aristotelianism in Some of Calvin's and Beza's Expository and Exegetical Writings on the Doctrine of the Trinity with Particular Reference to the Terms *ousia* and *hypostasis*." In

Histoire de l'exégèse au XVIe siècle, ed. O. Fatio and P. Fraenkel, 351-60. Geneva: Librairie Droz, 1978.

―――――. "Polemic, Exegetical Tradition, and Ontology: Bucer's Interpretation of John 6:52, 53, and 64 Before and After the Wittenberg Concord." In *The Bible in the Sixteenth Century*, ed. David C. Steinmetz, 167-80. Durham: Duke University Press, 1990.

―――――. "Nicolas Durand de Villegagnon contre Calvin: le *Consensus Tigurinus* et la Présence Réelle." In *Calvin et ses Contemporains*, ed. Olivier Millet, 163-78. Cahiers d'Humanisme et Renaissance Vol. 53. Geneva: Librairie Droz, 1998.

Badcock, Gary D. *Light of Truth and Fire of Love: A Theology of the Holy Spirit*. Grand Rapids: Eerdmans, 1997.

Bagchi, D. V. N. "Sic et Non: Luther and Scholasticism." In *Protestant Scholasticism: Essays in Reassessment*, ed. Carl R. Trueman and R. S. Clark, 3-15. Carlisle: Paternoster Press, 1999.

Bahmann, Manfred K. "Calvin's Controversy with Certain 'Half-Papists.'" *Hartford Quarterly* 5 (1964/65): 27-41.

Baker, J. Wayne. *Heinrich Bullinger and the Covenant: the Other Reformed Tradition*. Athens: Ohio University Press, 1980.

Balke, W. "The Word of God and Experientia according to Calvin." In *Calvinus Ecclesiae Doctor*, ed. W. H. Neuser, 19-31. Kampen: Uitgeversmaatschappij J. H. Kok B. V., 1978.

Balserak, Jon. *Divinity Compromised: A Study of Divine Accommodation in the Thought of John Calvin*. Studies in Early Modern Religious Reforms 5; Berlin/Heidelberg/Dordrecht/New York: Springer, 2006.

Barrett, C. K. *A Commentary on the Epistle to the Romans*. Black's New Testament Commentaries. London: A. & C. Black, 1957.

―――――. "Paul and the Introspective Conscience." In *The Bible, the Reformation and the Church: Essays in Honour of James Atkinson*, ed. W. Peter Stephens, 36-48. Journal for the Study of the New Testament Supplement Series 105. Sheffield: Sheffield Academic Press, 1995.

Barth, Karl. *Church Dogmatics* II/1, ed. Geoffrey W. Bromiley and Thomas F. Torrance. Edinburgh: T. & T. Clark, 1957.

―――――. *Church Dogmatics* IV/1-3, ed. Geoffrey W. Bromiley and Thomas F. Torrance. Edinburgh: T. & T. Clark, 1962.

―――――. *The Theology of Calvin*. Translated by Geoffrey W. Bromiley. Grand Rapids: Eerdmans, 1995.

Battenhouse, R. W. "The Doctrine of Man in Calvin and in Renaissance Platonism." *Journal of the History of Ideas* 9 (1948): 447-71.

Battles, Ford Lewis. *The Piety of John Calvin. An Anthology Illustrative of the Spirituality of the Reformer of Geneva.* Grand Rapids: Baker, 1978.
_____. "Calculus Fidei." In *Calvinus Ecclesia Doctor*, ed. W. H. Neuser, 85-110. Kampen: Uitgeversmaatschappij J. H. Kok B. V., 1978.
_____. *Interpreting John Calvin*, ed. Robert Benedetto. Grand Rapids: Baker/H. Henry Meeter Center for Calvin Studies, 1996.
Bauke, Hermann. *Die Probleme Der Theologie Calvins.* Leipzig: J. C. Hinrichs'schen Buchhandlung, 1922.
Bavaud, G. "La doctrine de la justification d'après saint Augustin et la Rèforme." *Revue des Ètudes Augustiniennes* 5 (1959): 21-32.
_____. "Les rapports de la grâce et du libre arbitre." *Verbum Caro* 14 (1960): 328-38.
_____. "La doctrine de la justification d'après Calvin et le Concile de Trente." *Verbum Caro* 22 (1968): 83-92.
Beckmann, Joachim. *Vom Sakrament bei Calvin: Die Sakramentslehre Calvins in ihren Beziehungen zu Augustin.* Tübingen: J. C. B. Mohr, 1926.
Beeke, Joel R. *Assurance of Faith: Calvin, English Puritanism, and the Dutch Second Reformation.* New York: Peter Lang, 1991.
Beesley, Alan. "An unpublished source of the Book of Common Prayer: Peter Martyr Vermigli's Adhortatio ad Coenam Domini Mysticam." *Journal of Ecclesiastical History* 19 (1968): 83-8.
Bell, M. Charles. "Calvin and the Extent of the Atonement." *Evangelical Quarterly* 55 (1983): 115-23.
_____. "Was Calvin a Calvinist." *Scottish Journal of Theology* 36 (1983): 535-40.
_____. *Calvin and Scottish Theology: The Doctrine of Assurance.* Edinburgh: Handsel Press, 1985.
Bell, Theo. "Calvin and Luther on Bernard of Clairvaux." *Calvin Theological Journal* 34 (1999): 370–95.
Bell, Thomas J. "The Eucharistic Theologies of *Lauda Sion* and Thomas Aquinas's *Summa Theologiae*." *The Thomist* 57 (1993): 179-83.
Benoit, Jean-Daniel. "The History and Development of the *Institutio*: How Calvin Worked." In *John Calvin: A Collection of Distinguished Essays*, ed. G. E. Duffield, 102-17. Grand Rapids: Eerdmans, 1966.
_____. *Calvin in his Letters: A Study of Calvin's Pastoral Counselling, Mainly from his Letters.* Translated by Richard Haig. Appleford: Sutton Courtenay Press, 1991.
Bente, F. "The Osiandrian Controversy." In *Concordia Triglotta*, cols 152a-61b.

Berkouwer, G. C. *Faith and Justification*. Translated by Lewis B. Smedes. Grand Rapids: Eerdmans, 1954.
———. *The Sacraments*. Translated by Hugo Bekker. Grand Rapids: Eerdmans, 1969.
Bierma, Lyle D. "Federal Theology in the Sixteenth Century: Two Traditions?" *Westminster Theological Journal* 45 (1983): 304-21.
———. *German Calvinism in the Confessional Age: The Covenant Theology of Caspar Olevianus*. Grand Rapids: Baker, 1996.
———. "What Hath Wittenberg to do with Heidelberg? Philip Melanchthon and the Heidelberg Catechism." In *Melanchthon in Europe: His Work and Influence Beyond Wittenberg*, ed. Karin Maag, 103-21. Grand Rapids: Baker, 1999.
Bihary, Michael, ed. *Bibliographia Calviniana: Calvins Werke und ihre Übersetzungen / Calvin's Works and their Translations 1850-1997*. 3rd revised and enlarged edition. Prague, 2000.
Billings, J. Todd. "United to God through Christ: Assessing Calvin on the Question of Deification." *Harvard Theological Review* 98 (2005): 315-334.
Bizer, Ernst. *Fides ex Auditu: Eine Untersuchung über die Entdeeckung der Gerechtigkeit Gottes durch Martin Luther*. 2nd ed. Neukirchen: Neukirchener Verlag, 1961.
Bluhm, Heinz. *Luther: Translator of Paul: Studies in Romans and Galatians*. New York: Peter Lang, 1984.
Bohatec, Josef B. "Calvin et l'humanisme." *Revue Historique* 183 (1938): 207-41; 184 (1939): 71-104.
———. *Budé und Calvin: Studien zur Gedankenwelt des französischen Frühhumanismus*. Graz, Austria: Hermann Bohlaus, 1950.
Boisset, J. *Sagesse et Sainteté dans la pensée de Calvin. Essai sur l'humanisme du Réformateur*. Paris, 1959.
———. "Justification et Sanctification chez Calvin." In *Calvinus Theologus*, ed. W. H. Neuser, 131-48. Amsterdam: Neukirchener Verlag, 1976.
Böttger, Paul C. "Die Christusgemeinschaft als Grundlage der Applikation." In Böttger, *Calvins Institutio als Erbauungs buch. Versuch einer literarischen Analyse*, 31-54. Neukirchener: Neukirchener Verlag, 1990.
———. "Einzelanalyse der Institutio von 1536 und von 1559." In Böttger, *Calvins Institutio als Erbauungs buch. Versuch einer literarischen Analyse*, 55-142. Neukirchener: Neukirchener Verlag, 1990.
Bouwsma, William J. *Calvinism as Theologia Rhetorica: Protocol of the Fifty-Fourth Colloquy (Colloquy 54)*. Berkeley: Center for Hermeneutical Studies in Hellenistic and Modern Culture, 1986.

_____. "The Spirituality of John Calvin." In *Christian Spirituality: High Middle Ages and Reformation*, ed. Jill Raitt, 318-33. New York: Crossroad, 1987.

_____. *John Calvin: A Sixteenth Century Portrait.* New York: Oxford University Press, 1988.

Braaten, Carl E. and Robert W. Jenson, eds. *Union with Christ: The New Finnish Interpretation of Luther.* Grand Rapids: Eerdmans, 1998.

Brady, T. A., Heiko A. Oberman, and James D. Tracy, eds. *Handbook of European History 1400-1600: Late Middle Ages, Renaissance and Reformation.* 2 vols. Leiden: E. J. Brill, 1995; Grand Rapids: Eerdmans, 1996.

Bray, John S. "The Value of Works in the Theology of Calvin and Beza." *Sixteenth Century Journal* 4 (1973): 77-86.

Breen, Quirinus. "John Calvin and the Rhetorical Tradition." *Church History* 26 (1957): 3-21.

_____. *John Calvin: A Study in French Humanism.* 2nd ed. Hamden: Archon Books, 1968.

_____. *Christianity and Humanism: Studies in the History of Ideas.* Grand Rapids: Eerdmans, 1968.

Brglez, H. A. "Saving Union with Christ in the Theology of John Calvin: A Critical Study." Ph.D. diss., University of Aberdeen, 1993.

Bromiley, Geoffrey W. "The Doctrine of Justification in Luther." *Evangelical Quarterly* 24 (1952): 91-100.

Brug, John F. "The Lutheran-Catholic Statement of Justification." *Wisconsin Lutheran Quarterly* (Winter, 1984): 66-70.

_____. "Osiandrianism – Then and Now: Justification through Christ Dwelling in Us." Privately Published Paper, Wisconsin Lutheran Seminary, 2001.

Brunner, Emil. *Das Wirken des Heiligen Geistes.* Zurich, 1935.

Brunner, Peter. *Vom Glauben bei Calvin.* Tübingen: J. C. B. Mohr, 1925.

Bryant, Barry E. "Trinity and Hymnody: the Doctrine of the Trinity in the Hymns of Charles Wesley." Paper read at the Conference on Trinitarian Theology, Institute of Systematic Theology, Kings College, University of London, 26 September 1990. Web version edited by Michael Mattei and published in 2000 by the Wesley Center for Applied Theology, Northwest Nazarene University, Nampa, ID, http://wesley.nnu.edu/WesleyanTheology/theojrnl/21-25/25-13.htm.

Bulman, James M. "The Place of Knowledge in Calvin's View of Faith." *Review and Expositor* 50 (1953): 323-29.

Büsser, Fritz. "Bullinger as Calvin's Model in Biblical Exposition: An Examination of Calvin's Preface to the Epistle to the Romans." In

In Honor of John Calvin, 1509-64, ed. J. Furcha, 64-95. Montreal: Faculty of Religious Studies, McGill University, 1987.

Butin, Philip Walker. *Reformed Ecclesiology: Trinitarian Grace According to Calvin*. Studies in Reformed Theology and History 2.1. Princeton Theological Seminary, Winter, 1994.

_____. *Revelation, Redemption, and Response: Calvin's Trinitarian Understanding of the Divine-Human Relationship*. New York: Oxford University Press, 1995.

_____. "A Response to 'Constructing Tradition: Schleiermacher, Hodge and the Theological Legacy of John Calvin.'" In *The Legacy of John Calvin*, ed. David Foxgrover, 176-81. Grand Rapids: CRC Product Services for the Calvin Studies Society, 2000.

Cappelli, A. *Lexicon abbreviaturarum: Dizionario di abbreviature latine ed italiane*. 6th ed. Milan, 1985.

Carpenter, Craig B. "A Question of Union with Christ? Calvin and Trent on Justification." *Westminster Theological Journal* 64 (2002): 363-86.

Casteel, Theodore W. "Calvin and Trent: Calvin's Reaction to The Council of Trent in the Context of his Conciliar Thought." *Harvard Theological Review* 63 (1970): 91-117.

Chadwick, Owen. *The Reformation*. Revised edition, London: Penguin Books Ltd., 1972.

Chester, T. J. "The Relationship Between Eschatology and Mission in the Theology of Jürgen Moltmann and in Recent Evangelical Social Concern." Ph.D. diss., University of Wales, 1997.

Chin, Clive S. "*Unio Mystica* and *Imitatio Christi*: The Two-Dimensional Nature of John Calvin's Spirituality." Ph.D. diss., Dallas Theological Seminary, 2002.

Citron, Bernhard. *New Birth: A Study of the Evangelical Doctrine of Conversion in the Protestant Fathers*. Edinburgh: Edinburgh University Press/Clarke and Irwin, 1951.

Clifford, Alan C. "Calvin on Justification" in Clifford, *Calvinus: Authentic Calvinism A Clarification*, 83-7 (Appendix IV). Norwich: Charenton Reformed Publishing, 1996.

Clines, David J. A. "Job and the Spirituality of the Reformation." In *The Bible, the Reformation and the Church: Essays in Honour of James Atkinson*, ed. W. Peter Stephens, 49-72. Journal for the Study of the New Testament Supplement Series 105. Sheffield: Sheffield Academic Press, 1995.

Coates, Thomas. "John Calvin's Doctrine of Justification." *Concordia Theological Monthly* 34 (1963): 325-34.

Compier, Don H. "The Independent Pupil: Calvin's Transformation of Erasmus' Theological Hermeneutics." *Westminster Theological Journal* 54 (1992): 217-33.

Corda, Salvatore. *Veritas Sacramenti: A Study in Vermigli's Doctrine of the Lord's Supper.* Zurich: Theologischer Verlag, 1975.
Cottret, Bernhard. *Calvin: A Biography.* Translated by M. Wallace McDonald. Grand Rapids: Eerdmans; Edinburgh: T. & T. Clark, 2000.
Cranfield, C. E. B. *A Critical and Exegetical Commentary on the Epistle to the Romans.* 6th ed. 2 vols. International Cricital Commentary. Edinburgh: T. & T. Clark, 1975, 1979.
Cross, Richard. "Catholic, Calvinist, and Lutheran Doctrines of the Eucharistic Presence: A Brief Note towards a Rapprochement." *International Journal of Systematic Theology* 4 (2002): 301-18.
Cunningham, William. *The Reformers and the Theology of the Reformation.* Edinburgh: Clark, 1862; rep. Edinburgh: Banner of Truth Trust, 1967.
_____. *Historical Theology.* 2 vols. London: Banner of Truth Trust, 1969.
Dankbaar, W. F. "Calvijns Oordeel over het Concilie van Trente, inzonderheid inzake het Rechtvaardigingsdecreet." *Nederlands Archief voor Kerkgeschiedenis* 45 (1963): 79-112; rep. in *Hervormers en Humanisten,* 67-99. Amsterdam: Ton Bolland, 1978.
_____. *De Sacramentsleer van Calvijn.* Amsterdam: H. J. Paris, 1941.
Davies, Glenn N. *Faith and Obedience in Romans: A Study in Romans 1-4.* Journal for the Study of the New Testament Supp. 39. Sheffield: JSOT/Sheffield Academic Press, 1990.
Davis, Thomas J. "Not 'Hidden and Far Off': The Bodily Aspect of Salvation and Its Implications for Understanding the Body in Calvin's Theology." *Calvin Theological Journal* 29 (1994): 406-18.
_____. *The Clearest Promises of God: the Development of Calvin's Eucharistic Teaching.* AMS Studies in Religion 1. New York: AMS Press, 1995.
D'Avray, David. *Medieval Marriage Sermons: Mass Communication in a Culture without Print.* Oxford: Oxford University Press, 2001.
_____. *Medieval Marriage: Symbolism and Society.* Oxford: Oxford University Press, 2005.
Dean, Albert Clarke. "The Institutes of 1539 and the Letter to the Romans." M.Th. thesis, Union Theological Seminary, 1953.
De Kroon, Marijn. *Martin Bucer und Johannes Calvin: Reformatorische Perspektiven Einleitung und Texte.* Translated by Hartmut Rudolph. Göttingen: Vandenhoeck & Ruprecht, 1991.
_____. *The Honour of God and Human Salvation: Calvin's Theology According to His Institutes.* Translated by John Vriend and Lyle D. Bierma. Edinburgh: T. & T. Clark, 2001.

De Lubac, Henri. *Exègése médiévale: Les quatre sens de l'Ecriture*. 4 vols. Paris: Aubier, 1954-1964.

Demura, Akira. "Two Commentaries on the Epistle to the Romans: Calvin and Oecolampadius." In *Calvinus Sincerioris Religionis Vindex*, ed. W. H. Neuser, 165-88. Kirksville: Sixteenth Century Journal Publications, 1997.

De Ru, G. *De Rechtvaardiging bij Augustinus: Vergeleken met de leer der iustificatio bij Luther en Calvijn*. Wageningen: H. Veenman & Zonen, 1966.

DeVries, Dawn. "The Incarnation and the Sacramental World: Calvin's and Schleiermacher's Sermons on Luke 2." In *Toward the Future of Reformed Theology: Tasks, Topics, Traditions*, ed. David Willis and Michael Welker, 386-405. Grand Rapids: Eerdmans, 1999.

Dols, P. M. E. *Bibliographie der Moderne Devotie*. Nimegen, 1941.

Donnelly, John Patrick. *Calvinism and Scholasticism in Vermigli's Doctrine of Man and Grace*. Leiden: E. J. Brill, 1976.

_____ and Robert M. Kingdon, eds., *A Bibliography of the Works of Peter Martyr Vermigli*. Kirksville: Sixteenth Century Journal Publishers, 1990.

_____. "Calvinist Thomism." *Viator* 7 (1976): 441-55.

Dorman, Ted. "Review of *Union with Christ: The New Finnish Interpretation of Luther*, edited by C. E. Braaten and R. W. Jenson." *First Things* 98 (1999): 49-53.

Dörries, Hermann. "Calvin und Lefèvre." *Zeitschrift für Kirchengeschichte* 44 (1925): 544-81.

Douglas, R. M. *Jacopo Sadoleto 1477-1545, Humanist and Reformer*. Cambridge: Harvard University Press, 1959.

Douglass, Jane Dempsey. *Justification in Late Medieval Preaching: A Study of John Geiler of Kaisersberg*. Studies in Medieval and Reformation Thought 1. Leiden: E. J. Brill, 1966.

Doumerge, Emile. *Jean Calvin: les hommes et les choses de son temps*. 7 vols. Lausanne: Georges Bridel et Cie: 1899-1927.

_____. *La piété réformée d'après Calvin*. Paris, 1907.

Dowey, Edward A., Jr. *The Knowledge of God in Calvin's Theology*. 2nd ed. New York: Columbia University Press, 1965; expanded edition, Grand Rapids: Eerdmans, 1994.

_____. "The Structure of Calvin's Theological Thought as Influenced by the Two-fold Knowledge of God." *Calvinus Ecclesiae Genevensis Custus*, ed. W. H. Neuser, 135-48. New York: Peter Lang, 1984.

Doyle, Robert C. "The Context of Moral Decision Making in the Writings of John Calvin: The Christological Ethics of Eschatological Order." Ph.D. diss., University of Aberdeen, 1981.

———. "The Preaching of Repentance in John Calvin: Repentance and Union with Christ." In *God Who Is Rich In Mercy: Essays Presented to D. B. Knox*, ed. P. T. O'Brien and D. G. Peterson, 287-321. Homebush West: Anzea Publishers, 1986.

Dupuy, Michel. "Union à Dieu." In *Dictionnaire de Spiritualité Ascétique et Mystique Doctrine et Histoire*, 17 vols. Originally edited by M. Viller, et al; continued by A. Derville, et al. Vol. 16, cols. 40-61. Paris: Beauchesne, 1994.

Duran, André. *Le mysticisme de Calvin d'aprés l'Institution chrétienne.* Montauban, 1900.

Ebeling, Gerhard. *Luther.* Translated by R. A. Wilson. Philadelphia: Fortress Press, 1972.

Edmondson, Stephen. *Calvin's Christology.* Cambridge: Cambridge University Press, 2004.

———. "Christ and History: Hermeneutical Convergence in Calvin and its Challenge to Biblical Theology." *Modern Theology* 21 (2005): 3-36.

———. "The Biblical Historical Structure of Calvin's *Institutes*." *Scottish Journal of Theology* 59 (2006): 1-13.

Eire, Carlos. *War Against the Idols: The Reformation of Worship from Erasmus to Calvin.* Cambridge: Cambridge University Press, 1986.

Elder, E. Rozanne, ed. *The Spirituality of Western Christendom, II: The Roots of the Modern Christian Tradition.* Cistercian studies series, no. 55. Kalamazoo: Cistercian Publications, 1984.

Elwood, Christopher. *The Body Broken: the Calvinist Doctrine of the Eucharist and the Symbolization of Power in Sixteenth-Century France.* New York: Oxford University Press, 1999.

Emerson, E. H. "Calvin and Covenant Theology." *Church History* 25 (1956): 136-44.

Emery, Kent, Jr. "Mysticism and the Coincidence of Opposites in Sixteenth- and Seventeenth-Century France." *Journal of the History of Ideas* 45 (1984): 3-23.

Emmen, E. *De Christologie van Calvijn.* Amsterdam: H. J. Paris, 1935.

Engel, Mary Potter. *Calvin's Perspectival Anthropology.* Atlanta: Scholars Press, 1988.

Evans, G. R. "Calvin on Signs: an Augustinian Dilemma." *Renaissance Studies* 3 (1989): 35-45.

———. *The Language and Logic of the Bible*, 2 vols. Cambridge: Cambridge University Press, 1984-85.

Evans, William Borden. "Imputation and Impartation: the Problem of Union with Christ in Nineteenth Century American Reformed Theology." Ph.D. diss., Vanderbilt University, 1996.

Faber, Jelle. "The Saving Work of the Holy Spirit in Calvin." In *Essays in Reformed Doctrine*, 282-91. Neerlandia, Alberta, Canada: Inheritance Publications, 1990.

―――――. "Imago Dei in Calvin: Calvin's Doctrine of Man as the Image of God by Virtue of Creation." In *Essays in Reformed Doctrine*, 227-50. Neerlandia, Alberta, Canada: Inheritance Publications, 1990.

―――――. "Imago Dei in Calvin: Calvin's Doctrine of Man as the Image of God in Connection with Sin and Restoration." In *Essays in Reformed Doctrine*, 251-81. Neerlandia, Alberta, Canada: Inheritance Publications, 1990.

Farmer, Craig. *The Gospel of John in the Sixteenth Century: The Johannine Exegesis of Wolfgang Musculus*. New York: Oxford University Press, 1997.

Farthing, John L. *Thomas Aquinas and Gabriel Biel: Interpretations of St. Thomas Aquinas in German Nominalism on the Eve of the Reformation*. Durham: Duke University Press, 1988.

Fatio, Olivier and Pierre Fraenkel, eds. *Histoire de l'Exégèse au XVIe Siècle: Textes du Colloque International Genève, 1976*. Geneva: Librairie Droz, 1978.

Feenstra, Ronald J. "Calvin versus Osiander on Justification." Paper submitted to seminar on Calvin's *Institutes* conducted by Ford Lewis Battles, Grand Rapids, Calvin Theological Seminary, 1978.

Feld, Helmut. "Die Wiedergeburt des Paulinismus im Europäischen Humanismus." In *Catholica: Vierteljahresschrift für Oekumenische Theologie* vol. 36, 294-327. Münster: Aschendorff, 1982.

―――――. "Um die Reinere Lehre des Evangeliums: Calvins Kontroverse mit Sadoleto 1539." *Catholica* 36 (1982): 150-80.

Ferguson, Sinclair. *The Holy Spirit*. Downers Grove: InterVarsity Press, 1996.

―――――. "Calvin on the Lord's Supper and Communion with Christ." In *Serving the Word of God: Celebrating the Life and Ministry of James Philip*, ed. David Stay and David Wright, 203-17. Edinburgh: Christian Focus and Rutherford House, 2002.

Fitzer, Joseph. "The Augustinian Roots of Calvin's Eucharistic Thought." *Augustinian Studies* 7 (1976): 69-98.

Fligge, Jörg Rainer. "Herzog Albrecht von Preussen und der Osiandrismus." Ph.D. diss., Friedrich-Wilhelms University in Bonn, 1972.

―――――. "Zur Interpretation der osiandrischen Theologie Herzog Albrechts v. Preussen." *Archiv für Reformationsgeschichte* 64 (1973): 245-80.

Flogaus, Reinhard. "Luther versus Melanchthon? Zur Frage der Einheit der Wittenberger Reformation in der

Rechtfertigungslehre." *Archiv für Reformationsgeschichte* 91 (2000): 6-46.

Forell, George W. *Luther's Disputations as a Key to his Theology.* University of Iowa, privately printed.

Foxgrover, David, ed. *Calvin and Spirituality.* Papers Presented at the 10th Colloquium of the Calvin Studies Society, May 18-20, 1995, Calvin Theological Seminary, Grand Rapids, Michigan. Grand Rapids: CRC Product Services for the Calvin Studies Society, 1998.

⎯⎯⎯, ed. *The Legacy of John Calvin.* Papers Presented at the 12th Colloquium of the Calvin Studies Society, April 22-24, 1999, Union Theological Seminary, Richmond, Virginia. Grand Rapids: CRC Product Services for the Calvin Studies Society, 2000.

⎯⎯⎯. "The Humanity of Christ: Within Proper Limits." In *Calviniana: Ideas and Influence of Jean Calvin*, 93-105. Sixteenth Century Essays and Studies 10. Kirksville: Sixteenth Century Journal Publishers, 1988.

Fredrich, Edward C. "Osiander – a Man for All Churches in an Ecumenical Age." Paper Presented at the Metropolitan North-South Pastoral Conference, St. James, Milwaukee, MN, November 17, 1980.

Freedman, Joseph S. "Aristotle and the Content of Philosophy Instruction at Central European Schools and Universities during the Reformation Era (1500-1650)." *Proceedings of the American Philosophical Society* 137 (1993): 213-53.

Froehlich, Karlfried. "Justification Language and Grace: The Charge of Pelagianism in the Middle Ages." In *Probing the Reformed Tradition: Historical Studies in Honor of Edward A. Dowey*, ed. Elsie Anne McKee and Brian G. Armstrong, 21-47. Louisville: Westminster/John Knox Press, 1989.

⎯⎯⎯. "Which Paul? Observations on the Image of the Apostle in the History of Biblical Exegesis." In *New Perspectives on Historical Theology: Essays in Memory of John Meyendorff*, ed. Bradley Nassif, 279-99. Grand Rapids: Eerdmans, 1996.

Frye, Roland M. "Calvin's Theological Use of Figurative Language." In *John Calvin and the Church: A Prism of Reform*, ed. Timothy George, 172-94. Louisville: Westminster/John Knox Press, 1990.

Fuchs, Eric. *La Morale Selon Calvin.* Paris: Les Éditions du Cerf, 1986.

Gaffin, Richard. B., Jr. "Biblical Theology and the Westminster Standards." *Westminster Theological Journal* 65 (2003): 165-79.

Gamble, Richard C. "Brevitas et Facilitas: Toward an Understanding of Calvin's Hermeneutic." *Westminster Theological Journal* 47 (1985): 1-17.

⎯⎯⎯. "Exposition and Method in Calvin." *Westminster Theological Journal* 49 (1987): 153-65.

_____. "Calvin as Theologian and Exegete: Is There Anything New?" *Calvin Theological Journal* 23 (1988): 178-94.

_____. "Calvin's Theological Method: Word and Spirit, A Case Study." In *Calviniana: Ideas and Influence of Jean Calvin*, ed. Robert V. Schnucker, 63-75. Kirksville: Sixteenth Century Essay and Studies, 1988.

_____. "Calvin's Theological Method: The Case of Caroli." In *Calvin: Erbe und Auftrag, Festschrift for W. H. Neuser*, ed. W. van't Spijker, 130-37. Kampen: Kok Pharos Publishing House, 1991.

_____. "Current Trends in Calvin Research, 1982-90." In *Calvinus Sacrae Scripturae Professor*, ed. W. H. Neuser, 91-112. Grand Rapids: Eerdmans, 1994.

_____. "Calvin and Sixteenth-Century Spirituality: Comparison with the Anabaptists." In *Calvin and Spirituality*, ed. David Foxgrover, 31-51. Grand Rapids: CRC Product Services for the Calvin Studies Society, 1998.

_____, ed. *Articles on Calvin and Calvinism*. 14 vols. New York and London: Garland Publishing Company, 1992.

Ganoczy, Alexandre and Klaus Müller. *Calvins Handschriftliche Annotationen zu Chrysostomus: Ein Beitrag zur Hermeneutik Calvins*. Wiesbaden: Franz Steiner, 1981.

Ganoczy Alexandre and Stefan Scheld. *Herrschaft-Tugend-Vorsehung*. Wiesbaden: Franz Steiner, 1982.

_____. *Die Hermeneutik Calvins: Geistesgeschichtliche Voraussetzungen und Grundzüge*. Wiesbaden: Franz Steiner, 1983.

Ganoczy, Alexandre. *Calvin, Théologien de l'Eglise et du Ministère*. Paris: Les Éditions du Cerf, 1964.

_____. *Ecclesia Ministrans*. Wiesbaden: Franz Steiner, 1968.

_____. *La Bibliothèque de l'Académie de Calvin*. Geneva: Librairie Droz, 1969.

_____. "Calvin als paulinischer Theologe." In *Calvinus Theologus*, ed. W. H. Neuser, 36-69. Neukirchen: Neukirchener, 1976.

_____. *The Young Calvin*. Translated by David Foxgrover and Wade Provo. Philadelphia: Westminster Press, 1987.

_____. "Observations on Calvin's Trinitarian Doctrine of Grace." Translated by Keith Crim. In *Probing the Reformed Tradition: Historical Studies in Honor of Edward A. Dowey*, ed. Elsie Anne McKee and Brian G. Armstrong, 96-107. Louisville: Westminster/John Knox Press, 1989.

Garcia, Mark A. "Imputation and the Christology of Union with Christ: Calvin, Osiander, and the Contemporary Quest for a Reformed Model." *Westminster Theological Journal* 68:2 (2006): 219-51.

George, Timothy. *Theology of the Reformers*. Nashville: Broadman Press, 1988.

_____, ed. *John Calvin and the Church: A Prism of Reform*. Louisville: Westminster/John Knox Press, 1990.

_____. "John Calvin and the Agreement of Zurich (1549)." In *John Calvin and the Church: A Prism of Reform*, ed. Timothy George, 42-58. Louisville: Westminster/John Knox Press, 1990.

_____. "The Atonement in Martin Luther's Theology." In *The Glory of the Atonement: Biblical, Theological and Practical Perspectives*, ed. Charles E. Hill and Frank A. James, III, 263-78. Downers Grove: InterVarsity Press, 2004.

Gerrish, Brian A. "The Flesh of the Son of Man: John W. Nevin on the Church and the Eucharist." In Gerrish, *Tradition in the Modern World: Reformed Theology in the Nineteenth Century*, 49-70. Chicago: University of Chicago Press, 1978.

_____. *The Old Protestantism and the New: Essays on the Reformation Heritage*. Chicago: University of Chicago Press/Edinburgh: T. & T. Clark, 1982.

_____. *Grace and Gratitude: The Eucharistic Theology of John Calvin*. Edinburgh: T. & T. Clark, 1993.

_____. *Continuing the Reformation: Essays on Modern Religious Thought*. Chicago: University of Chicago Press, 1993.

_____. "Eucharist," s.v. In *Oxford Encyclopedia of the Reformation*, ed. Hans J. Hillerbrand, vol. 2, cols. 71b-81a.

_____. "Constructing Tradition: Schleiermacher, Hodge, and the Theological Legacy of Calvin." In *The Legacy of John Calvin*, ed. David Foxgrover, 158-75.

_____. "Calvin's Eucharistic Piety." In *Calvin and Spirituality*, ed. David Foxgrover, 52-65. Grand Rapids: CRC Product Services for the Calvin Studies Society, 1998.

Gilson, Etienne. *Christian Philosophy in the Middle Ages*. London: Sheed and Ward, 1955.

Girardin, Benoit. *Rhetorique et théologique: Calvin, le Commentaire de l'Epître aux Romains*. Paris: Beauchesne, 1979.

Gleason, E. G. *Gasparo Contarini*. Berkeley: University of California Press, 1993.

Gleason, Randall C. *John Calvin and John Owen on Mortification: A Comparative Study in Reformed Spirituality*. New York: Peter Lang, 1995.

Gluckler, I. R. "Faith and Works: A Comparative Study of the Doctrine of Justification by Faith and the Ethics of Good Works in the Theologies of Martin Luther, Huldrych Zwingli, and Martin Bucer." M.Th. diss., University of Aberdeen, 1992.

Godfrey, W. Robert. "Reformed Thought on the Extent of the Atonement to 1618." *Westminster Theological Journal* 37 (1974-75): 133-71.
Godsey, John D. "The Interpretation of Romans in the History of the Christian Faith." *Interpretation* 34 (1980): 3-16.
Göhler, Alfred. *Calvins Lehre von der Heiligung.* Münich: Chr. Kaiser, 1934.
Gollwitzer, Helmut. *Coena Domini.* Münich: Chr. Kaiser, 1937.
Gorday, Peter. *Principles of Patristic Exegesis: Romans 9-11 in Origen, John Chrysostom, and Augustine.* New York and Toronto: Edwin Mellen Press, 1983.
Gordh, George. "Calvin's Conception of Faith." *Review and Expositor* 50 (1953): 207-15.
Goumaz, L. *La doctrine du salut (doctrina salutis) d'après les commentaires de Jean Calvin sur le Nouveau Testament.* Lausanne-Paris, 1917.
Graafland, C. "Hat Calvin einen Ordo Salutis Gelehrt." In *Calvinus Ecclesiae Genevensis Custos,* ed. W. H. Neuser, 221-44. Frankfurt: Peter Lang, 1984.
Greef, Wulfert de. *The Writings of John Calvin: An Introductory Guide.* Translated by Lyle D. Bierma. Leicester: Apollos; Grand Rapids: Baker, 1993.
Green, Lowell C. "Faith, Righteousness, and Justification: New Light on Their Development under Luther and Melanchton." *Sixteenth Century Journal* 4 (1972): 65-86.
―――. "Melanchthon's Relation to Scholasticism." In *Protestant Scholasticism: Essays in Reassessment,* ed. Carl R. Trueman and R. S. Clark, 273-88. Carlisle: Paternoster Press, 1999.
Gregory, Thomas. "Union with Christ the Ground of Justification." *Opening and Closing Addresses to the New College Theological Society, Session 1882-83,* 33-50. Edinburgh: Lorimer & Gillies, 1883.
Greschat, Martin. "Bucer, Martin," s.v. Translated by Wolfgang Katenz. In *Oxford Encyclopedia of the Reformation,* ed. Hans J. Hillerbrand, vol. 1, cols. 221b-24a.
Grislis, Egil. "Calvin's Doctrine of Baptism." *Church History* 31 (1962): 46-65.
Gründler, Otto. "John Calvin: Ingrafting into Christ." In *The Spirituality of Western Christendom,* ed. E. Rozanne Elder, 169-87. Kalamazoo: Cistercian Publications, 1976.
Gunton, Colin. *Intellect and Action: Elucidations on Christian Theology and the Life of Faith.* Edinburgh: T. & T. Clark, 2000.
Hagen, Kenneth. *Hebrews Commentating from Erasmus to Bèze: 1516-1598.* Beiträge zur Geschichte der Biblischen Exegese 23. Tübingen: J. C. B. Mohr (Paul Siebeck), 1981.

Haldane, Robert. *The Epistle to the Romans*. 1835-39; rep. London: Banner of Truth Trust, 1980.
Hall, Basil. *Humanists and Protestants 1500-1900*. Edinburgh: T. & T. Clark, 1990.
??????. *John Calvin: Humanist and Theologian*. London: Routledge and Kegan Paul, 1956.
??????. "Calvin Against the Calvinists." In *John Calvin: A Collection of Distinguished Essays*, ed. Gervase E. Duffield, 19-37. Grand Rapids: Eerdmans, 1966.
Hall, Charles A. M. *With the Spirit's Sword: The Drama of Spiritual Warfare in the Theology of John Calvin*. Basel Studies in Theology 3. Richmond: John Knox Press, 1970.
Hamann, Henry P. "The Righteousness of Faith Before God." In *A Contemporary Look at the Formula of Concord*, ed. Robert D. Preus and Wilbert H. Rosin, 137-62. St. Louis: Concordia Publishing House, 1978.
Hamm, Berndt. *Promissio, Pactum, Ordinatio. Freiheit und Selbstbindung Gottes in der scholastischen Gnadenlehre*. Tübingen: J. C. B. Mohr, 1977.
Hampson, Daphne. *Christian Contradictions: The Structures of Lutheran and Catholic Thought*. Cambridge: Cambridge University Press, 2001.
Hanna, Eleanor B. "Biblical Interpretation and Sacramental Practice: John Calvin's Interpretation of John 6:51–58." *Worship* 73 (1999): 211–30.
Harbison, E. Harris. "Calvin's Sense of History." In *Christianity and History*, 270-88. Princeton: Princeton University Press, 1964.
Hart, Trevor. "Humankind in Christ and Christ in Humankind: Salvation as Participation in Our Substitute in the Theology of John Calvin." *Scottish Journal of Theology* 42 (1989): 67-84.
Hashagen, J. "Die Devotio Moderna in ihre Einwirkung auf Humanismus, Reformation, Gegenreformation und spätere Richtungen." *Zeitschrift für Kirchengeschichte* 55 (1936): 523-31.
Hauck, Wilhelm-Albert. *Calvin und die Rechtfertigung: Herzpunkte evangelischer Lehre nach Calvins reformatorischem Verständnis*. Gütersloh: C. Bertelsmann, 1938.
??????. *"Sunde" und "Erbsunde" Nach Calvin*. Heidelberg: Evangelischer Verlag Jakob Comtesse, 1939.
Hauke, Rainer. "Sola Dei iustitia. Die theozentrische Rechtfertigungslehre des Andreas Osiander (1498-1552): eine misslungene Belehrung der forensischen Rechtfertigungslehre?" In *Belehrter Glaube, Festschrift für Johannes Wirsching zum 65. Geburtstag*, ed. Elke Axmacher and Klaus Schwarzwäller, 101-32. Frankfurt, 1994.

_____. *Gott-Haben – um Gottes Willen: Andreas Osianders Theosisgedanke und die Diskussion um die Grundlagen der evangelisch verstandenen Rechtfertigung*. Kontexte. Neue Beiträge zur Historischen und Systematischen Theologie 30. Frankfurt am Main: Peter Lang, 1999.

Hausammann, Susi. *Römerbriefauslegung zwischen Humanismus und Reformation: Eine Studie zu Henrich Bullingers Römerbriefvorlesung von 1525*. Studien zur Dogmengeschichte und Systematischen Theologie 27. Zurich: Zwingli, 1970.

Hazlett, W. Ian P. "Calvin's Latin Preface to His Proposed French Edition of Chrysostom's Homilies: Translation and Commentary." In *Humanism and Reform: The Church in Europe, England, and Scotland, 1400-1643: Essays in Honour of James K. Cameron*, ed. James Kirk, 129-50. Studies in Church History. Subsidia 8. Cambridge: Blackwell Publishers, 1991.

Hebblethwaite, E. S. "The Theology of Rewards in English Printed Treatises and Sermons (c.1550-c.1650)." Ph.D. diss., University of Cambridge, 1992.

Helm, Paul. *Calvin and the Calvinists*. Edinburgh: Banner of Truth Trust, 1982.

_____. "Calvin and the Covenant: Unity and Continuity." *Evangelical Quarterly* 55 (1983): 65-81.

_____. *John Calvin's Ideas*. Oxford: OUP, 2004.

Hendrix, Scott H. "Deparentifying the Fathers: the Reformers and Patristic Authority." In *Auctoritas patrum: zur Rezeption der Kirchenväter im 15. und 16. Jahrhundert ; contributions on the reception of the Church Fathers in the 15th and 16th century*, ed. Leif Grane, Alfred Schindler, and Markus Wriedt, 55-68. Mainz: Verlag Philipp von Zabern, 1994.

Henninger, J. S. *Augustinus et doctrina de duplici iustitia*. Mödling, 1935.

Heppe, Heinrich. *Reformed Dogmatics: Set Out and Illustrated From the Sources*, ed. Ernst Bizer. Translated by G. T. Thomson. London: George Allen & Unwin, 1950.

Hesselink, I. John. "Calvin, the Holy Spirit, and Mystical Union." *Perspectives* 13 (1998): 15-18.

_____. "Review of *The Unaccommodated Calvin: Studies in the Foundation of a Theological Tradition* by Richard A. Muller." *Calvin Theological Journal* 37 (2002): 148-50.

_____. *Calvin's First Catechism: A Commentary*. Louisville: Westminster/John Knox Press, 1997.

_____. "The Role of the Holy Spirit in Calvin's Doctrine of the Sacraments." In *Essentialia et Hodierna*, 66-88. Acta Theologica 2002

Supplementum 3. Bloemfontein: Universiteit van die Oranje-Vrystaat, 2002.
Higman, Francis M. *The Style of John Calvin in his French Polemical Treatises.* London: Oxford University Press, 1967.
_____. *Lire et Découvrir: La Circulation des idées au temps de la Réforme.* Travaux d'Humanisme et Renaissance Vol. 326. Geneva: Librairie Droz, 1998.
Hillerbrand, Hans J., ed. *The Oxford Encyclopedia of the Reformation.* 4 vols. New York: Oxford University Press, 1996.
Hirsch, Emanuel. *Die Theologie des Andreas Osiander.* Göttingen: Vandenhoeck & Ruprecht, 1919.
Hobbs, R. Gerald. "Hebraica veritas *and* Traditio Apostolica: Saint Paul and the Interpretation of the Psalms in the Sixteenth Century." In *The Bible in the Sixteenth Century,* ed. David C. Steinmetz, 83-99. Durham: Duke University Press, 1982.
Hocutt, M. "Aristotle's Four Becauses." *Philosophy* 49 (1974): 385-99.
Hodge, Charles. "Doctrine of the Reformed Church on the Lord's Supper." *Princeton Review* 20 (1848): 227-78.
_____. *Systematic Theology.* 3 vols. 1871-1872; rep. Grand Rapids: Eerdmans, 1982.
_____. *A Commentary on Romans.* 1864; rep. London: Banner of Truth Trust, 1972.
Hoekema, Anthony A. "The Covenant of Grace in Calvin's Teaching." *Calvin Theological Journal* 2 (1967): 133-61.
Hoffman, Manfred. *Rhetoric and Theology: The Hermeneutic of Erasmus.* Toronto: University of Toronto Press, 1994.
Hoitenga, Dewey J., Jr. "Happiness for the Sake of Goodness: Calvin's Solution." In *Seeking Understanding: the Stob lectures, 1986-1998,* 320-41. The second of two Stob lectures delivered in 1994. Grand Rapids: Eerdmans, 2001.
_____. *John Calvin and the Will: A Critique and Corrective.* Grand Rapids: Baker, 1997.
Hoogland, Marvin P. *Calvin's Perspective on the Exaltation of Christ in Comparison with the Post-Reformation Doctrine of the Two States.* Kampen: J. H. Kok, 1966.
Hsia, R. Po-Chia. *Social Discipline in the Reformation: Central Europe 1550-1750.* London and New York: Routledge, 1989.
Hunt, J. A. "Calvin's Doctrine of Self-Denial and Conformity to Christ." M.Th. diss., University of Aberdeen, 1990.
Hyma, Albert. *The Brethren of the Common Life.* Grand Rapids: Eerdmans, 1950.
_____. *The Christian Renaissance: A History of the "Devotio Moderna."* New York: Hamden/Grand Rapids: Reformed Press, 1924.

Idel, Moshe and Bernard McGinn, eds. *Mystical Union in Judaism, Christianity, and Islam: An Ecumenical Dialogue.* New York: Continuum, 1996.

Ives, R. B. "An Early Effort toward Protestant-Catholic Conciliation: The Doctrine of Double Justification in the Sixteenth Century." *Gordon Review* 11 (1968-70): 99-110.

Jackson, B. Darrell. "The Theory of Signs in *De doctrina Christiana*." In *Augustine: A Collection of Critical Essays*, ed. R. A. Markus, 92-147. New York: Anchor Books, 1972.

Jackson, Pamela. "Eucharist," s.v. In *Augustine Through the Ages: An Encyclopedia*, ed. Allan D. Fitzgerald, et al., 330b-34b. Grand Rapids: Eerdmans, 1999.

Jacobs, Paul. *Prädestination und Verantwortlichkeit bei Calvin.* Kasel: Oncken, 1937.

James, Frank A., III. "A Late Medieval Parallel in Reformation Thought: *Gemina Praedestinatio* in Gregory of Rimini and Peter Martyr Vermigli." In *Via Augustini: Augustine in the Later Middle Ages, Renaissance and Reformation: Essays in Honor of Damasus Trapp, O.S.E.*, ed. Heiko A. Oberman and Frank A. James, III, 157-88. Leiden: E. J. Brill, 1991.

———. "Peter Martyr Vermigli." In *Historical Handbook of Major Biblical Interpreters*, ed. Donald McKim, 239-45. Downers Grove: InterVarsity Press, 1998.

———. *Peter Martyr Vermigli and Predestination: The Augustinian Inheritance of an Italian Reformer.* Oxford: Clarendon Press, 1998.

———. "Peter Martyr Vermigli: At the Crossroads of Late Medieval Scholasticism, Christian Humanism and Resurgent Augustinianism." In *Protestant Scholasticism: Essays in Reassessment*, ed. Carl R. Trueman and R. S. Clark, 62-78. Carlisle: Paternoster Press, 1999.

———. "Peter Martyr and the Reformed Doctrine of Justification." *Princeton Theological Review* (1999): 15-20.

———. "*De Iustificatione*: The Evolution of Peter Martyr Vermigli's Doctrine of Justification." Ph.D. diss., Westminster Theological Seminary, 2000.

———. "The Complex of Justification: Vermigli versus Pighius." In *Peter Martyr Vermigli: Humanism, Republicanism and Reformation*, ed. Emidio Campi and Frank A. James III, 45-58. Geneva: Librairie Droz, 2002.

Jansen, John Frederick. *Calvin's Doctrine of the Work of Christ.* London: James Clarke, 1956.

Jarrott, C. A. L. "John Colet on Justification." *Sixteenth Century Journal* 7 (1976): 59-72.

Jenson, Robert W. *Systematic Theology*, Vol. 2: *The Works of God*. Oxford: Oxford University Press, 1999.

———. "Response to Seifrid, Trueman, and Metzger on Finnish Luther Research." *Westminster Theological Journal* 65 (2003): 245-50.

Johnson, Galen. "The Development of John Calvin's Doctrine of Infant Baptism in Reaction to the Anabaptists." *Mennonite Quarterly Review* 73 (1999): 803–23.

Johnson, Harry. *The Humanity of the Savior: A Biblical and Historical Study of the Human Nature of Christ in Relation to Original Sin, with Special Reference to Its Soteriological Significance*. London: Epworth Press, 1962.

Jones, R. Tudur. "Union with Christ: The Existential Nerve of Puritan Piety." *Tyndale Bulletin* 41 (1990): 186-208.

Jones, Rufus Matthew. *Spiritual Reformers in the 16th and 17th Centuries*. London: Macmillan, 1914.

Kayayan, Éric. "Accommodation, Incarnation et Sacrement dans L'Institution de la Religion Chrétienne de Jean Calvin: L'utilisation de métaphores et de similitudes." *Revue d'Histoire et de Philosophie Religieuses* 75 (1995): 273-87.

———. "La Porteé Epistémologique de *la Métaphore du Miroir* dans l'Institution de la Religion Chrétienne de J. Calvin." *Revue d'Histoire et de Philosophie Religieuses* 77 (1997): 431-51.

Keller, Carl-A. *Calvin Mystique: Au cœur de la pensée du Réformateur*. Geneva: Labor et Fidès, 2001.

Kelly, J. N. D. *Early Christian Doctrines*. 4th ed. London, 1968.

Kendall, R. T. *Calvin and English Calvinism to 1649*. Oxford: Oxford University Press, 1979.

———. "The Puritan Modification of Calvin's Theology." In *John Calvin: His Influence in the Western World*, ed. W. Stanford Reid, 197-214. Grand Rapids: Zondervan, 1982.

Kennedy, Kevin Dixon. "Union with Christ as Key to John Calvin's Understanding of the Extent of the Atonement." Ph.D. diss., Southern Baptist Theological Seminary, 1999.

———. *Union with Christ and the Extent of the Atonement in Calvin*. Studies in Biblical Literature 48. New York: Peter Lang, 2002.

Kickel, Walter. *Verunft und Offenbarung bei Theodor Beza*. Neukirken: Neukirkener Verlag, 1967.

Kim, J. D. "Holiness in the Triune God: Calvin's Doctrine of Sanctification with Special Reference to the Eschatological Dialectic Between Its Objective and Subjective Aspects, and with Application to the Calvinist Doctrine of the Korean Presbyterian Church." Ph.D. diss., University of Bristol, 2002.

Kim, Jae Sung. "*Unio cum Christo*: The Work of the Holy Spirit in Calvin's Theology." Ph.D. diss., Westminster Theological Seminary, 1998.

Kim, Kwang-yul. "The Concept of Definitive Sanctification in John Calvin's Thought." *Chongshin Review* 2 (1997): 80-100.

Kingdon, Robert M., ed., with John Patrick Donnelly, S.J., *A Bibliography of the Works of Peter Martyr Vermigli*. Kirksville: Sixteenth Century Journal Publishers, 1990.

Kirk, Kenneth E. *The Vision of God: The Christian Doctrine of the Summum Bonum*. New York: Longmans, Green and Co., 1931.

Köhler, W. *Dogmengeschichte als Geschichte des christlichen Selbstbewusstseins*. Zürich and Leipzig, 1938; 3rd ed., 1951.

Kok, Joel Edward. "The Influence of Martin Bucer on John Calvin's Interpretation of Romans: A Comparative Case Study." Ph.D. diss., Duke University, 1993.

Kolb, Robert. "Dynamics of Party Conflict in the Saxon Late Reformation: Gnesio-Lutherans vs. Philippists." *The Journal of Modern History* 49, On Demand Supplement (1977): D1289-D1305.

———. *Andreae and the Formula of Concord: Six Sermons on the Way to Lutheran Unity*. St. Louis: Concordia Publishing House, 1977.

———. *Nikolaus von Amsdorf (1483-1565): Popular Polemics in the Preservation of Luther's Legacy*. Nieuwkoop: De Graaf, 1978.

———. "'Perilous Events and Troublesome Disturbances': the Role of Controversy in the Tradition of Luther to Lutheran Controversy." In *Pietas et Societas*, 181-201. Kirksville: Sixteenth Century Essays & Studies, 1985.

———. *For All the Saints: Changing Perceptions of Martyrdom and Sainthood in the Lutheran Reformation*. Macon: Mercer University Press, 1987.

———. "The Influence of Luther's Galatians Commentary of 1535 on Later Sixteenth-Century Lutheran Commentaries on Galatians." *Archiv für Reformationsgeschichte* 84 (1993): 156-84.

———. *Martin Luther as Prophet, Teacher, and Hero: Images of the Reformer, 1520-1620*. Carlisle: Paternoster/Grand Rapids: Baker, 1999.

———. "Patristic Citation as Homiletical Tool in the Vernacular Sermon of the German Late Reformation." In *Die Patristik in der Bibelexegese des 16. Jahrhunderts*, ed. David C. Steinmetz, 155-79. Wiesbaden: Harrassowitz Verlag, 1999.

———. "Contemporary Lutheran Understandings of the Doctrine of Justification: A Selective Glimpse." In *Justification: What's at Stake in the Current Debates*, ed. Mark Husbands and Daniel J. Trier, 153-76. Downers Grove: InterVarsity Press, 2004.

Kolfhaus, W. *Christusgemeinschaft bei Johannes Calvin*. Beiträge zur Geschichte und Lehre der Reformierten Kirche 3. Neukirchen: Buchhandlung des Erziehungsvereins, 1939.
_____. *Vom christlichen Leben nach Johannes Calvin*. Neukirchen: Buchhaulung des Eriziehungsvereins, 1949.
Kon, Ho Duk. "Incarnation According to Calvin and His Followers." In *The Word of God Stands Forever: Essays in Honor of Prof. Dr. Ui-Won Choy*, ed. Daniel H. Ryou, 409-69. Seoul: Christian Digest, 1997.
Köstlin, J. "Calvins *Institutio* nach Form und Inhalt, in ihrer Geschichtlichen Entwicklung." *Theologische Studien und Kritiken* (1868): 6-62; 410-86.
Kraus, Hans-Joachim. "Calvin's Exegetical Principles." *Interpretation* 31.4 (1977): 8-18.
Kreck, Walter. "Die Eigenart der Theologie Calvins." In *Calvin Studien 1959*, ed. J. Moltmann, 26-42. Neukirchen: Neukirchener Verlag, 1960.
Krey, Philip. "'The Old Law Prohibits the Hand and Not the Spirit': The Law and the Jews in Nicholas of Lyra's Romans Commentary of 1329." In *Nicholas of Lyra: the Senses of Scripture*, ed. Philip D. W. Krey and Lesley Smith, 251-66. Studies in the History of Christian Thought 90. Leiden: E. J. Brill, 2000.
Krusche, Werner. *Das Wirken des heiligen Geistes nach Calvin*. Göttingen: Vandenhoeck und Ruprecht, 1957.
Kuropka, Nicole. "Calvins Römerbriefwidmung und der *Consensus Piorum*." In *Calvin im Kontext der Schweizer Reformation*, ed. Peter Opitz, 147-67. Zürich: Theologischer Verlag Zürich, 2003.
Kuyper, Abraham. *The Work of the Holy Spirit*. Translated by Henry De Vries with an introduction by B. B. Warfield. New York: Funk and Wagnalls, 1900.
Lane, Anthony N. S. "Calvin's Doctrine of Assurance." *Vox Evangelica* 11 (1979): 32-54.
_____. "The Quest for the Historical Calvin." *Evangelical Quarterly* 55 (1983): 95-113.
_____. "Recent Calvin Literature: a Review Article." *Themelios* 16 (1991): 17-24.
_____. "Bernard of Clairvaux: A Forerunner of Calvin?" In *Bernardus Magister*, ed. John R. Summerfeldt, 533-45. Kalamazoo: Cistercian Publications, 1993.
_____. "Justification in Sixteenth-Century Patristic Anthologies." In *Auctoritas patrum: zur Rezeption der Kirchenväter im 15. und 16. Jahrhundert: contributions on the reception of the Church Fathers in the 15th and 16th century*, ed. Leif Grane, Alfred Schindler, and Markus Wriedt, 69-95. Mainz: Verlag Philipp von Zabern, 1994.

———. *Calvin and Bernard of Clairvaux.* Studies in Reformed Theology and History, New Series No. 1. Princeton: Princeton University Press, 1996.

———. *John Calvin: Student of the Church Fathers.* Edinburgh: T. & T. Clark, 1999.

———. *Justification by Faith in Catholic-Protestant Dialogue: An Evangelical Assessment.* Edinburgh: T. & T. Clark, 2002.

———. "Calvin and Article 5 of the Regensburg Colloquy." In *Calvinus Praeceptor Ecclesiae*, ed. Herman Selderhuis, 233-63. Geneva: Librairie Droz, 2004.

———. "Cardinal Contarini and Article 5 of the Regensburg Colloquy (1541)." In *Grenzgängeder Theologie*, ed. O. Meuffels and J. Bründl, 163-90. Münster: Lit Verlag, forthcoming 2004.

———. "Twofold Righteousness: A Key to the Doctrine of Justification? Reflections of Article 5 of the Regensburg Colloquy (1541)." In *Justification: What's At Stake in the Current Debates*, ed. Mark Husbands and Daniel J. Trier, 205-24. Downers Grove: InterVarsity Press, 2004.

———. "A Tale of Two Imperial Cities: Justification at Regensburg (1541) and Trent (1546/7)." Paper Delivered at the Rutherford House Dogmatics Conference, Edinburgh, 2003.

Lausberg, Heinrich. *Handbook of Literary Rhetoric: A Foundation for Literary Study*, ed. David E. Orton and R. Dean Anderson. Forward by George A. Kennedy. Translation of 2nd German ed. (1973) by Matthew T. Bliss, et al. 2 vols. Leiden: E. J. Brill, 1998.

Lawrenz, Carl J. "On Justification: Osiander's Doctrine of the Indwelling Christ." In *No Other Gospel: Essays in Commemoration of the 400th Anniversary of the Formula of Concord*, 149-73. Milwaukee: Northwestern Publication House, 1980.

Leith, John H. "Calvin's Theological Method and the Ambiguity in His Theology." In *Reformation Studies: Essays in Honor of Roland H. Bainton*, ed. Franklin H. Littell, 106-14; 265-6. Richmond: John Knox Press, 1962.

———. *An Introduction to the Reformed Tradition.* Atlanta: John Knox Press, 1977.

———. *John Calvin's Doctrine of the Christian Life.* Louisville: Westminster/John Knox Press, 1989.

Leithart, Peter. "Stoic Elements in Calvin's Doctrine of the Christian Life." *Westminster Theological Journal* 55 (1993): 31-54 (Part One); 191-208 (Part Two).

Lillback, Peter A. *The Binding of God: Calvin's Role in the Development of Covenant Theology.* Grand Rapids: Baker, 2001.

Lindbeck, George A. *The Church in a Postliberal Age*, ed. James J. Buckley. London: SCM Press, 2002.

Linder, Robert D. "Calvinism and Humanism: The First Generation." *Church History* 44 (1975): 167-81.
Lubac, Henri de. *Exégèse médiévale: les quatres sens de l'écriture.* 4 vols. Paris: Aubier, 1959-1964.
Lund, Eric, ed. *Documents From the History of Lutheranism, 1517-1750.* Minneapolis: Fortress Press, 2002.
Lüttge, Willy. *Die Rechtfertigungslehre Calvins und Ihre Bedeutung fur seine Frommigkeit.* Berlin: Reuther & Reichard, 1909.
Lyons, P. "Calvin's Doctrine of the Holy Spirit." Ph.D. diss., Belfast: Queen's University, 1985.
MacCulloch, Diarmaid. *Thomas Cranmer: A Life.* New Haven: Yale University Press, 1996.
MacGregor, Geddes. *Corpus Christi: The Nature of the Church according to the Reformed Tradition.* London: Macmillan Co. Ltd, 1959.
Mannermaa, Tuomo. "In ipsa fide Christus adest: Der Schnittpunkt zwischen lutherischer und orthodoxer Theologie." In *Der Im Glauben Gengenwärtige Christus: Rechtfertigung und Vergottung,* ed. Tuomo Mannermaa. Hannover: Lutherisches Verlaghaus, 1989.
_____. "Theosis as a Subject of Finnish Luther Research." *Pro Ecclesia* 4 (1995): 37-48.
Marcel, Pierre. "The Relation between Justification and Sanctification in Calvin's Thought." *Evangelical Quarterly* 27 (1955): 132-45.
Markus, R. A. "St. Augustine on Signs." In *Augustine: A Collection of Critical Essays,* ed. R. A. Markus, 61-91. New York: Anchor Books, 1972.
Marshall, Bruce D. "Justification as Declaration and Deification." *International Journal of Systematic Theology* 4 (2002): 3-28.
Marshall, I. Howard. "Sanctification in the Teaching of John Wesley and John Calvin." *Evangelical Quarterly* 34 (1962): 75-82.
Martin, Dennis D. "The Via Moderna, Humanism, and the Hermeneutics of Late Medieval Monastic Life." *Journal of the History of Ideas* 51 (1990): 179-97.
Matheson, Peter. *Cardinal Contarini at Regensburg.* Oxford: Oxford University Press, 1972.
_____. *The Rhetoric of the Reformation.* Edinburgh: T. & T. Clark, 1998.
Matter, E. Ann. *The Voice of My Beloved. The Song of Songs in Western Medieval Christianity.* Philadelphia: University of Pennsylvania Press, 1990.
Mautner, T. *A Dictionary of Philosophy.* Oxford: Blackwell, 1996.
Maxcey, Carl E. *Bona Opera: A Study in the Development of the Doctrine in Philip Melanchthon.* Nieuwkoop: B. de Graaf, 1980.

McClelland, J. C. (sic; see "McLelland" below). "The Reformed Doctrine of Predestination According to Peter Martyr." *Scottish Journal of Theology* 8 (1955): 255-71.

McGowen, Andrew Thomas Blake. "Calvin on Limited Atonement." In *The Federal Theology of Thomas Boston*, 48-53, 56-8. Rutherford Studies in Historical Theology. Edinburgh: Paternoster and Rutherford House, 1997.

McCormack, Bruce L. *For Us and Our Salvation: Incarnation and Atonement in the Reformed Tradition*. Studies in Reformed Theology and History 1. Princeton: Princeton Theological Seminary, Spring 1993.

_____. "What's at Stake in Current Debates over Justification? The Crisis of Protestantism in the West." In *Justification: What's at Stake in the Current Debates*, ed. Mark Husbands and Daniel J. Trier, 81-117. Downers Grove: InterVarsity Press, 2004.

McCoy, Charles Sherwood and J. Wayne Baker. *Fountainhead of Federalism: Heinrich Bullinger and the Covenantal Tradition*. Louisville: Westminster/John Knox Press, 1991.

McCue, James F. "The Doctrine of Transubstantiation from Berengar through Trent: The Point at Issue." *Harvard Theological Review* 61 (1968): 385-430.

McDonnell, Kilian. *John Calvin, the Church, and the Eucharist*. Princeton: Princeton University Press, 1967.

McGinn, Bernard. "Love, Knowledge, and Mystical Union in Western Christianity: Twelfth to Sixteenth Centuries." *Church History* 56 (1987): 7-24.

_____. *The Presence of God: A History of Western Christian Mysticism*. New York: Crossroad Publishing, 1994-.

_____. *The Foundations of Mysticism: Origins to the Fifth Century*. Vol. 1 of McGinn, *The Presence of God*. New York: Crossroad Pubishing, 1994.

_____. *The Growth of Mysticism: Gregory the Great through the Twelfth Century*. Vol. 2 of McGinn, *The Presence of God*. New York: Crossroad Publishing, 1996.

_____. *The Flowering of Mysticism: Men and Women in the New Mysticism (1200-1350)*. Vol. 3 of McGinn, *The Presence of God*. New York: Crossroad Publishing, 1998.

McGrath, Alister E. "The Anti-Pelagian Structure of 'Nominalist' Doctrines of Justification." *Ephemerides Theologicae Lovanienses* 57 (1981): 107-19.

_____. *Iustitia Dei: A History of the Christian Doctrine of Justification*. 2 vols. Cambridge: Cambridge University Press, 1986; 2nd ed. in one vol. 1998.

———. "Humanist Elements in the Early Reformed Doctrine of Justification." *Archiv für Reformationsgeschichte* 73 (1982): 5-19.

———. "The Righteousness of God from Augustine to Luther." *Studia Theologica* 36 (1982): 63-78.

———. "Mira et Nova Diffinitio Iustitiae: Luther and Scholastic Doctrines of Justification." *Archiv für Reformationsgeschichte* 74 (1983): 37-40.

———. "Reformation to Enlightenment." In *The History of Christian Theology. Vol. 1, The Science of Theology*, ed. Paul Avis, 107-229. Grand Rapids: Eerdmans, 1986.

———. "John Calvin and Late Medieval Thought: A Study in Late Medieval Influences upon Calvin's Theological Development." *Archiv für Reformationsgeschichte* 77 (1986): 58-78.

———. *The Intellectual Origins of the European Reformation*. Grand Rapids: Baker, 1987.

———. *Reformation Thought: An Introduction*. Oxford: Basil Blackwell, 1988.

———. *Justification by Faith*. Grand Rapids: Zondervan, 1988.

———. "Forerunners of the Reformation? A Critical Examination of the Evidence for Precursors of the Reformation Doctrines of Justification." *Harvard Theological Review* 75 (1982): 219-42.

———. *A Life of John Calvin: A Study in the Shaping of Western Culture*. Oxford: Blackwell, 1990.

McIntyre, John. *The Shape of Pneumatology: Studies in the Doctrine of the Holy Spirit*. Edinburgh: T. & T. Clark, 1997.

McKee, Elsie Anne. *John Calvin on the Diaconate and Liturgical Almsgiving*. Geneva: Librairie Droz, 1984.

———. *Elders and the Plural Ministry: The Role of Exegetical History in Illuminating John Calvin's Theology*. Geneva: Librairie Droz, 1988.

———. "Calvin's Exegesis of Romans 12:8 – Social, Accidental or Theological." *Calvin Theological Journal* 23 (1988): 6-18.

———. "Exegesis, Theology and Development in Calvin's *Institutio*: A Methodological Suggestion." In *Probing the Reformed Tradition: Historical Studies in Honor of Edward A. Dowey*, ed. Elsie Anne McKee and Brian G. Armstrong, 154-72. Louisville: Westminster/John Knox Press, 1989.

McLelland, Joseph C. (see "McClelland" [sic] above). *The Visible Words of God: An Exposition of the Sacramental Theology of Peter Martyr Vermigli*. Edinburgh: Oliver & Boyd, 1957.

———. "Calvinism Perfecting Thomism: Peter Martyr Vermigli's Question." *Scottish Journal of Theology* 31 (1978): 571-8.

———, ed. *Peter Martyr Vermigli and Italian Reform*. Waterloo: Wilfred Laurier University Press, 1981.

_____. "Renaissance in Theology: Calvin's 1536 Institutio – Fresh Start or False?" In *In Honor of John Calvin, 1509-64*, ed. E. J. Furcha, 154-74. Montreal: McGill University Press, 1987.

_____. "Meta-Zwingli or Anti-Zwingli? Bullinger and Calvin in Eucharistic Concord." In *Huldrych Zwingli, 1484-1531: A Lively Legacy of Reform*, ed. Edward J. Furcha, 179-96. ARC Supplement 2. Montreal: McGill University Faculty of Religious Studies, 1985.

_____ and G. E. Duffield, eds. *The Life, Early Letters & Eucharistic Writings of Peter Martyr*. Courtenay Library of Reformation Classics. Appleford: Sutton Courtenay Press, 1989.

McNair, Philip. *Peter Martyr in Italy: An Anatomy of Apostasy*. Oxford: Clarendon Press, 1967.

McNeil, John T. *The History and Character of Calvinism*. New York: Oxford University Press, 1954.

Metzger, Paul Louis. "Mystical Union with Christ: An Alternative to Blood Transfusions and Legal Fictions." *Westminster Theological Journal* 65 (2003): 201-14.

Miln, P. "Hommes d'une Bonne Cause: Calvin's Sermons on the Book of Job." Ph.D. diss., University of Nottingham, 1989.

Milner, Benjamin Charles. *Calvin's Doctrine of the Church*. Leiden: E. J. Brill, 1970.

Mönckeberg, Carl. *Ioachim Westphal und Iohannes Calvin*. Hamburg, 1865.

Mosser, Carl. "The Greatest Possible Blessing: Calvin and Deification." *Scottish Journal of Theology* 55 (2002): 36-57.

Muller, Richard A. "Christ in the Eschaton: Calvin and Moltmann on the Duration of the Munus Regium." *Harvard Theological Review* 74 (1981): 31-59.

_____. *A Dictionary of Latin and Greek Theological Terms*. Grand Rapids: Baker, 1985.

_____. *Christ and the Decree: Christology and Predestination in Reformed Theology from Calvin to Perkins*. Studies in Historical Theology 2. Durham: Labyrinth Press, 1986; paperback ed., Grand Rapids: Baker, 1988.

_____. "The Hermeneutic of Promise and Fulfillment in Calvin's Exegesis of the Old Testament Prophecies of the Kingdom." In *The Bible in the Sixteenth Century*, ed. David C. Steinmetz, 68-82. Duke Monographs in Medieval and Renaissance Studies 11. Durham: Duke University Press, 1990.

_____. "*Fides* and *Cognitio* in Relation to the Problem of Intellect and Will in the Theology of John Calvin." *Calvin Theological Journal* 25 (1990): 207-24. Also in Muller, *The Unaccommodated Calvin*, 159-73.

_____. and John. L. Thompson, eds., *Biblical Interpretation in the Era of the Reformation: Essays Presented to David Steinmetz in Honor of his Sixtieth Birthday*. Grand Rapids: Eerdmans, 1996.

_____. "In the Light of Orthodoxy: The 'Method and Disposition' of Calvin's *Institutio* from the Perspective of Calvin's Late-Sixteenth-Century Editors." *Sixteenth Century Journal* (1997): 1203-29.

_____. "'*Scimus enim quod lex spiritualis est*': Melanchthon and Calvin on the Interpretation of Romans 7:14-23." In *Philip Melanchthon (1497-1560) and the Commentary*, ed. Timothy J. Wengert and M. Patrick Graham, 216-37. Sheffield: Sheffield Academic Press, 1997.

_____. "Calvin, Beza, and the Exegetical History of Romans 13." In *Calvin and the State*, ed. Peter de Klerk, 139-70. Grand Rapids: Calvin Studies Society, 1993.

_____. "Directions in Current Calvin Research." *Calvin Studies IX*, ed. J. H. Leith and Robert A. Johnson, 70-87. Davidson College and Davidson Presbyterian Church, North Carolina, January 30-31, 1998.

_____. "*Ordo docendi:* Melanchthon and the Organization of Calvin's *Institutes*, 1536-1543." In *Melanchthon in Europe: His Work and Influence Beyond Wittenberg*, ed. Karin Maag, 123-40. Grand Rapids: Baker, 1999.

_____. "The Use and Abuse of a Document: Beza's *Tabula praedestinationis*, the Bolsec Controversy, and the Origins of Reformed Orthodoxy." In *Protestant Scholasticism: Essays in Reassessment*, ed. Carl R. Trueman and R. S. Clark, 33-61. Carlisle: Paternoster Press, 1999.

_____. "*Ad Fontes Argumentorum.* The Sources of Reformed Theology in the Seventeenth Century." Inaugural Lecture as Visiting Professor at the Faculty of Theology of Utrecht University. Utrechtse theologische Reeks 40. Utrecht: Universiteit Utrecht, 1999.

_____. *The Unaccommodated Calvin: Studies in the Foundation of a Theological Tradition*. New York: Oxford University Press, 2000.

_____. *After Calvin: Studies in the Development of a Theological Tradition*. Oxford: Oxford University Press, 2003.

_____. *Post-Reformation Reformed Dogmatics: The Rise and Development of Reformed Orthodoxy, ca. 1520 to ca. 1725*. 4 vols. Grand Rapids: Baker, 2003.

_____. "The Problem of Protestant Scholasticism – A Review and Definition." In *Reformation and Scholasticism: An Ecumenical Enterprise*, ed. Willem J. van Asselt and Eef Dekker, 45-64. Grand Rapids: Baker, 2001.

Müller, Johannes. *Martin Bucers Hermeneutik.* Quellen und Forschungen zur Reformationsgeschichte 32. Mohn: Gütersloh, 1965.

Murray, John. *The Epistle to the Romans.* 2 vols. New International Commentary on the New Testament. Grand Rapids: Eerdmans, 1960, 1965.

──────. *Collected Writings of John Murray.* 4 vols. Edinburgh: Banner of Truth Trust, 1976-83.

──────. "Calvin as Theologian and Expositor." In *Collected Writings of John Murray, Vol. 1: The Claims of Truth,* 305-11.

──────. "Calvin on the Sovereignty of God." In *Collected Writings of John Murray, Vol. 4: Studies in Theology,* 191-204.

Needham, Nick. "Peter Martyr and the Eucharistic Controversy." *Scottish Bulletin of Evangelical Theology* 17 (1999): 5-25.

Neuser, Wilhelm H. "Theologie des Wortes – Schrift, Verheibung und Evangelium bei Calvin." In *Calvinus Theologus,* ed. W. H. Neuser, 17-37. Neukirchen-Vluyn: Neukirchener Verlag, 1976.

──────, ed. *Calvinus Theologus.* Die Referate des Internationalen Kongresses für Calvinforschung, vom 16 bis 19 September 1974, Amsterdam. Neukirchen-Vluyn: Neukirchener Verlag, 1976.

──────, ed. *Calvinus Ecclesiae Doctor.* Die Referate des Internationalen Kongresses für Calvinforschung, vom 25 bis 28 September 1978, Amsterdam. Kampen: J. H. Kok, 1978.

──────, ed. *Calvinus Ecclesiae Genevensis Custos.* Die Referate des Internationalen Kongresses für Calvinforschung, vom 6 bis 9 September 1982, Geneva. Frankfurt am Main: Peter Lang, 1984.

──────, ed. *Calvinus Servus Christi.* Die Referate des Internationalen Kongresses für Calvinforschung, vom 25 bis 28 August 1986, Debrecen, Hungary. Budapest: Presseabteilung des Ráday-Kollegiums, 1988.

──────, ed. *Calvinus Sacrae Scripturae Professor / Calvin as Confessor of Holy Scripture.* Die Referate des Internationalen Kongresses für Calvinforschung, vom 20 bis 23 August 1990, Grand Rapids. Grand Rapids: Eerdmans, 1994.

──────, and Brian G. Armstrong, eds. *Calvinus sincerioris religionis vindix / Calvin as Protector of the Purer Religion.* Die Referate des Internationalen Kongresses für Calvinforschung, vom 13 bis 16 September 1994, Edinburgh. Sixteenth Century Essays and Studies 36. Kirksville: Sixteenth Century Journal Publishers, 1997.

──────. "Calvins Urteil über den Rechtfertigungsartikel des Regensburger Buches." In *Reformation und Humanismus,* ed. Martin Greschat and J. F. G. Goeters, 176-94. Witten: Luther-Verlag, 1969.

──────, ed. *Die Vorbereitung der Religionsgespräche von Worms und Regensburg 1540/41.* Neukirchen: Neukirchener Verlag, 1974.

Nevin, John W. *The Mystical Presence: A Vindication of the Reformed or Calvinistic Doctrine of the Holy Eucharist.* Philadelphia: J. B. Lippincott & Co., 1846.

─────────. "Doctrine of the Reformed Church on the Lord's Supper." *Mercersburg Review* 2 (1850): 421-548. Rep. in *The Mystical Presence and other Writings on the Eucharist*, ed. Bard Thompson and George H. Bricker. Philadelphia: United Church Press, 1966.

New Schaff-Herzog Encyclopedia of Religious Knowledge, ed. by Phillip Schaff; rev. ed. Samuel Macauley Jackson. 13 vols; rep. Grand Rapids: Baker, 1952.

Nicholls, John D. "Union with Christ: John Calvin on the Lord's Supper." In *Union and Communion*, ed. D. Moore-Crispin, P. Eveson, et al., 35-54. London: The Westminster Conference, 1979.

Nicole, Roger. "John Calvin's View of the Extent of the Atonement." *Westminster Theological Journal* 47 (1985): 197-225.

Niesel, Wilhelm. "Calvin wider Osianders Rechtfertigungslehre." *Zeitschrift für Kirchengeschichte* 46 (1927): 410-30.

─────────. *Calvins Lehre vom Abendmahl*. Munich: Chr. Kaiser, 1930.

─────────. *The Theology of Calvin*. Translated by Harold Knight. Philadelphia: Westminster Press, 1956.

─────────. *Reformed Symbolics*. Translated by D. Lewis. Edinburgh and London: Oliver and Boyd, 1962.

Nieter, J. T. A. *De controversia quae de Coena Sacra inter Westphalum et Calvinum fuit, dijudicatio*. Berlin, 1873.

Nischan, Bodo. "Ritual and Protestant Identity in Late Reformation Germany." In *Protestant History and Identity in Sixteenth-Century Europe, Vol. 2, The Later Reformation*, ed. Bruce Gordon, 142-58. Brookfield: Scholar Press, 1996.

Oberman, Heiko Augustinus. "Headwaters of the Reformation: Initia Lutheri – Initia Reformationis." In *Luther and the Dawn of the Modern Era*, ed. Heiko Oberman, 40-88. Leiden: E. J. Brill, 1974.

─────────. *The Dawn of the Reformation: Essays in Late Medieval and Early Reformation Thought*. Edinburgh: T. & T. Clark, 1986.

─────────. "Via Antiqua and Via Moderna: Late Medieval Prolegomena to Early Reformation Thought." *Journal of the History of Ideas* 48 (1987): 23-40.

─────────. *Forerunners of the Reformation: The Shape of Late Medieval Thought*. New York: Holt, Rinehart and Winston, 1966; rep. Philadelphia: Fortress Press, 1981.

─────────. *Masters of the Reformation: The Emergence of a New Intellectual Climate in Europe*. Translated by D. Martin. London: Cambridge University Press, 1981.

─────────. *The Reformation: Roots and Ramifications*. Edinburgh: T. & T. Clark, 1994.

_____. *The Harvest of Medieval Theology: Gabriel Biel and Late Medieval Nominalism*. Harvard, 1963; 3rd ed. rep. Grand Rapids: Baker, 2000.

_____. "The 'Extra' Dimension in the Theology of John Calvin." *Journal of Ecclesiastical History* 21 (1970): 43-64. Rep. in Oberman, *The Dawn of the Reformation*, 234-58.

_____. "'Iustitia Christi' and 'Iustitia Dei': Luther and the Scholastic Doctrines of Justification." In Oberman, *The Dawn of the Reformation*, 104-25.

_____. and Frank A. James, III, eds. *Via Augustini: Augustine in the Later Middle Ages, Renaissance and Reformation: Essays in Honor of Damasus Trapp, O.S.A.* Leiden: E. J. Brill, 1991.

_____. *Initia Calvini: The Matrix of Calvin's Reformation.* Mededelingen van de Afdeling Letterkunde, Nieuwe Reeks 54, no. 4. Amsterdam: Koninklijke Nederlandse Akademie van Wetenschappen, 1991. Rep. in *Calvinus Sacrae Scripturae Professor: Calvin as Confessor of Holy Scripture*, ed. W. H. Neuser, 113-54. Grand Rapids: Eerdmans, 1994.

_____. "The Meaning of Mysticism from Meister Eckhart to Martin Luther." In Oberman, *The Reformation: Roots and Ramifications*, 77-90.

Ocker, Christopher. *Biblical Poetics Before Humanism and Reformation.* Cambridge: Cambridge University Press, 2002.

Old, Hughes Oliphant. "Biblical Wisdom Theology and Calvin's Understanding of the Lord's Supper." In *Calvin Studies VI*, ed. John H. Leith, 111-36. Colloquium on Calvin Studies, Davidson College and Davidson Presbyterian Church, January, 1992.

_____. *The Reading and Preaching of the Scriptures in the Worship of the Christian Church, Vol. 4: The Age of the Reformation.* Grand Rapids: Eerdmans, 2002.

Olson, Jeannine Evelyn. "Review of *Union with Christ: John Calvin and the Mysticism of St. Bernard* by Dennis E. Tamburello." *Sixteenth Century Journal* 27 (1996): 957-9.

Osterhaven, M. Eugene. "Calvin on the Covenant." *Reformed Review* 33 (1980): 136-49.

Owen, John Michael. "The Angel of the Great Counsel of God and the Christology of the *Scots Confession* of 1560." *Scottish Journal of Theology* 55 (2002): 303-24.

Ozment, Steven E. *Homo Spiritualis: A Comparative Study of the Anthropology of Johannes Tauler, Jean Gerson, and Martin Luther (1509-16) in the Context of their Theological Thought.* Studies in Medieval and Reformation Thought 6. Leiden: E. J. Brill, 1969.

_____, ed. *The Reformation in Medieval Perspective.* Chicago: Quadrangle Books, 1971.

_____. *Mysticism and Dissent: Religious Ideology and Social Protest in the Sixteenth Century*. New Haven: Yale University Press, 1973.

_____. *The Age of Reform 1250-1550: An Intellectual and Religious History of Late Medieval and Reformation Europe*. New Haven: Yale University Press, 1980.

Pannenberg, Wolfhart. *Jesus – God and Man*. Translated by Lewis Wilckens and Duane Priebe. 2nd ed. Philadelphia: Westminster Press, 1977.

Parker, T. H. L. "The Approach to Calvin." *Evangelical Quarterly* 16 (1944): 165-72.

_____. *The Oracles of God: An Introduction to the Preaching of John Calvin*. London: Lutterworth Press, 1947; rep. London: Lutterworth Press/James Clarke, 2003.

_____. "Calvin's Doctrine of Justification." *Evangelical Quarterly* 24 (1952): 101-7.

_____. *The Doctrine of the Knowledge of God: A Study in the Theology of John Calvin*. 1952; rev. ed. Edinburgh: Oliver & Boyd, 1969.

_____. *Calvin's Doctrine of the Knowledge of God*. 2nd ed. Grand Rapids: Eerdmans, 1959.

_____. "Calvin the Biblical Expositor." *The Churchman* 78 (1964): 23-31.

_____. *Calvin's New Testament Commentaries*. London: SCM Press Ltd, 1971; 2nd ed. Grand Rapids: Eerdmans, 1993.

_____. "Calvin the Exegete: Change and Development." In *Calvinus Ecclesiae Doctor*, ed. W. H. Neuser, 33-46. Kampen: J. H. Kok, 1978.

_____. *Calvin's Old Testament Commentaries*. Edinburgh: T. & T. Clark, 1986.

_____. *John Calvin: A Biography*. Philadelphia: Westminster Press, 1975.

_____. *Commentaries on the Epistle to the Romans 1532-1542*. Edinburgh: T. & T. Clark, 1986.

_____. *Calvin: An Introduction to his Thought*. Louisville: Westminster/John Knox Press, 1995.

Partee, Charles. *Calvin and Classical Philosophy*. Leiden: E. J. Brill, 1977.

_____. "Calvin, Calvinism, and Philosophy: A Prolusion." *Reformed Review* 33 (1980): 129-35.

_____. "Calvin's Central Dogma Again." *Sixteenth Century Journal* 18 (1987): 191-9.

Payne, John B. "Erasmus: Interpreter of Romans." In *Sixteenth Century Essays and Studies*. 2 vols, ed. Carl S. Meyer, vol. 2, 1-35. St. Louis: Foundation for Reformation Research, 1971.

_____. "Erasmus and Lefèvre d'Étaples as Interpreters of Paul." *Archiv für Reformationsgeschichte* 65 (1974): 54-83.

_____. "Interpretations of Paul in the Reformation." *Encounter* 36 (1975): 196-211.

Pelikan, Jaroslav. *The Christian Tradition. Vol. 4: Reformation of Church and Dogma (1300-1700)*. Chicago: University of Chicago Press, 1984.

Pendergrass, Jan Noble. "Humanismus und Theologie in Johannes Altenstaigs *Opus ro conficiundis epistolis* (1512)." Paper for the Conference "'Germania Latina – latinitas teutonica': Politics, Science, and Humanist Culture from the Late Middle Ages to the Present," Munich, 2001.

Peter, Rodolphe and Jean-François Gilmont, eds. *Bibliotheca Calviniana: les oeuvres de Jean Calvin publiées au XVIe siècle*. 3 vols. Vols 1-2 ed. R. Peter and J.-F. Gilmont. Geneva: Librairie Droz, 1991-1994. Vol. 3 ed. R. Peter and J.-F. Gilmont with Christian Krieger. Geneva: Librairie Droz, 2000.

Peterson, Robert A. "Calvin's Doctrine of the Atonement." Ph.D. diss., Drew University, 1980.

_____. *Calvin's Doctrine of the Atonement*. Phillipsburg: Presbyterian and Reformed, 1983.

Pfnür, Vinzenz. "Die Einigung bei den Religionsgesprächen von Worms und Regensburg 1540/41 eine Täuschung?" In *Die Religionsgespräche der Reformationszeit*, ed. Gerhard Müller, 55-88. Gütersloh 1980.

Pin, Jean-Pierre. "Pour une analyse textuelle du catèchisme (1542) de Jean Calvin." In *Calvinus Ecclesiae Doctor*, ed. W. H. Neuser, 159-70. Kampen: Uitgeversmaatschappij J. H. Kok B. V., 1978.

Pitkin, Barbara. *What Pure Eyes Could See: Calvin's Doctrine of Faith in Its Exegetical Context*. New York: Oxford University Press, 1999.

Posset, Franz. "'Deification' in the German Spirituality of the Late Middle Ages and in Luther: An Ecumenical Historical Perspective." *Archiv für Reformationsgeschichte* 84 (1993): 103-25.

Post, R. R. *The Modern Devotion: Confrontation with Reformation and Humanism*. Studies in Medieval and Reformation Thought 3. Leiden: E. J. Brill, 1968.

Potter, Mary Lane. "The 'Whole Office of the Law' in the Theology of John Calvin." *Journal of Law and Religion* 3 (1985): 117-39.

Preus, Jacob A. O. "Martin Chemnitz on the Doctrine of Justification." Paper Presented at the Reformation Lectures, Bethany Lutheran College and Bethany Lutheran Theological Seminary, October 30, 1985, Lecture II.

Prins, R. "The Image of God in Adam and the Restoration of Man in Jesus Christ. A Study in Calvin." *Scottish Journal of Theology* 25 (1972): 32-44.

Pruett, Gordon E. "A Protestant Doctrine of the Eucharistic Presence." *Calvin Theological Journal* 10 (1975): 142-74.

Puckett, David L. *John Calvin's Exegesis of the Old Testament*. Louisville: Westminster/John Knox Press, 1995.

Quistrop, Heinrich. *Calvin's Doctrine of the Last Things*. Translated by Harold Knight. London: Lutterworth Press, 1955.

Rainbow, Jonathan H. "Double Grace: John Calvin's View of the Relationship of Justification and Sanctification." *Ex Auditu: An International Journal of Theological Interpretation of Scripture* 5 (1989): 99-105.

Raitt, Jill, Bernard McGinn, and John Meyendorff, eds. *Christian Spirituality II: High Middle Ages and Reformation*. New York: Crossroad Publishing, 1987. Vol. 17 of *World Spirituality: An Encyclopedic History of the Religious Quest*, ed. Ewert Cousins. New York: Crossroad Publishing.

Raitt, Jill. "Calvin's Use of Bernard of Clairvaux." *Archiv für Reformationsgeschichte* 72 (1981): 98-121.

Rankin, W. Duncan. "Carnal Union with Christ in the Theology of T. F. Torrance." Ph.D. diss., University of Edinburgh, 1997.

Realencycklopädie für protestantische Theologie und Kirche. 3rd ed. Leipzig, 1896-1913.

Redding, Graham. *Prayer and the Priesthood of Christ in the Reformed Tradition*. Edinburgh: T. & T. Clark, 2003.

Redman, Robert R., Jr. *Reformulating Reformed Theology: Jesus Christ in the Theology of Hugh Ross Mackintosh*. Lanham: University Press of America, 1997.

Reid, J. K. S. *Our Life in Christ*. London: SCM Press Ltd., 1963.

Reid, W. Stanford. "Bernard of Clairvaux in the Thought of John Calvin." *Westminster Theological Journal* 41 (1978-1979): 127-45.

Reuter, Karl. *Das Gründverständnis der Theologie Calvins, Unter Einbeziehung ihrer geschichtlichen Abhändigkeiten*. Neukirchen-Vluyn: Neukirchener Verlag, 1963.

_____. *Vom Scholaren bis zum jungen Reformator, Studien zum Werdegang Johannes Calvins*. Neukirchen-Vluyn: Neukirchener Verlag, 1981.

Richard, Lucien Joseph. *The Spirituality of John Calvin*. Atlanta: John Knox Press, 1974.

Ritschl, Albrecht. "Die Rechtfertigungslehre des Andreas Osiander." *Jahrbücher für Deutsche Theologie* 2 (1857): 795-829.

———. *A Critical History of the Christian Doctrine of Justification and Reconciliation.* Vol. 1. Translated by John S. Black. Edinburgh: Edmonston and Douglas, 1872.

———. *The Christian Doctrine of Justification and Reconciliation.* Vol. 3. Ed. H. R. Mackintosh and A. B. Macaulay. New York: Charles Scribner's Sons, 1900.

Ritschl, Otto. *Dogmengeschichte des Protestantismus.* Göttingen: Vandenhoeck & Ruprecht, 1926.

Rogers, Eugene F., Jr. "The Mystery of the Spirit in Three Traditions: Calvin, Rahner, Florensky Or, You *Keep* Wondering Where the Spirit Went." *Modern Theology* 19 (2003): 243-60.

Rorem, Paul E. "Calvin and Bullinger on the Lord's Supper, Part 1: The Impasse." *Lutheran Quarterly* 2, no. 2 (1988): 155-84.

———. "Calvin and Bullinger on the Lord's Supper, Part 2: The Agreement." *Lutheran Quarterly* 2, no. 3 (1988): 357-89.

———. "The *Consensus Tigurinus* (1549): Did Calvin Compromise?" In *Calvinus Sacrae Scripturae Professor,* ed. W. H. Neuser, 72-90. Grand Rapids: Eerdmans, 1994.

Rossall, Judith. "God's Activity and the Believer's Experience in the Theology of John Calvin." Ph.D. diss., University of Durham, 1991.

Roussel, M. Bernard. "Martin Bucer et Jacques Sadolet: la condorde possible." *Bulletin de la Société de l'histoire de protestantisme française* 22 (1976): 525-50.

Ruffini, Francesco. "Francesco Stancaro," s.v. In *Studi sui Reformatori Italiani di Francesco Ruffini,* ed. A. Bertoli, L. Furpo, and E. Ruffing, 215-7. Turin: Romella, 1955.

Rupp, Gordon. "Patterns of Salvation in the First Age of the Reformation." *Archiv für Reformationsgeschichte* 57 (1966): 52-66.

Rusch, William G. "How the Eastern Fathers Understood What the Western Church Meant by Justification." In *Justification by Faith,* ed. H. George Anderson, T. Austin Murphy, and Joseph A. Burgess, 131-41. Minneapolis: Augsburg, 1985.

Safire, William. "Invective's Comeback." *The New York Times,* Tuesday, April 29, 2003.

Sanday, William and A. C. Headlam. *A Critical and Exegetical Commentary on the Epistle to the Romans.* 5th ed. Edinburgh: T. & T. Clark, 1902.

Santmire, H. Paul. "Justification in Calvin's 1540 Romans Commentary." *Church History* 33 (1964): 294-313.

Schäfer, Rolf. "Melanchthons Hermeneutik im Römerbrief-Kommentar von 1532." *Zeitschrift für Theologie und Kirche* 60 (1963): 216-35.

Schaff, Philip, ed. *The Creeds of Christendom.* 3 Vols. New York: Harper & Brothers, 1877; rep. Grand Rapids: Baker, 1998.

Scheible, Heinz. "Melanchthon und Osiander über die Rechtfertigung: Zwei Versuche, Wahrheit zu formulieren." In *Reformation und Recht: Festgabe für Gottfried Seebass zum 65. Geburtstag*, ed. Irene Dingal, et al., 161-75. Gütersloh: Christian Kaiser, Gütersloher Verl.-Haus, 2002.

Scheld, Stefan. *Media Salutis: Zur Heilsvermittlung bei Calvin.* Wiesbaden: Franz Steiner Verlag, 1989.

Schilling, Heinz. *Konfessionskonflikt und Staatsbilding.* Gütersloh, 1981.

_____. *Religion, Political Culture and the Emergence of Early Modern Society: Essays in German and Dutch History.* Leiden: E. J. Brill, 1992.

_____. "Confessional Europe." In *Handbook of European History, 1400-1600*, Vol. 2, *Late Middle Ages, Renaissance, and Reformation: Visions, Programs, and Outcomes*, ed. Thomas A. Brady, Jr., Heiko A. Oberman, and James D. Tracy, 641-81. Leiden: E. J. Brill, 1995.

Schnueker, Robert V., ed. *Calviniana: Ideas and Influences of Jean Calvin.* Sixteenth Century Essays and Studies 10. Kirksville: Sixteenth Century Journal Publications, 1988.

Schreiner, Susan Elizabeth. "Through a Mirror Dimly: Calvin's Sermons on Job." *Calvin Theological Journal* 21 (1986): 175-93.

_____. "Exegesis and Double Justice in Calvin's Sermons on Job." *Church History* 58 (1989): 322-38.

_____. *The Theater of His Glory: Nature and the Natural Order in the Thought of John Calvin.* Durham: Labyrinth Press, 1991.

_____. "'The Spiritual Man Judges All Things': Calvin and the Exegetical Debates about Certainty in the Reformation." In *Biblical Interpretation in the Era of the Reformation: Essays Presented to David C. Steinmetz in Honor of his Sixtieth Birthday*, ed. Richard A. Muller and John L. Thompson, 189-215. Grand Rapids: Eerdmans, 1996.

Schulz, Hans. "Andreas Osianders reformatorische Lehre vom Eid." *Archiv für Reformationsgeschichte* 84 (1993): 185-205.

Schulze, L. F. *Calvin's Reply to Pighius.* Potchefstroom: Pro Rege Press, 1971.

Searle, Mark and Kenneth W. Stevenson. *Documents of the Marriage Liturgy.* Collegeville: Liturgical Press/Pueblo, 1992.

Seebass, Gottfried. *Das reformatorische Werk des Andreas Osiander.* Einzelarbeiten aus der Kirchengeschichte Bayerns 44. Nuremberg, 1967.

_____. "Zwei Schreiben von Andreas Osiander." *Mitteiliungen des Verins für Geschichte der Stadt Nürnberg* 57 (1970): 201-15.

_____. *Bibliographia Osiandrica: Bibliographie der gedruckten Schriften Andreas Osianders d. Ä., 1496-1552.* Nieuwkoop: B. de Graaf, 1971.

———. "Osiander, Andreas," s.v. In *Oxford Encylcopedia of the Reformation*, ed. Hans J. Hillerbrand. Vol. 3, cols. 183b-5a.

Seeberg, Reinhold. *Text-Book of the History of Doctrines*. Translated by C. E. Hay, II. Grand Rapids: Baker, 1954.

Seifrid, Mark A. "Paul, Luther, and Justification in Gal 2:15-21." *Westminster Theological Journal* 65 (2003): 215-30.

———. "Luther, Melanchthon and Paul on the Question of Imputation: Recommendations on a Current Debate." In *Justification: What's at Stake in the Current Debates*, ed. Mark Husbands and Daniel J. Trier, 137-52. Downers Grove: InterVarsity Press, 2004.

Selderhuis, Herman J., ed. *Calvinus Praeceptor Ecclesiae*. Papers of the International Congress on Calvin Research, Princeton, August 20-24, 2002. Geneva: Librairie Droz, 2004.

Selinger, Suzanne. *Calvin Against Himself: An Inquiry in Intellectual History*. Hamden: Archon Books, 1984.

Shepherd, Victor V. *The Nature and Function of Faith in the Theology of John Calvin*. Macon: Mercer University Press, 1983.

Siggins, Ian D. Kingston. *Martin Luther's Doctrine of Christ*. Yale Publications in Religion 14. London and New Haven: Yale University Press, 1970.

Sillem, C. H. W., ed. *Briefsammlung des hamburgischen Superintendenten Joachim Westphal aus den Jahren 1530 bis 1575*. Hamburg, 1903.

Smedes, Lewis. *All Things Made New*. Grand Rapids: Eerdmans, 1970.

Smith, C. S. "Calvin's Doctrine of Justification in Relation to the Sense of Sin and the Dialogue with Rome." M.Phil. thesis, London Bible College, 1993.

Snell, F. W. "The Place of Augustine in Calvin's Concept of Righteousness." Th.D. diss., Union Theological Seminary, 1968.

Souter, Alexander. *The Earliest Latin Commentaries on the Epistles of Paul*. Oxford: Clarendon Press, 1927.

Spinks, Bryan D. "Luther's Other Major Liturgical Reforms: 3. The Traubuchlein." *Liturgical Review* 10 (1980): 33-8.

———. "Calvin's Baptismal Theology and the Making of the Strasbourg and Geneva Baptismal Liturgies 1540 and 1542." *Scottish Journal of Theology* 48 (1995): 55-78.

Spitz, Lewis W. *The Renaissance and Reformation Movements*. 2 vols. St. Louis: Concordia Publishing House, 1971; rev. ed. 1987.

Stadtland, Tjarko. *Rechtfertigung und Heiligung bei Calvin*. Neukirchen: Neukirchener Verlag, 1972.

Steenkamp, Johan J. "A Review of the Concept of Progress in Calvin's Institutes." In *Calvin: Erbe und Auftrag, Festschrift for W. H.*

Neuser, ed. W. van't Spijker, 69-76. Kampen: Kok Pharos Publishing House, 1991.

Steinmetz, David C. *Misercordia Dei: The Theology of Johannes von Staupitz in its Late Medieval Setting*. Leiden: E. J. Brill, 1978.

_____. *Luther in Context*. Grand Rapids: Baker, 1995; 2nd ed., Grand Rapids: Baker, 2002.

_____. "Luther and Augustine on Romans 9." In Steinmetz, *Luther in Context*, 12-22. Grand Rapids: Baker, 2002.

_____. "Abraham and the Reformation." In Steinmetz, *Luther in Context*, 32-46. Grand Rapids: Baker, 2002.

_____. "Luther Among the Anti-Thomists." In Steinmetz, *Luther in Context*, 47-58. Grand Rapids: Baker, 2002.

_____. "Scripture and the Lord's Supper in Luther's Theology." In Steinmetz, *Luther in Context*, 72-84. Grand Rapids: Baker, 2002.

_____. "Luther and Calvin on Church and Tradition." In Steinmetz, *Luther in Context*, 85-97. Grand Rapids: Baker, 2002.

_____. "Luther and Calvin on the Banks of the Jabbok." In Steinmetz, *Luther in Context*, 156-68. Grand Rapids: Baker, 2002.

_____. "Calvin and the Patristic Exegesis of Paul." In *The Bible in the Sixteenth Century*, ed. David C. Steinmetz, 100-18. Durham: Duke University Press, 1990.

_____. "Calvin and His Lutheran Critics." *The Lutheran Quarterly* 4 (1990): 179-4; rev. in Steinmetz, *Calvin in Context*, 172-86.

_____. *Calvin in Context*. New York: Oxford University Press, 1995.

_____. *Reformers in the Wings*. Philadelphia: Fortress Press, 1971.

_____. "The Scholastic Calvin." In *Protestant Scholasticism: Essays in Reassessment*, ed. Carl R. Trueman and R. S. Clark, 16-30. Carlisle: Paternoster Press, 1999.

_____, ed. *The Bible in the Sixteenth Century*. Duke Monographs in Medieval and Renaissance Studies 11. Durham: Duke University Press, 1982.

Stephens, W. Peter. *The Holy Spirit in the Theology of Martin Bucer*. Cambridge: Cambridge University Press, 1970.

_____. "The Soteriological Motive in the Eucharistic Controversy." In *Calvin: Erbe und Auftrag: Festschrift für Wilhelm Neuser zu seinem 65. Geburstag*, ed. Willem van't Spijker, 203-13. Kampen: Kok, 1991.

Stevenson, Kenneth W. *Nuptial Blessing: A Study of Christian Marriage Rites*. New York: S.P.C.K., 1982; rep. New York: Oxford, 1983.

_____. *To Join Together: The Rite of Marriage*. Studies in the Reformed Rites of the Roman Catholic Church 5. New York: Pueblo, 1987.

Stiktberg, W. R. "The Mystical Element in the Theology of John Calvin." Ph.D. diss., Union Theological Seminary, New York, 1951.
Strehle, Stephen Alan. *Calvinism, Federalism, and Scholasticism: A Study of the Reformed Doctrine of Covenant*. Bern: Peter Lang, 1988.
──────. "Imputatio iustitiae: Its Origin in Melanchthon, its Opposition in Osiander." *Theologische Zeitschrift* 50 (1994): 201-19. Rev. in Strehle, *The Catholic Roots of the Protestant Gospel*, 66-85.
──────. *The Catholic Roots of the Protestant Gospel: Encounter between the Middle Ages and the Reformation*. Studies in the History of Christian Thought 60. Leiden: E. J. Brill, 1995.
Stuermann, Walter E. *A Critical Study of Calvin's Concept of Faith*. Tulsa: University of Tulsa, 1952.
Stupperich, Martin. *Osiander in Preussen, 1549-1552*. Berlin and New York: de Gruyter, 1973.
──────. "Das Augsburger Interim als apokalyptisches Geschehnis nach den Königsberger Schriften Andreas Osianders." *Archiv für Reformationsgeschichte* 64 (1973): 225-45.
Swierenga, R. P. "Calvin and the Council of Trent: A Reappraisal. Part II.," *Reformed Journal* 16 (1966): 19-21.
Tamburello, Dennis E. *Union with Christ: John Calvin and the Mysticism of St. Bernard*. Louisville: Westminster/John Knox Press, 1994.
──────. *Ordinary Mysticism*. New York: Paulist Press, 1996.
Tavard, George H. *The Starting Point of Calvin's Theology*. Grand Rapids: Eerdmans, 2000.
Taylor, Henry Osborn. *Thought and Expression in the Sixteenth Century*. 2 vols. New York: MacMillan, 1920.
Theologische Realenzyklopädie. Ed. Gerhard Krause and Gerhard Müller. 2 vols. Berlin: Walter de Gruyter, 1977-.
Thompson, John L. "Review of *Revelation, Redemption, and Response: Calvin's Trinitarian Understanding of the Divine-Human Relationship* by Philip Walker Butin." *The Expository Times* 107 (1995): 58.
──────. "The Survival of Allegorical Argumentation in Peter Martyr Vermigli's Old Testament Exegesis." In *Biblical Interpretation in the Era of the Reformation*, ed. Richard A. Muller and John L. Thompson, 255-71. Grand Rapids: Eerdmans, 1996.
Thompson, Matthew E. "Walther's Anti-Conventical Position: Its Roots in Pietism and Contemporary Application." *Lutheran Synod Quarterly* 42 (2002): 252-90.
Thompson, William M. "Viewing Justification Through Calvin's Eyes: An Ecumenical Experiment." *Theological Studies* 57 (1996): 447-66.
Tinker, Melvin. "Language, Symbols and Sacraments. Was Calvin's View of the Lord's Supper Right?" *Churchman* 112 (1998): 131–49.

Torrance, J. B. "The Vicarious Humanity and Priesthood of Christ in the Theology of John Calvin." In *Calvinus Ecclesiae Doctor*, ed. W. H. Neuser, 69-84. Kampen: Uitgeversmaatschappij J. H. Kok B. V., 1978.

———. "The Incarnation and 'Limited Atonement.'" *Evangelical Quarterly* 55 (1983): 83-94.

———. "The Concept of Federal Theology – Was Calvin a Federal Theologian." In *Calvinus Sacrae Scripturae Professor*, ed. W. H. Neuser, 15-40. Grand Rapids: Eerdmans, 1994.

Torrance, Thomas Forsyth. *Calvin's Doctrine of Man*. London: Lutterworth Press, 1949.

———. *Kingdom and Church*. London: Oliver & Boyd, 1956.

———. "Introduction." In *The School of Faith: The Catechisms of the Reformed Church*. Translated with an introduction by T. F. Torrance. London: James Clarke, 1959.

———. *Theology in Reconstruction*. London: SCM Press, 1965.

———. *The Hermeneutics of John Calvin*. Edinburgh: Scottish Academic Press, 1988.

Trinkaus, Charles. "Renaissance Problems in Calvin's Theology." *Studies in the Renaissance* 1 (1954): 59-80.

Troeltsch, Ernst. *The Social Teaching of the Christian Churches*. Translated by O. Wyon, II. New York: MacMillan Company, 1931.

Trueman, Carl R. and R. S. Clark, eds. *Protestant Scholasticism: Essays in Reassessment*. Carlisle: Paternoster Press, 1999.

Trueman, Carl R. "Is the Finnish Line a New Beginning? A Critical Assessment of the Reading of Luther Offered by the Helsinki Circle." *Westminster Theological Journal* 65 (2003): 231-44.

Trumper, Tim J. R. "An Historical Study of the Doctrine of Adoption in the Calvinistic Tradition." Ph.D. diss., University of Edinburgh, 2001.

Tylanda [sic, see "Tylenda" below], Joseph N. "Christ the Mediator: Calvin versus Stancaro." *Calvin Theological Journal* 8 (1973): 5-16.

Tylenda, Joseph N. "A Study in the Eucharistic Theologies of John Calvin, Reformer of Geneva, and of Max Thurian, Monk of Taize." Ph.D. diss., Pontifica Universitas Gregoriana, 1964.

———. "Calvin on Christ's True Presence in the Lord's Supper." *American Ecclesiastical Review* 155 (1966): 321-33.

———. "The Controversy on Christ the Mediator: Calvin's Second Reply to Stancaro." *Calvin Theological Journal* 8 (1973): 131-57.

———. "Calvin and Christ's Presence in the Supper – True or Real." *Scottish Journal of Theology* 27 (1974): 65-75.

———. "The Calvin-Westphal Exchange: The Genesis of Calvin's Treatises Against Westphal." *Calvin Theological Journal* 9 (1974): 182-209.

_____. "Calvin's Understanding of the Communication of Properties." *Westminster Theological Journal* 38 (1975): 54-65.

_____. "A Eucharistic Sacrifice in Calvin's Soteriology?" *Theological Studies* 37 (1976): 456-66.

_____. "The Ecumenical Intention of Calvin's Early Eucharistic Teaching." In *Reformatio Perennis: Essays on Calvin and the Reformation in Honor of Ford Lewis Battles*, ed. B. A. Gerrish, 27-47. Pittsburgh: Pickwick Press, 1981.

_____. "Calvin and Westphal: Two Eucharistic Theologies in Conflict." In *Calvin's Books: Festschrift dedicated to Peter De Klerk on the Occasion of his Seventieth Birthday*, ed. Wilhem H. Neuser, et al., 9-21. Heerenveen: J. J. Groen en Zoon, 1997.

Van Asselt, Willem J. and Eef Dekker, eds. *Reformation and Scholasticism: An Ecumenical Enterprise*. Grand Rapids: Baker, 2001.

_____. "Introduction." In *Reformation and Scholasticism: An Ecumenical Enterprise*, ed. Willem J. van Asselt and Eef Dekker, 11-43. Grand Rapids: Baker, 2001.

Van Buren, Paul. *Christ in Our Place: The Substitutionary Character of Calvin's Doctrine of Reconciliation*. Edinburgh and London: Oliver and Boyd, 1957.

Van Dyke, Leanne. "John McLeod Campbell's Doctrine of the Atonement: A Revision and Expansion of the Reformed Tradition." Ph.D. diss., Princeton Theological Seminary, 1992.

van't Spijker, Willem. "The Influence of Bucer on Calvin As Becomes Evident from the *Institutes*." In *John Calvin's Institutes: His Opus Magnum*, 106-32. Proceedings of the Second South African Congress for Calvin Research. Potchefstroom: Potchefstroom University for Christian Higher Education, 1986.

_____, ed. *Calvin: Erbe und Auftrag, Festschrift for W. H. Neuser*. Kampen: Kok Pharos Publishing House, 1991.

_____. "Die Lehre vom Heiligen Geist bei Bucer und Calvin." In *Calvinus Servus Christi*, ed. W. H. Neuser, 73-106. Budapest: Presseabteilung des Ráday-Kollegiums, 1988.

_____. "'Extra Nos' and 'In Nobis' bij Calvijn in pneumatologisch licht." *Theologia Reformata* 31 (1988): 271-91.

_____. "Bucer und Calvin." In *Martin Bucer and Sixteenth Century Europe: Actes du colloque de Strasbourg, 28-31 août 1991*, Vol. 1, ed. Christian Krieger and Marc Lienhard, 461-70. Leiden: E. J. Brill, 1993.

_____. *The Ecclesiastical Offices in the Thought of Martin Bucer*. Translated by John Vriend and Lyle Bierma. Leiden: E. J. Brill, 1996.

_____. "Reformation and Scholasticism." In *Reformation and Scholasticism: An Ecumenical Enterprise*, ed. Willem J. van Asselt and Eef Dekker, 79-98. Grand Rapids: Baker, 2001.

Venema, Cornelis Paul. "The Twofold Nature of the Gospel in Calvin's Theology: The 'Duplex Gratia Dei' and the Interpretation of Calvin's Theology." Ph.D. diss., Princeton Theological Seminary, 1985.

_____. *Heinrich Bullinger and the Doctrine of Predestination: Author of "the Other Reformed Tradition"?* Grand Rapids: Baker, 2002.

Vincent, G. "La thèologie calvinienne du sacrement a la lumière de la linguistique." In *Calvinus Ecclesiae Doctor*, ed. W. H. Neuser, 145-58. Kampen: Uitgeversmaatschappij J. H. Kok B. V., 1978.

Vinke, Rainer. "Osiander, Andreas," s.v. In *Contemporaries of Erasmus: A Biographical Register of the Renaissance and Reformation*, ed. Peter G. Bietenholz and Thomas B. Deutscher, vol. 3, 35-6.

Von Loewenich, Walther. *Duplex Iustitia: Luthers Stellung zu einer Unionsformel des 16. Jahrhunderts*. Wiesbaden: Steiner, 1972.

Vos, Antonie. "Scholasticism and Reformation." In *Reformation and Scholasticism: An Ecumenical Enterprise*, ed. Willem J. van Asselt and Eef Dekker, 99-119. Grand Rapids: Baker, 2001.

Walchenbach, John R. "John Calvin as Biblical Commentator: An Investigation into Calvin's Use of John Chrysostom as an Exegetical Tutor." Ph.D. diss., University of Pittsburgh, 1974.

Wallace, Ronald S. *Calvin's Doctrine of the Word and Sacrament*. Edinburgh: Oliver & Boyd, 1953; rep. Edinburgh: Scottish Academic Press Ltd, 1995.

_____. *Calvin's Doctrine of the Christian Life*. Edinburgh: Oliver & Boyd, 1959.

_____. "A Christian Theologian: Calvin's Approach to Theology." *Scottish Bulletin of Evangelical Theology* (Special Study) (1987): 123-50.

_____. *Calvin, Geneva, and the Reformation: A Study of Calvin as Social Reformer, Churchman, Pastor and Theologian*. Edinburgh: Scottish Academic Press, 1988.

Walker, G. S. M. "The Lord's Supper in the Theology and Practice of Calvin." In *John Calvin*, 131-48. Courtenay Studies in Reformation Theology 1. Appleford: Sutton Courtenay Press, 1966.

Walters, Gwyn. "The Doctrine of the Holy Spirit in John Calvin." Ph.D. diss., University of Edinburgh, 1949.

Walters, Gwenfair M. "The Atonement in Medieval Theology." In *The Glory of the Atonement: Biblical, Theological and Practical Perspectives*, ed. Charles E. Hill and Frank A. James, III, 239-62. Downers Grove: InterVarsity Press, 2004.

Warfield, Benjamin B. *Calvin and Calvinism.* New York: Oxford University Press/Philadelphia: Presbyterian and Reformed, 1931.

———. "On the Literary History of Calvin's 'Institutes'." *Presbyterian and Reformed Review* 10 (1899): 193-219. Rep. in Warfield, *Calvin and Calvinism,* 372-428.

———. "Calvin's Doctrine of the Trinity." In *Calvin and Augustine,* ed. S. Craig. Philadelphia: Presbyterian and Reformed, 1956.

Watanabe, Nobuo. "Calvin's Second Catechism: Its Predecessors and Its Environment." In *Calvinus Sacrae Scripturae Professor,* ed. W. H. Neuser, 224-32. Grand Rapids: Eerdmans, 1994.

Wawrykow, Joseph. "John Calvin and Condign Merit." *Archiv für Reformationsgeschichte* 83 (1992): 73-90.

Weber, Hans Emil. *Reformation, Orthodoxie und Rationalismus.* Gütersloh: Gerd Mohn, 1937.

Weir, David A. *The Origins of the Federal Theology in Sixteenth-Century Reformation Thought.* Oxford: Clarendon Press, 1990.

Weis, James. "Calvin versus Osiander on Justification." *Springfielder* 30 (1965): 31-47.

Wendel, François. *Calvin: The Origins and Development of His Religious Thought.* Translated by Phillip Mairet. New York: Harper and Row, 1963.

———. *Calvin et l'humanisme.* Paris: Presses Universitaires de France, 1976.

Wengert, Timothy J. and M. Patrick Graham, eds. *Philip Melanchthon (1497-1560) and the Commentary.* Sheffield: Sheffield Academic Press, 1997.

Wengert, Timothy J. *Law and Gospel: Philip Melanchthon's Debate with John Agricola of Eisleben over* Poenitentia. Grand Rapids: Baker, 1997.

———. "'We Will Feast Together in Heaven Forever': The Epistolary Friendship of John Calvin and Philip Melanchthon." In *Melanchthon in Europe: His Work and Influence Beyond Wittenberg,* ed. Karin Maag, 19-44. Grand Rapids: Baker, 1999.

Wernle, Paul. *Der Evangelische Glaube, Nach den Haupschriften der Reformation,* Vol. 3: *Calvin.* Tübingen: J. C. B. Mohr, 1919.

Wesche, Kenneth Paul. "Eastern Orthodox Spirituality: Union with God in *Theosis.*" *Theology Today* 56 (1999): 29-43.

Wilcox, Peter. "'The Restoration of the Church' in Calvin's 'Commentaries on Isaiah the Prophet'." *Archiv für Reformationsgeschichte* 85 (1994): 68-95.

———. "Evangelisation in the Thought and Practice of John Calvin." *Anvil* 12 (1995): 201-17.

———. "Conversion in the Thought and Experience of John Calvin." *Anvil* 14 (1997): 113-28.

Wiles, Maurice. *The Divine Apostle: The Interpretation of St. Paul's Epistles in the Early Church.* Cambridge: Cambridge University Press, 1967.

Wiley, David N. "The Church as the Elect in the Theology of Calvin." In *John Calvin and the Church: A Prism of Reform,* ed. Timothy George, 96-117. Louisville: Westminster/John Knox Press, 1990.

Williams, A. N. *The Ground of Union: Deification in Aquinas and Palamas.* New York: Oxford University Press, 1999.

Williams, George H. *The Radical Reformation.* Philadelphia: Westminster, 1962.

―――――. "Francis Stancaro's Schismatic Reformed Church, Centered in Dubets'ko in Ruthenia, 1559/61 – 1570." *Harvard Ukrainian Studies* 4 (1980): 931-57.

Willis-Watkins, E. David. "The Influence of Laelius Socinus on Calvin's Doctrines of the Merits of Christ and the Assurance of Faith." In *Italian Reformation Studies in Honor of Laelius Socinus,* ed. John A. Tedeschi. Florence: Felice le Monnier, 1965. Rep. in Gamble, ed., *Articles on Calvin and Calvinism,* vol. 5, 59-67.

―――――. *Calvin's Catholic Christology: The Function of the So-Called Extra Calvinisticum in Calvin's Theology.* Studies in Medieval and Reformation Thought 2. Leiden: E. J. Brill, 1966.

―――――. "Rhetoric and Responsibility in Calvin's Theology." In *The Context of Contemporary Theology: Essays in Honor of Paul Lehmann,* ed. A. J. McKelway and E. David Willis, 43-63. Atlanta: John Knox Press, 1974.

―――――. "A Reformed Doctrine of the Eucharist and Ministry and Its Implications for Roman Catholic Dialogues." *Journal of Ecumenical Studies* (1981): 295-305.

―――――. "Calvin's Use of 'Substantia'." In *Calvinus ecclesiae Genevensis custos,* ed. W. H. Neuser, 289-301. Frankfurt-am-Main, 1984.

―――――. "The *Unio Mystica* and the Assurance of Faith According to Calvin." In *Calvin: Erbe und Auftrag, Festschrift for W. H. Neuser,* ed. Willem van't Spijker, 77-84. Kampen: Kok Pharos Publishing House, 1991.

Wilson-Kastner, Patricia. "Andreas Osiander's Theology of Grace in the Perspective of the Influence of Augustine of Hippo." *Sixteenth Century Journal* 10 (1979): 72-91.

―――――. "Andreas Osiander's Probable Influence on Thomas Cranmer's Eucharistic Theology." *Sixteenth Century Journal* 14 (1983): 411-25.

Winroth, Anders. *The Making of Gratian's* Decretum. Cambridge: Cambridge University Press, 2000.

Woolsey, Andrew Alexander. "Unity and Continuity in Covenantal Thought: A Study in the Reformed Tradition to the Westminster Assembly." 2 vols. Ph.D. diss., University of Glasgow, 1988.

Wright, David F. "Calvin's Pentateuchal Criticism: Equity, Hardness of Heart, and Divine Accommodation in the Mosaic Harmony Commentary." *Calvin Theological Journal* 21 (1986): 33-50.

Yarnold, E. "*Duplex Iustitia*: The Sixteenth Century and the Twentieth." In *Christian Authority: Essays in Honour of Henry Chadwick*, ed. G. R. Evans, 207-13. Oxford: Clarendon Press, 1988.

Yoo, Jung Woo. "A Study of the Place and Importance of Good Works in Calvin's Soteriology." Th.D. diss., Asia United Theological University, 1998.

You, Hae Yong. "Bonaventure and John Calvin: The Restoration of the Image of God as a Mode of Spiritual Consummation." Ph.D. diss., Fordham University, 1992.

Ziesler, John. *Pauline Christianity.* Rev. ed., New York: Oxford University Press, 1990.

Zimmermann, Von Gunter. "Die Thesen Osianders zur Disputation 'de iustificatione'." *Kerygma und Dogma* 33 (1987): 224-44.

_____. "Calvins Auseinandersetzung mit Osianders Rechtfertigungslehre." *Kerygma und Dogma* 35 (1989): 236-56.

_____. *Prediger der Freiheit: Andreas Osiander und der Nürnberger Rat 1522-1548.* Mannheimer historische Forschungen Vol. 15. Mannheim: Palatium Verlag, 1999.

Zoepfl, Friedrich. *Johannes Altenstaig: Ein Gelehrtenleben aus der Zeit des Humanismus und der Reformation.* Münster in Westf.: Verlag der Aschendorffschen Verlagshandlung, 1918.

Zu Dohna, Lothar Graf. "Staupitz and Luther: Continuity and Breakthrough at the Beginning of the Reformation." In *Via Augustini: Augustine in the Later Middle Ages, Renaissance and Reformation: Essays in Honor of Damasus Trapp, O.S.E.*, ed. Heiko A. Oberman and Frank A. James, III, 116-29. Leiden: E. J. Brill, 1991.

Zumkeller, Adolar. "Der Terminus 'sola fides' bei Augustinus." In *Christian Authority: Essays in Honour of Henry Chadwick*, ed. G. R. Evans, 86-100. Oxford: Clarendon Press, 1988.

Scripture Index

Genesis
4:4-5, 7 – *99*
15:1 – *99*

Exodus
1:21 – *99*

Ruth
2:12 – *99*

2 Chronicles
15:7 – *99*

Psalms
17:24-25 – *99*
32:1 – *114*
118:112 – *99*
119 – *233*
127:23 – *99*

Proverbs
11:18 – *99*

Isaiah
9:6 – *212*
40:10 – *99*
53:11 – *211*

Jeremiah
23:5-6 – *212*
23:6 – *198, 204, 218*
31:16 – *99*

Ezekiel
18:17 – *263*
20:44 – *264*

Daniel
4:24 – *99*

Hosea
2:19 – *54*
10:12 – *99*

Matthew
5:12 – *99*
7:21 – *99*
9 – *84*
10:42 – *99*
16:24 – *129*
19:17 – *99*
20:4 – *99*
25:34 – *99*
25:35 – *99*

Mark
16:16 – *266*

Luke
6:23 – *99*
18:10 – *99*

John
2:1-25 – *54*
3:5 – *266*
4:36 – *99*
5:29 – *99*
6 – *173, 178, 179*
6:52 – *173*
6:53 – *173*
6:57 – *66*
6:64 – *173*
7 – *99*
8 – *99*
13:1-5 – *189*
14:20 – *20*
15:14 – *99*
17:21 – *257*

Romans

1 – 270
1- 4 – 126
1-11 – 126
1:17 – 217
2 – 6, 99, 105, 108, 110, 129, 130, 139, 142, 143, 271
2:6 – 99, 102, 104, 106, 108, 109
2:6-7 – 90, 98, 99, 136
2:7 – 99, 108
2:10 – 99
2:11 – 107
2:13 – 90, 99, 100, 101, 106
2:25 – 109
3 – 84, 105, 142, 218, 270
3-4 – 126
3:9 – 109
3:20 – 100, 101, 102
3:20-28 – 113, 117
3:20-31 – 90, 113
3:21 – 114, 115, 117
3:22 – 119
3:23 – 119
3:27 – 109
4 – 270
4:4 – 99
4:4-5 – 109
4:25 – 127, 131
5 – 97, 125, 126, 225, 235, 270
5:12 – 232
5-6 – 126
6 – 90, 93, 97, 119, 120, 122, 125, 126, 131, 143, 144, 235, 270, 271
6:1 – 98, 125, 235
6:2 – 125
6:4 – 127
6:5 – 127, 129
6:6 – 127
6:7 – 127
6:10 – 127
6:11 – 16
6:23 – 107, 127
7-10 – 126
7:14-23 – 95
8 – 6, 41, 90, 93, 108, 110, 130, 133, 136, 142, 143, 184, 186, 210, 249, 270
8:1-30 – 133
8:1 – 133
8:2 – 133, 134
8:3 – 133, 189
8:4 – 133, 135
8:6 – 133
8:8 – 133
8:9 – 133, 136, 172, 235
8:10 – 133
8:11 – 133
8:13 – 2, 133, 134, 136
8:14 – 133
8:15 – 133
8:17 – 137, 138, 140
8:23 – 133
8:26 – 238
8:28 – 133, 137
8:28-30 – 143, 255
8:29 – 89, 133, 140
8:29-30 – 108, 111, 142, 222
8:30 – 133, 266
9-11 – 113
9:32 – 109
10 – 270
10:5 – 109
11 – 126, 270
11:6 – 99, 109
12 – 271
13 – 98

1 Corinthians

1:9 – 277
1:13 – 232, 271
1:30 – 2, 165, 198, 205, 207, 217, 218, 219, 221, 223, 224, 226, 228, 236, 237, 239, 240, 241, 270
3 – 270, 271
3:8 – 99
4 – 271

Scripture Index

6 – *270*
6:13 – *232*
6:15 – *257*
6:15-16 – *232*
9 – *270*
9:17 – *99*
11 – *156, 265*
11:27 – *180, 182*
11:27-29 – *160, 180*
13:3 – *99*
15 – *271*
15:58 – *99*

2 Corinthians
1 – *271*
4 – *130, 270*
5 – *138, 270, 271*
5:10 – *99*
6 – *270*
9 – *271*

Galatians
2 – *271*
2:15-21 – *67*
3 – *270*
3:27 – *89*
4 – *271*
5 – *84, 270, 271*
5:6 – *99*
6:8 – *99*

Ephesians
1 – *270, 271*
2 – *270*
2:14 – *239*
4:15 – *89*
4:20 – *229*
5:5 – *99*
5:21-27 – *55*
5:29-30 – *257*
5:30 – *89*

Philippians
1:21 – *99*

2:12 – *99*
3 – *270*

Colossians
1 – *270, 271*
1:10 – *99*
1:22 – *229*
1:23 – *232*
3 – *271*
3:23-24 – *99*

1 Thessalonians
3 – *271*
4 – *271*
5 – *271*

2 Thessalonians
1 – *271*

1 Timothy
2 – *225*
6 – *271*

2 Timothy
1 – *270*
2 – *270*

Titus
2 – *270*
3 – *270*

Hebrews
2:7 – *122*
6:10 – *99*
12:14 – *266*
13:16 – *99*

1 Peter
3:21 – *233*

2 Peter
1:4 – *50, 258*
3:21 – *234*

1 John
2:2 – *189*
3:7 – *99*
5:18 – *263*

2 John
8 – *99*

Apocrypha

Wisdom
3:15 – *99*
5:16 – *99*
10:17 – *99*

Ecclesiasticus
2:8 – *99*
3:3 – *99*
9:10 – *99*
12:5 – *99*
16:15 – *99*

General Index

Abraham 95, 114
Adam 23, 96, 121-22, 142, 176, 189, 204, 219 n.64
adoption 4 n.6, 117, 126, 133 n.116, 134, 136-138, 138 n.127, 139-41, 185 n.111, 187 n.188, 229
Agricola, John 103, 206, 206 n.24
Altenstaig, Johannes 48-49
Ambrose 174, 270
Anabaptism 31
Andreae, Jacob 207
anthropology 95, 115, 145, 265
Aquinas, Thomas 49, 51, 60, 170-71, 177 n.89, 194
Aristotle 59, 118, 118 n.73, 146
Armstrong, Brian 21-24
Athanasius 50
Athenagoras 49
Augsburg Confession 198
Augustine 49, 51, 56-57, 59, 62, 90, 99 n.25, 105, 113-14, 149, 154, 157, 161, 174, 179-80, 182, 188-89, 194, 218, 218 n.60, 229, 270
Bahmann, Manfred K. 268, 268 n.25
baptism 39, 43, 54, 96-97, 120-21, 127-28, 142, 151-52, 214
Barth, Karl 12, 27, 122, 256, 265

Basil of Caesarea 50
Battles, Ford Lewis 22
Bauke, Herman 21-22
beatific vision 122
Bell, Charles 191
Berkouwer, G. C. 209, 209 n.35, 248
Bernard of Clairvaux 33, 62-63, 70-71
Beza, Theodor 159, 200 n.6, 215-16, 273, 283
Biel, Gabriel 48-49, 51, 59-60
Bizer, Ernst 217
body of Christ 5, 73 n.80, 115, 117, 128, 152, 155, 157, 162-66, 168, 170-71, 177, 179-81, 183, 185-86, 230-32, 233 n.93, 234, 274-75, 277, 283-85
Bolsec, Jerome 91, 139 n.130
Bonaventure 49, 51, 59
Bouwsma, William 22
Brenz, Johann 103, 205, 230
Brglez, H. A. 33, 34 n.76, 191
Brunner, Peter 13
Bucer, Martin 17 n.22, 31, 37-38, 38 n.86, 39, 78-80, 82, 91-92, 101-102, 105-106, 113, 141, 146, 156, 194, 259 n.9
Bullinger, Heinrich 38, 38 n.86, 74 n.85, 76, 76 n.89, 92, 156, 156 n.21, 231

Butin, Philip 25-26, 153 n.13
Cajetan, Thomas de Vio 92, 100
Calvin, John *passim; Bondage and Liberation of the Will* 77-78; *Catechism* 36, 131 n.109, 219-20; christology of 24-25, 34, 42, 172, 174-76, 179-80, 184, 193, 193 n.126, 194-95, 234, 236, 241, 255-56, 259, 265, 268; *Clear Explanation* 158; covenantal theology of 29-30, 262; *Commentary on 1Cor.* 2, n.3, 180-81, 226, 236, 239-40; *Commentary on Isaiah* 211-12; *Commentary on Romans* 2 n.3, 6, 36-39, 39 n.88, 40-41, 84, 90-95, 98, 106-107, 109-110, 113-14, 123, 125, 133, 138, 144, 146, 184, 210, 213, 235-36, 240, 249, 255-56, 268, 269-70; *Defense* 154, 156-57, 274; eucharistic theology and debates of 25, 28, 42, 45, 150-95, 198, 230, 234, 236, 243, 246-51, 256, 258, 267-68; exegesis/hermeneutics of 37-41, 108, 178, 236, 255; *Institutes* 1, 2 n.3, 3 n.5, 4 n.6 n.7, 17, 19-24, 31, 36-38, 39 n.88, 45, 70, 84, 89-91, 93, 106, 109-110, 112, 131 n.109, 146-47, 155, 158, 167, 174, 176, 204 n.17, 208, 210, 214, 219, 221, 221 n.67, 236, 238, 240, 249, 256-57, 262, 269-70, 278, 286; *Last Admonition* 158; mysticism of 71-74, 257-58; "replication principle" of 90, 133, 137, 139, 141, 141 n.133, 142-44, 144 n.136, 145-46, 152, 159-60, 193, 222 n.68, 255; *Second Defense* 157, 171; soteriology of 13, 16, 18, 23-25, 27, 29-32, 34, 39 n.88, 42-43, 45, 47, 93, 98, 118, 133, 143-45, 160-65, 170, 172-74, 176, 184-85, 188, 190, 192-93, 193 n.126, 194, 219, 221, 230, 234, 236, 238-39, 241, 250-51, 255-56, 259, 262, 264, 266-67, 269; spirituality of 12, 14, 30-32, 42, 70, 74; trinitarianism of 24-25, 34, 176
Catholic doctrine 70, 76, 100-101, 229, 258
cause (see also "primary cause" and "secondary causes") 55, 79, 102, 105, 109-111, 114, 117-18, 123-24, 131, 137-38, 146-47, 204, 255, 263-64, 266 n.22, 267 n.24, 282
Chalcedon, Council of 149, 162-63, 194
christology (see also "Calvin, John, christology of") 25,

General Index   347

49-51, 93 n.13, 122 nn.82-83, 128 n.102, 149, 162-63, 169-70, 174, 183, 194, 197-98, 212, 228 n.81, 230, 233, 242-43, 245-48, 250-51
Chrysostom, John 101, 180, 226, 226 n.77, 227 n.79, 270
Church (see also "body of Christ") 22, 51-52, 54-55, 64, 67, 73-74, 85, 151, 194, 230-31, 260, 262
Cicero 229
Clement of Alexandria 229
conditional language 6, 23, 46, 75, 77, 90, 99, 108, 119, 130, 137, 138 n.127, 142, 145, 255, 262
conscience 97-98, 114, 124, 133-34, 206, 248
Consensus Tigurinus 153-54, 173, 274
Contarini, Gasparo 82
cooperative grace 100, 105
covenant 29, 76-77, 183
cross/*crux* 61, 64, 125, 130-31, 137-40, 142-43
Cyril of Alexandria 50, 156, 218
Davis, Thomas J. 154, 167
D'Avray, David 53, 55, 73 n.81
Dean, Albert Clarke 270
death 96, 141, 237
death and resurrection (see also "Jesus Christ, death of" and "resurrection of") 120, 127-29, 131, 141-42

debitum 109 n.54
deification 50-51, 67 n.62, 174, 209, 257-58
De Kroon, Marijn 242, 242 n.108, 257-58, 258 n.6
De Reims, Pierre 54
Devotio Moderna 31, 120, 120 n.77, 144
divine essence 206, 219, 228, 233, 243-44
divine love 76, 95, 146, 224, 263
divinization (see "deification")
double justification 83, 141, 141 n.133, 146
Dowey, Edward A. 19-22
Doyle, Robert C. 18 n.23, 31
Dupuy, Michel 49-50
duplex cognitio 21-22
duplex gratia 3, 4, 4 n.6, 6, 12, 12 n.2, 14, 18, 22, 29-33, 36, 43, 46, 78, 126-27, 132-33, 135 n.121, 142 n.134, 151, 169, 190, 193, 219, 224, 235-36, 240, 252, 255, 265, 279, 286-87
duplex iustitia 5, 47, 58, 79, 141
duplex regeneratio 133
Eck, John 75, 82, 98-99, 107
elect 134, 173, 182, 187, 189, 256, 263, 275, 279-81, 285
election 16, 20, 79, 107, 137, 142, 147
engrafting 5, 71, 98, 120, 122, 127-29, 131, 141-43, 179

Erasmus, Desiderius 101, 101 n.29, 105, 121-22, 127, 200 n.6
eschaton 105, 113
eternal life 21, 79, 108, 110-13, 123, 130-31, 136, 141-43, 144 n.136, 145, 147, 152, 159, 179, 182, 207, 255, 260, 266
Eucharist (see also "Calvin, John, eucharistic theology and debates of") 6, 42-43, 53, 81, 85, 150, 161, 230, 259
Evans, G. R. 161
exemplar 95, 98, 130, 139, 144
Faber, Jelle 265
faith 5, 16-18, 20-21, 23, 27, 29, 33, 42, 50, 54-56, 58, 64-66, 68, 71, 75-77, 79, 83-84, 94-95, 98-100, 102-105, 108, 113-119, 123-25, 134, 136, 142, 144 n.136, 146, 150, 150 n.1, 152, 155, 155 n.16, 159, 163, 163 n.42, 168-71, 172 n.68, 173-74, 179-82, 187, 187 n.118, 188-89, 200, 203-205-207, 207 nn.26-27, 209-10, 219-23, 227-28, 235-39, 244 n.115, 245, 248-50, 256, 260, 262-64, 266, 275, 280-86
Feenstra, Ronald J. 210, 251
first causes (see "primary causes")
Flacius Illyricus, Matthew 201, 205-206, 215

forgiveness 98, 105, 114, 125-26, 133, 151, 184, 190, 193, 204-206, 234, 237, 252, 255, 260, 266
Formula of Concord 200-201, 207-208, 242
Friedrich, Johann 83
fruit 105, 114, 128, 130, 141, 165-66, 179, 194, 206, 216, 267 n.24, 277, 282
Gamble, Richard 40-41
Ganoczy, Alexandre 21-22, 27
Gentile, Valentine 233
Gerrish, Brian 182, 279 n.22, 286
Gerson, Jean 49, 51-52, 63, 65
Gleason, Randall C. 32
glorification 107-108, 110-11, 113, 137, 142-44, 147
God 95-96, 98-119, 122, 124-27, 129, 131-39, 142-43, 145-47, 149-52, 159, 162, 164, 167, 170, 175, 180, 183-84, 187-90, 198, 203-204, 207, 207 n.26, 212, 218-19, 222-29, 231, 233, 233 n.93, 236-37, 239, 242, 244-45, 255, 260, 263-64, 266, 275, 277, 280-81, 283, 285
God the Father 24-25, 50, 78, 176, 207, 225, 232-33, 247
Gorham, George C. 283-84
gospel 94-95, 103, 105, 107, 112-13, 123, 125-26, 159, 161, 206-207, 232, 241, 263, 268, 284

General Index

grace (see also *"duplex gratia"*) 27, 48, 52, 56-58, 60-61, 66-67, 76, 89, 95-101, 105, 111, 113-15, 118-20, 126, 128, 132, 135, 137-38, 142, 147, 150, 150 n.1, 151-52, 155, 161, 164-66, 169-70, 172 n.68, 173-74, 176, 181-83, 188, 190, 192, 205, 209, 216, 219-20, 223-24, 227-28, 237, 241, 244-46, 248, 252, 262, 262 n.16, 282-83
Gregory of Nyssa 49
Gregory of Rimini 49, 62
Grimani, Cardinal Marino 100-101
Gropper, Johann 82
Grynaeus, Simon 38
Guilliaud, Claude 100
habitus 80
Haresche, Philibert 100, 100 n.28
Hart, Trevor 13, 27, 191
Herborn, Nikolaus 107
Heshusius, Tilemann 42, 154, 156 n.19, 158, 159 nn.32-33, 166, 169-70, 183, 192, 193 n.126, 202, 213-15, 242, 243 n.109, 247
Hilary of Poitiers 174, 218
Hodge, Charles 267 n.24
Holy Spirit 3, 4, 5, 16, 18, 20-21, 24-25, 27-28, 42, 50, 71, 76, 79-80, 85, 89-90, 97-98, 108, 112-15, 117, 125-27, 129, 131, 133-41, 143-44, 144 n.136, 146, 149, 151, 154, 162-66, 168-70, 172-84, 187-90, 193-95, 208 n.31, 210, 214, 217, 219-21, 223, 225, 227, 229, 232-35, 235 n.100, 236, 238, 239 n.104, 244-45, 247-50, 255-56, 258, 263-64, 275-80, 282-83, 285-86
Hugh of St. Victor 51, 229
human nature 26, 54, 124, 128, 145
humiliation-exaltation pattern 98, 141, 142, 255 n.134, 144, 144 n.135
image of Christ 2, 138-39, 187, 204
image of God 111, 113, 138, 204, 229, 233 n.93, 234 n.98
imitatio Christi 74, 90, 120-22, 129-30, 136, 139, 141, 144, 144 n.136, 145
impartation 79
imputation 4 n.7, 54, 79, 82-85, 102, 104, 104 n.41, 106, 120, 123, 123 n.86, 124, 126, 132, 135, 135 n.122, 146, 151-52, 204-205, 244, 248, 250, 252
incarnational union (see "natural union")
inferior causes (see "secondary causes")
inheritance 111, 133 n.116, 137, 138 n.127, 141-43, 145, 147
Irenaeus 49
Irving, Edward 122

iustitia Dei/righteousness of God (see also "Jesus Christ, righteousness of/*iustitia Christi*") 56, 58, 60, 98, 102, 113-14, 117, 142, 212, 217, 223, 243, 244 n.115

Jacobs, Paul 13

James, Frank 79-80, 261, 261 n.13

Jenson, Robert W. 1 n.2, 67 n.62

Jesus Christ 3, 27, 42, 44, 47, 49-50, 52, 53, 59-60, 63-66, 68, 76, 84, 89, 95-98, 100-101, 108, 112-13, 115, 117-22, 128-29, 131, 133, 136-40, 142, 142 n.134, 143-46, 149-53, 155, 157, 159-61, 163-65, 167-89, 191-94, 198, 202, 204, 209-10, 213-14, 217, 219-23, 225, 227-28, 230-32, 234-39, 241-47, 249-51, 255-58, 264, 268, 277, 281; ascension of 163; death of 4, 31-32, 42, 100, 125-33, 169, 178, 234, 236, 243; divinity of 54, 55, 161, 163, 169, 194, 204, 205 n.19, 212, 218, 230, 242, 247; humanity of 149, 161, 163, 169, 175, 177, 191-92, 194, 205 n.19, 213, 230, 245, 247, 249; incarnation of 26, 100, 185, 212; as Mediator 149, 163-64, 174-76, 178 n.92, 179, 205, 216, 250, 255, 275, 281; resurrection of 4, 31-32, 42, 100, 129-33; righteousness of/*iustitia Christi* 58, 60-61, 77, 81, 85, 104, 118, 123, 142, 142 n.134, 146, 169, 194, 203-204, 206-207, 223, 225, 260, 264; union with *passim*

justification 2, 4, 4 n.6 n.7, 5-7, 12-14, 20-24, 26-32, 39, 43-46, 47, 53, 58-62, 64-65, 68, 70-71, 74-86, 94-98, 100-102, 104, 104 n.41, 105-107, 113-20, 122, 125-27, 131-33, 133 n.116, 134, 136, 139-40, 142 n.134, 145, 146, 149, 151, 153, 160, 162-65, 168-69, 172-73, 184, 187 n.118, 189-90, 193-94, 197-201, 201 n.9, 202-205, 205 n.19, 207 n.27, 208 n.31, 211, 213, 213 n.46, 216-18, 218 n.61, 220-21, 223-24, 225 n.73, 227-29, 235, 235 n.100, 236-38, 239 n.104, 241-44, 244 n.115, 245-48, 250-52, 255-56, 258-61, 261 nn.12-13, 262-64, 266-67, 267 n.24, 268, 274-75, 278-87

Karlstadt, Andreas Bodenstein von 150

Keller, Carl-A. 71, 213 n.46, 257-58

Kennedy, Kevin Dixon 192

kingdom 151

knowledge of God 18, 20, 21, 48
koinonia 50
Kok, Joel 101, 105
Kolb, Robert 201
Kolfhaus, W. 13, 33, 71
Kreck, Walter 13
Kuyper, Abraham 257
Lane, Anthony N. S. 5 n.12, 83, 83 n.115, 84, 84 n.118, 193 n.126, 227 n.79
law 13, 50, 53, 59-60, 66, 75-77, 96, 100-101, 103, 103 n.38, 104 n.41, 107, 113-15, 118, 122, 125-26, 134-35, 206-207, 219-20
Lefèvre d'Étaples, Jacques 101, 105, 121-22
Lillback, Peter 29-30, 76-77, 78 n.97
Lombard, Peter 59, 161, 205, 270
Lord's Supper (see also "Eucharist") 149-51, 153, 157, 159-60, 163-66, 168, 170, 172, 174, 177-84, 188, 194, 210, 210 n.39, 214-15, 242, 245-46, 249-51, 258
love (see also "divine love") 51-52, 61, 64, 83-84
Lucretius 229
Luther, Martin 29-30, 44, 47, 53, 56, 58-67, 67 n.62, 68, 73-78, 78 n.97, 80-86, 93, 98, 103, 117, 150, 155, 197, 198 n.2, 200, 200 n.6, 201-202, 204, 217-18, 242;

Freedom of a Christian 65-66, 258, 262
Lutheranism 7, 13, 30, 42, 45, 105, 145, 158, 160, 162-63, 165-66, 168-71, 173-74, 176-77, 180-81, 185, 192-94, 197-201, 205, 207-10, 213-16, 229, 230, 241-43, 245-48, 250-52, 256-61, 277
manducatio impiorum 160, 160 n.36, 165, 168 n.58, 170-71, 173-74, 177, 179-80, 182-83, 185, 192-94, 256-57
Manichaeism 233, 243
Major, John 69 n.65
Marburg Colloquy 150, 202
marriage 53-57, 64-66, 68, 72-73, 73 n.80
marriage sermons 53-54, 61
marriage union with Christ 65-66
McGinn, Bernard 62
McGrath, Alister E. 57
McKee, Elsie Anne 262, 269
McLelland, J. C. 280
medieval nominalism (late) 48, 61, 67
medieval theology and religion (see also "mysticism") 35, 47-48, 53, 55, 57-63, 68, 85, 101, 114, 116-17, 120, 161, 170, 180, 183
Melanchthon, Philip 7, 24, 31, 37-38, 38 n.86, 39 44, 67 n.62, 78 n.97, 81-82, 95 n.19, 101-103, 103 n.38,

104, 104 n.41, 105-107, 113, 120, 122, 122 n.42, 123-25, 132, 135 nn.121-22, 138 n.127, 140 n.132, 141, 145, 155, 199, 204-207, 213-17, 248, 250, 259, 259 n.10, 260; necessity principle of 122-25

merit/*meritum* 52, 59-60, 76-77, 82, 93 n.15, 98, 99 n.23, 103, 109 n.54, 184, 206, 239, 255-56, 260-65

model (see "*exemplar*")

Mörlin, Joachim 205-206, 218 n.61

mortification 4, 14, 120, 122-23, 125, 127-28, 130-33, 151, 265

Muller, Richard A. 3 n.5, 174, 175 n.81, 191

Musculus, Wolfgang 256

mysticism 47-48, 51, 53, 55-56, 61-65, 67, 68-69, 71-72, 72 n.77, 73, 73 n.80, 74, 85, 120-21, 257-58

mystic union (see "*unio mystica*")

natural union with Christ 185-87, 187 n.118, 188, 190-91, 256, 273 n.1, 275-76, 278-79, 279 n.22, 280-82

necessity 30-31, 36, 56, 80-82, 85-86, 90, 95, 97, 101 n.31, 104, 104 n.41, 106, 112, 122-24, 131, 138, 138 n.127, 143, 145, 145 n.136, 160, 163 n.42, 175 n.78, 193-94, 206, 228, 230, 239, 241, 266, 266 n.22, 267

Neo-Platonism 50

Niesel, Wilhelm 12, 17, 209, 250, 261 n.12

obedience 59-60, 76, 80, 86, 93 n.15, 99, 103-104, 104 n.41, 105, 107, 109, 111, 115, 118, 123-24, 137, 138 n.127, 139, 141-142, 142 n.134, 143-46, 151-52, 160, 169, 194, 206-207, 225, 225 n.73, 236, 241, 243, 255

Oberman, Heiko A. 53, 55, 57-61, 63, 65, 170 n.62

Ockham, William 60

ontology 22, 72 n.77, 85, 128 n.104, 149, 162, 176, 204-205, 225, 227, 241-43, 247-49, 275, 277

ordo 108-111, 117, 131, 137, 141-42, 142 n.134, 145, 222 n.68, 255

Origen 95 n.19, 101

Osiander, Andreas 2, 7, 43-45, 72, 74, 86, 91 n. 3, 103, 158, 195, 197-99, 199 n.4, 200, 200 n.6, 201-204, 204 n.17, 205-218, 223-29, 233-34, 236, 239-52, 256-57, 259, 265, 268

Owen, John Michael 212

Ozment, Steven 58, 63

Parker, T. H. L. 13, 19, 21, 38, 41, 91-93, 100, 212 n.43

Partee, Charles 18

Paul, the Apostle 6, 36, 39 n.87, 59, 79 n.101, 89-90, 92-103, 106-109, 109 n.53, 111, 112 n.58, 113-14, 119, 119 n.76, 120-26, 126 n.95, 126 n.97, 129-33, 135-137, 139-40, 142-43, 198, 207, 217, 219, 222 n.68, 224-27, 232, 237, 241, 262, 277
Payne, John B. 122
Pelagius 95 n.19
Pelikan, Jaroslav 202-204, 252
Pflug, Julius 82
Pharisees 122
Pighius, Albert 77, 91
Pistorius, Johann 82
predestination 91, 137, 259
prevenient grace 60
primary cause 102, 137-38, 145-46
Pseudo-Dionysius 50
Quintilian 229
Rankin, Duncan 28, 33, 43, 185, 275 n.5, 278 n.19, 279, 279 n.21, 280, 280 n.28, 281, 286
reconciliation to God 55, 58, 117, 131-32, 190, 228, 275, 277, 279, 281-85
Redding, Graham 192
redemption 4, 18, 21, 26, 29, 93, 120, 178, 198, 206, 219, 222, 227, 237, 255, 267, 280-81
Reformation 7, 22, 24, 35, 40, 44, 62, 65, 74, 85-86, 101, 114, 118 n.73, 119, 123, 149, 154, 198, 216, 221, 241, 252, 259, 261, 264, 266, 274
regeneration 4 n.7, 20, 22, 31, 80, 82, 96-97, 107 n.51, 111, 126, 133-36, 151, 173, 204, 221, 224, 235, 237, 265, 279, 281
Regensburg Colloquy 5, 5 n.12, 81-84
Renaissance 22, 24, 40
renewal 80, 85, 105-107, 117, 120, 123, 124 n.88, 127 n.99, 128, 134, 151, 168, 190, 193, 204, 206, 244, 246, 248
repentance 4 n.7, 31, 125, 182, 266 n.22
replication (see "Calvin, John, 'replication principle' of")
res 149, 151, 161, 161 n.39, 162, 166-67, 171, 173, 179, 189, 256
resurrection, day of 238
reward (see also "merit") 77-78, 98-99, 99 n.23, 102, 102 n.32, 103, 104 n.41, 105-108, 109 n.53, 110, 112, 118, 136, 141, 142 n.134, 143, 145, 255
righteousness (see also "Jesus Christ, righteousness of") 2, 23, 56, 58, 60, 66, 68, 75, 77, 79, 81-85, 95-97, 105-106, 106 n.45, 112-15, 117-19, 119 n.76, 123, 126, 126 n.97, 127 n.98, 129 n.107, 131-32, 134, 136, 145, 151,

159, 170, 184, 198, 204, 206-208, 211, 214, 216-18, 221-25, 227-28, 234, 236-39, 241, 243-48, 252, 268
Rihel, Wendelin 91
Rupp, Gordon 256
sacramentarians 155, 157
sacraments 6, 16-17, 29, 42-43, 55, 60, 64, 97 n.21, 149-50, 150 n.1, 151-53, 156 n.19, 159-62, 163 n.42, 164-67, 167 n.56, 168, 171, 173, 179, 182-84, 187 n.118, 188, 190, 193, 195, 245
Sadoleto, Jacques 82, 102, 102 n.37, 168, 220, 230, 231 n.90, 240
salvation 89, 101-102, 109-112, 114, 126, 130-32, 137-43, 145-46, 149-50, 152-53, 159-60, 162-65, 174, 177-78, 184, 188, 190, 192-95, 198, 205, 208, 213-14, 220, 223-24, 235, 237, 239, 241-42, 245, 247-49, 251-52, 255, 260-62, 266, 278, 281
salvation, economy of 2
sanctification 2, 4, 4 n.6 n.7, 5-7, 12-13, 21-24, 26-32, 39, 43, 45-46, 75, 77, 80, 83-85, 96-98, 102, 104, 104 n.41, 105, 113, 120-21, 125-26, 126 n.95, 126 n.97, 127, 127 n.100, 132-33, 133 n.116, 134, 136, 142 n.134, 143-46, 151, 153, 160, 162-65, 168-69, 172-73, 184, 187 n.118,

190, 193-94, 198, 204-206, 207 n.27, 208 n.31, 209-10, 219-24, 227-28, 234-35, 235 n.100, 236-39, 239 n.104, 140-41, 247-48, 250-52, 255-58, 262-64, 267-68, 274-86
scholasticism 68
Schwenckfeld, Caspar 158
Scots Confession 212
Scotus, John Duns 49, 51, 59-60, 170 n.62
secondary causes 102, 111, 142, 147
Sedgwick, Obadiah 266
Selnecker, Nikolaus 202
Seneca 229
Servetus, Michael 91, 153, 233, 242 n.108
signa 149, 151, 155, 161, 161 n.39, 162, 167-69, 171, 173, 179, 188-89, 192, 256
sin 23, 63, 85, 95-97, 114-17, 122, 125, 125 n.94, 126, 127 n.98, 128 n.103, 132-35, 135 n.121, 136, 151, 173, 184, 187, 190, 193, 201, 204, 206-207, 229, 232, 234-37, 252, 260, 266
Smedes, Lewis 209, 209 n.35
sola Scriptura 40
sons of God 112-13, 134, 137, 139, 144 n.136, 263
soul 20, 54-55, 63-66, 68, 152, 163, 192, 221, 233 n.95, 275
Smalcald Articles 197

soteriology (see also "Calvin, John, soteriology of") 3, 6, 11, 23, 27, 58-59, 61-62, 65, 72 n.77, 74, 77, 90, 96, 98, 114-16, 117, 120, 143, 149, 198, 228 n.81, 246-47, 258, 267-68
Spangenberg, Cyriakus 218
spiritual union with Christ 186-87, 187 n.118, 188-90, 224, 256-57, 275-76, 278-282, 285-86
Stancaro, Francesco 205, 205 n.19
Staupitz, Johannes von 62
Steinmetz, David C. 74
Stephens, W. Peter 79, 149-50
Stevenson, Kenneth 73
suffering 64, 98, 133 n.116, 136-38, 138 n.127, 139-42, 142 n.134, 143-44, 234, 255, 265
Tamburello, Dennis E. 16, 33, 43, 70-72, 74, 257, 279, 279 nn.22-23, 280 n.28, 280-81, 286
Tauler, Johannes 62-63, 65
Tertullian 27, 233 n.94
Theologia Deutsch 72
Torrance, J. B. 191
Torrance, T. F. 13, 185, 185 n.111, 191, 278, 280
transubstantiation 155, 171, 181
Trent, Council of 5, 77, 81, 90-91, 93 n.15, 114, 114 n.60, 115, 115 n.63, 116, 116 n.68, 117, 118 n.73, 141-42
tribunal of God 117
Trumper, Tim J. R. 43
Tylenda, Joseph N. 157-58
ubiquitarianism 149, 160, 162, 166, 172, 180, 184, 194, 197, 230, 242-45, 247-48, 250
ultimate cause (see "primary cause")
unio Christi-duplex gratia model 3, 6, 12, 30, 34, 42-43, 78, 90, 153, 160, 163, 184, 194, 198 n.2, 213, 219, 238, 241, 246, 250, 256-57, 260-61, 261 n.12, 267
unio mystica 57, 62, 65, 67, 70-71, 72 n.77, 74, 186-87, 187 n.118, 188, 190, 192, 224, 256-57, 278-80, 282
Ursinus, Zacharias 266
Ussher, James 218 n.60
van't Spijker, Willem 258
Venema, Cornelis Paul 12-14, 22, 34 n.76
Vermigli, Peter Martyr 28, 43, 79-80, 108-109 n.53, 156, 185, 185 n.112, 186, 186 n.116, 187, 187 n.118, 189, 192, 194, 230, 261, 261 n.13, 273-78, 280-86
Via Moderna 57
vivification 4, 14, 120, 124-25, 127-28, 130-31, 133, 172, 176, 181, 184, 193, 213
Walchenbach, John Robert 226

Wallace, Ronald S. 16
Wendel, François 14, n.11, 15, 15 n.13, 200, 209, 251, 257 n.3
Westminster Assembly 266
Westphal, Joachim 42, 154, 154 n.15, 155-56, 156 n.19, 157-58, 165-66, 169, 171-72, 174, 177-78, 182, 210, 213, 215, 242, 247-48
Wigand, Johannes 202
will 20, 59-60, 91, 101, 124, 143
Willis-Watkins, E. David 17, 27-28, 34, 278
Word of God 150, 152, 159, 161, 176, 183, 208 n.31
works 26, 29-31, 36, 55-56, 60, 90, 93 n.15, 98-99, 99 n.25, 100-101, 101 n.31, 103, 103 n.38, 104, 104 n.41, 105-106, 106 nn.41-42, 107, 107 n.51, 108, 108 n.53, 109, 109 n.53, 110-19, 119 n.76, 121, 123-25, 133 n.116, 137-39, 141, 141 n.133, 142-43, 145, 145 n.136, 146-47, 151, 165, 168-69, 184, 193-94, 205-206, 221-23, 228, 230, 237, 239, 241, 252, 255, 259-64, 266-68
Zimmermann, Von Gunter 209
Zwingli, Ulrich 150, 155 n.16, 200 n.6

Studies in Christian History and Thought
(All titles uniform with this volume)
Dates in bold are of projected publication

David Bebbington
Holiness in Nineteenth-Century England
David Bebbington stresses the relationship of movements of spirituality to changes in their cultural setting, especially the legacies of the Enlightenment and Romanticism. He shows that these broad shifts in ideological mood had a profound effect on the ways in which piety was conceptualized and practised. Holiness was intimately bound up with the spirit of the age.

2000 / 0-85364-981-2 / viii + 98pp

J. William Black
Reformation Pastors
Richard Baxter and the Ideal of the Reformed Pastor
This work examines Richard Baxter's *Gildas Salvianus, The Reformed Pastor* (1656) and explores each aspect of his pastoral strategy in light of his own concern for 'reformation' and in the broader context of Edwardian, Elizabethan and early Stuart pastoral ideals and practice.

2003 / 1-84227-190-3 / xxii + 308pp

James Bruce
Prophecy, Miracles, Angels, *and* Heavenly Light?
The Eschatology, Pneumatology and Missiology of Adomnán's Life of Columba
This book surveys approaches to the marvellous in hagiography, providing the first critique of Plummer's hypothesis of Irish saga origin. It then analyses the uniquely systematized phenomena in the *Life of Columba* from Adomnán's seventh-century theological perspective, identifying the coming of the eschatological Kingdom as the key to understanding.

2004 / 1-84227-227-6 / xviii + 286pp

Colin J. Bulley
The Priesthood of Some Believers
Developments from the General to the Special Priesthood in the Christian Literature of the First Three Centuries
The first in-depth treatment of early Christian texts on the priesthood of all believers shows that the developing priesthood of the ordained related closely to the division between laity and clergy and had deleterious effects on the practice of the general priesthood.

2000 / 1-84227-034-6 / xii + 336pp

Anthony R. Cross (ed.)
Ecumenism and History
Studies in Honour of John H.Y. Briggs
This collection of essays examines the inter-relationships between the two fields in which Professor Briggs has contributed so much: history—particularly Baptist and Nonconformist—and the ecumenical movement. With contributions from colleagues and former research students from Britain, Europe and North America, *Ecumenism and History* provides wide-ranging studies in important aspects of Christian history, theology and ecumenical studies.

2002 / 1-84227-135-0 / xx + 362pp

Maggi Dawn
Confessions of an Inquiring Spirit
Form as Constitutive of Meaning in S.T. Coleridge's Theological Writing
This study of Coleridge's *Confessions* focuses on its confessional, epistolary and fragmentary form, suggesting that attention to these features significantly affects its interpretation. Bringing a close study of these three literary forms, the author suggests ways in which they nuance the text with particular understandings of the Trinity, and of a kenotic christology. Some parallels are drawn between Romantic and postmodern dilemmas concerning the authority of the biblical text.

2006 / 1-84227-255-1 / approx. 224 pp

Ruth Gouldbourne
The Flesh and the Feminine
Gender and Theology in the Writings of Caspar Schwenckfeld
Caspar Schwenckfeld and his movement exemplify one of the radical communities of the sixteenth century. Challenging theological and liturgical norms, they also found themselves challenging social and particularly gender assumptions. In this book, the issues of the relationship between radical theology and the understanding of gender are considered.

2005 / 1-84227-048-6 / approx. 304pp

Crawford Gribben
Puritan Millennialism
Literature and Theology, 1550–1682
Puritan Millennialism surveys the growth, impact and eventual decline of puritan millennialism throughout England, Scotland and Ireland, arguing that it was much more diverse than has frequently been suggested. This Paternoster edition is revised and extended from the original 2000 text.

2007 / 1-84227-372-8 / approx. 320pp

Galen K. Johnson
Prisoner of Conscience
John Bunyan on Self, Community and Christian Faith

This is an interdisciplinary study of John Bunyan's understanding of conscience across his autobiographical, theological and fictional writings, investigating whether conscience always deserves fidelity, and how Bunyan's view of conscience affects his relationship both to modern Western individualism and historic Christianity.

2003 / 1-84227-223-3 / xvi + 236pp

R.T. Kendall
Calvin and English Calvinism to 1649

The author's thesis is that those who formed the Westminster Confession of Faith, which is regarded as Calvinism, in fact departed from John Calvin on two points: (1) the extent of the atonement and (2) the ground of assurance of salvation.

1997 / 0-85364-827-1 / xii + 264pp

Timothy Larsen
Friends of Religious Equality
Nonconformist Politics in Mid-Victorian England

During the middle decades of the nineteenth century the English Nonconformist community developed a coherent political philosophy of its own, of which a central tenet was the principle of religious equality (in contrast to the stereotype of Evangelical Dissenters). The Dissenting community fought for the civil rights of Roman Catholics, non-Christians and even atheists on an issue of principle which had its flowering in the enthusiastic and undivided support which Nonconformity gave to the campaign for Jewish emancipation. This reissued study examines the political efforts and ideas of English Nonconformists during the period, covering the whole range of national issues raised, from state education to the Crimean War. It offers a case study of a theologically conservative group defending religious pluralism in the civic sphere, showing that the concept of religious equality was a grand vision at the centre of the political philosophy of the Dissenters.

2007 / 1-84227-402-3 / x + 300pp

Byung-Ho Moon
Christ the Mediator of the Law
Calvin's Christological Understanding of the Law as the Rule of Living and Life-Giving

This book explores the coherence between Christology and soteriology in Calvin's theology of the law, examining its intellectual origins and his position on the concept and extent of Christ's mediation of the law. A comparative study between Calvin and contemporary Reformers—Luther, Bucer, Melancthon and Bullinger—and his opponent Michael Servetus is made for the purpose of pointing out the unique feature of Calvin's Christological understanding of the law.

2005 / 1-84227-318-3 / approx. 370pp

John Eifion Morgan-Wynne
Holy Spirit and Religious Experience in Christian Writings, c.AD 90–200

This study examines how far Christians in the third to fifth generations (c.AD 90–200) attributed their sense of encounter with the divine presence, their sense of illumination in the truth or guidance in decision-making, and their sense of ethical empowerment to the activity of the Holy Spirit in their lives.

2005 / 1-84227-319-1 / approx. 350pp

James I. Packer
The Redemption and Restoration of Man in the Thought of Richard Baxter

James I. Packer provides a full and sympathetic exposition of Richard Baxter's doctrine of humanity, created and fallen; its redemption by Christ Jesus; and its restoration in the image of God through the obedience of faith by the power of the Holy Spirit.

2002 / 1-84227-147-4 / 432pp

Andrew Partington,
Church and State
The Contribution of the Church of England Bishops to the House of Lords during the Thatcher Years

In *Church and State*, Andrew Partington argues that the contribution of the Church of England bishops to the House of Lords during the Thatcher years was overwhelmingly critical of the government; failed to have a significant influence in the public realm; was inefficient, being undertaken by a minority of those eligible to sit on the Bench of Bishops; and was insufficiently moral and spiritual in its content to be distinctive. On the basis of this, and the likely reduction of the number of places available for Church of England bishops in a fully reformed Second Chamber, the author argues for an evolution in the Church of England's approach to the service of its bishops in the House of Lords. He proposes the Church of England works to overcome the genuine obstacles which hinder busy diocesan bishops from contributing to the debates of the House of Lords and to its life more informally.

2005 / 1-84227-334-5 / approx. 324pp

Michael Pasquarello III
God's Ploughman
Hugh Latimer: A 'Preaching Life' (1490–1555)

This construction of a 'preaching life' situates Hugh Latimer within the larger religious, political and intellectual world of late medieval England. Neither biography, intellectual history, nor analysis of discrete sermon texts, this book is a work of homiletic history which draws from the details of Latimer's milieu to construct an interpretive framework for the preaching performances that formed the core of his identity as a religious reformer. Its goal is to illumine the practical wisdom embodied in the content, form and style of Latimer's preaching, and to recapture a sense of its overarching purpose, movement, and transforming force during the reform of sixteenth-century England.

2006 / 1-84227-336-1 / approx. 250pp

Alan P.F. Sell
Enlightenment, Ecumenism, Evangel
Theological Themes and Thinkers 1550–2000

This book consists of papers in which such interlocking topics as the Enlightenment, the problem of authority, the development of doctrine, spirituality, ecumenism, theological method and the heart of the gospel are discussed. Issues of significance to the church at large are explored with special reference to writers from the Reformed and Dissenting traditions.

2005 / 1-84227-330-2 / xviii + 422pp

Alan P.F. Sell
Hinterland Theology
Some Reformed and Dissenting Adjustments

Many books have been written on theology's 'giants' and significant trends, but what of those lesser-known writers who adjusted to them? In this book some hinterland theologians of the British Reformed and Dissenting traditions, who followed in the wake of toleration, the Evangelical Revival, the rise of modern biblical criticism and Karl Barth, are allowed to have their say. They include Thomas Ridgley, Ralph Wardlaw, T.V. Tymms and N.H.G. Robinson.

2006 / 1-84227-331-0 / approx. 350pp

Alan P.F. Sell and Anthony R. Cross (eds)
Protestant Nonconformity in the Twentieth Century

In this collection of essays scholars representative of a number of Nonconformist traditions reflect thematically on Nonconformists' life and witness during the twentieth century. Among the subjects reviewed are biblical studies, theology, worship, evangelism and spirituality, and ecumenism. Over and above its immediate interest, this collection provides a marker to future scholars and others wishing to know how some of their forebears assessed Nonconformity's contribution to a variety of fields during the century leading up to Christianity's third millennium.

2003 / 1-84227-221-7 / x + 398pp

Mark Smith
Religion in Industrial Society
Oldham and Saddleworth 1740–1865

This book analyses the way British churches sought to meet the challenge of industrialization and urbanization during the period 1740–1865. Working from a case-study of Oldham and Saddleworth, Mark Smith challenges the received view that the Anglican Church in the eighteenth century was characterized by complacency and inertia, and reveals Anglicanism's vigorous and creative response to the new conditions. He reassesses the significance of the centrally directed church reforms of the mid-nineteenth century, and emphasizes the importance of local energy and enthusiasm. Charting the growth of denominational pluralism in Oldham and Saddleworth, Dr Smith compares the strengths and weaknesses of the various Anglican and Nonconformist approaches to promoting church growth. He also demonstrates the extent to which all the churches participated in a common culture shaped by the influence of evangelicalism, and shows that active co-operation between the churches rather than denominational conflict dominated. This revised and updated edition of Dr Smith's challenging and original study makes an important contribution both to the social history of religion and to urban studies.

2006 / 1-84227-335-3 / approx. 300pp

Martin Sutherland
Peace, Toleration and Decay
The Ecclesiology of Later Stuart Dissent
This fresh analysis brings to light the complexity and fragility of the later Stuart Nonconformist consensus. Recent findings on wider seventeenth-century thought are incorporated into a new picture of the dynamics of Dissent and the roots of evangelicalism.
2003 / 1-84227-152-0 / xxii + 216pp

G. Michael Thomas
The Extent of the Atonement
A Dilemma for Reformed Theology from Calvin to the Consensus
A study of the way Reformed theology addressed the question, 'Did Christ die for all, or for the elect only?', commencing with John Calvin, and including debates with Lutheranism, the Synod of Dort and the teaching of Moïse Amyraut.
1997 / 0-85364-828-X / x + 278pp

David M. Thompson
Baptism, Church and Society in Britain from the Evangelical Revival to *Baptism, Eucharist and Ministry*
The theology and practice of baptism have not received the attention they deserve. How important is faith? What does baptismal regeneration mean? Is baptism a bond of unity between Christians? This book discusses the theology of baptism and popular belief and practice in England and Wales from the Evangelical Revival to the publication of the World Council of Churches' consensus statement on *Baptism, Eucharist and Ministry* (1982).
2005 / 1-84227-393-0 / approx. 224pp

Mark D. Thompson
A Sure Ground on Which to Stand
The Relation of Authority and Interpretive Method of Luther's Approach to Scripture
The best interpreter of Luther is Luther himself. Unfortunately many modern studies have superimposed contemporary agendas upon this sixteenth-century Reformer's writings. This fresh study examines Luther's own words to find an explanation for his robust confidence in the Scriptures, a confidence that generated the famous 'stand' at Worms in 1521.
2004 / 1-84227-145-8 / xvi + 322pp

Carl R. Trueman and R.S. Clark (eds)
Protestant Scholasticism
Essays in Reassessment

Traditionally Protestant theology, between Luther's early reforming career and the dawn of the Enlightenment, has been seen in terms of decline and fall into the wastelands of rationalism and scholastic speculation. In this volume a number of scholars question such an interpretation. The editors argue that the development of post-Reformation Protestantism can only be understood when a proper historical model of doctrinal change is adopted. This historical concern underlies the subsequent studies of theologians such as Calvin, Beza, Olevian, Baxter, and the two Turrentini. The result is a significantly different reading of the development of Protestant Orthodoxy, one which both challenges the older scholarly interpretations and clichés about the relationship of Protestantism to, among other things, scholasticism and rationalism, and which demonstrates the fruitfulness of the new, historical approach.

1999 / 0-85364-853-0 / xx + 344pp

Shawn D. Wright
Our Sovereign Refuge
The Pastoral Theology of Theodore Beza

Our Sovereign Refuge is a study of the pastoral theology of the Protestant reformer who inherited the mantle of leadership in the Reformed church from John Calvin. Countering a common view of Beza as supremely a 'scholastic' theologian who deviated from Calvin's biblical focus, Wright uncovers a new portrait. He was not a cold and rigid academic theologian obsessed with probing the eternal decrees of God. Rather, by placing him in his pastoral context and by noting his concerns in his pastoral and biblical treatises, Wright shows that Beza was fundamentally a committed Christian who was troubled by the vicissitudes of life in the second half of the sixteenth century. He believed that the biblical truth of the supreme sovereignty of God alone could support Christians on their earthly pilgrimage to heaven. This pastoral and personal portrait forms the heart of Wright's argument.

2004 / 1-84227-252-7 / xviii + 308pp

Paternoster
9 Holdom Avenue,
Bletchley,
Milton Keynes MK1 1QR,
United Kingdom
Web: www.authenticmedia.co.uk/paternoster

www.ingramcontent.com/pod-product-compliance
Lightning Source LLC
Chambersburg PA
CBHW071232290426
44108CB00013B/1382